150 Best Recession-Proof Jobs

Part of JIST's Best Jobs® Series

The Editors @ JIST **and Laurence Shatkin, Ph.D.**

Also in JIST's Best Jobs Series

jist Works

America's Career Publisher®

150 Best Recession-Proof Jobs

© 2009 by JIST Publishing

Published by JIST Works, an imprint of JIST Publishing
7321 Shadeland Station, Suite 200
Indianapolis, IN 46256-3923

Phone: 800-648-JIST   Fax: 877-454-7839
E-mail: info@jist.com   Web site: www.jist.com

Some Other Books by the Authors

The Editors at JIST

EZ Occupational Outlook Handbook
Salary Facts Handbook
Enhanced Occupational Outlook Handbook
Guide to America's Federal Jobs
Health-Care CareerVision Book and DVD

Laurence Shatkin

90-Minute College Major Matcher

Quantity discounts are available for JIST products. Have future editions of JIST books automatically delivered to you on publication through our convenient standing order program. Please call 800-648-JIST or visit www.jist.com for a free catalog and more information.

Visit www.jist.com for information on JIST, free job search information, tables of contents, sample pages, and ordering information on our many products.

Acquisitions Editor: Susan Pines
Development Editor: Stephanie Koutek
Cover and Interior Designer: Aleata Halbig

Cover Photograph: Yin Yang, iStock photo
Proofreaders: Chuck Hutchinson, Jeanne Clark
Indexer: Cheryl Lenser

Printed in the United States of America

13 12 11 10 09 08   9 8 7 6 5 4 3 2

Library of Congress Cataloging-in-Publication Data

150 best recession-proof jobs / the editors at JIST and Laurence Shatkin.
      p. cm. -- (Jist's best jobs series)
   Includes index.
   ISBN 978-1-59357-623-3 (alk. paper)
  1. Occupations--United States. 2. Vocational guidance--United States. 3.
  Job descriptions. I. Shatkin, Laurence. II. JIST Publishing. III. Title:
  One hundred fifty best recession-proof jobs.
  HF5382.5.U5A594 2009
  331.7020973--dc22

                                    2008038415

ISBN 978-1-59357-623-3

This Is a Big Book, But It Is Very Easy to Use

Are you tired of riding the economic roller coaster? This book can help you plan for a job that is not likely to be affected by ups and downs in the economy.

Every few years the United States economy goes into a slowdown. Experienced workers lose their jobs and young people leaving school have a hard time finding work.

But some jobs are considered recession-proof because they meet needs that are not diminished even during hard times. These jobs are the focus of this book.

Here you'll find lists of good jobs that are selected and ordered to emphasize those with the highest earnings and the highest demand for workers. Specialized lists arrange these jobs by the level of education or training required and by interest fields. You can also see lists of industries, states, and metropolitan areas where the recession-proof jobs are most densely clustered.

Every job is described in detail later in the book, so you can explore the jobs that interest you the most. You'll learn the major work tasks, all the important skills, educational programs, fastest-growing industries, and many other informative facts.

You'll also find tips about how to recession-proof your career—ideas that can help you get ahead in both good times and bad.

Using this book, you'll be surprised how quickly you'll get new ideas for careers that are good bets for an unsteady economy and can suit you in many other ways.

Some Things You Can Do with This Book

- Identify recession-proof jobs that don't require you to get additional training or education, perhaps as options for retirement or a second career.
- Develop long-term career plans that may require additional training, education, or experience.
- Explore and select a training or educational program that relates to a career objective unlikely to be affected by economic downturns.
- Prepare for interviews by learning how to connect your work preferences to your career goal.

These are a few of the many ways you can use this book. We hope you find it as interesting to browse as we did to put together. We have tried to make it easy to use and as interesting as occupational information can be.

When you are done with this book, pass it along or tell someone else about it. We wish you well in your career and in your life.

Credits and Acknowledgments: While the authors created this book, it is based on the work of many others. The occupational information is based on data obtained from the U.S. Department of Labor and the U.S. Census Bureau. These sources provide the most authoritative occupational information available. The job titles and their related descriptions are from the O*NET database, which was developed by researchers and developers under the direction of the U.S. Department of Labor. They, in turn, were assisted by thousands of employers who provided details on the nature of work in the many thousands of job samplings used in the database's development. We used the most recent version of the O*NET database, release 12.0. We appreciate and thank the staff of the U.S. Department of Labor for their efforts and expertise in providing such a rich source of data.

Table of Contents

Summary of Major Sections

Introduction. A short overview to help you better understand and use the book. *Starts on page 1.*

Part I. Recession-Proof Your Career. Explains what a recession is, what makes a job recession-proof, and strategies for keeping your job during hard times or bouncing back from job loss. These suggestions are useful for your career no matter what shape the economy is in. *Starts on page 19.*

Part II. The Best Jobs Lists: Jobs Not Sensitive to Recessions. Very useful for exploring career options! Lists are arranged into easy-to-use groups. The first list presents the 150 best recession-proof jobs overall. Additional lists give the 40 best-paying recession-proof jobs, the 40 fastest-growing recession-proof jobs, and the 40 recession-proof jobs with the most openings. More-specialized lists follow, presenting jobs that have a high concentration of certain kinds of workers and jobs by level of education or training and by interest area. The column starting at right presents all the list titles. *Starts on page 25.*

Part III. Descriptions of the Best Recession-Proof Jobs. Provides complete descriptions of the jobs that appear on the lists in Part II. Each description contains information on work tasks, skills, education and training required, earnings, projected growth, fastest-growing industries, job duties, related knowledge and courses, working conditions, and many other details. *Starts on page 115.*

Appendix A. Resources for Further Exploration. A helpful list of resources to learn more about recession-proof careers. *Starts on page 403.*

Appendix B. The GOE Interest Areas and Work Groups. This list of the 16 GOE Interest Areas and Work Groups can help you narrow down your career interests. *Starts on page 405.*

Appendix C. Skills Referenced in This Book. Provides definitions of the skills listed in the job descriptions in Part III. *Starts on page 410.*

Appendix D. Knowledge Areas Referenced in This Book. Provides definitions of the knowledges/courses listed in the job descriptions in Part III. *Starts on page 412.*

Detailed Table of Contents

Introduction

Not everybody will want to read this introduction. You may want to skip this background information and go directly to Part I, which discusses how to recession-proof your career, or Part II, which lists the best recession-proof jobs.

But if you want to understand how (and why) we put this book together, where the information comes from, and what makes a job "recession-proof" and "best," this introduction can answer many questions.

How This Book Can Help You in Both Good and Bad Economic Times

When you choose a career and prepare for it, you want some assurances that you will be able to find work in the career. You can improve your chances by focusing on careers that have a good job outlook. The U.S. Department of Labor projects the future demand for various occupations, and you can choose one that is expected to grow and take on many new workers. But keep in mind that these labor-market forecasts are like a Midwestern weather forecast that says the days will get warmer over the course of March. Yes, the weather will be warmer by March 31, but during those 31 days there will be cold spells, maybe even snowstorms.

The economy also has ups and downs. Despite the efforts of the wizards at the Federal Reserve Bank, the economy tends to experience a repeated sequence called *the business cycle*. During an upswing in the cycle, businesses invest in equipment, build up inventory, and—most important for your career decision—hire workers. As long as the economic outlook remains optimistic, businesses expect to gain greater productivity from their new equipment, sell their newly created inventory, and find work for their new employees. But eventually, for one economic reason or another, the outlook becomes gloomy. Businesses stop buying new equipment and may even shut down facilities; they slash prices and sell off their inventory; and they reduce payroll expenses by laying off workers and not hiring replacements for those who leave.

Some occupations and industries are less sensitive than others to these swings of the business cycle because they produce goods or perform services that are necessary no matter which way the economy is trending. This book focuses on those recession-proof jobs and industries.

1

If you look around you and see a tempest-tossed economy or have reason to think one is coming soon—or if you consider that a recession is certain to arrive eventually—this book can help you identify jobs and industries that can likely weather the storm.

But this book can also be useful during good economic times, because many of the jobs included here can serve as stepping-stones to more economically sensitive jobs that may be worth the risk of pursuing when the economy is booming. For example, take our 16th-ranked recession-proof job, Environmental Engineers. Unlike most other engineering jobs, this job is considered a good bet during hard times. You may gain experience in this occupation even when other engineers are being laid off. Then, when the economy improves, you may have acquired enough skills and knowledge to be ready for a job in engineering management—a more insecure position, but perhaps worth the risk because of its higher pay (on average, about 50 percent higher). You might then try to move into a recession-proof industry, such as utilities, to reduce the chances that your job will be threatened by the next economic downturn.

Business cycles are not the only forces that can affect your job security. Certain long-term trends such as automation, the aging of the population, and increased global competition for energy can make your job either more or less vulnerable to downsizing and shrinking job opportunities. The lists of recession-proof jobs in Part II of this book are based on both short- and long-term trends. Keep in mind, however, that a trend is only an average of the changes that occur. Part I of this book offers suggestions for how you can exceed the average so that employers will not want to lay you off, even during hard times.

Where the Information Came From

The information we used in creating this book came mostly from databases created by the U.S. Department of Labor:

* We started with economic information from the Bureau of Labor Statistics (BLS). These figures are reported under a classifying system called Standard Occupational Classification (SOC), which organizes the U.S. workforce into approximately 800 job titles. Based on these economic figures, we were able to determine which jobs are most likely to have good opportunities even during recessions. Some other information reported under SOC titles included figures on the number of part-time and self-employed workers in each job and on the level of education required.

* To obtain additional information, we linked the SOC job titles to titles in the O*NET (Occupational Information Network) database, which is now the primary source of detailed information on occupations. The Labor Department updates O*NET regularly, and we used the most recent version available: O*NET release 12. Data from O*NET allowed us to determine the personality types associated with jobs, as well as the important skills, types of knowledge, and work conditions. Because O*NET uses a slightly different set of job titles than SOC, we had to match similar titles. In a few cases,

we could not obtain data about each of these topics for every occupation. Nevertheless, the information we report here is the most reliable data we could obtain.

❋ We used the Classification of Instructional Programs, a system developed by the U.S. Department of Education, to cross-reference the education or training programs related to each job.

Of course, information in a database format can be boring and even confusing, so we did many things to help make the data useful and present it to you in a form that is easy to understand.

How the Best Recession-Proof Jobs Were Selected

The Bureau of Labor Statistics, our main source of career information, provides projections of job growth and annual job openings for about 750 individual occupations. However, the BLS does not attempt to predict recessions or boom times when it makes these projections. Rather, the BLS bases its projections on the *average* growth and openings over a 10-year period (currently, the period from 2006 to 2016).

Therefore, to choose 150 recession-proof jobs for this book, we could not rely simply on job-growth projections averaged out over a decade. We followed this procedure:

1. To select the jobs that are least likely to be affected by a recession, we followed the ratings given by an article in the *Occupational Outlook Quarterly (OOQ)*, a BLS publication. It rates jobs on a three-point scale, from 0 to 3, for "economic sensitivity," which means how closely the jobs have, in the past, prospered or suffered along with the economy. For an additional check, we consulted the 2008–2009 edition of the *Occupational Outlook Handbook,* another BLS publication, focusing on the outlook statements given for the occupations. When necessary, we adjusted the sensitivity ratings for some jobs. Because many of the job titles are very diverse collections of jobs—for example, Actors, Producers, and Directors—we did not automatically assume that all the related specific titles deserve to share the same numerical rating for economic sensitivity. To determine separate ratings in these cases, we performed a statistical analysis comparing the historical ups and downs in the workforce size of occupations with the ups and downs in the national economy. For each job in these cases, we also considered the economic outlook projected between 2006 and 2016.

2. In some cases, we did not need to disaggregate groups of rated occupations because the full set of economic figures that we needed for creating the lists in Part II was available only at a high level of aggregation. For example, job outlook information was available for one occupation called Physicians and Surgeons rather than for the eight related SOC occupations and for one college teaching job called Postsecondary Teachers rather than for 39 professorial SOC titles.

3. Our initial list of jobs with complete economic data—economic sensitivity ratings, earnings figures, and projections for growth and job openings—consisted of 711 titles. Of these, 682 also had the full range of noneconomic information—work tasks, skills, and work conditions—needed for a reasonably complete description in this book.

4. Next, we eliminated 49 jobs with annual median earnings of less than $20,270, which is the earnings level that exceeds that of the lowest 25 percent of wage-earners. Although some of these jobs may employ many workers, even in a recession, their low pay makes them unlikely to be of interest to the readers of this book. Admittedly, some of the jobs that do appear in this book—such as Embalmers or Pest Control Workers—may be unappealing to you for other reasons, but we'll leave it to you to decide how you feel about other aspects of jobs. We also eliminated 14 jobs that cannot be considered best jobs because they are expected to employ fewer than 500 workers per year and to shrink rather than grow in workforce size. Even if they are unaffected by recession, they offer little job opportunity. The list at this point included 619 jobs.

5. To limit the list to recession-proof jobs, we selected only the 171 jobs rated 0 on economic sensitivity in the *OOQ* article, plus 13 jobs rated 1 with outstanding projected job growth between 2006 and 2016.

6. Next, we eliminated occupations that are at high risk for being offshored—meaning that the work can readily be done by people in foreign countries. Four of the occupations on our list at this point were identified as vulnerable to offshoring in a 2006 BLS publication called *Occupational Projections and Training Data*: Computer Software Engineers, Applications; Computer Software Engineers, Systems Software; Customer Service Representatives; and Medical Transcriptionists. Some of these offshorable jobs have very good employment outlook through 2016, but their long-term security is questionable, so they cannot be considered recession-proof. The list now included 180 jobs.

7. We ranked the 180 recession-proof jobs three times, based on these major criteria: median annual earnings, projected growth through 2016, and number of job openings projected per year.

8. We then added the three numerical rankings for each job to calculate its overall score.

9. To emphasize jobs that tend to pay more, are likely to grow more rapidly, and have more job openings, we selected the 150 job titles with the best total overall scores.

For example, the recession-proof job with the best combined score for earnings, growth, and number of job openings is Computer Systems Analysts, so this job is listed first even though it is not the best-paying recession-proof job (which is Physicians and Surgeons), the fastest-growing job (which is Network Systems and Data Communications Analysts), or the job with the most openings (which is Nursing Aides, Orderlies, and Attendants).

Why This Book Has More Than 150 Job Descriptions

We didn't think you would mind that this book actually provides information on more than 150 jobs. We combined several jobs to create the lists in Part II, as mentioned earlier, but in Part III we describe these jobs separately. This means that although we used 150 job titles to construct the lists, Part III actually has a total of 205 job descriptions.

Understand the Limits of the Data in This Book

In this book, we used the most reliable and up-to-date information available on earnings, projected growth, number of openings, and other topics. The earnings data came from the U.S. Department of Labor's Bureau of Labor Statistics. As you look at the figures, keep in mind that they are estimates. They give you a general idea about the number of workers employed, annual earnings, rate of job growth, and annual job openings.

Understand that a problem with such data is that it describes an average. Just as there is no precisely average person, there is no such thing as a statistically average example of a particular job. We say this because data, while helpful, can also be misleading.

Take, for example, the yearly earnings information in this book. This is highly reliable data obtained from a very large U.S. working population sample by the Bureau of Labor Statistics. It tells us the average annual pay received as of May 2006 by people in various job titles (actually, it is the median annual pay, which means that half earned more and half less).

This sounds great, except that half of all people in that occupation earned less than that amount. For example, people who are new to the occupation or with only a few years of work experience often earn much less than the median amount. People who live in rural areas or who work for smaller employers typically earn less than those who do similar work in cities (where the cost of living is higher) or for bigger employers. People in certain areas of the country earn less than those in others. Other factors also influence how much you are likely to earn in a given job in your area. For example, Aircraft Mechanics and Service Technicians in the Detroit–Warren–Livonia, Michigan, metropolitan area have median earnings of $52,640, probably because Northwest Airlines has a hub at Detroit and their mechanics are unionized. By comparison, the New Haven, Connecticut, metropolitan area has no major airline hub and only a small aircraft service facility with nonunionized workers; Aircraft Mechanics and Service Technicians there earn a median of only $26,830.

Beginning wages also vary greatly, depending not only on location and size of employer, but also on what skills and educational credentials a new hire brings to the job.

Also keep in mind that the figures for job growth and number of openings are projections by labor economists—their best guesses about what we can expect between now and 2016. The same is true for the identification of jobs that are expected to be recession-proof. They are not guarantees. A catastrophic economic downturn, war, or technological breakthrough could change the actual outcome.

Finally, don't forget that the job market consists of both job openings and job *seekers*. The figures on job growth and openings don't tell you how many people will be competing with you to be hired. The Department of Labor does not publish figures on the supply of job candidates, so we are unable to tell you about the level of competition you can expect. Competition is an important issue that you should research for any tentative career goal. The *Occupational Outlook Handbook* provides informative statements for many occupations. You should speak to people who educate or train tomorrow's workers; they probably have a good idea of how many graduates find rewarding employment and how quickly. People in the workforce also can provide insights into this issue. Use your critical thinking skills to evaluate what people tell you. For example, educators or trainers may be trying to recruit you, whereas people in the workforce may be trying to discourage you from competing. Get a variety of opinions to balance out possible biases.

So, in reviewing the information in this book, please understand the limitations of the data. You need to use common sense in career decision making as in most other things in life. We hope that, by using that approach, you find the information helpful and interesting.

The Data Complexities

For those of you who like details, we present some of the complexities inherent in our sources of information and what we did to make sense of them here. You don't need to know this to use the book, so jump to the next section of the Introduction if you are bored with details.

We selected the jobs on the basis of economic data, and we include information on earnings, projected growth, and number of job openings for each job throughout this book.

Selection of Recession-Proof Jobs, Industries, States, and Metropolitan Areas

Nuclear physicist Niels Bohr once remarked, "Prediction is very difficult, especially about the future." Nobody has developed a foolproof way to determine which jobs, industries, or locations will offer the best opportunities during future recessions; but to create the lists in Part II of this book, we used the best measures available.

The economic sensitivity ratings we used to select recession-proof jobs were taken from an article that appeared in the fall 2004 issue of the *Occupational Outlook Quarterly:* "Matching Yourself to the World of Work: 2004," by Henry T. Kasper, an economist in the Office of Occupational Statistics and Employment Projections. A table in the article rates approximately 280 occupations on "economic sensitivity," based on how the occupations historically have fluctuated—or not fluctuated—in step with the economy as a whole.

Because the article is several years old and different economic trends may have emerged since it was written, we compared the ratings in the article to outlook statements in the

2008–2009 edition of the *Occupational Outlook Handbook*. In a few cases we detected inconsistencies and corrected the ratings to reflect the more recent information.

The job titles we were working with at this point were a mix of specific SOC occupations and aggregated titles such as Counselors, which represents six specific SOC titles. To determine separate ratings for the separate SOC jobs that made up the aggregated titles, we analyzed the historical behavior of individual occupations, using a statistical procedure patterned after one performed by two BLS economists who determined which industries are most economically sensitive ("Which Industries Are Sensitive to Business Cycles?" by Jay Berman and Janet Pfleeger, *Monthly Labor Review*, February 1997). To measure the historical ups and downs of occupations, we used figures on workforce size from the BLS; comparable annual figures were available from 1999 to 2006. To measure fluctuations in the economy as a whole, we used annual figures for gross domestic product (GDP) during the same years from the Bureau of Economic Analysis, Department of Commerce. The 1999–2006 time span included the technology boom of the late 1990s as well as the recession of 2001. For each occupation, we computed a figure that technically is called the Pearson product-moment coefficient of correlation and that indicates how closely the fluctuations in workforce size followed the fluctuations in the economy as a whole. These correlation figures enabled us to make ratings for specific occupations where necessary. Afterward, we had sensitivity ratings for more than 700 SOC occupations.

The historical approach, which we and the BLS economists relied on to estimate the economic sensitivity of jobs, has one major limitation: The past U.S. economy is not exactly the same as the future U.S. economy. The makeup of the economy and the forces that buffet it change, so each business cycle is somewhat different from the one that came before. The technology boom of the late 1990s and the recession that followed did not raise and lower exactly the same industries and jobs as the boom and bust that followed. For example, it seems likely that construction jobs will be more seriously affected by the downturn of 2008 than they were by the recession of 2001. In a future recession, some other sector of the economy may suffer the most severe setbacks.

Therefore, we tempered the historical approach to assigning ratings by considering the BLS projections for job growth and number of job openings. These projections (discussed in greater detail later in this section) are based on trends in the economy that are expected to continue in the future. For example, with the aging of the population, the health-care industry will play a larger role in the economy over the next decade than it did during the past decade, so it will be less sensitive to economic downturns than ever before. Computers and other high-tech devices have become ingrained in our lives, yet college enrollments in technology majors are not increasing; therefore, it seems likely that future recessions will not cause great competition among computer specialists, as did the recession of 2001.

One way we used these projections was to assign ratings to specific occupations that were aggregated within large job titles in the article by Kasper. For example, Kasper gave the rating of 0 (zero) to the job title "Social Workers," but when we examined the projections for the four kinds of social workers that the BLS covers, we decided to give one of them a rating of 1.

The other way we used these projections was when we discarded jobs that cannot be considered recession-proof. We kept not only jobs rated 0, but also jobs rated 1 for which the projected growth is greater than 23.5 percent. Only about 8 percent of the jobs that the BLS covers are expected to have job growth this high, so although these jobs rated 1 have some economic sensitivity, they can be considered safe bets over the coming decade even during a recession. The 23.5 percent figure represents one standard deviation above the mean figure for all occupations, a statistical measure that isolates the truly high performers in a group.

To determine the most recession-proof industries, states, and metropolitan areas for the bonus lists in Part II, we ranked the items by the degree to which the 150 recession-proof jobs are concentrated. That is, we calculated the percentage of the total workforce of the industries, states, and metro areas that is employed in the 150 best recession-proof jobs. The assumption is that where these jobs make up the biggest chunk of the workforce, future recessions will have the smallest impact. These 150 jobs were rated recession-proof by the BLS largely because they are clustered in industries that are expected to do comparatively well during future recessions, and industries tend to be clustered in certain states and metro areas.

Earnings

The employment security agency of each state gathers information on earnings for various jobs and forwards it to the U.S. Bureau of Labor Statistics. This information is organized in standardized ways by a BLS program called Occupational Employment Statistics (OES). To keep the earnings for the various jobs and regions comparable, the OES screens out certain types of earnings and includes others, so the OES earnings we use in this book represent straight-time gross pay exclusive of premium pay. More specifically, the OES earnings include the job's base rate; cost-of-living allowances; guaranteed pay; hazardous-duty pay; incentive pay, including commissions and production bonuses; on-call pay; and tips. They do not include back pay, jury duty pay, overtime pay, severance pay, shift differentials, nonproduction bonuses, or tuition reimbursements. Also, self-employed workers are not included in the estimates, and they can be a significant segment in certain occupations. When data on annual earnings for an occupation is highly unreliable, OES does not report a figure, which meant that we reluctantly had to exclude from this book a few occupations such as Actors.

For each job, we report three facts related to earnings:

* The Annual Earnings figure shows the median earnings (half earn more, half earn less).
* The Beginning Wage figure shows the 10th percentile earnings (the figure that exceeds the earnings of the lowest 10 percent of the workers). This is a rough approximation of what a beginning worker may be offered.
* The Earnings Growth Potential statement represents the gap between the 10th percentile and the median. This information answers the question, "If I started at the beginning wage and then got a raise that took me up to the median, how much of a pay boost (in

percentage terms) would that be?" If this would be a big boost, the job has great potential for increasing your earnings as you gain experience and skills. If the boost would be small, you probably will need to move on to another occupation to improve your earnings substantially. Rather than use a percentage figure, which might be hard to hard to interpret, we use a verbal tag to express the Earnings Growth Potential: "very low" when the percentage is less than 25%, "low" for 25–35%, "medium" for 35%–40%, "high" for 40%–50%, and "very high" for any figure higher than 50%. For the highest-paying jobs, those for which BLS reports the median earnings as "more than $145,600," we are unable to calculate a figure for Earnings Growth Potential. The great majority of jobs in this book have very high earnings growth potential.

The median earnings for all workers in all occupations were $30,400 in May 2006. The 150 recession-proof jobs in this book were chosen partly on the basis of good earnings, so their average is a respectable $45,247. (This is a weighted average, which means that jobs with larger workforces are given greater weight in the computation. It also is based on the assumption that a job with income reported as "more than $145,600" pays exactly $145,600, so the actual average is somewhat higher.)

The beginning (that is, 10th percentile) wage for all occupations in May 2006 was $15,500. For the 150 recession-proof jobs, the weighted average is an impressive $28,078.

The earnings data from the OES survey is reported under the Standard Occupational Classification (SOC) system. As discussed earlier, these are the job titles we use in the lists in Part II, but in Part III we cross-reference these titles to O*NET job titles so that we can provide O*NET-derived information on many useful topics. In some cases, an SOC title cross-references to more than one O*NET job title. For example, the SOC title Fire Fighters, which we use in Part II, is linked to two jobs described in Part III: Forest Fire Fighters and Municipal Fire Fighters. Because earnings data is available only for the combined job title Fire Fighters, in Part III you will find the same earnings figure, $41,190, reported for both kinds of fire fighters. In reality, there probably is a difference in what the two kinds of fire fighters earn, but this is the best information available.

Projected Growth and Number of Job Openings

This information comes from the Office of Occupational Statistics and Employment Projections, a program within the Bureau of Labor Statistics that develops information about projected trends in the nation's labor market for the next 10 years. As mentioned earlier, the most recent projections available cover the years 2006 to 2016. The projections are based on information about people moving into and out of occupations. The BLS uses data from various sources in projecting the growth and number of openings for each job title; some data comes from the Census Bureau's Current Population Survey and some comes from an OES survey. The projections assume that there will be no major war, depression, or other economic upheaval. They do assume that recessions may occur, in keeping with the business cycles we have experienced for several decades, but because they cover 10 years, they are intended to provide an average of both the good times and the bad times.

Like the earnings figures, the figures on projected growth and job openings are reported according to the SOC classification, so again you will find that some of the SOC jobs that we use in Part II crosswalk to more than one O*NET job in Part III. To continue the example we used earlier, the BLS reports growth (12.1 percent) and openings (18,887) for one SOC occupation called Fire Fighters, but in Part III of this book we report these figures separately for the O*NET occupations Forest Fire Fighters and Municipal Fire Fighters. In Part III, when you see that Forest Fire Fighters is described as having 12.1 percent projected growth and 18,887 projected job openings and Municipal Fire Fighters is described with the same two numbers, you should realize that the 12.1 percent rate of projected growth represents the *average* of these two occupations—one may actually experience higher growth than the other—and that these two occupations will *share* the 18,887 projected openings.

While salary figures are fairly straightforward, you may not know what to make of job-growth figures. For example, is a projected growth of 15 percent good or bad? Keep in mind that the average (mean) growth projected for all occupations by the Bureau of Labor Statistics is 10.4 percent. One-quarter of the SOC occupations have a growth projection of 3.2 percent or lower. Growth of 11.6 percent is the median, meaning that half of the occupations have more, half less. Only one-quarter of the occupations have growth projected at more than 17.4 percent.

Because the jobs in this book were selected as "best" partly on the basis of job growth, their mean growth is 16.7 percent, which compares favorably to the mean for all jobs. Among these 150 jobs, the job ranked 37th by projected growth has a figure of 23.6 percent, the job ranked 75th (the median) has a projected growth of 14.6 percent, and the job ranked 112th has a projected growth of 10.3 percent.

The number of job openings for the 150 recession-proof jobs is considerably lower than the national average for all occupations. The BLS projects an average of about 35,000 job openings per year for the 750 occupations that it studies, but for the 150 occupations included in this book, the average is about 24,000 openings. The job ranked 37th for job openings has a figure of about 27,000 annual openings, the job ranked 75th (the median) has about 8,300 openings projected, and the job ranked 112th has about 3,000 openings projected.

However, keep in mind that figures for job openings depend on how the BLS defines an occupation. Consider the occupation Detectives and Criminal Investigators, which employs a workforce of more than 100,000 people and is expected to provide almost 15,000 job openings each year. The BLS regards this as one occupation when it reports figures for earnings and job projections, but O*NET divides it into four separate occupations: Police Detectives; Police Identification and Records Officers; Criminal Investigators and Special Agents; and Immigration and Customs Inspectors. If the BLS employment-projection tables were to list these as four separate occupations and divide the 15,000 openings among them, the average number of openings for all occupations would be smaller. So it follows that because the way the BLS defines occupations is somewhat arbitrary, any "average" figure for job openings is also somewhat arbitrary.

Perhaps you're wondering why we present figures on both job growth *and* number of openings. Aren't these two ways of saying the same thing? Actually, you need to know both. Consider the occupation Hydrologists, which is projected to grow at the outstanding rate of 24.3 percent. There should be lots of opportunities in such a fast-growing job, right? Not exactly. This is a tiny occupation, with only about 8,000 people currently employed, so although it is growing rapidly, it will not create many new jobs (about 900 per year). Now consider Secondary School Teachers, Except Special and Vocational Education. This occupation is growing at the sluggish rate of 5.6 percent, held back by stagnating high school enrollments. Nevertheless, this is a huge occupation that employs more than one million workers, so although its growth rate is unimpressive, it is expected to take on more than 93,000 new workers each year as existing workers retire, die, or move on to other jobs. That's why we base our selection of the best jobs on both of these economic indicators and why you should pay attention to both when you scan our lists of best jobs.

Other Job Characteristics

Like the figures for earnings, some of the other figures that describe jobs in this book are shared by more than one job title. Usually this is the case for occupations that are so small that the BLS does not release separate statistics for them. For example, the occupation Cardiovascular Technologists and Technicians has a total workforce of only about 45,000 workers, so the BLS does not report a specific figure for the percentage of women workers. In this case, we had to use the figure that the BLS reports for a group of occupations it calls Diagnostic Related Technologists and Technicians. We relied on this same figure for three other jobs: Diagnostic Medical Sonographers, Nuclear Medicine Technologists, and Radiologic Technologists and Technicians. You may notice similar figure-sharing among related jobs in the lists that show percentages of workers in specific age brackets.

How This Book Is Organized

The information in this book about best recession-proof jobs moves from the general to the highly specific.

Part I. Recession-Proof Your Career

What exactly is a recession? Part I defines the term and explains why some jobs and industries are barely affected by recessions. Unfortunately, even jobs that seem recession-proof can sometimes be threatened by layoffs, so we offer several suggestions for how to make yourself essential to your employer and how to be a resilient worker who can bounce back from a layoff. These pointers can be helpful for improving your career prospects in boom times as well as in recessions.

Part II. The Best Jobs Lists

For many people, the 75 lists in Part II constitute the book's most interesting feature. Here you can see titles of the 150 recession-proof jobs that have the best combination of high salaries, fast growth, and plentiful job openings. You can see which jobs are best in terms of each of these factors combined and considered separately. Additional lists highlight jobs with a high percentage of female, male, part-time, and self-employed workers. Look in the Table of Contents for a complete list of lists. Although there are a lot of lists, they are not difficult to understand because they have clear titles and are organized into groupings of related lists.

Depending on your situation, some of the lists in Part II will interest you more than others. For example, if you are young, you may be interested in the best-paying recession-proof jobs that employ high percentages of people age 16–24. Other lists show jobs within interest groupings, personality types, levels of education, or other ways that you might find helpful in exploring your career options.

Whatever your situation, we suggest you use the lists that make sense for you to help explore career options. Following are the names of each group of lists along with short comments on each group. You will find additional information in a brief introduction provided at the beginning of each group of lists in Part II.

Best Recession-Proof Jobs Overall: Jobs with the Highest Pay, Fastest Growth, and Most Openings

Four lists are in this group, and they are the ones that most people want to see first. The first list presents the top 150 recession-proof job titles in order of their combined scores for earnings, growth, and number of job openings. Three more lists in this group are extracted from the 150 best and present the 50 jobs with the highest earnings, the 50 jobs projected to grow most rapidly, and the 50 jobs with the most openings.

Best Recession-Proof Jobs Listed by Demographic

This group of lists presents interesting information for various types of people based on data from the U.S. Census Bureau. The lists are arranged into groups for workers age 16–24, workers 55 and older, part-time workers, self-employed workers, women, and men. We created five lists for each group, basing the last four on the jobs selected for the first list:

* The recession-proof jobs having the highest percentage of people of each type
* The 25 jobs with the highest combined scores for earnings, growth, and number of openings
* The 25 jobs with the highest earnings
* The 25 jobs with the highest growth rates
* The 25 jobs with the largest number of openings

Best Recession-Proof Jobs Sorted by Education or Training Required

We created separate lists for each level of education, training, and experience as defined by the U.S. Department of Labor. We put each of the top 150 job titles into one of the lists based on the kind of preparation required for entry. Jobs within these lists are presented in order of their total combined scores for earnings, growth, and number of openings. The lists include recession-proof jobs in these groupings:

- Short-term on-the-job training
- Moderate-term on-the-job training
- Long-term on-the-job training
- Work experience in a related job
- Postsecondary vocational training
- Associate degree
- Bachelor's degree
- Work experience plus degree
- Master's degree
- Doctoral degree
- First professional degree

Best Recession-Proof Jobs Sorted by Interests

These lists organize the 150 best jobs into groups based on interests. Within each list, jobs are presented in order of their total scores for earnings, growth, and number of openings. Here are the 16 interest areas used in these lists: Agriculture and Natural Resources; Architecture and Construction; Arts and Communication; Business and Administration; Education and Training; Finance and Insurance; Government and Public Administration; Health Science; Hospitality, Tourism, and Recreation; Human Service; Information Technology; Law and Public Safety; Manufacturing; Retail and Wholesale Sales and Service; Scientific Research, Engineering, and Mathematics; and Transportation, Distribution, and Logistics.

Best Recession-Proof Jobs Sorted by Personality Types

These lists organize the 150 best jobs into six personality types described in the introduction to the lists: Realistic, Investigative, Artistic, Social, Enterprising, and Conventional. The jobs within each list are presented in order of their total scores for earnings, growth, and number of openings.

Bonus Lists: The Most Recession-Proof Industries, States, and Metropolitan Areas

Job opportunities vary according to what industry you work in and where you're located. These lists highlight the industries, states, and metropolitan areas that have the highest concentrations of recession-proof jobs.

Bonus Lists: The 10 Most Recession-Proof Skills and Knowledges/ Courses

One list shows the most important transferable skills required for the 150 recession-proof jobs, listed in order of importance. The other list shows the most important knowledges required for the jobs, also listed in order of importance. These knowledges may be thought of either as courses you might take or as topics to learn about informally.

Bonus Lists: Best Recession-Sensitive Jobs

These lists focus on jobs that are *not* considered recession-proof, although some of them are only moderately sensitive to economic downturns. The first list presents the top 150 recession-sensitive job titles in order of their combined scores for earnings, growth, and number of job openings. Three more lists in this group are extracted from the 150 best and present the 50 jobs with the highest earnings, the 50 jobs projected to grow most rapidly, and the 50 jobs with the most openings. You may want to consider the more promising jobs in these lists as possible career moves during good times.

Part III: Descriptions of the Best Recession-Proof Jobs

This part contains descriptions of all 205 O*NET job titles related to the 150 best recession-proof jobs, using a format that is informative yet compact and easy to read. The descriptions contain statistics such as earnings and projected percent of growth, lists such as major skills and work tasks, and key descriptors such as personality type and interest field. Because the jobs in this section are arranged in alphabetical order, you can easily find a job that you've identified from Part II and that you want to learn more about.

In some cases, a job title in Part II cross-references to two or more job titles in Part III. For example, if you look up Physicians and Surgeons in Part III, you'll find a note telling you to look at the descriptions for Anesthesiologists and six other medical specializations. That's why there are 205 descriptions in Part III rather than 150.

As discussed earlier in this introduction, we used the most current information from a variety of government sources to create the descriptions. Although we've tried to make the descriptions easy to understand, the sample that follows—with an explanation of each of its parts—may help you better understand and use the descriptions.

Job Title →

Chiropractors

Data Elements →

- ❀ Education/Training Required: First professional degree
- ❀ Annual Earnings: $65,220
- ❀ Beginning Wage: $32,670
- ❀ Earnings Growth Potential: Very high
- ❀ Growth: 14.4%
- ❀ Annual Job Openings: 3,179
- ❀ Self-Employed: 51.7%
- ❀ Part-Time: 23.6%

Industry Information →

Industries with Greatest Employment: Ambulatory Health Care Services.

Highest-Growth Industries (Projected Growth for this Job): Ambulatory Health Care Services (23.4%).

Lowest-Growth Industries (Projected Growth for this Job): Hospitals, Public and Private (12.2%).

Fastest-Growing Metropolitan Areas →

Fastest-Growing Metropolitan Areas (Recent Growth for this Job): Grand Rapids–Wyoming, MI (125.0%); Atlanta–Sandy Springs–Marietta, GA (71.1%); Washington–Arlington–Alexandria, DC–VA–MD–WV (48.6%); Los Angeles–Long Beach–Santa Ana, CA (48.3%); Sioux Falls, SD (40.0%).

Other Considerations for Job Security →

Other Considerations for Job Security: Job prospects for new chiropractors are expected to be good. In this occupation, replacement needs arise almost entirely from retirements. Chiropractors usually remain in the occupation until they retire; few transfer to other occupations. Establishing a new practice will be easiest in areas with a low concentration of chiropractors. Employment is expected to grow faster than average because of increasing consumer demand for alternative health care. Demand for chiropractic treatment, however, is related to the ability of patients to pay, either directly or through health insurance. Although more insurance plans now cover chiropractic services, the extent of such coverage varies among plans.

Summary Description and Tasks →

Adjust spinal column and other articulations of the body to correct abnormalities believed to be caused by interference with the nervous system. Examine patient to determine nature and extent of disorder. Manipulate spine or other involved area. May utilize supplementary measures, such as exercise, rest, water, light, heat, and nutritional therapy. Perform a series of manual adjustments to the spine or other articulations of the body to correct the musculoskeletal system. Evaluate the functioning of the neuromuscularskeletal system and the spine, using systems of chiropractic diagnosis. Diagnose health problems by reviewing patients' health and medical histories; questioning, observing, and examining patients; and interpreting X rays. Maintain accurate case histories of patients. Advise patients about recommended courses of treatment. Obtain and record patients' medical histories. Analyze X rays to locate the sources of patients' difficulties and to rule out fractures or diseases as sources of problems. Counsel patients about nutrition, exercise, sleeping habits, stress management, and other matters. Arrange for diagnostic X rays to be taken. Consult with and refer patients to appropriate health practitioners when necessary. Suggest and apply the use of supports such as straps, tapes, bandages, and braces if necessary.

Personality Type: Investigative.

Personality Type →

GOE Information →

GOE—Interest Area: 08. Health Science. **Work Group:** 08.04. Health Specialties. **Other Jobs in this Work Group:** Optometrists; Podiatrists.

Skills →

Skills: Science; Management of Financial Resources; Social Perceptiveness; Persuasion; Service Orientation; Management of Personnel Resources.

Education/Training Program(s) →

Education and Training Program: Chiropractic (DC). **Related Knowledge/Courses:** Medicine and Dentistry; Therapy and Counseling; Biology; Psychology; Sales and Marketing; Personnel and Human Resources.

Work Environment →

Work Environment: Indoors; disease or infections; standing; using hands on objects, tools, or controls; bending or twisting the body; repetitive motions.

Here are some details on each of the major parts of the job descriptions you will find in Part III:

⊛ **Job Title:** This is the job title for the job as defined by the U.S. Department of Labor and used in its O*NET database.

⊛ **Data Elements:** The information comes from various U.S. Department of Labor and Census Bureau databases, as explained elsewhere in this introduction.

⊛ **Industries with Greatest Employment:** These are the industries that each employ more than 10 percent of the workforce, ordered with the biggest employers first. Although these industries employ many workers, not all of them are growing fast; in fact, sometimes one of these industries is also listed for the topic "Lowest-Growth Industries."

⊛ **Highest-Growth Industries (Projected Growth for This Job):** These industries are expected to show the greatest employment increases for this job between 2006 and 2016. The figure in parentheses shows the projected amount of growth. The fastest-growing industries are listed first, and the list includes all industries offering more than 15 percent growth for the job. For a few booming high-tech jobs, we abbreviated the list. A few jobs exist in only one industry—for example, all Postal Service Clerks work for the Postal Service—so we were unable to list any industries where there is significant growth.

⊛ **Lowest-Growth Industries (Projected Growth for This Job):** We listed as many as 10 industries with projected growth of less than 15 percent for the occupation. The industries appear in ascending order of growth. Again, for some one-industry jobs, we could not list any low-growth industries here.

⊛ **Fastest-Growing Metropolitan Areas (Recent Growth for This Job):** These are the metropolitan areas in which the workforce for the job grew fastest between 2005 and 2006. (Unfortunately, it is not possible to obtain comparable figures for projected *future* job growth for all metro areas.) The percentage of growth appears in parentheses, and we list as many as five metro areas with recent growth over 10 percent. Keep in mind that recent growth may not continue.

⊛ **Other Considerations for Job Security:** This information, based on the *Occupational Outlook Handbook*, explains the factors that are expected to affect opportunities for job-seekers. Note that these comments apply to the period of time from 2006 to 2016.

⊛ **Summary Description and Tasks:** The boldfaced sentence provides a summary description of the occupation. It is followed by a listing of tasks generally performed by people who work in this job. This information comes from the O*NET database but, where necessary, has been edited to avoid exceeding 2,200 characters.

⊛ **Personality Type:** The O*NET database assigns each job to its most closely related personality type. You can find more information on the personality types as well as a brief definition of each type in the introduction to the lists of jobs based on personality types in Part II.

❋ **GOE Information:** This information cross-references the Guide for Occupational Exploration (GOE), a system developed by the U.S. Department of Labor that organizes jobs based on interests. We use the groups from the *New Guide for Occupational Exploration*, Fourth Edition, as published by JIST. That book uses a set of interest areas based on the 16 career clusters developed by the U.S. Department of Education and used in various career information systems. Here we include the major Interest Area the job fits into, its more-specific Work Group, and a list of related O*NET job titles that are in this same GOE Work Group. This information will help you identify other job titles that have similar interests or require similar skills, but note that not all jobs in a work group are equally good bets for riding out a recession. You can find a list of the GOE Interest Areas and Work Groups in Appendix B.

❋ **Skills:** For each job, we included the skills whose level-of-performance scores exceeded the average for all jobs by the greatest amount and whose ratings on the importance scale were higher than very low. We included as many as six such skills for each job, and we ranked them by the extent to which their rating exceeds the average. Appendix C contains the definitions of the skills.

❋ **Education/Training Program(s):** This part of the job description provides the name of the educational or training program(s) for the job. It will help you identify sources of formal or informal training for a job that interests you. To get this information, we adapted a crosswalk created by the National Center for O*NET Development to connect information in the Classification of Instructional Programs (CIP) to the O*NET job titles we used in this book. We made various changes to connect the O*NET job titles to the education or training programs related to them and also modified the names of some education and training programs so that they would be more easily understood. In 21 cases, we abbreviated the listing of related programs for the sake of space; such entries end with "others."

❋ **Related Knowledge/Courses:** This entry can help you understand the most important knowledge areas that are required for a job and the types of courses or programs you will likely need to take to prepare for it. We used information in the O*NET database for this entry. For each job, we identified any knowledge area with a rating that was higher than the average rating for that knowledge area for all jobs; then we listed as many as six in descending order. Definitions of the knowledge areas are in Appendix D.

❋ **Work Environment:** We included any work condition with a rating that exceeds the midpoint of the rating scale. The order does not indicate their frequency on the job. Consider whether you like these conditions and whether any of these conditions would make you uncomfortable. Keep in mind that when hazards are present (such as contaminants), protective equipment and procedures are provided to keep you safe.

Getting all the information we used in the job descriptions was not a simple process, and it is not always perfect. Even so, we used the best and most recent sources of data we could find, and we think that our efforts will be helpful to many people.

PART I

Recession-Proof Your Career

Nobody's job is 100 percent secure, but you can take steps to reduce your chances of being laid off in the event of an economic downturn and to increase your chances of bouncing back if you are laid off anyway. You can **recession-proof your career** by choosing the right occupation, choosing the right job within that occupation, making yourself the indispensable employee within that job, and being resilient enough to be able to rebound from a job loss. The ideas in this part of the book can be valuable for your career, no matter whether the economy is booming or stagnating.

Recession Defined

Economists keep track of the health of the U.S. economy by calculating a measure called the *gross domestic product* (GDP), which is defined as the total market value of all goods and services produced within the economy during a certain time period. The GDP grows at an unsteady rate from month to month, so economists look at how it changes over each three-month period—one-quarter of the year—to get a clear sense of how the GDP is trending. As the population continues to increase, economic activity normally increases, so most of the time the quarterly GDP climbs upward. But every few years, for various reasons, we experience an economic slowdown in which the GDP drops for two or more quarters, and that is the official definition of a recession.

Economists can't add up the GDP for a period of time until after that time is past, so they can't officially know that we're in a recession until *after* we've been in one for at least half a year. Likewise, we can't know officially that we have recovered from a recession until we have already experienced one quarter of solid growth. That is why, when the economy seems to be slowing, you will often hear economists, politicians, and business leaders disagreeing about whether we're really in a recession and about when the recession is over. These official pronouncements matter only for the history books; what matters to you is what's happening to the economy right now, the effects you can see even as the recession happens.

One of the most important economic effects of a recession is a slowdown of hiring. Employers who are facing reduced demand usually do not want to take on new workers or replace departing workers. Even when business starts to grow again, employers may want to find ways to keep their payroll expenses low and may try to increase productivity through methods other than hiring. Some of these methods are automating work tasks, offshoring work to lower-paid workers in foreign countries, hiring part-time or temporary workers (often without benefits), or asking current employees to work longer hours. These practices became so common during the period of economic growth following the 2001 recession that it was often called a "jobless recovery."

Therefore, if you need to work for a living, you should be concerned about how to identify a job that will be less threatened than most by economic downturns. After you identify that job and are hired, you also should be concerned about ways to improve your job security. This part of the book is intended to help you with these two concerns.

Identify a Recession-Proof Industry and Occupation

It used to be a common belief among economy-watchers that the best indicator of the current state of the economy is production of corrugated cardboard. Almost everything that businesses produce and that you buy is shipped in a cardboard box; when the economy cools down, cardboard is in less demand, and when the economy heats up, cardboard boxes are everywhere. It follows that when cardboard box–makers are out of work, many of the rest of us will soon be out of work. This idea is no longer as fashionable as it once was because an increasing amount of economic activity consists of services such as health care, education, information, and financial transactions, none of which is delivered in a box. Also, each year more goods we buy are imported from foreign countries and have been boxed overseas.

Although cardboard box–makers may not be the job to watch, it is still true that employment in certain occupations tends to go up and down in step with changes in the economy, whereas employment remains steady in certain other occupations even during hard times. In this book, we concentrate on the latter.

Some jobs are recession-proof because they provide goods or services that are essential to everyday life. For example, you'll find Water and Liquid Waste Treatment Plant and System Operators in the list of recession-proof jobs because in even the most dire economic times, people need to drink, wash, and flush. Technology is unlikely to develop a useful substitute for water or to make human operators unnecessary at the water purification and treatment plants, and imported bottled water can serve only a tiny fraction of the need, so the job is also not sensitive to any foreseeable long-term economic trends. Some other jobs that serve basic needs are Power Plant Operators, Pest Control Workers, and Clergy. It is often said that death and taxes are certainties, so you should not be surprised to find that our list includes Embalmers, Funeral Attendants, Funeral Directors, and Tax Examiners, Collectors, and Revenue Agents.

Some other recession-proof jobs protect us from harm and make the justice system work: Air Traffic Controllers, Occupational Health and Safety Technicians, Police and Sheriff's Patrol

Officers, Fire Fighters, Court Reporters, and Correctional Officers and Jailers. The fact that many of these workers are employed by government, rather than by private businesses, adds to their security. Ever since Ronald Reagan, governments have tried to trim their payrolls so they can cut taxes, but the protective functions of government mostly have been unaffected or have even expanded. Homeland security has become a big segment in the already large protective services industry.

One of the most useful ways to identify recession-proof jobs is to look for other recession-proof industries. The health-care industry employs more people than any other industry and also accounts for more of the recession-proof jobs than any other. Many of us have health-care coverage of some kind, so the ups and downs of the economy have only small effects on our ability to pay medical bills. Furthermore, as the population ages, the need for health care will increase. However, not every health-care occupation is recession-proof. Dental-care insurance is not as widespread as basic health-care insurance, and often the policies cover only semiannual cleanings, not the more expensive procedures. As a result, dentists' earnings, if not their jobs, suffer during economic slowdowns.

Like health care, education is an industry that creates many recession-proof jobs. Children are required to attend school no matter what shape the economy is in, and most teachers are employed by government. Teachers of baby boom age are expected to retire over the coming two decades, creating many job openings. Also, as our workplaces are becoming more filled with technology and with immigrant workers, adults are increasingly in need of night classes and on-site training, creating another long-term trend of job openings in education. In fact, adult education actually *increases* during recessions as employers become more demanding and people work on upgrading their skills.

Finally, technology has become so much a part of our daily lives that it's not as sensitive to the economy as it used to be. For example, the Internet has become a utility almost as essential as telephone service. On the other hand, many occupations in this industry can easily be performed by workers in low-wage foreign countries, and during hard times employers tend to offshore these jobs. Therefore, if you want to work in this industry, you should look for a job (such as Systems Analysts) that requires workers to deal with on-site problems and to work collaboratively in ways that are difficult for foreign workers to do. At the top of our list of the 150 best recession-proof jobs you'll find a few high-tech jobs that are less likely than most to be offshored.

If job security is important to you, you should not only work in a recession-proof occupation but also try to find work in a recession-proof industry. For example, more than 3,000 Budget Analysts are employed in the Transportation Equipment Manufacturing industry, but this industry (like most manufacturing industries) is sensitive to economic downturns. The approximately 8,100 Budget Analysts working in the Educational Services industry are probably more secure in their jobs (although they earn about 25 percent less). One of the bonus lists in Part II identifies industries that have a high concentration of recession-proof jobs and that are probably more secure than most.

Even workers in recession-*sensitive* occupations often can gain a certain amount of security by finding employment in a recession-proof industry. For example, the education industry employs many people who aren't teachers; the health-care industry employs many people who never come near a patient; the high-tech industry employs many people who aren't engineers or technicians. Even if you are uninterested in any of the recession-proof jobs in this book, you may want to look for work in an industry that has a good outlook. For example, the bonus list of best recession-*sensitive* jobs in Part II features Management Analysts as the fifth-best job. The job is rated 1 (on a scale from 0 to 3) for recession sensitivity, but you could gain security in this occupation by taking a position in a large hospital or university.

Limitations of Forecasts

All of this book's forecasts of recession-proof jobs and industries are based on well-known economic trends, but economists know only what they know and tend to be unaware of what they don't know. One such unknown factor is a new technology that drastically changes the way people can do their jobs. For example, the invention of the phonograph severely reduced the number of jobs for musicians, musical instrument makers, and music teachers because live performance no longer was the only way to listen to music. On the other hand, the new technology also created jobs. Record companies formed, and for decades every downtown business district or shopping mall had at least one record store, providing jobs that didn't exist before Thomas Edison's invention. Now we're seeing a drastic loss of jobs in the music distribution business because the way we obtain music has changed again, this time the result of the Internet. The Internet will certainly destroy jobs in many fields, but it also will create many jobs.

The lesson to take away is that a recession is not the only economic event or trend that can threaten your job, and therefore even a recession-proof job or industry is not a guarantee of lifetime employability. But this book focuses on the jobs and industries that appear to be best suited for the economic trends that currently are well understood.

Also, *even if every job-related prediction in this book turns out to be inaccurate,* the following tips will be useful because they can help you hang onto a threatened job or shift to a new job with minimal disruption to your life.

Be the Irreplaceable Worker

Sometimes jobs are threatened by short-term or local events. For example, if you live in a town where the economy is dominated by a steel mill and the mill shuts down, your job may be threatened even if you are working as a dental hygienist, school bus driver, or librarian. One of the bonus lists in Part II shows the metropolitan areas where the recession-proof jobs are most densely clustered, and moving to one of these areas may help you avoid a local downturn.

More commonly, jobs are threatened because a particular business gets into trouble even though the economy is in good shape. Perhaps a manager makes some very bad decisions, a competitor captures a large market share, or an essential raw material suddenly jumps in price. Now the employer has to decide how to cut costs to stay in business, and the most obvious way is to get rid of some workers.

Even a prosperous business may need to lay off workers. Let's say the business is so successful that a larger company sees it as an excellent investment and acquires it. But now some of the jobs in the new subsidiary are redundant because the parent company already has staff to perform those business functions. The result: layoffs.

Whatever the reason for layoffs, you may be able to hang onto your job *if you're irreplaceable.* You need to be so vital to the business that it can't go on without you. Here are some techniques to be the irreplaceable worker:

* **Focus on the core mission of the business.** Many businesses diversify and serve several functions, but usually there's a central mission that makes money and determines whether the business will succeed or fail. Identify that central function and play a role in it. Identify the skills the business needs for future development of this function and acquire them.

* **Be exceptionally productive.** This doesn't necessarily mean working longer hours. It's more important to find a task or role you can handle that goes beyond your job description. Here again, skills are important because they are the key to productivity.

* **Be visible.** In many businesses, the person whose office is next to the boss's tends to get the best performance appraisals. If you don't have that office, find ways to make your accomplishments known; don't wait for performance-appraisal season. For example, start an in-house Web page, newsletter, or bulletin board showcasing the project you're working on and soliciting suggestions from people outside the project. This will encourage them to buy into the project and make your efforts look not purely self-promotional. If you have a work-at-home arrangement, find reasons to show up at the office regularly or make lunch dates.

* **Acquire a mentor.** Find someone who really knows the business; be helpful; and ask a lot of very specific questions, including questions about how to improve your work. Give public credit to the mentor for the advice you get.

* **Be pleasant.** Back-stabbing may seem like a way to get ahead, but it can hurt you in the long run. Abrasiveness may make you stand out, but for the wrong reasons. If you really can't get along with some people in your work group, try to be transferred to one where you'll fit in better.

Be a Resilient Worker

For one reason or another, you may lose your job or get stuck in a dead-end job even while following the preceding tips. So the other strategy for recession-proofing your career is to *be resilient,* or be able to bounce back quickly. Here's how:

❋ **Specialize and focus on a specific goal.** After a few years in an occupation or industry, find a niche that is not overcrowded and is related to your core skills; then, acquire the specialized skills to excel in that role. In a tight job market, employers are more interested in someone with the perfect fit of skills than in a generalist. Your niche may be at the intersection of two very different skills; for example, you may be the chemist who is an ace computer programmer or the police officer who is an inspiring teacher.

❋ **Be visible beyond your workplace.** Join a professional organization, find something missing from its services, and put yourself in that key role. Start a blog or be active in commenting on a prominent blog; this is a readily available way to become known by people with connections in your industry. Become a brand; in the same way that Volvo is known as The Car that is Crashworthy and Wal-Mart is known as The Store with Low Prices, become known as The Person Who _____ [fill in the blank].

❋ **Keep your resume up to date.** Do more than list your current job title. Be sure to include a recent accomplishment so you don't look as though your career has been coasting. Make sure that your skills are easy to identify.

❋ **Keep your skills up to date.** The particular skills needed by your industry and for your targeted role will vary, but the bonus list of recession-proof skills and knowledges in Part II may give you some ideas about the capabilities that will be most valued in the emerging economy.

❋ **Believe in yourself.** Every job you hold is just one scene in the drama that is your life. If one episode is going badly or ends suddenly, it doesn't have to turn the whole arc of your career into a tragedy. Instead, think of the setback as a plot complication or as an adventure.

When you rebound from a job loss, it may be into another job in the same occupation, or perhaps you'll be open to the idea of moving into an occupation that usually is unaffected by economic downturns. If you're considering the latter, turn the page and start scanning the lists of the best recession-proof jobs.

PART II

The Best Jobs Lists: Jobs Not Sensitive to Recessions

This part contains many interesting lists, and it's a good place for you to start using the book. Here are some suggestions for using the lists to explore career options that are likely to be less sensitive than most to economic slowdowns:

❋ The table of contents at the beginning of this book presents a complete listing of the list titles in this section. You can browse the lists or use the table of contents to find those that interest you most.

❋ We gave the lists clear titles, so most require little explanation. We provide comments for each group of lists.

❋ As you review the lists of jobs, one or more of the jobs may appeal to you enough that you want to seek additional information. As this happens, mark that job (or, if someone else will be using this book, write it on a separate sheet of paper) so that you can look up the description of the job in Part III.

❋ Keep in mind that all jobs in these lists meet our basic criteria for being included in this book, as explained in the introduction. All lists, therefore, contain jobs that are considered not sensitive to recessions, with emphasis on occupations that have high pay, high growth, or large numbers of openings. These last three economic measures are easily quantified and are often presented in lists of best jobs in the newspapers and other media. Although earnings, growth, and openings are important, you also should consider other factors in your career planning. Obviously, you are considering the chances of riding out a recession in the job; that's why you're reading this book. Other examples of factors to consider are location, liking the people you work with, and having opportunities to be creative. Many other factors that may help define the ideal job for you are difficult or impossible to quantify and thus aren't used in this book, so you need to consider the importance of these issues yourself.

❋ All data used to create these lists comes from the U.S. Department of Labor and the Census Bureau. The earnings figures are based on the average annual pay received by full-time workers. Because the earnings represent the national averages, actual pay rates can vary greatly by location, amount of previous work experience, and other factors.

Some Details on the Lists

The sources of the information we used in constructing these lists are presented in this book's introduction. Here are some additional details on how we created the lists:

❋ Some jobs have the same scores for one or more data elements. For example, in the category of fastest-growing, two jobs—Environmental Engineers and Occupational Therapist Assistants—are expected to grow at the same rate, 25.4 percent. Therefore, we ordered these two jobs alphabetically, and their order has no other significance. Avoiding these ties was impossible, so understand simply that the difference of several positions on a list may not mean as much as it seems.

❋ Likewise, it is unwise to place too much emphasis on small differences in outlook information: projections for job growth and job openings. For example, Secondary School Teachers, Except Special and Vocational Education, are projected to have 93,166 job openings per year, whereas 92,977 openings are projected for Medical Assistants. This is a difference of only 189 jobs spread over the entire United States, and of course it is only a projection. Before 2007, the Bureau of Labor Statistics rounded these projections to the nearest 1,000 and would have assigned these two occupations the same figure (93,000), which would have given Medical Assistants the higher rank on the basis of alphabetical ordering. So, again, keep in mind that small differences of position on a list aren't very significant.

❋ Some job titles represent combinations of two or more closely related jobs. For example, here in Part II you will find a job called Clinical, Counseling, and School Psychologists. The U.S. Department of Labor provides data on earnings, job growth, and job openings for this job title, so it is useful for the purposes of these lists. In Part III, however, where you'll turn to find more detailed information about the jobs on these lists, you can find separate descriptions of the jobs Clinical Psychologists, Counseling Psychologists, and School Psychologists. That level of detail is more appropriate for that section of the book.

Best Recession-Proof Jobs Overall: Jobs with the Highest Pay, Fastest Growth, and Most Openings

The four lists that follow are the most important lists in this book. The first list presents the jobs meeting the criteria for this book with the highest combined scores for pay, growth, and number of openings. These are very appealing lists because they represent recession-proof jobs that have the very highest quantifiable measures from our labor market. The 150 jobs in the first list are the basis for all the job lists in Part II and are described in detail in Part III.

The three additional sets of lists present 50 jobs with the highest scores on each of three measures: annual earnings, projected percentage growth, and largest number of openings.

The 150 Best Recession-Proof Jobs Overall

Most people want to see this list first. You can see the recession-proof jobs with the highest overall combined ratings for earnings, projected growth, and number of openings. (The section in the introduction on "How the Best Recession-Proof Jobs Were Selected" explains in detail how we rated jobs to assemble this list.)

The top 20 positions on the list are dominated by jobs in health care and technology, but if you look farther down the list you'll notice many jobs in education, counseling, law enforcement, and transportation. Some fields aren't well represented, however, because they tend to experience layoffs and hiring freezes during hard times. Thus, you'll find few jobs in construction, management, sales, or travel.

A look at the list will clarify how we ordered the jobs. The occupation with the best total score was Computer Systems Analysts, so it tops the list. Coming in at second place is another high-tech job, Network Systems and Data Communications Analysts. Although it offers considerably faster job growth than the top-ranked job, its average earnings are $5,000 less per year and its expected job openings are just over half those of Computer Systems Analysts, so it had a lower total score. The other occupations follow in descending order based on their total scores. Many jobs had tied scores and were simply listed one after another, so often only very small or even no differences exist between the scores of jobs that are near each other on the list. All other job lists in this book (other than the bonus lists) use these jobs as their source list. You can find descriptions for each of these jobs in Part III, beginning on page 115. If a job appeals to you, or if you're not sure what it is, find it alphabetically in Part III and read the description.

The 150 Best Recession-Proof Jobs Overall

Job	Annual Earnings	Percent Growth	Annual Openings
1. Computer Systems Analysts	$69,760	29.0%	63,166
2. Network Systems and Data Communications Analysts	$64,600	53.4%	35,086
3. Network and Computer Systems Administrators	$62,130	27.0%	37,010
4. Registered Nurses	$57,280	23.5%	233,499
5. Teachers, Postsecondary	$57,770	22.9%	237,478
6. Physical Therapists	$66,200	27.1%	12,072
7. Physicians and Surgeons	more than $145,600	14.2%	38,027
8. Dental Hygienists	$62,800	30.1%	10,433
9. Pharmacists	$94,520	21.7%	16,358
10. Medical and Health Services Managers	$73,340	16.4%	31,877
11. Physician Assistants	$74,980	27.0%	7,147
12. Veterinarians	$71,990	35.0%	5,301
13. Database Administrators	$64,670	28.6%	8,258

(continued)

(continued)

The 150 Best Recession-Proof Jobs Overall

Job	Annual Earnings	Percent Growth	Annual Openings
14. Social and Community Service Managers	$52,070	24.7%	23,788
15. Instructional Coordinators	$52,790	22.5%	21,294
16. Environmental Engineers	$69,940	25.4%	5,003
17. Education Administrators, Postsecondary	$73,990	14.2%	17,121
18. Occupational Therapists	$60,470	23.1%	8,338
19. Public Relations Specialists	$47,350	17.6%	51,216
20. Environmental Scientists and Specialists, Including Health	$56,100	25.1%	6,961
21. Detectives and Criminal Investigators	$58,260	17.3%	14,746
22. Actuaries	$82,800	23.7%	3,245
23. Medical Assistants	$26,290	35.4%	92,977
24. Mental Health Counselors	$34,380	30.0%	24,103
25. Substance Abuse and Behavioral Disorder Counselors	$34,040	34.3%	20,821
26. Social and Human Service Assistants	$25,580	33.6%	80,142
27. Educational, Vocational, and School Counselors	$47,530	12.6%	54,025
28. Health Educators	$41,330	26.2%	13,707
29. Clinical, Counseling, and School Psychologists	$59,440	15.8%	8,309
30. Medical and Public Health Social Workers	$43,040	24.2%	16,429
31. Education Administrators, Elementary and Secondary School	$77,740	7.6%	27,143
32. Mental Health and Substance Abuse Social Workers	$35,410	29.9%	17,289
33. Self-Enrichment Education Teachers	$33,440	23.1%	64,449
34. Pharmacy Technicians	$25,630	32.0%	54,453
35. Clergy	$39,680	18.9%	35,092
36. Dental Assistants	$30,220	29.2%	29,482
37. Geoscientists, Except Hydrologists and Geographers	$72,660	21.9%	2,471
38. Child, Family, and School Social Workers	$37,480	19.1%	35,402
39. Kindergarten Teachers, Except Special Education	$43,580	16.3%	27,603
40. Middle School Teachers, Except Special and Vocational Education	$46,300	11.2%	75,270
41. Correctional Officers and Jailers	$35,760	16.9%	56,579
42. Radiologic Technologists and Technicians	$48,170	15.1%	12,836
43. Marriage and Family Therapists	$43,210	29.8%	5,953
44. Physical Therapist Assistants	$41,360	32.4%	5,957
45. Radiation Therapists	$66,170	24.8%	1,461
46. Preschool Teachers, Except Special Education	$22,680	26.3%	78,172
47. Surgical Technologists	$36,080	24.5%	15,365
48. Police and Sheriff's Patrol Officers	$47,460	10.8%	37,842
49. Licensed Practical and Licensed Vocational Nurses	$36,550	14.0%	70,610

The 150 Best Recession-Proof Jobs Overall

Job	Annual Earnings	Percent Growth	Annual Openings
50. Special Education Teachers, Middle School	$47,650	15.8%	8,846
51. Automotive Service Technicians and Mechanics	$33,780	14.3%	97,350
52. Respiratory Therapists	$47,420	22.6%	5,563
53. Secondary School Teachers, Except Special and Vocational Education	$47,740	5.6%	93,166
54. Speech-Language Pathologists	$57,710	10.6%	11,160
55. Diagnostic Medical Sonographers	$57,160	19.1%	3,211
56. First-Line Supervisors/Managers of Police and Detectives	$69,310	9.2%	9,373
57. Medical and Clinical Laboratory Technologists	$49,700	12.4%	11,457
58. Veterinary Technologists and Technicians	$26,780	41.0%	14,674
59. Hydrologists	$66,260	24.3%	687
60. Adult Literacy, Remedial Education, and GED Teachers and Instructors	$43,910	14.2%	17,340
61. Rehabilitation Counselors	$29,200	23.0%	32,081
62. Claims Adjusters, Examiners, and Investigators	$50,660	8.9%	22,024
63. Education Administrators, Preschool and Child Care Center/Program	$37,740	23.5%	8,113
64. Chiropractors	$65,220	14.4%	3,179
65. Cardiovascular Technologists and Technicians	$42,300	25.5%	3,550
66. Nursing Aides, Orderlies, and Attendants	$22,180	18.2%	321,036
67. Medical Records and Health Information Technicians	$28,030	17.8%	39,048
68. Court Reporters	$45,610	24.5%	2,620
69. Industrial-Organizational Psychologists	$86,420	21.3%	118
70. Interpreters and Translators	$35,560	23.6%	6,630
71. First-Line Supervisors/Managers of Fire Fighting and Prevention Workers	$62,900	11.5%	3,771
72. Occupational Therapist Assistants	$42,060	25.4%	2,634
73. Automotive Body and Related Repairers	$35,180	11.6%	37,469
74. Optometrists	$91,040	11.3%	1,789
75. Fire Fighters	$41,190	12.1%	18,887
76. First-Line Supervisors/Managers of Correctional Officers	$52,580	12.5%	4,180
77. Coaches and Scouts	$26,950	14.6%	51,100
78. Probation Officers and Correctional Treatment Specialists	$42,500	10.9%	18,335
79. Emergency Medical Technicians and Paramedics	$27,070	19.2%	19,513
80. Massage Therapists	$33,400	20.3%	9,193
81. Athletes and Sports Competitors	$41,060	19.2%	4,293
82. Audio and Video Equipment Technicians	$34,840	24.2%	4,681

(continued)

(continued)

The 150 Best Recession-Proof Jobs Overall

Job	Annual Earnings	Percent Growth	Annual Openings
83. Environmental Engineering Technicians	$40,560	24.8%	2,162
84. Funeral Directors	$49,620	12.5%	3,939
85. Librarians	$49,060	3.6%	18,945
86. Maintenance and Repair Workers, General	$31,910	10.1%	165,502
87. Nuclear Medicine Technologists	$62,300	14.8%	1,290
88. Budget Analysts	$61,430	7.1%	6,423
89. Special Education Teachers, Secondary School	$48,330	8.5%	10,601
90. Bus Drivers, Transit and Intercity	$32,090	12.5%	27,100
91. Curators	$46,300	23.3%	1,416
92. Private Detectives and Investigators	$33,750	18.2%	7,329
93. Air Traffic Controllers	$117,240	10.2%	1,213
94. Statisticians	$65,720	8.5%	3,433
95. Water and Liquid Waste Treatment Plant and System Operators	$36,070	13.8%	9,575
96. Editors	$46,990	2.3%	20,193
97. Medical and Clinical Laboratory Technicians	$32,840	15.0%	10,866
98. Insurance Underwriters	$52,350	6.3%	6,880
99. Police, Fire, and Ambulance Dispatchers	$31,470	13.6%	17,628
100. Athletic Trainers	$36,560	24.3%	1,669
101. Film and Video Editors	$46,670	12.7%	2,707
102. Gaming Surveillance Officers and Gaming Investigators	$27,130	33.6%	2,124
103. Podiatrists	$108,220	9.5%	648
104. Teacher Assistants	$20,740	10.4%	193,986
105. Judges, Magistrate Judges, and Magistrates	$101,690	5.1%	1,567
106. Mathematicians	$86,930	10.2%	473
107. Economists	$77,010	7.5%	1,555
108. Taxi Drivers and Chauffeurs	$20,350	13.0%	35,954
109. Interviewers, Except Eligibility and Loan	$26,290	9.5%	54,060
110. Postal Service Mail Carriers	$44,350	1.0%	16,710
111. Anthropologists and Archeologists	$49,930	15.0%	446
112. Dietitians and Nutritionists	$46,980	8.6%	4,996
113. Bus Drivers, School	$24,820	9.3%	59,809
114. Computer, Automated Teller, and Office Machine Repairers	$36,480	3.0%	22,330
115. Electrical and Electronics Repairers, Commercial and Industrial Equipment	$45,180	6.8%	6,607
116. Insurance Appraisers, Auto Damage	$49,180	12.5%	1,030
117. Nuclear Power Reactor Operators	$69,370	10.6%	233

The 150 Best Recession-Proof Jobs Overall

Job	Annual Earnings	Percent Growth	Annual Openings
118. Vocational Education Teachers, Secondary School	$48,690	–4.6%	7,639
119. Automotive Glass Installers and Repairers	$30,720	18.7%	3,457
120. Physical Therapist Aides	$22,060	24.4%	4,092
121. Pest Control Workers	$27,880	15.5%	6,006
122. Medical Equipment Preparers	$25,950	14.2%	8,363
123. Library Technicians	$26,560	8.5%	29,075
124. Audiologists	$57,120	9.8%	980
125. Political Scientists	$90,140	5.3%	318
126. Inspectors, Testers, Sorters, Samplers, and Weighers	$29,420	–7.0%	75,361
127. Embalmers	$37,840	14.3%	1,660
128. Sociologists	$60,290	10.0%	403
129. Food Scientists and Technologists	$53,810	10.3%	663
130. Ambulance Drivers and Attendants, Except Emergency Medical Technicians	$20,370	21.7%	3,703
131. Arbitrators, Mediators, and Conciliators	$49,490	10.6%	546
132. Power Plant Operators	$55,000	2.7%	1,796
133. Tax Examiners, Collectors, and Revenue Agents	$45,620	2.1%	4,465
134. Soil and Plant Scientists	$56,080	8.4%	850
135. Fire Inspectors and Investigators	$48,050	11.0%	644
136. Administrative Law Judges, Adjudicators, and Hearing Officers	$72,600	0.1%	794
137. Archivists	$40,730	14.4%	795
138. Museum Technicians and Conservators	$34,340	15.9%	1,341
139. Postal Service Mail Sorters, Processors, and Processing Machine Operators	$43,900	–8.4%	6,855
140. Dietetic Technicians	$24,040	14.8%	4,062
141. Funeral Attendants	$20,350	14.3%	6,034
142. Postal Service Clerks	$44,800	1.2%	3,703
143. Electrical and Electronics Repairers, Powerhouse, Substation, and Relay	$57,400	–4.7%	1,591
144. Hazardous Materials Removal Workers	$35,450	11.2%	1,933
145. Postmasters and Mail Superintendents	$55,790	–0.8%	1,627
146. Bailiffs	$34,210	11.2%	2,223
147. Library Assistants, Clerical	$21,640	7.9%	18,961
148. Animal Control Workers	$27,910	12.5%	3,377
149. Broadcast Technicians	$30,690	12.1%	2,955
150. Animal Scientists	$47,800	9.8%	299

The 50 Best-Paying Recession-Proof Jobs

On the following list you'll find the 50 best-paying jobs that met our criteria for this book. This list is appealing, for obvious reasons.

It shouldn't be a big surprise to learn that most of the highest-paying jobs require advanced levels of education, training, or experience. For example, a bachelor's degree or higher is needed for all but one of the top 20 jobs—and in that exceptional job, Air Traffic Controllers, almost one-third of the workers have a bachelor's. In fact, most of these top 20 jobs require an *additional* degree or work experience beyond the bachelor's. Although the top 20 jobs may not appeal to you for various reasons, you are likely to find others that will among the top 50 jobs with the highest earnings.

Keep in mind that the earnings reflect the national average for all workers in the occupation. This is an important consideration because starting pay in the job is usually much less than the pay that workers can earn with several years of experience. Earnings also vary significantly by region of the country, so actual pay in your area could be substantially different.

The 50 Best-Paying Recession-Proof Jobs

Job	Annual Earnings
1. Physicians and Surgeons	more than $145,600
2. Air Traffic Controllers	$117,240
3. Podiatrists	$108,220
4. Judges, Magistrate Judges, and Magistrates	$101,690
5. Pharmacists	$94,520
6. Optometrists	$91,040
7. Political Scientists	$90,140
8. Mathematicians	$86,930
9. Industrial-Organizational Psychologists	$86,420
10. Actuaries	$82,800
11. Education Administrators, Elementary and Secondary School	$77,740
12. Economists	$77,010
13. Physician Assistants	$74,980
14. Education Administrators, Postsecondary	$73,990
15. Medical and Health Services Managers	$73,340
16. Geoscientists, Except Hydrologists and Geographers	$72,660
17. Administrative Law Judges, Adjudicators, and Hearing Officers	$72,600
18. Veterinarians	$71,990
19. Environmental Engineers	$69,940
20. Computer Systems Analysts	$69,760
21. Nuclear Power Reactor Operators	$69,370

The 50 Best-Paying Recession-Proof Jobs

Job	Annual Earnings
22. First-Line Supervisors/Managers of Police and Detectives	$69,310
23. Hydrologists	$66,260
24. Physical Therapists	$66,200
25. Radiation Therapists	$66,170
26. Statisticians	$65,720
27. Chiropractors	$65,220
28. Database Administrators	$64,670
29. Network Systems and Data Communications Analysts	$64,600
30. First-Line Supervisors/Managers of Fire Fighting and Prevention Workers	$62,900
31. Dental Hygienists	$62,800
32. Nuclear Medicine Technologists	$62,300
33. Network and Computer Systems Administrators	$62,130
34. Budget Analysts	$61,430
35. Occupational Therapists	$60,470
36. Sociologists	$60,290
37. Clinical, Counseling, and School Psychologists	$59,440
38. Detectives and Criminal Investigators	$58,260
39. Teachers, Postsecondary	$57,770
40. Speech-Language Pathologists	$57,710
41. Electrical and Electronics Repairers, Powerhouse, Substation, and Relay	$57,400
42. Registered Nurses	$57,280
43. Diagnostic Medical Sonographers	$57,160
44. Audiologists	$57,120
45. Environmental Scientists and Specialists, Including Health	$56,100
46. Soil and Plant Scientists	$56,080
47. Postmasters and Mail Superintendents	$55,790
48. Power Plant Operators	$55,000
49. Food Scientists and Technologists	$53,810
50. Instructional Coordinators	$52,790

The 50 Fastest-Growing Recession-Proof Jobs

From the list of the 150 best recession-proof jobs, this list shows the 50 jobs projected to have the highest percentage increase in the numbers of people employed through 2016.

The top of this list is dominated by jobs in health care, social services, and technology, but these jobs cover a wide range of levels of training and education, and many other fields are represented elsewhere in the list.

The 50 Fastest-Growing Recession-Proof Jobs

Job	Percent Growth
1. Network Systems and Data Communications Analysts	53.4%
2. Veterinary Technologists and Technicians	41.0%
3. Medical Assistants	35.4%
4. Veterinarians	35.0%
5. Substance Abuse and Behavioral Disorder Counselors	34.3%
6. Gaming Surveillance Officers and Gaming Investigators	33.6%
7. Social and Human Service Assistants	33.6%
8. Physical Therapist Assistants	32.4%
9. Pharmacy Technicians	32.0%
10. Dental Hygienists	30.1%
11. Mental Health Counselors	30.0%
12. Mental Health and Substance Abuse Social Workers	29.9%
13. Marriage and Family Therapists	29.8%
14. Dental Assistants	29.2%
15. Computer Systems Analysts	29.0%
16. Database Administrators	28.6%
17. Physical Therapists	27.1%
18. Network and Computer Systems Administrators	27.0%
19. Physician Assistants	27.0%
20. Preschool Teachers, Except Special Education	26.3%
21. Health Educators	26.2%
22. Cardiovascular Technologists and Technicians	25.5%
23. Environmental Engineers	25.4%
24. Occupational Therapist Assistants	25.4%
25. Environmental Scientists and Specialists, Including Health	25.1%
26. Environmental Engineering Technicians	24.8%
27. Radiation Therapists	24.8%
28. Social and Community Service Managers	24.7%
29. Court Reporters	24.5%
30. Surgical Technologists	24.5%
31. Physical Therapist Aides	24.4%
32. Athletic Trainers	24.3%
33. Hydrologists	24.3%
34. Audio and Video Equipment Technicians	24.2%
35. Medical and Public Health Social Workers	24.2%
36. Actuaries	23.7%
37. Interpreters and Translators	23.6%
38. Education Administrators, Preschool and Child Care Center/Program	23.5%

The 50 Fastest-Growing Recession-Proof Jobs

Job	Percent Growth
39. Registered Nurses	23.5%
40. Curators	23.3%
41. Occupational Therapists	23.1%
42. Self-Enrichment Education Teachers	23.1%
43. Rehabilitation Counselors	23.0%
44. Teachers, Postsecondary	22.9%
45. Respiratory Therapists	22.6%
46. Instructional Coordinators	22.5%
47. Geoscientists, Except Hydrologists and Geographers	21.9%
48. Ambulance Drivers and Attendants, Except Emergency Medical Technicians	21.7%
49. Pharmacists	21.7%
50. Industrial-Organizational Psychologists	21.3%

The 50 Recession-Proof Jobs with the Most Openings

From the list of 150 best recession-proof jobs, this list shows the 50 jobs projected to have the largest number of job openings per year through 2016. Keep in mind that these figures for job openings are average yearly openings over a 10-year period. Although these jobs are considered not sensitive to economic fluctuations, the number of openings is likely to vary somewhat from year to year.

Jobs with many openings present several advantages that you may find attractive. Employment can be easier to obtain, particularly for those just entering the job market. These jobs may also offer more opportunities to move from one employer to another with relative ease. Although some of these jobs have average or below-average pay, some also pay quite well and can provide good long-term career opportunities. This list is especially noteworthy because many of the jobs require only on-the-job training.

The 50 Recession-Proof Jobs with the Most Openings

Job	Annual Openings
1. Nursing Aides, Orderlies, and Attendants	321,036
2. Teachers, Postsecondary	237,478
3. Registered Nurses	233,499
4. Teacher Assistants	193,986
5. Maintenance and Repair Workers, General	165,502

(continued)

(continued)

The 50 Recession-Proof Jobs with the Most Openings

Job	Annual Openings
6. Automotive Service Technicians and Mechanics	97,350
7. Secondary School Teachers, Except Special and Vocational Education	93,166
8. Medical Assistants	92,977
9. Social and Human Service Assistants	80,142
10. Preschool Teachers, Except Special Education	78,172
11. Inspectors, Testers, Sorters, Samplers, and Weighers	75,361
12. Middle School Teachers, Except Special and Vocational Education	75,270
13. Licensed Practical and Licensed Vocational Nurses	70,610
14. Self-Enrichment Education Teachers	64,449
15. Computer Systems Analysts	63,166
16. Bus Drivers, School	59,809
17. Correctional Officers and Jailers	56,579
18. Pharmacy Technicians	54,453
19. Interviewers, Except Eligibility and Loan	54,060
20. Educational, Vocational, and School Counselors	54,025
21. Public Relations Specialists	51,216
22. Coaches and Scouts	51,100
23. Medical Records and Health Information Technicians	39,048
24. Physicians and Surgeons	38,027
25. Police and Sheriff's Patrol Officers	37,842
26. Automotive Body and Related Repairers	37,469
27. Network and Computer Systems Administrators	37,010
28. Taxi Drivers and Chauffeurs	35,954
29. Child, Family, and School Social Workers	35,402
30. Clergy	35,092
31. Network Systems and Data Communications Analysts	35,086
32. Rehabilitation Counselors	32,081
33. Medical and Health Services Managers	31,877
34. Dental Assistants	29,482
35. Library Technicians	29,075
36. Kindergarten Teachers, Except Special Education	27,603
37. Education Administrators, Elementary and Secondary School	27,143
38. Bus Drivers, Transit and Intercity	27,100
39. Mental Health Counselors	24,103
40. Social and Community Service Managers	23,788
41. Computer, Automated Teller, and Office Machine Repairers	22,330
42. Claims Adjusters, Examiners, and Investigators	22,024

The 50 Recession-Proof Jobs with the Most Openings

Job	Annual Openings
43. Instructional Coordinators	21,294
44. Substance Abuse and Behavioral Disorder Counselors	20,821
45. Editors	20,193
46. Emergency Medical Technicians and Paramedics	19,513
47. Library Assistants, Clerical	18,961
48. Librarians	18,945
49. Fire Fighters	18,887
50. Probation Officers and Correctional Treatment Specialists	18,335

Best Recession-Proof Jobs Lists by Demographic

We decided it would be interesting to include lists in this section that show what sorts of jobs different types of people are most likely to have. For example, what recession-proof jobs have the highest percentage of men or young workers? We're not saying that men or young people should consider these jobs over others, but it is interesting information to know.

In some cases, the lists can give you ideas for jobs to consider that you might otherwise overlook. For example, perhaps women should consider some jobs that traditionally have high percentages of men in them. Or older workers might consider some jobs typically held by young people. Although these aren't obvious ways of using these lists, the lists may give you some good ideas of jobs to consider. The lists may also help you identify jobs that work well for others in your situation—for example, jobs with plentiful opportunities for part-time work, if that's something you want to do.

All lists in this section were created through a similar process. We began with the 150 best recession-proof jobs. Next, we sorted those jobs in order of the primary criterion for each set of lists. For example, we sorted the 150 jobs based on the percentage of workers age 55 and over from highest to lowest percentage, and then selected the jobs with a high percentage (98 jobs with a percentage greater than 15). From this initial list of jobs with a high percentage of each type of worker, we created four more-specialized lists:

* 25 Best Jobs Overall (the subset of jobs that have the highest combined scores for earnings, growth rate, and number of openings)
* 25 Best-Paying Jobs
* 25 Fastest-Growing Jobs
* 25 Jobs with the Most Openings

Again, each of these four lists includes only jobs that have high percentages of different types of workers. The same basic process was used to create all the lists in this section, although in one demographic the number of jobs is less than 25. The lists are very interesting, and we hope you find them helpful.

Best Recession-Proof Jobs with the Highest Percentage of Workers Age 16–24

These jobs have higher percentages (more than 15 percent) of workers between the ages of 16 and 24. Young people are found in almost all jobs, but those with higher percentages of young people may present more opportunities for initial entry. On the other hand, jobs with a large showing of young people also tend to be economically sensitive, so it's no coincidence that the following lists are the shortest in this section, with only 22 jobs.

Best Recession-Proof Jobs with the Highest Percentage of Workers Age 16–24	
Job	Percent Age 16–24
1. Athletes and Sports Competitors	34.5%
2. Coaches and Scouts	34.5%
3. Library Technicians	32.5%
4. Library Assistants, Clerical	28.5%
5. Ambulance Drivers and Attendants, Except Emergency Medical Technicians	26.4%
6. Dietetic Technicians	24.7%
7. Pharmacy Technicians	24.7%
8. Surgical Technologists	24.7%
9. Veterinary Technologists and Technicians	24.7%
10. Hazardous Materials Removal Workers	22.6%
11. Interviewers, Except Eligibility and Loan	20.9%
12. Medical Assistants	19.5%
13. Medical Equipment Preparers	19.5%
14. Automotive Glass Installers and Repairers	19.1%
15. Automotive Body and Related Repairers	19.0%
16. Dental Assistants	18.5%
17. Nursing Aides, Orderlies, and Attendants	17.8%
18. Adult Literacy, Remedial Education, and GED Teachers and Instructors	17.4%
19. Self-Enrichment Education Teachers	17.4%
20. Emergency Medical Technicians and Paramedics	17.3%
21. Automotive Service Technicians and Mechanics	16.2%
22. Gaming Surveillance Officers and Gaming Investigators	16.2%

The jobs in the following four lists are derived from the preceding list of the recession-proof jobs with the highest percentage of workers age 16–24.

Best Recession-Proof Jobs Overall with a High Percentage of Workers Age 16–24

Job	Percent Age 16–24	Annual Earnings	Percent Growth	Annual Openings
1. Self-Enrichment Education Teachers	17.4%	$33,440	23.1%	64,449
2. Medical Assistants	19.5%	$26,290	35.4%	92,977
3. Automotive Service Technicians and Mechanics	16.2%	$33,780	14.3%	97,350
4. Dental Assistants	18.5%	$30,220	29.2%	29,482
5. Surgical Technologists	24.7%	$36,080	24.5%	15,365
6. Pharmacy Technicians	24.7%	$25,630	32.0%	54,453
7. Athletes and Sports Competitors	34.5%	$41,060	19.2%	4,293
8. Veterinary Technologists and Technicians	24.7%	$26,780	41.0%	14,674
9. Adult Literacy, Remedial Education, and GED Teachers and Instructors	17.4%	$43,910	14.2%	17,340
10. Automotive Body and Related Repairers	19.0%	$35,180	11.6%	37,469
11. Emergency Medical Technicians and Paramedics	17.3%	$27,070	19.2%	19,513
12. Coaches and Scouts	34.5%	$26,950	14.6%	51,100
13. Nursing Aides, Orderlies, and Attendants	17.8%	$22,180	18.2%	321,036
14. Gaming Surveillance Officers and Gaming Investigators	16.2%	$27,130	33.6%	2,124
15. Automotive Glass Installers and Repairers	19.1%	$30,720	18.7%	3,457
16. Interviewers, Except Eligibility and Loan	20.9%	$26,290	9.5%	54,060
17. Hazardous Materials Removal Workers	22.6%	$35,450	11.2%	1,933
18. Library Technicians	32.5%	$26,560	8.5%	29,075
19. Ambulance Drivers and Attendants, Except Emergency Medical Technicians	26.4%	$20,370	21.7%	3,703
20. Medical Equipment Preparers	19.5%	$25,950	14.2%	8,363
21. Dietetic Technicians	24.7%	$24,040	14.8%	4,062
22. Library Assistants, Clerical	28.5%	$21,640	7.9%	18,961

Best-Paying Recession-Proof Jobs for Workers Age 16–24

Job	Percent Age 16–24	Annual Earnings
1. Adult Literacy, Remedial Education, and GED Teachers and Instructors	17.4%	$43,910
2. Athletes and Sports Competitors	34.5%	$41,060

(continued)

(continued)

Best-Paying Recession-Proof Jobs for Workers Age 16–24

Job	Percent Age 16–24	Annual Earnings
3. Surgical Technologists	24.7%	$36,080
4. Hazardous Materials Removal Workers	22.6%	$35,450
5. Automotive Body and Related Repairers	19.0%	$35,180
6. Automotive Service Technicians and Mechanics	16.2%	$33,780
7. Self-Enrichment Education Teachers	17.4%	$33,440
8. Automotive Glass Installers and Repairers	19.1%	$30,720
9. Dental Assistants	18.5%	$30,220
10. Gaming Surveillance Officers and Gaming Investigators	16.2%	$27,130
11. Emergency Medical Technicians and Paramedics	17.3%	$27,070
12. Coaches and Scouts	34.5%	$26,950
13. Veterinary Technologists and Technicians	24.7%	$26,780
14. Library Technicians	32.5%	$26,560
15. Interviewers, Except Eligibility and Loan	20.9%	$26,290
16. Medical Assistants	19.5%	$26,290
17. Medical Equipment Preparers	19.5%	$25,950
18. Pharmacy Technicians	24.7%	$25,630
19. Dietetic Technicians	24.7%	$24,040
20. Nursing Aides, Orderlies, and Attendants	17.8%	$22,180
21. Library Assistants, Clerical	28.5%	$21,640
22. Ambulance Drivers and Attendants, Except Emergency Medical Technicians	26.4%	$20,370

Fastest-Growing Recession-Proof Jobs for Workers Age 16–24

Job	Percent Age 16–24	Percent Growth
1. Veterinary Technologists and Technicians	24.7%	41.0%
2. Medical Assistants	19.5%	35.4%
3. Gaming Surveillance Officers and Gaming Investigators	16.2%	33.6%
4. Pharmacy Technicians	24.7%	32.0%
5. Dental Assistants	18.5%	29.2%
6. Surgical Technologists	24.7%	24.5%
7. Self-Enrichment Education Teachers	17.4%	23.1%
8. Ambulance Drivers and Attendants, Except Emergency Medical Technicians	26.4%	21.7%
9. Athletes and Sports Competitors	34.5%	19.2%

Fastest-Growing Recession-Proof Jobs for Workers Age 16–24

Job	Percent Age 16–24	Percent Growth
10. Emergency Medical Technicians and Paramedics	17.3%	19.2%
11. Automotive Glass Installers and Repairers	19.1%	18.7%
12. Nursing Aides, Orderlies, and Attendants	17.8%	18.2%
13. Dietetic Technicians	24.7%	14.8%
14. Coaches and Scouts	34.5%	14.6%
15. Automotive Service Technicians and Mechanics	16.2%	14.3%
16. Adult Literacy, Remedial Education, and GED Teachers and Instructors	17.4%	14.2%
17. Medical Equipment Preparers	19.5%	14.2%
18. Automotive Body and Related Repairers	19.0%	11.6%
19. Hazardous Materials Removal Workers	22.6%	11.2%
20. Interviewers, Except Eligibility and Loan	20.9%	9.5%
21. Library Technicians	32.5%	8.5%
22. Library Assistants, Clerical	28.5%	7.9%

Recession-Proof Jobs with the Most Openings for Workers Age 16–24

Job	Percent Age 16–24	Annual Openings
1. Nursing Aides, Orderlies, and Attendants	17.8%	321,036
2. Automotive Service Technicians and Mechanics	16.2%	97,350
3. Medical Assistants	19.5%	92,977
4. Self-Enrichment Education Teachers	17.4%	64,449
5. Pharmacy Technicians	24.7%	54,453
6. Interviewers, Except Eligibility and Loan	20.9%	54,060
7. Coaches and Scouts	34.5%	51,100
8. Automotive Body and Related Repairers	19.0%	37,469
9. Dental Assistants	18.5%	29,482
10. Library Technicians	32.5%	29,075
11. Emergency Medical Technicians and Paramedics	17.3%	19,513
12. Library Assistants, Clerical	28.5%	18,961
13. Adult Literacy, Remedial Education, and GED Teachers and Instructors	17.4%	17,340
14. Surgical Technologists	24.7%	15,365
15. Veterinary Technologists and Technicians	24.7%	14,674
16. Medical Equipment Preparers	19.5%	8,363
17. Athletes and Sports Competitors	34.5%	4,293
18. Dietetic Technicians	24.7%	4,062

(continued)

(continued)

Recession-Proof Jobs with the Most Openings for Workers Age 16–24

Job	Percent Age 16–24	Annual Openings
19. Ambulance Drivers and Attendants, Except Emergency Medical Technicians	26.4%	3,703
20. Automotive Glass Installers and Repairers	19.1%	3,457
21. Gaming Surveillance Officers and Gaming Investigators	16.2%	2,124
22. Hazardous Materials Removal Workers	22.6%	1,933

Best Recession-Proof Jobs with a High Percentage of Workers Age 55 and Over

We created the following list by identifying the best recession-proof jobs in which more than 15 percent of workers are age 55 and over.

You may be surprised to note that 98 of the best 150 jobs meet this cutoff, whereas only 22 employ the same percentage of people age 16–24. Obviously, the older age bracket has a much greater presence in recession-proof jobs. One reason is that we selected our 150 best jobs partly by eliminating all jobs with annual earnings of less than $20,270, so a lot of entry-level jobs with high concentrations of young people were among those removed. Also, many of the recession-proof jobs require advanced education or years of work experience—credentials that people younger than 25 are unlikely to have on their resumes. Finally, over the course of a working lifetime, people tend to lose recession-sensitive jobs when economic downturns strike, and the jobs they find during those hard times tend to be available because they're recession-proof. By the time these workers reach age 55 and have weathered several recessions, they are more likely to have settled into a recession-proof occupation.

Best Recession-Proof Jobs with the Highest Percentage of Workers Age 55 and Over

Job	Percent Age 55 and Over
1. Clergy	42.0%
2. Librarians	39.0%
3. Bus Drivers, School	38.2%
4. Bus Drivers, Transit and Intercity	38.2%
5. Sociologists	37.8%
6. Clinical, Counseling, and School Psychologists	35.0%
7. Industrial-Organizational Psychologists	35.0%

Best Recession-Proof Jobs with the Highest Percentage of Workers Age 55 and Over

Job	Percent Age 55 and Over
8. Archivists	32.5%
9. Curators	32.5%
10. Museum Technicians and Conservators	32.5%
11. Taxi Drivers and Chauffeurs	31.4%
12. Funeral Directors	31.0%
13. Private Detectives and Investigators	30.4%
14. Instructional Coordinators	30.4%
15. Postal Service Clerks	29.8%
16. Teachers, Postsecondary	29.0%
17. Education Administrators, Elementary and Secondary School	28.7%
18. Education Administrators, Postsecondary	28.7%
19. Education Administrators, Preschool and Child Care Center/Program	28.7%
20. Veterinarians	28.4%
21. Administrative Law Judges, Adjudicators, and Hearing Officers	27.8%
22. Arbitrators, Mediators, and Conciliators	27.8%
23. Judges, Magistrate Judges, and Magistrates	27.8%
24. Physicians and Surgeons	27.2%
25. Medical Records and Health Information Technicians	26.1%
26. Electrical and Electronics Repairers, Commercial and Industrial Equipment	26.0%
27. Electrical and Electronics Repairers, Powerhouse, Substation, and Relay	26.0%
28. Library Assistants, Clerical	25.7%
29. Audiologists	25.6%
30. Educational, Vocational, and School Counselors	25.3%
31. Maintenance and Repair Workers, General	25.3%
32. Marriage and Family Therapists	25.3%
33. Mental Health Counselors	25.3%
34. Rehabilitation Counselors	25.3%
35. Social and Community Service Managers	25.3%
36. Substance Abuse and Behavioral Disorder Counselors	25.3%
37. Gaming Surveillance Officers and Gaming Investigators	24.9%
38. Postal Service Mail Sorters, Processors, and Processing Machine Operators	24.8%
39. Medical and Health Services Managers	24.7%
40. Optometrists	24.6%
41. Postal Service Mail Carriers	24.2%
42. Budget Analysts	23.0%

(continued)

(continued)

Best Recession-Proof Jobs with the Highest Percentage of Workers Age 55 and Over

Job	Percent Age 55 and Over
43. Environmental Scientists and Specialists, Including Health	22.6%
44. Geoscientists, Except Hydrologists and Geographers	22.6%
45. Hydrologists	22.6%
46. Pharmacists	22.5%
47. Secondary School Teachers, Except Special and Vocational Education	22.2%
48. Vocational Education Teachers, Secondary School	22.2%
49. Adult Literacy, Remedial Education, and GED Teachers and Instructors	22.1%
50. Economists	22.1%
51. Self-Enrichment Education Teachers	22.1%
52. Interviewers, Except Eligibility and Loan	22.0%
53. Licensed Practical and Licensed Vocational Nurses	22.0%
54. Middle School Teachers, Except Special and Vocational Education	22.0%
55. Fire Inspectors and Investigators	21.6%
56. Tax Examiners, Collectors, and Revenue Agents	21.5%
57. Embalmers	21.4%
58. Anthropologists and Archeologists	21.2%
59. Political Scientists	21.2%
60. Registered Nurses	21.0%
61. Database Administrators	20.0%
62. Hazardous Materials Removal Workers	20.0%
63. Mathematicians	20.0%
64. Child, Family, and School Social Workers	19.9%
65. Medical and Public Health Social Workers	19.9%
66. Mental Health and Substance Abuse Social Workers	19.9%
67. Water and Liquid Waste Treatment Plant and System Operators	19.9%
68. Medical and Clinical Laboratory Technicians	19.8%
69. Medical and Clinical Laboratory Technologists	19.8%
70. Statisticians	19.7%
71. Environmental Engineering Technicians	19.6%
72. Special Education Teachers, Middle School	19.5%
73. Special Education Teachers, Secondary School	19.5%
74. Occupational Therapist Assistants	19.0%
75. Claims Adjusters, Examiners, and Investigators	18.9%
76. Insurance Appraisers, Auto Damage	18.9%
77. Interpreters and Translators	18.7%

Best Recession-Proof Jobs with the Highest Percentage of Workers Age 55 and Over

Job	Percent Age 55 and Over
78. Inspectors, Testers, Sorters, Samplers, and Weighers	18.5%
79. Athletic Trainers	18.4%
80. Automotive Body and Related Repairers	18.4%
81. Health Educators	18.3%
82. Probation Officers and Correctional Treatment Specialists	18.3%
83. Social and Human Service Assistants	18.3%
84. Court Reporters	18.2%
85. Ambulance Drivers and Attendants, Except Emergency Medical Technicians	18.1%
86. Editors	18.0%
87. Public Relations Specialists	17.6%
88. Chiropractors	17.5%
89. Library Technicians	17.5%
90. Nursing Aides, Orderlies, and Attendants	17.5%
91. Dietitians and Nutritionists	17.3%
92. Teacher Assistants	17.3%
93. Respiratory Therapists	17.1%
94. Speech-Language Pathologists	17.1%
95. First-Line Supervisors/Managers of Fire Fighting and Prevention Workers	16.8%
96. Environmental Engineers	16.2%
97. Nuclear Power Reactor Operators	16.0%
98. Power Plant Operators	16.0%

The jobs in the following four lists are derived from the preceding list of the recession-proof jobs with the highest percentage of workers age 55 and over.

Best Recession-Proof Jobs Overall with a High Percentage of Workers Age 55 and Over

Job	Percent Age 55 and Over	Annual Earnings	Percent Growth	Annual Openings
1. Registered Nurses	21.0%	$57,280	23.5%	233,499
2. Teachers, Postsecondary	29.0%	$57,770	22.9%	237,478
3. Physicians and Surgeons	27.2% more than	$145,600	14.2%	38,027
4. Medical and Health Services Managers	24.7%	$73,340	16.4%	31,877
5. Pharmacists	22.5%	$94,520	21.7%	16,358
6. Social and Community Service Managers	25.3%	$52,070	24.7%	23,788

(continued)

Best Recession-Proof Jobs Overall with a High Percentage of Workers Age 55 and Over

Job	Percent Age 55 and Over	Annual Earnings	Percent Growth	Annual Openings
7. Veterinarians	28.4%	$71,990	35.0%	5,301
8. Database Administrators	20.0%	$64,670	28.6%	8,258
9. Environmental Engineers	16.2%	$69,940	25.4%	5,003
10. Instructional Coordinators	30.4%	$52,790	22.5%	21,294
11. Education Administrators, Postsecondary	28.7%	$73,990	14.2%	17,121
12. Environmental Scientists and Specialists, Including Health	22.6%	$56,100	25.1%	6,961
13. Public Relations Specialists	17.6%	$47,350	17.6%	51,216
14. Social and Human Service Assistants	18.3%	$25,580	33.6%	80,142
15. Mental Health Counselors	25.3%	$34,380	30.0%	24,103
16. Clinical, Counseling, and School Psychologists	35.0%	$59,440	15.8%	8,309
17. Educational, Vocational, and School Counselors	25.3%	$47,530	12.6%	54,025
18. Geoscientists, Except Hydrologists and Geographers	22.6%	$72,660	21.9%	2,471
19. Substance Abuse and Behavioral Disorder Counselors	25.3%	$34,040	34.3%	20,821
20. Education Administrators, Elementary and Secondary School	28.7%	$77,740	7.6%	27,143
21. Health Educators	18.3%	$41,330	26.2%	13,707
22. Self-Enrichment Education Teachers	22.1%	$33,440	23.1%	64,449
23. Medical and Public Health Social Workers	19.9%	$43,040	24.2%	16,429
24. Mental Health and Substance Abuse Social Workers	19.9%	$35,410	29.9%	17,289
25. Clergy	42.0%	$39,680	18.9%	35,092

Best-Paying Recession-Proof Jobs for Workers Age 55 and Over

Job	Percent Age 55 and Over	Annual Earnings
1. Physicians and Surgeons	27.2%	more than $145,600
2. Judges, Magistrate Judges, and Magistrates	27.8%	$101,690
3. Pharmacists	22.5%	$94,520
4. Optometrists	24.6%	$91,040
5. Political Scientists	21.2%	$90,140
6. Mathematicians	20.0%	$86,930

Best-Paying Recession-Proof Jobs for Workers Age 55 and Over

Job	Percent Age 55 and Over	Annual Earnings
7. Industrial-Organizational Psychologists	35.0%	$86,420
8. Education Administrators, Elementary and Secondary School	28.7%	$77,740
9. Economists	22.1%	$77,010
10. Education Administrators, Postsecondary	28.7%	$73,990
11. Medical and Health Services Managers	24.7%	$73,340
12. Geoscientists, Except Hydrologists and Geographers	22.6%	$72,660
13. Administrative Law Judges, Adjudicators, and Hearing Officers	27.8%	$72,600
14. Veterinarians	28.4%	$71,990
15. Environmental Engineers	16.2%	$69,940
16. Nuclear Power Reactor Operators	16.0%	$69,370
17. Hydrologists	22.6%	$66,260
18. Statisticians	19.7%	$65,720
19. Chiropractors	17.5%	$65,220
20. Database Administrators	20.0%	$64,670
21. First-Line Supervisors/Managers of Fire Fighting and Prevention Workers	16.8%	$62,900
22. Budget Analysts	23.0%	$61,430
23. Sociologists	37.8%	$60,290
24. Clinical, Counseling, and School Psychologists	35.0%	$59,440
25. Teachers, Postsecondary	29.0%	$57,770

Fastest-Growing Recession-Proof Jobs for Workers Age 55 and Over

Job	Percent Age 55 and Over	Percent Growth
1. Veterinarians	28.4%	35.0%
2. Substance Abuse and Behavioral Disorder Counselors	25.3%	34.3%
3. Gaming Surveillance Officers and Gaming Investigators	24.9%	33.6%
4. Social and Human Service Assistants	18.3%	33.6%
5. Mental Health Counselors	25.3%	30.0%
6. Mental Health and Substance Abuse Social Workers	19.9%	29.9%
7. Marriage and Family Therapists	25.3%	29.8%
8. Database Administrators	20.0%	28.6%
9. Health Educators	18.3%	26.2%
10. Environmental Engineers	16.2%	25.4%

(continued)

(continued)

Fastest-Growing Recession-Proof Jobs for Workers Age 55 and Over

Job	Percent Age 55 and Over	Percent Growth
11. Occupational Therapist Assistants	19.0%	25.4%
12. Environmental Scientists and Specialists, Including Health	22.6%	25.1%
13. Environmental Engineering Technicians	19.6%	24.8%
14. Social and Community Service Managers	25.3%	24.7%
15. Court Reporters	18.2%	24.5%
16. Athletic Trainers	18.4%	24.3%
17. Hydrologists	22.6%	24.3%
18. Medical and Public Health Social Workers	19.9%	24.2%
19. Interpreters and Translators	18.7%	23.6%
20. Education Administrators, Preschool and Child Care Center/Program	28.7%	23.5%
21. Registered Nurses	21.0%	23.5%
22. Curators	32.5%	23.3%
23. Self-Enrichment Education Teachers	22.1%	23.1%
24. Rehabilitation Counselors	25.3%	23.0%
25. Teachers, Postsecondary	29.0%	22.9%

Recession-Proof Jobs with the Most Openings for Workers Age 55 and Over

Job	Percent Age 55 and Over	Annual Openings
1. Nursing Aides, Orderlies, and Attendants	17.5%	321,036
2. Teachers, Postsecondary	29.0%	237,478
3. Registered Nurses	21.0%	233,499
4. Teacher Assistants	17.3%	193,986
5. Maintenance and Repair Workers, General	25.3%	165,502
6. Secondary School Teachers, Except Special and Vocational Education	22.2%	93,166
7. Social and Human Service Assistants	18.3%	80,142
8. Inspectors, Testers, Sorters, Samplers, and Weighers	18.5%	75,361
9. Middle School Teachers, Except Special and Vocational Education	22.0%	75,270
10. Licensed Practical and Licensed Vocational Nurses	22.0%	70,610
11. Self-Enrichment Education Teachers	22.1%	64,449
12. Bus Drivers, School	38.2%	59,809
13. Interviewers, Except Eligibility and Loan	22.0%	54,060

Recession-Proof Jobs with the Most Openings for Workers Age 55 and Over

Job	Percent Age 55 and Over	Annual Openings
14. Educational, Vocational, and School Counselors	25.3%	54,025
15. Public Relations Specialists	17.6%	51,216
16. Medical Records and Health Information Technicians	26.1%	39,048
17. Physicians and Surgeons	27.2%	38,027
18. Automotive Body and Related Repairers	18.4%	37,469
19. Taxi Drivers and Chauffeurs	31.4%	35,954
20. Child, Family, and School Social Workers	19.9%	35,402
21. Clergy	42.0%	35,092
22. Rehabilitation Counselors	25.3%	32,081
23. Medical and Health Services Managers	24.7%	31,877
24. Library Technicians	17.5%	29,075
25. Education Administrators, Elementary and Secondary School	28.7%	27,143

Best Recession-Proof Jobs with a High Percentage of Part-Time Workers

Health care and education are the main industries represented in the following lists of the recession-proof jobs with high percentages (more than 20 percent) of part-time workers.

In some cases, people work part time because they want the freedom of time this arrangement can provide, but others may do so because they can't find full-time employment in these jobs. These folks may work in other full- or part-time jobs to make ends meet. If you want to work part time now or in the future, these lists will help you identify recession-proof jobs that are more likely to provide that opportunity. If you want full-time work, the lists may also help you identify recession-proof jobs for which such opportunities are more difficult to find. In either case, it's good information to know in advance.

Note: The earnings estimates in the following lists are based on a survey of both part-time and full-time workers. On average, part-time workers earn about 10 percent less per hour than full-time workers.

Best Recession-Proof Jobs with the Highest Percentage of Part-Time Workers

Job	Percent Part-Time Workers
1. Library Technicians	65.0%
2. Dental Hygienists	58.7%
3. Library Assistants, Clerical	52.5%
4. Massage Therapists	42.9%
5. Adult Literacy, Remedial Education, and GED Teachers and Instructors	41.3%
6. Self-Enrichment Education Teachers	41.3%
7. Athletes and Sports Competitors	39.1%
8. Coaches and Scouts	39.1%
9. Teacher Assistants	38.0%
10. Dental Assistants	35.7%
11. Bus Drivers, School	34.1%
12. Bus Drivers, Transit and Intercity	34.1%
13. Occupational Therapists	29.8%
14. Interpreters and Translators	28.5%
15. Audiologists	28.3%
16. Teachers, Postsecondary	27.8%
17. Physical Therapist Aides	27.1%
18. Physical Therapist Assistants	27.1%
19. Dietitians and Nutritionists	27.0%
20. Kindergarten Teachers, Except Special Education	25.1%
21. Preschool Teachers, Except Special Education	25.1%
22. Speech-Language Pathologists	24.6%
23. Clinical, Counseling, and School Psychologists	24.0%
24. Industrial-Organizational Psychologists	24.0%
25. Nursing Aides, Orderlies, and Attendants	24.0%
26. Sociologists	24.0%
27. Chiropractors	23.6%
28. Podiatrists	23.6%
29. Interviewers, Except Eligibility and Loan	23.4%
30. Medical Assistants	23.2%
31. Medical Equipment Preparers	23.2%
32. Physical Therapists	22.7%
33. Registered Nurses	21.8%
34. Embalmers	21.6%
35. Funeral Attendants	21.6%

Best Recession-Proof Jobs with the Highest Percentage of Part-Time Workers

Job	Percent Part-Time Workers
36. Librarians	21.2%
37. Dietetic Technicians	20.8%
38. Optometrists	20.8%
39. Pharmacy Technicians	20.8%
40. Surgical Technologists	20.8%
41. Veterinary Technologists and Technicians	20.8%
42. Anthropologists and Archeologists	20.1%
43. Political Scientists	20.1%

The jobs in the following four lists are derived from the preceding list of the recession-proof jobs with the highest percentage of part-time workers.

Best Overall Part-Time Recession-Proof Jobs

Job	Percent Part-Time Workers	Annual Earnings	Percent Growth	Annual Openings
1. Registered Nurses	21.8%	$57,280	23.5%	233,499
2. Teachers, Postsecondary	27.8%	$57,770	22.9%	237,478
3. Physical Therapists	22.7%	$66,200	27.1%	12,072
4. Dental Hygienists	58.7%	$62,800	30.1%	10,433
5. Medical Assistants	23.2%	$26,290	35.4%	92,977
6. Self-Enrichment Education Teachers	41.3%	$33,440	23.1%	64,449
7. Dental Assistants	35.7%	$30,220	29.2%	29,482
8. Occupational Therapists	29.8%	$60,470	23.1%	8,338
9. Pharmacy Technicians	20.8%	$25,630	32.0%	54,453
10. Surgical Technologists	20.8%	$36,080	24.5%	15,365
11. Veterinary Technologists and Technicians	20.8%	$26,780	41.0%	14,674
12. Preschool Teachers, Except Special Education	25.1%	$22,680	26.3%	78,172
13. Kindergarten Teachers, Except Special Education	25.1%	$43,580	16.3%	27,603
14. Physical Therapist Assistants	27.1%	$41,360	32.4%	5,957
15. Clinical, Counseling, and School Psychologists	24.0%	$59,440	15.8%	8,309
16. Nursing Aides, Orderlies, and Attendants	24.0%	$22,180	18.2%	321,036
17. Industrial-Organizational Psychologists	24.0%	$86,420	21.3%	118
18. Interpreters and Translators	28.5%	$35,560	23.6%	6,630

(continued)

(continued)

Best Overall Part-Time Recession-Proof Jobs

Job	Percent Part-Time Workers	Annual Earnings	Percent Growth	Annual Openings
19. Adult Literacy, Remedial Education, and GED Teachers and Instructors	41.3%	$43,910	14.2%	17,340
20. Coaches and Scouts	39.1%	$26,950	14.6%	51,100
21. Chiropractors	23.6%	$65,220	14.4%	3,179
22. Speech-Language Pathologists	24.6%	$57,710	10.6%	11,160
23. Massage Therapists	42.9%	$33,400	20.3%	9,193
24. Optometrists	20.8%	$91,040	11.3%	1,789
25. Athletes and Sports Competitors	39.1%	$41,060	19.2%	4,293

Best-Paying Part-Time Recession-Proof Jobs

Job	Percent Part-Time Workers	Annual Earnings
1. Podiatrists	23.6%	$108,220
2. Optometrists	20.8%	$91,040
3. Political Scientists	20.1%	$90,140
4. Industrial-Organizational Psychologists	24.0%	$86,420
5. Physical Therapists	22.7%	$66,200
6. Chiropractors	23.6%	$65,220
7. Dental Hygienists	58.7%	$62,800
8. Occupational Therapists	29.8%	$60,470
9. Sociologists	24.0%	$60,290
10. Clinical, Counseling, and School Psychologists	24.0%	$59,440
11. Teachers, Postsecondary	27.8%	$57,770
12. Speech-Language Pathologists	24.6%	$57,710
13. Registered Nurses	21.8%	$57,280
14. Audiologists	28.3%	$57,120
15. Anthropologists and Archeologists	20.1%	$49,930
16. Librarians	21.2%	$49,060
17. Dietitians and Nutritionists	27.0%	$46,980
18. Adult Literacy, Remedial Education, and GED Teachers and Instructors	41.3%	$43,910
19. Kindergarten Teachers, Except Special Education	25.1%	$43,580
20. Physical Therapist Assistants	27.1%	$41,360

Best-Paying Part-Time Recession-Proof Jobs

Job	Percent Part-Time Workers	Annual Earnings
21. Athletes and Sports Competitors	39.1%	$41,060
22. Embalmers	21.6%	$37,840
23. Surgical Technologists	20.8%	$36,080
24. Interpreters and Translators	28.5%	$35,560
25. Self-Enrichment Education Teachers	41.3%	$33,440

Fastest-Growing Part-Time Recession-Proof Jobs

Job	Percent Part-Time Workers	Percent Growth
1. Veterinary Technologists and Technicians	20.8%	41.0%
2. Medical Assistants	23.2%	35.4%
3. Physical Therapist Assistants	27.1%	32.4%
4. Pharmacy Technicians	20.8%	32.0%
5. Dental Hygienists	58.7%	30.1%
6. Dental Assistants	35.7%	29.2%
7. Physical Therapists	22.7%	27.1%
8. Preschool Teachers, Except Special Education	25.1%	26.3%
9. Surgical Technologists	20.8%	24.5%
10. Physical Therapist Aides	27.1%	24.4%
11. Interpreters and Translators	28.5%	23.6%
12. Registered Nurses	21.8%	23.5%
13. Occupational Therapists	29.8%	23.1%
14. Self-Enrichment Education Teachers	41.3%	23.1%
15. Teachers, Postsecondary	27.8%	22.9%
16. Industrial-Organizational Psychologists	24.0%	21.3%
17. Massage Therapists	42.9%	20.3%
18. Athletes and Sports Competitors	39.1%	19.2%
19. Nursing Aides, Orderlies, and Attendants	24.0%	18.2%
20. Kindergarten Teachers, Except Special Education	25.1%	16.3%
21. Clinical, Counseling, and School Psychologists	24.0%	15.8%
22. Anthropologists and Archeologists	20.1%	15.0%
23. Dietetic Technicians	20.8%	14.8%
24. Coaches and Scouts	39.1%	14.6%
25. Chiropractors	23.6%	14.4%

Part-Time Recession-Proof Jobs with the Most Openings

Job	Percent Part-Time Workers	Annual Openings
1. Nursing Aides, Orderlies, and Attendants	24.0%	321,036
2. Teachers, Postsecondary	27.8%	237,478
3. Registered Nurses	21.8%	233,499
4. Teacher Assistants	38.0%	193,986
5. Medical Assistants	23.2%	92,977
6. Preschool Teachers, Except Special Education	25.1%	78,172
7. Self-Enrichment Education Teachers	41.3%	64,449
8. Bus Drivers, School	34.1%	59,809
9. Pharmacy Technicians	20.8%	54,453
10. Interviewers, Except Eligibility and Loan	23.4%	54,060
11. Coaches and Scouts	39.1%	51,100
12. Dental Assistants	35.7%	29,482
13. Library Technicians	65.0%	29,075
14. Kindergarten Teachers, Except Special Education	25.1%	27,603
15. Bus Drivers, Transit and Intercity	34.1%	27,100
16. Library Assistants, Clerical	52.5%	18,961
17. Librarians	21.2%	18,945
18. Adult Literacy, Remedial Education, and GED Teachers and Instructors	41.3%	17,340
19. Surgical Technologists	20.8%	15,365
20. Veterinary Technologists and Technicians	20.8%	14,674
21. Physical Therapists	22.7%	12,072
22. Speech-Language Pathologists	24.6%	11,160
23. Dental Hygienists	58.7%	10,433
24. Massage Therapists	42.9%	9,193
25. Medical Equipment Preparers	23.2%	8,363

Best Recession-Proof Jobs with a High Percentage of Self-Employed Workers

About 8 percent of all working people are self-employed. Although you may think of the self-employed as having similar jobs, they actually work in an enormous range of situations, fields, and work environments that you may not have considered.

Among the self-employed are people who own small or large businesses, as many dentists and funeral directors do; people working on a contract basis for one or more employers, as many editors do; people running home consulting or other businesses; and people in many other situations. They may go to the same worksite every day, as commercial and industrial designers do; visit multiple employers during the course of a week, as many translators do; or do most of their work from home. Some work part time, others full time, some as a way to have fun, some so they can spend time with their kids or go to school.

The point is that there is an enormous range of situations, and one of them could make sense for you now or in the future.

The following list contains recession-proof jobs in which more than 10 percent of the workers are self-employed.

Best Recession-Proof Jobs with the Highest Percentage of Self-Employed Workers

Job	Percent Self-Employed Workers
1. Massage Therapists	64.0%
2. Chiropractors	51.7%
3. Industrial-Organizational Psychologists	39.3%
4. Clinical, Counseling, and School Psychologists	34.2%
5. Private Detectives and Investigators	29.7%
6. Taxi Drivers and Chauffeurs	29.5%
7. Athletes and Sports Competitors	27.0%
8. Optometrists	25.5%
9. Podiatrists	23.9%
10. Coaches and Scouts	22.7%
11. Interpreters and Translators	21.6%
12. Self-Enrichment Education Teachers	21.5%
13. Automotive Glass Installers and Repairers	20.7%
14. Computer, Automated Teller, and Office Machine Repairers	19.7%
15. Funeral Directors	19.7%
16. Soil and Plant Scientists	19.5%
17. Network Systems and Data Communications Analysts	17.5%
18. Veterinarians	17.1%
19. Automotive Service Technicians and Mechanics	16.8%
20. Food Scientists and Technologists	16.3%
21. Film and Video Editors	15.9%
22. Physicians and Surgeons	14.7%
23. Automotive Body and Related Repairers	14.1%
24. Editors	13.4%
25. Audio and Video Equipment Technicians	12.8%
26. Broadcast Technicians	12.4%
27. Audiologists	10.2%

The jobs in the following four lists are derived from the preceding list of the recession-proof jobs with the highest percentage of self-employed workers. Where the following lists give earnings estimates, keep in mind that these figures are based on a survey that *doesn't include self-employed workers*. The median earnings for self-employed workers in these occupations may be significantly higher or lower.

Best Recession-Proof Jobs Overall with a High Percentage of Self-Employed Workers

Job	Percent Self-Employed Workers	Annual Earnings	Percent Growth	Annual Openings
1. Network Systems and Data Communications Analysts	17.5%	$64,600	53.4%	35,086
2. Physicians and Surgeons	14.7%	more than $145,600	14.2%	38,027
3. Veterinarians	17.1%	$71,990	35.0%	5,301
4. Self-Enrichment Education Teachers	21.5%	$33,440	23.1%	64,449
5. Clinical, Counseling, and School Psychologists	34.2%	$59,440	15.8%	8,309
6. Interpreters and Translators	21.6%	$35,560	23.6%	6,630
7. Automotive Service Technicians and Mechanics	16.8%	$33,780	14.3%	97,350
8. Audio and Video Equipment Technicians	12.8%	$34,840	24.2%	4,681
9. Industrial-Organizational Psychologists	39.3%	$86,420	21.3%	118
10. Chiropractors	51.7%	$65,220	14.4%	3,179
11. Athletes and Sports Competitors	27.0%	$41,060	19.2%	4,293
12. Massage Therapists	64.0%	$33,400	20.3%	9,193
13. Coaches and Scouts	22.7%	$26,950	14.6%	51,100
14. Automotive Body and Related Repairers	14.1%	$35,180	11.6%	37,469
15. Private Detectives and Investigators	29.7%	$33,750	18.2%	7,329
16. Optometrists	25.5%	$91,040	11.3%	1,789
17. Funeral Directors	19.7%	$49,620	12.5%	3,939
18. Editors	13.4%	$46,990	2.3%	20,193
19. Taxi Drivers and Chauffeurs	29.5%	$20,350	13.0%	35,954
20. Computer, Automated Teller, and Office Machine Repairers	19.7%	$36,480	3.0%	22,330
21. Automotive Glass Installers and Repairers	20.7%	$30,720	18.7%	3,457
22. Film and Video Editors	15.9%	$46,670	12.7%	2,707
23. Podiatrists	23.9%	$108,220	9.5%	648
24. Audiologists	10.2%	$57,120	9.8%	980
25. Food Scientists and Technologists	16.3%	$53,810	10.3%	663

Best-Paying Recession-Proof Jobs for Self-Employed Workers

Job	Percent Self-Employed Workers	Annual Earnings
1. Physicians and Surgeons	14.7% more than	$145,600
2. Podiatrists	23.9%	$108,220
3. Optometrists	25.5%	$91,040
4. Industrial-Organizational Psychologists	39.3%	$86,420
5. Veterinarians	17.1%	$71,990
6. Chiropractors	51.7%	$65,220
7. Network Systems and Data Communications Analysts	17.5%	$64,600
8. Clinical, Counseling, and School Psychologists	34.2%	$59,440
9. Audiologists	10.2%	$57,120
10. Soil and Plant Scientists	19.5%	$56,080
11. Food Scientists and Technologists	16.3%	$53,810
12. Funeral Directors	19.7%	$49,620
13. Editors	13.4%	$46,990
14. Film and Video Editors	15.9%	$46,670
15. Athletes and Sports Competitors	27.0%	$41,060
16. Computer, Automated Teller, and Office Machine Repairers	19.7%	$36,480
17. Interpreters and Translators	21.6%	$35,560
18. Automotive Body and Related Repairers	14.1%	$35,180
19. Audio and Video Equipment Technicians	12.8%	$34,840
20. Automotive Service Technicians and Mechanics	16.8%	$33,780
21. Private Detectives and Investigators	29.7%	$33,750
22. Self-Enrichment Education Teachers	21.5%	$33,440
23. Massage Therapists	64.0%	$33,400
24. Automotive Glass Installers and Repairers	20.7%	$30,720
25. Broadcast Technicians	12.4%	$30,690

Fastest-Growing Recession-Proof Jobs for Self-Employed Workers

Job	Percent Self-Employed Workers	Percent Growth
1. Network Systems and Data Communications Analysts	17.5%	53.4%
2. Veterinarians	17.1%	35.0%
3. Audio and Video Equipment Technicians	12.8%	24.2%

(continued)

(continued)

Fastest-Growing Recession-Proof Jobs for Self-Employed Workers

Job	Percent Self-Employed Workers	Percent Growth
4. Interpreters and Translators	21.6%	23.6%
5. Self-Enrichment Education Teachers	21.5%	23.1%
6. Industrial-Organizational Psychologists	39.3%	21.3%
7. Massage Therapists	64.0%	20.3%
8. Athletes and Sports Competitors	27.0%	19.2%
9. Automotive Glass Installers and Repairers	20.7%	18.7%
10. Private Detectives and Investigators	29.7%	18.2%
11. Clinical, Counseling, and School Psychologists	34.2%	15.8%
12. Coaches and Scouts	22.7%	14.6%
13. Chiropractors	51.7%	14.4%
14. Automotive Service Technicians and Mechanics	16.8%	14.3%
15. Physicians and Surgeons	14.7%	14.2%
16. Taxi Drivers and Chauffeurs	29.5%	13.0%
17. Film and Video Editors	15.9%	12.7%
18. Funeral Directors	19.7%	12.5%
19. Broadcast Technicians	12.4%	12.1%
20. Automotive Body and Related Repairers	14.1%	11.6%
21. Optometrists	25.5%	11.3%
22. Food Scientists and Technologists	16.3%	10.3%
23. Audiologists	10.2%	9.8%
24. Podiatrists	23.9%	9.5%
25. Soil and Plant Scientists	19.5%	8.4%

Recession-Proof Jobs with the Most Openings for Self-Employed Workers

Job	Percent Self-Employed Workers	Annual Openings
1. Automotive Service Technicians and Mechanics	16.8%	97,350
2. Self-Enrichment Education Teachers	21.5%	64,449
3. Coaches and Scouts	22.7%	51,100
4. Physicians and Surgeons	14.7%	38,027
5. Automotive Body and Related Repairers	14.1%	37,469
6. Taxi Drivers and Chauffeurs	29.5%	35,954

Recession-Proof Jobs with the Most Openings for Self-Employed Workers

Job	Percent Self-Employed Workers	Annual Openings
7. Network Systems and Data Communications Analysts	17.5%	35,086
8. Computer, Automated Teller, and Office Machine Repairers	19.7%	22,330
9. Editors	13.4%	20,193
10. Massage Therapists	64.0%	9,193
11. Clinical, Counseling, and School Psychologists	34.2%	8,309
12. Private Detectives and Investigators	29.7%	7,329
13. Interpreters and Translators	21.6%	6,630
14. Veterinarians	17.1%	5,301
15. Audio and Video Equipment Technicians	12.8%	4,681
16. Athletes and Sports Competitors	27.0%	4,293
17. Funeral Directors	19.7%	3,939
18. Automotive Glass Installers and Repairers	20.7%	3,457
19. Chiropractors	51.7%	3,179
20. Broadcast Technicians	12.4%	2,955
21. Film and Video Editors	15.9%	2,707
22. Optometrists	25.5%	1,789
23. Audiologists	10.2%	980
24. Soil and Plant Scientists	19.5%	850
25. Food Scientists and Technologists	16.3%	663

Best Recession-Proof Jobs Employing a High Percentage of Women

To create the 10 lists that follow, we sorted the 150 best recession-proof jobs according to the percentages of women and men in the workforce. We knew we would create some controversy when we first included the best jobs lists with high percentages (more than 70 percent) of men and women in an earlier *Best Jobs* book. But these lists aren't meant to restrict women or men from considering job options; our reason for including these lists is exactly the opposite. We hope the lists help people see possibilities that they might not otherwise have considered.

The fact is that jobs with high percentages of women or high percentages of men offer good opportunities for both men and women if they want to do one of these jobs. So we suggest that women browse the lists of recession-proof jobs that employ high percentages of men and that men browse the lists of recession-proof jobs with high percentages of women. There are jobs in both sets of lists that pay well, and women or men who are interested in them and who have or can obtain the necessary education and training should consider them.

It is interesting to compare the two sets of recession-proof jobs—those with the highest percentage of men and those with the highest percentage of women—in terms of the economic measures that we use to rank these lists. Sadly, the male-dominated jobs have higher average earnings than the female-dominated jobs: $41,035 compared to $37,846. On the other hand, the female-dominated jobs are expected to grow faster (an average of 19.5 percent compared to 15.4 percent) and to provide many more annual job openings (an average of 34,650 compared to 20,967). That's largely because female-dominated jobs are clustered in the booming health-care and education fields.

Best Recession-Proof Jobs Employing the Highest Percentage of Women

Job	Percent Women
1. Dental Hygienists	98.6%
2. Kindergarten Teachers, Except Special Education	97.7%
3. Preschool Teachers, Except Special Education	97.7%
4. Dental Assistants	95.4%
5. Speech-Language Pathologists	95.3%
6. Licensed Practical and Licensed Vocational Nurses	94.2%
7. Teacher Assistants	92.3%
8. Medical Records and Health Information Technicians	92.0%
9. Registered Nurses	91.3%
10. Dietitians and Nutritionists	91.0%
11. Medical Assistants	90.4%
12. Medical Equipment Preparers	90.4%
13. Occupational Therapists	90.3%
14. Occupational Therapist Assistants	89.4%
15. Nursing Aides, Orderlies, and Attendants	88.9%
16. Library Assistants, Clerical	87.9%
17. Librarians	84.2%
18. Massage Therapists	84.1%
19. Special Education Teachers, Middle School	83.5%
20. Special Education Teachers, Secondary School	83.5%
21. Child, Family, and School Social Workers	82.6%
22. Medical and Public Health Social Workers	82.6%
23. Mental Health and Substance Abuse Social Workers	82.6%
24. Middle School Teachers, Except Special and Vocational Education	82.2%
25. Interviewers, Except Eligibility and Loan	82.1%
26. Dietetic Technicians	80.1%
27. Pharmacy Technicians	80.1%
28. Surgical Technologists	80.1%
29. Veterinary Technologists and Technicians	80.1%

Best Recession-Proof Jobs Employing the Highest Percentage of Women

Job	Percent Women
30. Audiologists	79.6%
31. Physical Therapist Aides	78.4%
32. Physical Therapist Assistants	78.4%
33. Medical and Clinical Laboratory Technicians	78.1%
34. Medical and Clinical Laboratory Technologists	78.1%
35. Court Reporters	76.8%
36. Radiation Therapists	74.1%
37. Athletic Trainers	73.4%
38. Cardiovascular Technologists and Technicians	72.9%
39. Diagnostic Medical Sonographers	72.9%
40. Nuclear Medicine Technologists	72.9%
41. Radiologic Technologists and Technicians	72.9%
42. Archivists	72.4%
43. Curators	72.4%
44. Library Technicians	72.4%
45. Museum Technicians and Conservators	72.4%
46. Physician Assistants	71.7%
47. Health Educators	70.5%
48. Probation Officers and Correctional Treatment Specialists	70.5%
49. Social and Human Service Assistants	70.5%

The jobs in the following four lists are derived from the preceding list of the recession-proof jobs employing the highest percentage of women.

Best Recession-Proof Jobs Overall Employing a High Percentage of Women

Job	Percent Women	Annual Earnings	Percent Growth	Annual Openings
1. Registered Nurses	91.3%	$57,280	23.5%	233,499
2. Dental Hygienists	98.6%	$62,800	30.1%	10,433
3. Physician Assistants	71.7%	$74,980	27.0%	7,147
4. Medical Assistants	90.4%	$26,290	35.4%	92,977
5. Social and Human Service Assistants	70.5%	$25,580	33.6%	80,142
6. Dental Assistants	95.4%	$30,220	29.2%	29,482
7. Pharmacy Technicians	80.1%	$25,630	32.0%	54,453

(continued)

(continued)

Best Recession-Proof Jobs Overall Employing a High Percentage of Women

Job	Percent Women	Annual Earnings	Percent Growth	Annual Openings
8. Mental Health and Substance Abuse Social Workers	82.6%	$35,410	29.9%	17,289
9. Health Educators	70.5%	$41,330	26.2%	13,707
10. Medical and Public Health Social Workers	82.6%	$43,040	24.2%	16,429
11. Occupational Therapists	90.3%	$60,470	23.1%	8,338
12. Radiation Therapists	74.1%	$66,170	24.8%	1,461
13. Veterinary Technologists and Technicians	80.1%	$26,780	41.0%	14,674
14. Preschool Teachers, Except Special Education	97.7%	$22,680	26.3%	78,172
15. Kindergarten Teachers, Except Special Education	97.7%	$43,580	16.3%	27,603
16. Middle School Teachers, Except Special and Vocational Education	82.2%	$46,300	11.2%	75,270
17. Child, Family, and School Social Workers	82.6%	$37,480	19.1%	35,402
18. Physical Therapist Assistants	78.4%	$41,360	32.4%	5,957
19. Surgical Technologists	80.1%	$36,080	24.5%	15,365
20. Radiologic Technologists and Technicians	72.9%	$48,170	15.1%	12,836
21. Diagnostic Medical Sonographers	72.9%	$57,160	19.1%	3,211
22. Cardiovascular Technologists and Technicians	72.9%	$42,300	25.5%	3,550
23. Medical and Clinical Laboratory Technologists	78.1%	$49,700	12.4%	11,457
24. Nursing Aides, Orderlies, and Attendants	88.9%	$22,180	18.2%	321,036
25. Speech-Language Pathologists	95.3%	$57,710	10.6%	11,160

Best-Paying Recession-Proof Jobs Employing a High Percentage of Women

Job	Percent Women	Annual Earnings
1. Physician Assistants	71.7%	$74,980
2. Radiation Therapists	74.1%	$66,170
3. Dental Hygienists	98.6%	$62,800
4. Nuclear Medicine Technologists	72.9%	$62,300
5. Occupational Therapists	90.3%	$60,470
6. Speech-Language Pathologists	95.3%	$57,710
7. Registered Nurses	91.3%	$57,280
8. Diagnostic Medical Sonographers	72.9%	$57,160

Best-Paying Recession-Proof Jobs Employing a High Percentage of Women

Job	Percent Women	Annual Earnings
9. Audiologists	79.6%	$57,120
10. Medical and Clinical Laboratory Technologists	78.1%	$49,700
11. Librarians	84.2%	$49,060
12. Special Education Teachers, Secondary School	83.5%	$48,330
13. Radiologic Technologists and Technicians	72.9%	$48,170
14. Special Education Teachers, Middle School	83.5%	$47,650
15. Dietitians and Nutritionists	91.0%	$46,980
16. Curators	72.4%	$46,300
17. Middle School Teachers, Except Special and Vocational Education	82.2%	$46,300
18. Court Reporters	76.8%	$45,610
19. Kindergarten Teachers, Except Special Education	97.7%	$43,580
20. Medical and Public Health Social Workers	82.6%	$43,040
21. Probation Officers and Correctional Treatment Specialists	70.5%	$42,500
22. Cardiovascular Technologists and Technicians	72.9%	$42,300
23. Occupational Therapist Assistants	89.4%	$42,060
24. Physical Therapist Assistants	78.4%	$41,360
25. Health Educators	70.5%	$41,330

Fastest-Growing Recession-Proof Jobs Employing a High Percentage of Women

Job	Percent Women	Percent Growth
1. Veterinary Technologists and Technicians	80.1%	41.0%
2. Medical Assistants	90.4%	35.4%
3. Social and Human Service Assistants	70.5%	33.6%
4. Physical Therapist Assistants	78.4%	32.4%
5. Pharmacy Technicians	80.1%	32.0%
6. Dental Hygienists	98.6%	30.1%
7. Mental Health and Substance Abuse Social Workers	82.6%	29.9%
8. Dental Assistants	95.4%	29.2%
9. Physician Assistants	71.7%	27.0%
10. Preschool Teachers, Except Special Education	97.7%	26.3%
11. Health Educators	70.5%	26.2%
12. Cardiovascular Technologists and Technicians	72.9%	25.5%

(continued)

(continued)

Fastest-Growing Recession-Proof Jobs
Employing a High Percentage of Women

Job	Percent Women	Percent Growth
13. Occupational Therapist Assistants	89.4%	25.4%
14. Radiation Therapists	74.1%	24.8%
15. Court Reporters	76.8%	24.5%
16. Surgical Technologists	80.1%	24.5%
17. Physical Therapist Aides	78.4%	24.4%
18. Athletic Trainers	73.4%	24.3%
19. Medical and Public Health Social Workers	82.6%	24.2%
20. Registered Nurses	91.3%	23.5%
21. Curators	72.4%	23.3%
22. Occupational Therapists	90.3%	23.1%
23. Massage Therapists	84.1%	20.3%
24. Child, Family, and School Social Workers	82.6%	19.1%
25. Diagnostic Medical Sonographers	72.9%	19.1%

Recession-Proof Jobs with the Most Openings
Employing a High Percentage of Women

Job	Percent Women	Annual Openings
1. Nursing Aides, Orderlies, and Attendants	88.9%	321,036
2. Registered Nurses	91.3%	233,499
3. Teacher Assistants	92.3%	193,986
4. Medical Assistants	90.4%	92,977
5. Social and Human Service Assistants	70.5%	80,142
6. Preschool Teachers, Except Special Education	97.7%	78,172
7. Middle School Teachers, Except Special and Vocational Education	82.2%	75,270
8. Licensed Practical and Licensed Vocational Nurses	94.2%	70,610
9. Pharmacy Technicians	80.1%	54,453
10. Interviewers, Except Eligibility and Loan	82.1%	54,060
11. Medical Records and Health Information Technicians	92.0%	39,048
12. Child, Family, and School Social Workers	82.6%	35,402
13. Dental Assistants	95.4%	29,482
14. Library Technicians	72.4%	29,075

Recession-Proof Jobs with the Most Openings Employing a High Percentage of Women

Job	Percent Women	Annual Openings
15. Kindergarten Teachers, Except Special Education	97.7%	27,603
16. Library Assistants, Clerical	87.9%	18,961
17. Librarians	84.2%	18,945
18. Probation Officers and Correctional Treatment Specialists	70.5%	18,335
19. Mental Health and Substance Abuse Social Workers	82.6%	17,289
20. Medical and Public Health Social Workers	82.6%	16,429
21. Surgical Technologists	80.1%	15,365
22. Veterinary Technologists and Technicians	80.1%	14,674
23. Health Educators	70.5%	13,707
24. Radiologic Technologists and Technicians	72.9%	12,836
25. Medical and Clinical Laboratory Technologists	78.1%	11,457

Best Recession-Proof Jobs Employing a High Percentage of Men

If you haven't already read the intro to the previous group of lists, Best Recession-Proof Jobs Employing a High Percentage of Women, consider doing so. Much of the content there applies to these lists as well.

We didn't include these groups of lists with the assumption that men should consider only recession-proof jobs with high percentages of men or that women should consider only recession-proof jobs with high percentages of women. Instead, these lists are here because we think they are interesting and perhaps helpful in considering nontraditional career options. For example, some men would do very well in and enjoy some of the jobs with high percentages of women but may not have considered them seriously. Similarly, some women would very much enjoy and do well in some jobs that traditionally have been held by high percentages of men. We hope that these lists help you consider options that you simply didn't seriously consider because of gender stereotypes.

In the jobs on the following lists, more than 70 percent of the workers are men, but increasing numbers of women are entering many of these jobs.

Best Recession-Proof Jobs Employing the Highest Percentage of Men

Job	Percent Men
1. Automotive Body and Related Repairers	99.4%
2. Automotive Glass Installers and Repairers	99.4%
3. Automotive Service Technicians and Mechanics	98.4%
4. Pest Control Workers	97.8%
5. Nuclear Power Reactor Operators	97.7%
6. Power Plant Operators	97.7%
7. Fire Fighters	96.5%
8. Maintenance and Repair Workers, General	96.0%
9. Water and Liquid Waste Treatment Plant and System Operators	96.0%
10. First-Line Supervisors/Managers of Fire Fighting and Prevention Workers	92.8%
11. Computer, Automated Teller, and Office Machine Repairers	90.3%
12. Environmental Engineering Technicians	90.1%
13. Clergy	87.2%
14. Police and Sheriff's Patrol Officers	87.2%
15. Air Traffic Controllers	87.0%
16. Environmental Engineers	85.5%
17. Electrical and Electronics Repairers, Commercial and Industrial Equipment	84.8%
18. First-Line Supervisors/Managers of Police and Detectives	84.5%
19. Audio and Video Equipment Technicians	84.4%
20. Film and Video Editors	84.4%
21. Taxi Drivers and Chauffeurs	84.0%
22. Network and Computer Systems Administrators	83.4%
23. Environmental Scientists and Specialists, Including Health	78.0%
24. Fire Inspectors and Investigators	77.7%
25. Gaming Surveillance Officers and Gaming Investigators	77.0%
26. Chiropractors	76.9%
27. Network Systems and Data Communications Analysts	74.5%
28. Detectives and Criminal Investigators	74.0%
29. Mathematicians	73.3%
30. Statisticians	73.3%
31. Ambulance Drivers and Attendants, Except Emergency Medical Technicians	72.0%
32. Correctional Officers and Jailers	71.8%

The jobs in the following four lists are derived from the preceding list of the recession-proof jobs employing the highest percentage of men.

Best Recession-Proof Jobs Overall Employing a High Percentage of Men

Job	Percent Men	Annual Earnings	Percent Growth	Annual Openings
1. Network Systems and Data Communications Analysts	74.5%	$64,600	53.4%	35,086
2. Network and Computer Systems Administrators	83.4%	$62,130	27.0%	37,010
3. Environmental Engineers	85.5%	$69,940	25.4%	5,003
4. Environmental Scientists and Specialists, Including Health	78.0%	$56,100	25.1%	6,961
5. Detectives and Criminal Investigators	74.0%	$58,260	17.3%	14,746
6. Clergy	87.2%	$39,680	18.9%	35,092
7. Correctional Officers and Jailers	71.8%	$35,760	16.9%	56,579
8. Police and Sheriff's Patrol Officers	87.2%	$47,460	10.8%	37,842
9. Automotive Service Technicians and Mechanics	98.4%	$33,780	14.3%	97,350
10. Chiropractors	76.9%	$65,220	14.4%	3,179
11. First-Line Supervisors/Managers of Police and Detectives	84.5%	$69,310	9.2%	9,373
12. Fire Fighters	96.5%	$41,190	12.1%	18,887
13. Automotive Body and Related Repairers	99.4%	$35,180	11.6%	37,469
14. First-Line Supervisors/Managers of Fire Fighting and Prevention Workers	92.8%	$62,900	11.5%	3,771
15. Audio and Video Equipment Technicians	84.4%	$34,840	24.2%	4,681
16. Environmental Engineering Technicians	90.1%	$40,560	24.8%	2,162
17. Water and Liquid Waste Treatment Plant and System Operators	96.0%	$36,070	13.8%	9,575
18. Air Traffic Controllers	87.0%	$117,240	10.2%	1,213
19. Maintenance and Repair Workers, General	96.0%	$31,910	10.1%	165,502
20. Taxi Drivers and Chauffeurs	84.0%	$20,350	13.0%	35,954
21. Mathematicians	73.3%	$86,930	10.2%	473
22. Statisticians	73.3%	$65,720	8.5%	3,433
23. Film and Video Editors	84.4%	$46,670	12.7%	2,707
24. Gaming Surveillance Officers and Gaming Investigators	77.0%	$27,130	33.6%	2,124
25. Pest Control Workers	97.8%	$27,880	15.5%	6,006

Best-Paying Recession-Proof Jobs Employing a High Percentage of Men

Job	Percent Men	Annual Earnings
1. Air Traffic Controllers	87.0%	$117,240
2. Mathematicians	73.3%	$86,930
3. Environmental Engineers	85.5%	$69,940
4. Nuclear Power Reactor Operators	97.7%	$69,370
5. First-Line Supervisors/Managers of Police and Detectives	84.5%	$69,310
6. Statisticians	73.3%	$65,720
7. Chiropractors	76.9%	$65,220
8. Network Systems and Data Communications Analysts	74.5%	$64,600
9. First-Line Supervisors/Managers of Fire Fighting and Prevention Workers	92.8%	$62,900
10. Network and Computer Systems Administrators	83.4%	$62,130
11. Detectives and Criminal Investigators	74.0%	$58,260
12. Environmental Scientists and Specialists, Including Health	78.0%	$56,100
13. Power Plant Operators	97.7%	$55,000
14. Fire Inspectors and Investigators	77.7%	$48,050
15. Police and Sheriff's Patrol Officers	87.2%	$47,460
16. Film and Video Editors	84.4%	$46,670
17. Electrical and Electronics Repairers, Commercial and Industrial Equipment	84.8%	$45,180
18. Fire Fighters	96.5%	$41,190
19. Environmental Engineering Technicians	90.1%	$40,560
20. Clergy	87.2%	$39,680
21. Computer, Automated Teller, and Office Machine Repairers	90.3%	$36,480
22. Water and Liquid Waste Treatment Plant and System Operators	96.0%	$36,070
23. Correctional Officers and Jailers	71.8%	$35,760
24. Automotive Body and Related Repairers	99.4%	$35,180
25. Audio and Video Equipment Technicians	84.4%	$34,840

Fastest-Growing Recession-Proof Jobs Employing a High Percentage of Men

Job	Percent Men	Percent Growth
1. Network Systems and Data Communications Analysts	74.5%	53.4%
2. Gaming Surveillance Officers and Gaming Investigators	77.0%	33.6%
3. Network and Computer Systems Administrators	83.4%	27.0%
4. Environmental Engineers	85.5%	25.4%
5. Environmental Scientists and Specialists, Including Health	78.0%	25.1%

Fastest-Growing Recession-Proof Jobs Employing a High Percentage of Men

Job	Percent Men	Percent Growth
6. Environmental Engineering Technicians	90.1%	24.8%
7. Audio and Video Equipment Technicians	84.4%	24.2%
8. Ambulance Drivers and Attendants, Except Emergency Medical Technicians	72.0%	21.7%
9. Clergy	87.2%	18.9%
10. Automotive Glass Installers and Repairers	99.4%	18.7%
11. Detectives and Criminal Investigators	74.0%	17.3%
12. Correctional Officers and Jailers	71.8%	16.9%
13. Pest Control Workers	97.8%	15.5%
14. Chiropractors	76.9%	14.4%
15. Automotive Service Technicians and Mechanics	98.4%	14.3%
16. Water and Liquid Waste Treatment Plant and System Operators	96.0%	13.8%
17. Taxi Drivers and Chauffeurs	84.0%	13.0%
18. Film and Video Editors	84.4%	12.7%
19. Fire Fighters	96.5%	12.1%
20. Automotive Body and Related Repairers	99.4%	11.6%
21. First-Line Supervisors/Managers of Fire Fighting and Prevention Workers	92.8%	11.5%
22. Fire Inspectors and Investigators	77.7%	11.0%
23. Police and Sheriff's Patrol Officers	87.2%	10.8%
24. Nuclear Power Reactor Operators	97.7%	10.6%
25. Air Traffic Controllers	87.0%	10.2%

Recession-Proof Jobs with the Most Openings Employing a High Percentage of Men

Job	Percent Men	Annual Openings
1. Maintenance and Repair Workers, General	96.0%	165,502
2. Automotive Service Technicians and Mechanics	98.4%	97,350
3. Correctional Officers and Jailers	71.8%	56,579
4. Police and Sheriff's Patrol Officers	87.2%	37,842
5. Automotive Body and Related Repairers	99.4%	37,469
6. Network and Computer Systems Administrators	83.4%	37,010
7. Taxi Drivers and Chauffeurs	84.0%	35,954
8. Clergy	87.2%	35,092

(continued)

(continued)

Recession-Proof Jobs with the Most Openings Employing a High Percentage of Men		
Job	Percent Men	Annual Openings
9. Network Systems and Data Communications Analysts	74.5%	35,086
10. Computer, Automated Teller, and Office Machine Repairers	90.3%	22,330
11. Fire Fighters	96.5%	18,887
12. Detectives and Criminal Investigators	74.0%	14,746
13. Water and Liquid Waste Treatment Plant and System Operators	96.0%	9,575
14. First-Line Supervisors/Managers of Police and Detectives	84.5%	9,373
15. Environmental Scientists and Specialists, Including Health	78.0%	6,961
16. Electrical and Electronics Repairers, Commercial and Industrial Equipment	84.8%	6,607
17. Pest Control Workers	97.8%	6,006
18. Environmental Engineers	85.5%	5,003
19. Audio and Video Equipment Technicians	84.4%	4,681
20. First-Line Supervisors/Managers of Fire Fighting and Prevention Workers	92.8%	3,771
21. Ambulance Drivers and Attendants, Except Emergency Medical Technicians	72.0%	3,703
22. Automotive Glass Installers and Repairers	99.4%	3,457
23. Statisticians	73.3%	3,433
24. Chiropractors	76.9%	3,179
25. Film and Video Editors	84.4%	2,707

Best Recession-Proof Jobs Sorted by Education or Training Required

The lists in this section organize the 150 best recession-proof jobs into groups based on the education or training typically required for entry. Unlike in many of the previous sections, here we don't include separate lists for highest pay, growth, or number of openings. Instead, we provide one list that includes all the best recession-proof jobs that fit into each of the education levels and that ranks them by their total combined score for earnings, growth, and number of openings.

These lists can help you identify a job with higher earnings or upward mobility but with a similar level of education to the job you now hold. For example, you will find jobs within the same level of education that require similar skills, yet one pays significantly better than the other, is projected to grow more rapidly, or has significantly more job openings per year. This information can help you leverage your present skills and experience into jobs that might provide better long-term career opportunities.

You can also use these lists to explore possible job options if you were to get additional training, education, or work experience. For example, you can use these lists to identify recession-proof occupations that offer high potential and then look into the education or training required to get the jobs that interest you most.

The lists can also help you when you plan your education. For example, you might be thinking about a job helping people who are trying to overcome obstacles in their lives, but you aren't sure exactly what kind of work you want to do. The lists show that Rehabilitation Counselors need a master's degree and earn $29,200, while Probation Officers and Correctional Treatment Specialists need only a bachelor's degree but earn an average of $42,500. If you want higher earnings without lengthy training, this information might make a difference in your choice.

The Education Levels

The U.S. Department of Labor defines the training and education levels used in this set of lists as follows:

* **Short-term on-the-job training:** It is possible to work in these occupations and achieve an average level of performance within a few days or weeks through on-the-job training.

* **Moderate-term on-the-job training:** Occupations requiring this type of training can be performed adequately after a one- to 12-month period of combined on-the-job and informal training. Typically, untrained workers observe experienced workers performing tasks and are gradually moved into progressively more difficult assignments.

* **Long-term on-the-job training:** This training requires more than 12 months of on-the-job training or combined work experience and formal classroom instruction. This includes occupations that use formal apprenticeships for training workers that may take up to four years. It also includes intensive occupation-specific, employer-sponsored training, such as police academies. Furthermore, it includes occupations that require natural talent that must be developed over many years.

* **Work experience in a related occupation:** This type of job requires experience in a related occupation. For example, police detectives are selected based on their experience as police patrol officers.

* **Postsecondary vocational training:** This requirement can vary from training that involves a few months to usually less than one year. In a few instances, as many as four years of training may be required.

* **Associate degree:** This degree usually requires two years of full-time academic work beyond high school.

* **Bachelor's degree:** This degree requires approximately four to five years of full-time academic work beyond high school.

* **Work experience, plus degree:** Jobs in this category are often management-related and require some experience in a related nonmanagerial position.

⊛ **Master's degree:** Completion of a master's degree usually requires one to two years of full-time study beyond the bachelor's degree.

⊛ **Doctoral degree:** This degree normally requires two or more years of full-time academic work beyond the bachelor's degree.

⊛ **First professional degree:** This type of degree normally requires a minimum of two years of education beyond the bachelor's degree and frequently requires three years.

Another Warning About the Data

We warned you in the introduction to use caution in interpreting the data we use, and we want to do it again here. The occupational data we use is the most accurate available anywhere, but it has its limitations. The education or training requirements for entry into a job are those typically required as a minimum, but some people working in those jobs may have considerably more or different credentials. For example, although a bachelor's degree plus work experience is considered the usual requirement for Medical and Health Services Managers, almost half of the people working in this occupation don't have a bachelor's. On the other hand, Police and Sheriff's Patrol Officers usually need to have completed only long-term on-the-job training (at a police academy), but almost one-third of these workers are college graduates.

Similarly, you need to be cautious about assuming that more education or training always leads to higher income. It is true that people with jobs that require long-term on-the-job training typically earn more than people with jobs that require short-term on-the-job training. (For the jobs in this book, the difference is an average of $43,192 versus an average of $26,851.) However, some people with short-term on-the-job training do earn more than the average for the highest-paying occupations listed in this book; furthermore, some people with long-term on-the-job training earn much less than the average shown in this book—this is particularly true early in a person's career.

So as you browse the following lists, please use them as a way to be encouraged rather than discouraged. Education and training are very important for success in the labor market of the future, but so are ability, drive, initiative, and—yes—luck.

Having said this, we encourage you to get as much education and training as you can. You used to be able to get your schooling and then close the schoolbooks forever, but this isn't a good attitude to have now, especially in the recession-proof jobs, which tend to use technology that is constantly advancing. You will probably need to continue learning new things throughout your working life. This can be done by going to school, which is a good thing for many people to do. But other workers may learn through workshops, adult education programs, certification programs, employer training, professional conferences, Internet training, or reading related books and magazines.

Best Recession-Proof Jobs Requiring Short-Term On-the-Job Training

Job	Annual Earnings	Percent Growth	Annual Openings
1. Interviewers, Except Eligibility and Loan	$26,290	9.5%	54,060
2. Medical Equipment Preparers	$25,950	14.2%	8,363
3. Teacher Assistants	$20,740	10.4%	193,986
4. Physical Therapist Aides	$22,060	24.4%	4,092
5. Postal Service Mail Carriers	$44,350	1.0%	16,710
6. Taxi Drivers and Chauffeurs	$20,350	13.0%	35,954
7. Library Assistants, Clerical	$21,640	7.9%	18,961
8. Funeral Attendants	$20,350	14.3%	6,034
9. Postal Service Clerks	$44,800	1.2%	3,703
10. Postal Service Mail Sorters, Processors, and Processing Machine Operators	$43,900	–8.4%	6,855

Best Recession-Proof Jobs Requiring Moderate-Term On-the-Job Training

Job	Annual Earnings	Percent Growth	Annual Openings
1. Correctional Officers and Jailers	$35,760	16.9%	56,579
2. Medical Assistants	$26,290	35.4%	92,977
3. Social and Human Service Assistants	$25,580	33.6%	80,142
4. Dental Assistants	$30,220	29.2%	29,482
5. Maintenance and Repair Workers, General	$31,910	10.1%	165,502
6. Bus Drivers, Transit and Intercity	$32,090	12.5%	27,100
7. Pharmacy Technicians	$25,630	32.0%	54,453
8. Police, Fire, and Ambulance Dispatchers	$31,470	13.6%	17,628
9. Gaming Surveillance Officers and Gaming Investigators	$27,130	33.6%	2,124
10. Inspectors, Testers, Sorters, Samplers, and Weighers	$29,420	–7.0%	75,361
11. Bailiffs	$34,210	11.2%	2,223
12. Pest Control Workers	$27,880	15.5%	6,006
13. Hazardous Materials Removal Workers	$35,450	11.2%	1,933
14. Animal Control Workers	$27,910	12.5%	3,377
15. Ambulance Drivers and Attendants, Except Emergency Medical Technicians	$20,370	21.7%	3,703
16. Bus Drivers, School	$24,820	9.3%	59,809

Best Recession-Proof Jobs Requiring Long-Term On-the-Job Training

Job	Annual Earnings	Percent Growth	Annual Openings
1. Police and Sheriff's Patrol Officers	$47,460	10.8%	37,842
2. Fire Fighters	$41,190	12.1%	18,887
3. Interpreters and Translators	$35,560	23.6%	6,630
4. Athletes and Sports Competitors	$41,060	19.2%	4,293
5. Coaches and Scouts	$26,950	14.6%	51,100
6. Audio and Video Equipment Technicians	$34,840	24.2%	4,681
7. Claims Adjusters, Examiners, and Investigators	$50,660	8.9%	22,024
8. Water and Liquid Waste Treatment Plant and System Operators	$36,070	13.8%	9,575
9. Automotive Body and Related Repairers	$35,180	11.6%	37,469
10. Air Traffic Controllers	$117,240	10.2%	1,213
11. Nuclear Power Reactor Operators	$69,370	10.6%	233
12. Automotive Glass Installers and Repairers	$30,720	18.7%	3,457
13. Power Plant Operators	$55,000	2.7%	1,796

Best Recession-Proof Jobs Requiring Work Experience in a Related Occupation

Job	Annual Earnings	Percent Growth	Annual Openings
1. Detectives and Criminal Investigators	$58,260	17.3%	14,746
2. Self-Enrichment Education Teachers	$33,440	23.1%	64,449
3. First-Line Supervisors/Managers of Police and Detectives	$69,310	9.2%	9,373
4. First-Line Supervisors/Managers of Fire Fighting and Prevention Workers	$62,900	11.5%	3,771
5. Private Detectives and Investigators	$33,750	18.2%	7,329
6. First-Line Supervisors/Managers of Correctional Officers	$52,580	12.5%	4,180
7. Postmasters and Mail Superintendents	$55,790	−0.8%	1,627
8. Fire Inspectors and Investigators	$48,050	11.0%	644

Best Recession-Proof Jobs Requiring Postsecondary Vocational Training

Job	Annual Earnings	Percent Growth	Annual Openings
1. Court Reporters	$45,610	24.5%	2,620
2. Preschool Teachers, Except Special Education	$22,680	26.3%	78,172

Best Recession-Proof Jobs Requiring Postsecondary Vocational Training

Job	Annual Earnings	Percent Growth	Annual Openings
3. Surgical Technologists	$36,080	24.5%	15,365
4. Automotive Service Technicians and Mechanics	$33,780	14.3%	97,350
5. Licensed Practical and Licensed Vocational Nurses	$36,550	14.0%	70,610
6. Nursing Aides, Orderlies, and Attendants	$22,180	18.2%	321,036
7. Emergency Medical Technicians and Paramedics	$27,070	19.2%	19,513
8. Massage Therapists	$33,400	20.3%	9,193
9. Embalmers	$37,840	14.3%	1,660
10. Computer, Automated Teller, and Office Machine Repairers	$36,480	3.0%	22,330
11. Electrical and Electronics Repairers, Commercial and Industrial Equipment	$45,180	6.8%	6,607
12. Insurance Appraisers, Auto Damage	$49,180	12.5%	1,030
13. Library Technicians	$26,560	8.5%	29,075
14. Electrical and Electronics Repairers, Powerhouse, Substation, and Relay	$57,400	–4.7%	1,591
15. Dietetic Technicians	$24,040	14.8%	4,062

Best Recession-Proof Jobs Requiring an Associate Degree

Job	Annual Earnings	Percent Growth	Annual Openings
1. Dental Hygienists	$62,800	30.1%	10,433
2. Registered Nurses	$57,280	23.5%	233,499
3. Physical Therapist Assistants	$41,360	32.4%	5,957
4. Veterinary Technologists and Technicians	$26,780	41.0%	14,674
5. Radiation Therapists	$66,170	24.8%	1,461
6. Cardiovascular Technologists and Technicians	$42,300	25.5%	3,550
7. Radiologic Technologists and Technicians	$48,170	15.1%	12,836
8. Respiratory Therapists	$47,420	22.6%	5,563
9. Diagnostic Medical Sonographers	$57,160	19.1%	3,211
10. Medical Records and Health Information Technicians	$28,030	17.8%	39,048
11. Occupational Therapist Assistants	$42,060	25.4%	2,634
12. Funeral Directors	$49,620	12.5%	3,939
13. Medical and Clinical Laboratory Technicians	$32,840	15.0%	10,866
14. Environmental Engineering Technicians	$40,560	24.8%	2,162
15. Nuclear Medicine Technologists	$62,300	14.8%	1,290
16. Broadcast Technicians	$30,690	12.1%	2,955

Best Recession-Proof Jobs Requiring a Bachelor's Degree

Job	Annual Earnings	Percent Growth	Annual Openings
1. Secondary School Teachers, Except Special and Vocational Education	$47,740	5.6%	93,166
2. Middle School Teachers, Except Special and Vocational Education	$46,300	11.2%	75,270
3. Computer Systems Analysts	$69,760	29.0%	63,166
4. Public Relations Specialists	$47,350	17.6%	51,216
5. Network and Computer Systems Administrators	$62,130	27.0%	37,010
6. Child, Family, and School Social Workers	$37,480	19.1%	35,402
7. Network Systems and Data Communications Analysts	$64,600	53.4%	35,086
8. Kindergarten Teachers, Except Special Education	$43,580	16.3%	27,603
9. Social and Community Service Managers	$52,070	24.7%	23,788
10. Substance Abuse and Behavioral Disorder Counselors	$34,040	34.3%	20,821
11. Editors	$46,990	2.3%	20,193
12. Probation Officers and Correctional Treatment Specialists	$42,500	10.9%	18,335
13. Adult Literacy, Remedial Education, and GED Teachers and Instructors	$43,910	14.2%	17,340
14. Medical and Public Health Social Workers	$43,040	24.2%	16,429
15. Health Educators	$41,330	26.2%	13,707
16. Medical and Clinical Laboratory Technologists	$49,700	12.4%	11,457
17. Special Education Teachers, Secondary School	$48,330	8.5%	10,601
18. Special Education Teachers, Middle School	$47,650	15.8%	8,846
19. Database Administrators	$64,670	28.6%	8,258
20. Insurance Underwriters	$52,350	6.3%	6,880
21. Budget Analysts	$61,430	7.1%	6,423
22. Environmental Engineers	$69,940	25.4%	5,003
23. Dietitians and Nutritionists	$46,980	8.6%	4,996
24. Tax Examiners, Collectors, and Revenue Agents	$45,620	2.1%	4,465
25. Film and Video Editors	$46,670	12.7%	2,707
26. Athletic Trainers	$36,560	24.3%	1,669
27. Museum Technicians and Conservators	$34,340	15.9%	1,341
28. Soil and Plant Scientists	$56,080	8.4%	850
29. Food Scientists and Technologists	$53,810	10.3%	663
30. Animal Scientists	$47,800	9.8%	299

150 Best Recession-Proof Jobs © JIST Works

Best Recession-Proof Jobs Requiring Work Experience Plus Degree

Job	Annual Earnings	Percent Growth	Annual Openings
1. Actuaries	$82,800	23.7%	3,245
2. Medical and Health Services Managers	$73,340	16.4%	31,877
3. Education Administrators, Elementary and Secondary School	$77,740	7.6%	27,143
4. Education Administrators, Postsecondary	$73,990	14.2%	17,121
5. Education Administrators, Preschool and Child Care Center/Program	$37,740	23.5%	8,113
6. Judges, Magistrate Judges, and Magistrates	$101,690	5.1%	1,567
7. Arbitrators, Mediators, and Conciliators	$49,490	10.6%	546
8. Administrative Law Judges, Adjudicators, and Hearing Officers	$72,600	0.1%	794
9. Vocational Education Teachers, Secondary School	$48,690	–4.6%	7,639

Best Recession-Proof Jobs Requiring a Master's Degree

Job	Annual Earnings	Percent Growth	Annual Openings
1. Physical Therapists	$66,200	27.1%	12,072
2. Physician Assistants	$74,980	27.0%	7,147
3. Mental Health Counselors	$34,380	30.0%	24,103
4. Occupational Therapists	$60,470	23.1%	8,338
5. Instructional Coordinators	$52,790	22.5%	21,294
6. Environmental Scientists and Specialists, Including Health	$56,100	25.1%	6,961
7. Mental Health and Substance Abuse Social Workers	$35,410	29.9%	17,289
8. Geoscientists, Except Hydrologists and Geographers	$72,660	21.9%	2,471
9. Hydrologists	$66,260	24.3%	687
10. Educational, Vocational, and School Counselors	$47,530	12.6%	54,025
11. Marriage and Family Therapists	$43,210	29.8%	5,953
12. Clergy	$39,680	18.9%	35,092
13. Rehabilitation Counselors	$29,200	23.0%	32,081
14. Industrial-Organizational Psychologists	$86,420	21.3%	118
15. Speech-Language Pathologists	$57,710	10.6%	11,160
16. Economists	$77,010	7.5%	1,555
17. Curators	$46,300	23.3%	1,416
18. Statisticians	$65,720	8.5%	3,433
19. Librarians	$49,060	3.6%	18,945

(continued)

(continued)

Best Recession-Proof Jobs Requiring a Master's Degree

Job	Annual Earnings	Percent Growth	Annual Openings
20. Political Scientists	$90,140	5.3%	318
21. Anthropologists and Archeologists	$49,930	15.0%	446
22. Sociologists	$60,290	10.0%	403
23. Archivists	$40,730	14.4%	795

Best Recession-Proof Jobs Requiring a Doctoral Degree

Job	Annual Earnings	Percent Growth	Annual Openings
1. Teachers, Postsecondary	$57,770	22.9%	237,478
2. Clinical, Counseling, and School Psychologists	$59,440	15.8%	8,309
3. Mathematicians	$86,930	10.2%	473

Best Recession-Proof Jobs Requiring a First Professional Degree

Job	Annual Earnings	Percent Growth	Annual Openings
1. Physicians and Surgeons	more than $145,600	14.2%	38,027
2. Pharmacists	$94,520	21.7%	16,358
3. Veterinarians	$71,990	35.0%	5,301
4. Chiropractors	$65,220	14.4%	3,179
5. Optometrists	$91,040	11.3%	1,789
6. Podiatrists	$108,220	9.5%	648
7. Audiologists	$57,120	9.8%	980

Best Recession-Proof Jobs Sorted by Interests

This group of lists organizes the 150 best recession-proof jobs into 16 interest areas. You can use these lists to identify jobs quickly based on your interests. Within each interest area, jobs are listed in order of their combined score on earnings, job growth, and job openings, from highest to lowest.

Find the interest area or areas that appeal to you most and review the recession-proof jobs in those areas. When you find jobs you want to explore in more detail, look up their descriptions in Part III. You can also review interest areas in which you've had past experience, education, or training to see whether other jobs in those areas would meet your current requirements.

Note: The 16 interest areas used in these lists are those used in the *New Guide for Occupational Exploration*, Fourth Edition, published by JIST. The original GOE was developed by the U.S. Department of Labor as an intuitive way to assist in career exploration. The 16 interest areas used in the *New GOE* are based on the 16 career clusters that the U.S. Department of Education's Office of Vocational and Adult Education developed around 1999 and that many states now use to organize their career-oriented programs and career information.

Descriptions for the 16 Interest Areas

Brief descriptions follow for the 16 interest areas we use in the lists. The descriptions are from the *New Guide for Occupational Exploration,* Fourth Edition. Some of them refer to jobs (as examples) that aren't included in this book.

Also note that in most cases we put each of the 150 best jobs into only one interest area list, the one its related O*NET job fits into best. However, many jobs could be included in more than one list, so consider reviewing several interest areas to find jobs that you might otherwise overlook. Some of the 150 recession-proof jobs link to two or more jobs in the O*NET database and do appear in more than one interest area.

For a detailed outline of the interest areas that shows the work groups classified into each interest area, see Appendix B.

❀ **Agriculture and Natural Resources:** *An interest in working with plants, animals, forests, or mineral resources for agriculture, horticulture, conservation, extraction, and other purposes.* You can satisfy this interest by working in farming, landscaping, forestry, fishing, mining, and related fields. You may like doing physical work outdoors, such as on a farm or ranch, in a forest, or on a drilling rig. If you have a scientific curiosity, you could study plants and animals or analyze biological or rock samples in a lab. If you have management ability, you could own, operate, or manage a fish hatchery, a landscaping business, or a greenhouse.

❀ **Architecture and Construction:** *An interest in designing, assembling, and maintaining components of buildings and other structures.* You may want to be part of the team of architects, drafters, and others who design buildings and render the plans. If construction interests you, you might find fulfillment in the many building projects being undertaken at all times. If you like to organize and plan, you can find careers in managing these projects. Or you can play a more direct role in putting up and finishing buildings by doing jobs such as plumbing, carpentry, masonry, painting, or roofing, either as a skilled craftsworker or as a helper. You can prepare the building site by operating heavy equipment or installing, maintaining, and repairing vital building equipment and systems such as electricity and heating.

❋ **Arts and Communication:** *An interest in creatively expressing feelings or ideas, in communicating news or information, or in performing.* You can satisfy this interest in creative, verbal, or performing activities. For example, if you enjoy literature, perhaps writing or editing would appeal to you. Journalism and public relations are other fields for people who like to use their writing or speaking skills. Do you prefer to work in the performing arts? If so, you could direct or perform in drama, music, or dance. If you especially enjoy the visual arts, you could create paintings, sculpture, or ceramics or design products or visual displays. A flair for technology might lead you to specialize in photography, broadcast production, or dispatching.

❋ **Business and Administration:** *An interest in making a business organization or function run smoothly.* You can satisfy this interest by working in a position of leadership or by specializing in a function that contributes to the overall effort in a business, a nonprofit organization, or a government agency. If you especially enjoy working with people, you may find fulfillment from working in human resources. An interest in numbers may lead you to consider accounting, finance, budgeting, billing, or financial record-keeping. A job as an administrative assistant may interest you if you like a variety of tasks in a busy environment. If you are good with details and word processing, you may enjoy a job as a secretary or data-entry clerk. Or perhaps you would do well as the manager of a business.

❋ **Education and Training:** *An interest in helping people learn.* You can satisfy this interest by teaching students, who may be preschoolers, retirees, or any age in between. You may specialize in a particular academic field or work with learners of a particular age, with a particular interest, or with a particular learning problem. Working in a library or museum may give you an opportunity to expand people's understanding of the world.

❋ **Finance and Insurance:** *An interest in helping businesses and people be assured of a financially secure future.* You can satisfy this interest by working in a financial or insurance business in a leadership or support role. If you like gathering and analyzing information, you may find fulfillment as an insurance adjuster or financial analyst. Or you may deal with information at the clerical level as a banking or insurance clerk or in person-to-person situations providing customer service. Another way to interact with people is to sell financial or insurance services that will meet their needs.

❋ **Government and Public Administration:** *An interest in helping a government agency serve the needs of the public.* You can satisfy this interest by working in a position of leadership or by specializing in a function that contributes to the role of government. You may help protect the public by working as an inspector or examiner to enforce standards. If you enjoy using clerical skills, you could work as a clerk in a law court or government office. Or perhaps you prefer the top-down perspective of a government executive or urban planner.

❋ **Health Science:** *An interest in helping people and animals be healthy.* You can satisfy this interest by working on a health-care team as a doctor, therapist, or nurse. You might specialize in one of the many different parts of the body (such as the teeth or eyes) or in one of the many different types of care. Or you may want to be a generalist who deals with the whole patient. If you like technology, you might find satisfaction working with

X rays or new diagnostic methods. You might work with healthy people, helping them eat right. If you enjoy working with animals, you might care for them and keep them healthy.

❋ **Hospitality, Tourism, and Recreation:** *An interest in catering to the personal wishes and needs of others so that they can enjoy a clean environment, good food and drink, comfortable lodging away from home, and recreation.* You can satisfy this interest by providing services for the convenience, care, and pampering of others in hotels, restaurants, airplanes, beauty parlors, and so on. You may want to use your love of cooking as a chef. If you like working with people, you may want to provide personal services by being a travel guide, a flight attendant, a concierge, a hairdresser, or a waiter. You may want to work in cleaning and building services if you like a clean environment. If you enjoy sports or games, you could work for an athletic team or casino.

❋ **Human Service:** *An interest in improving people's social, mental, emotional, or spiritual well-being.* You can satisfy this interest as a counselor, social worker, or religious worker who helps people sort out their complicated lives or solve personal problems. You may work as a caretaker for very young people or the elderly. Or you may interview people to help identify the social services they need.

❋ **Information Technology:** *An interest in designing, developing, managing, and supporting information systems.* You can satisfy this interest by working with hardware, software, multimedia, or integrated systems. If you like to use your organizational skills, you might work as a systems or database administrator. Or you can solve complex problems as a software engineer or systems analyst. If you enjoy getting your hands on hardware, you might find work servicing computers, peripherals, and information-intense machines such as cash registers and ATMs.

❋ **Law and Public Safety:** *An interest in upholding people's rights or in protecting people and property by using authority, inspecting, or investigating.* You can satisfy this interest by working in law, law enforcement, fire fighting, the military, and related fields. For example, if you enjoy mental challenge and intrigue, you could investigate crimes or fires for a living. If you enjoy working with verbal skills and research skills, you may want to defend citizens in court or research deeds, wills, and other legal documents. If you want to help people in critical situations, you may want to fight fires, work as a police officer, or become a paramedic. Or, if you want more routine work in public safety, perhaps a job in guarding, patrolling, or inspecting would appeal to you. If you have management ability, you could seek a leadership position in law enforcement and the protective services. Work in the military gives you a chance to use technical and leadership skills while serving your country.

❋ **Manufacturing:** *An interest in processing materials into intermediate or final products or maintaining and repairing products by using machines or hand tools.* You can satisfy this interest by working in one of many industries that mass-produce goods or by working for a utility that distributes electric power or other resources. You might enjoy manual work, using your hands or hand tools in highly skilled jobs such as assembling engines or electronic equipment. If you enjoy making machines run efficiently or fixing them when they break down, you could seek a job installing or repairing such devices as copiers, aircraft engines, cars, or watches. Perhaps you prefer to set up or operate machines used to manufacture products made of food, glass, or paper. You could enjoy cutting and grinding metal and plastic parts to desired shapes and measurements. Or you may want to operate equipment in systems that provide water and process wastewater. You may like inspecting, sorting, counting, or weighing products. Another option is to work with your hands and machinery to move boxes and freight in a warehouse. If leadership appeals to you, you could manage people engaged in production and repair.

⁕ **Retail and Wholesale Sales and Service:** *An interest in bringing others to a particular point of view by personal persuasion and by sales and promotional techniques.* You can satisfy this interest in various jobs that involve persuasion and selling. If you like using knowledge of science, you may enjoy selling pharmaceutical, medical, or electronic products or services. Real estate offers several kinds of sales jobs as well. If you like speaking on the phone, you could work as a telemarketer. Or you may enjoy selling apparel and other merchandise in a retail setting. If you prefer to help people, you may want a job in customer service.

⁕ **Scientific Research, Engineering, and Mathematics:** *An interest in discovering, collecting, and analyzing information about the natural world; in applying scientific research findings to problems in medicine, the life sciences, human behavior, and the natural sciences; in imagining and manipulating quantitative data; and in applying technology to manufacturing, transportation, and other economic activities.* You can satisfy this interest by working with the knowledge and processes of the sciences. You may enjoy researching and developing new knowledge in mathematics, or perhaps solving problems in the physical, life, or social sciences would appeal to you. You may want to study engineering and help create new machines, processes, and structures. If you want to work with scientific equipment and procedures, you could seek a job in a research or testing laboratory.

⁕ **Transportation, Distribution, and Logistics:** *An interest in operations that move people or materials.* You can satisfy this interest by managing a transportation service, by helping vehicles keep on their assigned schedules and routes, or by driving or piloting a vehicle. If you enjoy taking responsibility, perhaps managing a rail line would appeal to you. If you work well with details and can take pressure on the job, you might consider being an air traffic controller. Or would you rather get out on the highway, on the water, or up in the air? If so, you could drive a truck from state to state, be employed on a ship, or fly a crop duster over a cornfield. If you prefer to stay closer to home, you could drive a delivery van, taxi, or school bus. You can use your physical strength to load freight and arrange it so that it gets to its destination in one piece.

Best Recession-Proof Jobs for People Interested in Agriculture and Natural Resources

Job	Annual Earnings	Percent Growth	Annual Openings
1. Environmental Engineers	$69,940	25.4%	5,003
2. Pest Control Workers	$27,880	15.5%	6,006
3. Food Scientists and Technologists	$53,810	10.3%	663
4. Soil and Plant Scientists	$56,080	8.4%	850
5. Animal Scientists	$47,800	9.8%	299

Best Recession-Proof Jobs for People Interested in Architecture and Construction

Job	Annual Earnings	Percent Growth	Annual Openings
1. Hazardous Materials Removal Workers	$35,450	11.2%	1,933
2. Maintenance and Repair Workers, General	$31,910	10.1%	165,502
3. Electrical and Electronics Repairers, Powerhouse, Substation, and Relay	$57,400	−4.7%	1,591

Best Recession-Proof Jobs for People Interested in Arts and Communication

Job	Annual Earnings	Percent Growth	Annual Openings
1. Public Relations Specialists	$47,350	17.6%	51,216
2. Interpreters and Translators	$35,560	23.6%	6,630
3. Audio and Video Equipment Technicians	$34,840	24.2%	4,681
4. Editors	$46,990	2.3%	20,193
5. Police, Fire, and Ambulance Dispatchers	$31,470	13.6%	17,628
6. Air Traffic Controllers	$117,240	10.2%	1,213
7. Film and Video Editors	$46,670	12.7%	2,707
8. Broadcast Technicians	$30,690	12.1%	2,955

Best Recession-Proof Jobs for People Interested in Business and Administration

Job	Annual Earnings	Percent Growth	Annual Openings
1. Budget Analysts	$61,430	7.1%	6,423
2. Postal Service Clerks	$44,800	1.2%	3,703
3. Postal Service Mail Sorters, Processors, and Processing Machine Operators	$43,900	–8.4%	6,855

Best Recession-Proof Jobs for People Interested in Education and Training

Job	Annual Earnings	Percent Growth	Annual Openings
1. Teachers, Postsecondary	$57,770	22.9%	237,478
2. Instructional Coordinators	$52,790	22.5%	21,294
3. Preschool Teachers, Except Special Education	$22,680	26.3%	78,172
4. Education Administrators, Postsecondary	$73,990	14.2%	17,121
5. Self-Enrichment Education Teachers	$33,440	23.1%	64,449
6. Education Administrators, Elementary and Secondary School	$77,740	7.6%	27,143
7. Educational, Vocational, and School Counselors	$47,530	12.6%	54,025
8. Kindergarten Teachers, Except Special Education	$43,580	16.3%	27,603
9. Middle School Teachers, Except Special and Vocational Education	$46,300	11.2%	75,270
10. Secondary School Teachers, Except Special and Vocational Education	$47,740	5.6%	93,166
11. Health Educators	$41,330	26.2%	13,707
12. Curators	$46,300	23.3%	1,416
13. Special Education Teachers, Middle School	$47,650	15.8%	8,846
14. Adult Literacy, Remedial Education, and GED Teachers and Instructors	$43,910	14.2%	17,340
15. Education Administrators, Preschool and Child Care Center/Program	$37,740	23.5%	8,113
16. Librarians	$49,060	3.6%	18,945
17. Special Education Teachers, Secondary School	$48,330	8.5%	10,601
18. Teacher Assistants	$20,740	10.4%	193,986
19. Library Technicians	$26,560	8.5%	29,075
20. Museum Technicians and Conservators	$34,340	15.9%	1,341
21. Vocational Education Teachers, Secondary School	$48,690	–4.6%	7,639
22. Archivists	$40,730	14.4%	795
23. Library Assistants, Clerical	$21,640	7.9%	18,961

Best Recession-Proof Jobs for People Interested in Finance and Insurance

Job	Annual Earnings	Percent Growth	Annual Openings
1. Claims Adjusters, Examiners, and Investigators	$50,660	8.9%	22,024
2. Insurance Underwriters	$52,350	6.3%	6,880
3. Insurance Appraisers, Auto Damage	$49,180	12.5%	1,030

Best Recession-Proof Jobs for People Interested in Government and Public Administration

Job	Annual Earnings	Percent Growth	Annual Openings
1. Social and Community Service Managers	$52,070	24.7%	23,788
2. Tax Examiners, Collectors, and Revenue Agents	$45,620	2.1%	4,465
3. Court Reporters	$45,610	24.5%	2,620

Best Recession-Proof Jobs for People Interested in Health Science

Job	Annual Earnings	Percent Growth	Annual Openings
1. Physical Therapists	$66,200	27.1%	12,072
2. Pharmacists	$94,520	21.7%	16,358
3. Registered Nurses	$57,280	23.5%	233,499
4. Dental Hygienists	$62,800	30.1%	10,433
5. Veterinarians	$71,990	35.0%	5,301
6. Physician Assistants	$74,980	27.0%	7,147
7. Medical and Health Services Managers	$73,340	16.4%	31,877
8. Medical Assistants	$26,290	35.4%	92,977
9. Physicians and Surgeons	more than $145,600	14.2%	38,027
10. Pharmacy Technicians	$25,630	32.0%	54,453
11. Veterinary Technologists and Technicians	$26,780	41.0%	14,674
12. Dental Assistants	$30,220	29.2%	29,482
13. Occupational Therapists	$60,470	23.1%	8,338
14. Physical Therapist Assistants	$41,360	32.4%	5,957
15. Surgical Technologists	$36,080	24.5%	15,365
16. Radiation Therapists	$66,170	24.8%	1,461
17. Radiologic Technologists and Technicians	$48,170	15.1%	12,836

(continued)

(continued)

Best Recession-Proof Jobs for People Interested in Health Science

Job	Annual Earnings	Percent Growth	Annual Openings
18. Cardiovascular Technologists and Technicians	$42,300	25.5%	3,550
19. Medical Records and Health Information Technicians	$28,030	17.8%	39,048
20. Nursing Aides, Orderlies, and Attendants	$22,180	18.2%	321,036
21. Respiratory Therapists	$47,420	22.6%	5,563
22. Licensed Practical and Licensed Vocational Nurses	$36,550	14.0%	70,610
23. Occupational Therapist Assistants	$42,060	25.4%	2,634
24. Speech-Language Pathologists	$57,710	10.6%	11,160
25. Diagnostic Medical Sonographers	$57,160	19.1%	3,211
26. Medical and Clinical Laboratory Technologists	$49,700	12.4%	11,457
27. Massage Therapists	$33,400	20.3%	9,193
28. Chiropractors	$65,220	14.4%	3,179
29. Optometrists	$91,040	11.3%	1,789
30. Medical and Clinical Laboratory Technicians	$32,840	15.0%	10,866
31. Athletic Trainers	$36,560	24.3%	1,669
32. Nuclear Medicine Technologists	$62,300	14.8%	1,290
33. Podiatrists	$108,220	9.5%	648
34. Physical Therapist Aides	$22,060	24.4%	4,092
35. Dietitians and Nutritionists	$46,980	8.6%	4,996
36. Medical Equipment Preparers	$25,950	14.2%	8,363
37. Embalmers	$37,840	14.3%	1,660
38. Audiologists	$57,120	9.8%	980
39. Dietetic Technicians	$24,040	14.8%	4,062

Best Recession-Proof Jobs for People Interested in Hospitality, Tourism, and Recreation

Job	Annual Earnings	Percent Growth	Annual Openings
1. Athletes and Sports Competitors	$41,060	19.2%	4,293
2. Coaches and Scouts	$26,950	14.6%	51,100

Best Recession-Proof Jobs for People Interested in Human Service

Job	Annual Earnings	Percent Growth	Annual Openings
1. Social and Human Service Assistants	$25,580	33.6%	80,142
2. Child, Family, and School Social Workers	$37,480	19.1%	35,402
3. Mental Health Counselors	$34,380	30.0%	24,103
4. Substance Abuse and Behavioral Disorder Counselors	$34,040	34.3%	20,821
5. Clergy	$39,680	18.9%	35,092
6. Medical and Public Health Social Workers	$43,040	24.2%	16,429
7. Marriage and Family Therapists	$43,210	29.8%	5,953
8. Mental Health and Substance Abuse Social Workers	$35,410	29.9%	17,289
9. Clinical, Counseling, and School Psychologists	$59,440	15.8%	8,309
10. Rehabilitation Counselors	$29,200	23.0%	32,081
11. Probation Officers and Correctional Treatment Specialists	$42,500	10.9%	18,335
12. Interviewers, Except Eligibility and Loan	$26,290	9.5%	54,060
13. Funeral Attendants	$20,350	14.3%	6,034

Best Recession-Proof Jobs for People Interested in Information Technology

Job	Annual Earnings	Percent Growth	Annual Openings
1. Computer Systems Analysts	$69,760	29.0%	63,166
2. Network Systems and Data Communications Analysts	$64,600	53.4%	35,086
3. Database Administrators	$64,670	28.6%	8,258
4. Network and Computer Systems Administrators	$62,130	27.0%	37,010
5. Computer, Automated Teller, and Office Machine Repairers	$36,480	3.0%	22,330

Best Recession-Proof Jobs for People Interested in Law and Public Safety

Job	Annual Earnings	Percent Growth	Annual Openings
1. Detectives and Criminal Investigators	$58,260	17.3%	14,746
2. Correctional Officers and Jailers	$35,760	16.9%	56,579
3. First-Line Supervisors/Managers of Correctional Officers	$52,580	12.5%	4,180

(continued)

(continued)

Best Recession-Proof Jobs for People Interested in Law and Public Safety

Job	Annual Earnings	Percent Growth	Annual Openings
4. Emergency Medical Technicians and Paramedics	$27,070	19.2%	19,513
5. Fire Fighters	$41,190	12.1%	18,887
6. First-Line Supervisors/Managers of Fire Fighting and Prevention Workers	$62,900	11.5%	3,771
7. First-Line Supervisors/Managers of Police and Detectives	$69,310	9.2%	9,373
8. Police and Sheriff's Patrol Officers	$47,460	10.8%	37,842
9. Private Detectives and Investigators	$33,750	18.2%	7,329
10. Gaming Surveillance Officers and Gaming Investigators	$27,130	33.6%	2,124
11. Judges, Magistrate Judges, and Magistrates	$101,690	5.1%	1,567
12. Animal Control Workers	$27,910	12.5%	3,377
13. Administrative Law Judges, Adjudicators, and Hearing Officers	$72,600	0.1%	794
14. Bailiffs	$34,210	11.2%	2,223
15. Fire Inspectors and Investigators	$48,050	11.0%	644
16. Arbitrators, Mediators, and Conciliators	$49,490	10.6%	546

Best Recession-Proof Jobs for People Interested in Manufacturing

Job	Annual Earnings	Percent Growth	Annual Openings
1. Automotive Service Technicians and Mechanics	$33,780	14.3%	97,350
2. Water and Liquid Waste Treatment Plant and System Operators	$36,070	13.8%	9,575
3. Automotive Body and Related Repairers	$35,180	11.6%	37,469
4. Automotive Glass Installers and Repairers	$30,720	18.7%	3,457
5. Electrical and Electronics Repairers, Commercial and Industrial Equipment	$45,180	6.8%	6,607
6. Nuclear Power Reactor Operators	$69,370	10.6%	233
7. Power Plant Operators	$55,000	2.7%	1,796
8. Inspectors, Testers, Sorters, Samplers, and Weighers	$29,420	−7.0%	75,361

Best Recession-Proof Jobs for People Interested in Retail and Wholesale Sales and Service

Job	Annual Earnings	Percent Growth	Annual Openings
1. Funeral Directors	$49,620	12.5%	3,939

Best Recession-Proof Jobs for People Interested in Scientific Research, Engineering, and Mathematics

Job	Annual Earnings	Percent Growth	Annual Openings
1. Actuaries	$82,800	23.7%	3,245
2. Environmental Scientists and Specialists, Including Health	$56,100	25.1%	6,961
3. Geoscientists, Except Hydrologists and Geographers	$72,660	21.9%	2,471
4. Hydrologists	$66,260	24.3%	687
5. Mathematicians	$86,930	10.2%	473
6. Environmental Engineering Technicians	$40,560	24.8%	2,162
7. Industrial-Organizational Psychologists	$86,420	21.3%	118
8. Statisticians	$65,720	8.5%	3,433
9. Economists	$77,010	7.5%	1,555
10. Political Scientists	$90,140	5.3%	318
11. Anthropologists and Archeologists	$49,930	15.0%	446
12. Sociologists	$60,290	10.0%	403

Best Recession-Proof Jobs for People Interested in Transportation, Distribution, and Logistics

Job	Annual Earnings	Percent Growth	Annual Openings
1. Bus Drivers, School	$24,820	9.3%	59,809
2. Bus Drivers, Transit and Intercity	$32,090	12.5%	27,100
3. Taxi Drivers and Chauffeurs	$20,350	13.0%	35,954
4. Postal Service Mail Carriers	$44,350	1.0%	16,710
5. Ambulance Drivers and Attendants, Except Emergency Medical Technicians	$20,370	21.7%	3,703
6. Postmasters and Mail Superintendents	$55,790	–0.8%	1,627

Best Recession-Proof Jobs Sorted by Personality Types

These lists organize the 150 best recession-proof jobs into groups matching six personality types: Realistic, Investigative, Artistic, Social, Enterprising, and Conventional. This system was developed by John L. Holland and is used in the *Self-Directed Search* (SDS) and other career assessment inventories and information systems.

If you have used one of these career inventories or systems, the lists will help you identify jobs that most closely match these personality types. Even if you haven't used one of these systems, the concept of personality types and the jobs related to them can help you identify recession-proof jobs that suit the type of person you are.

As we did for the education levels, we have created only one list for each personality type. We've ranked the recession-proof jobs within each personality type based on their total combined scores for earnings, growth, and annual job openings. Each job is listed in the one personality type its related O*NET job most closely matches, even though it might also fit into others. Some of the jobs in the list correspond to two or more O*NET jobs linked to different personality types, so you may notice that these jobs appear on two or more lists below. Consider reviewing the jobs for more than one personality type so that you don't overlook possible jobs that would interest you.

Also, note that we didn't have data to crosswalk 10 of the 150 best jobs to their related personality type, so the following best jobs don't appear on the lists in this section:

* Diagnostic Medical Sonographers
* Environmental Engineering Technicians
* Environmental Engineers
* First-Line Supervisors/Managers of Correctional Officers
* Gaming Surveillance Officers and Gaming Investigators
* Marriage and Family Therapists
* Massage Therapists
* Postal Service Mail Sorters, Processors, and Processing Machine Operators
* Rehabilitation Counselors
* Veterinary Technologists and Technicians

It should come as no surprise that the smallest list in this set, with only seven jobs, is the list for the Artistic personality type. Jobs in the arts are highly competitive even during good times, and during recessions people and institutions tend to cut back on their expenditures for the arts.

Descriptions of the Six Personality Types

Following are brief descriptions for each of the six personality types used in the lists. Select the two or three descriptions that most closely describe you and then use the lists to identify jobs that best fit these personality types.

❋ **Realistic:** These occupations frequently involve work activities that include practical, hands-on problems and solutions. They often deal with plants; animals; and real-world materials such as wood, tools, and machinery. Many of the occupations require working outside and don't involve a lot of paperwork or working closely with others.

❋ **Investigative:** These occupations frequently involve working with ideas and require an extensive amount of thinking. These occupations can involve searching for facts and figuring out problems mentally.

❋ **Artistic:** These occupations frequently involve working with forms, designs, and patterns. They often require self-expression, and the work can be done without following a clear set of rules.

❋ **Social:** These occupations frequently involve working with, communicating with, and teaching people. These occupations often involve helping or providing service to others.

❋ **Enterprising:** These occupations frequently involve starting up and carrying out projects. These occupations can involve leading people and making many decisions. They sometimes require risk taking and often deal with business.

❋ **Conventional:** These occupations frequently involve following set procedures and routines. These occupations can include working with data and details more than with ideas. Usually there is a clear line of authority to follow.

Best Recession-Proof Jobs for People with a Realistic Personality Type

Job	Annual Earnings	Percent Growth	Annual Openings
1. Correctional Officers and Jailers	$35,760	16.9%	56,579
2. Radiologic Technologists and Technicians	$48,170	15.1%	12,836
3. Surgical Technologists	$36,080	24.5%	15,365
4. Automotive Service Technicians and Mechanics	$33,780	14.3%	97,350
5. Fire Fighters	$41,190	12.1%	18,887
6. Automotive Body and Related Repairers	$35,180	11.6%	37,469
7. Medical and Clinical Laboratory Technicians	$32,840	15.0%	10,866
8. Water and Liquid Waste Treatment Plant and System Operators	$36,070	13.8%	9,575
9. First-Line Supervisors/Managers of Fire Fighting and Prevention Workers	$62,900	11.5%	3,771
10. Bus Drivers, Transit and Intercity	$32,090	12.5%	27,100

(continued)

(continued)

Best Recession-Proof Jobs for People with a Realistic Personality Type

Job	Annual Earnings	Percent Growth	Annual Openings
11. Embalmers	$37,840	14.3%	1,660
12. Maintenance and Repair Workers, General	$31,910	10.1%	165,502
13. Automotive Glass Installers and Repairers	$30,720	18.7%	3,457
14. Computer, Automated Teller, and Office Machine Repairers	$36,480	3.0%	22,330
15. Electrical and Electronics Repairers, Commercial and Industrial Equipment	$45,180	6.8%	6,607
16. Pest Control Workers	$27,880	15.5%	6,006
17. Taxi Drivers and Chauffeurs	$20,350	13.0%	35,954
18. Nuclear Power Reactor Operators	$69,370	10.6%	233
19. Medical Equipment Preparers	$25,950	14.2%	8,363
20. Bus Drivers, School	$24,820	9.3%	59,809
21. Inspectors, Testers, Sorters, Samplers, and Weighers	$29,420	–7.0%	75,361
22. Power Plant Operators	$55,000	2.7%	1,796
23. Electrical and Electronics Repairers, Powerhouse, Substation, and Relay	$57,400	–4.7%	1,591
24. Hazardous Materials Removal Workers	$35,450	11.2%	1,933
25. Broadcast Technicians	$30,690	12.1%	2,955

Best Recession-Proof Jobs for People with an Investigative Personality Type

Job	Annual Earnings	Percent Growth	Annual Openings
1. Computer Systems Analysts	$69,760	29.0%	63,166
2. Pharmacists	$94,520	21.7%	16,358
3. Network Systems and Data Communications Analysts	$64,600	53.4%	35,086
4. Physician Assistants	$74,980	27.0%	7,147
5. Physicians and Surgeons	more than $145,600	14.2%	38,027
6. Veterinarians	$71,990	35.0%	5,301
7. Network and Computer Systems Administrators	$62,130	27.0%	37,010
8. Database Administrators	$64,670	28.6%	8,258
9. Geoscientists, Except Hydrologists and Geographers	$72,660	21.9%	2,471
10. Environmental Scientists and Specialists, Including Health	$56,100	25.1%	6,961
11. Clinical, Counseling, and School Psychologists	$59,440	15.8%	8,309
12. Optometrists	$91,040	11.3%	1,789

Best Recession-Proof Jobs for People with an Investigative Personality Type

Job	Annual Earnings	Percent Growth	Annual Openings
13. Hydrologists	$66,260	24.3%	687
14. Chiropractors	$65,220	14.4%	3,179
15. Respiratory Therapists	$47,420	22.6%	5,563
16. Industrial-Organizational Psychologists	$86,420	21.3%	118
17. Cardiovascular Technologists and Technicians	$42,300	25.5%	3,550
18. Medical and Clinical Laboratory Technologists	$49,700	12.4%	11,457
19. Nuclear Medicine Technologists	$62,300	14.8%	1,290
20. Mathematicians	$86,930	10.2%	473
21. Economists	$77,010	7.5%	1,555
22. Statisticians	$65,720	8.5%	3,433
23. Political Scientists	$90,140	5.3%	318
24. Anthropologists and Archeologists	$49,930	15.0%	446
25. Dietitians and Nutritionists	$46,980	8.6%	4,996
26. Archivists	$40,730	14.4%	795
27. Food Scientists and Technologists	$53,810	10.3%	663
28. Sociologists	$60,290	10.0%	403
29. Soil and Plant Scientists	$56,080	8.4%	850
30. Fire Inspectors and Investigators	$48,050	11.0%	644
31. Animal Scientists	$47,800	9.8%	299

Best Recession-Proof Jobs for People with an Artistic Personality Type

Job	Annual Earnings	Percent Growth	Annual Openings
1. Librarians	$49,060	3.6%	18,945
2. Editors	$46,990	2.3%	20,193
3. Court Reporters	$45,610	24.5%	2,620
4. Interpreters and Translators	$35,560	23.6%	6,630
5. Film and Video Editors	$46,670	12.7%	2,707
6. Curators	$46,300	23.3%	1,416
7. Museum Technicians and Conservators	$34,340	15.9%	1,341

Best Recession-Proof Jobs for People with a Social Personality Type

Job	Annual Earnings	Percent Growth	Annual Openings
1. Registered Nurses	$57,280	23.5%	233,499
2. Teachers, Postsecondary	$57,770	22.9%	237,478
3. Physical Therapists	$66,200	27.1%	12,072
4. Dental Hygienists	$62,800	30.1%	10,433
5. Social and Community Service Managers	$52,070	24.7%	23,788
6. Medical Assistants	$26,290	35.4%	92,977
7. Social and Human Service Assistants	$25,580	33.6%	80,142
8. Instructional Coordinators	$52,790	22.5%	21,294
9. Mental Health Counselors	$34,380	30.0%	24,103
10. Substance Abuse and Behavioral Disorder Counselors	$34,040	34.3%	20,821
11. Occupational Therapists	$60,470	23.1%	8,338
12. Dental Assistants	$30,220	29.2%	29,482
13. Preschool Teachers, Except Special Education	$22,680	26.3%	78,172
14. Radiation Therapists	$66,170	24.8%	1,461
15. Educational, Vocational, and School Counselors	$47,530	12.6%	54,025
16. Health Educators	$41,330	26.2%	13,707
17. Mental Health and Substance Abuse Social Workers	$35,410	29.9%	17,289
18. Education Administrators, Elementary and Secondary School	$77,740	7.6%	27,143
19. Kindergarten Teachers, Except Special Education	$43,580	16.3%	27,603
20. Medical and Public Health Social Workers	$43,040	24.2%	16,429
21. Middle School Teachers, Except Special and Vocational Education	$46,300	11.2%	75,270
22. Self-Enrichment Education Teachers	$33,440	23.1%	64,449
23. Child, Family, and School Social Workers	$37,480	19.1%	35,402
24. Clergy	$39,680	18.9%	35,092
25. Physical Therapist Assistants	$41,360	32.4%	5,957
26. Secondary School Teachers, Except Special and Vocational Education	$47,740	5.6%	93,166
27. Clinical, Counseling, and School Psychologists	$59,440	15.8%	8,309
28. Police and Sheriff's Patrol Officers	$47,460	10.8%	37,842
29. Nursing Aides, Orderlies, and Attendants	$22,180	18.2%	321,036
30. Licensed Practical and Licensed Vocational Nurses	$36,550	14.0%	70,610
31. Adult Literacy, Remedial Education, and GED Teachers and Instructors	$43,910	14.2%	17,340
32. Special Education Teachers, Middle School	$47,650	15.8%	8,846
33. Occupational Therapist Assistants	$42,060	25.4%	2,634
34. Speech-Language Pathologists	$57,710	10.6%	11,160

Best Recession-Proof Jobs for People with a Social Personality Type

Job	Annual Earnings	Percent Growth	Annual Openings
35. Education Administrators, Preschool and Child Care Center/Program	$37,740	23.5%	8,113
36. Emergency Medical Technicians and Paramedics	$27,070	19.2%	19,513
37. Probation Officers and Correctional Treatment Specialists	$42,500	10.9%	18,335
38. Athletic Trainers	$36,560	24.3%	1,669
39. Special Education Teachers, Secondary School	$48,330	8.5%	10,601
40. Teacher Assistants	$20,740	10.4%	193,986
41. Podiatrists	$108,220	9.5%	648
42. Police, Fire, and Ambulance Dispatchers	$31,470	13.6%	17,628
43. Vocational Education Teachers, Secondary School	$48,690	−4.6%	7,639
44. Physical Therapist Aides	$22,060	24.4%	4,092
45. Audiologists	$57,120	9.8%	980
46. Ambulance Drivers and Attendants, Except Emergency Medical Technicians	$20,370	21.7%	3,703
47. Dietetic Technicians	$24,040	14.8%	4,062
48. Bailiffs	$34,210	11.2%	2,223
49. Animal Control Workers	$27,910	12.5%	3,377
50. Funeral Attendants	$20,350	14.3%	6,034

Best Recession-Proof Jobs for People with an Enterprising Personality Type

Job	Annual Earnings	Percent Growth	Annual Openings
1. Medical and Health Services Managers	$73,340	16.4%	31,877
2. Education Administrators, Postsecondary	$73,990	14.2%	17,121
3. Public Relations Specialists	$47,350	17.6%	51,216
4. Detectives and Criminal Investigators	$58,260	17.3%	14,746
5. Athletes and Sports Competitors	$41,060	19.2%	4,293
6. Coaches and Scouts	$26,950	14.6%	51,100
7. First-Line Supervisors/Managers of Police and Detectives	$69,310	9.2%	9,373
8. Claims Adjusters, Examiners, and Investigators	$50,660	8.9%	22,024
9. Private Detectives and Investigators	$33,750	18.2%	7,329
10. Judges, Magistrate Judges, and Magistrates	$101,690	5.1%	1,567
11. Funeral Directors	$49,620	12.5%	3,939

(continued)

(continued)

Best Recession-Proof Jobs for People with an Enterprising Personality Type

Job	Annual Earnings	Percent Growth	Annual Openings
12. Administrative Law Judges, Adjudicators, and Hearing Officers	$72,600	0.1%	794
13. Postmasters and Mail Superintendents	$55,790	–0.8%	1,627
14. Arbitrators, Mediators, and Conciliators	$49,490	10.6%	546

Best Recession-Proof Jobs for People with a Conventional Personality Type

Job	Annual Earnings	Percent Growth	Annual Openings
1. Detectives and Criminal Investigators	$58,260	17.3%	14,746
2. Pharmacy Technicians	$25,630	32.0%	54,453
3. Actuaries	$82,800	23.7%	3,245
4. Medical Records and Health Information Technicians	$28,030	17.8%	39,048
5. Claims Adjusters, Examiners, and Investigators	$50,660	8.9%	22,024
6. Air Traffic Controllers	$117,240	10.2%	1,213
7. Audio and Video Equipment Technicians	$34,840	24.2%	4,681
8. Budget Analysts	$61,430	7.1%	6,423
9. Interviewers, Except Eligibility and Loan	$26,290	9.5%	54,060
10. Insurance Underwriters	$52,350	6.3%	6,880
11. Insurance Appraisers, Auto Damage	$49,180	12.5%	1,030
12. Library Technicians	$26,560	8.5%	29,075
13. Fire Inspectors and Investigators	$48,050	11.0%	644
14. Library Assistants, Clerical	$21,640	7.9%	18,961
15. Postal Service Mail Carriers	$44,350	1.0%	16,710
16. Tax Examiners, Collectors, and Revenue Agents	$45,620	2.1%	4,465
17. Postal Service Clerks	$44,800	1.2%	3,703

Bonus Lists: The Most Recession-Proof Industries, States, and Metropolitan Areas

If you read Part I of this book, you know that you can improve your chances of staying employed during recessions by choosing not just the right occupation, but also the right industry and the right location. The following lists can help you make these additional choices. To create the lists, we ranked industries, states, and metropolitan areas to identify those with the greatest concentrations of recession-proof jobs. In the following lists, the degree of concentration is expressed as the percentage of the total workforce of the industry, state, or metro area workforce that is employed in the 150 best recession-proof jobs.

The 10 Most Recession-Proof Industries

Industries with a high concentration of recession-proof jobs may be less sensitive to economic downturns. In fact, even workers in recession-sensitive occupations may be able to ride out an economic downturn if they're working in an industry that tends to grow at a steady rate. That's why you may be interested in the following list of industries where the recession-proof jobs are most highly concentrated. We limited the list to 10 items because any additional industries would have only a small concentration of recession-proof jobs.

The 10 Most Recession-Proof Industries

Industry	Percentage of Workers in Recession-Proof Jobs
1. Transit and Ground Passenger Transportation	15.5%
2. Hospitals, Public and Private	13.1%
3. Ambulatory Health Care Services	10.6%
4. Nursing and Residential Care Facilities	10.4%
5. Educational Services, Public and Private	10.2%
6. Other Information Services	9.7%
7. Social Assistance	8.3%
8. Repair and Maintenance	6.8%
9. Religious, Grantmaking, Civic, Professional, and Similar Organizations	6.6%
10. Insurance Carriers and Related Activities	4.3%

The States Ranked by Concentration of Recession-Proof Jobs

Recessions strike different geographic regions with different degrees of severity. We looked at the 50 states, plus the District of Columbia, to see where the recession-proof jobs are most highly concentrated. You may find more economic stability in the states near the top of the list. However, notice that there isn't a great amount of variation between the states, with the exception of Nevada. The drop in air travel following 9/11 hurt Nevada badly and made planners there acutely aware of the state's sensitivity to recession and other economic upsets; since then, they have been working to diversify Nevada's industries. You can take away a lesson from Nevada's experience: Beware of locating in a region that depends on a highly limited set of industries.

The States Ranked by Concentration of Recession-Proof Jobs

State	Percentage of Workers in Recession-Proof Jobs
1. Maine	7.3%
2. Massachusetts	7.1%
3. Connecticut	7.0%
4. Vermont	7.0%
5. New York	6.7%
6. West Virginia	6.7%
7. Mississippi	6.6%
8. Pennsylvania	6.6%
9. New Jersey	6.5%
10. Oklahoma	6.4%
11. Rhode Island	6.4%
12. Maryland	6.3%
13. Missouri	6.3%
14. South Dakota	6.3%
15. Kansas	6.2%
16. Louisiana	6.2%
17. Nebraska	6.2%
18. New Hampshire	6.2%
19. New Mexico	6.2%
20. Arkansas	6.1%
21. Iowa	6.1%
22. Kentucky	6.1%
23. Montana	6.1%
24. North Dakota	6.1%
25. Alaska	6.0%

The States Ranked by Concentration of Recession-Proof Jobs

State	Percentage of Workers in Recession-Proof Jobs
26. North Carolina	6.0%
27. Ohio	6.0%
28. Virginia	6.0%
29. Alabama	5.9%
30. Michigan	5.9%
31. Tennessee	5.9%
32. Texas	5.9%
33. Washington	5.9%
34. Wyoming	5.9%
35. Delaware	5.8%
36. Georgia	5.8%
37. Minnesota	5.8%
38. South Carolina	5.8%
39. Wisconsin	5.8%
40. Hawaii	5.7%
41. Illinois	5.7%
42. Colorado	5.6%
43. Florida	5.6%
44. Indiana	5.6%
45. District of Columbia	5.5%
46. Idaho	5.5%
47. Oregon	5.5%
48. California	5.4%
49. Utah	5.4%
50. Arizona	5.2%
51. Nevada	3.9%

The 25 Most Recession-Proof Metropolitan Areas

To create the following list, we calculated the concentration of recession-proof jobs in approximately 350 metropolitan areas and identified the 25 with the highest concentration. It's no accident that four of these metro areas are state capitals; occupations with many government workers tend to be more recession-proof. It seems reasonable to conclude that government centers are the exceptions to the rule that it's unwise to locate in a one-industry town.

Notice that, even in the top-listed metro areas, the percentage of workers in recession-proof jobs isn't very high. Nevertheless, these metro areas are probably more economically stable than the lowest-listed metro areas; for the lowest-listed five, the concentration is lower than 3 percent.

The 25 Most Recession-Proof Metropolitan Areas	
Metro Area	Ratio of Recession-Proof Jobs to All Jobs
1. New Bedford, MA	8.5%
2. Worcester, MA–CT	8.5%
3. Waterbury, CT	8.3%
4. Duluth, MN–WI	8.2%
5. Utica–Rome, NY	8.2%
6. Springfield, MA–CT	8.1%
7. Vineland–Millville–Bridgeton, NJ	8.1%
8. Hartford–West Hartford–East Hartford, CT	8.0%
9. Killeen–Temple–Fort Hood, TX	8.0%
10. New Haven, CT	7.9%
11. Albany–Schenectady–Troy, NY	7.8%
12. Barnstable Town, MA	7.8%
13. Olympia, WA	7.7%
14. Johnstown, PA	7.6%
15. Poughkeepsie–Newburgh–Middletown, NY	7.6%
16. Topeka, KS	7.6%
17. Augusta–Richmond County, GA–SC	7.5%
18. Huntington–Ashland, WV–KY–OH	7.5%
19. Kingston, NY	7.5%
20. Leominster–Fitchburg–Gardner, MA	7.5%
21. McAllen–Edinburg–Mission, TX	7.5%
22. Monroe, LA	7.5%
23. Portland–South Portland–Biddeford, ME	7.5%
24. Youngstown–Warren–Boardman, OH–PA	7.5%
25. Binghamton, NY	7.4%

Bonus Lists: The 10 Most Recession-Proof Skills and Knowledges/Courses

Part I of this book emphasizes the importance of developing your skills as a way of making your job recession-proof. Some skills are highly specific to a particular job, such as mastery of a specialized software application. But other skills are transferable from many jobs to many others; they are especially valuable because they can be useful in a wide variety of work situations.

The O*NET database identifies the transferable skills for each occupation, and you can see the most important skills for any of the 150 recession-proof jobs by looking at the job descriptions in Part III. However, we thought it would be especially useful to regard the 150 recession-proof jobs together *as a group* and find the 10 most important skills for them. Because these 10 skills are associated with recession-proof jobs that have good economic rewards, they may be the most valuable skills of all. The name of the skill may not communicate its full meaning, so we also provide O*NET's definition of each skill.

The 10 Most Recession-Proof Skills

Skill	Definition
1. Social Perceptiveness	Being aware of others' reactions and understanding why they react the way they do
2. Writing	Communicating effectively with others in writing as indicated by the needs of the audience
3. Reading Comprehension	Understanding written sentences and paragraphs in work-related documents
4. Service Orientation	Actively looking for ways to help people
5. Persuasion	Persuading others to approach things differently
6. Active Listening	Listening to what other people are saying and asking questions as appropriate
7. Critical Thinking	Using logic and analysis to identify the strengths and weaknesses of different approaches
8. Speaking	Talking to others to effectively convey information
9. Learning Strategies	Using multiple approaches when learning or teaching new things
10. Instructing	Teaching others how to do something

Each occupation in the O*NET database is also rated on features called *knowledges*. One way of looking at these is as subjects that you might study in school and college or as topics that you might become informed about through your work.

As we did for transferable skills, we looked at which knowledges are most important for the 150 recession-proof jobs, and the results of our analysis are very interesting. The top 10 recession-proof knowledges that emerged are closely linked to the relatively secure fields of health care and education. Also, most of these knowledges tend to be applied in situations where workers and clients meet face to face, so the work tasks cannot be shipped to workers in a foreign country. The names of the knowledges are fairly straightforward, but we provide definitions for all of them.

The 10 Most Recession-Proof Knowledges/Courses

Skill	Definition
1. Therapy and Counseling	Information and techniques needed to rehabilitate physical and mental ailments and to provide career guidance, including alternative treatments, rehabilitation equipment and its proper use, and methods to evaluate treatment effects
2. Psychology	Human behavior and performance, mental processes, psychological research methods, and the assessment and treatment of behavioral and affective disorders
3. Sociology and Anthropology	Group behavior and dynamics; societal trends and influences; and cultures and their history, migrations, ethnicity, and origins
4. Philosophy and Theology	Different philosophical systems and religions, including their basic principles, values, ethics, ways of thinking, customs, and practices and their impact on human culture
5. Education and Training	Instructional methods and training techniques, including curriculum design principles, learning theory, group and individual teaching techniques, design of individual development plans, and test design principles
6. Medicine and Dentistry	Information and techniques needed to diagnose and treat injuries, diseases, and deformities; these include symptoms, treatment alternatives, drug properties and interactions, and preventive health-care measures
7. English Language	The structure and content of the English language, including the meaning and spelling of words, rules of composition, and grammar
8. Biology	Plant and animal living tissue, cells, organisms, and entities, including their functions, interdependencies, and interactions with each other and the environment
9. Communications and Media	Media production, communication, and dissemination techniques and methods, including alternative ways to inform and entertain via written, oral, and visual media
10. History and Archeology	Past historical events and their causes, indicators, and impact on particular civilizations and cultures

Bonus Lists: The Best Recession-Sensitive Jobs

When the economy is humming along at a good pace, you may want to consider taking a job that's not recession-proof. The pay or other satisfactions in the recession-*sensitive* job may be better than you can get from a more secure job. Or the job may be a way for you to establish your credentials in a new industry or develop new skills that you can use in a recession-proof job later, when the economic scene worsens.

So you may want to consider the most rewarding jobs in the following set of lists, even though they are more sensitive to economic downturns—in some cases, much more sensitive—than the 150 jobs that make up the other lists in this book. We created this list using the exact same criteria that we used for the 150 recession-proof jobs (for details, see the introduction), except that for this list we drew from the pool of occupations that are *not* rated very low on economic sensitivity. On the following lists you'll see the sensitivity rating for each job next to the job title. The ratings range from 1 (somewhat sensitive) to 3 (very sensitive).

Note: For 21 of these ratings, the number is followed by the letter F, which indicates that the job is at risk for offshoring; employers can find ways to have the work done in low-wage foreign countries rather than by Americans.

The 150 Best Recession-Sensitive Jobs Overall

These jobs have the highest combined ratings for earnings, projected growth, and number of openings, and the jobs rated 1 have only moderate sensitivity to recession. The top of the list is dominated by jobs in management and technology, but you can also find jobs for business specialists, technicians, and many other kinds of workers. Unlike the 150 recession-proof jobs, these 150 recession-sensitive jobs are *not* described in Part III of this book, but in Appendix A you'll find a list of sources you can use to learn more about them.

Risk-taking does not necessarily lead to greater rewards. When we compared these 150 recession-sensitive jobs to the 150 best recession-proof jobs, we found that the recession-sensitive jobs pay *less,* an average of $46,698 compared to $52,967 for the recession-proof jobs. Projected job growth also isn't as good for the recession-sensitive jobs: 13.2 percent compared to 16.7 percent for the recession-proof jobs. However, the recession-sensitive jobs offer more job openings, an average of 53,484 job openings per year, compared to 24,443 for the recession-proof jobs. So consider pursuing these jobs if you can accept somewhat higher long-range unemployment risks in exchange for greater short-term availability of jobs.

The 150 Best Recession-Sensitive Jobs Overall

Job	Economic Sensitivity Rating	Annual Earnings	Percent Growth	Annual Openings
1. Computer Software Engineers, Applications	1F	$79,780	44.6%	58,690
2. Management Analysts	1	$68,050	21.9%	125,669
3. Computer Software Engineers, Systems Software	3F	$85,370	28.2%	33,139
4. Securities, Commodities, and Financial Services Sales Agents	3	$68,500	24.8%	47,750

(continued)

(continued)

The 150 Best Recession-Sensitive Jobs Overall

Job	Economic Sensitivity Rating	Annual Earnings	Percent Growth	Annual Openings
5. Financial Analysts	3	$66,590	33.8%	29,317
6. Computer and Information Systems Managers	3	$101,580	16.4%	30,887
7. Accountants and Auditors	1	$54,630	17.7%	134,463
8. Financial Managers	3	$90,970	12.6%	57,589
9. Market Research Analysts	2	$58,820	20.1%	45,015
10. Construction Managers	1	$73,700	15.7%	44,158
11. Personal Financial Advisors	1	$66,120	41.0%	17,114
12. Lawyers	1	$102,470	11.0%	49,445
13. Cost Estimators	1	$52,940	18.5%	38,379
14. Marketing Managers	1	$98,720	14.4%	20,189
15. Civil Engineers	1	$68,600	18.0%	15,979
16. Sales Representatives, Wholesale and Manufacturing, Technical and Scientific Products	1	$64,440	12.4%	43,469
17. Industrial Engineers	3	$68,620	20.3%	11,272
18. Training and Development Specialists	2	$47,830	18.3%	35,862
19. Elementary School Teachers, Except Special Education	2	$45,570	13.6%	181,612
20. Sales Managers	2	$91,560	10.2%	36,392
21. Multi-Media Artists and Animators	1F	$51,350	25.8%	13,182
22. Medical Scientists, Except Epidemiologists	2F	$61,680	20.2%	10,596
23. Compensation, Benefits, and Job Analysis Specialists	1	$50,230	18.4%	18,761
24. Loan Officers	2	$51,760	11.5%	54,237
25. Advertising Sales Agents	1	$42,750	20.3%	29,233
26. Surveyors	1	$48,290	23.7%	14,305
27. Insurance Sales Agents	1	$43,870	12.9%	64,162
28. Paralegals and Legal Assistants	1	$43,040	22.2%	22,756
29. Architects, Except Landscape and Naval	2F	$64,150	17.7%	11,324
30. Employment, Recruitment, and Placement Specialists	1	$42,420	18.4%	33,588
31. Special Education Teachers, Preschool, Kindergarten, and Elementary School	1	$46,360	19.6%	20,049
32. Property, Real Estate, and Community Association Managers	1	$43,070	15.1%	49,916
33. Administrative Services Managers	1	$67,690	11.7%	19,513
34. Computer Support Specialists	1F	$41,470	12.9%	97,334
35. Executive Secretaries and Administrative Assistants	1	$37,240	14.8%	235,314

The 150 Best Recession-Sensitive Jobs Overall

Job	Economic Sensitivity Rating	Annual Earnings	Percent Growth	Annual Openings
36. First-Line Supervisors/Managers of Construction Trades and Extraction Workers	1	$53,850	9.1%	82,923
37. Writers and Authors	2	$48,640	12.8%	24,023
38. Technical Writers	2	$58,050	19.5%	7,498
39. Public Relations Managers	3	$82,180	16.9%	5,781
40. Real Estate Brokers	3	$60,790	11.1%	18,689
41. Construction and Building Inspectors	1	$46,570	18.2%	12,606
42. Sales Representatives, Wholesale and Manufacturing, Except Technical and Scientific Products	2	$49,610	8.4%	156,215
43. Customer Service Representatives	2F	$28,330	24.8%	600,937
44. Plumbers, Pipefitters, and Steamfitters	3	$42,770	10.6%	68,643
45. Computer and Information Scientists, Research	1F	$93,950	21.5%	2,901
46. Bill and Account Collectors	1F	$29,050	22.9%	118,709
47. General and Operations Managers	1	$85,230	1.5%	112,072
48. Airline Pilots, Copilots, and Flight Engineers	1	$141,090	12.9%	4,073
49. First-Line Supervisors/Managers of Landscaping, Lawn Service, and Groundskeeping Workers	1	$37,300	17.6%	18,956
50. Real Estate Sales Agents	1	$39,760	10.6%	61,232
51. Compensation and Benefits Managers	2	$74,750	12.0%	6,121
52. Interior Designers	2	$42,260	19.5%	8,434
53. Legal Secretaries	2	$38,190	11.7%	38,682
54. Meeting and Convention Planners	2	$42,180	19.9%	8,318
55. Carpenters	2	$36,550	10.3%	223,225
56. Training and Development Managers	2	$80,250	15.6%	3,759
57. Truck Drivers, Heavy and Tractor-Trailer	1	$35,040	10.4%	279,032
58. Environmental Science and Protection Technicians, Including Health	1	$38,090	28.0%	8,404
59. First-Line Supervisors/Managers of Non-Retail Sales Workers	1	$65,510	3.7%	48,883
60. Producers and Directors	1	$56,310	11.1%	8,992
61. Bookkeeping, Accounting, and Auditing Clerks	2F	$30,560	12.5%	286,854
62. Electricians	1	$43,610	7.4%	79,083
63. First-Line Supervisors/Managers of Personal Service Workers	1	$32,800	15.5%	37,555
64. Dentists, General	1	$132,140	9.2%	7,106
65. Flight Attendants	1	$53,780	10.6%	10,773

(continued)

(continued)

The 150 Best Recession-Sensitive Jobs Overall

Job	Economic Sensitivity Rating	Annual Earnings	Percent Growth	Annual Openings
66. First-Line Supervisors/Managers of Transportation and Material-Moving Machine and Vehicle Operators	2	$48,330	10.2%	16,580
67. Brokerage Clerks	1	$36,390	20.0%	10,826
68. Art Directors	1	$68,100	9.0%	9,719
69. Chief Executives	2 more than	$145,600	2.0%	21,209
70. First-Line Supervisors/Managers of Mechanics, Installers, and Repairers	1	$53,890	7.3%	24,361
71. Aerospace Engineers	1F	$87,610	10.2%	6,498
72. Roofers	2	$32,260	14.3%	38,398
73. Biomedical Engineers	2F	$73,930	21.1%	1,804
74. First-Line Supervisors/Managers of Office and Administrative Support Workers	1	$43,510	5.8%	138,420
75. Bus and Truck Mechanics and Diesel Engine Specialists	1	$37,660	11.5%	25,428
76. Fitness Trainers and Aerobics Instructors	1	$25,910	26.8%	51,235
77. Painters, Construction and Maintenance	1	$31,190	11.8%	101,140
78. Appraisers and Assessors of Real Estate	1	$44,460	16.9%	6,493
79. Biological Technicians	1F	$35,710	16.0%	15,374
80. Directors, Religious Activities and Education	1	$34,260	19.7%	11,463
81. Natural Sciences Managers	2	$100,080	11.4%	3,661
82. Medical Secretaries	1	$28,090	16.7%	60,659
83. Chemists	1F	$59,870	9.1%	9,024
84. First-Line Supervisors/Managers of Helpers, Laborers, and Material Movers, Hand	1	$39,570	12.5%	13,877
85. Engineering Managers	1	$105,430	7.3%	7,404
86. Cargo and Freight Agents	1	$37,110	16.5%	9,967
87. Aircraft Mechanics and Service Technicians	1F	$47,740	10.6%	9,708
88. Gaming Supervisors	1	$41,160	23.4%	4,602
89. Mobile Heavy Equipment Mechanics, Except Engines	2	$40,440	12.3%	11,037
90. Sales Engineers	1	$77,720	8.5%	7,371
91. Forensic Science Technicians	1	$45,330	30.7%	3,074
92. Cartographers and Photogrammetrists	2	$48,240	20.3%	2,823
93. Graphic Designers	2F	$39,900	9.8%	26,968
94. Operations Research Analysts	2	$64,650	10.6%	5,727
95. Brickmasons and Blockmasons	2	$42,980	9.7%	17,569

The 150 Best Recession-Sensitive Jobs Overall

Job	Economic Sensitivity Rating	Annual Earnings	Percent Growth	Annual Openings
96. Aircraft Structure, Surfaces, Rigging, and Systems Assemblers	1	$45,410	12.8%	6,550
97. Food Service Managers	1	$43,020	5.0%	59,302
98. Captains, Mates, and Pilots of Water Vessels	2	$53,430	17.9%	2,665
99. Cement Masons and Concrete Finishers	2	$32,650	11.4%	34,625
100. Industrial Machinery Mechanics	1	$41,050	9.0%	23,361
101. Operating Engineers and Other Construction Equipment Operators	2	$36,890	8.4%	55,468
102. Receptionists and Information Clerks	1	$22,900	17.2%	334,124
103. Biochemists and Biophysicists	2F	$76,320	15.9%	1,637
104. Tile and Marble Setters	2	$36,590	15.4%	9,066
105. First-Line Supervisors/Managers of Housekeeping and Janitorial Workers	2	$31,290	12.7%	30,613
106. Music Directors and Composers	1	$39,750	12.9%	8,597
107. Transportation, Storage, and Distribution Managers	2	$73,080	8.3%	6,994
108. Mechanical Engineers	2F	$69,850	4.2%	12,394
109. Landscape Architects	1	$55,140	16.4%	2,342
110. Landscaping and Groundskeeping Workers	2	$21,260	18.1%	307,138
111. Heating, Air Conditioning, and Refrigeration Mechanics and Installers	1	$37,660	8.7%	29,719
112. Office Clerks, General	1	$23,710	12.6%	765,803
113. Gaming Managers	3	$62,820	24.4%	549
114. Human Resources Assistants, Except Payroll and Timekeeping	1	$33,750	11.3%	18,647
115. Surveying and Mapping Technicians	2	$32,340	19.4%	8,299
116. Security Guards	2	$21,530	16.9%	222,085
117. Security and Fire Alarm Systems Installers	2	$34,810	20.2%	5,729
118. Electrical Engineers	2F	$75,930	6.3%	6,806
119. First-Line Supervisors/Managers of Food Preparation and Serving Workers	3	$26,980	11.3%	154,175
120. Computer Programmers	3F	$65,510	–4.1%	27,937
121. Construction Laborers	2	$26,320	10.9%	257,407
122. Urban and Regional Planners	1	$56,630	14.5%	1,967
123. Transportation Inspectors	2	$50,390	16.4%	2,122
124. Lodging Managers	2	$42,320	12.2%	5,529
125. Production, Planning, and Expediting Clerks	3	$38,620	4.2%	52,735
126. Sheet Metal Workers	1	$37,360	6.7%	31,677

(continued)

(continued)

The 150 Best Recession-Sensitive Jobs Overall

Job	Economic Sensitivity Rating	Annual Earnings	Percent Growth	Annual Openings
127. Agents and Business Managers of Artists, Performers, and Athletes	1	$64,500	9.6%	3,940
128. Compliance Officers, Except Agriculture, Construction, Health and Safety, and Transportation	1	$47,050	4.9%	15,841
129. Medical Equipment Repairers	1	$40,580	21.7%	2,351
130. Drywall and Ceiling Tile Installers	1	$36,140	7.3%	30,945
131. Purchasing Managers	1	$81,570	3.4%	7,243
132. Tellers	1	$22,140	13.5%	146,077
133. First-Line Supervisors/Managers of Retail Sales Workers	2	$33,960	4.2%	221,241
134. Industrial Engineering Technicians	1	$46,810	9.9%	6,172
135. Purchasing Agents, Except Wholesale, Retail, and Farm Products	1F	$50,730	0.1%	22,349
136. First-Line Supervisors/Managers of Production and Operating Workers	1	$47,300	−4.8%	46,144
137. Farm, Ranch, and Other Agricultural Managers	1	$52,070	1.1%	18,101
138. Financial Examiners	1	$65,370	10.7%	2,449
139. Civil Engineering Technicians	2	$40,560	10.2%	7,499
140. Industrial Production Managers	1	$77,670	−5.9%	14,889
141. Telecommunications Equipment Installers and Repairers, Except Line Installers	1	$52,430	2.5%	13,541
142. Telecommunications Line Installers and Repairers	1	$46,280	4.6%	14,719
143. Architectural and Civil Drafters	1F	$41,960	6.1%	16,238
144. Commercial Pilots	1	$57,480	13.2%	1,425
145. Boilermakers	1	$46,960	14.0%	2,333
146. Electrical and Electronic Engineering Technicians	1F	$50,660	3.6%	12,583
147. Demonstrators and Product Promoters	1	$22,150	18.0%	32,779
148. Sailors and Marine Oilers	3	$30,630	15.7%	8,600
149. Electronics Engineers, Except Computer	2F	$81,050	3.7%	5,699
150. Ship Engineers	3	$54,820	14.1%	1,102

The 50 Best-Paying Recession-Sensitive Jobs

To create the following list, we sorted the 150 recession-sensitive jobs to find the highest-paying 50. Like all our earnings figures, the figures in this list represent national averages; actual earnings vary considerably, depending on your level of experience, the industry you're working in, and your geographical location.

The 50 Best-Paying Recession-Sensitive Jobs

Job	Economic Sensitivity Rating	Annual Earnings
1. Chief Executives	2 ..... more than	$145,600
2. Airline Pilots, Copilots, and Flight Engineers	1	$141,090
3. Dentists, General	1	$132,140
4. Engineering Managers	1	$105,430
5. Lawyers	1	$102,470
6. Computer and Information Systems Managers	3	$101,580
7. Natural Sciences Managers	2	$100,080
8. Marketing Managers	1	$98,720
9. Computer and Information Scientists, Research	1F	$93,950
10. Sales Managers	2	$91,560
11. Financial Managers	3	$90,970
12. Aerospace Engineers	1F	$87,610
13. Computer Software Engineers, Systems Software	3F	$85,370
14. General and Operations Managers	1	$85,230
15. Public Relations Managers	3	$82,180
16. Purchasing Managers	1	$81,570
17. Electronics Engineers, Except Computer	2F	$81,050
18. Training and Development Managers	2	$80,250
19. Computer Software Engineers, Applications	1F	$79,780
20. Sales Engineers	1	$77,720
21. Industrial Production Managers	1	$77,670
22. Biochemists and Biophysicists	2F	$76,320
23. Electrical Engineers	2F	$75,930
24. Compensation and Benefits Managers	2	$74,750
25. Biomedical Engineers	2F	$73,930
26. Construction Managers	1	$73,700
27. Transportation, Storage, and Distribution Managers	2	$73,080
28. Mechanical Engineers	2F	$69,850
29. Industrial Engineers	3	$68,620
30. Civil Engineers	1	$68,600
31. Securities, Commodities, and Financial Services Sales Agents	3	$68,500
32. Art Directors	1	$68,100
33. Management Analysts	1	$68,050
34. Administrative Services Managers	1	$67,690
35. Financial Analysts	3	$66,590
36. Personal Financial Advisors	1	$66,120

(continued)

(continued)

The 50 Best-Paying Recession-Sensitive Jobs

Job	Economic Sensitivity Rating	Annual Earnings
37. Computer Programmers	3F	$65,510
38. First-Line Supervisors/Managers of Non-Retail Sales Workers	1	$65,510
39. Financial Examiners	1	$65,370
40. Operations Research Analysts	2	$64,650
41. Agents and Business Managers of Artists, Performers, and Athletes	1	$64,500
42. Sales Representatives, Wholesale and Manufacturing, Technical and Scientific Products	1	$64,440
43. Architects, Except Landscape and Naval	2F	$64,150
44. Gaming Managers	3	$62,820
45. Medical Scientists, Except Epidemiologists	2F	$61,680
46. Real Estate Brokers	3	$60,790
47. Chemists	1F	$59,870
48. Market Research Analysts	2	$58,820
49. Technical Writers	2	$58,050
50. Commercial Pilots	1	$57,480

The 50 Fastest-Growing Recession-Sensitive Jobs

Although the recession-sensitive jobs aren't expected to grow as fast on average as the recession-proof jobs, many of them are booming. The following list shows the 50 jobs that are projected to have the highest percentage increase in the numbers of people employed through 2016. Some of the fastest-growing jobs have a high rating (3) for sensitivity to recession, and some run a risk of offshoring, but others are only moderately sensitive.

The 50 Fastest-Growing Recession-Sensitive Jobs

Job	Economic Sensitivity Rating	Percent Growth
1. Computer Software Engineers, Applications	1F	44.6%
2. Personal Financial Advisors	1	41.0%
3. Financial Analysts	3	33.8%
4. Forensic Science Technicians	1	30.7%
5. Computer Software Engineers, Systems Software	3F	28.2%
6. Environmental Science and Protection Technicians, Including Health	1	28.0%

The 50 Fastest-Growing Recession-Sensitive Jobs

Job	Economic Sensitivity Rating	Percent Growth
7. Fitness Trainers and Aerobics Instructors	1	26.8%
8. Multi-Media Artists and Animators	1F	25.8%
9. Customer Service Representatives	2F	24.8%
10. Securities, Commodities, and Financial Services Sales Agents	3	24.8%
11. Gaming Managers	3	24.4%
12. Surveyors	1	23.7%
13. Gaming Supervisors	1	23.4%
14. Bill and Account Collectors	1F	22.9%
15. Paralegals and Legal Assistants	1	22.2%
16. Management Analysts	1	21.9%
17. Medical Equipment Repairers	1	21.7%
18. Computer and Information Scientists, Research	1F	21.5%
19. Biomedical Engineers	2F	21.1%
20. Advertising Sales Agents	1	20.3%
21. Cartographers and Photogrammetrists	2	20.3%
22. Industrial Engineers	3	20.3%
23. Medical Scientists, Except Epidemiologists	2F	20.2%
24. Security and Fire Alarm Systems Installers	2	20.2%
25. Market Research Analysts	2	20.1%
26. Brokerage Clerks	1	20.0%
27. Meeting and Convention Planners	2	19.9%
28. Directors, Religious Activities and Education	1	19.7%
29. Special Education Teachers, Preschool, Kindergarten, and Elementary School	1	19.6%
30. Interior Designers	2	19.5%
31. Technical Writers	2	19.5%
32. Surveying and Mapping Technicians	2	19.4%
33. Cost Estimators	1	18.5%
34. Compensation, Benefits, and Job Analysis Specialists	1	18.4%
35. Employment, Recruitment, and Placement Specialists	1	18.4%
36. Training and Development Specialists	2	18.3%
37. Construction and Building Inspectors	1	18.2%
38. Landscaping and Groundskeeping Workers	2	18.1%
39. Civil Engineers	1	18.0%
40. Demonstrators and Product Promoters	1	18.0%
41. Captains, Mates, and Pilots of Water Vessels	2	17.9%
42. Accountants and Auditors	1	17.7%

(continued)

The 50 Fastest-Growing Recession-Sensitive Jobs

Job	Economic Sensitivity Rating	Percent Growth
43. Architects, Except Landscape and Naval	2F	17.7%
44. First-Line Supervisors/Managers of Landscaping, Lawn Service, and Groundskeeping Workers	1	17.6%
45. Receptionists and Information Clerks	1	17.2%
46. Appraisers and Assessors of Real Estate	1	16.9%
47. Public Relations Managers	3	16.9%
48. Security Guards	2	16.9%
49. Medical Secretaries	1	16.7%
50. Cargo and Freight Agents	1	16.5%

The 50 Recession-Sensitive Jobs with the Most Openings

We sorted the list of 150 best recession-sensitive jobs to identify the 50 jobs that are projected to have the largest number of job openings per year through 2016. The list is an interesting mix of managers, business specialists, and technicians.

The 50 Recession-Sensitive Jobs with the Most Openings

Job	Economic Sensitivity Rating	Annual Openings
1. Office Clerks, General	1	765,803
2. Customer Service Representatives	2F	600,937
3. Receptionists and Information Clerks	1	334,124
4. Landscaping and Groundskeeping Workers	2	307,138
5. Bookkeeping, Accounting, and Auditing Clerks	2F	286,854
6. Truck Drivers, Heavy and Tractor-Trailer	1	279,032
7. Construction Laborers	2	257,407
8. Executive Secretaries and Administrative Assistants	1	235,314
9. Carpenters	2	223,225
10. Security Guards	2	222,085
11. First-Line Supervisors/Managers of Retail Sales Workers	2	221,241
12. Elementary School Teachers, Except Special Education	2	181,612

The 50 Recession-Sensitive Jobs with the Most Openings

Job	Economic Sensitivity Rating	Annual Openings
13. Sales Representatives, Wholesale and Manufacturing, Except Technical and Scientific Products	2	156,215
14. First-Line Supervisors/Managers of Food Preparation and Serving Workers	3	154,175
15. Tellers	1	146,077
16. First-Line Supervisors/Managers of Office and Administrative Support Workers	1	138,420
17. Accountants and Auditors	1	134,463
18. Management Analysts	1	125,669
19. Bill and Account Collectors	1F	118,709
20. General and Operations Managers	1	112,072
21. Painters, Construction and Maintenance	1	101,140
22. Computer Support Specialists	1F	97,334
23. First-Line Supervisors/Managers of Construction Trades and Extraction Workers	1	82,923
24. Electricians	1	79,083
25. Plumbers, Pipefitters, and Steamfitters	3	68,643
26. Insurance Sales Agents	1	64,162
27. Real Estate Sales Agents	1	61,232
28. Medical Secretaries	1	60,659
29. Food Service Managers	1	59,302
30. Computer Software Engineers, Applications	1F	58,690
31. Financial Managers	3	57,589
32. Operating Engineers and Other Construction Equipment Operators	2	55,468
33. Loan Officers	2	54,237
34. Production, Planning, and Expediting Clerks	3	52,735
35. Fitness Trainers and Aerobics Instructors	1	51,235
36. Property, Real Estate, and Community Association Managers	1	49,916
37. Lawyers	1	49,445
38. First-Line Supervisors/Managers of Non-Retail Sales Workers	1	48,883
39. Securities, Commodities, and Financial Services Sales Agents	3	47,750
40. First-Line Supervisors/Managers of Production and Operating Workers	1	46,144
41. Market Research Analysts	2	45,015
42. Construction Managers	1	44,158
43. Sales Representatives, Wholesale and Manufacturing, Technical and Scientific Products	1	43,469
44. Legal Secretaries	2	38,682

(continued)

(continued)

The 50 Recession-Sensitive Jobs with the Most Openings

Job	Economic Sensitivity Rating	Annual Openings
45. Roofers	2	38,398
46. Cost Estimators	1	38,379
47. First-Line Supervisors/Managers of Personal Service Workers	1	37,555
48. Sales Managers	2	36,392
49. Training and Development Specialists	2	35,862
50. Cement Masons and Concrete Finishers	2	34,625

PART III

Descriptions of the Best Recession-Proof Jobs

This part provides descriptions for all the jobs included in one or more of the lists in Part II. The book's introduction gives more details on how to use and interpret the job descriptions, but here is some additional information:

⚜ Job descriptions are arranged in alphabetical order by job title. This approach allows you to find a description quickly if you know its correct title from one of the lists in Part II.

⚜ In some cases, a job title that appears in Part II is linked to two or more different job titles in Part III. For example, if you look for the job title Automotive Service Technicians and Mechanics, you will find it listed here alphabetically, but a note will tell you to see the descriptions for Automotive Master Mechanics and Automotive Specialty Technicians. Because these job titles are also listed alphabetically, you can find the descriptions easily.

⚜ The job title Physicians and Surgeons, as used in the Part II lists, represents seven jobs in Part III: Anesthesiologists; Family and General Practitioners; Internists, General; Obstetricians and Gynecologists; Pediatricians, General; Psychiatrists; and Surgeons. Likewise, the job title Teachers, Postsecondary, represents 36 occupational titles described here: Agricultural Sciences Teachers, Postsecondary; Anthropology and Archeology Teachers, Postsecondary; Architecture Teachers, Postsecondary; Area, Ethnic, and Cultural Studies Teachers, Postsecondary; Art, Drama, and Music Teachers, Postsecondary; Atmospheric, Earth, Marine, and Space Sciences Teachers, Postsecondary; Biological Science Teachers, Postsecondary; Business Teachers, Postsecondary; Chemistry Teachers, Postsecondary; Communications Teachers, Postsecondary; Computer Science Teachers, Postsecondary; Criminal Justice and Law Enforcement Teachers, Postsecondary; Economics Teachers, Postsecondary; Education Teachers, Postsecondary; Engineering Teachers, Postsecondary; English Language and Literature Teachers, Postsecondary; Environmental Science Teachers, Postsecondary; Foreign Language and Literature Teachers, Postsecondary; Forestry and Conservation Science Teachers, Postsecondary; Geography Teachers, Postsecondary; Graduate Teaching Assistants; Health Specialties Teachers, Postsecondary; History Teachers, Postsecondary; Home Economics Teachers, Postsecondary; Law Teachers, Postsecondary; Library Science Teachers, Postsecondary; Mathematical Science Teachers,

Postsecondary; Nursing Instructors and Teachers, Postsecondary; Philosophy and Religion Teachers, Postsecondary; Physics Teachers, Postsecondary; Political Science Teachers, Postsecondary; Psychology Teachers, Postsecondary; Recreation and Fitness Studies Teachers, Postsecondary; Social Work Teachers, Postsecondary; Sociology Teachers, Postsecondary; and Vocational Education Teachers, Postsecondary.

❋ Consider the job descriptions in this section as a first step in career exploration. When you find a job that interests you, turn to Appendix A for suggestions about resources for further exploration.

❋ If you are using this section to browse for interesting options, we suggest that you begin with the Table of Contents. Part II features many interesting lists that will help you identify job titles to explore in more detail. If you have not browsed the lists in Part II, consider spending some time there. The lists are interesting and will help you identify job titles you can find described in the material that follows. The job titles in Part III are also listed in the Table of Contents.

Actuaries

- ❋ Education/Training Required: Work experience plus degree
- ❋ Annual Earnings: $82,800
- ❋ Beginning Wage: $46,470
- ❋ Earnings Growth Potential: Very high
- ❋ Growth: 23.7%
- ❋ Annual Job Openings: 3,245
- ❋ Self-Employed: 0.0%
- ❋ Part-Time: 5.9%

Industries with Greatest Employment: Insurance Carriers and Related Activities; Professional, Scientific, and Technical Services; Management of Companies and Enterprises.

Highest-Growth Industries (Projected Growth for This Job): Professional, Scientific, and Technical Services (75.7%); Securities, Commodity Contracts, and Other Financial Investments and Related Activities (44.1%); Management of Companies and Enterprises (38.3%); Administrative and Support Services (26.5%); Funds, Trusts, and Other Financial Vehicles (23.3%).

Lowest-Growth Industries (Projected Growth for This Job): Insurance Carriers and Related Activities (5.4%); Credit Intermediation and Related Activities (10.8%).

Fastest-Growing Metropolitan Areas (Recent Growth for This Job): Detroit–Warren–Livonia, MI (82.6%); Indianapolis–Carmel, IN (64.3%); Columbus, OH (54.5%); New Haven, CT (50.0%); Portland–Vancouver–Beaverton, OR–WA (42.9%).

Other Considerations for Job Security: Opportunities for actuaries should be good, particularly for those who have passed at least one or two of the initial exams. Candidates with additional knowledge or experience, such as computer programming skills, will be particularly attractive to employers. Most jobs in this occupation are located in urban areas, but opportunities vary by geographic location. Steady demand by the insurance industry should ensure that actuarial jobs in this key industry will remain stable through 2016.

Analyze statistical data, such as mortality, accident, sickness, disability, and retirement rates, and construct probability tables to forecast risk and liability for payment of future benefits. May ascertain premium rates required and cash reserves necessary to ensure payment of future benefits. Ascertain premium rates required and cash reserves and liabilities necessary to ensure payment of future benefits. Analyze statistical information to estimate mortality, accident, sickness, disability, and retirement rates. Design, review, and help administer insurance, annuity, and pension plans, determining financial soundness and calculating premiums. Collaborate with programmers, underwriters, accountants, claims experts, and senior management to help companies develop plans for new lines of business or for improving existing business. Determine or help determine company policy and explain complex technical matters to company executives, government officials, shareholders, policyholders, or the public. Testify before public agencies on proposed legislation affecting businesses. Provide advice to clients on a contract basis, working as a consultant. Testify in court as expert witness or to provide legal evidence on matters such as the value of potential lifetime earnings of a person who is disabled or killed in an accident. Construct probability tables for events such as fires, natural disasters, and unemployment, based on analysis of statistical data and other pertinent information. Determine policy contract provisions for each type of insurance. Manage credit and help price corporate security offerings. Provide expertise to help financial institutions manage risks and maximize returns associated with investment products or credit offerings. Determine equitable basis for distributing surplus earnings under participating insurance and annuity contracts in mutual companies. Explain changes in contract provisions to customers.

Personality Type: Conventional.

GOE—Interest Area: 15. Scientific Research, Engineering, and Mathematics. **Work Group:** 15.06.

Mathematics and Data Analysis. **Other Jobs in this Work Group:** Mathematical Technicians; Mathematicians; Social Science Research Assistants; Statistical Assistants; Statisticians.

Skills: Programming; Mathematics; Complex Problem Solving; Active Learning; Operations Analysis; Quality Control Analysis.

Education and Training Program: Actuarial Science. **Related Knowledge/Courses:** Mathematics; Economics and Accounting; Sales and Marketing; Computers and Electronics; Personnel and Human Resources; Law and Government.

Work Environment: Indoors; sitting; using hands on objects, tools, or controls; repetitive motions.

Administrative Law Judges, Adjudicators, and Hearing Officers

- ❈ Education/Training Required: Work experience plus degree
- ❈ Annual Earnings: $72,600
- ❈ Beginning Wage: $36,190
- ❈ Earnings Growth Potential: High
- ❈ Growth: 0.1%
- ❈ Annual Job Openings: 794
- ❈ Self-Employed: 0.0%
- ❈ Part-Time: 5.9%

Industries with Greatest Employment: State Government, excluding Education and Hospitals; Local Government, excluding Education and Hospitals.

Highest-Growth Industries (Projected Growth for This Job): None met the criteria.

Lowest-Growth Industries (Projected Growth for This Job): None met the criteria.

Fastest-Growing Metropolitan Areas (Recent Growth for This Job): Austin–Round Rock, TX (87.5%); Phoenix–Mesa–Scottsdale, AZ (81.3%); Chicago–Naperville–Joliet, IL–IN–WI (52.0%); Philadelphia–Camden–Wilmington, PA–NJ–DE–MD (27.8%); Dallas–Fort Worth–Arlington, TX (16.7%).

Other Considerations for Job Security: Most job openings will arise as judges retire. However, additional openings will occur when new judgeships are authorized by law or when judges are elevated to higher judicial offices. Budgetary pressures at all levels of government are expected to hold down the hiring of judges, despite rising caseloads, particularly in federal courts. However, the continued need to cope with crime and settle disputes, as well as the public's willingness to go to court to settle disputes, should spur demand for judges. Also, economic growth is expected to lead to more business contracts and transactions and, thus, more legal disputes.

Conduct hearings to decide or recommend decisions on claims concerning government programs or other government-related matters and prepare decisions. Determine penalties or the existence and the amount of liability or recommend the acceptance or rejection of claims or compromise settlements. Prepare written opinions and decisions. Review and evaluate data on documents such as claim applications, birth or death certificates, and physician or employer records. Research and analyze laws, regulations, policies, and precedent decisions to prepare for hearings and to determine conclusions. Confer with individuals or organizations involved in cases to obtain relevant information. Recommend the acceptance or rejection of claims or compromise settlements according to laws, regulations, policies, and precedent decisions. Explain to claimants how they can appeal rulings that go against them. Monitor and direct the activities of trials and hearings to ensure that they are conducted fairly and that courts administer justice while safeguarding the legal rights of all involved parties. Authorize payment of valid claims and determine method of payment. Conduct hearings to review and decide claims regarding issues such as social program eligibility, environmental protection, and enforcement of health and safety regulations. Rule on exceptions, motions, and admissibility of evidence. Determine existence and amount of liability according to current laws, administrative and judicial precedents, and available evidence. Issue subpoenas and administer oaths in preparation for formal hearings. Conduct studies of appeals procedures in field agencies to ensure adherence to legal requirements and to facilitate determination of cases.

Personality Type: Enterprising.

GOE—Interest Area: 12. Law and Public Safety. **Work Group:** 12.02. Legal Practice and Justice Administration. **Other Jobs in this Work Group:** Arbitrators, Mediators, and Conciliators; Judges, Magistrate Judges, and Magistrates; Lawyers.

Skills: Judgment and Decision Making; Reading Comprehension; Active Listening; Social Perceptiveness; Time Management; Writing.

Education and Training Programs: Law (LL.B., J.D.); Legal Professions and Studies, Other. **Related Knowledge/Courses:** Law and Government; Medicine and Dentistry; Psychology; Therapy and Counseling; Biology; Customer and Personal Service.

Work Environment: Indoors; sitting.

Adult Literacy, Remedial Education, and GED Teachers and Instructors

- ❋ Education/Training Required: Bachelor's degree
- ❋ Annual Earnings: $43,910
- ❋ Beginning Wage: $24,610
- ❋ Earnings Growth Potential: Very high
- ❋ Growth: 14.2%
- ❋ Annual Job Openings: 17,340
- ❋ Self-Employed: 0.0%
- ❋ Part-Time: 41.3%

Industries with Greatest Employment: Educational Services, Public and Private; Social Assistance.

Highest-Growth Industries (Projected Growth for This Job): Social Assistance (40.1%); Administrative and Support Services (36.3%); Amusement, Gambling, and Recreation Industries (30.4%); Nursing and Residential Care Facilities (25.5%); Religious, Grantmaking, Civic, Professional, and Similar Organizations (17.2%).

Lowest-Growth Industries (Projected Growth for This Job): Private Households (5.1%); Educational Services, Public and Private (11.7%).

Fastest-Growing Metropolitan Areas (Recent Growth for This Job): Salt Lake City, UT (325.0%); Oklahoma City, OK (100.0%); Poughkeepsie–Newburgh–Middletown, NY (100.0%); Baltimore–Towson, MD (88.9%); Columbus, OH (88.0%).

Other Considerations for Job Security: Job opportunities are expected to be favorable, particularly for teachers of English to speakers of other languages, and especially in states with large populations of residents who have limited English skills—such as California, Florida, Texas, and New York. The demand for adult literacy and basic and secondary education tends to be greater when the economy softens, because then employers can be more selective. Also, adult education classes often are subject to changes in funding levels. In particular, budget pressures may limit federal funding of adult education, which may cause programs to rely more on volunteers if other organizations and governments don't make up the difference. Other factors such as immigration policies and the relative prosperity of the United States compared with other countries also may have an impact on the number of immigrants entering this country and, consequently, the demand for ESOL teachers.

Teach or instruct out-of-school youths and adults in remedial education classes, preparatory classes for the General Educational Development test, literacy, or English as a second language. Teaching may or may not take place in a traditional educational institution. Adapt teaching methods and instructional materials to meet students' varying needs, abilities, and interests. Observe and evaluate students' work to determine progress and make suggestions for improvement. Instruct students individually and in groups, using various teaching methods such as lectures, discussions, and demonstrations. Plan and conduct activities for a balanced program of instruction, demonstration, and work time that provides students with opportunities to observe, question, and investigate. Maintain accurate and complete student records as required by laws or administrative policies. Prepare materials and classrooms for class activities. Establish clear objectives for all lessons, units, and projects and communicate those objectives to students. Conduct classes, workshops, and demonstrations to teach principles, techniques, or methods in subjects such as basic English language skills, life skills, and workforce entry skills. Prepare students for further education by encouraging them to explore learning opportunities and to persevere with challenging tasks. Establish and enforce rules for behavior and procedures for maintaining order among the students for whom they are responsible. Provide information, guidance, and preparation for the General Equivalency Diploma (GED) examination. Assign and grade classwork and homework. Observe students to determine qualifications, limitations, abilities, interests, and other individual characteristics. Register, orient, and assess new students according to standards and procedures. Prepare and implement remedial programs for students requiring extra help. Prepare and administer written, oral, and performance tests and issue grades in accordance with performance. Use computers, audiovisual aids, and other equipment and materials to supplement presentations. Prepare objectives and outlines for courses of study, following curriculum guidelines or requirements of states and schools. Guide and counsel students with adjustment or academic problems or special academic interests. Enforce administration policies and rules governing students.

Personality Type: Social.

GOE—Interest Area: 05. Education and Training. **Work Group:** 05.03. Postsecondary and Adult Teaching and Instructing. **Other Jobs in this Work Group:** Agricultural Sciences Teachers, Postsecondary; Anthropology and Archeology Teachers, Postsecondary; Architecture Teachers, Postsecondary; Area, Ethnic, and Cultural Studies Teachers, Postsecondary; Art, Drama, and Music Teachers, Postsecondary; Atmospheric, Earth, Marine, and Space Sciences Teachers, Postsecondary; Biological Science Teachers, Postsecondary; Business Teachers, Postsecondary; Chemistry Teachers, Postsecondary; Communications Teachers, Postsecondary; Computer Science Teachers, Postsecondary; Criminal Justice and Law Enforcement Teachers, Postsecondary; Economics Teachers, Postsecondary; Education Teachers, Postsecondary; Engineering Teachers, Postsecondary; English Language and Literature Teachers, Postsecondary; Environmental Science Teachers, Postsecondary; Farm and Home Management Advisors; Foreign Language and Literature Teachers, Postsecondary; Forestry and Conservation Science Teachers, Postsecondary; Geography Teachers, Postsecondary; Graduate Teaching Assistants; Health Specialties Teachers, Postsecondary; History Teachers, Postsecondary; Home Economics Teachers, Postsecondary; Law Teachers, Postsecondary; Library Science Teachers, Postsecondary; Mathematical Science Teachers, Postsecondary; Nursing Instructors and Teachers, Postsecondary; Philosophy and Religion Teachers, Postsecondary; Physics Teachers, Postsecondary; Political Science Teachers, Postsecondary; Psychology Teachers, Postsecondary; Recreation and Fitness Studies Teachers, Postsecondary; Self-Enrichment Education Teachers; Social Work Teachers, Postsecondary; Sociology Teachers, Postsecondary; Vocational Education Teachers, Postsecondary.

Skills: Instructing; Social Perceptiveness; Learning Strategies; Service Orientation; Speaking; Monitoring.

Education and Training Programs: Bilingual and Multilingual Education; Multicultural Education; Adult and Continuing Education and Teaching; Teaching English as a Second or Foreign Language/ESL Language Instructor; Teaching French as a Second or Foreign Language; Adult Literacy Tutor/Instructor; Linguistics of ASL and Other Sign Languages. **Related Knowledge/Courses:** History and Archeology; Sociology and Anthropology; Therapy and Counseling; Education and Training; Geography; English Language.

Work Environment: Indoors; more often standing than sitting.

Agricultural Sciences Teachers, Postsecondary

* Education/Training Required: Doctoral degree
* Annual Earnings: $75,140
* Beginning Wage: $41,440
* Earnings Growth Potential: Very high
* Growth: 22.9%
* Annual Job Openings: 237,478
* Self-Employed: 0.4%
* Part-Time: 27.8%

Our sources did not provide separate job openings data for this occupation. The job openings listed here are shared with 35 other postsecondary teaching occupations. For a complete list, see the beginning of this section.

Industries with Greatest Employment: Educational Services, Public and Private.

Highest-Growth Industries (Projected Growth for This Job): Administrative and Support Services (48.3%); Amusement, Gambling, and Recreation Industries (45.3%); Social Assistance (38.6%); Support Activities for Transportation (32.8%); Religious, Grantmaking, Civic, Professional, and Similar Organizations (29.9%); Professional, Scientific, and Technical Services (28.8%); Management of Companies and Enterprises (26.8%); Educational Services, Public and Private (22.9%); Hospitals, Public and Private (21.4%); Personal and Laundry Services (21.0%).

Lowest-Growth Industries (Projected Growth for This Job): Other Information Services (7.4%); Sporting Goods, Hobby, Book, and Music Stores (13.3%); Performing Arts, Spectator Sports, and Related Industries (13.4%); Insurance Carriers and Related Activities (13.9%).

Fastest-Growing Metropolitan Area (Recent Growth for This Job): Miami–Fort Lauderdale–Miami Beach, FL (60.8%).

Other Considerations for Job Security: Retirements of current postsecondary teachers should create numerous openings for all types of postsecondary teachers, so job opportunities are generally expected to be very good. Because students attend postsecondary institutions to prepare themselves for careers, the best job prospects for postsecondary teachers are likely to be in rapidly growing fields, such as agricultural sciences, that offer many nonacademic career options. Community colleges and other institutions offering career and technical education have been among the most rapidly growing and are expected to offer some of the best opportunities for postsecondary teachers.

Teach courses in the agricultural sciences, including agronomy, dairy sciences, fisheries management, horticultural sciences, poultry sciences, range management, and agricultural soil conservation. Prepare course materials such as syllabi, homework assignments, and handouts. Evaluate and grade students' classwork, laboratory work, assignments, and papers. Keep abreast of developments in agriculture by reading current literature, talking with colleagues, and participating in professional conferences. Prepare and deliver lectures to undergraduate and/or graduate students on topics such as crop production, plant genetics, and soil chemistry. Initiate, facilitate, and moderate classroom discussions. Conduct research in a particular field of knowledge and publish findings in professional journals, books, and/or electronic media. Supervise laboratory sessions and fieldwork and coordinate laboratory operations. Supervise undergraduate and/or graduate teaching, internships, and research work. Compile, administer, and grade examinations or assign this work to others. Advise students on academic and vocational curricula and on career issues. Plan, evaluate, and revise curricula, course content, course materials, and instructional methods. Maintain student attendance records, grades, and other required records. Write grant proposals to procure external research funding. Collaborate with colleagues to address teaching and research issues. Maintain regularly scheduled office hours to advise and assist students. Participate in student recruitment, registration, and placement activities. Select and obtain materials and supplies such as textbooks and laboratory equipment. Act as advisers to student organizations. Participate in campus and community events. Serve on academic or administrative committees that deal with institutional policies, departmental matters, and academic issues. Provide professional consulting services to government and/or industry. Perform administrative duties such as serving as department head. Compile bibliographies of specialized materials for outside reading assignments.

Personality Type: Investigative.

GOE—Interest Area: 05. Education and Training. **Work Group:** 05.03. Postsecondary and Adult Teaching and Instructing. **Other Jobs in this Work Group:** Adult Literacy, Remedial Education, and GED Teachers and Instructors; Anthropology and Archeology Teachers, Postsecondary; Architecture Teachers, Postsecondary; Area, Ethnic, and Cultural Studies Teachers, Postsecondary; Art, Drama, and Music Teachers, Postsecondary; Atmospheric, Earth, Marine, and Space Sciences Teachers, Postsecondary; Biological Science Teachers, Postsecondary; Business Teachers, Postsecondary; Chemistry Teachers, Postsecondary; Communications Teachers, Postsecondary; Computer Science Teachers, Postsecondary; Criminal Justice and Law Enforcement Teachers, Postsecondary; Economics Teachers, Postsecondary; Education Teachers, Postsecondary; Engineering Teachers, Postsecondary; English Language and Literature Teachers, Postsecondary; Environmental Science Teachers, Postsecondary; Farm and Home Management Advisors; Foreign Language and Literature Teachers, Postsecondary; Forestry and Conservation Science Teachers, Postsecondary; Geography Teachers, Postsecondary; Graduate Teaching Assistants; Health Specialties Teachers, Postsecondary; History Teachers, Postsecondary; Home Economics Teachers, Postsecondary; Law Teachers, Postsecondary; Library Science Teachers, Postsecondary; Mathematical Science Teachers, Postsecondary; Nursing Instructors and Teachers, Postsecondary; Philosophy and Religion Teachers, Postsecondary; Physics Teachers, Postsecondary; Political Science Teachers, Postsecondary; Psychology Teachers, Postsecondary; Recreation and Fitness Studies Teachers,

Postsecondary; Self-Enrichment Education Teachers; Social Work Teachers, Postsecondary; Sociology Teachers, Postsecondary; Vocational Education Teachers, Postsecondary.

Skills: Science; Management of Financial Resources; Writing; Reading Comprehension; Instructing; Complex Problem Solving.

Education and Training Programs: Agriculture, General; Agricultural Business and Management, General; Agribusiness/Agricultural Business Operations; Agricultural Economics; Farm/Farm and Ranch Management; Agricultural/Farm Supplies Retailing and Wholesaling; Agricultural Business and Management, Other; Agricultural Mechanization, General; Agricultural Power Machinery Operation; Agricultural Mechanization, Other; others. **Related Knowledge/Courses:** Biology; Food Production; Education and Training; Geography; Chemistry; Communications and Media.

Work Environment: Indoors; sitting.

Air Traffic Controllers

- ❋ **Education/Training Required:** Long-term on-the-job training
- ❋ **Annual Earnings:** $117,240
- ❋ **Beginning Wage:** $59,410
- ❋ **Earnings Growth Potential:** Very high
- ❋ **Growth:** 10.2%
- ❋ **Annual Job Openings:** 1,213
- ❋ **Self-Employed:** 0.0%
- ❋ **Part-Time:** 2.1%

Industries with Greatest Employment: Support Activities for Transportation; Administrative and Support Services.

Highest-Growth Industries (Projected Growth for This Job): Administrative and Support Services (34.8%); Support Activities for Transportation (20.3%).

Lowest-Growth Industries (Projected Growth for This Job): None met the criteria.

Fastest-Growing Metropolitan Areas (Recent Growth for This Job): Houston–Sugar Land–Baytown, TX (38.6%); Colorado Springs, CO (33.3%); Las Vegas–Paradise, NV (33.3%); Omaha–Council Bluffs, NE–IA (25.0%); Philadelphia–Camden–Wilmington, PA–NJ–DE–MD (23.1%).

Other Considerations for Job Security: Most job opportunities are expected as the result of replacement needs from workers leaving the occupation. The majority of today's air traffic controllers will be eligible to retire over the next decade, although not all are expected to do so. Nevertheless, replacement needs will result in job opportunities each year for those graduating from the FAA training programs. Despite the increasing number of jobs coming open, competition to get into the FAA training programs is expected to remain keen, as there generally are many more applicants to get into the schools than there are openings, but those who graduate have good prospects of getting a job as a controller. Air traffic controllers who continue to meet proficiency and medical requirements enjoy more job security than do most workers. The demand for air travel and the workloads of air traffic controllers decline during recessions, but controllers seldom are laid off.

Control air traffic on and within vicinity of airport and movement of air traffic between altitude sectors and control centers according to established procedures and policies. Authorize, regulate, and control commercial airline flights according to government or company regulations to expedite and ensure flight safety. Issue landing and take-off authorizations and instructions. Monitor and direct the movement of aircraft within an assigned air space and on the ground at airports to minimize delays and maximize safety. Monitor aircraft within a specific airspace, using radar, computer equipment, and visual references. Inform pilots about nearby planes as well as potentially hazardous conditions such as weather, wind speed and direction, and visibility problems. Provide flight path changes or directions to emergency landing fields for pilots traveling in bad weather or in emergency situations. Alert airport emergency services in cases of emergency and when aircraft are experiencing difficulties. Direct pilots to runways when space is available or direct them to maintain a traffic pattern until there is space for them to land. Transfer control of departing flights to traffic control centers and accept control of arriving flights. Direct ground traffic, including taxiing aircraft, maintenance and baggage vehicles, and airport workers. Determine the timing and procedures for flight vector changes. Maintain radio and telephone contact with adjacent control towers, terminal control units, and other area control centers to coordinate aircraft movement. Contact pilots by radio to provide meteorological, navigational, and other information. Initiate and coordinate searches for missing aircraft. Check conditions and traffic at different altitudes in response to pilots' requests for altitude changes. Relay to control centers such air traffic information as courses, altitudes, and expected arrival times. Compile information about flights from flight plans, pilot reports, radar, and observations. Inspect, adjust, and control radio equipment and airport lights. Conduct pre-flight briefings on weather conditions, suggested routes, altitudes, indications of turbulence, and other flight safety information. Analyze factors such as weather reports, fuel requirements, and maps to determine air routes. Organize flight plans and traffic management plans to prepare for planes about to enter assigned airspace.

Personality Type: Conventional.

GOE—Interest Area: 03. Arts and Communication. **Work Group:** 03.10. Communications Technology. **Other Jobs in this Work Group:** Airfield Operations Specialists; Dispatchers, Except Police, Fire, and Ambulance; Police, Fire, and Ambulance Dispatchers; Telephone Operators.

Skills: Operation and Control; Operation Monitoring; Complex Problem Solving; Coordination; Active Listening; Instructing.

Education and Training Program: Air Traffic Controller Training. **Related Knowledge/Courses:** Transportation; Geography; Telecommunications; Public Safety and Security; Physics; Education and Training.

Work Environment: Indoors; noisy; sitting; using hands on objects, tools, or controls; repetitive motions.

Ambulance Drivers and Attendants, Except Emergency Medical Technicians

* ❈ Education/Training Required: Moderate-term on-the-job training
* ❈ Annual Earnings: $20,370
* ❈ Beginning Wage: $14,140
* ❈ Earnings Growth Potential: Very high
* ❈ Growth: 21.7%
* ❈ Annual Job Openings: 3,703
* ❈ Self-Employed: 0.1%
* ❈ Part-Time: 16.9%

Industries with Greatest Employment: Ambulatory Health Care Services; Transit and Ground Passenger Transportation; Hospitals, Public and Private.

Highest-Growth Industries (Projected Growth for This Job): Ambulatory Health Care Services (27.6%); Transit and Ground Passenger Transportation (19.7%).

Lowest-Growth Industries (Projected Growth for This Job): Food and Beverage Stores (9.1%); Hospitals, Public and Private (10.2%).

Fastest-Growing Metropolitan Areas (Recent Growth for This Job): St. Louis, MO–IL (157.1%); Dallas–Fort Worth–Arlington, TX (100.0%); Cleveland–Elyria–Mentor, OH (63.6%); Phoenix–Mesa–Scottsdale, AZ (61.1%); Los Angeles–Long Beach–Santa Ana, CA (58.1%).

Other Considerations for Job Security: No data available.

Drive ambulance or assist ambulance driver in transporting sick, injured, or convalescent persons. Assist in lifting patients. Drive ambulances or assist ambulance drivers in transporting sick, injured, or convalescent persons. Remove and replace soiled linens and equipment to maintain sanitary conditions. Accompany and assist emergency medical technicians on calls. Place patients on stretchers and load stretchers into ambulances, usually with assistance from other attendants. Earn and maintain appropriate certifications. Replace supplies and disposable items on ambulances. Report facts concerning accidents or emergencies to hospital personnel or law-enforcement officials. Administer first aid such as bandaging, splinting, and administering oxygen. Restrain or shackle violent patients.

Personality Type: Social.

GOE—Interest Area: 16. Transportation, Distribution, and Logistics. **Work Group:** 16.06. Other Services Requiring Driving. **Other Jobs in this Work Group:** Bus Drivers, School; Bus Drivers, Transit and Intercity; Couriers and Messengers; Driver/Sales Workers; Parking Lot Attendants; Postal Service Mail Carriers; Taxi Drivers and Chauffeurs.

Skills: Equipment Maintenance; Operation Monitoring; Operation and Control; Repairing; Technology Design; Equipment Selection.

Education and Training Program: Emergency Medical Technology/Technician (EMT Paramedic). **Related Knowledge/Courses:** Transportation; Psychology; Medicine and Dentistry; Customer and Personal Service; Telecommunications; Public Safety and Security.

Work Environment: Outdoors; noisy; very hot or cold; disease or infections; sitting; using hands on objects, tools, or controls.

Anesthesiologists

* Education/Training Required: First professional degree
* Annual Earnings: More than $145,600
* Beginning Wage: $114,200
* Earnings Growth Potential: Cannot be calculated.
* Growth: 14.2%
* Annual Job Openings: 38,027
* Self-Employed: 14.7%
* Part-Time: 8.1%

Our sources did not provide separate job openings data for this occupation. The job openings listed here are shared with Family and General Practitioners; Internists, General; Obstetricians and Gynecologists; Pediatricians, General; Psychiatrists; and Surgeons.

Industries with Greatest Employment: Ambulatory Health Care Services; Hospitals, Public and Private.

Highest-Growth Industries (Projected Growth for This Job): Social Assistance (58.6%); Administrative and Support Services (26.8%); Professional, Scientific, and Technical Services (22.6%); Nursing and Residential Care Facilities (21.0%); Ambulatory Health Care Services (19.4%); Religious, Grantmaking, Civic, Professional, and Similar Organizations (16.7%); Management of Companies and Enterprises (15.3%).

Lowest-Growth Industries (Projected Growth for This Job): Insurance Carriers and Related Activities (4.6%); Health and Personal Care Stores (5.3%); Hospitals, Public and Private (9.9%); Educational Services, Public and Private (11.8%).

Fastest-Growing Metropolitan Areas (Recent Growth for This Job): St. Louis, MO–IL (12.5%); Louisville–Jefferson County, KY–IN (12.5%); Tampa–St. Petersburg–Clearwater, FL (12.2%); San Juan–Caguas–Guaynabo, PR (11.3%); New York–Northern New Jersey–Long Island, NY–NJ–PA (11.1%).

Other Considerations for Job Security: Opportunities for individuals interested in becoming physicians and surgeons are expected to be very good. Unlike their predecessors, new physicians are much less likely to enter solo practice and more likely to take salaried jobs in group medical practices, clinics, and health networks. Reports of shortages in some specialties, such as general or family practice, internal medicine, and OB/GYN, or in rural or low-income areas should attract new entrants, encouraging schools to expand programs and hospitals to increase available residency slots. However, because physician training is so lengthy, employment change happens gradually. Opportunities should be particularly good in rural and low-income areas, as some physicians find these areas unattractive because of less control over work hours, isolation from medical colleagues, or other reasons.

Administer anesthetics during surgery or other medical procedures. Administer anesthetic or sedation during medical procedures, using local, intravenous, spinal, or caudal methods. Monitor patient before, during, and after anesthesia and counteract adverse reactions or complications. Provide and maintain life support and airway management and help prepare patients for emergency surgery. Record type and amount of anesthesia and patient condition throughout procedure. Examine patient; obtain medical history; and use diagnostic tests to determine risk during surgical, obstetrical, and other medical procedures. Position patient on operating table to maximize patient comfort and surgical accessibility. Decide when patients have recovered or stabilized enough to be sent to another room or ward or to be sent home following outpatient surgery. Coordinate administration of anesthetics with surgeons during operation. Confer with other medical professionals to determine type and method of anesthetic or sedation to render patient insensible to pain. Coordinate and direct work of nurses, medical technicians, and other health-care providers. Order laboratory tests, X rays, and other diagnostic procedures. Diagnose illnesses, using examinations, tests, and reports. Manage anesthesiological services, coordinating them with other medical activities and formulating plans and procedures. Provide medical care and consultation in many settings, prescribing medication and treatment and referring patients for surgery. Inform students and staff of types and methods of anesthesia administration, signs of complications, and emergency methods to counteract reactions. Schedule and maintain use of surgical suite, including operating, wash-up, and waiting rooms and anesthetic and sterilizing equipment. Instruct individuals and groups on ways to preserve health and prevent disease. Conduct medical research to aid in controlling and curing disease, to investigate new medications, and to develop and test new medical techniques.

Personality Type: Investigative.

GOE—Interest Area: 08. Health Science. **Work Group:** 08.02. Medicine and Surgery. **Other Jobs in this Work Group:** Family and General Practitioners; Internists, General; Medical Assistants; Medical Transcriptionists; Obstetricians and Gynecologists; Pediatricians, General; Pharmacists; Pharmacy Aides; Pharmacy Technicians; Physician Assistants; Psychiatrists; Registered Nurses; Surgeons; Surgical Technologists.

Skills: Operation Monitoring; Science; Operation and Control; Judgment and Decision Making; Monitoring; Complex Problem Solving.

Education and Training Programs: Anesthesiology; Critical Care Anesthesiology. **Related Knowledge/Courses:** Medicine and Dentistry; Biology; Chemistry; Psychology; Physics; Therapy and Counseling.

Work Environment: Indoors; contaminants; radiation; disease or infections; standing; using hands on objects, tools, or controls.

Animal Control Workers

- ❋ Education/Training Required: Moderate-term on-the-job training
- ❋ Annual Earnings: $27,910
- ❋ Beginning Wage: $17,160
- ❋ Earnings Growth Potential: Very high
- ❋ Growth: 12.5%
- ❋ Annual Job Openings: 3,377
- ❋ Self-Employed: 0.1%
- ❋ Part-Time: 15.1%

Industries with Greatest Employment: Religious, Grantmaking, Civic, Professional, and Similar Organizations.

Highest-Growth Industries (Projected Growth for This Job): None met the criteria.

Lowest-Growth Industries (Projected Growth for This Job): Fishing, Hunting, and Trapping (–22.9%); Educational Services, Public and Private (8.5%); Religious, Grantmaking, Civic, Professional, and Similar Organizations (14.8%).

Fastest-Growing Metropolitan Areas (Recent Growth for This Job): Bridgeport–Stamford–Norwalk, CT (83.3%); Springfield, MA–CT (75.0%); Phoenix–Mesa–Scottsdale, AZ (64.3%); Tampa–St. Petersburg–Clearwater, FL (57.1%); Houston–Sugar Land–Baytown, TX (42.9%).

Other Considerations for Job Security: No data available.

Handle animals for the purpose of investigations of mistreatment or control of abandoned, dangerous, or unattended animals. Investigate reports of animal attacks or animal cruelty, interviewing witnesses, collecting evidence, and writing reports. Capture and remove stray, uncontrolled, or abused animals from undesirable conditions, using nets, nooses, or tranquilizer darts as necessary. Examine animals for injuries or malnutrition and arrange for any necessary medical treatment. Remove captured animals from animal-control service vehicles and place them in shelter cages or other enclosures. Euthanize rabid, unclaimed, or severely injured animals. Supply animals with food, water, and personal care. Clean facilities and equipment such as dog pens and animal control trucks. Prepare for prosecutions related to animal treatment and give evidence in court. Contact animal owners to inform them that their pets are at animal-holding facilities. Educate the public about animal welfare and animal-control laws and regulations. Write reports of activities and maintain files of impoundments and dispositions of animals. Issue warnings or citations in connection with animal-related offenses or contact police to report violations and request arrests. Answer inquiries from the public concerning animal-control operations. Examine animal licenses and inspect establishments housing animals for compliance with laws. Organize the adoption of unclaimed animals. Train police officers in dog handling and training techniques for tracking, crowd control, and narcotics and bomb detection.

Personality Type: Social.

GOE—Interest Area: 12. Law and Public Safety. **Work Group:** 12.05. Safety and Security. **Other Jobs in this Work Group:** Crossing Guards; Gaming Surveillance Officers and Gaming Investigators; Lifeguards, Ski Patrol, and Other Recreational Protective Service Workers; Private Detectives and Investigators; Security Guards; Transportation Security Screeners.

Skills: No data available.

Education and Training Program: Security and Protective Services, Other. **Related Knowledge/Courses:** Public Safety and Security; Law and Government; Biology; Customer and Personal Service; Telecommunications; Communications and Media.

Work Environment: More often outdoors than indoors; contaminants; disease or infections; minor burns, cuts, bites, or stings; using hands on objects, tools, or controls.

Animal Scientists

- ❋ Education/Training Required: Bachelor's degree
- ❋ Annual Earnings: $47,800
- ❋ Beginning Wage: $31,540
- ❋ Earnings Growth Potential: Very high
- ❋ Growth: 9.8%
- ❋ Annual Job Openings: 299
- ❋ Self-Employed: 9.0%
- ❋ Part-Time: 11.4%

Industries with Greatest Employment: Educational Services, Public and Private; Professional, Scientific, and Technical Services.

Highest-Growth Industries (Projected Growth for This Job): Professional, Scientific, and Technical Services (18.2%).

Lowest-Growth Industries (Projected Growth for This Job): Food Manufacturing (3.8%); Support Activities for Agriculture and Forestry (7.4%); Educational Services, Public and Private (11.9%).

Fastest-Growing Metropolitan Areas (Recent Growth for This Job): No data available.

Other Considerations for Job Security: Animal scientists, like other agricultural scientists, will be needed to balance increased agricultural output with protection and preservation of soil, water, and ecosystems. Opportunities should be good for scientists with a master's degree, particularly those seeking applied research positions in a laboratory. Those with a Ph.D. will experience the best opportunities, especially in basic research and teaching positions at colleges and universities. Graduates with a bachelor's degree can sometimes work in applied research and product development positions under the guidance of a doctoral scientist. Employment of animal scientists is relatively stable during periods of economic recession. Layoffs are less likely among animal scientists than in some other occupations because food is a staple item and its demand fluctuates very little with economic activity.

Conduct research in the genetics, nutrition, reproduction, growth, and development of domestic farm animals. Conduct research concerning animal nutrition, breeding, or management to improve products or processes. Advise producers about improved products and techniques that could enhance their animal production efforts. Study nutritional requirements of animals and nutritive values of animal feed materials. Study effects of management practices, processing methods, feed, or environmental conditions on quality and quantity of animal products, such as eggs and milk. Develop improved practices in feeding, housing, sanitation, or parasite and disease control of animals. Research and control animal selection and breeding practices to increase production efficiency and improve animal quality. Determine genetic composition of animal populations and heritability of traits, utilizing principles of genetics. Crossbreed animals with existing strains or cross strains to obtain new combinations of desirable characteristics.

Personality Type: Investigative.

GOE—Interest Area: 01. Agriculture and Natural Resources. **Work Group:** 01.02. Resource Science/Engineering for Plants, Animals, and the Environment. **Other Jobs in this Work Group:** Agricultural Engineers; Conservation Scientists; Environmental Engineers; Foresters; Mining and Geological Engineers, Including Mining Safety Engineers; Petroleum Engineers; Range Managers; Soil and Plant Scientists; Soil and Water Conservationists; Zoologists and Wildlife Biologists.

Skills: Science; Management of Financial Resources; Systems Analysis; Writing; Complex Problem Solving; Reading Comprehension.

Education and Training Programs: Agriculture, General; Animal Sciences, General; Agricultural Animal Breeding; Animal Health; Animal Nutrition; Dairy Science; Poultry Science; Animal Sciences, Other; Range Science and Management. **Related Knowledge/Courses:** Food Production; Biology; Chemistry; Education and Training; Mathematics; Physics.

Work Environment: More often indoors than outdoors; sitting.

Anthropologists

* Education/Training Required: Master's degree
* Annual Earnings: $49,930
* Beginning Wage: $28,940
* Earnings Growth Potential: Very high
* Growth: 15.0%
* Annual Job Openings: 446
* Self-Employed: 6.1%
* Part-Time: 20.1%

Our sources did not provide separate job openings data for this occupation. The job openings listed here are shared with Archeologists.

Industries with Greatest Employment: Professional, Scientific, and Technical Services.

Highest-Growth Industries (Projected Growth for This Job): Museums, Historical Sites, and Similar Institutions (36.2%); Professional, Scientific, and Technical Services (27.8%).

Lowest-Growth Industries (Projected Growth for This Job): Educational Services, Public and Private (11.8%).

Fastest-Growing Metropolitan Areas (Recent Growth for This Job): Austin–Round Rock, TX (128.6%); Flagstaff, AZ (100.0%); New Orleans–Metairie–Kenner, LA (25.0%); Anchorage, AK (20.0%).

Other Considerations for Job Security: Job seekers may face competition, and those with higher educational attainment will have the best prospects. Anthropologists will experience most of their job growth in the management, scientific, and technical consulting services industry. Anthropologists who work as consultants apply anthropological knowledge and methods to problems ranging from economic development issues to forensics. There will be keen competition for tenured positions as university faculty.

Research, evaluate, and establish public policy concerning the origins of humans; their physical, social, linguistic, and cultural development; and their behavior, as well as the cultures, organizations, and institutions they have created. Collect information and make judgments through observation, interviews, and the review of documents. Plan and direct research to characterize and compare the economic, demographic, health-care, social, political, linguistic, and religious institutions of distinct cultural groups, communities, and organizations. Write about and present research findings for various specialized and general audiences. Advise government agencies, private organizations, and communities regarding proposed programs, plans, and policies and their potential impacts on cultural institutions, organizations, and communities. Identify culturally specific beliefs and practices affecting health status and access to services for distinct populations and communities in collaboration with medical and public health officials. Build and use text-based database management systems to support the analysis of detailed first-hand observational records, or "field notes." Develop intervention procedures, utilizing techniques such as individual and focus-group interviews, consultations, and participant observation of social interaction. Construct and test data-collection methods. Explain the origins and physical, social, or cultural development of humans, including physical attributes, cultural traditions, beliefs, languages, resource management practices, and settlement patterns. Conduct participatory action research in communities and organizations to assess how work is done and to design work systems, technologies, and environments. Train others in the application of ethnographic research methods to solve problems in organizational effectiveness, communications, technology development, policy making, and program planning. Formulate general rules that describe and predict the development and behavior of cultures and social institutions. Collaborate with economic development planners to decide on the implementation of proposed development policies, plans, and programs

based on culturally institutionalized barriers and facilitating circumstances. Create data records for use in describing and analyzing social patterns and processes, using photography, videography, and audio recordings.

Personality Type: Investigative.

GOE—Interest Area: 15. Scientific Research, Engineering, and Mathematics. **Work Group:** 15.04. Social Sciences. **Other Jobs in this Work Group:** Anthropologists and Archeologists; Archeologists; Economists; Historians; Industrial-Organizational Psychologists; Political Scientists; School Psychologists; Sociologists.

Skills: Writing; Social Perceptiveness; Science; Complex Problem Solving; Systems Evaluation; Systems Analysis.

Education and Training Programs: Anthropology; Physical Anthropology. **Related Knowledge/Courses:** Sociology and Anthropology; History and Archeology; Foreign Language; Philosophy and Theology; Geography; Biology.

Work Environment: Indoors; sitting.

Anthropologists and Archeologists

See *Anthropologists and Archeologists, described separately.*

Anthropology and Archeology Teachers, Postsecondary

* Education/Training Required: Doctoral degree
* Annual Earnings: $62,820
* Beginning Wage: $37,590
* Earnings Growth Potential: Very high
* Growth: 22.9%
* Annual Job Openings: 237,478
* Self-Employed: 0.4%
* Part-Time: 27.8%

Our sources did not provide separate job openings data for this occupation. The job openings listed here are shared with 35 other postsecondary teaching occupations. For a complete list, see the beginning of this section.

Industries with Greatest Employment: Educational Services, Public and Private.

Highest-Growth Industries (Projected Growth for This Job): Administrative and Support Services (48.3%); Amusement, Gambling, and Recreation Industries (45.3%); Social Assistance (38.6%); Support Activities for Transportation (32.8%); Religious, Grantmaking, Civic, Professional, and Similar Organizations (29.9%); Professional, Scientific, and Technical Services (28.8%); Management of Companies and Enterprises (26.8%); Educational Services, Public and Private (22.9%); Hospitals, Public and Private (21.4%); Personal and Laundry Services (21.0%).

Lowest-Growth Industries (Projected Growth for This Job): Other Information Services (7.4%); Sporting Goods, Hobby, Book, and Music Stores (13.3%); Performing Arts, Spectator Sports, and Related Industries (13.4%); Insurance Carriers and Related Activities (13.9%).

Fastest-Growing Metropolitan Areas (Recent Growth for This Job): Tampa–St. Petersburg–Clearwater, FL (75.0%); Denver–Aurora, CO (66.7%); New York–Northern New Jersey–Long Island, NY–NJ–PA (62.5%).

Other Considerations for Job Security: Retirements of current postsecondary teachers should create numerous openings for all types of postsecondary teachers, so job opportunities are generally expected to be very good. However, because students attend postsecondary institutions to prepare themselves for careers, the best job prospects for postsecondary teachers are likely to be in rapidly growing fields that offer many nonacademic career options—unlike anthropology and archeology. Community colleges and other institutions offering career and technical education have been among the most rapidly growing and are expected to offer some of the best opportunities for postsecondary teachers.

Teach courses in anthropology or archeology. Conduct research in a particular field of knowledge and publish findings in professional journals, books, and electronic media. Keep abreast of developments in their field by reading current literature, talking with colleagues, and participating in professional conferences. Prepare and deliver lectures to undergraduate and graduate students on topics such as research methods, urban anthropology, and language and culture. Evaluate and grade students' classwork, assignments, and papers. Initiate, facilitate, and moderate classroom discussions. Write grant proposals to procure external research funding. Supervise undergraduate and/or graduate teaching, internships, and research work. Prepare course materials such as syllabi, homework assignments, and handouts. Compile, administer, and grade examinations or assign this work to others. Supervise students' laboratory work or fieldwork. Plan, evaluate, and revise curricula, course content, course materials, and methods of instruction. Advise students on academic and vocational curricula, career issues, and laboratory and field research. Maintain student attendance records, grades, and other required records. Maintain regularly scheduled office hours to advise and assist students. Collaborate with colleagues to address teaching and research issues. Compile bibliographies of specialized materials for outside reading assignments. Perform administrative duties such as serving as department head. Select and obtain materials and supplies such as textbooks and laboratory equipment. Serve on academic or administrative committees that deal with institutional policies, departmental matters, and academic issues. Participate in student recruitment, registration, and placement activities. Participate in campus and community events. Provide professional consulting services to government and industry. Act as adviser to student organizations.

Personality Type: Social.

GOE—Interest Area: 05. Education and Training. **Work Group:** 05.03. Postsecondary and Adult Teaching and Instructing. **Other Jobs in this Work Group:** Adult Literacy, Remedial Education, and GED Teachers and Instructors; Agricultural

Sciences Teachers, Postsecondary; Architecture Teachers, Postsecondary; Area, Ethnic, and Cultural Studies Teachers, Postsecondary; Art, Drama, and Music Teachers, Postsecondary; Atmospheric, Earth, Marine, and Space Sciences Teachers, Postsecondary; Biological Science Teachers, Postsecondary; Business Teachers, Postsecondary; Chemistry Teachers, Postsecondary; Communications Teachers, Postsecondary; Computer Science Teachers, Postsecondary; Criminal Justice and Law Enforcement Teachers, Postsecondary; Economics Teachers, Postsecondary; Education Teachers, Postsecondary; Engineering Teachers, Postsecondary; English Language and Literature Teachers, Postsecondary; Environmental Science Teachers, Postsecondary; Farm and Home Management Advisors; Foreign Language and Literature Teachers, Postsecondary; Forestry and Conservation Science Teachers, Postsecondary; Geography Teachers, Postsecondary; Graduate Teaching Assistants; Health Specialties Teachers, Postsecondary; History Teachers, Postsecondary; Home Economics Teachers, Postsecondary; Law Teachers, Postsecondary; Library Science Teachers, Postsecondary; Mathematical Science Teachers, Postsecondary; Nursing Instructors and Teachers, Postsecondary; Philosophy and Religion Teachers, Postsecondary; Physics Teachers, Postsecondary; Political Science Teachers, Postsecondary; Psychology Teachers, Postsecondary; Recreation and Fitness Studies Teachers, Postsecondary; Self-Enrichment Education Teachers; Social Work Teachers, Postsecondary; Sociology Teachers, Postsecondary; Vocational Education Teachers, Postsecondary.

Skills: Science; Writing; Critical Thinking; Reading Comprehension; Active Learning; Instructing.

Education and Training Programs: Social Science Teacher Education; Anthropology; Physical Anthropology; Archeology. **Related Knowledge/Courses:** Sociology and Anthropology; History and Archeology; Geography; Foreign Language; Philosophy and Theology; English Language.

Work Environment: Indoors; sitting.

Arbitrators, Mediators, and Conciliators

* Education/Training Required: Work experience plus degree
* Annual Earnings: $49,490
* Beginning Wage: $28,090
* Earnings Growth Potential: Very high
* Growth: 10.6%
* Annual Job Openings: 546
* Self-Employed: 0.0%
* Part-Time: 5.9%

Industries with Greatest Employment: Professional, Scientific, and Technical Services; Management of Companies and Enterprises.

Highest-Growth Industries (Projected Growth for This Job): Administrative and Support Services (35.8%); Professional, Scientific, and Technical Services (19.5%); Management of Companies and Enterprises (15.5%).

Lowest-Growth Industries (Projected Growth for This Job): Hospitals, Public and Private (6.7%); Educational Services, Public and Private (10.9%).

Fastest-Growing Metropolitan Areas (Recent Growth for This Job): Philadelphia–Camden–Wilmington, PA–NJ–DE–MD (250.0%); Chicago–Naperville–Joliet, IL–IN–WI (85.7%); St. Louis, MO–IL (83.3%); Los Angeles–Long Beach–Santa Ana, CA (50.0%); Hartford–West Hartford–East Hartford, CT (40.0%).

Other Considerations for Job Security: Many individuals and businesses try to avoid litigation, which can involve lengthy delays, high costs, unwanted publicity, and ill will. Arbitration and other alternatives to litigation usually are faster, less expensive, and more conclusive, spurring demand for the services of arbitrators, mediators, and conciliators. Demand also will continue to increase for arbitrators, mediators, and conciliators as all jurisdictions now have some type of alternative dispute resolution program. Some jurisdictions have programs requiring disputants to meet with a mediator in certain circumstances, such as when attempting to resolve child custody issues.

Facilitate negotiation and conflict resolution through dialogue. Resolve conflicts outside of the court system by mutual consent of parties involved. Use mediation techniques to facilitate communication between disputants, to further parties' understanding of different perspectives, and to guide parties toward mutual agreement. Set up appointments for parties to meet for mediation. Rule on exceptions, motions, and admissibility of evidence. Prepare written opinions and decisions regarding cases. Notify claimants of denied claims and appeal rights. Issue subpoenas and administer oaths to prepare for formal hearings. Authorize payment of valid claims. Organize and deliver public presentations about mediation to organizations such as community agencies and schools. Conduct studies of appeals procedures to ensure adherence to legal requirements and to facilitate disposition of cases. Arrange and conduct hearings to obtain information and evidence relative to disposition of claims. Determine existence and amount of liability according to evidence, laws, and administrative and judicial precedents. Review and evaluate information from documents such as claim applications, birth or death certificates, and physician or employer records. Analyze evidence and apply relevant laws, regulations, policies, and precedents to reach conclusions. Conduct initial meetings with disputants to outline the arbitration process, settle procedural matters such as fees, and determine details such as witness numbers and time requirements. Confer with disputants to clarify issues, identify underlying concerns, and develop an understanding of their respective needs and interests. Interview claimants, agents, or witnesses to obtain information about disputed issues. Participate in court proceedings. Prepare settlement agreements for disputants to sign. Recommend acceptance or rejection of compromise settlement offers. Research laws, regulations, policies, and precedent decisions to prepare for hearings.

Personality Type: Enterprising.

GOE—Interest Area: 12. Law and Public Safety. **Work Group:** 12.02. Legal Practice and Justice Administration. **Other Jobs in this Work Group:** Administrative Law Judges, Adjudicators, and Hearing Officers; Judges, Magistrate Judges, and Magistrates; Lawyers.

Skills: Negotiation; Active Listening; Persuasion; Judgment and Decision Making; Social Perceptiveness; Complex Problem Solving.

Education and Training Programs: Law (LL.B., J.D.); Legal Professions and Studies, Other. **Related Knowledge/Courses:** Sociology and Anthropology; Therapy and Counseling; Law and Government; Personnel and Human Resources; Psychology; Philosophy and Theology.

Work Environment: Indoors; sitting.

Archeologists

* Education/Training Required: Master's degree
* Annual Earnings: $49,930
* Beginning Wage: $28,940
* Earnings Growth Potential: Very high
* Growth: 15.0%
* Annual Job Openings: 446
* Self-Employed: 6.1%
* Part-Time: 20.1%

Our sources did not provide separate job openings data for this occupation. The job openings listed here are shared with Anthropologists.

Industries with Greatest Employment: Professional, Scientific, and Technical Services.

Highest-Growth Industries (Projected Growth for This Job): Museums, Historical Sites, and Similar Institutions (36.2%); Professional, Scientific, and Technical Services (27.8%).

Lowest-Growth Industries (Projected Growth for This Job): Educational Services, Public and Private (11.8%).

Fastest-Growing Metropolitan Areas (Recent Growth for This Job): Austin–Round Rock, TX (128.6%); Flagstaff, AZ (100.0%); New Orleans–Metairie–Kenner, LA (25.0%); Anchorage, AK (20.0%).

Other Considerations for Job Security: Job seekers may face competition, and those with higher educational attainment will have the best prospects. As construction projects increase, more archaeologists will be needed to monitor the work, ensuring that historical sites and artifacts are preserved. Some people with degrees in archaeology will find opportunities as university faculty rather than as applied archaeologists. Although there will be keen competition for tenured positions, the number of faculty expected to retire over the decade and the increasing number of part-time or short-term faculty positions will lead to better opportunities in colleges and universities than in the past.

Conduct research to reconstruct record of past human life and culture from human remains, artifacts, architectural features, and structures recovered through excavation, underwater recovery, or other means of discovery. Write, present, and publish reports that record site history, methodology, and artifact analysis results, along with recommendations for conserving and interpreting findings. Compare findings from one site with archeological data from other sites to find similarities or differences. Research, survey, or assess sites of past societies and cultures in search of answers to specific research questions. Study objects and structures recovered by excavation to identify, date, and authenticate them and to interpret their significance. Develop and test theories concerning the origin and development of past cultures. Consult site reports, existing artifacts, and topographic maps to identify archeological sites. Create a grid of each site and draw and update maps of unit profiles, stratum surfaces, features, and findings. Record the exact locations and conditions of artifacts uncovered in diggings or surveys, using drawings and photographs as necessary. Assess archeological sites for resource management, development, or conservation purposes and recommend methods for site protection. Describe artifacts' physical properties or attributes, such as the materials from which artifacts are made and their size, shape, function, and decoration. Teach archeology at colleges and universities. Collect artifacts made of stone, bone, metal, and other materials, placing them in bags and marking them to show where they were found. Create artifact typologies to organize and make sense of past material cultures. Lead field training sites and train field staff, students, and volunteers in excavation methods. Clean, restore, and preserve artifacts.

Personality Type: Investigative.

GOE—Interest Area: 15. Scientific Research, Engineering, and Mathematics. **Work Group:** 15.04. Social Sciences. **Other Jobs in this Work Group:** Anthropologists; Anthropologists and Archeologists; Economists; Historians; Industrial-Organizational Psychologists; Political Scientists; School Psychologists; Sociologists.

Skills: Science; Management of Financial Resources; Management of Personnel Resources; Writing; Reading Comprehension; Active Learning.

Education and Training Program: Archeology. **Related Knowledge/Courses:** History and Archeology; Sociology and Anthropology; Geography; Philosophy and Theology; Foreign Language; English Language.

Work Environment: More often indoors than outdoors; sitting; using hands on objects, tools, or controls.

Architecture Teachers, Postsecondary

✴ Education/Training Required: Doctoral degree
✴ Annual Earnings: $64,620
✴ Beginning Wage: $37,670
✴ Earnings Growth Potential: Very high
✴ Growth: 22.9%
✴ Annual Job Openings: 237,478
✴ Self-Employed: 0.4%
✴ Part-Time: 27.8%

Our sources did not provide separate job openings data for this occupation. The job openings listed here are shared with 35 other postsecondary teaching occupations. For a complete list, see the beginning of this section.

Industries with Greatest Employment: Educational Services, Public and Private.

Highest-Growth Industries (Projected Growth for This Job): Administrative and Support Services (48.3%); Amusement, Gambling, and Recreation Industries (45.3%); Social Assistance (38.6%); Support Activities for Transportation (32.8%); Religious, Grantmaking, Civic, Professional, and Similar Organizations (29.9%); Professional, Scientific, and Technical Services (28.8%); Management of Companies and Enterprises (26.8%); Educational Services, Public and Private (22.9%); Hospitals, Public and Private (21.4%); Personal and Laundry Services (21.0%).

Lowest-Growth Industries (Projected Growth for This Job): Other Information Services (7.4%); Sporting Goods, Hobby, Book, and Music Stores (13.3%); Performing Arts, Spectator Sports, and Related Industries (13.4%); Insurance Carriers and Related Activities (13.9%).

Fastest-Growing Metropolitan Areas (Recent Growth for This Job): None growing over 10 percent.

Other Considerations for Job Security: Retirements of current postsecondary teachers should create numerous openings for all types of postsecondary teachers, so job opportunities are generally expected to be very good. Because students attend postsecondary institutions to prepare themselves for careers, the best job prospects for postsecondary teachers are likely to be in rapidly growing fields that offer many nonacademic career options. Community colleges and other institutions offering career and technical education have been among the most rapidly growing and are expected to offer some of the best opportunities for postsecondary teachers.

Teach courses in architecture and architectural design, such as architectural environmental design, interior architecture/design, and landscape architecture. Evaluate and grade students' work, including work performed in design studios. Prepare and deliver lectures to undergraduate and/or graduate students on topics such as architectural design methods, aesthetics and design, and structures and materials. Prepare course materials such as syllabi, homework assignments, and handouts. Initiate, facilitate, and moderate classroom discussions. Plan, evaluate, and revise curricula, course content, course materials, and methods of instruction. Keep abreast of developments in their field by reading current literature, talking with colleagues, and participating in professional conferences. Maintain student attendance records, grades, and other required records. Maintain regularly scheduled office hours to advise and assist students. Compile, administer, and grade examinations or assign this work to others. Conduct research in a particular field of knowledge and publish findings in professional journals, books, and/or electronic media. Supervise undergraduate and/or graduate teaching, internships, and research work. Advise students on academic and vocational curricula and on career issues. Collaborate with colleagues to address teaching and research issues. Compile bibliographies of specialized materials for outside reading assignments. Serve on academic or administrative committees that deal with institutional policies, departmental matters, and academic issues. Participate in student recruitment, registration, and placement activities. Select and obtain materials and supplies such as textbooks and laboratory equipment.

Write grant proposals to procure external research funding. Provide professional consulting services to government and/or industry. Perform administrative duties such as serving as department head. Act as advisers to student organizations. Participate in campus and community events.

Personality Type: No data available.

GOE—Interest Area: 05. Education and Training. **Work Group:** 05.03. Postsecondary and Adult Teaching and Instructing. **Other Jobs in this Work Group:** Adult Literacy, Remedial Education, and GED Teachers and Instructors; Agricultural Sciences Teachers, Postsecondary; Anthropology and Archeology Teachers, Postsecondary; Area, Ethnic, and Cultural Studies Teachers, Postsecondary; Art, Drama, and Music Teachers, Postsecondary; Atmospheric, Earth, Marine, and Space Sciences Teachers, Postsecondary; Biological Science Teachers, Postsecondary; Business Teachers, Postsecondary; Chemistry Teachers, Postsecondary; Communications Teachers, Postsecondary; Computer Science Teachers, Postsecondary; Criminal Justice and Law Enforcement Teachers, Postsecondary; Economics Teachers, Postsecondary; Education Teachers, Postsecondary; Engineering Teachers, Postsecondary; English Language and Literature Teachers, Postsecondary; Environmental Science Teachers, Postsecondary; Farm and Home Management Advisors; Foreign Language and Literature Teachers, Postsecondary; Forestry and Conservation Science Teachers, Postsecondary; Geography Teachers, Postsecondary; Graduate Teaching Assistants; Health Specialties Teachers, Postsecondary; History Teachers, Postsecondary; Home Economics Teachers, Postsecondary; Law Teachers, Postsecondary; Library Science Teachers, Postsecondary; Mathematical Science Teachers, Postsecondary; Nursing Instructors and Teachers, Postsecondary; Philosophy and Religion Teachers, Postsecondary; Physics Teachers, Postsecondary; Political Science Teachers, Postsecondary; Psychology Teachers, Postsecondary; Recreation and Fitness Studies Teachers, Postsecondary; Self-Enrichment Education Teachers; Social Work Teachers, Postsecondary; Sociology Teachers, Postsecondary; Vocational Education Teachers, Postsecondary.

Skills: Technology Design; Instructing; Operations Analysis; Writing; Complex Problem Solving; Speaking.

Education and Training Programs: Architecture (BArch, BA/BS, MArch, MA/MS, PhD); City/Urban, Community and Regional Planning; Environmental Design/Architecture; Interior Architecture; Landscape Architecture (BS, BSLA, BLA, MSLA, MLA, PhD); Teacher Education and Professional Development, Specific Subject Areas, Other; Architectural Engineering. **Related Knowledge/Courses:** Fine Arts; Design; Building and Construction; History and Archeology; Philosophy and Theology; Geography.

Work Environment: Indoors; sitting.

Archivists

* Education/Training Required: Master's degree
* Annual Earnings: $40,730
* Beginning Wage: $23,890
* Earnings Growth Potential: Very high
* Growth: 14.4%
* Annual Job Openings: 795
* Self-Employed: 1.3%
* Part-Time: 18.4%

Industries with Greatest Employment: Educational Services, Public and Private; Museums, Historical Sites, and Similar Institutions; Professional, Scientific, and Technical Services.

Highest-Growth Industries (Projected Growth for This Job): Museums, Historical Sites, and Similar Institutions (36.2%); Administrative and Support Services (31.8%); Performing Arts, Spectator Sports, and Related Industries (28.8%).

Lowest-Growth Industries (Projected Growth for This Job): Publishing Industries (except Internet) (–8.6%); Professional, Scientific, and Technical Services (11.0%); Educational Services, Public and Private (11.9%); Management of Companies and Enterprises (14.7%).

Fastest-Growing Metropolitan Areas (Recent Growth for This Job): Washington–Arlington–Alexandria, DC–VA–MD–WV (125.0%); Seattle–Tacoma–Bellevue, WA (114.3%); Buffalo–Niagara Falls, NY (60.0%); San Francisco–Oakland–Fremont, CA (50.0%); Salt Lake City, UT (33.3%).

Other Considerations for Job Security: Keen competition is expected because qualified applicants generally outnumber job openings. Demand for archivists who specialize in electronic records and records management will grow more rapidly than the demand for archivists who specialize in older media formats. Graduates with highly specialized training, such as master's degrees in both library science and history, with a concentration in archives or records management and extensive computer skills, should have the best opportunities for jobs as archivists.

Appraise, edit, and direct safekeeping of permanent records and historically valuable documents. Participate in research activities based on archival materials. Create and maintain accessible, retrievable computer archives and databases, incorporating current advances in electric information storage technology. Organize archival records and develop classification systems to facilitate access to archival materials. Authenticate and appraise historical documents and archival materials. Provide reference services and assistance for users needing archival materials. Direct activities of workers who assist in arranging, cataloging, exhibiting, and maintaining collections of valuable materials. Prepare archival records, such as document descriptions, to allow easy access to information. Preserve records, documents, and objects, copying records to film, videotape, audiotape, disk, or computer formats as necessary. Establish and administer policy guidelines concerning public access and use of materials. Locate new materials and direct their acquisition and display. Research and record the origins and historical significance of archival materials. Specialize in an area of history or technology, researching topics or items relevant to collections to determine what should be retained or acquired. Coordinate educational and public outreach programs such as tours, workshops, lectures, and classes. Select and edit documents for publication and display, applying knowledge of subject, literary expression, and presentation techniques.

Personality Type: Investigative.

GOE—Interest Area: 05. Education and Training. **Work Group:** 05.05. Archival and Museum Services. **Other Jobs in this Work Group:** Audio-Visual Collections Specialists; Curators; Museum Technicians and Conservators.

Skills: No data available.

Education and Training Programs: Historic Preservation and Conservation; Cultural Resource Management and Policy Analysis; Historic Preservation and Conservation, Other; Museology/Museum Studies; Art History, Criticism, and Conservation; Public/Applied History and Archival Administration. **Related Knowledge/Courses:** Clerical Studies; History and Archeology; Computers and Electronics; English Language; Administration and Management; Customer and Personal Service.

Work Environment: Indoors; sitting.

Area, Ethnic, and Cultural Studies Teachers, Postsecondary

- Education/Training Required: Doctoral degree
- Annual Earnings: $56,380
- Beginning Wage: $31,770
- Earnings Growth Potential: Very high
- Growth: 22.9%
- Annual Job Openings: 237,478
- Self-Employed: 0.4%
- Part-Time: 27.8%

Our sources did not provide separate job openings data for this occupation. The job openings listed here are shared with 35 other postsecondary teaching occupations. For a complete list, see the beginning of this section.

Industries with Greatest Employment: Educational Services, Public and Private.

Highest-Growth Industries (Projected Growth for This Job): Administrative and Support Services (48.3%); Amusement, Gambling, and Recreation Industries (45.3%); Social Assistance (38.6%); Support Activities for Transportation (32.8%); Religious, Grantmaking, Civic, Professional, and Similar Organizations (29.9%); Professional, Scientific, and Technical Services (28.8%); Management of Companies and Enterprises (26.8%); Educational Services, Public and Private (22.9%); Hospitals, Public and Private (21.4%); Personal and Laundry Services (21.0%).

Lowest-Growth Industries (Projected Growth for This Job): Other Information Services (7.4%); Sporting Goods, Hobby, Book, and Music Stores (13.3%); Performing Arts, Spectator Sports, and Related Industries (13.4%); Insurance Carriers and Related Activities (13.9%).

Fastest-Growing Metropolitan Areas (Recent Growth for This Job): Riverside–San Bernardino–Ontario, CA (60.0%); Columbus, OH (55.6%); New York–Northern New Jersey–Long Island, NY–NJ–PA (50.0%); Pittsburgh, PA (50.0%); Durham, NC (50.0%).

Other Considerations for Job Security: Retirements of current postsecondary teachers should create numerous openings for all types of postsecondary teachers, so job opportunities are generally expected to be very good. However, because students attend postsecondary institutions to prepare themselves for careers, the best job prospects for postsecondary teachers are likely to be in rapidly growing fields that offer many nonacademic career options—unlike area, ethnic, and cultural studies. Community colleges and other institutions offering career and technical education have been among the most rapidly growing and are expected to offer some of the best opportunities for postsecondary teachers.

Teach courses pertaining to the culture and development of an area (e.g., Latin America), an ethnic group, or any other group (e.g., women's studies, urban affairs). Keep abreast of developments in their field by reading current literature, talking with colleagues, and participating in professional conferences. Conduct research in a particular field of knowledge and publish findings in professional journals, books, and/or electronic media. Evaluate and grade students' classwork, assignments, and papers. Prepare course materials such as syllabi, homework assignments, and handouts. Prepare and deliver lectures to undergraduate and/or graduate students on topics such as race and ethnic relations, gender studies, and cross-cultural perspectives. Initiate, facilitate, and moderate classroom discussions. Compile, administer, and grade examinations or assign this work to others. Maintain regularly scheduled office hours to advise and assist students. Plan, evaluate, and revise curricula, course content, course materials, and methods of instruction. Maintain student attendance records, grades, and other required records. Advise students on academic and vocational curricula and on career issues. Supervise undergraduate and/or graduate teaching, internships, and research work. Select and obtain materials and supplies such as textbooks. Collaborate with colleagues to address teaching and research issues. Serve on academic or administrative committees that deal with institutional policies, departmental matters, and academic issues. Compile bibliographies of specialized materials for outside reading assignments. Write grant proposals to procure external research funding. Participate in campus and community events. Participate in student recruitment, registration, and placement activities. Act as advisers to student organizations. Incorporate experiential/site visit components into courses. Perform administrative duties such as serving as department head. Provide professional consulting services to government and/or industry.

Personality Type: Social.

GOE—Interest Area: 05. Education and Training. **Work Group:** 05.03. Postsecondary and Adult Teaching and Instructing. **Other Jobs in this Work Group:** Adult Literacy, Remedial Education, and GED Teachers and Instructors; Agricultural Sciences Teachers, Postsecondary; Anthropology and Archeology Teachers, Postsecondary; Architecture Teachers, Postsecondary; Art, Drama, and Music Teachers,

Postsecondary; Atmospheric, Earth, Marine, and Space Sciences Teachers, Postsecondary; Biological Science Teachers, Postsecondary; Business Teachers, Postsecondary; Chemistry Teachers, Postsecondary; Communications Teachers, Postsecondary; Computer Science Teachers, Postsecondary; Criminal Justice and Law Enforcement Teachers, Postsecondary; Economics Teachers, Postsecondary; Education Teachers, Postsecondary; Engineering Teachers, Postsecondary; English Language and Literature Teachers, Postsecondary; Environmental Science Teachers, Postsecondary; Farm and Home Management Advisors; Foreign Language and Literature Teachers, Postsecondary; Forestry and Conservation Science Teachers, Postsecondary; Geography Teachers, Postsecondary; Graduate Teaching Assistants; Health Specialties Teachers, Postsecondary; History Teachers, Postsecondary; Home Economics Teachers, Postsecondary; Law Teachers, Postsecondary; Library Science Teachers, Postsecondary; Mathematical Science Teachers, Postsecondary; Nursing Instructors and Teachers, Postsecondary; Philosophy and Religion Teachers, Postsecondary; Physics Teachers, Postsecondary; Political Science Teachers, Postsecondary; Psychology Teachers, Postsecondary; Recreation and Fitness Studies Teachers, Postsecondary; Self-Enrichment Education Teachers; Social Work Teachers, Postsecondary; Sociology Teachers, Postsecondary; Vocational Education Teachers, Postsecondary.

Skills: Writing; Critical Thinking; Instructing; Persuasion; Active Learning; Learning Strategies.

Education and Training Programs: African Studies; American/United States Studies/Civilization; Asian Studies/Civilization; East Asian Studies; Central/Middle and Eastern European Studies; European Studies/Civilization; Latin American Studies; Near and Middle Eastern Studies; Pacific Area/Pacific Rim Studies; Russian Studies; Scandinavian Studies; South Asian Studies; Southeast Asian Studies; Western European Studies; others. **Related Knowledge/ Courses:** History and Archeology; Sociology and Anthropology; Foreign Language; Philosophy and Theology; Geography; Education and Training.

Work Environment: Indoors; sitting.

Art, Drama, and Music Teachers, Postsecondary

* Education/Training Required: Doctoral degree
* Annual Earnings: $53,160
* Beginning Wage: $29,290
* Earnings Growth Potential: Very high
* Growth: 22.9%
* Annual Job Openings: 237,478
* Self-Employed: 0.4%
* Part-Time: 27.8%

Our sources did not provide separate job openings data for this occupation. The job openings listed here are shared with 35 other postsecondary teaching occupations. For a complete list, see the beginning of this section.

Industries with Greatest Employment: Educational Services, Public and Private.

Highest-Growth Industries (Projected Growth for This Job): Administrative and Support Services (48.3%); Amusement, Gambling, and Recreation Industries (45.3%); Social Assistance (38.6%); Support Activities for Transportation (32.8%); Religious, Grantmaking, Civic, Professional, and Similar Organizations (29.9%); Professional, Scientific, and Technical Services (28.8%); Management of Companies and Enterprises (26.8%); Educational Services, Public and Private (22.9%); Hospitals, Public and Private (21.4%); Personal and Laundry Services (21.0%).

Lowest-Growth Industries (Projected Growth for This Job): Other Information Services (7.4%); Sporting Goods, Hobby, Book, and Music Stores (13.3%); Performing Arts, Spectator Sports, and Related Industries (13.4%); Insurance Carriers and Related Activities (13.9%).

Fastest-Growing Metropolitan Areas (Recent Growth for This Job): Rochester, NY (29.4%); Lancaster, PA (28.6%); Scranton–Wilkes-Barre, PA (25.5%); San Antonio, TX (20.8%); Portland–Vancouver–Beaverton, OR–WA (20.0%).

Other Considerations for Job Security: Retirements of current postsecondary teachers should create numerous openings for all types of postsecondary teachers, so job opportunities are generally expected to be very good. However, because students attend postsecondary institutions to prepare themselves for careers, the best job prospects for postsecondary teachers are likely to be in rapidly growing fields that offer many nonacademic career options. Community colleges and other institutions offering career and technical education have been among the most rapidly growing and are expected to offer some of the best opportunities for postsecondary teachers.

Teach courses in drama; music; and the arts, including fine and applied art, such as painting and sculpture, or design and crafts. Evaluate and grade students' classwork, performances, projects, assignments, and papers. Explain and demonstrate artistic techniques. Prepare students for performances, exams, or assessments. Prepare and deliver lectures to undergraduate or graduate students on topics such as acting techniques, fundamentals of music, and art history. Organize performance groups and direct their rehearsals. Prepare course materials such as syllabi, homework assignments, and handouts. Initiate, facilitate, and moderate classroom discussions. Keep abreast of developments in their field by reading current literature, talking with colleagues, and participating in professional conferences. Advise students on academic and vocational curricula and on career issues. Maintain student attendance records, grades, and other required records. Conduct research in a particular field of knowledge and publish findings in professional journals, books, or electronic media. Supervise undergraduate and/or graduate teaching, internships, and research work. Plan, evaluate, and revise curricula, course content, course materials, and methods of instruction. Maintain regularly scheduled office hours to advise and assist students. Compile, administer, and grade examinations or assign this work to others. Participate in student recruitment, registration, and placement activities. Select and obtain materials and supplies such as textbooks and performance pieces. Collaborate with colleagues to address teaching and research issues. Serve on academic or administrative committees that deal with institutional policies, departmental matters, and academic issues. Participate in campus and community events. Keep students informed of community events such as plays and concerts. Compile bibliographies of specialized materials for outside reading assignments. Display students' work in schools, galleries, and exhibitions. Perform administrative duties such as serving as department head. Act as advisers to student organizations. Write grant proposals to procure external research funding. Provide professional consulting services to government or industry.

Personality Type: Artistic.

GOE—Interest Area: 05. Education and Training. **Work Group:** 05.03. Postsecondary and Adult Teaching and Instructing. **Other Jobs in this Work Group:** Adult Literacy, Remedial Education, and GED Teachers and Instructors; Agricultural Sciences Teachers, Postsecondary; Anthropology and Archeology Teachers, Postsecondary; Architecture Teachers, Postsecondary; Area, Ethnic, and Cultural Studies Teachers, Postsecondary; Atmospheric, Earth, Marine, and Space Sciences Teachers, Postsecondary; Biological Science Teachers, Postsecondary; Business Teachers, Postsecondary; Chemistry Teachers, Postsecondary; Communications Teachers, Postsecondary; Computer Science Teachers, Postsecondary; Criminal Justice and Law Enforcement Teachers, Postsecondary; Economics Teachers, Postsecondary; Education Teachers, Postsecondary; Engineering Teachers, Postsecondary; English Language and Literature Teachers, Postsecondary; Environmental Science Teachers, Postsecondary; Farm and Home Management Advisors; Foreign Language and Literature Teachers, Postsecondary; Forestry and Conservation Science Teachers, Postsecondary; Geography Teachers, Postsecondary; Graduate Teaching Assistants; Health Specialties Teachers, Postsecondary; History Teachers, Postsecondary; Home Economics Teachers, Postsecondary; Law Teachers, Postsecondary; Library Science Teachers, Postsecondary; Mathematical Science Teachers, Postsecondary; Nursing Instructors and Teachers, Postsecondary; Philosophy and Religion Teachers, Postsecondary; Physics Teachers, Postsecondary; Political Science Teachers,

Postsecondary; Psychology Teachers, Postsecondary; Recreation and Fitness Studies Teachers, Postsecondary; Self-Enrichment Education Teachers; Social Work Teachers, Postsecondary; Sociology Teachers, Postsecondary; Vocational Education Teachers, Postsecondary.

Skills: Instructing; Social Perceptiveness; Speaking; Persuasion; Active Listening; Learning Strategies.

Education and Training Programs: Visual and Performing Arts, General; Crafts/Craft Design, Folk Art and Artisanry; Dance, General; Design and Visual Communications, General; Industrial Design; Commercial Photography; Fashion/Apparel Design; Interior Design; Graphic Design; Design and Applied Arts, Other; Drama and Dramatics/Theatre Arts, General; Technical Theatre/Theatre Design and Technology; Playwriting and Screenwriting; others. **Related Knowledge/Courses:** Fine Arts; History and Archeology; Philosophy and Theology; Education and Training; Communications and Media; Sociology and Anthropology.

Work Environment: Indoors; noisy; sitting.

Athletes and Sports Competitors

- ❋ Education/Training Required: Long-term on-the-job training
- ❋ Annual Earnings: $41,060
- ❋ Beginning Wage: $14,570
- ❋ Earnings Growth Potential: Medium
- ❋ Growth: 19.2%
- ❋ Annual Job Openings: 4,293
- ❋ Self-Employed: 27.0%
- ❋ Part-Time: 39.1%

Industries with Greatest Employment: Performing Arts, Spectator Sports, and Related Industries; Amusement, Gambling, and Recreation Industries.

Highest-Growth Industries (Projected Growth for This Job): Amusement, Gambling, and Recreation Industries (29.9%); Performing Arts, Spectator

Sports, and Related Industries (24.1%); Educational Services, Public and Private (21.9%).

Lowest-Growth Industries (Projected Growth for This Job): None met the criteria.

Fastest-Growing Metropolitan Areas (Recent Growth for This Job): Cape Coral–Fort Myers, FL (200.0%); Hartford–West Hartford–East Hartford, CT (150.0%); Miami–Fort Lauderdale–Miami Beach, FL (57.9%); Washington–Arlington–Alexandria, DC–VA–MD–WV (45.8%); Chicago–Naperville–Joliet, IL–IN–WI (43.1%).

Other Considerations for Job Security: Competition for professional athlete jobs will continue to be extremely intense. Opportunities to make a living as a professional in individual sports such as golf or tennis may grow as new tournaments are established and as prize money distributed to participants increases. Because most professional athletes' careers last only a few years due to debilitating injuries and age, annual replacement needs for these jobs is high, creating some job opportunities. However, the talented young men and women who dream of becoming sports superstars greatly outnumber the number of openings.

Compete in athletic events. Lead teams by serving as captains. Receive instructions from coaches and other sports staff before events and discuss their performance afterward. Participate in athletic events and competitive sports according to established rules and regulations. Maintain optimum physical fitness levels by training regularly, following nutrition plans, and consulting with health professionals. Exercise and practice under the direction of athletic trainers or professional coaches to develop skills, improve physical condition, and prepare for competitions. Attend scheduled practice and training sessions. Assess performance following athletic competition, identifying strengths and weaknesses and making adjustments to improve future performance. Maintain equipment used in a particular sport. Represent teams or professional sports clubs, performing such activities as meeting with members of the media, making speeches, or participating in charity events.

Personality Type: Enterprising.

GOE—Interest Area: 09. Hospitality, Tourism, and Recreation. **Work Group:** 09.06. Sports. **Other Jobs in this Work Group:** Coaches and Scouts; Umpires, Referees, and Other Sports Officials.

Skills: No data available.

Education and Training Program: Health and Physical Education, General. **Related Knowledge/Courses:** Therapy and Counseling; Communications and Media; Psychology; Sales and Marketing; Personnel and Human Resources.

Work Environment: Indoors; very hot or cold; keeping or regaining balance; using hands on objects, tools, or controls; bending or twisting the body; repetitive motions.

Athletic Trainers

- ❋ Education/Training Required: Bachelor's degree
- ❋ Annual Earnings: $36,560
- ❋ Beginning Wage: $21,940
- ❋ Earnings Growth Potential: Very high
- ❋ Growth: 24.3%
- ❋ Annual Job Openings: 1,669
- ❋ Self-Employed: 2.4%
- ❋ Part-Time: 8.0%

Industries with Greatest Employment: Educational Services, Public and Private; Amusement, Gambling, and Recreation Industries; Ambulatory Health Care Services; Hospitals, Public and Private.

Highest-Growth Industries (Projected Growth for This Job): Ambulatory Health Care Services (37.6%); Amusement, Gambling, and Recreation Industries (32.7%); Nursing and Residential Care Facilities (27.2%); Performing Arts, Spectator Sports, and Related Industries (22.7%); Hospitals, Public and Private (22.3%); Religious, Grantmaking, Civic, Professional, and Similar Organizations (17.6%); Educational Services, Public and Private (15.3%).

Lowest-Growth Industries (Projected Growth for This Job): None met the criteria.

Fastest-Growing Metropolitan Areas (Recent Growth for This Job): Phoenix–Mesa–Scottsdale, AZ (114.3%); Los Angeles–Long Beach–Santa Ana, CA (96.4%); Akron, OH (66.7%); Denver–Aurora, CO (63.6%); Sacramento–Arden–Arcade–Roseville, CA (50.0%).

Other Considerations for Job Security: Job prospects should be good for athletic trainers in the health-care industry. Those looking for a position with a sports team, however, may face competition. Because of relatively low turnover, the settings with the best job prospects will be the ones that are expected to have the most job growth, primarily positions in the heath-care industry and fitness and recreational sports centers. Additional job opportunities are expected in elementary and secondary schools as more positions are created. Some of these positions also will require teaching responsibilities. There will be more competition for positions within colleges and universities as well as in professional sports clubs. The occupation is expected to continue to change over the next decade, including more administrative responsibilities, adapting to new technology, and working with larger populations, and job seekers must be able to adapt to these changes.

Evaluate, advise, and treat athletes to assist recovery from injury, avoid injury, or maintain peak physical fitness. Conduct an initial assessment of an athlete's injury or illness to provide emergency or continued care and to determine whether he or she should be referred to physicians for definitive diagnosis and treatment. Care for athletic injuries, using physical therapy equipment, techniques, and medication. Evaluate athletes' readiness to play and provide participation clearances when necessary and warranted. Apply protective or injury-preventive devices such as tape, bandages, or braces to body parts such as ankles, fingers, or wrists. Assess and report the progress of recovering athletes to coaches and physicians. Collaborate with physicians to develop and implement comprehensive rehabilitation programs for athletic injuries. Advise athletes on the proper use of equipment. Plan and implement comprehensive athletic injury and illness prevention programs. Develop training programs and routines designed to improve athletic performance. Travel with athletic teams to be available at sporting events. Instruct coaches, athletes, parents, medical personnel, and community members in the care and prevention of athletic injuries. Inspect playing fields to locate any items that could injure players. Conduct research and provide instruction on subject matter related to athletic training or sports medicine. Recommend special diets to improve athletes' health, increase their stamina, or alter their weight. Massage body parts to relieve soreness, strains, and bruises. Confer with coaches to select protective equipment. Accompany injured athletes to hospitals. Perform team-support duties such as running errands, maintaining equipment, and stocking supplies. Lead stretching exercises for team members before games and practices.

Personality Type: Social.

GOE—Interest Area: 08. Health Science. **Work Group:** 08.09. Health Protection and Promotion. **Other Jobs in this Work Group:** Dietetic Technicians; Dietitians and Nutritionists; Embalmers.

Skills: Social Perceptiveness; Science; Management of Material Resources; Management of Personnel Resources; Management of Financial Resources; Time Management.

Education and Training Program: Athletic Training/Trainer. **Related Knowledge/Courses:** Therapy and Counseling; Medicine and Dentistry; Biology; Psychology; Sociology and Anthropology; Physics.

Work Environment: More often indoors than outdoors; very hot or cold; contaminants; disease or infections; standing.

Atmospheric, Earth, Marine, and Space Sciences Teachers, Postsecondary

* Education/Training Required: Doctoral degree
* Annual Earnings: $69,300
* Beginning Wage: $37,330
* Earnings Growth Potential: Very high
* Growth: 22.9%
* Annual Job Openings: 237,478
* Self-Employed: 0.4%
* Part-Time: 27.8%

Our sources did not provide separate job openings data for this occupation. The job openings listed here are shared with 35 other postsecondary teaching occupations. For a complete list, see the beginning of this section.

Industries with Greatest Employment: Educational Services, Public and Private.

Highest-Growth Industries (Projected Growth for This Job): Administrative and Support Services (48.3%); Amusement, Gambling, and Recreation Industries (45.3%); Social Assistance (38.6%); Support Activities for Transportation (32.8%); Religious, Grantmaking, Civic, Professional, and Similar Organizations (29.9%); Professional, Scientific, and Technical Services (28.8%); Management of Companies and Enterprises (26.8%); Educational Services, Public and Private (22.9%); Hospitals, Public and Private (21.4%); Personal and Laundry Services (21.0%).

Lowest-Growth Industries (Projected Growth for This Job): Other Information Services (7.4%); Sporting Goods, Hobby, Book, and Music Stores (13.3%); Performing Arts, Spectator Sports, and Related Industries (13.4%); Insurance Carriers and Related Activities (13.9%).

Fastest-Growing Metropolitan Areas (Recent Growth for This Job): None growing over 10 percent.

Other Considerations for Job Security: Retirements of current postsecondary teachers should create numerous openings for all types of postsecondary teachers, so job opportunities are generally expected to be very good. Because students attend postsecondary institutions to prepare themselves for careers, the best job prospects for postsecondary teachers are likely to be in rapidly growing fields that offer many nonacademic career options. Community colleges and other institutions offering career and technical education have been among the most rapidly growing and are expected to offer some of the best opportunities for postsecondary teachers.

Teach courses in the physical sciences, except chemistry and physics. Conduct research in a particular field of knowledge and publish findings in professional journals, books, and/or electronic media. Write grant proposals to procure external research funding. Keep abreast of developments in their field by reading current literature, talking with colleagues, and participating in professional conferences. Supervise undergraduate and/or graduate teaching, internships, and research work. Prepare and deliver lectures to undergraduate and/or graduate students on topics such as structural geology, micrometeorology, and atmospheric thermodynamics. Supervise laboratory work and fieldwork. Evaluate and grade students' classwork, assignments, and papers. Prepare course materials such as syllabi, homework assignments, and handouts. Collaborate with colleagues to address teaching and research issues. Compile, administer, and grade examinations or assign this work to others. Plan, evaluate, and revise curricula, course content, course materials, and methods of instruction. Initiate, facilitate, and moderate classroom discussions. Maintain regularly scheduled office hours to advise and assist students. Advise students on academic and vocational curricula and on career issues. Maintain student attendance records, grades, and other required records. Participate in student recruitment, registration, and placement activities. Perform administrative duties such as serving as department head. Select and obtain materials and supplies such as textbooks and laboratory equipment. Serve on academic or administrative committees that deal with institutional policies, departmental matters, and academic issues. Compile bibliographies of specialized materials for outside reading assignments. Provide professional consulting services to government and/or industry. Act as adviser to student organizations. Participate in campus and community events.

Personality Type: No data available.

GOE—Interest Area: 05. Education and Training. **Work Group:** 05.03. Postsecondary and Adult Teaching and Instructing. **Other Jobs in this Work Group:** Adult Literacy, Remedial Education, and GED Teachers and Instructors; Agricultural Sciences Teachers, Postsecondary; Anthropology and Archeology Teachers, Postsecondary; Architecture Teachers, Postsecondary; Area, Ethnic, and Cultural Studies Teachers, Postsecondary; Art, Drama, and Music Teachers, Postsecondary; Biological Science Teachers, Postsecondary; Business Teachers, Postsecondary; Chemistry Teachers, Postsecondary; Communications Teachers, Postsecondary; Computer Science Teachers, Postsecondary; Criminal Justice and Law Enforcement Teachers, Postsecondary; Economics Teachers, Postsecondary; Education Teachers, Postsecondary; Engineering Teachers, Postsecondary; English Language and Literature Teachers, Postsecondary; Environmental Science Teachers, Postsecondary; Farm and Home Management Advisors; Foreign Language and Literature Teachers, Postsecondary; Forestry and Conservation Science Teachers, Postsecondary; Geography Teachers, Postsecondary; Graduate Teaching Assistants; Health Specialties Teachers, Postsecondary; History Teachers, Postsecondary; Home Economics Teachers, Postsecondary; Law Teachers, Postsecondary; Library Science Teachers, Postsecondary; Mathematical Science Teachers, Postsecondary; Nursing Instructors and Teachers, Postsecondary; Philosophy and Religion Teachers, Postsecondary; Physics Teachers, Postsecondary; Political Science Teachers, Postsecondary; Psychology Teachers, Postsecondary; Recreation and Fitness Studies Teachers, Postsecondary; Self-Enrichment Education Teachers; Social Work Teachers, Postsecondary; Sociology Teachers, Postsecondary; Vocational Education Teachers, Postsecondary.

Skills: Science; Programming; Mathematics; Management of Financial Resources; Complex Problem Solving; Writing.

Education and Training Programs: Science Teacher Education/General Science Teacher Education; Physics Teacher Education; Astronomy; Astrophysics; Planetary Astronomy and Science; Atmospheric Sciences and Meteorology, General; Atmospheric Chemistry and Climatology; Atmospheric Physics and Dynamics; Meteorology; Atmospheric Sciences and Meteorology, Other; Geology/Earth Science, General; Geochemistry; Geophysics and Seismology; others. **Related Knowledge/Courses:** Physics; Geography; Chemistry; Biology; Mathematics; Education and Training.

Work Environment: Indoors; sitting.

Audio and Video Equipment Technicians

- ✸ Education/Training Required: Long-term on-the-job training
- ✸ Annual Earnings: $34,840
- ✸ Beginning Wage: $19,980
- ✸ Earnings Growth Potential: Very high
- ✸ Growth: 24.2%
- ✸ Annual Job Openings: 4,681
- ✸ Self-Employed: 12.8%
- ✸ Part-Time: 12.9%

Industries with Greatest Employment: Motion Picture, Video, and Sound Recording Industries; Educational Services, Public and Private; Performing Arts, Spectator Sports, and Related Industries; Broadcasting (except Internet); Rental and Leasing Services.

Highest-Growth Industries (Projected Growth for This Job): Telecommunications (42.0%); Performing Arts, Spectator Sports, and Related Industries (37.8%); Professional, Scientific, and Technical Services (33.5%); Religious, Grantmaking, Civic, Professional, and Similar Organizations (31.3%); Credit Intermediation and Related Activities (31.0%); Merchant Wholesalers, Durable Goods (29.3%); Accommodation, Including Hotels and Motels (28.0%); Real Estate (27.2%); Rental and Leasing Services (26.8%); Management of Companies and Enterprises (26.7%); Hospitals, Public and Private (21.8%); Educational Services, Public and Private (21.7%); Motion Picture, Video, and Sound Recording Industries (15.8%); Specialty Trade Contractors (15.4%).

Lowest-Growth Industries (Projected Growth for This Job): Publishing Industries except Internet (0.0%); Electronics and Appliance Stores (0.8%); Computer and Electronic Product Manufacturing (7.5%); Broadcasting (except Internet) (13.3%); Food Services and Drinking Places (14.5%).

Fastest-Growing Metropolitan Areas (Recent Growth for This Job): Anchorage, AK (183.3%); Akron, OH (100.0%); Scranton–Wilkes-Barre, PA (100.0%); Kansas City, MO–KS (90.5%); Albany–Schenectady–Troy, NY (90.0%).

Other Considerations for Job Security: Employment is expected to grow faster than average because these workers will have to set up audio and video equipment and also maintain and repair it. People seeking entry-level jobs are expected to face keen competition in major metropolitan areas, where pay generally is higher and the number of qualified job seekers typically exceeds the number of openings. Prospects for entry-level positions are expected to be better in small cities and towns for beginners with appropriate training.

Set up or set up and operate audio and video equipment, including microphones, sound speakers, video screens, projectors, video monitors, recording equipment, connecting wires and cables, sound and mixing boards, and related electronic equipment for concerts, sports events, meetings and conventions, presentations, and news conferences. May also set up and operate associated spotlights and other custom lighting systems. Notify supervisors when major equipment repairs are needed. Monitor incoming and outgoing pictures and sound feeds to ensure quality; notify directors of any possible problems. Mix and regulate sound inputs and feeds or coordinate audio feeds with television pictures. Install, adjust, and operate electronic equipment used to record, edit, and transmit radio and television programs, cable programs, and motion pictures. Design layouts of audio and video equipment and perform upgrades and maintenance. Perform minor repairs and routine cleaning of audio and video equipment. Diagnose and resolve media system problems in classrooms. Switch sources of video input from one camera or studio to another, from film to live programming, or from network to local programming. Meet with directors and senior members of camera crews to discuss assignments and determine filming sequences, camera movements, and picture composition. Construct and position properties, sets, lighting equipment, and other equipment. Compress, digitize, duplicate, and store audio and video data. Obtain, set up, and load videotapes for scheduled productions or broadcasts. Edit videotapes by erasing and removing portions of programs and adding video or sound as required. Direct and coordinate activities of assistants and other personnel during production. Plan and develop pre-production ideas into outlines, scripts, storyboards, and graphics, using own ideas or specifications of assignments. Maintain inventories of audiotapes and videotapes and related supplies. Determine formats, approaches, content, levels, and media to effectively meet objectives within budgetary constraints, utilizing research, knowledge, and training. Record and edit audio material such as movie soundtracks, using audio recording and editing equipment. Inform users of audiotaping and videotaping service policies and procedures. Obtain and preview musical performance programs before events to become familiar with the order and approximate times of pieces. Produce rough and finished graphics and graphic designs. Locate and secure settings, properties, effects, and other production necessities.

Personality Type: Conventional.

GOE—Interest Area: 03. Arts and Communication. **Work Group:** 03.09. Media Technology. **Other Jobs in this Work Group:** Broadcast Technicians; Camera Operators, Television, Video, and Motion Picture; Film and Video Editors; Multi-Media Artists and Animators; Photographers; Radio Operators; Sound Engineering Technicians.

Skills: Installation; Operation and Control; Equipment Maintenance; Troubleshooting; Operation Monitoring; Repairing.

Education and Training Programs: Agricultural Communication/Journalism; Photographic and Film/Video Technology/Technician and Assistant; Recording Arts Technology/Technician. **Related Knowledge/Courses:** Computers and Electronics; Telecommunications; Engineering and Technology; Communications and Media; Mechanical Devices; Physics.

Work Environment: Indoors; standing; using hands on objects, tools, or controls.

Audiologists

* Education/Training Required: First professional degree
* Annual Earnings: $57,120
* Beginning Wage: $38,370
* Earnings Growth Potential: Very high
* Growth: 9.8%
* Annual Job Openings: 980
* Self-Employed: 10.2%
* Part-Time: 28.3%

Industries with Greatest Employment: Ambulatory Health Care Services; Health and Personal Care Stores; Educational Services, Public and Private; Hospitals, Public and Private.

Highest-Growth Industries (Projected Growth for This Job): Professional, Scientific, and Technical Services (21.1%); Nursing and Residential Care Facilities (18.2%).

Lowest-Growth Industries (Projected Growth for This Job): Health and Personal Care Stores (–3.3%); Computer and Electronic Product Manufacturing (0.0%); Educational Services, Public and Private (4.0%); Hospitals, Public and Private (9.5%); Ambulatory Health Care Services (14.6%).

Fastest-Growing Metropolitan Areas (Recent Growth for This Job): Charlotte–Gastonia–Concord, NC–SC (100.0%); Denver–Aurora, CO (66.7%); Bridgeport–Stamford–Norwalk, CT (50.0%); Buffalo–Niagara Falls, NY (40.0%); Memphis, TN–MS–AR (33.3%).

Other Considerations for Job Security: Employment in educational services will increase (altlhough slowly) along with growth in elementary and secondary school enrollments, including enrollment of special education students. Growth in employment of audiologists will be moderated by limitations on reimbursements made by third-party payers for the tests and services they provide. Job prospects will be favorable for those possessing the Au.D. degree. Only a few job openings for audiologists will arise from the need to replace those who leave the occupation, because the occupation is relatively small and workers tend to stay in this occupation until they retire.

Assess and treat persons with hearing and related disorders. May fit hearing aids and provide auditory training. May perform research related to hearing problems. Evaluate hearing and speech/language disorders to determine diagnoses and courses of treatment. Administer hearing or speech/language evaluations, tests, or examinations to patients to collect information on type and degree of impairment, using specialized instruments and electronic equipment. Fit and dispense assistive devices, such as hearing aids. Maintain client records at all stages, including initial evaluation and discharge. Refer clients to additional medical or educational services if needed. Counsel and instruct clients in techniques to improve hearing or speech impairment, including sign language or lipreading. Monitor clients' progress and discharge them from treatment when goals are attained. Plan and conduct treatment programs for clients' hearing or speech problems, consulting with physicians, nurses, psychologists, and other health-care personnel as necessary. Recommend assistive devices according to clients' needs or nature of impairments. Participate in conferences or training to update or share knowledge of new hearing or speech disorder treatment methods or technologies. Instruct clients, parents, teachers, or employers in how to avoid behavior patterns that lead to miscommunication. Examine and clean patients' ear canals. Advise educators or other medical staff on speech or hearing topics. Educate and supervise audiology students and health-care personnel. Fit and tune cochlear implants, providing rehabilitation for adjustment to listening with implant amplification systems. Work with multidisciplinary teams to assess and rehabilitate recipients of implanted hearing devices. Develop and supervise hearing screening programs. Conduct or direct research on hearing or speech topics and report findings to help in the development of procedures, technology, or treatments. Measure noise levels in workplaces and conduct hearing protection programs in industry, schools, and communities.

Personality Type: Social.

GOE—Interest Area: 08. Health Science. **Work Group:** 08.07. Medical Therapy. **Other Jobs in this Work Group:** Massage Therapists; Occupational Therapist Aides; Occupational Therapist Assistants; Occupational Therapists; Physical Therapist Aides; Physical Therapist Assistants; Physical Therapists; Radiation Therapists; Recreational Therapists; Respiratory Therapists; Respiratory Therapy Technicians; Speech-Language Pathologists.

Skills: Science; Social Perceptiveness; Service Orientation; Persuasion; Equipment Selection; Reading Comprehension.

Education and Training Programs: Communication Disorders, General; Audiology/Audiologist and Hearing Sciences; Audiology/Audiologist and Speech-Language Pathology/Pathologist; Communication Disorders Sciences and Services, Other. **Related Knowledge/Courses:** Therapy and Counseling; Medicine and Dentistry; Psychology; Sales and Marketing; Customer and Personal Service; Sociology and Anthropology.

Work Environment: Indoors; disease or infections; sitting; using hands on objects, tools, or controls.

Automotive Body and Related Repairers

* Education/Training Required: Long-term on-the-job training
* Annual Earnings: $35,180
* Beginning Wage: $21,000
* Earnings Growth Potential: Very high
* Growth: 11.6%
* Annual Job Openings: 37,469
* Self-Employed: 14.1%
* Part-Time: 5.6%

Industries with Greatest Employment: Repair and Maintenance; Motor Vehicle and Parts Dealers.

Highest-Growth Industries (Projected Growth for This Job): Administrative and Support Services (29.9%); Repair and Maintenance (17.2%); Management of Companies and Enterprises (15.3%).

Lowest-Growth Industries (Projected Growth for This Job): Gasoline Stations (–10.4%); Transportation Equipment Manufacturing (–7.0%); Motor Vehicle and Parts Dealers (2.4%); Educational Services, Public and Private (7.3%); Specialty Trade Contractors (11.1%); Support Activities for Transportation (11.7%); Transit and Ground Passenger Transportation (12.5%); Truck Transportation (12.9%); Merchant Wholesalers, Durable Goods (13.4%); Wholesale Electronic Markets and Agents and Brokers (13.4%).

Fastest-Growing Metropolitan Areas (Recent Growth for This Job): Knoxville, TN (110.0%); Springfield, IL (100.0%); Florence–Muscle Shoals, AL (83.3%); Athens–Clarke County, GA (75.0%); Harrisonburg, VA (75.0%).

Other Considerations for Job Security: Employment growth will create some opportunities, but the need to replace experienced repairers who transfer to other occupations or who retire or stop working for other reasons will account for the majority of job openings over the next 10 years. Opportunities will be excellent for people with formal training in automotive body repair and refinishing. Those without any training or experience in automotive body refinishing or collision repair—before or after high school—will face competition for these jobs. Experienced body repairers are rarely laid off during a general slowdown in the economy, as the automotive repair business isn't very sensitive to changes in economic conditions. Although repair of minor dents and crumpled fenders is often put off when drivers have less money, major body damage must be repaired before a vehicle can be driven safely.

Repair and refinish automotive vehicle bodies and straighten vehicle frames. File, grind, sand, and smooth filled or repaired surfaces, using power tools and hand tools. Sand body areas to be painted and cover bumpers, windows, and trim with masking tape or paper to protect them from the paint. Follow supervisors' instructions as to which parts to restore or replace and how much time a job should take. Remove damaged sections of vehicles, using metal-cutting guns, air grinders, and wrenches, and install replacement parts, using wrenches or welding equipment. Cut and tape plastic separating film to outside repair areas to avoid damaging surrounding surfaces during repair procedure and remove tape and wash surfaces after repairs are complete. Prime and paint repaired surfaces, using paint spray guns and motorized sanders. Inspect repaired vehicles for dimensional accuracy and test-drive them to ensure proper alignment and handling. Mix polyester resins and hardeners to be used in restoring damaged areas. Chain or clamp frames and sections to alignment machines that use hydraulic pressure to align damaged components. Fill small dents that cannot be worked out with plastic or solder. Fit and weld replacement parts into place, using wrenches and welding equipment, and grind down welds to smooth them, using power grinders and other tools. Position dolly blocks against surfaces of dented areas and beat opposite surfaces to remove dents, using hammers. Remove damaged panels and identify the family and properties of the plastic used on a vehicle. Review damage reports, prepare or review repair cost estimates, and plan work to be performed. Remove small pits and dimples in body metal, using pick hammers and punches. Remove upholstery, accessories, electrical window- and seat-operating equipment, and trim to gain access to vehicle bodies and fenders. Clean work areas, using air hoses, to remove damaged material and discarded fiberglass strips used in repair procedures. Adjust or align headlights, wheels, and brake systems. Apply heat to plastic panels, using hot-air welding guns or immersion in hot water, and press the softened panels back into shape by hand. Soak fiberglass matting in resin mixtures and apply layers of matting over repair areas to specified thicknesses.

Personality Type: Realistic.

GOE—Interest Area: 13. Manufacturing. **Work Group:** 13.14. Vehicle and Facility Mechanical Work. **Other Jobs in this Work Group:** Aircraft Mechanics and Service Technicians; Aircraft Structure, Surfaces, Rigging, and Systems Assemblers; Automotive Glass Installers and Repairers; Automotive Master Mechanics; Automotive Service Technicians and Mechanics; Automotive Specialty Technicians; Bus and Truck Mechanics and Diesel Engine Specialists; Farm Equipment Mechanics; Fiberglass Laminators and Fabricators; Mobile Heavy Equipment Mechanics, Except Engines; Motorboat Mechanics; Motorcycle Mechanics; Outdoor Power Equipment and Other Small Engine Mechanics; Rail Car Repairers; Recreational Vehicle Service Technicians; Tire Repairers and Changers.

Skills: No data available.

Education and Training Program: Autobody/Collision and Repair Technology/Technician. **Related Knowledge/Courses:** Mechanical Devices; Building and Construction; Chemistry; Production and Processing; Administration and Management; Transportation.

Work Environment: Noisy; contaminants; hazardous equipment; standing; using hands on objects, tools, or controls; repetitive motions.

Automotive Glass Installers and Repairers

- ❋ Education/Training Required: Long-term on-the-job training
- ❋ Annual Earnings: $30,720
- ❋ Beginning Wage: $19,120
- ❋ Earnings Growth Potential: Very high
- ❋ Growth: 18.7%
- ❋ Annual Job Openings: 3,457
- ❋ Self-Employed: 20.7%
- ❋ Part-Time: 4.5%

Industries with Greatest Employment: Repair and Maintenance; Motor Vehicle and Parts Dealers.

Highest-Growth Industries (Projected Growth for This Job): Building Material and Garden Equipment and Supplies Dealers (27.8%).

Lowest-Growth Industries (Projected Growth for This Job): Transportation Equipment Manufacturing (–2.2%); Motor Vehicle and Parts Dealers (7.5%); Specialty Trade Contractors (12.6%); Rental and Leasing Services (13.4%); Merchant Wholesalers, Durable Goods (13.6%); Repair and Maintenance (14.1%).

Fastest-Growing Metropolitan Areas (Recent Growth for This Job): Worcester, MA–CT (66.7%); New York–Northern New Jersey–Long Island, NY–NJ–PA (27.3%); San Juan–Caguas–Guaynabo, PR (18.2%); Minneapolis–St. Paul–Bloomington, MN–WI (17.1%); Chicago–Naperville–Joliet, IL–IN–WI (11.8%).

Other Considerations for Job Security: Employment growth will create some opportunities, but the need to replace experienced repairers who transfer to other occupations or who retire or stop working for other reasons will account for the majority of job openings over the next 10 years. Opportunities will be excellent for people with formal training in automotive glass installation and repair. Those without any training or experience—before or after high school—will face competition for these jobs.

Experienced automotive glass repairers are rarely laid off during a general slowdown in the economy as the automotive repair business isn't very sensitive to changes in economic conditions. Damaged automotive glass must be repaired before a vehicle can be driven safely.

Replace or repair broken windshields and window glass in motor vehicles. Remove all dirt, foreign matter, and loose glass from damaged areas; then apply primer along windshield or window edges and allow it to dry. Install replacement glass in vehicles after old glass has been removed and all necessary preparations have been made. Allow all glass parts installed with urethane ample time to cure, taking temperature and humidity into account. Prime all scratches on pinch welds with primer and allow primed scratches to dry. Obtain windshields or windows for specific automobile makes and models from stock and examine them for defects before installation. Apply a bead of urethane around the perimeter of each pinch weld and dress the remaining urethane on the pinch welds so that it is of uniform level and thickness all the way around. Check for moisture or contamination in damaged areas, dry out any moisture before making repairs, and keep damaged areas dry until repairs are complete. Select appropriate tools, safety equipment, and parts according to job requirements. Remove broken or damaged glass windshields or window glass from motor vehicles, using hand tools to remove screws from frames holding glass. Remove all moldings, clips, windshield wipers, screws, bolts, and inside A-pillar moldings; then lower headliners before beginning installation or repair work. Install, repair, and replace safety glass and related materials, such as back glass heating elements, on vehicles and equipment. Install rubber channeling strips around edges of glass or frames to weatherproof windows or to prevent rattling. Hold cut or uneven edges of glass against automated abrasive belts to shape or smooth edges. Cut flat safety glass according to specified patterns or perform precision pattern-making and glass-cutting to custom-fit replacement windows. Replace or adjust motorized or manual window-raising mechanisms. Install new foam dams on pinch welds if required. Cool or warm glass in the event of temperature extremes. Replace all moldings, clips, windshield wipers, and other parts that were removed before glass replacement or repair.

Personality Type: Realistic.

GOE—Interest Area: 13. Manufacturing. **Work Group:** 13.14. Vehicle and Facility Mechanical Work. **Other Jobs in this Work Group:** Aircraft Mechanics and Service Technicians; Aircraft Structure, Surfaces, Rigging, and Systems Assemblers; Automotive Body and Related Repairers; Automotive Master Mechanics; Automotive Service Technicians and Mechanics; Automotive Specialty Technicians; Bus and Truck Mechanics and Diesel Engine Specialists; Farm Equipment Mechanics; Fiberglass Laminators and Fabricators; Mobile Heavy Equipment Mechanics, Except Engines; Motorboat Mechanics; Motorcycle Mechanics; Outdoor Power Equipment and Other Small Engine Mechanics; Rail Car Repairers; Recreational Vehicle Service Technicians; Tire Repairers and Changers.

Skills: No data available.

Education and Training Program: Autobody/Collision and Repair Technology/Technician. **Related Knowledge/Courses:** Mechanical Devices; Production and Processing; Customer and Personal Service; Administration and Management; Sales and Marketing; Transportation.

Work Environment: Outdoors; very hot or cold; contaminants; cramped work space, awkward positions; standing; using hands on objects, tools, or controls.

Automotive Master Mechanics

* Education/Training Required: Postsecondary vocational training
* Annual Earnings: $33,780
* Beginning Wage: $19,070
* Earnings Growth Potential: Very high
* Growth: 14.3%
* Annual Job Openings: 97,350
* Self-Employed: 16.8%
* Part-Time: 5.6%

Our sources did not provide separate job openings data for this occupation. The job openings listed here are shared with Automotive Specialty Technicians.

Industries with Greatest Employment: Motor Vehicle and Parts Dealers; Repair and Maintenance.

Highest-Growth Industries (Projected Growth for This Job): Warehousing and Storage (33.6%); Professional, Scientific, and Technical Services (33.1%); Amusement, Gambling, and Recreation Industries (30.8%); Waste Management and Remediation Services (27.9%); Ambulatory Health Care Services (27.8%); Administrative and Support Services (26.7%); Performing Arts, Spectator Sports, and Related Industries (24.5%); Social Assistance (22.9%); Repair and Maintenance (22.0%); Religious, Grantmaking, Civic, Professional, and Similar Organizations (18.8%); Accommodation, Including Hotels and Motels (15.9%); Motor Vehicle and Parts Dealers (15.5%); Management of Companies and Enterprises (15.3%).

Lowest-Growth Industries (Projected Growth for This Job): Plastics and Rubber Products Manufacturing (–23.6%); Nonstore Retailers (–20.7%); Gasoline Stations (–19.4%); Transportation Equipment Manufacturing (–14.0%); Fabricated Metal Product Manufacturing (–13.3%); Machinery Manufacturing (–10.5%); Utilities (–8.9%); Merchant Wholesalers, Nondurable Goods (–8.2%); Chemical Manufacturing (–7.6%); Telecommunications (–7.6%).

Fastest-Growing Metropolitan Areas (Recent Growth for This Job): Dalton, GA (125.0%); Danville, IL (75.0%); Yauco, PR (66.7%); Farmington, NM (58.1%); Kankakee–Bradley, IL (56.5%).

Other Considerations for Job Security: In addition to openings from growth, many job openings will be created by the need to replace a growing number of retiring technicians. Job opportunities in this occupation are expected to be very good for those who complete high school or postsecondary automotive training programs and who earn ASE certification. Some employers report difficulty in finding workers with the right skills. People with good diagnostic and problem-solving abilities, as well as training in basic electronics and computer courses, are expected to have the best opportunities. Those without formal automotive training are likely to face competition for entry-level jobs. Most people who enter this occupation can expect steady work, even during economic downturns. Although car owners tend to postpone maintenance and repair on their vehicles when their budgets are strained, employers usually cut back on hiring new workers during economic downturns rather than let experienced workers go.

Repair automobiles, trucks, buses, and other vehicles. Master mechanics repair virtually any part on the vehicle or specialize in the transmission system. Examine vehicles to determine extent of damage or malfunctions. Test-drive vehicles and test components and systems, using equipment such as infrared engine analyzers, compression gauges, and computerized diagnostic devices. Repair, reline, replace, and adjust brakes. Review work orders and discuss work with supervisors. Follow checklists to ensure all important parts are examined, including belts, hoses, steering systems, spark plugs, brake and fuel systems, wheel bearings, and other potentially troublesome areas. Plan work procedures, using charts, technical manuals, and experience. Test and adjust repaired systems to meet manufacturers' performance specifications. Confer with customers to obtain descriptions of vehicle problems and to discuss work to be performed and future repair requirements. Perform routine and scheduled maintenance services such as oil changes, lubrications, and tune-ups. Disassemble units and inspect parts for wear, using micrometers, calipers, and gauges. Overhaul or replace carburetors, blowers, generators, distributors, starters, and pumps. Repair and service air conditioning, heating, engine-cooling, and electrical systems. Repair or replace parts such as pistons, rods, gears, valves, and bearings. Tear down, repair, and rebuild faulty assemblies such as power systems, steering systems, and linkages. Rewire ignition systems, lights, and instrument panels. Repair radiator leaks. Install and repair accessories such as radios, heaters, mirrors, and windshield wipers. Repair manual and automatic transmissions. Repair or replace shock absorbers. Align vehicles' front ends. Rebuild parts such as crankshafts and cylinder blocks. Repair damaged automobile bodies. Replace and adjust headlights.

Personality Type: Realistic.

GOE—Interest Area: 13. Manufacturing. **Work Group:** 13.14. Vehicle and Facility Mechanical Work. **Other Jobs in this Work Group:** Aircraft Mechanics and Service Technicians; Aircraft Structure, Surfaces, Rigging, and Systems Assemblers; Automotive Body and Related Repairers; Automotive Glass Installers and Repairers; Automotive Service Technicians and Mechanics; Automotive Specialty Technicians; Bus and Truck Mechanics and Diesel Engine Specialists; Farm Equipment Mechanics; Fiberglass Laminators and Fabricators; Mobile Heavy Equipment Mechanics, Except Engines; Motorboat Mechanics; Motorcycle Mechanics; Outdoor Power Equipment and Other Small Engine Mechanics; Rail Car Repairers; Recreational Vehicle Service Technicians; Tire Repairers and Changers.

Skills: Repairing; Troubleshooting; Installation; Equipment Maintenance; Operation Monitoring; Complex Problem Solving.

Education and Training Programs: Automotive Engineering Technology/Technician; Automobile/Automotive Mechanics Technology/Technician; Medium/Heavy Vehicle and Truck Technology/Technician. **Related Knowledge/Courses:** Mechanical Devices; Physics; Computers and Electronics;

Engineering and Technology; Chemistry; Public Safety and Security.

Work Environment: Noisy; contaminants; hazardous equipment; minor burns, cuts, bites, or stings; standing; using hands on objects, tools, or controls.

Automotive Service Technicians and Mechanics

See *Automotive Master Mechanics and Automotive Specialty Technicians, described separately.*

Automotive Specialty Technicians

* Education/Training Required: Postsecondary vocational training
* Annual Earnings: $33,780
* Beginning Wage: $19,070
* Earnings Growth Potential: Very high
* Growth: 14.3%
* Annual Job Openings: 97,350
* Self-Employed: 16.8%
* Part-Time: 5.6%

Our sources did not provide separate job openings data for this occupation. The job openings listed here are shared with Automotive Master Mechanics.

Industries with Greatest Employment: Motor Vehicle and Parts Dealers; Repair and Maintenance.

Highest-Growth Industries (Projected Growth for This Job): Warehousing and Storage (33.6%); Professional, Scientific, and Technical Services (33.1%); Amusement, Gambling, and Recreation Industries (30.8%); Waste Management and Remediation Services (27.9%); Ambulatory Health Care Services (27.8%); Administrative and Support Services (26.7%); Performing Arts, Spectator Sports, and Related Industries (24.5%); Social Assistance (22.9%); Repair and Maintenance (22.0%); Religious, Grantmaking, Civic, Professional, and Similar Organizations (18.8%); Accommodation, Including

Hotels and Motels (15.9%); Motor Vehicle and Parts Dealers (15.5%); Management of Companies and Enterprises (15.3%).

Lowest-Growth Industries (Projected Growth for This Job): Plastics and Rubber Products Manufacturing (–23.6%); Nonstore Retailers (–20.7%); Gasoline Stations (–19.4%); Transportation Equipment Manufacturing (–14.0%); Fabricated Metal Product Manufacturing (–13.3%); Machinery Manufacturing (–10.5%); Utilities (–8.9%); Merchant Wholesalers, Nondurable Goods (–8.2%); Chemical Manufacturing (–7.6%); Telecommunications (–7.6%).

Fastest-Growing Metropolitan Areas (Recent Growth for This Job): Dalton, GA (125.0%); Danville, IL (75.0%); Yauco, PR (66.7%); Farmington, NM (58.1%); Kankakee–Bradley, IL (56.5%).

Other Considerations for Job Security: In addition to openings from growth, many job openings will be created by the need to replace a growing number of retiring technicians. Job opportunities in this occupation are expected to be very good for those who complete high school or postsecondary automotive training programs and who earn ASE certification. Some employers report difficulty in finding workers with the right skills. People with good diagnostic and problem-solving abilities, as well as training in basic electronics and computer courses, are expected to have the best opportunities. Those without formal automotive training are likely to face competition for entry-level jobs. Most people who enter this occupation can expect steady work, even during economic downturns. Although car owners tend to postpone maintenance and repair on their vehicles when their budgets are strained, employers usually cut back on hiring new workers during economic downturns rather than let experienced workers go.

Repair only one system or component on a vehicle, such as brakes, suspension, or radiator. Examine vehicles, compile estimates of repair costs, and secure customers' approval to perform repairs. Repair, overhaul, and adjust automobile brake systems. Use electronic test equipment to locate and correct malfunctions in fuel, ignition, and emissions control systems. Repair and replace defective ball joint suspensions, brake shoes, and wheel bearings. Inspect and test new vehicles for damage; then record findings so that necessary repairs can be made. Test electronic computer components in automobiles to ensure that they are working properly. Tune automobile engines to ensure proper and efficient functioning. Install and repair air conditioners and service components such as compressors, condensers, and controls. Repair, replace, and adjust defective carburetor parts and gasoline filters. Remove and replace defective mufflers and tailpipes. Repair and replace automobile leaf springs. Rebuild, repair, and test automotive fuel injection units. Align and repair wheels, axles, frames, torsion bars, and steering mechanisms of automobiles, using special alignment equipment and wheel-balancing machines. Repair, install, and adjust hydraulic and electromagnetic automatic lift mechanisms used to raise and lower automobile windows, seats, and tops. Repair and rebuild clutch systems. Convert vehicle fuel systems from gasoline to butane gas operations and repair and service operating butane fuel units.

Personality Type: Realistic.

GOE—Interest Area: 13. Manufacturing. **Work Group:** 13.14. Vehicle and Facility Mechanical Work. **Other Jobs in this Work Group:** Aircraft Mechanics and Service Technicians; Aircraft Structure, Surfaces, Rigging, and Systems Assemblers; Automotive Body and Related Repairers; Automotive Glass Installers and Repairers; Automotive Master Mechanics; Automotive Service Technicians and Mechanics; Bus and Truck Mechanics and Diesel Engine Specialists; Farm Equipment Mechanics; Fiberglass Laminators and Fabricators; Mobile Heavy Equipment Mechanics, Except Engines; Motorboat Mechanics; Motorcycle Mechanics; Outdoor Power Equipment and Other Small Engine Mechanics; Rail Car Repairers; Recreational Vehicle Service Technicians; Tire Repairers and Changers.

Skills: Repairing; Operation Monitoring; Troubleshooting; Equipment Maintenance; Installation; Equipment Selection.

Education and Training Programs: Automotive Engineering Technology/Technician; Vehicle Emissions Inspection and Maintenance Technology/Technician; Alternative Fuel Vehicle Technology/Technician. **Related Knowledge/Courses:** Mechanical Devices; Physics; Engineering and Technology; Customer and Personal Service; Sales and Marketing; Administration and Management.

Work Environment: Contaminants; cramped work space, awkward positions; minor burns, cuts, bites, or stings; standing; using hands on objects, tools, or controls; bending or twisting the body.

Bailiffs

- ✻ Education/Training Required: Moderate-term on-the-job training
- ✻ Annual Earnings: $34,210
- ✻ Beginning Wage: $18,390
- ✻ Earnings Growth Potential: Very high
- ✻ Growth: 11.2%
- ✻ Annual Job Openings: 2,223
- ✻ Self-Employed: 0.0%
- ✻ Part-Time: 1.8%

Industries with Greatest Employment: State Government, excluding Education and Hospitals; Local Government, excluding Education and Hospitals.

Highest-Growth Industries (Projected Growth for This Job): None met the criteria.

Lowest-Growth Industries (Projected Growth for This Job): None met the criteria.

Fastest-Growing Metropolitan Areas (Recent Growth for This Job): Baton Rouge, LA (83.3%); Buffalo–Niagara Falls, NY (60.0%); Atlanta–Sandy Springs–Marietta, GA (50.0%); Utica–Rome, NY (50.0%); Denver–Aurora, CO (40.0%).

Other Considerations for Job Security: Outlook information for bailiffs is subsumed under the information for correctional officers. Job opportunities for correctional officers are expected to be excellent. The need to replace correctional officers who transfer to other occupations, retire, or leave the labor force, coupled with rising employment demand, will generate thousands of job openings each year. This situation is expected to continue. Layoffs of correctional officers are rare because of increasing offender populations.

Maintain order in courts of law. Collect and retain unauthorized firearms from persons entering courtroom. Maintain order in courtroom during trial and guard jury from outside contact. Guard lodging of sequestered jury. Provide jury escort to restaurant and other areas outside of courtroom to prevent jury contact with the public. Enforce courtroom rules of behavior and warn persons not to smoke or disturb court procedure. Report need for police or medical assistance to sheriff's office. Check courtroom for security and cleanliness and assure availability of sundry supplies for use of judge. Announce entrance of judge. Stop people from entering courtroom while judge charges jury.

Personality Type: Social.

GOE—Interest Area: 12. Law and Public Safety. **Work Group:** 12.04. Law Enforcement and Public Safety. **Other Jobs in this Work Group:** Correctional Officers and Jailers; Criminal Investigators and Special Agents; Detectives and Criminal Investigators; Fire Investigators; Forensic Science Technicians; Parking Enforcement Workers; Police and Sheriff's Patrol Officers; Police Detectives; Police Identification and Records Officers; Police Patrol Officers; Sheriffs and Deputy Sheriffs; Transit and Railroad Police.

Skills: No data available.

Education and Training Program: Criminal Justice/Police Science. **Related Knowledge/Courses:** Public Safety and Security; Law and Government; Philosophy and Theology; Customer and Personal Service; Psychology; Sociology and Anthropology.

Work Environment: Indoors; contaminants; disease or infections; sitting.

Biological Science Teachers, Postsecondary

* Education/Training Required: Doctoral degree
* Annual Earnings: $69,210
* Beginning Wage: $37,620
* Earnings Growth Potential: Very high
* Growth: 22.9%
* Annual Job Openings: 237,478
* Self-Employed: 0.4%
* Part-Time: 27.8%

Our sources did not provide separate job openings data for this occupation. The job openings listed here are shared with 35 other postsecondary teaching occupations. For a complete list, see the beginning of this section.

Industries with Greatest Employment: Educational Services, Public and Private.

Highest-Growth Industries (Projected Growth for This Job): Administrative and Support Services (48.3%); Amusement, Gambling, and Recreation Industries (45.3%); Social Assistance (38.6%); Support Activities for Transportation (32.8%); Religious, Grantmaking, Civic, Professional, and Similar Organizations (29.9%); Professional, Scientific, and Technical Services (28.8%); Management of Companies and Enterprises (26.8%); Educational Services, Public and Private (22.9%); Hospitals, Public and Private (21.4%); Personal and Laundry Services (21.0%).

Lowest-Growth Industries (Projected Growth for This Job): Other Information Services (7.4%); Sporting Goods, Hobby, Book, and Music Stores (13.3%); Performing Arts, Spectator Sports, and Related Industries (13.4%); Insurance Carriers and Related Activities (13.9%).

Fastest-Growing Metropolitan Areas (Recent Growth for This Job): Manchester, NH (50.0%); Toledo, OH (48.9%); Phoenix–Mesa–Scottsdale, AZ (46.7%); San Jose–Sunnyvale–Santa Clara, CA (33.3%); Winston-Salem, NC (33.3%).

Other Considerations for Job Security: Retirements of current postsecondary teachers should create numerous openings for all types of postsecondary teachers, so job opportunities are generally expected to be very good. Because students attend postsecondary institutions to prepare themselves for careers, the best job prospects for postsecondary teachers are likely to be in rapidly growing fields that offer many nonacademic career options, including the biological sciences. Community colleges and other institutions offering career and technical education have been among the most rapidly growing and are expected to offer some of the best opportunities for postsecondary teachers.

Teach courses in biological sciences. Prepare and deliver lectures to undergraduate and/or graduate students on topics such as molecular biology, marine biology, and botany. Evaluate and grade students' classwork, laboratory work, assignments, and papers. Prepare course materials such as syllabi, homework assignments, and handouts. Compile, administer, and grade examinations or assign this work to others. Supervise students' laboratory work. Keep abreast of developments in their field by reading current literature, talking with colleagues, and participating in professional conferences. Maintain student attendance records, grades, and other required records. Initiate, facilitate, and moderate classroom discussions. Plan, evaluate, and revise curricula, course content, course materials, and methods of instruction. Advise students on academic and vocational curricula and on career issues. Maintain regularly scheduled office hours to advise and assist students. Supervise undergraduate and/or graduate teaching, internships, and research work. Select and obtain materials and supplies such as textbooks and laboratory equipment. Collaborate with colleagues to address teaching and research issues. Conduct research in a particular field of knowledge and publish findings in professional journals, books, and/or electronic media. Serve on academic or administrative committees that deal with institutional policies, departmental matters, and academic issues. Participate in student recruitment, registration, and placement activities. Write grant proposals to procure external research funding.

Perform administrative duties such as serving as department head. Act as advisers to student organizations. Compile bibliographies of specialized materials for outside reading assignments. Participate in campus and community events. Provide professional consulting services to government and/or industry.

Personality Type: Investigative.

GOE—Interest Area: 05. Education and Training. **Work Group:** 05.03. Postsecondary and Adult Teaching and Instructing. **Other Jobs in this Work Group:** Adult Literacy, Remedial Education, and GED Teachers and Instructors; Agricultural Sciences Teachers, Postsecondary; Anthropology and Archeology Teachers, Postsecondary; Architecture Teachers, Postsecondary; Area, Ethnic, and Cultural Studies Teachers, Postsecondary; Art, Drama, and Music Teachers, Postsecondary; Atmospheric, Earth, Marine, and Space Sciences Teachers, Postsecondary; Business Teachers, Postsecondary; Chemistry Teachers, Postsecondary; Communications Teachers, Postsecondary; Computer Science Teachers, Postsecondary; Criminal Justice and Law Enforcement Teachers, Postsecondary; Economics Teachers, Postsecondary; Education Teachers, Postsecondary; Engineering Teachers, Postsecondary; English Language and Literature Teachers, Postsecondary; Environmental Science Teachers, Postsecondary; Farm and Home Management Advisors; Foreign Language and Literature Teachers, Postsecondary; Forestry and Conservation Science Teachers, Postsecondary; Geography Teachers, Postsecondary; Graduate Teaching Assistants; Health Specialties Teachers, Postsecondary; History Teachers, Postsecondary; Home Economics Teachers, Postsecondary; Law Teachers, Postsecondary; Library Science Teachers, Postsecondary; Mathematical Science Teachers, Postsecondary; Nursing Instructors and Teachers, Postsecondary; Philosophy and Religion Teachers, Postsecondary; Physics Teachers, Postsecondary; Political Science Teachers, Postsecondary; Psychology Teachers, Postsecondary; Recreation and Fitness Studies Teachers, Postsecondary; Self-Enrichment Education Teachers; Social Work Teachers, Postsecondary; Sociology Teachers, Postsecondary; Vocational Education Teachers, Postsecondary.

Skills: Science; Instructing; Writing; Reading Comprehension; Learning Strategies; Speaking.

Education and Training Programs: Biology/Biological Sciences, General; Biochemistry; Biophysics; Molecular Biology; Radiation Biology/Radiobiology; Botany/Plant Biology; Plant Pathology/Phytopathology; Plant Physiology; Cell/Cellular Biology and Histology; Anatomy; Microbiology, General; Virology; Parasitology; Immunology; Zoology/Animal Biology; Entomology; Animal Physiology; others. **Related Knowledge/Courses:** Biology; Chemistry; Education and Training; Medicine and Dentistry; Physics; English Language.

Work Environment: Indoors; more often sitting than standing.

Broadcast Technicians

- ❋ Education/Training Required: Associate degree
- ❋ Annual Earnings: $30,690
- ❋ Beginning Wage: $15,680
- ❋ Earnings Growth Potential: Very high
- ❋ Growth: 12.1%
- ❋ Annual Job Openings: 2,955
- ❋ Self-Employed: 12.4%
- ❋ Part-Time: 12.9%

Industries with Greatest Employment: Broadcasting (except Internet); Educational Services, Public and Private.

Highest-Growth Industries (Projected Growth for This Job): Telecommunications (34.3%); Performing Arts, Spectator Sports, and Related Industries (33.1%); Religious, Grantmaking, Civic, Professional, and Similar Organizations (19.8%); Professional, Scientific, and Technical Services (17.3%); Management of Companies and Enterprises (15.6%).

Lowest-Growth Industries (Projected Growth for This Job): Educational Services, Public and Private (10.7%); Broadcasting (except Internet) (12.2%); Rental and Leasing Services (12.9%); Motion Picture, Video, and Sound Recording Industries (14.5%).

Fastest-Growing Metropolitan Areas (Recent Growth for This Job): Portland–South Portland–Biddeford, ME (140.0%); Scranton–Wilkes-Barre, PA (133.3%); Sacramento–Arden–Arcade–Roseville, CA (109.1%); Cape Coral–Fort Myers, FL (100.0%); Yakima, WA (100.0%).

Other Considerations for Job Security: People seeking entry-level jobs as broadcast technicians in broadcasting are expected to face keen competition in major metropolitan areas, where pay generally is higher and the number of qualified jobseekers typically exceeds the number of openings. Prospects for entry-level positions are expected to be better in small cities and towns for beginners with appropriate training. In addition to employment growth, job openings will result from the need to replace experienced technicians who leave this field. Some of these workers leave for other jobs that require knowledge of electronics, such as computer repairer or industrial machinery repairer.

Set up, operate, and maintain the electronic equipment used to transmit radio and television programs. Control audio equipment to regulate volume level and quality of sound during radio and television broadcasts. Operate radio transmitter to broadcast radio and television programs. Maintain programming logs as required by station management and the Federal Communications Commission. Control audio equipment to regulate the volume and sound quality during radio and television broadcasts. Monitor strength, clarity, and reliability of incoming and outgoing signals and adjust equipment as necessary to maintain quality broadcasts. Regulate the fidelity, brightness, and contrast of video transmissions, using video console control panels. Observe monitors and converse with station personnel to determine audio and video levels and to ascertain that programs are airing. Preview scheduled programs to ensure that signals are functioning and programs are ready for transmission. Select sources from which programming will be received or through which programming will be transmitted. Report equipment problems, ensure that repairs are made; make emergency repairs to equipment when necessary and possible. Record sound onto tape or film for radio or television, checking its quality and making adjustments where necessary. Align antennae with receiving dishes to obtain the clearest signal for transmission of broadcasts from field locations. Substitute programs in cases where signals fail. Organize recording sessions and prepare areas such as radio booths and television stations for recording. Perform preventive and minor equipment maintenance, using hand tools. Instruct trainees in how to use television production equipment, film events, and how to copy and edit graphics or sound onto videotape. Schedule programming or read television programming logs to determine which programs are to be recorded or aired. Edit broadcast material electronically, using computers. Give technical directions to other personnel during filming. Set up and operate portable field transmission equipment outside the studio. Determine the number, type, and approximate location of microphones needed for best sound recording or transmission quality and position them appropriately. Design and modify equipment to employer specifications. Prepare reports outlining past and future programs, including content.

Personality Type: Realistic.

GOE—Interest Area: 03. Arts and Communication. **Work Group:** 03.09. Media Technology. **Other Jobs in this Work Group:** Audio and Video Equipment Technicians; Camera Operators, Television, Video, and Motion Picture; Film and Video Editors; Multi-Media Artists and Animators; Photographers; Radio Operators; Sound Engineering Technicians.

Skills: Operation Monitoring; Operation and Control; Troubleshooting; Installation; Equipment Maintenance; Repairing.

Education and Training Programs: Communications Technology/Technician; Radio and Television Broadcasting Technology/Technician; Audiovisual Communications Technologies/Technicians, Other. **Related Knowledge/Courses:** Telecommunications; Communications and Media; Engineering and Technology; Computers and Electronics; Mechanical Devices; Production and Processing.

Work Environment: Indoors; noisy; sitting; using hands on objects, tools, or controls.

Budget Analysts

- ❋ Education/Training Required: Bachelor's degree
- ❋ Annual Earnings: $61,430
- ❋ Beginning Wage: $40,070
- ❋ Earnings Growth Potential: Very high
- ❋ Growth: 7.1%
- ❋ Annual Job Openings: 6,423
- ❋ Self-Employed: 0.0%
- ❋ Part-Time: 3.2%

Industries with Greatest Employment: Educational Services, Public and Private; Professional, Scientific, and Technical Services; Management of Companies and Enterprises; Transportation Equipment Manufacturing; Computer and Electronic Product Manufacturing.

Highest-Growth Industries (Projected Growth for This Job): Securities, Commodity Contracts, and Other Financial Investments and Related Activities (47.4%); Social Assistance (41.6%); Professional, Scientific, and Technical Services (38.5%); Administrative and Support Services (29.0%); Waste Management and Remediation Services (27.9%); Ambulatory Health Care Services (22.4%); Real Estate (19.8%); Chemical Manufacturing (18.9%); Broadcasting (except Internet) (17.9%); Accommodation, Including Hotels and Motels (16.7%); Merchant Wholesalers, Durable Goods (15.9%); Management of Companies and Enterprises (15.3%); Religious, Grantmaking, Civic, Professional, and Similar Organizations (15.3%).

Lowest-Growth Industries (Projected Growth for This Job): Internet Service Providers, Web Search Portals, and Data Processing Services (–18.6%); Rail Transportation (–13.9%); Machinery Manufacturing (–13.3%); Fabricated Metal Product Manufacturing (–11.6%); Telecommunications (–8.8%); Computer and Electronic Product Manufacturing

(–8.6%); Utilities (–7.2%); Miscellaneous Manufacturing (–5.3%); Food Manufacturing (–1.7%); Oil and Gas Extraction (–1.7%).

Fastest-Growing Metropolitan Areas (Recent Growth for This Job): Santa Fe, NM (100.0%); Youngstown–Warren–Boardman, OH–PA (66.7%); Salt Lake City, UT (64.3%); Raleigh–Cary, NC (62.5%); Albuquerque, NM (60.9%).

Other Considerations for Job Security: Job prospects should generally be good, especially for applicants with a master's degree. Employment growth will be driven by the continuing demand for sound financial analysis in both public and private sectors. Familiarity with spreadsheet, database, data mining, financial analysis, and graphics software packages should enhance a jobseeker's prospects. Because of the importance of financial analysis, and because financial and budget reports must be completed during all phases of the business cycle, budget analysts usually are less vulnerable to layoffs than many other types of workers.

Examine budget estimates for completeness, accuracy, and conformance with procedures and regulations. Analyze budgeting and accounting reports for the purpose of maintaining expenditure controls. Direct the preparation of regular and special budget reports. Consult with managers to ensure that budget adjustments are made in accordance with program changes. Match appropriations for specific programs with appropriations for broader programs, including items for emergency funds. Provide advice and technical assistance with cost analysis, fiscal allocation, and budget preparation. Summarize budgets and submit recommendations for the approval or disapproval of funds requests. Seek new ways to improve efficiency and increase profits. Review operating budgets to analyze trends affecting budget needs. Perform cost-benefit analyses to compare operating programs, review financial requests, or explore alternative financing methods. Interpret budget directives and establish policies for carrying out directives. Compile and analyze accounting records and other data to determine the financial resources required to implement a program. Testify before examining and fund-granting authorities, clarifying and promoting the proposed budgets.

Personality Type: Conventional.

GOE—Interest Area: 04. Business and Administration. **Work Group:** 04.05. Accounting, Auditing, and Analytical Support. **Other Jobs in this Work Group:** Accountants; Accountants and Auditors; Auditors; Industrial Engineering Technicians; Logisticians; Management Analysts; Operations Research Analysts.

Skills: Management of Financial Resources; Mathematics; Operations Analysis; Quality Control Analysis; Complex Problem Solving; Monitoring.

Education and Training Programs: Accounting; Finance, General. **Related Knowledge/Courses:** Economics and Accounting; Administration and Management; Clerical Studies; Computers and Electronics; Mathematics; Personnel and Human Resources.

Work Environment: Indoors; sitting.

Bus Drivers, School

- ❀ Education/Training Required: Moderate-term on-the-job training
- ❀ Annual Earnings: $24,820
- ❀ Beginning Wage: $13,690
- ❀ Earnings Growth Potential: Very high
- ❀ Growth: 9.3%
- ❀ Annual Job Openings: 59,809
- ❀ Self-Employed: 1.4%
- ❀ Part-Time: 34.1%

Industries with Greatest Employment: Educational Services, Public and Private; Transit and Ground Passenger Transportation.

Highest-Growth Industries (Projected Growth for This Job): Social Assistance (39.5%); Nursing and Residential Care Facilities (35.8%); Ambulatory Health Care Services (28.0%); Administrative and Support Services (27.0%); Religious, Grantmaking, Civic, Professional, and Similar Organizations (15.6%); Management of Companies and Enterprises (15.3%).

Lowest-Growth Industries (Projected Growth for This Job): Hospitals, Public and Private (–4.7%); Educational Services, Public and Private (5.5%); Real Estate (10.6%); Transit and Ground Passenger Transportation (10.8%); Support Activities for Transportation (13.7%).

Fastest-Growing Metropolitan Areas (Recent Growth for This Job): Redding, CA (111.1%); Flagstaff, AZ (81.8%); Michigan City–La Porte, IN (66.7%); Cumberland, MD–WV (53.3%); Hot Springs, AR (50.0%).

Other Considerations for Job Security: People seeking jobs as bus drivers likely will have good opportunities. Employment growth will create jobs, but most job openings are expected because of the need to replace workers who take jobs in other occupations or who retire or leave the occupation for other reasons. Individuals who have good driving records and who are willing to work a part-time or irregular schedule probably will have the best job prospects. School bus driving jobs, particularly in rapidly growing suburban areas, should be easiest to acquire because most are part-time positions with high turnover and less training required than for other bus-driving jobs. School bus drivers seldom work during the summer or school holidays.

Transport students or special clients, such as the elderly or persons with disabilities. Ensure adherence to safety rules. May assist passengers in boarding or exiting. Follow safety rules as students board and exit buses and as they cross streets near bus stops. Comply with traffic regulations to operate vehicles safely and courteously. Check the condition of a vehicle's tires, brakes, windshield wipers, lights, oil, fuel, water, and safety equipment to ensure that everything is in working order. Maintain order among pupils during trips to ensure safety. Pick up and drop off students at regularly scheduled neighborhood locations, following strict time schedules. Report any bus malfunctions or needed repairs. Drive gasoline, diesel, or electrically powered multi-passenger vehicles to transport students between neighborhoods, schools, and school activities. Prepare and submit reports that may include the number of passengers or trips, hours worked, mileage, fuel consumption, and fares received. Maintain knowledge of first-aid procedures. Keep bus interiors clean for passengers. Read maps and follow written and verbal geographic directions. Report delays, accidents, or other traffic and transportation situations, using telephones or mobile two-way radios. Regulate heating, lighting, and ventilation systems for passenger comfort. Escort small children across roads and highways. Make minor repairs to vehicles.

Personality Type: Realistic.

GOE—Interest Area: 16. Transportation, Distribution, and Logistics. **Work Group:** 16.06. Other Services Requiring Driving. **Other Jobs in this Work Group:** Ambulance Drivers and Attendants, Except Emergency Medical Technicians; Bus Drivers, Transit and Intercity; Couriers and Messengers; Driver/Sales Workers; Parking Lot Attendants; Postal Service Mail Carriers; Taxi Drivers and Chauffeurs.

Skills: No data available.

Education and Training Program: Truck and Bus Driver/Commercial Vehicle Operation. **Related Knowledge/Courses:** Transportation; Psychology; Public Safety and Security.

Work Environment: Noisy; contaminants; disease or infections; sitting; using hands on objects, tools, or controls; repetitive motions.

Bus Drivers, Transit and Intercity

- ✸ Education/Training Required: Moderate-term on-the-job training
- ✸ Annual Earnings: $32,090
- ✸ Beginning Wage: $19,270
- ✸ Earnings Growth Potential: Very high
- ✸ Growth: 12.5%
- ✸ Annual Job Openings: 27,100
- ✸ Self-Employed: 1.3%
- ✸ Part-Time: 34.1%

Industries with Greatest Employment: Transit and Ground Passenger Transportation.

Highest-Growth Industries (Projected Growth for This Job): Amusement, Gambling, and Recreation Industries (45.0%); Social Assistance (42.0%); Nursing and Residential Care Facilities (40.9%); Museums, Historical Sites, and Similar Institutions (36.0%); Ambulatory Health Care Services (35.2%); Scenic and Sightseeing Transportation (34.5%); Religious, Grantmaking, Civic, Professional, and Similar Organizations (18.9%).

Lowest-Growth Industries (Projected Growth for This Job): Food and Beverage Stores (5.1%); Educational Services, Public and Private (9.5%); Hospitals, Public and Private (10.2%); Performing Arts, Spectator Sports, and Related Industries (11.0%); Support Activities for Transportation (12.8%); Transit and Ground Passenger Transportation (12.8%); Merchant Wholesalers, Durable Goods (14.7%).

Fastest-Growing Metropolitan Areas (Recent Growth for This Job): Scranton–Wilkes-Barre, PA (157.1%); Indianapolis–Carmel, IN (150.0%); Lancaster, PA (135.7%); Appleton, WI (66.7%); Youngstown–Warren–Boardman, OH–PA (62.5%).

Other Considerations for Job Security: People seeking jobs as bus drivers likely will have good opportunities. Individuals who have good driving records and who are willing to work a part-time or irregular schedule probably will have the best job prospects. Those seeking higher-paying public transit bus driver positions may encounter competition. Opportunities for intercity driving positions should be good, although employment prospects for motor coach drivers will depend on tourism, which fluctuates with the economy. Full-time bus drivers rarely are laid off during recessions. In local transit and intercity bus systems, if the number of passengers decreases, employers might reduce the hours of part-time bus drivers or consolidate routes because fewer buses would be required. Seasonal layoffs are common.

Drive bus or motor coach, including regular route operations, charters, and private carriage. May assist passengers with baggage. May collect fares or tickets. Inspect vehicles and check gas, oil, and water levels before departure. Drive vehicles over specified routes or to specified destinations according to time schedules to transport passengers, complying with traffic regulations. Park vehicles at loading areas so that passengers can board. Assist passengers with baggage and collect tickets or cash fares. Report delays or accidents. Advise passengers to be seated and orderly while on vehicles. Regulate heating, lighting, and ventilating systems for passenger comfort. Load and unload baggage in baggage compartments. Record cash receipts and ticket fares. Make minor repairs to vehicle and change tires.

Personality Type: Realistic.

GOE—Interest Area: 16. Transportation, Distribution, and Logistics. **Work Group:** 16.06. Other Services Requiring Driving. **Other Jobs in this Work Group:** Ambulance Drivers and Attendants, Except Emergency Medical Technicians; Bus Drivers, School; Couriers and Messengers; Driver/Sales Workers; Parking Lot Attendants; Postal Service Mail Carriers; Taxi Drivers and Chauffeurs.

Skills: No data available.

Education and Training Program: Truck and Bus Driver/Commercial Vehicle Operation. **Related Knowledge/Courses:** Transportation; Geography; Public Safety and Security; Psychology; Customer and Personal Service; Law and Government.

Work Environment: Outdoors; noisy; contaminants; sitting; using hands on objects, tools, or controls; repetitive motions.

Business Teachers, Postsecondary

* Education/Training Required: Doctoral degree
* Annual Earnings: $62,040
* Beginning Wage: $31,780
* Earnings Growth Potential: Very high
* Growth: 22.9%
* Annual Job Openings: 237,478
* Self-Employed: 0.4%
* Part-Time: 27.8%

Our sources did not provide separate job openings data for this occupation. The job openings listed here are shared with 35 other postsecondary teaching occupations. For a complete list, see the beginning of this section.

Industries with Greatest Employment: Educational Services, Public and Private.

Highest-Growth Industries (Projected Growth for This Job): Administrative and Support Services (48.3%); Amusement, Gambling, and Recreation Industries (45.3%); Social Assistance (38.6%); Support Activities for Transportation (32.8%); Religious, Grantmaking, Civic, Professional, and Similar Organizations (29.9%); Professional, Scientific, and Technical Services (28.8%); Management of Companies and Enterprises (26.8%); Educational Services, Public and Private (22.9%); Hospitals, Public and Private (21.4%); Personal and Laundry Services (21.0%).

Lowest-Growth Industries (Projected Growth for This Job): Other Information Services (7.4%); Sporting Goods, Hobby, Book, and Music Stores (13.3%); Performing Arts, Spectator Sports, and Related Industries (13.4%); Insurance Carriers and Related Activities (13.9%).

Fastest-Growing Metropolitan Areas (Recent Growth for This Job): Denver–Aurora, CO (225.0%); Pittsburgh, PA (140.0%); Miami–Fort

Lauderdale–Miami Beach, FL (100.0%); Savannah, GA (53.8%); Milwaukee–Waukesha–West Allis, WI (50.0%).

Other Considerations for Job Security: Retirements of current postsecondary teachers should create numerous openings for all types of postsecondary teachers, so job opportunities are generally expected to be very good. Because students attend postsecondary institutions to prepare themselves for careers, the best job prospects for postsecondary teachers are likely to be in rapidly growing fields that offer many nonacademic career options. Business is one of the most rapidly growing of these fields. Community colleges and other institutions offering career and technical education have been among the most rapidly growing and are expected to offer some of the best opportunities for postsecondary teachers.

Teach courses in business administration and management, such as accounting, finance, human resources, labor relations, marketing, and operations research. Prepare and deliver lectures to undergraduate and/or graduate students on topics such as financial accounting, principles of marketing, and operations management. Evaluate and grade students' classwork, assignments, and papers. Compile, administer, and grade examinations or assign this work to others. Prepare course materials such as syllabi, homework assignments, and handouts. Maintain student attendance records, grades, and other required records. Initiate, facilitate, and moderate classroom discussions. Plan, evaluate, and revise curricula, course content, course materials, and methods of instruction. Keep abreast of developments in their field by reading current literature, talking with colleagues, and participating in professional organizations and conferences. Maintain regularly scheduled office hours to advise and assist students. Advise students on academic and vocational curricula and on career issues. Select and obtain materials and supplies such as textbooks. Collaborate with colleagues to address teaching and research issues. Collaborate with members of the business community to improve programs, to develop new programs, and to provide student access to learning opportunities such as internships. Participate in student recruitment, registration, and placement activities. Serve on academic or administrative committees that deal with institutional policies, departmental matters, and academic issues. Participate in campus and community events. Compile bibliographies of specialized materials for outside reading assignments. Perform administrative duties such as serving as department head. Supervise undergraduate and/or graduate teaching, internships, and research work. Conduct research in a particular field of knowledge and publish findings in professional journals, books, and/or electronic media. Act as advisers to student organizations. Provide professional consulting services to government and/or industry. Write grant proposals to procure external research funding.

Personality Type: No data available.

GOE—Interest Area: 05. Education and Training. **Work Group:** 05.03. Postsecondary and Adult Teaching and Instructing. **Other Jobs in this Work Group:** Adult Literacy, Remedial Education, and GED Teachers and Instructors; Agricultural Sciences Teachers, Postsecondary; Anthropology and Archeology Teachers, Postsecondary; Architecture Teachers, Postsecondary; Area, Ethnic, and Cultural Studies Teachers, Postsecondary; Art, Drama, and Music Teachers, Postsecondary; Atmospheric, Earth, Marine, and Space Sciences Teachers, Postsecondary; Biological Science Teachers, Postsecondary; Chemistry Teachers, Postsecondary; Communications Teachers, Postsecondary; Computer Science Teachers, Postsecondary; Criminal Justice and Law Enforcement Teachers, Postsecondary; Economics Teachers, Postsecondary; Education Teachers, Postsecondary; Engineering Teachers, Postsecondary; English Language and Literature Teachers, Postsecondary; Environmental Science Teachers, Postsecondary; Farm and Home Management Advisors; Foreign Language and Literature Teachers, Postsecondary; Forestry and Conservation Science Teachers, Postsecondary; Geography Teachers, Postsecondary; Graduate Teaching Assistants; Health Specialties Teachers, Postsecondary; History Teachers, Postsecondary; Home Economics Teachers, Postsecondary;

Law Teachers, Postsecondary; Library Science Teachers, Postsecondary; Mathematical Science Teachers, Postsecondary; Nursing Instructors and Teachers, Postsecondary; Philosophy and Religion Teachers, Postsecondary; Physics Teachers, Postsecondary; Political Science Teachers, Postsecondary; Psychology Teachers, Postsecondary; Recreation and Fitness Studies Teachers, Postsecondary; Self-Enrichment Education Teachers; Social Work Teachers, Postsecondary; Sociology Teachers, Postsecondary; Vocational Education Teachers, Postsecondary.

Skills: Instructing; Learning Strategies; Writing; Monitoring; Speaking; Active Learning.

Education and Training Programs: Business Teacher Education; Business/Commerce, General; Business Administration and Management, General; Purchasing, Procurement/Acquisitions and Contracts Management; Logistics and Materials Management; Operations Management and Supervision; Accounting; Business/Corporate Communications; Entrepreneurship/Entrepreneurial Studies; Franchising and Franchise Operations; Finance, General; others. **Related Knowledge/Courses:** Economics and Accounting; Education and Training; Sociology and Anthropology; Sales and Marketing; English Language; Philosophy and Theology.

Work Environment: Indoors; sitting.

Cardiovascular Technologists and Technicians

- ❋ Education/Training Required: Associate degree
- ❋ Annual Earnings: $42,300
- ❋ Beginning Wage: $23,670
- ❋ Earnings Growth Potential: Very high
- ❋ Growth: 25.5%
- ❋ Annual Job Openings: 3,550
- ❋ Self-Employed: 1.1%
- ❋ Part-Time: 17.3%

Industries with Greatest Employment: Hospitals, Public and Private.

Highest-Growth Industries (Projected Growth for This Job): Administrative and Support Services (39.3%); Management of Companies and Enterprises (25.9%); Educational Services, Public and Private (23.0%); Hospitals, Public and Private (22.1%).

Lowest-Growth Industries (Projected Growth for This Job): None met the criteria.

Fastest-Growing Metropolitan Areas (Recent Growth for This Job): Palm Bay–Melbourne–Titusville, FL (60.0%); Hartford–West Hartford–East Hartford, CT (54.5%); Lafayette, LA (50.0%); Bridgeport–Stamford–Norwalk, CT (40.0%); Port St. Lucie–Fort Pierce, FL (40.0%).

Other Considerations for Job Security: Technologists and technicians trained to perform certain procedures will be in particular demand. Growth will occur as the population ages, because older people have a higher incidence of heart disease and other complications of the heart and vascular system. Employment of vascular technologists and echocardiographers will grow as advances in vascular technology and sonography reduce the need for more costly and invasive procedures. Electrophysiology is also becoming a rapidly growing specialty. However, fewer electrocardiogram (EKG) technicians will be needed, as hospitals train nursing aides and others to perform basic EKG procedures. Individuals trained in Holter monitoring and stress testing are expected to have more favorable job prospects than those who can perform only a basic EKG.

Conduct diagnostic tests on pulmonary or cardiovascular systems of patients. May conduct or assist in electrocardiograms, cardiac catheterizations, pulmonary-functions, lung capacity, and similar tests. Monitor patients' blood pressure and heart rate, using EKG equipment, during diagnostic and therapeutic procedures to notify the physician if something appears wrong. Monitor patients' comfort and safety during tests, alerting physicians to abnormalities or changes in patient responses. Explain testing procedures to patient to obtain cooperation and reduce anxiety. Prepare reports of diagnostic procedures for interpretation by physician. Observe gauges, recorders, and video screens of data analysis system during imaging of cardiovascular system. Conduct EKG, phonocardiogram, echocardiogram, stress testing, or other cardiovascular tests to record patients' cardiac activity, using specialized electronic test equipment, recording devices, and laboratory instruments. Obtain and record patient identification, medical history, or test results. Prepare and position patients for testing. Attach electrodes to patients' chests, arms, and legs; connect electrodes to leads from EKG machine; and operate EKG machine to obtain a reading. Adjust equipment and controls according to physicians' orders or established protocol. Check, test, and maintain cardiology equipment, making minor repairs when necessary, to ensure proper operation. Supervise and train other cardiology technologists and students. Assist physicians in diagnosis and treatment of cardiac and peripheral vascular treatments—for example, assisting with balloon angioplasties to treat blood vessel blockages. Operate diagnostic imaging equipment to produce contrast-enhanced radiographs of heart and cardiovascular system. Inject contrast medium into patients' blood vessels. Observe ultrasound display screen and listen to signals to record vascular information such as blood pressure, limb volume changes, oxygen saturation, and cerebral circulation. Assess cardiac physiology and calculate valve areas from blood-flow velocity measurements. Compare measurements of heart wall thickness and chamber sizes to standard norms to identify abnormalities. Activate fluoroscope and camera to produce images used to guide catheter through cardiovascular system.

Personality Type: Investigative.

GOE—Interest Area: 08. Health Science. **Work Group:** 08.06. Medical Technology. **Other Jobs in this Work Group:** Biological Technicians; Diagnostic Medical Sonographers; Medical and Clinical Laboratory Technicians; Medical and Clinical Laboratory Technologists; Medical Equipment Preparers; Medical Records and Health Information Technicians; Nuclear Medicine Technologists; Opticians,

Dispensing; Orthotists and Prosthetists; Radiologic Technicians; Radiologic Technologists; Radiologic Technologists and Technicians.

Skills: Operation Monitoring; Science; Equipment Maintenance; Operation and Control; Management of Material Resources; Equipment Selection.

Education and Training Programs: Cardiovascular Technology/Technologist; Electrocardiograph Technology/Technician; Perfusion Technology/Perfusionist; Cardiopulmonary Technology/Technologist. **Related Knowledge/Courses:** Medicine and Dentistry; Customer and Personal Service; Psychology; Physics; Biology; Therapy and Counseling.

Work Environment: Indoors; radiation; disease or infections; standing; walking and running; using hands on objects, tools, or controls.

Chemistry Teachers, Postsecondary

* Education/Training Required: Doctoral degree
* Annual Earnings: $61,220
* Beginning Wage: $36,160
* Earnings Growth Potential: Very high
* Growth: 22.9%
* Annual Job Openings: 237,478
* Self-Employed: 0.4%
* Part-Time: 27.8%

Our sources did not provide separate job openings data for this occupation. The job openings listed here are shared with 35 other postsecondary teaching occupations. For a complete list, see the beginning of this section.

Industries with Greatest Employment: Educational Services, Public and Private.

Highest-Growth Industries (Projected Growth for This Job): Administrative and Support Services (48.3%); Amusement, Gambling, and Recreation Industries (45.3%); Social Assistance (38.6%); Support Activities for Transportation (32.8%); Religious, Grantmaking, Civic, Professional, and Similar

Organizations (29.9%); Professional, Scientific, and Technical Services (28.8%); Management of Companies and Enterprises (26.8%); Educational Services, Public and Private (22.9%); Hospitals, Public and Private (21.4%); Personal and Laundry Services (21.0%).

Lowest-Growth Industries (Projected Growth for This Job): Other Information Services (7.4%); Sporting Goods, Hobby, Book, and Music Stores (13.3%); Performing Arts, Spectator Sports, and Related Industries (13.4%); Insurance Carriers and Related Activities (13.9%).

Fastest-Growing Metropolitan Areas (Recent Growth for This Job): None growing over 10 percent.

Other Considerations for Job Security: Retirements of current postsecondary teachers should create numerous openings for all types of postsecondary teachers, so job opportunities are generally expected to be very good. Because students attend postsecondary institutions to prepare themselves for careers, the best job prospects for postsecondary teachers are likely to be in rapidly growing fields that offer many nonacademic career options. Chemistry is a key part of the curriculum for health-care majors. Community colleges and other institutions offering career and technical education have been among the most rapidly growing and are expected to offer some of the best opportunities for postsecondary teachers.

Teach courses pertaining to the chemical and physical properties and compositional changes of substances. Work may include instruction in the methods of qualitative and quantitative chemical analysis. Includes both teachers primarily engaged in teaching and those who do a combination of teaching and research. Prepare and deliver lectures to undergraduate and/or graduate students on topics such as organic chemistry, analytical chemistry, and chemical separation. Supervise students' laboratory work. Evaluate and grade students' classwork, laboratory performance, assignments, and papers. Compile, administer, and grade examinations or assign this work to others. Maintain student attendance records, grades, and other required records. Prepare course materials such as syllabi, homework assignments, and handouts. Maintain regularly scheduled office hours to advise and assist students. Plan, evaluate, and revise curricula, course content, course materials, and methods of instruction. Supervise undergraduate and/or graduate teaching, internships, and research work. Keep abreast of developments in the field by reading current literature, talking with colleagues, and participating in professional conferences. Initiate, facilitate, and moderate classroom discussions. Select and obtain materials and supplies such as textbooks and laboratory equipment. Conduct research in a particular field of knowledge and publish findings in professional journals, books, and/or electronic media. Advise students on academic and vocational curricula and on career issues. Collaborate with colleagues to address teaching and research issues. Serve on academic or administrative committees that deal with institutional policies, departmental matters, and academic issues. Write grant proposals to procure external research funding. Participate in student recruitment, registration, and placement activities. Prepare and submit required reports related to instruction. Perform administrative duties such as serving as a department head. Act as advisers to student organizations. Compile bibliographies of specialized materials for outside reading assignments. Participate in campus and community events. Provide professional consulting services to government and/or industry.

Personality Type: Investigative.

GOE—Interest Area: 05. Education and Training. **Work Group:** 05.03. Postsecondary and Adult Teaching and Instructing. **Other Jobs in this Work Group:** Adult Literacy, Remedial Education, and GED Teachers and Instructors; Agricultural Sciences Teachers, Postsecondary; Anthropology and Archeology Teachers, Postsecondary; Architecture Teachers, Postsecondary; Area, Ethnic, and Cultural Studies Teachers, Postsecondary; Art, Drama, and Music Teachers, Postsecondary; Atmospheric, Earth, Marine, and Space Sciences Teachers, Postsecondary; Biological Science Teachers, Postsecondary; Business

Teachers, Postsecondary; Communications Teachers, Postsecondary; Computer Science Teachers, Postsecondary; Criminal Justice and Law Enforcement Teachers, Postsecondary; Economics Teachers, Postsecondary; Education Teachers, Postsecondary; Engineering Teachers, Postsecondary; English Language and Literature Teachers, Postsecondary; Environmental Science Teachers, Postsecondary; Farm and Home Management Advisors; Foreign Language and Literature Teachers, Postsecondary; Forestry and Conservation Science Teachers, Postsecondary; Geography Teachers, Postsecondary; Graduate Teaching Assistants; Health Specialties Teachers, Postsecondary; History Teachers, Postsecondary; Home Economics Teachers, Postsecondary; Law Teachers, Postsecondary; Library Science Teachers, Postsecondary; Mathematical Science Teachers, Postsecondary; Nursing Instructors and Teachers, Postsecondary; Philosophy and Religion Teachers, Postsecondary; Physics Teachers, Postsecondary; Political Science Teachers, Postsecondary; Psychology Teachers, Postsecondary; Recreation and Fitness Studies Teachers, Postsecondary; Self-Enrichment Education Teachers; Social Work Teachers, Postsecondary; Sociology Teachers, Postsecondary; Vocational Education Teachers, Postsecondary.

Skills: Science; Mathematics; Instructing; Writing; Reading Comprehension; Active Learning.

Education and Training Programs: Chemistry, General; Analytical Chemistry; Inorganic Chemistry; Organic Chemistry; Physical and Theoretical Chemistry; Polymer Chemistry; Chemical Physics; Chemistry, Other; Geochemistry. **Related Knowledge/Courses:** Chemistry; Biology; Physics; Education and Training; Mathematics; English Language.

Work Environment: Indoors; contaminants; hazardous conditions; sitting.

Child, Family, and School Social Workers

* Education/Training Required: Bachelor's degree
* Annual Earnings: $37,480
* Beginning Wage: $24,480
* Earnings Growth Potential: Very high
* Growth: 19.1%
* Annual Job Openings: 35,402
* Self-Employed: 2.8%
* Part-Time: 9.4%

Industries with Greatest Employment: Social Assistance; Educational Services, Public and Private; Nursing and Residential Care Facilities; Religious, Grantmaking, Civic, Professional, and Similar Organizations; Ambulatory Health Care Services.

Highest-Growth Industries (Projected Growth for This Job): Social Assistance (54.0%); Administrative and Support Services (28.0%); Ambulatory Health Care Services (22.6%); Nursing and Residential Care Facilities (21.3%); Management of Companies and Enterprises (15.3%); Religious, Grantmaking, Civic, Professional, and Similar Organizations (15.2%).

Lowest-Growth Industries (Projected Growth for This Job): Hospitals, Public and Private (1.5%); Educational Services, Public and Private (7.4%); Professional, Scientific, and Technical Services (13.4%).

Fastest-Growing Metropolitan Areas (Recent Growth for This Job): Birmingham–Hoover, AL (173.7%); Longview, TX (140.0%); Terre Haute, IN (113.3%); Huntsville, AL (111.8%); Gainesville, FL (107.7%).

Other Considerations for Job Security: Job prospects are generally expected to be favorable. Social workers, particularly family social workers, will be needed to assist in finding the best care for the aging and to support their families. Furthermore, demand for school social workers will increase and lead to more jobs as efforts are expanded to respond to rising student enrollments as well as the continued emphasis on integrating disabled children into the general school population. There could be competition for school social work jobs in some areas because of the limited number of openings. The availability of federal, state, and local funding will be a major factor in determining the actual job growth in schools. The demand for child and family social workers may also be tied to the availability of government funding.

Provide social services and assistance to improve the social and psychological functioning of children and their families and to maximize the family well-being and the academic functioning of children. May assist single parents, arrange adoptions, and find foster homes for abandoned or abused children. In schools, they address such problems as teenage pregnancy, misbehavior, and truancy. May also advise teachers on how to deal with problem children. Interview clients individually, in families, or in groups, assessing their situations, capabilities, and problems, to determine what services are required to meet their needs. Counsel individuals, groups, families, or communities regarding issues including mental health, poverty, unemployment, substance abuse, physical abuse, rehabilitation, social adjustment, child care, or medical care. Maintain case history records and prepare reports. Counsel students whose behavior, school progress, or mental or physical impairment indicate a need for assistance, diagnosing students' problems and arranging for needed services. Consult with parents, teachers, and other school personnel to determine causes of problems such as truancy and misbehavior and to implement solutions. Counsel parents with child rearing problems, interviewing the child and family to determine whether further action is required. Develop and review service plans in consultation with clients and perform follow-ups assessing the quantity and quality of services provided. Collect supplementary information needed to assist clients, such as employment records, medical records, or school reports. Address legal issues, such as child abuse and discipline, assisting with hearings and providing testimony to inform custody arrangements. Provide, find, or arrange for support services, such as child care, homemaker service, prenatal care, substance abuse treatment, job training, counseling, or parenting classes, to prevent more serious problems from developing. Refer clients to community resources for services such as job placement, debt counseling, legal aid, housing, medical treatment, or financial assistance and provide concrete information, such as where to go and how to apply. Arrange for medical, psychiatric, and other tests that may disclose causes of difficulties and indicate remedial measures. Work in child and adolescent residential institutions. Administer welfare programs. Evaluate personal characteristics and home conditions of foster home or adoption applicants. Serve as liaisons between students, homes, schools, family services, child guidance clinics, courts, protective services, doctors, and other contacts to help children who face problems such as disabilities, abuse, or poverty.

Personality Type: Social.

GOE—Interest Area: 10. Human Service. **Work Group:** 10.01. Counseling and Social Work. **Other Jobs in this Work Group:** Clinical Psychologists; Clinical, Counseling, and School Psychologists; Counseling Psychologists; Marriage and Family Therapists; Medical and Public Health Social Workers; Mental Health and Substance Abuse Social Workers; Mental Health Counselors; Probation Officers and Correctional Treatment Specialists; Rehabilitation Counselors; Residential Advisors; Social and Human Service Assistants; Substance Abuse and Behavioral Disorder Counselors.

Skills: Social Perceptiveness; Service Orientation; Speaking; Monitoring; Writing; Negotiation.

Education and Training Programs: Juvenile Corrections; Social Work; Youth Services/Administration. **Related Knowledge/Courses:** Therapy and Counseling; Psychology; Sociology and Anthropology; Philosophy and Theology; Customer and Personal Service; Law and Government.

Work Environment: Indoors; sitting.

Chiropractors

- ❋ Education/Training Required: First professional degree
- ❋ Annual Earnings: $65,220
- ❋ Beginning Wage: $32,670
- ❋ Earnings Growth Potential: Very high
- ❋ Growth: 14.4%
- ❋ Annual Job Openings: 3,179
- ❋ Self-Employed: 51.7%
- ❋ Part-Time: 23.6%

Industries with Greatest Employment: Ambulatory Health Care Services.

Highest-Growth Industries (Projected Growth for This Job): Ambulatory Health Care Services (23.4%).

Lowest-Growth Industries (Projected Growth for This Job): Hospitals, Public and Private (12.2%).

Fastest-Growing Metropolitan Areas (Recent Growth for This Job): Grand Rapids–Wyoming, MI (125.0%); Atlanta–Sandy Springs–Marietta, GA (71.1%); Washington–Arlington–Alexandria, DC–VA–MD–WV (48.6%); Los Angeles–Long Beach–Santa Ana, CA (48.3%); Sioux Falls, SD (40.0%).

Other Considerations for Job Security: Job prospects for new chiropractors are expected to be good. In this occupation, replacement needs arise almost entirely from retirements. Chiropractors usually remain in the occupation until they retire; few transfer to other occupations. Establishing a new practice will be easiest in areas with a low concentration of chiropractors. Employment is expected to grow faster than average because of increasing consumer demand for alternative health care. Demand for chiropractic treatment, however, is related to the ability of patients to pay, either directly or through health insurance. Although more insurance plans now cover chiropractic services, the extent of such coverage varies among plans.

Adjust spinal column and other articulations of the body to correct abnormalities believed to be caused by interference with the nervous system. Examine patient to determine nature and extent of disorder. Manipulate spine or other involved area. May utilize supplementary measures, such as exercise, rest, water, light, heat, and nutritional therapy. Perform a series of manual adjustments to the spine or other articulations of the body to correct the musculoskeletal system. Evaluate the functioning of the neuromuscularskeletal system and the spine, using systems of chiropractic diagnosis. Diagnose health problems by reviewing patients' health and medical histories; questioning, observing, and examining patients; and interpreting X rays. Maintain accurate case histories of patients. Advise patients about recommended courses of treatment. Obtain and record patients' medical histories. Analyze X rays to locate the sources of patients' difficulties and to rule out fractures or diseases as sources of problems. Counsel patients about nutrition, exercise, sleeping habits, stress management, and other matters. Arrange for diagnostic X rays to be taken. Consult with and refer patients to appropriate health practitioners when necessary. Suggest and apply the use of supports such as straps, tapes, bandages, and braces if necessary.

Personality Type: Investigative.

GOE—Interest Area: 08. Health Science. **Work Group:** 08.04. Health Specialties. **Other Jobs in this Work Group:** Optometrists; Podiatrists.

Skills: Science; Management of Financial Resources; Social Perceptiveness; Persuasion; Service Orientation; Management of Personnel Resources.

Education and Training Program: Chiropractic (DC). **Related Knowledge/Courses:** Medicine and Dentistry; Therapy and Counseling; Biology; Psychology; Sales and Marketing; Personnel and Human Resources.

Work Environment: Indoors; disease or infections; standing; using hands on objects, tools, or controls; bending or twisting the body; repetitive motions.

Claims Adjusters, Examiners, and Investigators

See *Claims Examiners, Property and Casualty Insurance, and Insurance Adjusters, Examiners, and Investigators, described separately.*

Claims Examiners, Property and Casualty Insurance

* Education/Training Required: Long-term on-the-job training
* Annual Earnings: $50,660
* Beginning Wage: $30,890
* Earnings Growth Potential: Very high
* Growth: 8.9%
* Annual Job Openings: 22,024
* Self-Employed: 3.5%
* Part-Time: 4.0%

Our sources did not provide separate job openings data for this occupation. The job openings listed here are shared with Insurance Adjusters, Examiners, and Investigators.

Industries with Greatest Employment: Insurance Carriers and Related Activities.

Highest-Growth Industries (Projected Growth for This Job): Professional, Scientific, and Technical Services (48.0%); Securities, Commodity Contracts, and Other Financial Investments and Related Activities (44.8%); Social Assistance (44.3%); Internet Service Providers, Web Search Portals, and Data Processing Services (35.2%); Administrative and Support Services (27.7%); Real Estate (26.4%); Ambulatory Health Care Services (24.5%); Funds, Trusts, and Other Financial Vehicles (23.7%); Religious, Grantmaking, Civic, Professional, and Similar Organizations (17.7%); Repair and Maintenance (16.7%); Management of Companies and Enterprises (15.3%).

Lowest-Growth Industries (Projected Growth for This Job): Rail Transportation (–14.0%); Utilities (–11.1%); Hospitals, Public and Private (9.6%); Insurance Carriers and Related Activities (10.8%); Educational Services, Public and Private (11.8%); Truck Transportation (12.7%); Rental and Leasing Services (14.0%).

Fastest-Growing Metropolitan Areas (Recent Growth for This Job): Deltona–Daytona Beach–Ormond Beach, FL (233.3%); Beaumont–Port Arthur, TX (225.0%); Goldsboro, NC (200.0%); Tuscaloosa, AL (175.0%); Sarasota–Bradenton–Venice, FL (114.3%).

Other Considerations for Job Security: Competition for investigator jobs will remain keen because the occupation attracts many qualified people, including retirees from law enforcement and the military and experienced claims adjusters and examiners who choose to get an investigator license. Heightened media and public awareness of insurance fraud also may attract qualified candidates to this occupation. Many insurance carriers are downsizing their claims staff in an effort to contain costs. Technology, such as the Internet, reduces the amount of time it takes investigators to perform background checks, allowing them to handle more cases.

Review settled insurance claims to determine that payments and settlements have been made in accordance with company practices and procedures. Report overpayments, underpayments, and other irregularities. Confer with legal counsel on claims requiring litigation. Investigate, evaluate, and settle claims, applying technical knowledge and human relations skills to effect fair and prompt disposal of cases and to contribute to a reduced loss ratio. Pay and process claims within designated authority level. Adjust reserves or provide reserve recommendations to ensure that reserve activities are consistent with corporate policies. Enter claim payments, reserves, and new claims on computer system, inputting concise yet sufficient file documentation. Resolve complex severe exposure claims, using high service-oriented file handling. Maintain claim files such as records of settled claims and an inventory of claims requiring detailed analysis. Verify and analyze data used in settling claims to ensure that claims are valid and that settlements are made according to company practices and procedures. Examine claims investigated by insurance adjusters, further investigating questionable claims to determine whether to authorize payments. Present cases and participate in their discussion at claim committee meetings. Contact or interview claimants, doctors, medical specialists, or employers to get additional information. Confer with legal counsel on claims requiring litigation. Report overpayments, underpayments, and other irregularities. Communicate with reinsurance brokers to obtain information necessary for processing claims. Supervise claims adjusters to ensure that adjusters have followed proper methods. Conduct detailed bill reviews to implement sound litigation management and expense control. Prepare reports to be submitted to company's data-processing department.

Personality Type: Conventional.

GOE—Interest Area: 06. Finance and Insurance. **Work Group:** 06.02. Finance/Insurance Investigation and Analysis. **Other Jobs in this Work Group:** Appraisers and Assessors of Real Estate; Appraisers, Real Estate; Assessors; Claims Adjusters, Examiners, and Investigators; Cost Estimators; Credit Analysts; Financial Analysts; Insurance Adjusters, Examiners, and Investigators; Insurance Appraisers, Auto Damage; Insurance Underwriters; Loan Counselors; Loan Officers; Market Research Analysts; Survey Researchers.

Skills: Judgment and Decision Making; Writing; Persuasion; Negotiation; Reading Comprehension; Critical Thinking.

Education and Training Program: Health/Medical Claims Examiner. **Related Knowledge/Courses:** Customer and Personal Service; Medicine and Dentistry; Clerical Studies; Law and Government; Computers and Electronics; English Language.

Work Environment: Indoors; sitting; using hands on objects, tools, or controls; repetitive motions.

Clergy

* Education/Training Required: Master's degree
* Annual Earnings: $39,680
* Beginning Wage: $20,730
* Earnings Growth Potential: Very high
* Growth: 18.9%
* Annual Job Openings: 35,092
* Self-Employed: 0.1%
* Part-Time: 10.0%

Industries with Greatest Employment: Religious, Grantmaking, Civic, Professional, and Similar Organizations.

Highest-Growth Industries (Projected Growth for This Job): Professional, Scientific, and Technical Services (55.1%); Ambulatory Health Care Services (53.2%); Social Assistance (36.6%); Administrative and Support Services (33.0%); Personal and Laundry Services (30.5%); Real Estate (22.1%); Nursing and Residential Care Facilities (21.4%); Religious, Grantmaking, Civic, Professional, and Similar Organizations (18.9%); Management of Companies and Enterprises (15.3%).

Lowest-Growth Industries (Projected Growth for This Job): Educational Services, Public and Private (9.2%); Hospitals, Public and Private (10.0%).

Fastest-Growing Metropolitan Areas (Recent Growth for This Job): Atlanta–Sandy Springs–Marietta, GA (133.3%); Jacksonville, FL (100.0%); Dayton, OH (77.8%); Houston–Sugar Land–Baytown, TX (75.0%); Evansville, IN–KY (66.7%).

Other Considerations for Job Security: No data available.

Conduct religious worship and perform other spiritual functions associated with beliefs and practices of religious faith or denomination. Provide spiritual and moral guidance and assistance to members. Pray and promote spirituality. Read from sacred texts such as the Bible, Torah, or Koran. Prepare and deliver sermons and other talks. Organize and lead regular religious services. Share information about religious issues by writing articles, giving speeches, or teaching. Instruct people who seek conversion to a particular faith. Visit people in homes, hospitals, and prisons to provide them with comfort and support. Counsel individuals and groups concerning their spiritual, emotional, and personal needs. Train leaders of church, community, and youth groups. Administer religious rites or ordinances. Study and interpret religious laws, doctrines, or traditions. Conduct special ceremonies such as weddings, funerals, and confirmations. Plan and lead religious education programs for congregation. Respond to requests for assistance during emergencies or crises. Devise ways in which congregation membership can be expanded. Collaborate with committees and individuals to address financial and administrative issues pertaining to congregation. Prepare people for participation in religious ceremonies. Perform administrative duties such as overseeing building management, ordering supplies, contracting for services and repairs, and supervising the work of staff members and volunteers. Refer people to community support services, psychologists, and doctors as necessary. Participate in fundraising activities to support congregation activities and facilities. Organize and engage in interfaith, community, civic, educational, and recreational activities sponsored by or related to their religion.

Personality Type: Social.

GOE—Interest Area: 10. Human Service. **Work Group:** 10.02. Religious Work. **Other Jobs in this Work Group:** Directors, Religious Activities and Education.

Skills: Management of Personnel Resources; Management of Financial Resources; Service Orientation; Negotiation; Judgment and Decision Making; Persuasion.

Education and Training Programs: Theology/Theological Studies; Divinity/Ministry (BD, MDiv.); Pre-Theology/Pre-Ministerial Studies; Rabbinical Studies; Theological and Ministerial Studies, Other; Pastoral Studies/Counseling; Youth Ministry; Pastoral Counseling and Specialized Ministries, Other; Theology and Religious Vocations, Other; Clinical Pastoral Counseling/Patient Counseling. **Related Knowledge/Courses:** Philosophy and Theology; Therapy and Counseling; Sociology and Anthropology; Psychology; Customer and Personal Service; Public Safety and Security.

Work Environment: Indoors; sitting.

Clinical Psychologists

* Education/Training Required: Doctoral degree
* Annual Earnings: $59,440
* Beginning Wage: $35,280
* Earnings Growth Potential: Very high
* Growth: 15.8%
* Annual Job Openings: 8,309
* Self-Employed: 34.2%
* Part-Time: 24.0%

Our sources did not provide separate job openings data for this occupation. The job openings listed here are shared with Counseling Psychologists and with School Psychologists.

Industries with Greatest Employment: Educational Services, Public and Private; Ambulatory Health Care Services; Hospitals, Public and Private; Social Assistance.

Highest-Growth Industries (Projected Growth for This Job): Social Assistance (56.2%); Professional, Scientific, and Technical Services (34.6%); Ambulatory Health Care Services (26.8%); Nursing and Residential Care Facilities (24.8%); Funds, Trusts, and Other Financial Vehicles (23.3%); Religious, Grantmaking, Civic, Professional, and Similar Organizations (19.4%); Management of Companies and Enterprises (15.2%).

Lowest-Growth Industries (Projected Growth for This Job): Hospitals, Public and Private (–3.5%); Educational Services, Public and Private (6.9%).

Fastest-Growing Metropolitan Areas (Recent Growth for This Job): Augusta–Richmond County, GA–SC (100.0%); Memphis, TN–MS–AR (100.0%); Peoria, IL (90.0%); Greenville, SC (87.5%); Oklahoma City, OK (86.2%).

Other Considerations for Job Security: Job prospects should be the best for people with a doctorate from a leading university. Master's degree holders will face keen competition for jobs. The rise in healthcare costs associated with unhealthy lifestyles, such as smoking, alcoholism, and obesity, has made prevention and treatment more critical. An increase in the number of employee assistance programs, which help workers deal with personal problems, also should lead to employment growth for clinical and counseling specialties. Clinical and counseling psychologists also will be needed to help people deal with depression and other mental disorders, marriage and family problems, job stress, and addiction. The growing number of elderly will increase the demand for psychologists trained in geropsychology to help people deal with the mental and physical changes that occur as individuals grow older. There also will be increased need for psychologists to work with returning veterans.

Diagnose or evaluate mental and emotional disorders of individuals through observation, interview, and psychological tests and formulate and administer programs of treatment. Identify psychological, emotional, or behavioral issues and diagnose disorders, using information obtained from interviews, tests, records, and reference materials. Develop and implement individual treatment plans, specifying type, frequency, intensity, and duration of therapy. Interact with clients to help them gain insight, define goals, and plan action to achieve effective personal, social, educational, and vocational development and adjustment. Discuss the treatment of problems with clients. Utilize a variety of treatment methods such as psychotherapy, hypnosis, behavior modification, stress-reduction therapy, psychodrama, and play therapy. Counsel individuals and groups regarding problems such as stress, substance abuse, and family situations to modify behavior or to improve personal, social, and vocational adjustment. Write reports on clients and maintain required paperwork. Evaluate the effectiveness of counseling or treatments and the accuracy and completeness of diagnoses; then modify plans and diagnoses as necessary. Obtain and study medical, psychological, social, and family histories by interviewing individuals, couples, or families and by reviewing records. Consult reference material such as textbooks, manuals, and journals to identify symptoms, make diagnoses, and develop approaches to treatment. Maintain current knowledge of relevant research. Observe individuals at play, in group interactions, or in other contexts to detect indications of mental deficiency, abnormal behavior, or maladjustment. Select, administer, score, and interpret psychological tests to obtain information on individuals' intelligence, achievements, interests, and personalities. Refer clients to other specialists, institutions, or support services as necessary. Develop, direct, and participate in training programs for staff and students. Provide psychological or administrative services and advice to private firms and community agencies regarding mental health programs or individual cases. Provide occupational, educational, and other information to individuals so that they can make educational and vocational plans.

Personality Type: Investigative.

GOE—Interest Area: 10. Human Service. **Work Group:** 10.01. Counseling and Social Work. **Other Jobs in this Work Group:** Child, Family, and School Social Workers; Clinical, Counseling, and School Psychologists; Counseling Psychologists; Marriage and Family Therapists; Medical and Public Health Social Workers; Mental Health and Substance Abuse Social Workers; Mental Health Counselors; Probation Officers and Correctional Treatment Specialists; Rehabilitation Counselors; Residential Advisors; Social and Human Service Assistants; Substance Abuse and Behavioral Disorder Counselors.

Skills: Social Perceptiveness; Service Orientation; Complex Problem Solving; Learning Strategies; Negotiation; Active Listening.

Education and Training Programs: Psychology, General; Clinical Psychology; Counseling Psychology; Developmental and Child Psychology; School

Psychology; Clinical Child Psychology; Psycho-analysis and Psychotherapy. **Related Knowledge/ Courses:** Therapy and Counseling; Psychology; Sociology and Anthropology; Philosophy and Theology; Customer and Personal Service; Medicine and Dentistry.

Work Environment: Indoors; sitting.

Clinical, Counseling, and School Psychologists

See *Clinical Psychologists, Counseling Psychologists, and School Psychologists, described separately.*

Coaches and Scouts

- ❋ Education/Training Required: Long-term on-the-job training
- ❋ Annual Earnings: $26,950
- ❋ Beginning Wage: $13,990
- ❋ Earnings Growth Potential: Very high
- ❋ Growth: 14.6%
- ❋ Annual Job Openings: 51,100
- ❋ Self-Employed: 22.7%
- ❋ Part-Time: 39.1%

Industries with Greatest Employment: Educational Services, Public and Private; Amusement, Gambling, and Recreation Industries.

Highest-Growth Industries (Projected Growth for This Job): Social Assistance (40.5%); Amusement, Gambling, and Recreation Industries (31.1%); Administrative and Support Services (28.6%); Performing Arts, Spectator Sports, and Related Industries (25.2%); Accommodation, Including Hotels and Motels (15.6%).

Lowest-Growth Industries (Projected Growth for This Job): Animal Production (–10.9%); Sporting Goods, Hobby, Book, and Music Stores (6.6%); Support Activities for Agriculture and Forestry (7.7%); Religious, Grantmaking, Civic, Professional, and Similar Organizations (13.1%).

Fastest-Growing Metropolitan Areas (Recent Growth for This Job): Holland–Grand Haven, MI (244.4%); Stockton, CA (242.9%); Gainesville, FL (142.9%); Ogden–Clearfield, UT (115.4%); Mount Vernon–Anacortes, WA (100.0%).

Other Considerations for Job Security: Persons who are state-certified to teach academic subjects in addition to physical education are likely to have the best prospects for obtaining coaching and instructor jobs. The need to replace the many high school coaches who change occupations or leave the labor force entirely also will provide some coaching opportunities. Competition should be keen for jobs as scouts, particularly for professional teams, because the number of available positions is limited.

Instruct or coach groups or individuals in the fundamentals of sports. Demonstrate techniques and methods of participation. May evaluate athletes' strengths and weaknesses as possible recruits or to improve athletes' techniques to prepare them for competition. Plan, organize, and conduct practice sessions. Provide training, direction, encouragement, and motivation to prepare athletes for games, competitive events, or tours. Identify and recruit potential athletes, arranging and offering incentives such as athletic scholarships. Plan strategies and choose team members for individual games or sports seasons. Plan and direct physical conditioning programs that will enable athletes to achieve maximum performance. Adjust coaching techniques based on athletes' strengths and weaknesses. File scouting reports that detail player assessments, provide recommendations on athlete recruitment, and identify locations and individuals to be targeted for future recruitment efforts. Keep records of athlete, team, and opposing team performance. Instruct individuals or groups in sports rules, game strategies, and performance principles such as specific ways of moving the body, hands, and feet to achieve desired results. Analyze strengths and weaknesses of opposing teams to develop game strategies. Evaluate athletes' skills and review performance records to determine their fitness and potential in a particular area of athletics. Keep abreast of changing rules, techniques, technologies, and philosophies relevant to their sport. Monitor athletes' use of equipment to ensure safe and proper use. Explain and enforce safety rules and regulations. Develop and arrange competition schedules and programs. Serve as organizer, leader, instructor, or referee for outdoor and indoor games such as volleyball, football, and soccer. Explain and demonstrate the use of sports and training equipment, such as trampolines or weights. Perform activities that support a team or a specific sport, such as meeting with media representatives and appearing at fundraising events. Arrange and conduct sports-related activities such as training camps, skill-improvement courses, clinics, or pre-season tryouts. Select, acquire, store, and issue equipment and other materials as necessary. Negotiate with professional athletes or their representatives to obtain services and arrange contracts.

Personality Type: Enterprising.

GOE—Interest Area: 09. Hospitality, Tourism, and Recreation. **Work Group:** 09.06. Sports. **Other Jobs in this Work Group:** Athletes and Sports Competitors; Umpires, Referees, and Other Sports Officials.

Skills: Management of Personnel Resources; Social Perceptiveness; Management of Financial Resources; Persuasion; Negotiation; Instructing.

Education and Training Programs: Physical Education Teaching and Coaching; Health and Physical Education, General; Sport and Fitness Administration/Management. **Related Knowledge/Courses:** Psychology; Therapy and Counseling; Education and Training; Sales and Marketing; Personnel and Human Resources; Sociology and Anthropology.

Work Environment: More often indoors than outdoors; noisy; standing; walking and running.

Communications Teachers, Postsecondary

- ❋ Education/Training Required: Doctoral degree
- ❋ Annual Earnings: $53,110
- ❋ Beginning Wage: $28,850
- ❋ Earnings Growth Potential: Very high
- ❋ Growth: 22.9%
- ❋ Annual Job Openings: 237,478
- ❋ Self-Employed: 0.4%
- ❋ Part-Time: 27.8%

Our sources did not provide separate job openings data for this occupation. The job openings listed here are shared with 35 other postsecondary teaching occupations. For a complete list, see the beginning of this section.

Industries with Greatest Employment: Educational Services, Public and Private.

Highest-Growth Industries (Projected Growth for This Job): Administrative and Support Services (48.3%); Amusement, Gambling, and Recreation Industries (45.3%); Social Assistance (38.6%); Support Activities for Transportation (32.8%); Religious, Grantmaking, Civic, Professional, and Similar Organizations (29.9%); Professional, Scientific, and Technical Services (28.8%); Management of Companies and Enterprises (26.8%); Educational Services, Public and Private (22.9%); Hospitals, Public and Private (21.4%); Personal and Laundry Services (21.0%).

Lowest-Growth Industries (Projected Growth for This Job): Other Information Services (7.4%); Sporting Goods, Hobby, Book, and Music Stores (13.3%); Performing Arts, Spectator Sports, and Related Industries (13.4%); Insurance Carriers and Related Activities (13.9%).

Fastest-Growing Metropolitan Areas (Recent Growth for This Job): Dallas–Fort Worth–Arlington, TX (22.0%); Harrisburg–Carlisle, PA (20.0%); St. Louis, MO–IL (16.7%); Cincinnati–Middletown, OH–KY–IN (16.3%); Augusta–Richmond County, GA–SC (11.1%).

Other Considerations for Job Security: Retirements of current postsecondary teachers should create numerous openings for all types of postsecondary teachers, so job opportunities are generally expected to be very good. Because students attend postsecondary institutions to prepare themselves for careers, the best job prospects for postsecondary teachers are likely to be in rapidly growing fields that offer many nonacademic career options. Community colleges and other institutions offering career and technical education have been among the most rapidly growing and are expected to offer some of the best opportunities for postsecondary teachers.

Teach courses in communications, such as organizational communications, public relations, radio/television broadcasting, and journalism. Evaluate and grade students' classwork, assignments, and papers. Prepare course materials such as syllabi, homework assignments, and handouts. Initiate, facilitate, and moderate classroom discussions. Prepare and deliver lectures to undergraduate or graduate students on topics such as public speaking, media criticism, and oral traditions. Compile, administer, and grade examinations or assign this work to others. Maintain student attendance records, grades, and other required records. Plan, evaluate, and revise curricula, course content, course materials, and methods of instruction. Maintain regularly scheduled office hours to advise and assist students. Keep abreast of developments in their field by reading current literature, talking with colleagues, and participating in professional conferences. Advise students on academic and vocational curricula and on career issues. Supervise undergraduate or graduate teaching, internships, and research work. Select and obtain materials and supplies such as textbooks. Collaborate with colleagues to address teaching and research issues. Conduct research in a particular field of knowledge and publish findings in professional journals, books, or electronic media. Participate in student recruitment, registration, and placement activities. Serve on academic or administrative committees that deal with institutional policies, departmental matters, and academic issues. Compile bibliographies of specialized materials for outside reading assignments. Act as advisers to student organizations. Participate in campus and community events. Perform administrative duties such as serving as department head. Write grant proposals to procure external research funding. Provide professional consulting services to government or industry.

Personality Type: No data available.

GOE—Interest Area: 05. Education and Training. **Work Group:** 05.03. Postsecondary and Adult Teaching and Instructing. **Other Jobs in this Work Group:** Adult Literacy, Remedial Education, and GED Teachers and Instructors; Agricultural Sciences Teachers, Postsecondary; Anthropology and Archeology Teachers, Postsecondary; Architecture Teachers, Postsecondary; Area, Ethnic, and Cultural Studies Teachers, Postsecondary; Art, Drama, and Music Teachers, Postsecondary; Atmospheric, Earth, Marine, and Space Sciences Teachers, Postsecondary; Biological Science Teachers, Postsecondary; Business Teachers, Postsecondary; Chemistry Teachers, Postsecondary; Computer Science Teachers, Postsecondary; Criminal Justice and Law Enforcement Teachers, Postsecondary; Economics Teachers, Postsecondary; Education Teachers, Postsecondary; Engineering Teachers, Postsecondary; English Language and Literature Teachers, Postsecondary; Environmental Science Teachers, Postsecondary; Farm and Home Management Advisors; Foreign Language and Literature Teachers, Postsecondary; Forestry and Conservation Science Teachers, Postsecondary; Geography Teachers, Postsecondary; Graduate Teaching Assistants; Health Specialties Teachers, Postsecondary; History Teachers, Postsecondary; Home Economics Teachers, Postsecondary; Law Teachers, Postsecondary; Library Science Teachers, Postsecondary; Mathematical Science Teachers, Postsecondary; Nursing Instructors and Teachers, Postsecondary; Philosophy and Religion Teachers, Postsecondary; Physics Teachers, Postsecondary; Political Science Teachers, Postsecondary; Psychology Teachers, Postsecondary; Recreation and Fitness Studies Teachers, Postsecondary; Self-Enrichment Education Teachers; Social Work Teachers, Postsecondary; Sociology Teachers, Postsecondary; Vocational Education Teachers, Postsecondary.

Skills: Instructing; Writing; Persuasion; Learning Strategies; Monitoring; Speaking.

Education and Training Programs: Communication Studies/Speech Communication and Rhetoric; Mass Communication/Media Studies; Journalism; Broadcast Journalism; Journalism, Other; Radio and Television; Digital Communication and Media/Multimedia; Public Relations/Image Management; Advertising; Political Communication; Health Communication; Communication, Journalism, and Related Programs, Other. **Related Knowledge/Courses:** Communications and Media; Education and Training; Philosophy and Theology; Sociology and Anthropology; English Language; History and Archeology.

Work Environment: Indoors; sitting.

Computer Science Teachers, Postsecondary

- ❊ Education/Training Required: Doctoral degree
- ❊ Annual Earnings: $57,620
- ❊ Beginning Wage: $32,130
- ❊ Earnings Growth Potential: Very high
- ❊ Growth: 22.9%
- ❊ Annual Job Openings: 237,478
- ❊ Self-Employed: 0.4%
- ❊ Part-Time: 27.8%

Our sources did not provide separate job openings data for this occupation. The job openings listed here are shared with 35 other postsecondary teaching occupations. For a complete list, see the beginning of this section.

Industries with Greatest Employment: Educational Services, Public and Private.

Highest-Growth Industries (Projected Growth for This Job): Administrative and Support Services (48.3%); Amusement, Gambling, and Recreation Industries (45.3%); Social Assistance (38.6%); Support Activities for Transportation (32.8%); Religious,

Grantmaking, Civic, Professional, and Similar Organizations (29.9%); Professional, Scientific, and Technical Services (28.8%); Management of Companies and Enterprises (26.8%); Educational Services, Public and Private (22.9%); Hospitals, Public and Private (21.4%); Personal and Laundry Services (21.0%).

Lowest-Growth Industries (Projected Growth for This Job): Other Information Services (7.4%); Sporting Goods, Hobby, Book, and Music Stores (13.3%); Performing Arts, Spectator Sports, and Related Industries (13.4%); Insurance Carriers and Related Activities (13.9%).

Fastest-Growing Metropolitan Areas (Recent Growth for This Job): Virginia Beach–Norfolk–Newport News, VA–NC (23.1%); Scranton–Wilkes-Barre, PA (20.0%); Indianapolis–Carmel, IN (20.0%); Joplin, MO (20.0%); Portland–Vancouver–Beaverton, OR–WA (18.0%).

Other Considerations for Job Security: Retirements of current postsecondary teachers should create numerous openings for all types of postsecondary teachers, so job opportunities are generally expected to be very good. However, because students attend postsecondary institutions to prepare themselves for careers, the best job prospects for postsecondary teachers are likely to be in rapidly growing fields that offer many nonacademic career options. Computer science courses are commonly required as part of many business, science, and technology majors. Community colleges and other institutions offering career and technical education have been among the most rapidly growing and are expected to offer some of the best opportunities for postsecondary teachers.

Teach courses in computer science. May specialize in a field of computer science, such as the design and function of computers or operations and research analysis. Evaluate and grade students' classwork, laboratory work, assignments, and papers. Maintain student attendance records, grades, and other required records. Prepare and deliver lectures to undergraduate and/or graduate students on topics such as programming, data structures, and software design. Prepare course materials such as syllabi, homework assignments, and handouts. Compile, administer, and grade examinations or assign this work to others. Keep abreast of developments in their field by reading current literature, talking with colleagues, and participating in professional conferences. Initiate, facilitate, and moderate classroom discussions. Plan, evaluate, and revise curricula, course content, course materials, and methods of instruction. Supervise students' laboratory work. Maintain regularly scheduled office hours to advise and assist students. Select and obtain materials and supplies such as textbooks and laboratory equipment. Advise students on academic and vocational curricula and on career issues. Participate in student recruitment, registration, and placement activities. Collaborate with colleagues to address teaching and research issues. Serve on academic or administrative committees that deal with institutional policies, departmental matters, and academic issues. Act as advisers to student organizations. Supervise undergraduate and/or graduate teaching, internships, and research work. Perform administrative duties such as serving as department head. Conduct research in a particular field of knowledge and publish findings in professional journals, books, and/or electronic media. Direct research of other teachers or of graduate students working for advanced academic degrees. Provide professional consulting services to government and/or industry. Participate in campus and community events. Compile bibliographies of specialized materials for outside reading assignments. Write grant proposals to procure external research funding.

Personality Type: Investigative.

GOE—Interest Area: 05. Education and Training. **Work Group:** 05.03. Postsecondary and Adult Teaching and Instructing. **Other Jobs in this Work Group:** Adult Literacy, Remedial Education, and GED Teachers and Instructors; Agricultural Sciences Teachers, Postsecondary; Anthropology and Archeology Teachers, Postsecondary; Architecture Teachers, Postsecondary; Area, Ethnic, and Cultural Studies Teachers, Postsecondary; Art, Drama, and Music Teachers, Postsecondary; Atmospheric, Earth, Marine, and Space Sciences Teachers, Postsecondary; Biological Science Teachers, Postsecondary; Business Teachers, Postsecondary; Chemistry Teachers, Postsecondary; Communications Teachers, Postsecondary; Criminal Justice and Law Enforcement Teachers, Postsecondary; Economics Teachers, Postsecondary; Education Teachers, Postsecondary; Engineering Teachers, Postsecondary; English Language and Literature Teachers, Postsecondary; Environmental Science Teachers, Postsecondary; Farm and Home Management Advisors; Foreign Language and Literature Teachers, Postsecondary; Forestry and Conservation Science Teachers, Postsecondary; Geography Teachers, Postsecondary; Graduate Teaching Assistants; Health Specialties Teachers, Postsecondary; History Teachers, Postsecondary; Home Economics Teachers, Postsecondary; Law Teachers, Postsecondary; Library Science Teachers, Postsecondary; Mathematical Science Teachers, Postsecondary; Nursing Instructors and Teachers, Postsecondary; Philosophy and Religion Teachers, Postsecondary; Physics Teachers, Postsecondary; Political Science Teachers, Postsecondary; Psychology Teachers, Postsecondary; Recreation and Fitness Studies Teachers, Postsecondary; Self-Enrichment Education Teachers; Social Work Teachers, Postsecondary; Sociology Teachers, Postsecondary; Vocational Education Teachers, Postsecondary.

Skills: Programming; Instructing; Technology Design; Operations Analysis; Mathematics; Learning Strategies.

Education and Training Programs: Computer and Information Sciences, General; Computer Programming/Programmer, General; Information Science/Studies; Computer Systems Analysis/Analyst; Computer Science. **Related Knowledge/Courses:** Computers and Electronics; Education and Training; Telecommunications; Mathematics; Engineering and Technology; English Language.

Work Environment: Indoors; sitting.

Computer Security Specialists

* Education/Training Required: Bachelor's degree
* Annual Earnings: $62,130
* Beginning Wage: $38,610
* Earnings Growth Potential: Very high
* Growth: 27.0%
* Annual Job Openings: 37,010
* Self-Employed: 0.4%
* Part-Time: 3.1%

Our sources did not provide separate job openings data for this occupation. The job openings listed here are shared with Network and Computer Systems Administrators.

Industries with Greatest Employment: Professional, Scientific, and Technical Services; Educational Services, Public and Private; Management of Companies and Enterprises; Telecommunications; Credit Intermediation and Related Activities.

Highest-Growth Industries (Projected Growth for This Job): Amusement, Gambling, and Recreation Industries (66.1%); Social Assistance (58.3%); Securities, Commodity Contracts, and Other Financial Investments and Related Activities (58.2%); Internet Publishing and Broadcasting (54.3%); Museums, Historical Sites, and Similar Institutions (49.6%); Professional, Scientific, and Technical Services (47.2%); Warehousing and Storage (46.9%); Personal and Laundry Services (40.4%); Lessors of Nonfinancial Intangible Assets (except Copyrighted Works) (40.1%); Building Material and Garden Equipment and Supplies Dealers (39.8%); Waste Management and Remediation Services (39.7%); Administrative and Support Services (39.0%); Ambulatory Health Care Services (38.7%); Performing Arts, Spectator Sports, and Related Industries (38.0%); Nursing and Residential Care Facilities (37.4%); Support Activities for Transportation (34.5%); Water Transportation (33.7%); Real Estate (32.9%); Nonstore Retailers (31.7%); Religious, Grantmaking, Civic, Professional, and Similar Organizations (30.4%); others.

Lowest-Growth Industries (Projected Growth for This Job): Apparel Manufacturing (–51.5%); Textile Mills (–23.5%); Primary Metal Manufacturing (–20.6%); Petroleum and Coal Products Manufacturing (–16.8%); Paper Manufacturing (–15.8%); Printing and Related Support Activities (–12.8%); Electronics and Appliance Stores (–10.4%); Electrical Equipment, Appliance, and Component Manufacturing (–6.2%); Machinery Manufacturing (–5.5%); Rail Transportation (–5.5%).

Fastest-Growing Metropolitan Areas (Recent Growth for This Job): Billings, MT (150.0%); Altoona, PA (125.0%); Jackson, MS (113.8%); Dalton, GA (100.0%); Lawton, OK (75.0%).

Other Considerations for Job Security: Strong employment growth combined with a limited supply of qualified workers will result in excellent employment prospects for this occupation and a high demand for their skills. Demand for computer security specialists will grow as businesses and government continue to invest heavily in "cyber security," protecting vital computer networks and electronic infrastructures from attack. Job prospects should be best for college graduates with the latest technological skills, particularly graduates who have supplemented their formal education with relevant work experience. Employers will continue to seek computer specialists who possess strong fundamental computer skills combined with good interpersonal and communication skills. Due to the demand for computer support specialists and systems administrators over the next decade, those with strong computer skills but no college degree should continue to qualify for some entry-level positions.

Plan, coordinate, and implement security measures for information systems to regulate access to computer data files and prevent unauthorized modification, destruction, or disclosure of information. Train users and promote security awareness to ensure system security and to improve server and network efficiency. Develop plans to safeguard computer files against accidental or unauthorized modification, destruction, or disclosure and to meet emergency data-processing needs. Confer with users to discuss issues such as computer data access needs, security violations, and programming changes. Monitor current reports of computer viruses to determine when to update virus protection systems. Modify computer security files to incorporate new software, correct errors, or change individual access status. Coordinate implementation of computer system plan with establishment personnel and outside vendors. Monitor use of data files and regulate access to safeguard information in computer files. Perform risk assessments and execute tests of data-processing system to ensure functioning of data-processing activities and security measures. Encrypt data transmissions and erect firewalls to conceal confidential information as it is being transmitted and to keep out tainted digital transfers. Document computer security and emergency measures policies, procedures, and tests. Review violations of computer security procedures and discuss procedures with violators to ensure that violations aren't repeated. Maintain permanent fleet cryptologic and carry-on direct support systems required in special land, sea surface, and subsurface operations.

Personality Type: Investigative.

GOE—Interest Area: 11. Information Technology. **Work Group:** 11.02. Information Technology Specialties. **Other Jobs in this Work Group:** Computer and Information Scientists, Research; Computer Operators; Computer Programmers; Computer Software Engineers, Applications; Computer Software Engineers, Systems Software; Computer Support Specialists; Computer Systems Analysts; Computer Systems Engineers/Architects; Database Administrators; Network Designers; Network Systems and Data Communications Analysts; Software Quality Assurance Engineers and Testers; Web Administrators; Web Developers.

Skills: Systems Evaluation; Systems Analysis; Programming; Installation; Management of Material Resources; Operations Analysis.

Education and Training Programs: Computer and Information Sciences, General; Information Science/Studies; Computer Systems Analysis/Analyst;

Computer Systems Networking and Telecommunications; System Administration/Administrator; System, Networking, and LAN/WAN Management/Manager; Computer and Information Systems Security; Computer and Information Sciences and Support Services, Other. **Related Knowledge/Courses:** Computers and Electronics; Telecommunications; Engineering and Technology; Design; Education and Training; Communications and Media.

Work Environment: Indoors; sitting.

Computer Systems Analysts

* Education/Training Required: Bachelor's degree
* Annual Earnings: $69,760
* Beginning Wage: $42,780
* Earnings Growth Potential: Very high
* Growth: 29.0%
* Annual Job Openings: 63,166
* Self-Employed: 5.8%
* Part-Time: 5.6%

Industries with Greatest Employment: Professional, Scientific, and Technical Services; Management of Companies and Enterprises; Insurance Carriers and Related Activities; Educational Services, Public and Private; Merchant Wholesalers, Durable Goods.

Highest-Growth Industries (Projected Growth for This Job): Amusement, Gambling, and Recreation Industries (63.0%); Social Assistance (60.3%); Securities, Commodity Contracts, and Other Financial Investments and Related Activities (58.4%); Internet Publishing and Broadcasting (54.3%); Museums, Historical Sites, and Similar Institutions (51.0%); Professional, Scientific, and Technical Services (49.6%); Warehousing and Storage (46.9%); Personal and Laundry Services (44.0%); Waste Management and Remediation Services (42.6%); Funds, Trusts, and Other Financial Vehicles (40.3%); Lessors of Nonfinancial Intangible Assets (Except Copyrighted Works) (40.1%); Administrative and Support

Services (38.6%); Ambulatory Health Care Services (38.0%); Nonstore Retailers (36.5%); Internet Service Providers, Web Search Portals, and Data Processing Services (36.3%); Support Activities for Transportation (35.4%); Publishing Industries (Except Internet) (34.7%); Nursing and Residential Care Facilities (32.7%); Real Estate (31.2%); Performing Arts, Spectator Sports, and Related Industries (31.1%); others.

Lowest-Growth Industries (Projected Growth for This Job): Crop Production (–27.1%); Pipeline Transportation (–26.2%); Primary Metal Manufacturing (–22.3%); Paper Manufacturing (–17.6%); Petroleum and Coal Products Manufacturing (–16.9%); Electronics and Appliance Stores (–13.3%); Printing and Related Support Activities (–12.9%); Computer and Electronic Product Manufacturing (–8.8%); Miscellaneous Store Retailers (–8.0%); Rail Transportation (–8.0%).

Fastest-Growing Metropolitan Areas (Recent Growth for This Job): Tyler, TX (100.0%); Kalamazoo–Portage, MI (77.8%); Appleton, WI (71.4%); Rochester, MN (71.4%); Springfield, IL (63.0%).

Other Considerations for Job Security: Job prospects should be very good. Job growth won't be as rapid as during the preceding decade, however, as the information technology sector matures and as routine work is increasingly outsourced offshore to foreign countries with lower prevailing wages. Individuals with an advanced degree in computer science or computer engineering or with an MBA with a concentration in information systems should have the best prospects. College graduates with a bachelor's degree in computer science, computer engineering, information science, or management information systems also should enjoy very good prospects, particularly if they have supplemented their formal education with practical experience.

Analyze science, engineering, business, and all other data-processing problems for application to electronic data-processing systems. Analyze user requirements, procedures, and problems to automate or improve existing systems and review computer system capabilities, workflow, **and scheduling limitations. May analyze or recommend commercially available software. May supervise computer programmers.** Provide staff and users with assistance solving computer-related problems, such as malfunctions and program problems. Test, maintain, and monitor computer programs and systems, including coordinating the installation of computer programs and systems. Use object-oriented programming languages as well as client/server application development processes and multimedia and Internet technology. Confer with clients regarding the nature of the information processing or computation needs a computer program is to address. Coordinate and link computer systems within an organization to increase compatibility and so information can be shared. Consult with management to ensure agreement on system principles. Expand or modify system to serve new purposes or improve workflow. Interview or survey workers, observe job performance, or perform the job to determine what information is processed and how it is processed. Determine computer software or hardware needed to set up or alter system. Train staff and users to work with computer systems and programs. Analyze information processing or computation needs and plan and design computer systems, using techniques such as structured analysis, data modeling, and information engineering. Assess the usefulness of pre-developed application packages and adapt them to a user environment. Define the goals of the system and devise flow charts and diagrams describing logical operational steps of programs. Develop, document, and revise system design procedures, test procedures, and quality standards. Review and analyze computer printouts and performance indicators to locate code problems; correct errors by correcting codes. Recommend new equipment or software packages. Read manuals, periodicals, and technical reports to learn how to develop programs that meet staff and user requirements. Supervise computer programmers or other systems analysts or serve as project leaders for particular systems projects. Utilize computers in the analysis and solution of business problems such as development of integrated production and inventory control and cost-analysis systems.

Personality Type: Investigative.

GOE—Interest Area: 11. Information Technology. **Work Group:** 11.02. Information Technology Specialties. **Other Jobs in this Work Group:** Computer and Information Scientists, Research; Computer Operators; Computer Programmers; Computer Security Specialists; Computer Software Engineers, Applications; Computer Software Engineers, Systems Software; Computer Support Specialists; Computer Systems Engineers/Architects; Database Administrators; Network Designers; Network Systems and Data Communications Analysts; Software Quality Assurance Engineers and Testers; Web Administrators; Web Developers.

Skills: Installation; Quality Control Analysis; Systems Analysis; Programming; Technology Design; Troubleshooting.

Education and Training Programs: Computer and Information Sciences, General; Information Technology; Computer Systems Analysis/Analyst; Web/Multimedia Management and Webmaster. **Related Knowledge/Courses:** Computers and Electronics; Telecommunications; Design; Customer and Personal Service; Law and Government; Communications and Media.

Work Environment: Indoors; sitting.

Computer, Automated Teller, and Office Machine Repairers

- ❋ Education/Training Required: Postsecondary vocational training
- ❋ Annual Earnings: $36,480
- ❋ Beginning Wage: $22,150
- ❋ Earnings Growth Potential: Very high
- ❋ Growth: 3.0%
- ❋ Annual Job Openings: 22,330
- ❋ Self-Employed: 19.7%
- ❋ Part-Time: 9.0%

Industries with Greatest Employment: Merchant Wholesalers, Durable Goods; Electronics and Appliance Stores; Repair and Maintenance; Professional, Scientific, and Technical Services; Miscellaneous Store Retailers.

Highest-Growth Industries (Projected Growth for This Job): Professional, Scientific, and Technical Services (32.3%); Warehousing and Storage (30.0%); Personal and Laundry Services (26.4%); Administrative and Support Services (25.2%); Ambulatory Health Care Services (20.0%); Internet Service Providers, Web Search Portals, and Data Processing Services (19.3%); Rental and Leasing Services (18.8%); Publishing Industries (except Internet) (17.3%).

Lowest-Growth Industries (Projected Growth for This Job): Computer and Electronic Product Manufacturing (–31.4%); Printing and Related Support Activities (–22.9%); Chemical Manufacturing (–21.5%); Electronics and Appliance Stores (–20.8%); Miscellaneous Store Retailers (–19.5%); Machinery Manufacturing (–16.0%); Fabricated Metal Product Manufacturing (–11.7%); Repair and Maintenance (–11.3%); Specialty Trade Contractors (2.6%); Telecommunications (2.6%).

Fastest-Growing Metropolitan Areas (Recent Growth for This Job): Florence, SC (166.7%); Greensboro–High Point, NC (141.2%); Rocky Mount, NC (125.0%); Rochester, MN (122.2%); Asheville, NC (100.0%).

Other Considerations for Job Security: In addition to new job growth, a number of openings will result from the need to replace workers who retire or leave the occupation. Job prospects will be best for applicants with knowledge of electronics, formal training, and repair experience. Although computer equipment continues to become less expensive and more reliable, malfunctions still occur and can cause severe problems for users, most of whom lack the knowledge to make repairs. The relatively slow rate at which new ATMs are installed, and the fact that they are becoming easier to repair, will limit demand for ATM repairers. Because office machines are becoming more reliable, job growth in office machine repairers will be limited as well.

Repair, maintain, or install computers; word-processing systems; automated teller machines; and electronic office machines, such as duplicating and fax machines. Converse with customers to determine details of equipment problems. Reassemble machines after making repairs or replacing parts. Travel to customers' stores or offices to service machines or to provide emergency repair service. Reinstall software programs or adjust settings on existing software to fix machine malfunctions. Advise customers concerning equipment operation, maintenance, and programming. Assemble machines according to specifications, using hand tools, power tools, and measuring devices. Test new systems to ensure that they are in working order. Operate machines to test functioning of parts and mechanisms. Maintain records of equipment maintenance work and repairs. Install and configure new equipment, including operating software and peripheral equipment. Maintain parts inventories and order any additional parts needed for repairs. Update existing equipment, performing tasks such as installing updated circuit boards or additional memory. Test components and circuits of faulty equipment to locate defects, using oscilloscopes, signal generators, ammeters, voltmeters, or special diagnostic software programs. Align, adjust, and calibrate equipment according to specifications. Repair, adjust, or replace electrical and mechanical components and parts by using hand tools, power tools, and soldering or welding equipment. Complete repair bills, shop records, time cards, and expense reports. Disassemble machine to examine parts such as wires, gears, and bearings for wear and defects by using hand tools, power tools, and measuring devices. Clean, oil, and adjust mechanical parts to maintain machines' operating efficiency and to prevent breakdowns. Enter information into computers to copy programs from one electronic component to another or to draw, modify, or store schematics. Read specifications such as blueprints, charts, and schematics to determine machine settings and adjustments. Lay cable and hook up electrical connections between machines, power sources, and phone lines. Analyze equipment performance records to assess equipment functioning.

Personality Type: Realistic.

GOE—Interest Area: 11. Information Technology. **Work Group:** 11.03. Digital Equipment Repair. **Other Jobs in this Work Group:** Coin, Vending, and Amusement Machine Servicers and Repairers.

Skills: Installation; Repairing; Troubleshooting; Equipment Maintenance; Management of Material Resources; Programming.

Education and Training Programs: Business Machine Repair; Computer Installation and Repair Technology/Technician. **Related Knowledge/Courses:** Computers and Electronics; Telecommunications; Mechanical Devices; Customer and Personal Service; Engineering and Technology; Sales and Marketing.

Work Environment: Indoors; sitting; using hands on objects, tools, or controls; repetitive motions.

Correctional Officers and Jailers

* Education/Training Required: Moderate-term on-the-job training
* Annual Earnings: $35,760
* Beginning Wage: $23,600
* Earnings Growth Potential: Very high
* Growth: 16.9%
* Annual Job Openings: 56,579
* Self-Employed: 0.0%
* Part-Time: 1.8%

Industries with Greatest Employment: Administrative and Support Services.

Highest-Growth Industries (Projected Growth for This Job): Administrative and Support Services (49.8%); Nursing and Residential Care Facilities (17.6%).

Lowest-Growth Industries (Projected Growth for This Job): Hospitals, Public and Private (–21.3%).

Fastest-Growing Metropolitan Areas (Recent Growth for This Job): San Diego–Carlsbad–San Marcos, CA (67.9%); Jackson, MS (65.4%);

Morgantown, WV (56.5%); San Francisco–Oakland–Fremont, CA (52.9%); Omaha–Council Bluffs, NE–IA (44.2%).

Other Considerations for Job Security: Job opportunities for correctional officers are expected to be excellent. The need to replace correctional officers who transfer to other occupations, retire, or leave the labor force, coupled with rising employment demand, will generate thousands of job openings each year. This situation is expected to continue. Layoffs of correctional officers are rare because of increasing offender populations.

Guard inmates in penal or rehabilitative institution in accordance with established regulations and procedures. May guard prisoners in transit between jail, courtroom, prison, or other point. Includes deputy sheriffs and police who spend most of their time guarding prisoners in correctional institutions. Monitor conduct of prisoners according to established policies, regulations, and procedures to prevent escape or violence. Inspect conditions of locks, window bars, grills, doors, and gates at correctional facilities to ensure that they will prevent escapes. Search prisoners, cells, and vehicles for weapons, valuables, or drugs. Guard facility entrances to screen visitors. Search for and recapture escapees. Inspect mail for the presence of contraband. Take prisoners into custody and escort to locations within and outside of facility, such as visiting room, courtroom, or airport. Record information such as prisoner identification, charges, and incidences of inmate disturbance. Use weapons, handcuffs, and physical force to maintain discipline and order among prisoners. Conduct fire, safety, and sanitation inspections. Provide to supervisors oral and written reports of the quality and quantity of work performed by inmates, inmate disturbances and rule violations, and unusual occurrences. Settle disputes between inmates. Drive passenger vehicles and trucks used to transport inmates to other institutions, courtrooms, hospitals, and work sites. Arrange daily schedules for prisoners, including library visits, work assignments, family visits, and counseling appointments. Assign duties to inmates, providing instructions as needed. Issue clothing, tools, and other authorized items to inmates. Serve meals and distribute commissary items to prisoners. Investigate crimes that have occurred within an institution or assist police in their investigations of crimes and inmates. Maintain records of prisoners' identification and charges. Supervise and coordinate work of other correctional service officers. Sponsor inmate recreational activities such as newspapers and self-help groups.

Personality Type: Realistic.

GOE—Interest Area: 12. Law and Public Safety. **Work Group:** 12.04. Law Enforcement and Public Safety. **Other Jobs in this Work Group:** Bailiffs; Criminal Investigators and Special Agents; Detectives and Criminal Investigators; Fire Investigators; Forensic Science Technicians; Parking Enforcement Workers; Police and Sheriff's Patrol Officers; Police Detectives; Police Identification and Records Officers; Police Patrol Officers; Sheriffs and Deputy Sheriffs; Transit and Railroad Police.

Skills: Social Perceptiveness; Persuasion; Negotiation; Writing; Speaking; Monitoring.

Education and Training Programs: Corrections; Juvenile Corrections; Corrections and Criminal Justice, Other. **Related Knowledge/Courses:** Psychology; Public Safety and Security; Law and Government; Philosophy and Theology; Sociology and Anthropology; Therapy and Counseling.

Work Environment: More often indoors than outdoors; noisy; contaminants; disease or infections; standing.

Counseling Psychologists

* Education/Training Required: Doctoral degree
* Annual Earnings: $59,440
* Beginning Wage: $35,280
* Earnings Growth Potential: Very high
* Growth: 15.8%
* Annual Job Openings: 8,309
* Self-Employed: 34.2%
* Part-Time: 24.0%

Our sources did not provide separate job openings data for this occupation. The job openings listed here are shared with Clinical Psychologists and with School Psychologists.

Industries with Greatest Employment: Educational Services, Public and Private; Ambulatory Health Care Services; Hospitals, Public and Private; Social Assistance.

Highest-Growth Industries (Projected Growth for This Job): Social Assistance (56.2%); Professional, Scientific, and Technical Services (34.6%); Ambulatory Health Care Services (26.8%); Nursing and Residential Care Facilities (24.8%); Funds, Trusts, and Other Financial Vehicles (23.3%); Religious, Grantmaking, Civic, Professional, and Similar Organizations (19.4%); Management of Companies and Enterprises (15.2%).

Lowest-Growth Industries (Projected Growth for This Job): Hospitals, Public and Private (–3.5%); Educational Services, Public and Private (6.9%).

Fastest-Growing Metropolitan Areas (Recent Growth for This Job): Augusta–Richmond County, GA–SC (100.0%); Memphis, TN–MS–AR (100.0%); Peoria, IL (90.0%); Greenville, SC (87.5%); Oklahoma City, OK (86.2%).

Other Considerations for Job Security: Job prospects should be the best for people with a doctorate from a leading university. Master's degree holders will face keen competition for jobs. The rise in health-care costs associated with unhealthy lifestyles, such as smoking, alcoholism, and obesity, has made prevention and treatment more critical. An increase in the number of employee assistance programs, which help workers deal with personal problems, also should lead to employment growth for clinical and counseling specialties. Clinical and counseling psychologists also will be needed to help people deal with depression and other mental disorders, marriage and family problems, job stress, and addiction. The growing number of elderly will increase the demand for psychologists trained in geropsychology to help people deal with the mental and physical changes that occur as individuals grow older. There also will be increased need for psychologists to work with returning veterans.

Assess and evaluate individuals' problems through the use of case history, interview, and observation and provide individual or group counseling services to assist individuals in achieving more effective personal, social, educational, and vocational development and adjustment. Collect information about individuals or clients, using interviews, case histories, observational techniques, and other assessment methods. Counsel individuals, groups, or families to help them understand problems, define goals, and develop realistic action plans. Develop therapeutic and treatment plans based on clients' interests, abilities, and needs. Consult with other professionals to discuss therapies, treatments, counseling resources, or techniques and to share occupational information. Analyze data such as interview notes, test results, and reference manuals to identify symptoms and to diagnose the nature of clients' problems. Advise clients on how counseling could help them. Evaluate the results of counseling methods to determine the reliability and validity of treatments. Provide consulting services to schools, social service agencies, and businesses. Refer clients to specialists or to other institutions for noncounseling treatment of problems. Select, administer, and interpret psychological tests to assess intelligence, aptitudes, abilities, or interests. Conduct research to develop or improve diagnostic or therapeutic counseling techniques.

Personality Type: Social.

GOE—Interest Area: 10. Human Service. **Work Group:** 10.01. Counseling and Social Work. **Other Jobs in this Work Group:** Child, Family, and School Social Workers; Clinical Psychologists; Clinical, Counseling, and School Psychologists; Marriage and Family Therapists; Medical and Public Health Social Workers; Mental Health and Substance Abuse Social Workers; Mental Health Counselors; Probation Officers and Correctional Treatment Specialists; Rehabilitation Counselors; Residential Advisors; Social and Human Service Assistants; Substance Abuse and Behavioral Disorder Counselors.

Skills: Social Perceptiveness; Active Listening; Persuasion; Service Orientation; Negotiation; Monitoring.

Education and Training Programs: Psychology, General; Clinical Psychology; Counseling Psychology; Developmental and Child Psychology; School Psychology; Clinical Child Psychology; Psychoanalysis and Psychotherapy. **Related Knowledge/Courses:** Therapy and Counseling; Philosophy and Theology; Sociology and Anthropology; Psychology; English Language; Customer and Personal Service.

Work Environment: Indoors; sitting.

Court Reporters

- ✸ Education/Training Required: Postsecondary vocational training
- ✸ Annual Earnings: $45,610
- ✸ Beginning Wage: $23,430
- ✸ Earnings Growth Potential: Very high
- ✸ Growth: 24.5%
- ✸ Annual Job Openings: 2,620
- ✸ Self-Employed: 7.9%
- ✸ Part-Time: 13.6%

Industries with Greatest Employment: Administrative and Support Services.

Highest-Growth Industries (Projected Growth for This Job): Administrative and Support Services (56.3%).

Lowest-Growth Industries (Projected Growth for This Job): None met the criteria.

Fastest-Growing Metropolitan Areas (Recent Growth for This Job): Atlanta–Sandy Springs–Marietta, GA (147.4%); Baton Rouge, LA (36.4%); Cedar Rapids, IA (33.3%); Oklahoma City, OK (27.3%).

Other Considerations for Job Security: Job opportunities should be excellent, especially for those with certification. Demand for court reporter services will be spurred by the continuing need for accurate transcription of proceedings in courts and in pretrial depositions, by the growing need to create captions for live television, and by the need to provide other real-time broadcast captioning and translating services for the deaf and hard of hearing.

Use verbatim methods and equipment to capture, store, retrieve, and transcribe pretrial and trial proceedings or other information. Includes stenocaptioners who operate computerized stenographic captioning equipment to provide captions of live or prerecorded broadcasts for hearing-impaired viewers. Take notes in shorthand or use a stenotype or shorthand machine that prints letters on a paper tape. Provide transcripts of proceedings upon request of judges, lawyers, or the public. Record verbatim proceedings of courts, legislative assemblies, committee meetings, and other proceedings, using computerized recording equipment, electronic stenograph machines, or stenomasks. Transcribe recorded proceedings in accordance with established formats. Ask speakers to clarify inaudible statements. File a legible transcript of records of a court case with the court clerk's office. File and store shorthand notes of court session. Respond to requests during court sessions to read portions of the proceedings already recorded. Record depositions and other proceedings for attorneys. Verify accuracy of transcripts by checking copies against original records of proceedings and accuracy of rulings by checking with judges. Record symbols on computer disks or CD-ROM; then translate and display them as text in computer-aided transcription process.

Personality Type: Artistic.

GOE—Interest Area: 07. Government and Public Administration. **Work Group:** 07.04. Public Administration Clerical Support. **Other Jobs in this Work Group:** Court Clerks; Court, Municipal, and License Clerks; License Clerks; Municipal Clerks.

Skills: Reading Comprehension; Active Listening; Equipment Selection; Operation and Control; Equipment Maintenance; Operation Monitoring.

Education and Training Program: Court Reporting/Court Reporter. **Related Knowledge/Courses:** Clerical Studies; English Language; Law and Government; Computers and Electronics; Production and Processing; Customer and Personal Service.

Work Environment: Indoors; noisy; sitting; using hands on objects, tools, or controls; repetitive motions.

Criminal Investigators and Special Agents

- ❋ Education/Training Required: Work experience in a related occupation
- ❋ Annual Earnings: $58,260
- ❋ Beginning Wage: $34,480
- ❋ Earnings Growth Potential: Very high
- ❋ Growth: 17.3%
- ❋ Annual Job Openings: 14,746
- ❋ Self-Employed: 0.3%
- ❋ Part-Time: 2.2%

Our sources did not provide separate job openings data for this occupation. The job openings listed here are shared with Immigration and Customs Inspectors; Police Detectives; and Police Identification and Records Officers.

Industries with Greatest Employment: Educational Services, Public and Private.

Highest-Growth Industries (Projected Growth for This Job): None met the criteria.

Lowest-Growth Industries (Projected Growth for This Job): Educational Services, Public and Private (11.9%).

Fastest-Growing Metropolitan Areas (Recent Growth for This Job): Brownsville–Harlingen, TX (366.7%); Las Cruces, NM (350.0%); Bellingham, WA (183.3%); Jackson, MS (172.7%); Tucson, AZ (121.3%).

Other Considerations for Job Security: Overall, opportunities in local police departments will be excellent for individuals who meet the psychological, personal, and physical qualifications. Competition for jobs in federal and state law-enforcement agencies will be higher than for jobs in local agencies. Less competition for jobs will occur in departments that offer relatively low salaries or those in urban communities where the crime rate is relatively high. Applicants with military experience or college training in police science will have the best opportunities in local and state departments. Applicants with a bachelor's degree and several years of law-enforcement or military experience, especially investigative experience, will have the best opportunities in federal agencies. The level of government spending determines the level of employment for police and detectives, but layoffs are rare because retirements enable most staffing cuts to be handled through attrition.

Investigate alleged or suspected criminal violations of federal, state, or local laws to determine whether evidence is sufficient to recommend prosecution. Record evidence and documents, using equipment such as cameras and photocopy machines. Obtain and verify evidence by interviewing and observing suspects and witnesses or by analyzing records. Examine records to locate links in chains of evidence or information. Prepare reports that detail investigation findings. Determine scope, timing, and direction of investigations. Collaborate with other offices and agencies to exchange information and coordinate activities. Testify before grand juries concerning criminal activity investigations. Analyze evidence in laboratories or in the field. Investigate organized crime, public corruption, financial crime, copyright infringement, civil rights violations, bank robbery, extortion, kidnapping, and other violations of federal or state statutes. Identify case issues and evidence needed, based on analysis of charges, complaints, or allegations of law violations. Obtain and use search and arrest warrants. Serve subpoenas or other official papers. Collaborate with other authorities on activities such as surveillance, transcription, and research. Develop relationships with informants to obtain information related to cases. Search for and collect evidence such as fingerprints, using investigative equipment. Collect and record physical information about arrested suspects, including fingerprints, height and weight measurements, and photographs. Compare crime scene fingerprints with those from suspects or fingerprint files to identify perpetrators, using computers. Administer counter-terrorism and counter-narcotics reward programs. Provide protection for individuals such as government leaders, political candidates, and visiting foreign dignitaries. Perform undercover assignments and maintain surveillance, including monitoring authorized wiretaps. Manage security programs designed to protect personnel, facilities, and information. Issue security clearances.

Personality Type: Enterprising.

GOE—Interest Area: 12. Law and Public Safety. **Work Group:** 12.04. Law Enforcement and Public Safety. **Other Jobs in this Work Group:** Bailiffs; Correctional Officers and Jailers; Detectives and Criminal Investigators; Fire Investigators; Forensic Science Technicians; Parking Enforcement Workers; Police and Sheriff's Patrol Officers; Police Detectives; Police Identification and Records Officers; Police Patrol Officers; Sheriffs and Deputy Sheriffs; Transit and Railroad Police.

Skills: Negotiation; Programming; Judgment and Decision Making; Operations Analysis; Service Orientation; Complex Problem Solving.

Education and Training Programs: Criminal Justice/Police Science; Criminalistics and Criminal Science. **Related Knowledge/Courses:** Law and Government; Psychology; Geography; Public Safety and Security; Clerical Studies; Telecommunications.

Work Environment: More often outdoors than indoors; noisy; very hot or cold; standing.

Criminal Justice and Law Enforcement Teachers, Postsecondary

* Education/Training Required: Doctoral degree
* Annual Earnings: $49,730
* Beginning Wage: $29,450
* Earnings Growth Potential: Very high
* Growth: 22.9%
* Annual Job Openings: 237,478
* Self-Employed: 0.4%
* Part-Time: 27.8%

Our sources did not provide separate job openings data for this occupation. The job openings listed here are shared with 35 other postsecondary teaching occupations. For a complete list, see the beginning of this section.

Industries with Greatest Employment: Educational Services, Public and Private.

Highest-Growth Industries (Projected Growth for This Job): Administrative and Support Services (48.3%); Amusement, Gambling, and Recreation Industries (45.3%); Social Assistance (38.6%); Support Activities for Transportation (32.8%); Religious, Grantmaking, Civic, Professional, and Similar Organizations (29.9%); Professional, Scientific, and Technical Services (28.8%); Management of Companies and Enterprises (26.8%); Educational Services, Public and Private (22.9%); Hospitals, Public and Private (21.4%); Personal and Laundry Services (21.0%).

Lowest-Growth Industries (Projected Growth for This Job): Other Information Services (7.4%);

Sporting Goods, Hobby, Book, and Music Stores (13.3%); Performing Arts, Spectator Sports, and Related Industries (13.4%); Insurance Carriers and Related Activities (13.9%).

Fastest-Growing Metropolitan Areas (Recent Growth for This Job): Houston–Sugar Land–Baytown, TX (33.3%); Milwaukee–Waukesha–West Allis, WI (25.0%); Greensboro–High Point, NC (20.0%); Boston–Cambridge–Quincy, MA–NH (20.0%); San Antonio, TX (16.7%).

Other Considerations for Job Security: Retirements of current postsecondary teachers should create numerous openings for all types of postsecondary teachers. However, because students attend postsecondary institutions to prepare themselves for careers, the best job prospects for postsecondary teachers are likely to be in rapidly growing fields that offer many nonacademic career options, such as criminal justice and law enforcement. Community colleges and other institutions offering career and technical education have been among the most rapidly growing and are expected to offer some of the best opportunities for postsecondary teachers.

Teach courses in criminal justice, corrections, and law-enforcement administration. Initiate, facilitate, and moderate classroom discussions. Keep abreast of developments in their field by reading current literature, talking with colleagues, and participating in professional conferences. Evaluate and grade students' classwork, assignments, and papers. Compile, administer, and grade examinations or assign this work to others. Prepare and deliver lectures to undergraduate or graduate students on topics such as criminal law, defensive policing, and investigation techniques. Prepare course materials such as syllabi, homework assignments, and handouts. Conduct research in a particular field of knowledge and publish findings in professional journals, books, and/or electronic media. Plan, evaluate, and revise curricula, course content, course materials, and methods of instruction. Supervise undergraduate and/or graduate teaching, internships, and research work. Maintain student attendance records, grades, and other required records. Select and obtain materials and supplies such as textbooks. Advise students on academic and vocational curricula and on career issues. Maintain regularly scheduled office hours to advise and assist students. Collaborate with colleagues to address teaching and research issues. Write grant proposals to procure external research funding. Serve on academic or administrative committees that deal with institutional policies, departmental matters, and academic issues. Compile bibliographies of specialized materials for outside reading assignments. Participate in student recruitment, registration, and placement activities. Provide professional consulting services to government and/or industry. Perform administrative duties such as serving as department head. Participate in campus and community events. Act as advisers to student organizations.

Personality Type: No data available.

GOE—Interest Area: 05. Education and Training. **Work Group:** 05.03. Postsecondary and Adult Teaching and Instructing. **Other Jobs in this Work Group:** Adult Literacy, Remedial Education, and GED Teachers and Instructors; Agricultural Sciences Teachers, Postsecondary; Anthropology and Archeology Teachers, Postsecondary; Architecture Teachers, Postsecondary; Area, Ethnic, and Cultural Studies Teachers, Postsecondary; Art, Drama, and Music Teachers, Postsecondary; Atmospheric, Earth, Marine, and Space Sciences Teachers, Postsecondary; Biological Science Teachers, Postsecondary; Business Teachers, Postsecondary; Chemistry Teachers, Postsecondary; Communications Teachers, Postsecondary; Computer Science Teachers, Postsecondary; Economics Teachers, Postsecondary; Education Teachers, Postsecondary; Engineering Teachers, Postsecondary; English Language and Literature Teachers, Postsecondary; Environmental Science Teachers, Postsecondary; Farm and Home Management Advisors; Foreign Language and Literature Teachers, Postsecondary; Forestry and Conservation Science Teachers, Postsecondary; Geography Teachers, Postsecondary; Graduate Teaching Assistants; Health Specialties Teachers, Postsecondary; History Teachers, Postsecondary; Home Economics Teachers, Postsecondary; Law Teachers, Postsecondary; Library Science Teachers, Postsecondary;

Mathematical Science Teachers, Postsecondary; Nursing Instructors and Teachers, Postsecondary; Philosophy and Religion Teachers, Postsecondary; Physics Teachers, Postsecondary; Political Science Teachers, Postsecondary; Psychology Teachers, Postsecondary; Recreation and Fitness Studies Teachers, Postsecondary; Self-Enrichment Education Teachers; Social Work Teachers, Postsecondary; Sociology Teachers, Postsecondary; Vocational Education Teachers, Postsecondary.

Skills: Writing; Critical Thinking; Instructing; Active Learning; Reading Comprehension; Persuasion.

Education and Training Programs: Teacher Education and Professional Development, Specific Subject Areas, Other; Corrections; Criminal Justice/Law Enforcement Administration; Criminal Justice/Safety Studies; Forensic Science and Technology; Criminal Justice/Police Science; Security and Loss Prevention Services; Juvenile Corrections; Criminalistics and Criminal Science; Corrections Administration; Corrections and Criminal Justice, Other. **Related Knowledge/Courses:** Sociology and Anthropology; Philosophy and Theology; History and Archeology; Law and Government; English Language; Education and Training.

Work Environment: Indoors; sitting.

Curators

- ❋ Education/Training Required: Master's degree
- ❋ Annual Earnings: $46,300
- ❋ Beginning Wage: $26,320
- ❋ Earnings Growth Potential: Very high
- ❋ Growth: 23.3%
- ❋ Annual Job Openings: 1,416
- ❋ Self-Employed: 1.3%
- ❋ Part-Time: 18.4%

Industries with Greatest Employment: Museums, Historical Sites, and Similar Institutions; Educational Services, Public and Private.

Highest-Growth Industries (Projected Growth for This Job): Museums, Historical Sites, and Similar Institutions (36.2%); Amusement, Gambling, and Recreation Industries (32.0%); Performing Arts, Spectator Sports, and Related Industries (22.4%).

Lowest-Growth Industries (Projected Growth for This Job): Other Information Services (–2.3%); Educational Services, Public and Private (12.0%); Religious, Grantmaking, Civic, Professional, and Similar Organizations (13.3%).

Fastest-Growing Metropolitan Areas (Recent Growth for This Job): Santa Barbara–Santa Maria, CA (200.0%); Louisville–Jefferson County, KY–IN (75.0%); Salt Lake City, UT (75.0%); Chicago–Naperville–Joliet, IL–IN–WI (71.4%); Worcester, MA–CT (66.7%).

Other Considerations for Job Security: Keen competition is expected because qualified applicants generally outnumber job openings. Curator jobs, in particular, are attractive to many people, and many applicants have the necessary training and subject knowledge. But because there are relatively few openings, candidates may have to work part time, as an intern, or even as a volunteer assistant curator or research associate after completing their formal education. Substantial work experience in collection management, research, exhibit design, or restoration, as well as database management skills, will be necessary for permanent status.

Administer affairs of museum and conduct research programs. Direct instructional, research, and public service activities of institution. Plan and organize the acquisition, storage, and exhibition of collections and related materials, including the selection of exhibition themes and designs. Develop and maintain an institution's registration, cataloging, and basic record-keeping systems, using computer databases. Provide information from the institution's holdings to other curators and to the public. Inspect premises to assess the need for repairs and to ensure that climate and pest-control issues are addressed. Train and supervise curatorial, fiscal, technical, research, and clerical staff, as well as volunteers or interns. Negotiate and authorize purchase, sale, exchange, or loan of collections. Plan and conduct special research projects in area of interest or expertise. Conduct or organize tours, workshops, and instructional sessions to acquaint individuals with an institution's facilities and materials. Confer with the board of directors to formulate and interpret policies, to determine budget requirements, and to plan overall operations. Attend meetings, conventions, and civic events to promote use of institution's services, to seek financing, and to maintain community alliances. Schedule events and organize details, including refreshment, entertainment, decorations, and the collection of any fees. Write and review grant proposals, journal articles, institutional reports, and publicity materials. Study, examine, and test acquisitions to authenticate their origin, composition, and history and to assess their current value. Arrange insurance coverage for objects on loan or for special exhibits and recommend changes in coverage for the entire collection. Establish specifications for reproductions and oversee their manufacture or select items from commercially available replica sources.

Personality Type: Artistic.

GOE—Interest Area: 05. Education and Training. **Work Group:** 05.05. Archival and Museum Services. **Other Jobs in this Work Group:** Archivists; Audio-Visual Collections Specialists; Museum Technicians and Conservators.

Skills: Management of Financial Resources; Management of Personnel Resources; Writing; Time Management; Speaking; Persuasion.

Education and Training Programs: Museology/Museum Studies; Art History, Criticism, and Conservation; Public/Applied History and Archival Administration. **Related Knowledge/Courses:** Fine Arts; History and Archeology; Clerical Studies; Sociology and Anthropology; Philosophy and Theology; Geography.

Work Environment: Indoors; sitting.

Database Administrators

- ❋ Education/Training Required: Bachelor's degree
- ❋ Annual Earnings: $64,670
- ❋ Beginning Wage: $37,350
- ❋ Earnings Growth Potential: Very high
- ❋ Growth: 28.6%
- ❋ Annual Job Openings: 8,258
- ❋ Self-Employed: 1.3%
- ❋ Part-Time: 5.3%

Industries with Greatest Employment: Professional, Scientific, and Technical Services; Educational Services, Public and Private; Management of Companies and Enterprises; Administrative and Support Services; Insurance Carriers and Related Activities.

Highest-Growth Industries (Projected Growth for This Job): Amusement, Gambling, and Recreation Industries (85.1%); Social Assistance (59.7%); Securities, Commodity Contracts, and Other Financial Investments and Related Activities (58.1%); Internet Publishing and Broadcasting (54.0%); Museums, Historical Sites, and Similar Institutions (49.3%); Professional, Scientific, and Technical Services (48.3%); Warehousing and Storage (46.9%); Waste Management and Remediation Services (43.1%); Administrative and Support Services (42.0%); Lessors of Nonfinancial Intangible Assets (Except Copyrighted Works) (40.2%); Funds, Trusts, and Other Financial Vehicles (39.8%); Ambulatory Health Care Services (37.2%); Support Activities for Transportation (36.4%); Nonstore Retailers (34.8%); Nursing and Residential Care Facilities (34.5%); Real Estate (33.2%); Religious, Grantmaking, Civic, Professional, and Similar Organizations (29.1%); Motion Picture, Video, and Sound Recording Industries (29.0%); Rental and Leasing Services (28.9%); Performing Arts, Spectator Sports, and Related Industries (28.2%); others.

Lowest-Growth Industries (Projected Growth for This Job): Pipeline Transportation (–26.8%);

Computer and Electronic Product Manufacturing (–13.8%); Electronics and Appliance Stores (–13.2%); Printing and Related Support Activities (–12.9%); Electrical Equipment, Appliance, and Component Manufacturing (–6.0%); Rail Transportation (–5.4%); Machinery Manufacturing (–4.3%); Fabricated Metal Product Manufacturing (–3.5%); Miscellaneous Store Retailers (–3.5%); Monetary Authorities–Central Bank (–3.5%).

Fastest-Growing Metropolitan Areas (Recent Growth for This Job): Santa Fe, NM (100.0%); Salt Lake City, UT (81.5%); Lynchburg, VA (75.0%); Naples–Marco Island, FL (75.0%); Salinas, CA (75.0%).

Other Considerations for Job Security: Database administrators are projected to be one of the fastest growing occupations over the next decade. Strong employment growth combined with a limited supply of qualified workers will result in excellent employment prospects for this occupation and a high demand for their skills. Expansion of electronic commerce—doing business on the Internet—and the continuing need to build and maintain databases that store critical information on customers, inventory, and projects are fueling demand for database administrators familiar with the latest technology. Individuals with an advanced degree in computer science or computer engineering or with an MBA with a concentration in information systems should enjoy favorable employment prospects. College graduates with a bachelor's degree in computer science, computer engineering, information science, or MIS also should enjoy favorable prospects, particularly if they have supplemented their formal education with practical experience.

Coordinate changes to computer databases; test and implement the database, applying knowledge of database management systems. May plan, coordinate, and implement security measures to safeguard computer databases. Develop standards and guidelines to guide the use and acquisition of software and to protect vulnerable information. Modify existing databases and database management systems or direct programmers and analysts to make changes.

Test programs or databases, correct errors, and make necessary modifications. Plan, coordinate, and implement security measures to safeguard information in computer files against accidental or unauthorized damage, modification, or disclosure. Approve, schedule, plan, and supervise the installation and testing of new products and improvements to computer systems, such as the installation of new database systems. Train users and answer questions. Establish and calculate optimum values for database parameters, using manuals and calculator. Specify users and user-access levels for each database segment. Develop data model describing data elements and how they are used, following procedures and using pen, template, or computer software. Develop methods for integrating different products so that they work properly together, such as customizing commercial databases to fit specific needs. Review project requests describing database user needs to estimate time and cost required to accomplish project. Review procedures in database management system manuals for making changes to database. Work as part of project team to coordinate database development and determine project scope and limitations. Select and enter codes to monitor database performance and to create production database. Identify and evaluate industry trends in database systems to serve as a source of information and advice for upper management. Write and code logical and physical database descriptions and specify database identifiers to management system or direct others in coding descriptions. Review workflow charts developed by programmer analyst to understand tasks computer will perform, such as updating records. Revise company definition of data as defined in data dictionary.

Personality Type: Investigative.

GOE—Interest Area: 11. Information Technology. **Work Group:** 11.02. Information Technology Specialties. **Other Jobs in this Work Group:** Computer and Information Scientists, Research; Computer Operators; Computer Programmers; Computer Security Specialists; Computer Software Engineers, Applications; Computer Software Engineers, Systems Software; Computer Support Specialists;

Computer Systems Analysts; Computer Systems Engineers/Architects; Network Designers; Network Systems and Data Communications Analysts; Software Quality Assurance Engineers and Testers; Web Administrators; Web Developers.

Skills: Troubleshooting; Systems Evaluation; Operations Analysis; Systems Analysis; Programming; Persuasion.

Education and Training Programs: Computer and Information Sciences, General; Computer Systems Analysis/Analyst; Data Modeling/Warehousing and Database Administration; Computer and Information Systems Security; Management Information Systems, General. **Related Knowledge/Courses:** Computers and Electronics; Economics and Accounting; Clerical Studies; Mathematics; Administration and Management; Telecommunications.

Work Environment: Indoors; noisy; sitting; using hands on objects, tools, or controls; repetitive motions.

Dental Assistants

- ❋ Education/Training Required: Moderate-term on-the-job training
- ❋ Annual Earnings: $30,220
- ❋ Beginning Wage: $20,530
- ❋ Earnings Growth Potential: Very high
- ❋ Growth: 29.2%
- ❋ Annual Job Openings: 29,482
- ❋ Self-Employed: 0.0%
- ❋ Part-Time: 35.7%

Industries with Greatest Employment: Ambulatory Health Care Services.

Highest-Growth Industries (Projected Growth for This Job): Ambulatory Health Care Services (30.4%); Administrative and Support Services (26.9%).

Lowest-Growth Industries (Projected Growth for This Job): Miscellaneous Manufacturing (1.9%); Hospitals, Public and Private (9.4%); Educational Services, Public and Private (11.7%).

Fastest-Growing Metropolitan Areas (Recent Growth for This Job): Muncie, IN (100.0%); Hattiesburg, MS (71.4%); Michigan City–La Porte, IN (60.0%); Des Moines–West Des Moines, IA (59.1%); Rockford, IL (59.1%).

Other Considerations for Job Security: Job prospects for dental assistants should be excellent. In addition to job openings due to employment growth, numerous job openings will arise out of the need to replace assistants who transfer to other occupations, retire, or leave for other reasons. Many opportunities for entry-level positions offer on-the-job training, but some dentists prefer to hire experienced assistants or those who have completed a dental-assisting program.

Assist dentist, set up patient and equipment, and keep records. Prepare patient, sterilize and disinfect instruments, set up instrument trays, prepare materials, and assist dentist during dental procedures. Expose dental diagnostic X rays. Record treatment information in patient records. Take and record medical and dental histories and vital signs of patients. Provide postoperative instructions prescribed by dentist. Assist dentist in management of medical and dental emergencies. Pour, trim, and polish study casts. Instruct patients in oral hygiene and plaque control programs. Make preliminary impressions for study casts and occlusal registrations for mounting them. Clean and polish removable appliances. Clean teeth, using dental instruments. Apply protective fluoride coating to teeth. Fabricate temporary restorations and custom impressions from preliminary impressions. Schedule appointments, prepare bills, and receive payment for dental services; complete insurance forms; and maintain records, manually or by using computer.

Personality Type: Social.

GOE—Interest Area: 08. Health Science. **Work Group:** 08.03. Dentistry. **Other Jobs in this Work Group:** Dental Hygienists; Dentists, General; Oral and Maxillofacial Surgeons; Orthodontists; Prosthodontists.

Skills: Equipment Maintenance; Operation and Control; Social Perceptiveness; Operation Monitoring; Management of Material Resources; Equipment Selection.

Education and Training Program: Dental Assisting/Assistant. **Related Knowledge/Courses:** Medicine and Dentistry; Chemistry; Clerical Studies; Customer and Personal Service; Psychology; Computers and Electronics.

Work Environment: Indoors; contaminants; disease or infections; using hands on objects, tools, or controls; bending or twisting the body; repetitive motions.

Dental Hygienists

* Education/Training Required: Associate degree
* Annual Earnings: $62,800
* Beginning Wage: $40,450
* Earnings Growth Potential: Very high
* Growth: 30.1%
* Annual Job Openings: 10,433
* Self-Employed: 0.1%
* Part-Time: 58.7%

Industries with Greatest Employment: Ambulatory Health Care Services.

Highest-Growth Industries (Projected Growth for This Job): Social Assistance (49.2%); Ambulatory Health Care Services (30.5%); Administrative and Support Services (26.7%).

Lowest-Growth Industries (Projected Growth for This Job): Hospitals, Public and Private (8.6%); Educational Services, Public and Private (11.0%).

Fastest-Growing Metropolitan Areas (Recent Growth for This Job): Canton–Massillon, OH (87.5%); Reading, PA (64.3%); Sioux City, IA–NE–SD (60.0%); Stockton, CA (52.6%); Oklahoma City, OK (44.7%).

Other Considerations for Job Security: Job prospects are expected to remain excellent. Older dentists, who have been less likely to employ dental hygienists, are leaving the occupation and will be replaced by recent graduates, who are more likely to employ one or more hygienists. Also, as dentists' workloads increase, they are expected to hire more hygienists to perform preventive dental care, such as cleaning, so that they can devote their own time to more complex procedures.

Clean teeth and examine oral areas, head, and neck for signs of oral disease. May educate patients on oral hygiene, take and develop X rays, or apply fluoride or sealants. Clean calcareous deposits, accretions, and stains from teeth and beneath margins of gums, using dental instruments. Feel and visually examine gums for sores and signs of disease. Chart conditions of decay and disease for diagnosis and treatment by dentist. Feel lymph nodes under patient's chin to detect swelling or tenderness that could indicate presence of oral cancer. Apply fluorides and other cavity-preventing agents to arrest dental decay. Examine gums, using probes, to locate periodontal recessed gums and signs of gum disease. Expose and develop X-ray film. Provide clinical services and health education to improve and maintain oral health of schoolchildren. Remove excess cement from coronal surfaces of teeth. Make impressions for study casts. Place, carve, and finish amalgam restorations. Administer local anesthetic agents. Conduct dental health clinics for community groups to augment services of dentist. Remove sutures and dressings. Place and remove rubber dams, matrices, and temporary restorations.

Personality Type: Social.

GOE—Interest Area: 08. Health Science. **Work Group:** 08.03. Dentistry. **Other Jobs in this Work Group:** Dental Assistants; Dentists, General; Oral and Maxillofacial Surgeons; Orthodontists; Prosthodontists.

Skills: Active Learning; Science; Time Management; Reading Comprehension; Persuasion; Social Perceptiveness.

Education and Training Program: Dental Hygiene/Hygienist. **Related Knowledge/Courses:** Biology; Medicine and Dentistry; Chemistry; Psychology; Therapy and Counseling; Sales and Marketing.

Work Environment: Indoors; radiation; disease or infections; sitting; using hands on objects, tools, or controls; repetitive motions.

Detectives and Criminal Investigators

See *Criminal Investigators and Special Agents; Immigration and Customs Inspectors; Police Detectives; and Police Identification and Records Officers, described separately.*

Diagnostic Medical Sonographers

* Education/Training Required: Associate degree
* Annual Earnings: $57,160
* Beginning Wage: $40,960
* Earnings Growth Potential: Very high
* Growth: 19.1%
* Annual Job Openings: 3,211
* Self-Employed: 1.1%
* Part-Time: 17.3%

Industries with Greatest Employment: Hospitals, Public and Private; Ambulatory Health Care Services.

Highest-Growth Industries (Projected Growth for This Job): Ambulatory Health Care Services (32.4%); Administrative and Support Services (28.8%).

Lowest-Growth Industries (Projected Growth for This Job): Hospitals, Public and Private (11.0%); Educational Services, Public and Private (11.8%).

Fastest-Growing Metropolitan Areas (Recent Growth for This Job): Cincinnati–Middletown, OH–KY–IN (94.1%); Hattiesburg, MS (66.7%); Tallahassee, FL (66.7%); Atlantic City, NJ (50.0%); Oxnard–Thousand Oaks–Ventura, CA (50.0%).

Other Considerations for Job Security: Job opportunities should be favorable. In addition to job openings from growth, some openings will arise from the need to replace sonographers who retire or leave the occupation permanently for some other reason. Sonographic technology is expected to evolve rapidly and to spawn many new sonography procedures, such as 3D- and 4D-sonography for use in obstetric and ophthalmologic diagnosis. However, high costs and federal approval may limit the rate at which some promising new technologies are adopted.

Produce ultrasonic recordings of internal organs for use by physicians. Decide which images to include, looking for differences between healthy and pathological areas. Observe screen during scan to ensure that image produced is satisfactory for diagnostic purposes, making adjustments to equipment as required. Observe and care for patients throughout examinations to ensure their safety and comfort. Provide sonogram and oral or written summary of technical findings to physician for use in medical diagnosis. Operate ultrasound equipment to produce and record images of the motion, shape, and composition of blood, organs, tissues, and bodily masses such as fluid accumulations. Select appropriate equipment settings and adjust patient positions to obtain the best sites and angles. Determine whether scope of exam should be extended based on findings. Process and code film from procedures and complete appropriate documentation. Obtain and record accurate patient history, including prior test results and information from physical examinations. Prepare patient for exam by explaining procedure, transferring them to ultrasound table, scrubbing skin and applying gel, and positioning them properly. Record and store suitable images, using camera unit connected to the ultrasound equipment. Coordinate work with physicians and other healthcare team members, including providing assistance during invasive procedures. Maintain records that include patient information; sonographs and interpretations; files of correspondence, publications, and regulations; or quality-assurance records such as pathology, biopsy, or post-operative reports. Perform legal and ethical duties, including preparing safety and accident reports, obtaining written consent from patient to perform invasive procedures, and reporting symptoms of abuse and neglect. Supervise and train students and other medical sonographers. Maintain stock and supplies, preparing supplies for special examinations and ordering supplies when necessary. Clean, check, and maintain sonographic equipment, submitting maintenance requests or performing minor repairs as necessary. Perform clerical duties such as scheduling exams and special procedures, keeping records, and archiving computerized images.

Personality Type: No data available.

GOE—Interest Area: 08. Health Science. **Work Group:** 08.06. Medical Technology. **Other Jobs in this Work Group:** Biological Technicians; Cardiovascular Technologists and Technicians; Medical and Clinical Laboratory Technicians; Medical and Clinical Laboratory Technologists; Medical Equipment Preparers; Medical Records and Health Information Technicians; Nuclear Medicine Technologists; Opticians, Dispensing; Orthotists and Prosthetists; Radiologic Technicians; Radiologic Technologists; Radiologic Technologists and Technicians.

Skills: Operation and Control; Reading Comprehension; Social Perceptiveness; Science; Learning Strategies; Active Listening.

Education and Training Programs: Diagnostic Medical Sonography/Sonographer and Ultrasound Technician; Allied Health Diagnostic, Intervention, and Treatment Professions, Other. **Related Knowledge/Courses:** Medicine and Dentistry; Biology; Physics; Therapy and Counseling; Clerical Studies; Education and Training.

Work Environment: Indoors; cramped work space, awkward positions; disease or infections; using hands on objects, tools, or controls; bending or twisting the body; repetitive motions.

Dietetic Technicians

- Education/Training Required: Postsecondary vocational training
- Annual Earnings: $24,040
- Beginning Wage: $15,720
- Earnings Growth Potential: Very high
- Growth: 14.8%
- Annual Job Openings: 4,062
- Self-Employed: 0.2%
- Part-Time: 20.8%

Industries with Greatest Employment: Hospitals, Public and Private; Nursing and Residential Care Facilities.

Highest-Growth Industries (Projected Growth for This Job): Social Assistance (52.7%); Ambulatory Health Care Services (28.2%); Nursing and Residential Care Facilities (20.2%); Religious, Grantmaking, Civic, Professional, and Similar Organizations (17.2%); Management of Companies and Enterprises (15.4%).

Lowest-Growth Industries (Projected Growth for This Job): Educational Services, Public and Private (8.1%); Hospitals, Public and Private (10.7%); Personal and Laundry Services (11.9%); Food Services and Drinking Places (14.0%).

Fastest-Growing Metropolitan Areas (Recent Growth for This Job): Boise City–Nampa, ID (80.0%); Oklahoma City, OK (71.4%); Columbus, OH (55.6%); Riverside–San Bernardino–Ontario, CA (50.0%); Fresno, CA (46.2%).

Other Considerations for Job Security: No data available.

Assist dietitians in the provision of food service and nutritional programs. Under the supervision of dietitians, may plan and produce meals based on established guidelines, teach principles of food and nutrition, or counsel individuals. Observe patient food intake and report progress and dietary problems to dietician. Prepare a major meal, following recipes and determining group food quantities. Analyze menus and recipes, standardize recipes, and test new products. Supervise food production and service or assist dietitians and nutritionists in food service supervision and planning. Obtain and evaluate dietary histories of individuals to plan nutritional programs. Plan menus and diets or guide individuals and families in food selection, preparation, and menu planning based on nutritional needs and established guidelines. Determine food and beverage costs and assist in implementing cost-control procedures. Develop job specifications, job descriptions, and work schedules. Select, schedule, and conduct orientation and in-service education programs. Provide dietitians with assistance researching food, nutrition, and food service systems. Deliver speeches on diet, nutrition, and health to promote healthy eating habits, as well as illness prevention and treatment. Refer patients to other relevant services to provide continuity of care.

Personality Type: Social.

GOE—Interest Area: 08. Health Science. **Work Group:** 08.09. Health Protection and Promotion. **Other Jobs in this Work Group:** Athletic Trainers; Dietitians and Nutritionists; Embalmers.

Skills: No data available.

Education and Training Programs: Foods, Nutrition, and Wellness Studies, General; Nutrition Sciences; Dietetics/Dietitian (RD); Dietetic Technician (DTR); Dietitian Assistant. **Related Knowledge/Courses:** Food Production; Medicine and Dentistry.

Work Environment: Indoors; disease or infections; minor burns, cuts, bites, or stings; standing; walking and running; repetitive motions.

Dietitians and Nutritionists

- ✳ Education/Training Required: Bachelor's degree
- ✳ Annual Earnings: $46,980
- ✳ Beginning Wage: $29,860
- ✳ Earnings Growth Potential: Very high
- ✳ Growth: 8.6%
- ✳ Annual Job Openings: 4,996
- ✳ Self-Employed: 7.9%
- ✳ Part-Time: 27.0%

Industries with Greatest Employment: Hospitals, Public and Private; Ambulatory Health Care Services; Nursing and Residential Care Facilities.

Highest-Growth Industries (Projected Growth for This Job): Social Assistance (51.4%); Professional, Scientific, and Technical Services (35.7%); Amusement, Gambling, and Recreation Industries (33.3%); Administrative and Support Services (30.6%); Ambulatory Health Care Services (28.9%); Religious, Grantmaking, Civic, Professional, and Similar Organizations (15.7%); Management of Companies and Enterprises (15.3%).

Lowest-Growth Industries (Projected Growth for This Job): Nursing and Residential Care Facilities (–0.2%); Hospitals, Public and Private (0.2%); Health and Personal Care Stores (8.0%); Educational Services, Public and Private (8.9%); Personal and Laundry Services (10.5%); Merchant Wholesalers, Nondurable Goods (12.3%); Real Estate (13.5%).

Fastest-Growing Metropolitan Areas (Recent Growth for This Job): Greenville, SC (133.3%); Lake Charles, LA (100.0%); Utica–Rome, NY (100.0%); Greenville, NC (80.0%); Riverside–San Bernardino–Ontario, CA (80.0%).

Other Considerations for Job Security: Overall, job opportunities will be good for dietitians and nutritionists, particularly for licensed and registered dietitians. Job opportunities should be particularly good in outpatient care facilities, offices of physicians, and food service management. Dietitians and nutritionists without a bachelor's degree will face keen competition for jobs. Dietitians with specialized training, an advanced degree, or certifications beyond the particular state's minimum requirement will experience the best job opportunities. Those specializing in renal and diabetic nutrition or gerontological nutrition will benefit from the growing number of diabetics and the aging of the population.

Plan and conduct food service or nutritional programs to assist in the promotion of health and control of disease. May supervise activities of a department providing quantity food services, counsel individuals, or conduct nutritional research. Assess nutritional needs, diet restrictions, and current health plans to develop and implement dietary-care plans and provide nutritional counseling. Consult with physicians and health-care personnel to determine nutritional needs and diet restrictions of patient or client. Advise patients and their families on nutritional principles, dietary plans and diet modifications, and food selection and preparation. Counsel individuals and groups on basic rules of good nutrition, healthy eating habits, and nutrition monitoring to improve their quality of life. Monitor food service operations to ensure conformance to nutritional, safety, sanitation, and quality standards. Coordinate recipe development and standardization and develop new menus for independent food service operations. Develop policies for food service or nutritional programs to assist in health promotion and disease control. Inspect meals served for conformance to prescribed diets and standards of palatability and appearance. Develop curriculum and prepare manuals, visual aids, course outlines, and other materials used in teaching. Prepare and administer budgets for food, equipment, and supplies. Purchase food in accordance with health and safety codes. Select, train, and supervise workers who plan, prepare, and serve meals. Manage quantity food service departments or clinical and community nutrition services. Coordinate diet counseling services. Advise food service managers and organizations on sanitation, safety procedures, menu development, budgeting, and planning to assist with the establishment, operation, and evaluation of food service facilities and nutrition programs. Organize, develop, analyze, test, and prepare special meals such as low-fat, low-cholesterol, or chemical-free meals. Plan, conduct, and evaluate dietary, nutritional, and epidemiological research. Plan and conduct training programs in dietetics, nutrition, and institutional management and administration for medical students, health-care personnel, and the general public. Make recommendations regarding public policy, such as nutrition labeling, food fortification, and nutrition standards for school programs.

Personality Type: Investigative.

GOE—Interest Area: 08. Health Science. **Work Group:** 08.09. Health Protection and Promotion. **Other Jobs in this Work Group:** Athletic Trainers; Dietetic Technicians; Embalmers.

Skills: Science; Writing; Social Perceptiveness; Instructing; Speaking; Reading Comprehension.

Education and Training Programs: Foods, Nutrition, and Wellness Studies, General; Human Nutrition; Foodservice Systems Administration/Management; Foods, Nutrition, and Related Services, Other; Nutrition Sciences; Dietetics/Dietitian (RD); Clinical Nutrition/Nutritionist; Dietetics and Clinical Nutrition Services, Other. **Related Knowledge/Courses:** Food Production; Therapy and Counseling; Sociology and Anthropology; Medicine and Dentistry; Philosophy and Theology; Psychology.

Work Environment: Indoors; more often sitting than standing.

Economics Teachers, Postsecondary

❋ Education/Training Required: Doctoral degree
❋ Annual Earnings: $71,850
❋ Beginning Wage: $38,630
❋ Earnings Growth Potential: Very high
❋ Growth: 22.9%
❋ Annual Job Openings: 237,478
❋ Self-Employed: 0.4%
❋ Part-Time: 27.8%

Our sources did not provide separate job openings data for this occupation. The job openings listed here are shared with 35 other postsecondary teaching occupations. For a complete list, see the beginning of this section.

Industries with Greatest Employment: Educational Services, Public and Private.

Highest-Growth Industries (Projected Growth for This Job): Administrative and Support Services (48.3%); Amusement, Gambling, and Recreation Industries (45.3%); Social Assistance (38.6%); Support Activities for Transportation (32.8%); Religious, Grantmaking, Civic, Professional, and Similar Organizations (29.9%); Professional, Scientific, and Technical Services (28.8%); Management of Companies and Enterprises (26.8%); Educational Services, Public and Private (22.9%); Hospitals, Public and Private (21.4%); Personal and Laundry Services (21.0%).

Lowest-Growth Industries (Projected Growth for This Job): Other Information Services (7.4%); Sporting Goods, Hobby, Book, and Music Stores (13.3%); Performing Arts, Spectator Sports, and Related Industries (13.4%); Insurance Carriers and Related Activities (13.9%).

Fastest-Growing Metropolitan Areas (Recent Growth for This Job): Virginia Beach–Norfolk–Newport News, VA–NC (50.0%); Cleveland–Elyria–Mentor, OH (50.0%); Kansas City, MO–KS (47.8%); Miami–Fort Lauderdale–Miami Beach, FL (40.0%); Riverside–San Bernardino–Ontario, CA (38.5%).

Other Considerations for Job Security: Retirements of current postsecondary teachers should create numerous openings for all types of postsecondary teachers, so job opportunities are generally expected to be very good. However, because students attend postsecondary institutions to prepare themselves for careers, the best job prospects for postsecondary teachers are likely to be in rapidly growing fields that offer many nonacademic career options. Economics courses are commonly required as part of business majors. Community colleges and other institutions offering career and technical education have been among the most rapidly growing and are expected to offer some of the best opportunities for postsecondary teachers.

Teach courses in economics. Prepare and deliver lectures to undergraduate and/or graduate students on topics such as econometrics, price theory, and macroeconomics. Prepare course materials such as syllabi, homework assignments, and handouts. Evaluate and grade students' classwork, assignments, and papers. Compile, administer, and grade examinations or assign this work to others. Keep abreast of developments in their field by reading current literature, talking with colleagues, and participating in professional conferences. Maintain student attendance records, grades, and other required records. Initiate, facilitate, and moderate classroom discussions. Maintain regularly scheduled office hours to advise and assist students. Select and obtain materials and supplies such as textbooks. Plan, evaluate, and revise curricula, course content, course materials, and methods of instruction. Conduct research in a particular field of knowledge and publish findings in professional journals, books, and/or electronic media. Supervise undergraduate and/or graduate teaching, internships, and research work. Advise students on academic and vocational curricula and on career issues. Serve on academic or administrative committees that deal with institutional policies, departmental matters, and academic issues. Collaborate with colleagues to address teaching and research issues. Compile bibliographies of specialized materials for outside reading assignments. Participate in student recruitment, registration, and placement activities. Perform administrative duties such as serving as department head. Write grant proposals to procure external research funding. Participate in campus and community events. Provide professional consulting services to government and/or industry. Act as advisers to student organizations.

Personality Type: Social.

GOE—Interest Area: 05. Education and Training. **Work Group:** 05.03. Postsecondary and Adult Teaching and Instructing. **Other Jobs in this Work Group:** Adult Literacy, Remedial Education, and GED Teachers and Instructors; Agricultural Sciences Teachers, Postsecondary; Anthropology and Archeology Teachers, Postsecondary; Architecture Teachers, Postsecondary; Area, Ethnic, and Cultural Studies Teachers, Postsecondary; Art, Drama, and Music Teachers, Postsecondary; Atmospheric, Earth, Marine, and Space Sciences Teachers, Postsecondary; Biological Science Teachers, Postsecondary; Business Teachers, Postsecondary; Chemistry Teachers, Postsecondary; Communications Teachers, Postsecondary; Computer Science Teachers, Postsecondary; Criminal Justice and Law Enforcement Teachers, Postsecondary; Education Teachers, Postsecondary; Engineering Teachers, Postsecondary; English Language and Literature Teachers, Postsecondary; Environmental Science Teachers, Postsecondary; Farm and Home Management Advisors; Foreign Language and Literature Teachers, Postsecondary; Forestry and Conservation Science Teachers, Postsecondary; Geography Teachers, Postsecondary; Graduate Teaching Assistants; Health Specialties Teachers, Postsecondary; History Teachers, Postsecondary; Home Economics Teachers, Postsecondary; Law Teachers, Postsecondary; Library Science Teachers, Postsecondary; Mathematical Science Teachers, Postsecondary; Nursing Instructors and Teachers, Postsecondary; Philosophy and Religion Teachers, Postsecondary; Physics Teachers, Postsecondary; Political Science Teachers, Postsecondary; Psychology Teachers, Postsecondary; Recreation and Fitness Studies Teachers, Postsecondary; Self-Enrichment Education Teachers; Social Work Teachers, Postsecondary; Sociology Teachers, Postsecondary; Vocational Education Teachers, Postsecondary.

Skills: Mathematics; Writing; Speaking; Instructing; Reading Comprehension; Critical Thinking.

Education and Training Programs: Social Science Teacher Education; Economics, General; Applied Economics; Econometrics and Quantitative Economics; Development Economics and International Development; International Economics; Economics, Other; Business/Managerial Economics. **Related Knowledge/Courses:** Economics and Accounting; History and Archeology; Mathematics; Education and Training; Philosophy and Theology; English Language.

Work Environment: Indoors; sitting.

Economists

* Education/Training Required: Master's degree
* Annual Earnings: $77,010
* Beginning Wage: $42,280
* Earnings Growth Potential: Very high
* Growth: 7.5%
* Annual Job Openings: 1,555
* Self-Employed: 6.5%
* Part-Time: 3.3%

Industries with Greatest Employment: Professional, Scientific, and Technical Services; Religious, Grantmaking, Civic, Professional, and Similar Organizations; Educational Services, Public and Private; Management of Companies and Enterprises.

Highest-Growth Industries (Projected Growth for This Job): Administrative and Support Services (35.9%); Securities, Commodity Contracts, and Other Financial Investments and Related Activities (34.2%); Professional, Scientific, and Technical Services (25.0%); Religious, Grantmaking, Civic, Professional, and Similar Organizations (18.4%); Management of Companies and Enterprises (15.2%).

Lowest-Growth Industries (Projected Growth for This Job): Monetary Authorities–Central Bank (–12.1%); Insurance Carriers and Related Activities (4.1%); Educational Services, Public and Private (11.3%); Credit Intermediation and Related Activities (12.4%).

Fastest-Growing Metropolitan Areas (Recent Growth for This Job): Little Rock–North Little Rock, AR (160.0%); San Antonio, TX (125.0%); Austin–Round Rock, TX (83.3%); Richmond, VA (37.5%); Charlotte–Gastonia–Concord, NC–SC (33.3%).

Other Considerations for Job Security: Job prospects will be best for those with graduate degrees in economics. Rising demand for economic analysis in virtually every industry should stem from the growing complexity of the global economy, the effects of competition on businesses, and increased reliance on quantitative methods for analyzing and forecasting business, sales, and other economic trends. Some corporations choose to hire economic consultants to fill these needs, rather than keep an economist on staff. This practice should result in more economists being employed in consulting services.

Conduct research, prepare reports, or formulate plans to aid in solution of economic problems arising from production and distribution of goods and services. May collect and process economic and statistical data, using econometric and sampling techniques. Study economic and statistical data in area of specialization, such as finance, labor, or agriculture. Provide advice and consultation on economic relationships to businesses, public and private agencies, and other employers. Compile, analyze, and report data to explain economic phenomena and forecast market trends, applying mathematical models and statistical techniques. Formulate recommendations, policies, or plans to solve economic problems or to interpret markets. Develop economic guidelines and standards and prepare points of view used in forecasting trends and formulating economic policy. Testify at regulatory or legislative hearings concerning the estimated effects of changes in legislation or public policy and present recommendations based on cost-benefit analyses. Supervise research projects and students' study projects. Forecast production and consumption of renewable resources and supply, consumption, and depletion of nonrenewable resources. Teach theories, principles, and methods of economics.

Personality Type: Investigative.

GOE—Interest Area: 15. Scientific Research, Engineering, and Mathematics. **Work Group:** 15.04. Social Sciences. **Other Jobs in this Work Group:** Anthropologists; Anthropologists and Archeologists; Archeologists; Historians; Industrial-Organizational Psychologists; Political Scientists; School Psychologists; Sociologists.

Skills: Mathematics; Programming; Persuasion; Judgment and Decision Making; Complex Problem Solving; Writing.

Education and Training Programs: Agricultural Economics; Economics, General; Applied Economics; Econometrics and Quantitative Economics; Development Economics and International Development; International Economics; Economics, Other; Business/Managerial Economics. **Related Knowledge/Courses:** Economics and Accounting; Mathematics; Geography; Sales and Marketing; Computers and Electronics; English Language.

Work Environment: Indoors; sitting.

Editors

- Education/Training Required: Bachelor's degree
- Annual Earnings: $46,990
- Beginning Wage: $27,340
- Earnings Growth Potential: Very high
- Growth: 2.3%
- Annual Job Openings: 20,193
- Self-Employed: 13.4%
- Part-Time: 14.6%

Industries with Greatest Employment: Publishing Industries (except Internet); Religious, Grantmaking,

Civic, Professional, and Similar Organizations; Professional, Scientific, and Technical Services.

Highest-Growth Industries (Projected Growth for This Job): Securities, Commodity Contracts, and Other Financial Investments and Related Activities (45.7%); Social Assistance (43.9%); Internet Publishing and Broadcasting (40.3%); Administrative and Support Services (36.6%); Museums, Historical Sites, and Similar Institutions (36.3%); Professional, Scientific, and Technical Services (29.0%); Nonstore Retailers (24.2%); Performing Arts, Spectator Sports, and Related Industries (21.2%); Motion Picture, Video, and Sound Recording Industries (16.2%); Management of Companies and Enterprises (15.3%).

Lowest-Growth Industries (Projected Growth for This Job): Printing and Related Support Activities (–20.7%); Sporting Goods, Hobby, Book, and Music Stores (–18.8%); Internet Service Providers, Web Search Portals, and Data Processing Services (–13.3%); Computer and Electronic Product Manufacturing (–11.8%); Publishing Industries (except Internet) (–10.6%); Other Information Services (–2.1%); Transportation Equipment Manufacturing (1.4%); Educational Services, Public and Private (3.8%); Broadcasting, except Internet (4.9%); Insurance Carriers and Related Activities (4.9%).

Fastest-Growing Metropolitan Areas (Recent Growth for This Job): Champaign–Urbana, IL (212.5%); Salt Lake City, UT (90.0%); Lakeland, FL (81.8%); Peoria, IL (60.0%); Niles–Benton Harbor, MI (50.0%).

Other Considerations for Job Security: Opportunities should be best for technical editors and those with training in a specialized field, such as law, medicine, or economics. Rapid growth and change in the high-technology and electronics industries result in a greater need for people to edit users' guides, instruction manuals, and training materials. In addition to job openings created by employment growth, some openings will arise as experienced workers retire, transfer to other occupations, or leave the labor force.

Perform variety of editorial duties, such as laying out, indexing, and revising content of written materials, in preparation for final publication. Prepare, rewrite, and edit copy to improve readability or supervise others who do this work. Read copy or proof to detect and correct errors in spelling, punctuation, and syntax. Allocate print space for story text, photos, and illustrations according to space parameters and copy significance, using knowledge of layout principles. Plan the contents of publications according to the publication's style, editorial policy, and publishing requirements. Verify facts, dates, and statistics, using standard reference sources. Review and approve proofs submitted by composing room before publication production. Develop story or content ideas, considering reader or audience appeal. Oversee publication production, including artwork, layout, computer typesetting, and printing, ensuring adherence to deadlines and budget requirements. Confer with management and editorial staff members regarding placement and emphasis of developing news stories. Assign topics, events, and stories to individual writers or reporters for coverage. Read, evaluate, and edit manuscripts or other materials submitted for publication and confer with authors regarding changes in content, style, organization, or publication. Monitor news-gathering operations to ensure utilization of all news sources, such as press releases, telephone contacts, radio, television, wire services, and other reporters. Meet frequently with artists, typesetters, layout personnel, marketing directors, and production managers to discuss projects and resolve problems. Supervise and coordinate work of reporters and other editors. Make manuscript acceptance or revision recommendations to the publisher. Select local, state, national, and international news items received from wire services based on assessment of items' significance and interest value. Interview and hire writers and reporters or negotiate contracts, royalties, and payments for authors or freelancers. Direct the policies and departments of newspapers, magazines, and other publishing establishments. Arrange for copyright permissions. Read material to determine index items and arrange them alphabetically or topically, indicating page or chapter location.

Personality Type: Artistic.

GOE—Interest Area: 03. Arts and Communication. **Work Group:** 03.02. Writing and Editing. **Other Jobs in this Work Group:** Copy Writers; Poets, Lyricists and Creative Writers; Technical Writers; Writers and Authors.

Skills: Writing; Reading Comprehension; Active Listening; Judgment and Decision Making; Persuasion; Critical Thinking.

Education and Training Programs: Mass Communication/Media Studies; Journalism; Broadcast Journalism; Publishing; Communication, Journalism, and Related Programs, Other; Family and Consumer Sciences/Human Sciences Communication; Creative Writing; Technical and Business Writing; Business/Corporate Communications. **Related Knowledge/Courses:** Communications and Media; History and Archeology; Geography; English Language; Sales and Marketing; Clerical Studies.

Work Environment: Indoors; sitting; using hands on objects, tools, or controls; repetitive motions.

Education Administrators, Elementary and Secondary School

- ✳ Education/Training Required: Work experience plus degree
- ✳ Annual Earnings: $77,740
- ✳ Beginning Wage: $51,320
- ✳ Earnings Growth Potential: Very high
- ✳ Growth: 7.6%
- ✳ Annual Job Openings: 27,143
- ✳ Self-Employed: 3.3%
- ✳ Part-Time: 8.3%

Industries with Greatest Employment: Educational Services, Public and Private.

Highest-Growth Industries (Projected Growth for This Job): Professional, Scientific, and Technical Services (51.8%); Social Assistance (33.6%); Administrative and Support Services (29.0%); Nursing and Residential Care Facilities (22.2%); Religious, Grantmaking, Civic, Professional, and Similar Organizations (19.9%).

Lowest-Growth Industries (Projected Growth for This Job): Hospitals, Public and Private (–3.6%); Educational Services, Public and Private (7.5%).

Fastest-Growing Metropolitan Areas (Recent Growth for This Job): Raleigh–Cary, NC (108.5%); Visalia–Porterville, CA (63.6%); Jefferson City, MO (50.0%); Salinas, CA (50.0%); Salisbury, MD (50.0%).

Other Considerations for Job Security: Job opportunities should be very good because a large proportion of education administrators are expected to retire over the next 10 years. Job growth will mainly depend on growth in enrollments of school-age children, but growth at the elementary and secondary level is expected to slow. Principals and assistant principals should have very favorable job prospects because the job has seen a sharp increase in responsibilities in recent years that has made the job more stressful and has discouraged some teachers from taking administrative positions. Enrollments are expected to increase the fastest in the West and the South, where the population is growing faster, and to decline or remain stable in the Northeast and the Midwest. School administrators also are in greater demand in rural and urban areas, where pay is generally lower than in the suburbs.

Plan, direct, or coordinate the academic, clerical, or auxiliary activities of public or private elementary or secondary-level schools. Review and approve new programs or recommend modifications to existing programs, submitting program proposals for school board approval as necessary. Prepare, maintain, or oversee the preparation and maintenance of attendance, activity, planning, or personnel reports and records. Confer with parents and staff to discuss educational activities, policies, and student behavioral or learning problems. Prepare and submit budget requests and recommendations or grant proposals to solicit program funding. Direct and coordinate school maintenance services and the use of school facilities. Counsel and provide guidance to students regarding personal, academic, vocational, or behavioral issues. Organize and direct committees of specialists, volunteers, and staff to provide technical and advisory assistance for programs. Teach classes or courses to students. Advocate for new schools to be built or for existing facilities to be repaired or remodeled. Plan and develop instructional methods and content for educational, vocational, or student activity programs. Develop partnerships with businesses, communities, and other organizations to help meet identified educational needs and to provide school-to-work programs. Direct and coordinate activities of teachers, administrators, and support staff at schools, public agencies, and institutions. Evaluate curricula, teaching methods, and programs to determine their effectiveness, efficiency, and utilization and to ensure that school activities comply with federal, state, and local regulations. Set educational standards and goals and help establish policies and procedures to carry them out. Recruit, hire, train, and evaluate primary and supplemental staff. Enforce discipline and attendance rules. Observe teaching methods and examine learning materials to evaluate and standardize curricula and teaching techniques and to determine areas where improvement is needed. Establish, coordinate, and oversee particular programs across school districts, such as programs to evaluate student academic achievement. Review and interpret government codes and develop programs to ensure adherence to codes and facility safety, security, and maintenance.

Personality Type: Social.

GOE—Interest Area: 05. Education and Training. **Work Group:** 05.01. Managerial Work in Education. **Other Jobs in this Work Group:** Education Administrators, Postsecondary; Education Administrators, Preschool and Child Care Center/Program; Instructional Coordinators.

Skills: Management of Personnel Resources; Management of Financial Resources; Negotiation; Systems Evaluation; Learning Strategies; Management of Material Resources.

Education and Training Programs: Educational Leadership and Administration, General;

Educational, Instructional, and Curriculum Supervision; Elementary and Middle School Administration/Principalship; Secondary School Administration/Principalship; Educational Administration and Supervision, Other. **Related Knowledge/Courses:** Therapy and Counseling; Education and Training; Personnel and Human Resources; Psychology; Sociology and Anthropology; History and Archeology.

Work Environment: Indoors; standing.

Education Administrators, Postsecondary

- ❀ Education/Training Required: Work experience plus degree
- ❀ Annual Earnings: $73,990
- ❀ Beginning Wage: $41,120
- ❀ Earnings Growth Potential: Very high
- ❀ Growth: 14.2%
- ❀ Annual Job Openings: 17,121
- ❀ Self-Employed: 3.3%
- ❀ Part-Time: 8.3%

Industries with Greatest Employment: Educational Services, Public and Private.

Highest-Growth Industries (Projected Growth for This Job): Professional, Scientific, and Technical Services (23.5%); Religious, Grantmaking, Civic, Professional, and Similar Organizations (22.5%); Management of Companies and Enterprises (18.2%).

Lowest-Growth Industries (Projected Growth for This Job): Hospitals, Public and Private (13.9%); Educational Services, Public and Private (14.4%).

Fastest-Growing Metropolitan Areas (Recent Growth for This Job): San Jose–Sunnyvale–Santa Clara, CA (65.2%); Bakersfield, CA (64.3%); Sacramento–Arden–Arcade–Roseville, CA (53.5%); San Antonio, TX (51.6%); Pittsburgh, PA (50.0%).

Other Considerations for Job Security: Job opportunities should be excellent because a large proportion of education administrators are expected to retire over the next 10 years. Job growth will mainly depend on enrollment growth, which will be especially fast at the postsecondary level, including private and for-profit institutions that serve adults. Enrollments are expected to increase the fastest in the West and the South, where the population is growing faster, and to decline or remain stable in the Northeast and the Midwest.

Plan, direct, or coordinate research, instructional, student administration and services, and other educational activities at postsecondary institutions, including universities, colleges, and junior and community colleges. Recruit, hire, train, and terminate departmental personnel. Plan, administer, and control budgets; maintain financial records; and produce financial reports. Represent institutions at community and campus events, in meetings with other institution personnel, and during accreditation processes. Participate in faculty and college committee activities. Provide assistance to faculty and staff in duties such as teaching classes, conducting orientation programs, issuing transcripts, and scheduling events. Establish operational policies and procedures and make any necessary modifications, based on analysis of operations, demographics, and other research information. Confer with other academic staff to explain and formulate admission requirements and course credit policies. Appoint individuals to faculty positions and evaluate their performance. Direct activities of administrative departments such as admissions, registration, and career services. Develop curricula and recommend curricula revisions and additions. Determine course schedules and coordinate teaching assignments and room assignments to ensure optimum use of buildings and equipment. Consult with government regulatory and licensing agencies to ensure the institution's conformance with applicable standards. Direct, coordinate, and evaluate the activities of personnel engaged in administering academic institutions, departments, and/or alumni organizations. Teach courses within their department. Participate in student recruitment, selection, and admission, making admissions recommendations when required to do so. Review student misconduct reports requiring disciplinary action and counsel students regarding such reports. Supervise coaches. Assess and collect tuition and fees. Direct scholarship, fellowship, and loan programs, performing activities such as selecting recipients and distributing aid. Coordinate the production and dissemination of university publications such as course catalogs and class schedules. Review registration statistics and consult with faculty officials to develop registration policies. Audit the financial status of student organizations and facility accounts.

Personality Type: Enterprising.

GOE—Interest Area: 05. Education and Training. **Work Group:** 05.01. Managerial Work in Education. **Other Jobs in this Work Group:** Education Administrators, Elementary and Secondary School; Education Administrators, Preschool and Child Care Center/Program; Instructional Coordinators.

Skills: Management of Personnel Resources; Management of Financial Resources; Systems Evaluation; Persuasion; Monitoring; Judgment and Decision Making.

Education and Training Programs: Educational Leadership and Administration, General; Educational, Instructional, and Curriculum Supervision; Higher Education/Higher Education Administration; Community College Education; Educational Administration and Supervision, Other. **Related Knowledge/Courses:** Personnel and Human Resources; Education and Training; Sociology and Anthropology; Administration and Management; Philosophy and Theology; English Language.

Work Environment: Indoors; sitting.

Education Administrators, Preschool and Child Care Center/ Program

- ❈ Education/Training Required: Work experience plus degree
- ❈ Annual Earnings: $37,740
- ❈ Beginning Wage: $24,470
- ❈ Earnings Growth Potential: Very high
- ❈ Growth: 23.5%
- ❈ Annual Job Openings: 8,113
- ❈ Self-Employed: 3.4%
- ❈ Part-Time: 8.3%

Industries with Greatest Employment: Social Assistance; Religious, Grantmaking, Civic, Professional, and Similar Organizations; Educational Services, Public and Private.

Highest-Growth Industries (Projected Growth for This Job): Professional, Scientific, and Technical Services (39.3%); Social Assistance (30.3%); Ambulatory Health Care Services (27.1%); Nursing and Residential Care Facilities (19.6%); Religious, Grantmaking, Civic, Professional, and Similar Organizations (17.6%); Management of Companies and Enterprises (15.2%).

Lowest-Growth Industries (Projected Growth for This Job): Educational Services, Public and Private (6.4%); Hospitals, Public and Private (9.9%).

Fastest-Growing Metropolitan Areas (Recent Growth for This Job): Greenville, NC (166.7%); Huntsville, AL (100.0%); Santa Rosa–Petaluma, CA (83.3%); Chico, CA (75.0%); Napa, CA (75.0%).

Other Considerations for Job Security: Job opportunities should be excellent because a large proportion of education administrators are expected to retire over the next 10 years. Job growth will mainly depend on enrollment growth, which will be especially fast at preschools and child-care centers. Enrollments are expected to increase the fastest in the West and the South, where the population is growing faster, and to decline or remain stable in the Northeast and the Midwest. School administrators also are in greater demand in rural and urban areas, where pay is generally lower than in the suburbs.

Plan, direct, or coordinate the academic and non-academic activities of preschool and child care centers or programs. Confer with parents and staff to discuss educational activities and policies and children's behavioral or learning problems. Prepare and maintain attendance, activity, planning, accounting, or personnel reports and records for officials and agencies or direct preparation and maintenance activities. Set educational standards and goals and help establish policies, procedures, and programs to carry them out. Monitor children's progress and provide children and teachers with assistance in resolving any problems. Determine allocations of funds for staff, supplies, materials, and equipment and authorize purchases. Recruit, hire, train, and evaluate primary and supplemental staff and recommend personnel actions for programs and services. Direct and coordinate activities of teachers or administrators at day-care centers, schools, public agencies, or institutions. Plan, direct, and monitor instructional methods and content of educational, vocational, or student activity programs. Review and interpret government codes and develop procedures to meet codes and to ensure facility safety, security, and maintenance. Determine the scope of educational program offerings and prepare drafts of program schedules and descriptions to estimate staffing and facility requirements. Review and evaluate new and current programs to determine their efficiency; effectiveness; and compliance with state, local, and federal regulations, and recommend any necessary modifications. Teach classes or courses or provide direct care to children. Prepare and submit budget requests or grant proposals to solicit program funding. Write articles, manuals, and other publications and assist in the distribution of promotional literature about programs and facilities. Collect and analyze survey data, regulatory information, and demographic and employment trends to forecast enrollment patterns and the need for curriculum changes. Inform businesses, community groups, and governmental agencies about educational needs, available programs, and program policies. Organize and direct committees of specialists, volunteers, and staff to provide technical and advisory assistance for programs.

Personality Type: Social.

GOE—Interest Area: 05. Education and Training. **Work Group:** 05.01. Managerial Work in Education. **Other Jobs in this Work Group:** Education Administrators, Elementary and Secondary School; Education Administrators, Postsecondary; Instructional Coordinators.

Skills: Management of Personnel Resources; Management of Financial Resources; Management of Material Resources; Learning Strategies; Monitoring; Social Perceptiveness.

Education and Training Programs: Educational Leadership and Administration, General; Educational, Instructional, and Curriculum Supervision; Elementary and Middle School Administration/Principalship; Educational Administration and Supervision, Other. **Related Knowledge/Courses:** Personnel and Human Resources; Education and Training; Clerical Studies; Philosophy and Theology; Therapy and Counseling; Sociology and Anthropology.

Work Environment: Indoors; standing.

Education Teachers, Postsecondary

- ❋ Education/Training Required: Doctoral degree
- ❋ Annual Earnings: $52,800
- ❋ Beginning Wage: $29,900
- ❋ Earnings Growth Potential: Very high
- ❋ Growth: 22.9%
- ❋ Annual Job Openings: 237,478
- ❋ Self-Employed: 0.4%
- ❋ Part-Time: 27.8%

Our sources did not provide separate job openings data for this occupation. The job openings listed here are shared with 35 other postsecondary teaching occupations. For a complete list, see the beginning of this section.

Industries with Greatest Employment: Educational Services, Public and Private.

Highest-Growth Industries (Projected Growth for This Job): Administrative and Support Services (48.3%); Amusement, Gambling, and Recreation Industries (45.3%); Social Assistance (38.6%); Support Activities for Transportation (32.8%); Religious, Grantmaking, Civic, Professional, and Similar Organizations (29.9%); Professional, Scientific, and Technical Services (28.8%); Management of Companies and Enterprises (26.8%); Educational Services, Public and Private (22.9%); Hospitals, Public and Private (21.4%); Personal and Laundry Services (21.0%).

Lowest-Growth Industries (Projected Growth for This Job): Other Information Services (7.4%); Sporting Goods, Hobby, Book, and Music Stores (13.3%); Performing Arts, Spectator Sports, and Related Industries (13.4%); Insurance Carriers and Related Activities (13.9%).

Fastest-Growing Metropolitan Areas (Recent Growth for This Job): Scranton–Wilkes-Barre, PA (15.8%); Atlanta–Sandy Springs–Marietta, GA (12.5%); San Antonio, TX (10.0%).

Other Considerations for Job Security: Retirements of current postsecondary teachers should create numerous openings for all types of postsecondary teachers, so job opportunities are generally expected to be very good. However, because students attend postsecondary institutions to prepare themselves for careers, and because the education industry is growing rapidly, many prospective teachers and teacher aides will attend colleges. Community colleges and other institutions offering career and technical education have been among the most rapidly growing and are expected to offer some of the best opportunities for postsecondary teachers.

Teach courses pertaining to education, such as counseling, curriculum, guidance, instruction, teacher education, and teaching English as a second language. Prepare course materials such as syllabi, homework assignments, and handouts. Prepare and deliver lectures to undergraduate and/or graduate students on topics such as children's literature, learning and development, and reading instruction. Initiate, facilitate, and moderate classroom discussions. Evaluate and grade students' classwork, assignments, and papers. Plan, evaluate, and revise curricula, course content, course materials, and methods of instruction. Supervise students' fieldwork, internships, and research work. Keep abreast of developments in their field by reading current literature, talking with colleagues, and participating in professional conferences. Advise students on academic and vocational curricula and on career issues. Maintain regularly scheduled office hours to advise and assist students. Maintain student attendance records, grades, and other required records. Collaborate with colleagues to address teaching and research issues. Compile, administer, and grade examinations or assign this work to others. Conduct research in a particular field of knowledge and publish findings in professional journals, books, or electronic media. Select and obtain materials and supplies such as textbooks. Participate in student recruitment, registration, and placement activities. Advise and instruct teachers employed in school systems by providing activities such as in-service seminars. Serve on academic or administrative committees that deal with institutional policies, departmental matters, and academic issues. Compile bibliographies of specialized materials for outside reading assignments. Write grant proposals to procure external research funding. Participate in campus and community events. Perform administrative duties such as serving as department head. Act as advisers to student organizations. Provide professional consulting services to government and/or industry.

Personality Type: No data available.

GOE—Interest Area: 05. Education and Training. **Work Group:** 05.03. Postsecondary and Adult Teaching and Instructing. **Other Jobs in this Work Group:** Adult Literacy, Remedial Education, and GED Teachers and Instructors; Agricultural Sciences Teachers, Postsecondary; Anthropology and Archeology Teachers, Postsecondary; Architecture Teachers, Postsecondary; Area, Ethnic, and Cultural Studies Teachers, Postsecondary; Art, Drama, and Music Teachers, Postsecondary; Atmospheric, Earth, Marine, and Space Sciences Teachers, Postsecondary; Biological Science Teachers, Postsecondary; Business Teachers, Postsecondary; Chemistry Teachers, Postsecondary; Communications Teachers, Postsecondary; Computer Science Teachers, Postsecondary; Criminal Justice and Law Enforcement Teachers, Postsecondary; Economics Teachers, Postsecondary; Engineering Teachers, Postsecondary; English Language and Literature Teachers, Postsecondary; Environmental Science Teachers, Postsecondary; Farm and Home Management Advisors; Foreign Language and Literature Teachers, Postsecondary; Forestry and Conservation Science Teachers, Postsecondary; Geography Teachers, Postsecondary; Graduate Teaching Assistants; Health Specialties Teachers, Postsecondary; History Teachers, Postsecondary; Home Economics Teachers, Postsecondary; Law Teachers, Postsecondary; Library Science Teachers, Postsecondary; Mathematical Science Teachers, Postsecondary; Nursing Instructors and Teachers, Postsecondary; Philosophy and Religion Teachers, Postsecondary; Physics Teachers, Postsecondary; Political Science Teachers, Postsecondary; Psychology Teachers, Postsecondary; Recreation and Fitness Studies Teachers, Postsecondary; Self-Enrichment Education Teachers; Social Work Teachers, Postsecondary; Sociology Teachers, Postsecondary; Vocational Education Teachers, Postsecondary.

Skills: Instructing; Learning Strategies; Writing; Social Perceptiveness; Speaking; Persuasion.

Education and Training Programs: Education, General; Indian/Native American Education; Social and Philosophical Foundations of Education; Agricultural Teacher Education; Art Teacher Education; Business Teacher Education; Driver and Safety Teacher Education; English/Language Arts Teacher Education; Foreign Language Teacher Education; Health Teacher Education; Family and Consumer Sciences/Home Economics Teacher Education; others. **Related Knowledge/Courses:** Therapy and Counseling; Education and Training; Sociology and Anthropology; Philosophy and Theology; Psychology; English Language.

Work Environment: Indoors; sitting.

Educational, Vocational, and School Counselors

* Education/Training Required: Master's degree
* Annual Earnings: $47,530
* Beginning Wage: $27,240
* Earnings Growth Potential: Very high
* Growth: 12.6%
* Annual Job Openings: 54,025
* Self-Employed: 6.1%
* Part-Time: 15.4%

Industries with Greatest Employment: Educational Services, Public and Private; Social Assistance.

Highest-Growth Industries (Projected Growth for This Job): Professional, Scientific, and Technical Services (46.3%); Social Assistance (32.9%); Ambulatory Health Care Services (26.2%); Nursing and Residential Care Facilities (22.3%); Religious, Grantmaking, Civic, Professional, and Similar Organizations (16.9%); Management of Companies and Enterprises (15.3%).

Lowest-Growth Industries (Projected Growth for This Job): Crop Production (–33.7%); Hospitals, Public and Private (–3.2%); Educational Services, Public and Private (10.3%); Insurance Carriers and Related Activities (11.1%); Accommodation, Including Hotels and Motels (12.6%).

Fastest-Growing Metropolitan Areas (Recent Growth for This Job): Indianapolis–Carmel, IN (331.6%); Napa, CA (125.0%); Chico, CA (94.4%); Spartanburg, SC (81.8%); Harrisonburg, VA (80.0%).

Other Considerations for Job Security: Demand for vocational or career counselors should grow as multiple job and career changes become common and as workers become increasingly aware of counseling services. Also, state and local governments will employ growing numbers of counselors to assist beneficiaries of welfare programs who exhaust their eligibility and must find jobs. Demand for school

counselors may increase due in large part to increases in student enrollments at postsecondary schools and colleges and as more states require elementary schools to employ counselors. Expansion of the responsibilities of school counselors should also lead to increases in their employment. Federal grants and subsidies may help to offset tight budgets and allow the reduction in student-to-counselor ratios to continue. For school counselors, job prospects should be good because many people are leaving the occupation to retire; however, opportunities may be more favorable in rural and urban areas, rather than the suburbs.

Counsel individuals and provide group educational and vocational guidance services. Counsel students regarding educational issues such as course and program selection, class scheduling, school adjustment, truancy, study habits, and career planning. Counsel individuals to help them understand and overcome personal, social, or behavioral problems affecting their educational or vocational situations. Maintain accurate and complete student records as required by laws, district policies, and administrative regulations. Confer with parents or guardians, teachers, other counselors, and administrators to resolve students' behavioral, academic, and other problems. Provide crisis intervention to students when difficult situations occur at schools. Identify cases involving domestic abuse or other family problems affecting students' development. Meet with parents and guardians to discuss their children's progress and to determine their priorities for their children and their resource needs. Prepare students for later educational experiences by encouraging them to explore learning opportunities and to persevere with challenging tasks. Encourage students and/or parents to seek additional assistance from mental-health professionals when necessary. Observe and evaluate students' performance, behavior, social development, and physical health. Enforce all administration policies and rules governing students. Meet with other professionals to discuss individual students' needs and progress. Provide students with information on such topics as college degree programs and admission requirements, financial-aid opportunities, trade and technical schools, and apprenticeship programs.

Evaluate individuals' abilities, interests, and personality characteristics, using tests, records, interviews, and professional sources. Collaborate with teachers and administrators in the development, evaluation, and revision of school programs. Establish and enforce behavioral rules and procedures to maintain order among students. Teach classes and present self-help or information sessions on subjects related to education and career planning. Attend professional meetings, educational conferences, and teacher training workshops to maintain and improve professional competence.

Personality Type: Social.

GOE—Interest Area: 05. Education and Training. **Work Group:** 05.06. Counseling, Health, and Fitness Education. **Other Jobs in this Work Group:** Fitness Trainers and Aerobics Instructors; Health Educators.

Skills: Social Perceptiveness; Service Orientation; Negotiation; Active Listening; Persuasion; Writing.

Education and Training Programs: Counselor Education/School Counseling and Guidance Services; College Student Counseling and Personnel Services. **Related Knowledge/Courses:** Therapy and Counseling; Psychology; Sociology and Anthropology; Education and Training; Philosophy and Theology; Clerical Studies.

Work Environment: Indoors; sitting.

Electrical and Electronics Repairers, Commercial and Industrial Equipment

❋ Education/Training Required: Postsecondary vocational training
❋ Annual Earnings: $45,180
❋ Beginning Wage: $27,940
❋ Earnings Growth Potential: Very high
❋ Growth: 6.8%
❋ Annual Job Openings: 6,607
❋ Self-Employed: 0.0%
❋ Part-Time: 0.6%

Industries with Greatest Employment: Merchant Wholesalers, Durable Goods; Computer and Electronic Product Manufacturing; Specialty Trade Contractors; Repair and Maintenance; Chemical Manufacturing.

Highest-Growth Industries (Projected Growth for This Job): Amusement, Gambling, and Recreation Industries (41.3%); Professional, Scientific, and Technical Services (34.6%); Telecommunications (30.6%); Support Activities for Transportation (27.1%); Rental and Leasing Services (24.0%); Management of Companies and Enterprises (23.0%); Merchant Wholesalers, Durable Goods (21.6%); Wholesale Electronic Markets and Agents and Brokers (20.9%); Construction of Buildings (19.5%); Broadcasting (except Internet) (18.7%); Hospitals, Public and Private (17.6%); Educational Services, Public and Private (16.2%).

Lowest-Growth Industries (Projected Growth for This Job): Pipeline Transportation (–30.1%); Textile Mills (–22.0%); Paper Manufacturing (–20.5%); Petroleum and Coal Products Manufacturing (–19.2%); Beverage and Tobacco Product Manufacturing (–17.2%); Printing and Related Support Activities (–15.6%); Fabricated Metal Product Manufacturing (–8.9%); Electrical Equipment, Appliance, and Component Manufacturing (–7.9%); Chemical Manufacturing (–6.5%); Machinery Manufacturing (–6.5%).

Fastest-Growing Metropolitan Areas (Recent Growth for This Job): Warner Robins, GA (163.6%); Anchorage, AK (116.7%); Augusta–Richmond County, GA–SC (116.7%); Anniston–Oxford, AL (112.5%); Wichita, KS (108.7%).

Other Considerations for Job Security: Job opportunities should be best for applicants with an associate degree in electronics, certification, and related experience. In addition to employment growth, the need to replace workers who transfer to other occupations or leave the labor force will result in some openings. Commercial and industrial equipment will become more sophisticated and will be used more frequently as businesses strive to lower costs by increasing and improving automation. Companies will install electronic controls, robots, sensors, and other equipment to automate processes such as assembly and testing. Also, as prices decline, this equipment will be used more frequently throughout a number of industries, including services, utilities, and construction, as well as manufacturing. Improved reliability of equipment shouldn't constrain employment growth, however: companies increasingly will rely on repairers because malfunctions that idle commercial and industrial equipment will continue to be costly.

Repair, test, adjust, or install electronic equipment, such as industrial controls, transmitters, and antennas. Perform scheduled preventive maintenance tasks, such as checking, cleaning, and repairing equipment, to detect and prevent problems. Examine work orders and converse with equipment operators to detect equipment problems and to ascertain whether mechanical or human errors contributed to the problems. Operate equipment to demonstrate proper use and to analyze malfunctions. Set up and test industrial equipment to ensure that it functions properly. Test faulty equipment to diagnose malfunctions, using test equipment and software and applying knowledge of the functional operation of electronic units and systems. Repair and adjust equipment, machines, and defective components, replacing worn parts such as gaskets and seals in watertight electrical equipment. Calibrate testing instruments and installed or repaired equipment to prescribed specifications. Advise management regarding customer satisfaction, product performance, and suggestions for product improvements. Study blueprints, schematics, manuals, and other specifications to determine installation procedures. Inspect components of industrial equipment for accurate assembly and installation and for defects such as loose connections and frayed wires. Maintain equipment logs that record performance problems, repairs, calibrations, and tests. Coordinate efforts with other workers involved in installing and maintaining equipment or components. Maintain inventory of spare parts. Consult with customers, supervisors, and engineers to plan layout of equipment and to resolve problems in system operation and maintenance. Install repaired equipment in various settings, such as industrial or military establishments. Send defective units to the manufacturer or to a specialized repair shop for repair. Determine feasibility of using standardized equipment and develop specifications for equipment required to perform additional functions. Enter information into computer to copy program or to draw, modify, or store schematics, applying knowledge of software package used. Sign overhaul documents for equipment replaced or repaired. Develop or modify industrial electronic devices, circuits, and equipment according to available specifications.

Personality Type: Realistic.

GOE—Interest Area: 13. Manufacturing. **Work Group:** 13.12. Electrical and Electronic Repair. **Other Jobs in this Work Group:** Avionics Technicians; Electric Motor, Power Tool, and Related Repairers; Electrical and Electronics Installers and Repairers, Transportation Equipment; Electronic Equipment Installers and Repairers, Motor Vehicles; Electronic Home Entertainment Equipment Installers and Repairers; Radio Mechanics.

Skills: Installation; Repairing; Operation Monitoring; Troubleshooting; Equipment Maintenance; Operation and Control.

Education and Training Programs: Computer Installation and Repair Technology/Technician; Industrial Electronics Technology/Technician. **Related**

Knowledge/Courses: Mechanical Devices; Computers and Electronics; Telecommunications; Engineering and Technology.

Work Environment: Indoors; noisy; cramped work space, awkward positions; hazardous conditions; standing; using hands on objects, tools, or controls.

Electrical and Electronics Repairers, Powerhouse, Substation, and Relay

* Education/Training Required: Postsecondary vocational training
* Annual Earnings: $57,400
* Beginning Wage: $40,390
* Earnings Growth Potential: Very high
* Growth: –4.7%
* Annual Job Openings: 1,591
* Self-Employed: 0.0%
* Part-Time: 0.6%

Industries with Greatest Employment: Utilities.

Highest-Growth Industries (Projected Growth for This Job): Management of Companies and Enterprises (15.1%).

Lowest-Growth Industries (Projected Growth for This Job): Pipeline Transportation (–32.9%); Utilities (–8.3%).

Fastest-Growing Metropolitan Areas (Recent Growth for This Job): Topeka, KS (33.3%); St. Louis, MO–IL (30.8%); San Juan–Caguas–Guaynabo, PR (21.1%); Pittsburgh, PA (10.0%).

Other Considerations for Job Security: Job opportunities should be best for applicants with an associate degree in electronics, certification, and related experience. Although employment is slowly declining, the need to replace workers who transfer to other occupations or leave the labor force will result in some openings. Consolidation and privatization in utilities industries should improve productivity, reducing

employment. Newer equipment will be more reliable and easier to repair, further limiting employment.

Inspect, test, repair, or maintain electrical equipment in generating stations, substations, and in-service relays. Construct, test, maintain, and repair substation relay and control systems. Inspect and test equipment and circuits to identify malfunctions or defects, using wiring diagrams and testing devices such as ohmmeters, voltmeters, or ammeters. Consult manuals, schematics, wiring diagrams, and engineering personnel to troubleshoot and solve equipment problems and to determine optimum equipment functioning. Notify facility personnel of equipment shutdowns. Open and close switches to isolate defective relays; then perform adjustments or repairs. Prepare and maintain records detailing tests, repairs, and maintenance. Analyze test data to diagnose malfunctions, to determine performance characteristics of systems, and to evaluate effects of system modifications. Test insulators and bushings of equipment by inducing voltage across insulation, testing current, and calculating insulation loss. Repair, replace, and clean equipment and components such as circuit breakers, brushes, and commutators. Disconnect voltage regulators, bolts, and screws and connect replacement regulators to high-voltage lines. Schedule and supervise the construction and testing of special devices and the implementation of unique monitoring or control systems. Run signal quality and connectivity tests for individual cables and record results. Schedule and supervise splicing or termination of cables in color-code order. Test oil in circuit breakers and transformers for dielectric strength, refilling oil periodically. Maintain inventories of spare parts for all equipment, requisitioning parts as necessary. Set forms and pour concrete footings for installation of heavy equipment.

Personality Type: Realistic.

GOE—Interest Area: 02. Architecture and Construction. **Work Group:** 02.05. Systems and Equipment Installation, Maintenance, and Repair. **Other Jobs in this Work Group:** Electrical Power-Line Installers and Repairers; Elevator Installers and

Repairers; Heating and Air Conditioning Mechanics and Installers; Maintenance and Repair Workers, General; Refrigeration Mechanics and Installers; Telecommunications Equipment Installers and Repairers, Except Line Installers; Telecommunications Line Installers and Repairers.

Skills: Installation; Repairing; Equipment Maintenance; Operation Monitoring; Troubleshooting; Operation and Control.

Education and Training Program: Mechanic and Repair Technologies/Technicians, Other. **Related Knowledge/Courses:** Mechanical Devices; Design; Telecommunications; Physics; Building and Construction; Public Safety and Security.

Work Environment: Outdoors; noisy; very bright or dim lighting; hazardous conditions; standing; using hands on objects, tools, or controls.

Embalmers

- ❋ Education/Training Required: Postsecondary vocational training
- ❋ Annual Earnings: $37,840
- ❋ Beginning Wage: $23,290
- ❋ Earnings Growth Potential: Very high
- ❋ Growth: 14.3%
- ❋ Annual Job Openings: 1,660
- ❋ Self-Employed: 0.7%
- ❋ Part-Time: 21.6%

Industries with Greatest Employment: Personal and Laundry Services.

Highest-Growth Industries (Projected Growth for This Job): None met the criteria.

Lowest-Growth Industries (Projected Growth for This Job): None met the criteria.

Fastest-Growing Metropolitan Areas (Recent Growth for This Job): St. Louis, MO–IL (83.3%); Virginia Beach–Norfolk–Newport News, VA–NC (18.2%); Los Angeles–Long Beach–Santa Ana, CA (11.1%).

Other Considerations for Job Security: No data available.

Prepare bodies for interment in conformity with legal requirements. Conform to laws of health and sanitation and ensure that legal requirements concerning embalming are met. Apply cosmetics to impart lifelike appearance to the deceased. Incise stomach and abdominal walls and probe internal organs, using trocar, to withdraw blood and waste matter from organs. Close incisions, using needles and sutures. Reshape or reconstruct disfigured or maimed bodies when necessary, using derma-surgery techniques and materials such as clay, cotton, plaster of paris, and wax. Make incisions in arms or thighs and drain blood from circulatory system and replace it with embalming fluid, using pump. Dress bodies and place them in caskets. Join lips, using needles and thread or wire. Conduct interviews to arrange for the preparation of obituary notices, to assist with the selection of caskets or urns, and to determine the location and time of burials or cremations. Perform the duties of funeral directors, including coordinating funeral activities. Attach trocar to pump-tube, start pump, and repeat probing to force embalming fluid into organs. Perform special procedures necessary for remains that are to be transported to other states or overseas or where death was caused by infectious disease. Maintain records such as itemized lists of clothing or valuables delivered with body and names of persons embalmed. Insert convex celluloid or cotton between eyeballs and eyelids to prevent slipping and sinking of eyelids. Wash and dry bodies, using germicidal soap and towels or hot air dryers. Arrange for transporting the deceased to another state for interment. Supervise funeral attendants and other funeral home staff. Pack body orifices with cotton saturated with embalming fluid to prevent escape of gases or waste matter. Assist with placing caskets in hearses and organize cemetery processions. Serve as pallbearers, attend visiting rooms, and provide other assistance to the bereaved. Direct casket and floral display placement and arrange guest seating. Arrange funeral home equipment and perform general maintenance. Assist coroners at death scenes or at autopsies, file police reports, and testify at inquests or in court if employed by a coroner.

Personality Type: Realistic.

GOE—Interest Area: 08. Health Science. **Work Group:** 08.09. Health Protection and Promotion. **Other Jobs in this Work Group:** Athletic Trainers; Dietetic Technicians; Dietitians and Nutritionists.

Skills: Science; Service Orientation; Management of Financial Resources; Management of Material Resources; Social Perceptiveness; Management of Personnel Resources.

Education and Training Programs: Funeral Service and Mortuary Science, General; Mortuary Science and Embalming/Embalmer. **Related Knowledge/Courses:** Chemistry; Biology; Philosophy and Theology; Customer and Personal Service; Therapy and Counseling; Medicine and Dentistry.

Work Environment: Indoors; contaminants; disease or infections; hazardous conditions; standing; using hands on objects, tools, or controls.

Emergency Medical Technicians and Paramedics

* ❋ Education/Training Required: Postsecondary vocational training
* ❋ Annual Earnings: $27,070
* ❋ Beginning Wage: $17,300
* ❋ Earnings Growth Potential: Very high
* ❋ Growth: 19.2%
* ❋ Annual Job Openings: 19,513
* ❋ Self-Employed: 0.2%
* ❋ Part-Time: 10.5%

Industries with Greatest Employment: Ambulatory Health Care Services; Hospitals, Public and Private.

Highest-Growth Industries (Projected Growth for This Job): Amusement, Gambling, and Recreation Industries (42.4%); Professional, Scientific, and Technical Services (39.7%); Administrative and Support Services (34.3%); Ambulatory Health Care Services (27.5%); Waste Management and Remediation Services (25.3%); Performing Arts, Spectator Sports, and Related Industries (24.3%); Transit and Ground Passenger Transportation (19.3%); Accommodation, Including Hotels and Motels (17.5%); Management of Companies and Enterprises (15.6%).

Lowest-Growth Industries (Projected Growth for This Job): Transportation Equipment Manufacturing (4.0%); Hospitals, Public and Private (10.8%); Health and Personal Care Stores (10.9%); Personal and Laundry Services (11.5%); Educational Services, Public and Private (13.2%); Air Transportation (13.5%).

Fastest-Growing Metropolitan Areas (Recent Growth for This Job): Burlington–South Burlington, VT (85.7%); Bridgeport–Stamford–Norwalk, CT (82.4%); Wichita Falls, TX (80.0%); Redding, CA (66.7%); Champaign–Urbana, IL (58.3%).

Other Considerations for Job Security: Job prospects should be favorable. Many job openings will arise from growth and from the need to replace workers who leave the occupation because of the limited potential for advancement, as well as the modest pay and benefits in private-sector jobs. Job opportunities should be best in private ambulance services. Competition will be greater for jobs in local government, including fire, police, and independent third-service rescue squad departments, which tend to have better salaries and benefits. EMTs and paramedics with advanced education and certifications, such as paramedic-level certification, should enjoy the most favorable job prospects as clients and patients demand higher levels of care before arriving at the hospital.

Assess injuries, administer emergency medical care, and extricate trapped individuals. Transport injured or sick persons to medical facilities. Administer first-aid treatment and life-support care to sick or injured persons in prehospital setting. Operate equipment such as electrocardiograms (EKGs), external defibrillators, and bag-valve mask resuscitators in advanced life-support environments. Assess nature and extent of illness or injury to establish and prioritize medical procedures. Maintain vehicles and medical and communication equipment and replenish first-aid equipment and supplies.

Observe, record, and report to physician the patient's condition or injury, the treatment provided, and reactions to drugs and treatment. Perform emergency diagnostic and treatment procedures, such as stomach suction, airway management, or heart monitoring, during ambulance ride. Administer drugs, orally or by injection, and perform intravenous procedures under a physician's direction. Comfort and reassure patients. Coordinate work with other emergency medical team members and police and fire department personnel. Communicate with dispatchers and treatment center personnel to provide information about situation, to arrange reception of victims, and to receive instructions for further treatment. Immobilize patient for placement on stretcher and ambulance transport, using backboard or other spinal immobilization device. Decontaminate ambulance interior following treatment of patient with infectious disease and report case to proper authorities. Drive mobile intensive care unit to specified location, following instructions from emergency medical dispatcher. Coordinate with treatment center personnel to obtain patients' vital statistics and medical history, to determine the circumstances of the emergency, and to administer emergency treatment.

Personality Type: Social.

GOE—Interest Area: 12. Law and Public Safety. **Work Group:** 12.06. Emergency Responding. **Other Jobs in this Work Group:** Fire Fighters; Forest Fire Fighters; Municipal Fire Fighters.

Skills: Equipment Maintenance; Operation Monitoring; Operation and Control; Service Orientation; Social Perceptiveness; Management of Personnel Resources.

Education and Training Programs: Emergency Care Attendant (EMT Ambulance); Emergency Medical Technology/Technician (EMT Paramedic). **Related Knowledge/Courses:** Medicine and Dentistry; Therapy and Counseling; Chemistry; Psychology; Customer and Personal Service; Biology.

Work Environment: Outdoors; noisy; very bright or dim lighting; contaminants; cramped work space, awkward positions; disease or infections.

Engineering Teachers, Postsecondary

* Education/Training Required: Doctoral degree
* Annual Earnings: $76,670
* Beginning Wage: $41,880
* Earnings Growth Potential: Very high
* Growth: 22.9%
* Annual Job Openings: 237,478
* Self-Employed: 0.4%
* Part-Time: 27.8%

Our sources did not provide separate job openings data for this occupation. The job openings listed here are shared with 35 other postsecondary teaching occupations. For a complete list, see the beginning of this section.

Industries with Greatest Employment: Educational Services, Public and Private.

Highest-Growth Industries (Projected Growth for This Job): Administrative and Support Services (48.3%); Amusement, Gambling, and Recreation Industries (45.3%); Social Assistance (38.6%); Support Activities for Transportation (32.8%); Religious, Grantmaking, Civic, Professional, and Similar Organizations (29.9%); Professional, Scientific, and Technical Services (28.8%); Management of Companies and Enterprises (26.8%); Educational Services, Public and Private (22.9%); Hospitals, Public and Private (21.4%); Personal and Laundry Services (21.0%).

Lowest-Growth Industries (Projected Growth for This Job): Other Information Services (7.4%); Sporting Goods, Hobby, Book, and Music Stores (13.3%); Performing Arts, Spectator Sports, and Related Industries (13.4%); Insurance Carriers and Related Activities (13.9%).

Fastest-Growing Metropolitan Areas (Recent Growth for This Job): Kansas City, MO–KS (66.7%); Palm Bay–Melbourne–Titusville, FL (44.4%); Riverside–San Bernardino–Ontario, CA (37.5%); Spokane, WA (25.0%).

E

Other Considerations for Job Security: Retirements of current postsecondary teachers should create numerous openings for all types of postsecondary teachers, so job opportunities are generally expected to be very good. However, because students attend postsecondary institutions to prepare themselves for careers, the best job prospects for postsecondary teachers are likely to be in rapidly growing fields that offer many nonacademic career options. Community colleges and other institutions offering career and technical education have been among the most rapidly growing and are expected to offer some of the best opportunities for postsecondary teachers.

Teach courses pertaining to the application of physical laws and principles of engineering for the development of machines, materials, instruments, processes, and services. Includes teachers of subjects such as chemical, civil, electrical, industrial, mechanical, mineral, and petroleum engineering. Includes both teachers primarily engaged in teaching and those who do both teaching and research. Prepare and deliver lectures to undergraduate and/or graduate students on topics such as mechanics, hydraulics, and robotics. Keep abreast of developments in their field by reading current literature, talking with colleagues, and participating in professional conferences. Supervise undergraduate and/or graduate teaching, internships, and research work. Evaluate and grade students' classwork, laboratory work, assignments, and papers. Conduct research in a particular field of knowledge and publish findings in professional journals, books, and/or electronic media. Prepare course materials such as syllabi, homework assignments, and handouts. Compile, administer, and grade examinations or assign this work to others. Write grant proposals to procure external research funding. Supervise students' laboratory work. Initiate, facilitate, and moderate class discussions. Maintain regularly scheduled office hours to advise and assist students. Plan, evaluate, and revise curricula, course content, course materials, and methods of instruction. Advise students on academic and vocational curricula and on career issues. Maintain student attendance records, grades, and other required records. Collaborate with colleagues to address teaching and research issues. Select and obtain materials and supplies such as textbooks and laboratory equipment. Participate in student recruitment, registration, and placement activities. Serve on academic or administrative committees that deal with institutional policies, departmental matters, and academic issues. Perform administrative duties such as serving as department head. Provide professional consulting services to government and/or industry. Compile bibliographies of specialized materials for outside reading assignments. Act as advisers to student organizations. Participate in campus and community events.

Personality Type: Investigative.

GOE—Interest Area: 05. Education and Training. **Work Group:** 05.03. Postsecondary and Adult Teaching and Instructing. **Other Jobs in this Work Group:** Adult Literacy, Remedial Education, and GED Teachers and Instructors; Agricultural Sciences Teachers, Postsecondary; Anthropology and Archeology Teachers, Postsecondary; Architecture Teachers, Postsecondary; Area, Ethnic, and Cultural Studies Teachers, Postsecondary; Art, Drama, and Music Teachers, Postsecondary; Atmospheric, Earth, Marine, and Space Sciences Teachers, Postsecondary; Biological Science Teachers, Postsecondary; Business Teachers, Postsecondary; Chemistry Teachers, Postsecondary; Communications Teachers, Postsecondary; Computer Science Teachers, Postsecondary; Criminal Justice and Law Enforcement Teachers, Postsecondary; Economics Teachers, Postsecondary; Education Teachers, Postsecondary; English Language and Literature Teachers, Postsecondary; Environmental Science Teachers, Postsecondary; Farm and Home Management Advisors; Foreign Language and Literature Teachers, Postsecondary; Forestry and Conservation Science Teachers, Postsecondary; Geography Teachers, Postsecondary; Graduate Teaching Assistants; Health Specialties Teachers, Postsecondary; History Teachers, Postsecondary; Home Economics Teachers, Postsecondary; Law Teachers, Postsecondary; Library Science Teachers, Postsecondary; Mathematical Science Teachers, Postsecondary; Nursing Instructors and Teachers,

Postsecondary; Philosophy and Religion Teachers, Postsecondary; Physics Teachers, Postsecondary; Political Science Teachers, Postsecondary; Psychology Teachers, Postsecondary; Recreation and Fitness Studies Teachers, Postsecondary; Self-Enrichment Education Teachers; Social Work Teachers, Postsecondary; Sociology Teachers, Postsecondary; Vocational Education Teachers, Postsecondary.

Skills: Science; Programming; Mathematics; Technology Design; Complex Problem Solving; Management of Financial Resources.

Education and Training Programs: Teacher Education and Professional Development, Specific Subject Areas, Other; Engineering, General; Aerospace, Aeronautical and Astronautical Engineering; Agricultural/Biological Engineering and Bioengineering; Architectural Engineering; Biomedical/Medical Engineering; Ceramic Sciences and Engineering; Chemical Engineering; Civil Engineering, General; Geotechnical Engineering; Structural Engineering; others. **Related Knowledge/Courses:** Engineering and Technology; Physics; Design; Mathematics; Education and Training; Telecommunications.

Work Environment: Indoors; sitting.

English Language and Literature Teachers, Postsecondary

- ✳ Education/Training Required: Doctoral degree
- ✳ Annual Earnings: $51,730
- ✳ Beginning Wage: $28,880
- ✳ Earnings Growth Potential: Very high
- ✳ Growth: 22.9%
- ✳ Annual Job Openings: 237,478
- ✳ Self-Employed: 0.4%
- ✳ Part-Time: 27.8%

Our sources did not provide separate job openings data for this occupation. The job openings listed here are shared with 35 other postsecondary teaching occupations. For a complete list, see the beginning of this section.

Industries with Greatest Employment: Educational Services, Public and Private.

Highest-Growth Industries (Projected Growth for This Job): Administrative and Support Services (48.3%); Amusement, Gambling, and Recreation Industries (45.3%); Social Assistance (38.6%); Support Activities for Transportation (32.8%); Religious, Grantmaking, Civic, Professional, and Similar Organizations (29.9%); Professional, Scientific, and Technical Services (28.8%); Management of Companies and Enterprises (26.8%); Educational Services, Public and Private (22.9%); Hospitals, Public and Private (21.4%); Personal and Laundry Services (21.0%).

Lowest-Growth Industries (Projected Growth for This Job): Other Information Services (7.4%); Sporting Goods, Hobby, Book, and Music Stores (13.3%); Performing Arts, Spectator Sports, and Related Industries (13.4%); Insurance Carriers and Related Activities (13.9%).

Fastest-Growing Metropolitan Areas (Recent Growth for This Job): Fort Wayne, IN (79.3%); Portland–Vancouver–Beaverton, OR–WA (57.1%); Lynchburg, VA (50.0%); Denver–Aurora, CO (50.0%); Greenville, SC (33.3%).

Other Considerations for Job Security: Retirements of current postsecondary teachers should create numerous openings for all types of postsecondary teachers, so job opportunities are generally expected to be very good. Because students attend postsecondary institutions to prepare themselves for careers, the best job prospects for postsecondary teachers are likely to be in rapidly growing fields that offer many nonacademic career options. English composition is a key part of the curriculum for most majors. Community colleges and other institutions offering career and technical education have been among the most rapidly growing and are expected to offer some of the best opportunities for postsecondary teachers.

Teach courses in English language and literature, including linguistics and comparative literature. Initiate, facilitate, and moderate classroom discussions. Evaluate and grade students' classwork, assignments, and papers. Prepare course materials such as syllabi, homework assignments, and handouts. Prepare and deliver lectures to undergraduate and graduate students on topics such as poetry, novel structure, and translation and adaptation. Maintain student attendance records, grades, and other required records. Plan, evaluate, and revise curricula, course content, course materials, and methods of instruction. Compile, administer, and grade examinations or assign this work to others. Maintain regularly scheduled office hours to advise and assist students. Keep abreast of developments in their field by reading current literature, talking with colleagues, and participating in professional conferences. Select and obtain materials and supplies such as textbooks. Advise students on academic and vocational curricula and on career issues. Conduct research in a particular field of knowledge and publish findings in professional journals, books, or electronic media. Collaborate with colleagues to address teaching and research issues. Serve on academic or administrative committees that deal with institutional policies, departmental matters, and academic issues. Participate in campus and community events. Participate in student recruitment, registration, and placement activities. Compile bibliographies of specialized materials for outside reading assignments. Supervise undergraduate and/or graduate teaching, internships, and research work. Provide assistance to students in college writing centers. Perform administrative duties such as serving as department head. Recruit, train, and supervise student writing instructors. Act as advisers to student organizations. Write grant proposals to procure external research funding. Provide professional consulting services to government or industry.

Personality Type: Artistic.

GOE—Interest Area: 05. Education and Training. **Work Group:** 05.03. Postsecondary and Adult Teaching and Instructing. **Other Jobs in this Work Group:** Adult Literacy, Remedial Education, and GED Teachers and Instructors; Agricultural Sciences Teachers, Postsecondary; Anthropology and Archeology Teachers, Postsecondary; Architecture Teachers, Postsecondary; Area, Ethnic, and Cultural Studies Teachers, Postsecondary; Art, Drama, and Music Teachers, Postsecondary; Atmospheric, Earth, Marine, and Space Sciences Teachers, Postsecondary; Biological Science Teachers, Postsecondary; Business Teachers, Postsecondary; Chemistry Teachers, Postsecondary; Communications Teachers, Postsecondary; Computer Science Teachers, Postsecondary; Criminal Justice and Law Enforcement Teachers, Postsecondary; Economics Teachers, Postsecondary; Education Teachers, Postsecondary; Engineering Teachers, Postsecondary; Environmental Science Teachers, Postsecondary; Farm and Home Management Advisors; Foreign Language and Literature Teachers, Postsecondary; Forestry and Conservation Science Teachers, Postsecondary; Geography Teachers, Postsecondary; Graduate Teaching Assistants; Health Specialties Teachers, Postsecondary; History Teachers, Postsecondary; Home Economics Teachers, Postsecondary; Law Teachers, Postsecondary; Library Science Teachers, Postsecondary; Mathematical Science Teachers, Postsecondary; Nursing Instructors and Teachers, Postsecondary; Philosophy and Religion Teachers, Postsecondary; Physics Teachers, Postsecondary; Political Science Teachers, Postsecondary; Psychology Teachers, Postsecondary; Recreation and Fitness Studies Teachers, Postsecondary; Self-Enrichment Education Teachers; Social Work Teachers, Postsecondary; Sociology Teachers, Postsecondary; Vocational Education Teachers, Postsecondary.

Skills: Instructing; Writing; Learning Strategies; Social Perceptiveness; Persuasion; Reading Comprehension.

Education and Training Programs: Comparative Literature; English Language and Literature, General; English Composition; Creative Writing; American Literature (United States); American Literature (Canadian); English Literature (British and Commonwealth); Technical and Business Writing; English Language and Literature/Letters, Other. **Related Knowledge/Courses:** Philosophy and Theology; English Language; History and Archeology; Education and Training; Fine Arts; Sociology and Anthropology.

Work Environment: Indoors; sitting.

Environmental Engineering Technicians

- ❋ Education/Training Required: Associate degree
- ❋ Annual Earnings: $40,560
- ❋ Beginning Wage: $25,110
- ❋ Earnings Growth Potential: Very high
- ❋ Growth: 24.8%
- ❋ Annual Job Openings: 2,162
- ❋ Self-Employed: 0.8%
- ❋ Part-Time: 5.9%

Industries with Greatest Employment: Professional, Scientific, and Technical Services; Waste Management and Remediation Services.

Highest-Growth Industries (Projected Growth for This Job): Waste Management and Remediation Services (38.7%); Professional, Scientific, and Technical Services (34.7%); Administrative and Support Services (26.5%); Management of Companies and Enterprises (15.6%).

Lowest-Growth Industries (Projected Growth for This Job): Paper Manufacturing (–30.2%); Primary Metal Manufacturing (–25.8%); Petroleum and Coal Products Manufacturing (–24.5%); Chemical Manufacturing (–15.0%); Electrical Equipment, Appliance, and Component Manufacturing (–14.3%); Machinery Manufacturing (–10.1%); Computer and Electronic Product Manufacturing (–8.9%); Utilities (–7.5%); Nonmetallic Mineral Product Manufacturing (1.3%); Transportation Equipment Manufacturing (1.3%).

Fastest-Growing Metropolitan Areas (Recent Growth for This Job): Albuquerque, NM (213.3%); San Diego–Carlsbad–San Marcos, CA (142.9%); Jackson, MS (133.3%); Pittsburgh, PA (133.3%); Cincinnati–Middletown, OH–KY–IN (71.4%).

Other Considerations for Job Security: More environmental engineering technicians will be needed to comply with environmental regulations and to develop methods of cleaning up existing hazards. A shift in emphasis toward preventing problems rather than controlling those that already exist, as well as increasing public health concerns resulting from population growth, also will spur demand. Opportunities will be best for individuals with an associate degree or extensive job training in engineering technology. As technology becomes more sophisticated, employers will continue to look for technicians who are skilled in new technology and require little additional training.

Apply theory and principles of environmental engineering to modify, test, and operate equipment and devices used in the prevention, control, and remediation of environmental pollution, including waste treatment and site remediation. May assist in the development of environmental pollution remediation devices under direction of engineer. Receive, set up, test, and decontaminate equipment. Maintain project logbook records and computer program files. Perform environmental quality work in field and office settings. Conduct pollution surveys, collecting and analyzing samples such as air and groundwater. Review technical documents to ensure completeness and conformance to requirements. Perform laboratory work such as logging numerical and visual observations, preparing and packaging samples, recording test results, and performing photo documentation. Review work plans to schedule activities. Obtain product information, identify vendors and suppliers, and order materials and equipment to maintain inventory. Arrange for the disposal of lead, asbestos, and other hazardous materials. Inspect facilities to monitor compliance with regulations governing substances such as asbestos, lead, and wastewater. Provide technical engineering support in the planning of projects such as wastewater treatment plants to ensure compliance with environmental regulations and policies. Improve chemical processes to reduce toxic emissions. Oversee support staff. Assist in the cleanup of hazardous material spills. Produce environmental assessment reports, tabulating data and preparing charts, graphs, and sketches. Maintain process parameters and evaluate process anomalies. Work with customers to assess the environmental impact of proposed construction and to develop pollution prevention programs. Perform statistical analysis and correction of air or water pollution data submitted by industry and other agencies. Develop work plans, including writing specifications and establishing material, manpower, and facilities needs.

Personality Type: No data available.

GOE—Interest Area: 15. Scientific Research, Engineering, and Mathematics. **Work Group:** 15.09. Engineering Technology. **Other Jobs in this Work Group:** Aerospace Engineering and Operations Technicians; Cartographers and Photogrammetrists; Civil Engineering Technicians; Electrical and Electronic Engineering Technicians; Electrical and Electronics Drafters; Electrical Drafters; Electrical Engineering Technicians; Electro-Mechanical Technicians; Electronic Drafters; Electronics Engineering Technicians; Mapping Technicians; Mechanical Drafters; Mechanical Engineering Technicians; Surveying and Mapping Technicians; Surveying Technicians.

Skills: Science; Repairing; Troubleshooting; Equipment Maintenance; Operation Monitoring; Mathematics.

Education and Training Programs: Environmental Engineering Technology/Environmental Technology; Hazardous Materials Information Systems Technology/Technician. **Related Knowledge/Courses:** Engineering and Technology; Building and Construction; Physics; Design; Biology; Chemistry.

Work Environment: More often indoors than outdoors; contaminants; hazardous conditions; hazardous equipment; standing.

Environmental Engineers

* Education/Training Required: Bachelor's degree
* Annual Earnings: $69,940
* Beginning Wage: $43,180
* Earnings Growth Potential: Very high
* Growth: 25.4%
* Annual Job Openings: 5,003
* Self-Employed: 2.7%
* Part-Time: 3.0%

Industries with Greatest Employment: Professional, Scientific, and Technical Services.

Highest-Growth Industries (Projected Growth for This Job): Professional, Scientific, and Technical Services (46.6%); Waste Management and Remediation Services (40.5%); Administrative and Support Services (33.7%); Religious, Grantmaking, Civic, Professional, and Similar Organizations (19.5%); Management of Companies and Enterprises (15.3%); Merchant Wholesalers, Nondurable Goods (15.1%).

Lowest-Growth Industries (Projected Growth for This Job): Pipeline Transportation (–33.7%); Primary Metal Manufacturing (–31.5%); Paper Manufacturing (–29.0%); Petroleum and Coal Products Manufacturing (–24.5%); Electrical Equipment, Appliance, and Component Manufacturing (–15.9%); Rail Transportation (–13.7%); Fabricated Metal Product Manufacturing (–13.5%); Machinery Manufacturing (–11.7%); Computer and Electronic Product Manufacturing (–11.6%); Food Manufacturing (–11.6%).

Fastest-Growing Metropolitan Areas (Recent Growth for This Job): Ann Arbor, MI (144.4%); San Diego–Carlsbad–San Marcos, CA (100.0%); Santa Rosa–Petaluma, CA (100.0%); Cincinnati–Middletown, OH–KY–IN (68.4%); Jacksonville, FL (57.9%).

Other Considerations for Job Security: More environmental engineers will be needed to comply with environmental regulations and to develop methods of cleaning up existing hazards. A shift in emphasis toward preventing problems rather than controlling those that already exist, as well as increasing public health concerns resulting from population growth, also are expected to spur demand for environmental engineers. Because of this employment growth, job opportunities should be good even as more students earn degrees. Although employment of environmental engineers should be less affected by economic conditions than most other types of engineers, a significant economic downturn could reduce the emphasis on environmental protection, reducing job opportunities.

Design, plan, or perform engineering duties in the prevention, control, and remediation of environmental health hazards, utilizing various engineering disciplines. Work may include waste treatment, site remediation, or pollution-control technology. Prepare, review, and update environmental investigation and recommendation reports. Collaborate with environmental scientists, planners, hazardous waste technicians, engineers, and other specialists and experts in law and business to address environmental problems. Obtain, update, and maintain plans, permits, and standard operating procedures. Provide technical-level support for environmental remediation and litigation projects, including remediation system design and determination of regulatory applicability. Monitor progress of environmental improvement programs. Inspect industrial and municipal facilities and programs to evaluate operational effectiveness and ensure compliance with environmental regulations. Provide administrative support for projects by collecting data, providing project documentation, training staff, and performing other general administrative duties. Develop proposed project objectives and targets and report to management on progress in attaining them. Advise corporations and government agencies of procedures to follow in cleaning up contaminated sites to protect people and the environment. Advise industries and government agencies about environmental policies and standards. Inform company employees and other interested parties of environmental issues. Assess the existing or potential environmental impact of land use projects on air, water, and land. Assist in budget implementation, forecasts, and administration. Develop site-specific health and safety protocols, such as spill contingency plans and methods for loading and transporting waste. Coordinate and manage environmental protection programs and projects, assigning and evaluating work. Serve as liaison with federal, state, and local agencies and officials on issues pertaining to solid and hazardous waste program requirements. Design systems, processes, and equipment for control, management, and remediation of water, air, and soil quality. Prepare hazardous waste manifests and land disposal restriction notifications. Serve on teams conducting multimedia inspections at complex facilities, providing assistance with planning, quality assurance, safety inspection protocols, and sampling.

Personality Type: No data available.

GOE—Interest Area: 01. Agriculture and Natural Resources. **Work Group:** 01.02. Resource Science/Engineering for Plants, Animals, and the Environment. **Other Jobs in this Work Group:** Agricultural Engineers; Animal Scientists; Conservation Scientists; Foresters; Mining and Geological Engineers, Including Mining Safety Engineers; Petroleum Engineers; Range Managers; Soil and Plant Scientists; Soil and Water Conservationists; Zoologists and Wildlife Biologists.

Skills: Science; Management of Financial Resources; Mathematics; Writing; Systems Analysis; Technology Design.

Education and Training Program: Environmental/Environmental Health Engineering. **Related Knowledge/Courses:** Biology; Chemistry; Engineering and Technology; Education and Training; Law and Government; Design.

Work Environment: Indoors; sitting.

Environmental Science Teachers, Postsecondary

* Education/Training Required: Doctoral degree
* Annual Earnings: $64,780
* Beginning Wage: $32,890
* Earnings Growth Potential: Very high
* Growth: 22.9%
* Annual Job Openings: 237,478
* Self-Employed: 0.4%
* Part-Time: 27.8%

Our sources did not provide separate job openings data for this occupation. The job openings listed here are shared with 35 other postsecondary teaching occupations. For a complete list, see the beginning of this section.

Industries with Greatest Employment: Educational Services, Public and Private.

Highest-Growth Industries (Projected Growth for This Job): Administrative and Support Services (48.3%); Amusement, Gambling, and Recreation Industries (45.3%); Social Assistance (38.6%); Support Activities for Transportation (32.8%); Religious, Grantmaking, Civic, Professional, and Similar Organizations (29.9%); Professional, Scientific, and Technical Services (28.8%); Management of Companies and Enterprises (26.8%); Educational Services, Public and Private (22.9%); Hospitals, Public and Private (21.4%); Personal and Laundry Services (21.0%).

Lowest-Growth Industries (Projected Growth for This Job): Other Information Services (7.4%); Sporting Goods, Hobby, Book, and Music Stores (13.3%); Performing Arts, Spectator Sports, and Related Industries (13.4%); Insurance Carriers and Related Activities (13.9%).

Fastest-Growing Metropolitan Areas (Recent Growth for This Job): Tampa–St. Petersburg–Clearwater, FL (14.3%); Washington–Arlington–Alexandria, DC–VA–MD–WV (14.3%).

Other Considerations for Job Security: Retirements of current postsecondary teachers should create numerous openings for all types of postsecondary teachers, so job opportunities are generally expected to be very good. Because students attend postsecondary institutions to prepare themselves for careers, the best job prospects for postsecondary teachers are likely to be in rapidly growing fields that offer many nonacademic career options. Community colleges and other institutions offering career and technical education have been among the most rapidly growing and are expected to offer some of the best opportunities for postsecondary teachers.

Teach courses in environmental science. Supervise undergraduate and/or graduate teaching, internships, and research work. Conduct research in a particular field of knowledge and publish findings in professional journals, books, and/or electronic media. Keep abreast of developments in their field by reading current literature, talking with colleagues, and participating in professional conferences. Evaluate and grade students' classwork, laboratory work, assignments, and papers. Write grant proposals to procure external research funding. Supervise students' laboratory work and fieldwork. Prepare course materials such as syllabi, homework assignments, and handouts. Plan, evaluate, and revise curricula, course content, course materials, and methods of instruction. Compile, administer, and grade examinations or assign this work to others. Initiate, facilitate, and moderate classroom discussions. Advise students on academic and vocational curricula and on career issues. Prepare and deliver lectures to undergraduate and/or graduate students on topics such as hazardous waste management, industrial safety, and environmental toxicology. Maintain student attendance records, grades, and other required records. Select and obtain materials and supplies such as textbooks and laboratory equipment. Maintain regularly scheduled office hours in order to advise and assist students. Collaborate with colleagues to address teaching and research issues. Perform administrative duties such as serving as department head. Participate in student recruitment, registration, and placement activities. Provide professional consulting services to government and/or industry. Serve on academic or administrative committees that deal with institutional policies, departmental matters, and academic issues. Compile bibliographies of specialized materials for outside reading assignments. Participate in campus and community events. Act as advisers to student organizations.

Personality Type: No data available.

GOE—Interest Area: 05. Education and Training. **Work Group:** 05.03. Postsecondary and Adult Teaching and Instructing. **Other Jobs in this Work Group:** Adult Literacy, Remedial Education, and GED Teachers and Instructors; Agricultural Sciences Teachers, Postsecondary; Anthropology and Archeology Teachers, Postsecondary; Architecture Teachers, Postsecondary; Area, Ethnic, and Cultural Studies Teachers, Postsecondary; Art, Drama, and Music Teachers, Postsecondary; Atmospheric, Earth, Marine, and Space Sciences Teachers, Postsecondary; Biological Science Teachers, Postsecondary; Business Teachers, Postsecondary; Chemistry Teachers, Postsecondary; Communications Teachers, Postsecondary; Computer Science Teachers, Postsecondary; Criminal Justice and Law Enforcement Teachers, Postsecondary; Economics Teachers, Postsecondary; Education Teachers, Postsecondary; Engineering Teachers, Postsecondary; English Language and Literature Teachers, Postsecondary; Farm and Home Management Advisors; Foreign Language and Literature Teachers, Postsecondary; Forestry and Conservation Science Teachers, Postsecondary; Geography Teachers, Postsecondary; Graduate Teaching Assistants; Health Specialties Teachers, Postsecondary; History Teachers, Postsecondary; Home Economics Teachers, Postsecondary; Law Teachers, Postsecondary; Library Science Teachers, Postsecondary; Mathematical Science Teachers, Postsecondary; Nursing Instructors and Teachers, Postsecondary; Philosophy and Religion Teachers, Postsecondary; Physics Teachers, Postsecondary; Political Science Teachers, Postsecondary; Psychology Teachers, Postsecondary; Recreation and Fitness Studies Teachers, Postsecondary; Self-Enrichment Education Teachers; Social Work Teachers, Postsecondary; Sociology Teachers, Postsecondary; Vocational Education Teachers, Postsecondary.

Skills: Science; Writing; Reading Comprehension; Instructing; Programming; Management of Financial Resources.

Education and Training Programs: Environmental Studies; Environmental Science; Science Teacher Education/General Science Teacher Education. **Related Knowledge/Courses:** Biology; Geography; Chemistry; Education and Training; Physics; History and Archeology.

Work Environment: Indoors; sitting.

Environmental Scientists and Specialists, Including Health

* Education/Training Required: Master's degree
* Annual Earnings: $56,100
* Beginning Wage: $34,590
* Earnings Growth Potential: Very high
* Growth: 25.1%
* Annual Job Openings: 6,961
* Self-Employed: 2.2%
* Part-Time: 5.3%

Industries with Greatest Employment: Professional, Scientific, and Technical Services; Educational Services, Public and Private.

Highest-Growth Industries (Projected Growth for This Job): Professional, Scientific, and Technical Services (54.3%); Administrative and Support Services (32.1%); Waste Management and Remediation Services (29.3%); Management of Companies and Enterprises (15.3%); Religious, Grantmaking, Civic, Professional, and Similar Organizations (15.2%).

Lowest-Growth Industries (Projected Growth for This Job): Paper Manufacturing (–29.1%); Chemical Manufacturing (–8.3%); Merchant Wholesalers, Nondurable Goods (–7.5%); Utilities (–6.9%); Oil and Gas Extraction (–1.7%); Transportation

Equipment Manufacturing (2.6%); Mining (except Oil and Gas) (5.1%); Hospitals, Public and Private (8.9%); Educational Services, Public and Private (11.8%).

Fastest-Growing Metropolitan Areas (Recent Growth for This Job): Austin–Round Rock, TX (92.7%); Albuquerque, NM (86.4%); Cleveland–Elyria–Mentor, OH (81.5%); Billings, MT (77.8%); Allentown–Bethlehem–Easton, PA–NJ (71.4%).

Other Considerations for Job Security: Job prospects for environmental scientists will be good. Because funding for federal and state geological surveys depends largely on political climate and current budget, job security for environmental scientists may vary. During periods of economic recession, layoffs of environmental scientists may occur in consulting firms; layoffs are much less likely in government.

Conduct research or perform investigation to identify, abate, or eliminate sources of pollutants or hazards that affect either the environment or the health of the population. By utilizing knowledge of various scientific disciplines, may collect, synthesize, study, report, and take action based on data derived from measurements or observations of air, food, soil, water, and other sources. Conduct environmental audits and inspections and investigations of violations. Evaluate violations or problems discovered during inspections to determine appropriate regulatory actions or to provide advice on the development and prosecution of regulatory cases. Communicate scientific and technical information through oral briefings, written documents, workshops, conferences, and public hearings. Review and implement environmental technical standards, guidelines, policies, and formal regulations that meet all appropriate requirements. Provide technical guidance, support, and oversight to environmental programs, industry, and the public. Provide advice on proper standards and regulations or the development of policies, strategies, and codes of practice for environmental management. Analyze data to determine validity, quality, and scientific significance and to interpret correlations between human activities and environmental effects. Collect, synthesize, and analyze data derived from pollution emission measurements, atmospheric monitoring, meteorological and mineralogical information, and soil or water samples. Determine data collection methods to be employed in research projects and surveys. Prepare charts or graphs from data samples, providing summary information on the environmental relevance of the data. Develop the technical portions of legal documents, administrative orders, or consent decrees. Investigate and report on accidents affecting the environment. Monitor environmental impacts of development activities. Supervise environmental technologists and technicians. Develop programs designed to obtain the most productive, nondamaging use of land. Research sources of pollution to determine their effects on the environment and to develop theories or methods of pollution abatement or control. Monitor effects of pollution and land degradation and recommend means of prevention or control. Design and direct studies to obtain technical environmental information about planned projects. Conduct applied research on topics such as waste control and treatment and pollution control methods.

Personality Type: Investigative.

GOE—Interest Area: 15. Scientific Research, Engineering, and Mathematics. **Work Group:** 15.03. Life Sciences. **Other Jobs in this Work Group:** Biochemists and Biophysicists; Biologists; Epidemiologists; Medical Scientists, Except Epidemiologists; Microbiologists.

Skills: Science; Service Orientation; Negotiation; Reading Comprehension; Coordination; Complex Problem Solving.

Education and Training Programs: Environmental Studies; Environmental Science. **Related Knowledge/Courses:** Biology; Geography; Chemistry; Law and Government; Engineering and Technology; Physics.

Work Environment: More often indoors than outdoors; noisy; sitting.

Family and General Practitioners

* Education/Training Required: First professional degree
* Annual Earnings: More than $145,600
* Beginning Wage: $69,990
* Earnings Growth Potential: Cannot be calculated.
* Growth: 14.2%
* Annual Job Openings: 38,027
* Self-Employed: 14.7%
* Part-Time: 8.1%

Our sources did not provide separate job openings data for this occupation. The job openings listed here are shared with Anesthesiologists; Internists, General; Obstetricians and Gynecologists; Pediatricians, General; Psychiatrists; and Surgeons.

Industries with Greatest Employment: Ambulatory Health Care Services; Hospitals, Public and Private.

Highest-Growth Industries (Projected Growth for This Job): Social Assistance (58.6%); Administrative and Support Services (26.8%); Professional, Scientific, and Technical Services (22.6%); Nursing and Residential Care Facilities (21.0%); Ambulatory Health Care Services (19.4%); Religious, Grantmaking, Civic, Professional, and Similar Organizations (16.7%); Management of Companies and Enterprises (15.3%).

Lowest-Growth Industries (Projected Growth for This Job): Insurance Carriers and Related Activities (4.6%); Health and Personal Care Stores (5.3%); Hospitals, Public and Private (9.9%); Educational Services, Public and Private (11.8%).

Fastest-Growing Metropolitan Areas (Recent Growth for This Job): New Haven, CT (10.4%); Kokomo, IN (10.3%); Anderson, IN (10.0%).

Other Considerations for Job Security: Opportunities for individuals interested in becoming physicians and surgeons are expected to be very good.

Unlike their predecessors, new physicians are much less likely to enter solo practice and more likely to take salaried jobs in group medical practices, clinics, and health networks. Reports of shortages in some specialties, such as general or family practice, internal medicine, and OB/GYN, or in rural or low-income areas should attract new entrants, encouraging schools to expand programs and hospitals to increase available residency slots. However, because physician training is so lengthy, employment change happens gradually. Opportunities should be particularly good in rural and low-income areas, as some physicians find these areas unattractive because of less control over work hours, isolation from medical colleagues, or other reasons.

Diagnose, treat, and help prevent diseases and injuries that commonly occur in the general population. Prescribe or administer treatment, therapy, medication, vaccination, and other specialized medical care to treat or prevent illness, disease, or injury. Order, perform, and interpret tests and analyze records, reports, and examination information to diagnose patients' condition. Monitor patients' conditions and progress and re-evaluate treatments as necessary. Explain procedures and discuss test results or prescribed treatments with patients. Collect, record, and maintain patient information, such as medical history, reports, and examination results. Advise patients and community members concerning diet, activity, hygiene, and disease prevention. Refer patients to medical specialists or other practitioners when necessary. Direct and coordinate activities of nurses, students, assistants, specialists, therapists, and other medical staff. Coordinate work with nurses, social workers, rehabilitation therapists, pharmacists, psychologists, and other health-care providers. Deliver babies. Operate on patients to remove, repair, or improve functioning of diseased or injured body parts and systems. Plan, implement, or administer health programs or standards in hospital, business, or community for information, prevention, or treatment of injury or illness. Prepare reports for government or management of birth, death, and disease statistics; workforce evaluations; or medical status of individuals. Conduct research to study anatomy and develop or test medications, treatments, or procedures to prevent or control disease or injury.

Personality Type: Investigative.

GOE—Interest Area: 08. Health Science. **Work Group:** 08.02. Medicine and Surgery. **Other Jobs in this Work Group:** Anesthesiologists; Internists, General; Medical Assistants; Medical Transcriptionists; Obstetricians and Gynecologists; Pediatricians, General; Pharmacists; Pharmacy Aides; Pharmacy Technicians; Physician Assistants; Psychiatrists; Registered Nurses; Surgeons; Surgical Technologists.

Skills: Science; Social Perceptiveness; Reading Comprehension; Complex Problem Solving; Persuasion; Service Orientation.

Education and Training Programs: Medicine (MD); Osteopathic Medicine/Osteopathy (DO); Family Medicine. **Related Knowledge/Courses:** Medicine and Dentistry; Biology; Therapy and Counseling; Psychology; Sociology and Anthropology; Chemistry.

Work Environment: Indoors; disease or infections; standing; using hands on objects, tools, or controls.

Film and Video Editors

- ❋ Education/Training Required: Bachelor's degree
- ❋ Annual Earnings: $46,670
- ❋ Beginning Wage: $22,710
- ❋ Earnings Growth Potential: High
- ❋ Growth: 12.7%
- ❋ Annual Job Openings: 2,707
- ❋ Self-Employed: 15.9%
- ❋ Part-Time: 18.9%

Industries with Greatest Employment: Motion Picture, Video, and Sound Recording Industries; Broadcasting (except Internet).

Highest-Growth Industries (Projected Growth for This Job): Telecommunications (36.2%); Performing Arts, Spectator Sports, and Related Industries (33.8%); Administrative and Support Services (25.9%); Professional, Scientific, and Technical Services (21.8%); Motion Picture, Video, and Sound Recording Industries (18.0%).

Lowest-Growth Industries (Projected Growth for This Job): Other Information Services (–2.2%); Computer and Electronic Product Manufacturing (–1.8%); Broadcasting (except Internet) (1.0%); Educational Services, Public and Private (10.8%); Merchant Wholesalers, Durable Goods (14.5%).

Fastest-Growing Metropolitan Areas (Recent Growth for This Job): Chicago–Naperville–Joliet, IL–IN–WI (137.0%); Salt Lake City, UT (100.0%); Miami–Fort Lauderdale–Miami Beach, FL (55.3%); Philadelphia–Camden–Wilmington, PA–NJ–DE–MD (54.5%); Honolulu, HI (50.0%).

Other Considerations for Job Security: Keen competition for jobs is expected due to the large number of people who want to enter the broadcasting and motion picture industries, where many camera operators and editors are employed. Those who succeed in landing a salaried job or attracting enough work to earn a living by freelancing are likely to be the most creative and highly motivated people, able to adapt to rapidly changing technologies and adept at operating a business. The change to digital cameras has increased the importance of strong computer skills. Those with the most experience and the most advanced computer skills will have the best job opportunities.

Edit motion picture soundtracks, film, and video. Cut shot sequences to different angles at specific points in scenes, making each individual cut as fluid and seamless as possible. Study scripts to become familiar with production concepts and requirements. Edit films and videotapes to insert music, dialog, and sound effects; to arrange films into sequences; and to correct errors, using editing equipment. Select and combine the most effective shots of each scene to form a logical and smoothly running story. Mark frames where a particular shot or piece of sound is to begin or end. Determine the specific audio and visual effects and music necessary to complete films. Verify key numbers and time codes on materials. Organize and string together raw footage into a continuous whole according to scripts or instructions of directors and producers. Review assembled films or edited videotapes on screens or monitors to determine whether corrections are necessary. Program computerized graphic effects. Review footage sequence by sequence to become familiar with it before assembling it into a final product. Set up and operate computer editing systems, electronic titling systems, video switching equipment, and digital video effects units to produce a final product. Record needed sounds or obtain them from sound effects libraries. Confer with producers and directors concerning layout or editing approaches needed to increase dramatic or entertainment value of productions. Manipulate plot, score, sound, and graphics to make the parts into a continuous whole, working closely with people in audio, visual, music, optical, or special effects departments. Supervise and coordinate activities of workers engaged in film editing, assembling, and recording activities. Trim film segments to specified lengths and reassemble segments in sequences that present stories with maximum effect. Develop postproduction models for films. Piece sounds together to develop film soundtracks. Conduct film screenings for directors and members of production staffs. Collaborate with music editors to select appropriate passages of music and develop production scores. Discuss the sound requirements of pictures with sound effects editors.

Personality Type: Artistic.

GOE—Interest Area: 03. Arts and Communication. **Work Group:** 03.09. Media Technology. **Other Jobs in this Work Group:** Audio and Video Equipment Technicians; Broadcast Technicians; Camera Operators, Television, Video, and Motion Picture; Multi-Media Artists and Animators; Photographers; Radio Operators; Sound Engineering Technicians.

Skills: Operation and Control; Equipment Selection; Equipment Maintenance; Operations Analysis; Installation; Operation Monitoring.

Education and Training Programs: Photojournalism; Radio and Television; Communications Technology/Technician; Radio and Television Broadcasting Technology/Technician; Audiovisual Communications Technologies/Technicians, Other; Cinematography and Film/Video Production. **Related Knowledge/Courses:** Fine Arts; Communications and Media; Design; Computers and Electronics; Telecommunications; English Language.

Work Environment: Indoors; sitting; using hands on objects, tools, or controls; repetitive motions.

Fire Fighters

See *Forest Fire Fighters and Municipal Fire Fighters, described separately.*

Fire Inspectors

- ❋ Education/Training Required: Work experience in a related occupation
- ❋ Annual Earnings: $48,050
- ❋ Beginning Wage: $29,840
- ❋ Earnings Growth Potential: Very high
- ❋ Growth: 11.0%
- ❋ Annual Job Openings: 644
- ❋ Self-Employed: 0.0%
- ❋ Part-Time: 2.2%

Our sources did not provide separate job openings data for this occupation. The job openings listed here are shared with Fire Investigators.

Industries with Greatest Employment: Administrative and Support Services; Educational Services, Public and Private; Specialty Trade Contractors.

Highest-Growth Industries (Projected Growth for This Job): Administrative and Support Services (26.5%).

Lowest-Growth Industries (Projected Growth for This Job): Educational Services, Public and Private (11.2%); Specialty Trade Contractors (12.7%).

Fastest-Growing Metropolitan Areas (Recent Growth for This Job): Columbus, OH (133.3%); Louisville–Jefferson County, KY–IN (125.0%); Kansas City, MO–KS (100.0%); Dallas–Fort Worth–Arlington, TX (68.8%); Minneapolis–St. Paul–Bloomington, MN–WI (63.6%).

Other Considerations for Job Security: Outlook information for fire inspectors is subsumed under the information for fire-fighting occupations. Prospective fire fighters are expected to face keen competition for available job openings. Many people are attracted to fire fighting because it is challenging and provides the opportunity to perform an essential public service; a high-school education is usually sufficient for entry; and a pension is usually guaranteed after 25 years of work. Consequently, the number of qualified applicants in most areas far exceeds the number of job openings, even though the written examination and physical requirements eliminate many applicants. This situation is expected to persist in coming years. Applicants with the best chances are those who are physically fit and score the highest on physical conditioning and mechanical aptitude exams. Those who have completed some fire-fighter education at a community college and have EMT or paramedic certification will have additional advantages.

Inspect buildings and equipment to detect fire hazards and enforce state and local regulations. Inspect buildings to locate hazardous conditions and fire code violations such as accumulations of combustible material, electrical wiring problems, and inadequate or nonfunctional fire exits. Identify corrective actions necessary to bring properties into compliance with applicable fire codes, laws, regulations, and standards and explain these measures to property owners or their representatives. Conduct inspections and acceptance testing of newly installed fire protection systems. Inspect and test fire-protection or fire-detection systems to verify that such systems are installed in accordance with appropriate laws, codes, ordinances, regulations, and standards. Conduct fire code compliance follow-ups to ensure that corrective actions have been taken in cases where violations were found. Inspect properties that store, handle, and use hazardous materials to ensure compliance with laws, codes, and regulations; issue hazardous materials permits to facilities found in compliance. Write detailed reports of fire inspections performed, fire code violations observed, and corrective recommendations offered. Review blueprints and plans for new or remodeled buildings to ensure that structures meet fire safety codes. Develop or review fire exit plans. Attend training classes to maintain current knowledge of fire prevention, safety, and fire-fighting procedures. Present and explain fire code requirements and fire prevention information to architects, contractors, attorneys, engineers, developers, fire service personnel, and the general public. Conduct fire exit drills to monitor and evaluate evacuation procedures. Inspect liquefied petroleum installations, storage containers, and transportation and delivery systems for compliance with fire laws. Search for clues as to the cause of a fire after the fire is completely extinguished. Develop and coordinate fire-prevention programs such as false alarm billing, fire inspection reporting, and hazardous materials management. Testify in court regarding fire code and fire safety issues. Recommend changes to fire prevention, inspection, and fire code endorsement procedures.

Personality Type: Conventional.

GOE—Interest Area: 07. Government and Public Administration. **Work Group:** 07.03. Regulations Enforcement. **Other Jobs in this Work Group:** Agricultural Inspectors; Aviation Inspectors; Compliance Officers, Except Agriculture, Construction, Health and Safety, and Transportation; Construction and Building Inspectors; Environmental Compliance Inspectors; Equal Opportunity Representatives and Officers; Financial Examiners; Fish and Game Wardens; Forest Fire Inspectors and Prevention Specialists; Freight and Cargo Inspectors; Government Property Inspectors and Investigators; Immigration and Customs Inspectors; Licensing Examiners and Inspectors; Nuclear Monitoring Technicians; Occupational Health and Safety Specialists; Occupational Health and Safety Technicians; Tax Examiners, Collectors, and Revenue Agents; Transportation Vehicle, Equipment, and Systems Inspectors, Except Aviation.

Skills: Science; Persuasion; Service Orientation; Negotiation; Operations Analysis; Operation Monitoring.

Education and Training Programs: Fire Protection and Safety Technology/Technician; Fire Science/Fire Fighting. **Related Knowledge/Courses:** Building and Construction; Public Safety and Security; Physics; Customer and Personal Service; Law and Government; Design.

Work Environment: More often outdoors than indoors; noisy; very hot or cold; very bright or dim lighting; hazardous equipment.

Fire Inspectors and Investigators

See *Fire Inspectors and Fire Investigators, described separately.*

Fire Investigators

* Education/Training Required: Work experience in a related occupation
* Annual Earnings: $48,050
* Beginning Wage: $29,840
* Earnings Growth Potential: Very high
* Growth: 11.0%
* Annual Job Openings: 644
* Self-Employed: 0.0%
* Part-Time: 2.2%

Our sources did not provide separate job openings data for this occupation. The job openings listed here are shared with Fire Inspectors.

Industries with Greatest Employment: Administrative and Support Services; Educational Services, Public and Private; Specialty Trade Contractors.

Highest-Growth Industries (Projected Growth for This Job): Administrative and Support Services (26.5%).

Lowest-Growth Industries (Projected Growth for This Job): Educational Services, Public and Private (11.2%); Specialty Trade Contractors (12.7%).

Fastest-Growing Metropolitan Areas (Recent Growth for This Job): Columbus, OH (133.3%); Louisville–Jefferson County, KY–IN (125.0%); Kansas City, MO–KS (100.0%); Dallas–Fort Worth–Arlington, TX (68.8%); Minneapolis–St. Paul–Bloomington, MN–WI (63.6%).

Other Considerations for Job Security: Outlook information for fire investigators is subsumed under the information for fire-fighting occupations. Prospective fire fighters are expected to face keen competition for available job openings. Many people are attracted to fire fighting because it is challenging and provides the opportunity to perform an essential public service; a high-school education is usually sufficient for entry; and a pension is usually guaranteed after 25 years of work. Consequently, the number of qualified applicants in most areas far exceeds the number of job openings, even though the written examination and physical requirements eliminate many applicants. This situation is expected to persist in coming years. Applicants with the best chances are those who are physically fit and score the highest on physical conditioning and mechanical aptitude exams. Those who have completed some fire-fighter education at a community college and have EMT or paramedic certification will have additional advantages.

Conduct investigations to determine causes of fires and explosions. Package collected pieces of evidence in securely closed containers such as bags, crates, or boxes to protect them. Examine fire sites and collect evidence such as glass, metal fragments, charred wood, and accelerant residue for use in determining the cause of a fire. Instruct children about the dangers of fire. Analyze evidence and other information to determine probable cause of fire or explosion. Photograph damage and evidence related to causes of fires or explosions to document investigation findings. Subpoena and interview witnesses, property owners, and building occupants to obtain information and sworn testimony. Swear out warrants and arrest and process suspected arsonists. Testify in court cases involving fires, suspected arson, and false alarms. Prepare and maintain reports of investigation results and records of convicted arsonists and arson suspects. Test sites and materials to establish facts such as burn patterns and flash points of materials, using test equipment. Conduct internal investigation to determine negligence and violation of laws and regulations by fire department employees. Dust evidence or portions of fire scenes for latent fingerprints.

Personality Type: Investigative.

GOE—Interest Area: 12. Law and Public Safety. **Work Group:** 12.04. Law Enforcement and Public Safety. **Other Jobs in this Work Group:** Bailiffs; Correctional Officers and Jailers; Criminal Investigators and Special Agents; Detectives and Criminal Investigators; Forensic Science Technicians; Parking Enforcement Workers; Police and Sheriff's Patrol Officers; Police Detectives; Police Identification and Records Officers; Police Patrol Officers; Sheriffs and Deputy Sheriffs; Transit and Railroad Police.

Skills: Management of Personnel Resources; Science; Equipment Maintenance; Operation and Control; Judgment and Decision Making; Repairing.

Education and Training Programs: Fire Protection and Safety Technology/Technician; Fire Science/Fire Fighting. **Related Knowledge/Courses:** Building and Construction; Public Safety and Security; Physics; Chemistry; Mechanical Devices; Law and Government.

Work Environment: Indoors; noisy; contaminants; hazardous conditions; hazardous equipment; using hands on objects, tools, or controls.

First-Line Supervisors/Managers of Correctional Officers

* Education/Training Required: Work experience in a related occupation
* Annual Earnings: $52,580
* Beginning Wage: $33,270
* Earnings Growth Potential: Very high
* Growth: 12.5%
* Annual Job Openings: 4,180
* Self-Employed: 0.0%
* Part-Time: 0.0%

Industries with Greatest Employment: Administrative and Support Services.

Highest-Growth Industries (Projected Growth for This Job): Administrative and Support Services (49.6%).

Lowest-Growth Industries (Projected Growth for This Job): Hospitals, Public and Private (–17.5%).

Fastest-Growing Metropolitan Areas (Recent Growth for This Job): Oklahoma City, OK (88.9%); Albany–Schenectady–Troy, NY (60.0%); Minneapolis–St. Paul–Bloomington, MN–WI (59.1%); Augusta–Richmond County, GA–SC (50.0%); Salem, OR (40.0%).

Other Considerations for Job Security: Job opportunities for correctional officers are expected to be excellent. The need to replace correctional officers who transfer to other occupations, retire, or leave the labor force, coupled with rising employment demand, will generate thousands of job openings each year. This situation is expected to continue. Layoffs of correctional officers are rare because of increasing offender populations.

Supervise and coordinate activities of correctional officers and jailers. Take, receive, and check periodic inmate counts. Maintain order, discipline, and security within assigned areas in accordance with relevant rules, regulations, policies, and laws. Respond to emergencies such as escapes. Maintain knowledge of, comply with, and enforce all institutional policies, rules, procedures, and regulations. Supervise and direct the work of correctional officers to ensure the safe custody, discipline, and welfare of inmates. Restrain, secure, and control offenders, using chemical agents, firearms, and other weapons of force as necessary. Supervise and perform searches of inmates and their quarters to locate contraband items. Monitor behavior of subordinates to ensure alert, courteous, and professional behavior toward inmates, parolees, fellow employees, visitors, and the public. Complete administrative paperwork and supervise the preparation and maintenance of records, forms, and reports. Instruct employees and provide on-the-job training. Conduct roll calls of correctional officers. Supervise activities such as searches, shakedowns, riot control, and institutional tours. Carry injured offenders or employees to safety and provide emergency first aid when necessary. Supervise and provide security for offenders performing tasks such as construction, maintenance, laundry, food service, and other industrial or agricultural operations. Develop work and security procedures. Set up employee work schedules. Resolve problems between inmates. Read and review offender information to identify issues that require special attention. Rate inmate behavior, promoting acceptable attitudes and behaviors to those with low ratings. Transfer and transport offenders on foot or by driving vehicles such as trailers, vans, and buses. Examine incoming and outgoing mail to ensure conformance with regulations. Convey correctional officers' and inmates' complaints to superiors.

Personality Type: No data available.

GOE—Interest Area: 12. Law and Public Safety. **Work Group:** 12.01. Managerial Work in Law and Public Safety. **Other Jobs in this Work Group:** Emergency Management Specialists; First-Line Supervisors/Managers of Fire Fighting and Prevention Workers; First-Line Supervisors/Managers of Police and Detectives; Forest Fire Fighting and Prevention Supervisors; Municipal Fire Fighting and Prevention Supervisors.

Skills: Management of Personnel Resources; Negotiation; Social Perceptiveness; Persuasion; Monitoring; Writing.

Education and Training Programs: Corrections; Corrections Administration. **Related Knowledge/Courses:** Public Safety and Security; Psychology; Therapy and Counseling; Personnel and Human Resources; Clerical Studies; Administration and Management.

Work Environment: More often indoors than outdoors; noisy; very bright or dim lighting; contaminants; disease or infections.

First-Line Supervisors/Managers of Fire Fighting and Prevention Workers

See *Forest Fire Fighting and Prevention Supervisors and Municipal Fire Fighting and Prevention Supervisors*, described separately.

First-Line Supervisors/Managers of Police and Detectives

* Education/Training Required: Work experience in a related occupation
* Annual Earnings: $69,310
* Beginning Wage: $41,260
* Earnings Growth Potential: Very high
* Growth: 9.2%
* Annual Job Openings: 9,373
* Self-Employed: 0.0%
* Part-Time: 0.8%

Industries with Greatest Employment: Educational Services, Public and Private.

Highest-Growth Industries (Projected Growth for This Job): None met the criteria.

Lowest-Growth Industries (Projected Growth for This Job): Hospitals, Public and Private (6.0%); Educational Services, Public and Private (11.7%).

Fastest-Growing Metropolitan Areas (Recent Growth for This Job): Monroe, LA (166.7%); Columbus, OH (131.6%); Lynchburg, VA (75.0%); Cleveland–Elyria–Mentor, OH (72.9%); Fresno, CA (66.7%).

Other Considerations for Job Security: Overall opportunities in local police departments will be excellent for individuals who meet the psychological, personal, and physical qualifications. There will be more competition for jobs in federal and state law enforcement agencies than for jobs in local agencies. Less competition for jobs will occur in departments that offer relatively low salaries or those in urban communities where the crime rate is relatively high. Applicants with military experience or college training in police science will have the best opportunities in local and state departments. Applicants with a bachelor's degree and several years of law enforcement or military experience, especially investigative experience, will have the best opportunities in federal agencies. The level of government spending determines the level of employment for police and detectives, but layoffs are rare because retirements enable most staffing cuts to be handled through attrition.

Supervise and coordinate activities of members of police force. Explain police operations to subordinates to assist them in performing their job duties. Inform personnel of changes in regulations and policies, implications of new or amended laws, and new techniques of police work. Supervise and coordinate the investigation of criminal cases, offering guidance and expertise to investigators and ensuring that procedures are conducted in accordance with laws and regulations. Investigate and resolve personnel problems within organization and charges of misconduct against staff. Train staff in proper police work procedures. Maintain logs; prepare reports; and direct the preparation, handling, and maintenance of departmental records. Monitor and evaluate the job performance of subordinates and authorize promotions and transfers. Direct collection, preparation, and handling of evidence and personal property of prisoners. Develop, implement, and revise departmental policies and procedures. Conduct raids and order detention of witnesses and suspects for questioning. Prepare work schedules and assign duties to subordinates. Discipline staff for violation of department rules and regulations. Cooperate with court personnel and officials from other law-enforcement agencies and testify in court as necessary. Review contents of written orders to ensure adherence to legal requirements. Inspect facilities, supplies, vehicles, and equipment to ensure conformance to standards. Prepare news releases and respond to police correspondence. Requisition and issue equipment and supplies. Meet with civic, educational, and community groups to develop community programs and events and to discuss law-enforcement subjects. Direct release or transfer of prisoners. Prepare budgets and manage expenditures of department funds.

Personality Type: Enterprising.

GOE—Interest Area: 12. Law and Public Safety. **Work Group:** 12.01. Managerial Work in Law and Public Safety. **Other Jobs in this Work Group:** Emergency Management Specialists; First-Line Supervisors/Managers of Correctional Officers; First-Line Supervisors/Managers of Fire Fighting and Prevention Workers; Forest Fire Fighting and Prevention Supervisors; Municipal Fire Fighting and Prevention Supervisors.

Skills: Management of Personnel Resources; Persuasion; Negotiation; Social Perceptiveness; Service Orientation; Monitoring.

Education and Training Programs: Corrections; Criminal Justice/Law Enforcement Administration; Criminal Justice/Safety Studies. **Related Knowledge/Courses:** Public Safety and Security; Psychology; Law and Government; Personnel and Human Resources; Telecommunications; Sociology and Anthropology.

Work Environment: More often outdoors than indoors; very hot or cold; very bright or dim lighting; hazardous equipment; sitting.

Food Scientists and Technologists

- ❋ Education/Training Required: Bachelor's degree
- ❋ Annual Earnings: $53,810
- ❋ Beginning Wage: $29,620
- ❋ Earnings Growth Potential: Very high
- ❋ Growth: 10.3%
- ❋ Annual Job Openings: 663
- ❋ Self-Employed: 16.3%
- ❋ Part-Time: 11.4%

Industries with Greatest Employment: Food Manufacturing; Professional, Scientific, and Technical Services; Educational Services, Public and Private; Management of Companies and Enterprises; Support Activities for Agriculture and Forestry.

Highest-Growth Industries (Projected Growth for This Job): Chemical Manufacturing (24.8%); Management of Companies and Enterprises (22.7%); Educational Services, Public and Private (19.0%); Professional, Scientific, and Technical Services (17.4%).

Lowest-Growth Industries (Projected Growth for This Job): Crop Production (–29.4%); Beverage and Tobacco Product Manufacturing (–8.3%); Food Manufacturing (5.5%); Merchant Wholesalers, Nondurable Goods (13.5%); Support Activities for Agriculture and Forestry (14.0%).

Fastest-Growing Metropolitan Areas (Recent Growth for This Job): Baltimore–Towson, MD (133.3%); Philadelphia–Camden–Wilmington, PA–NJ–DE–MD (100.0%); St. Louis, MO–IL (57.9%); Portland–Vancouver–Beaverton, OR–WA (50.0%); Washington–Arlington–Alexandria, DC–VA–MD–WV (42.9%).

Other Considerations for Job Security: Opportunities are expected to be good over the next decade, particularly for those holding a master's or doctoral degree. Employment of food scientists is relatively stable during periods of economic recession. Layoffs are less likely among food scientists than in some other occupations because food is a staple item and its demand fluctuates very little with economic activity.

Use chemistry, microbiology, engineering, and other sciences to study the principles underlying the processing and deterioration of foods; analyze food content to determine levels of vitamins, fat, sugar, and protein; discover new food sources; research ways to make processed foods safe, palatable, and healthful; and apply food science knowledge to determine the best ways to process, package, preserve, store, and distribute food. Test new products for flavor, texture, color, nutritional content, and adherence to government and industry standards. Check raw ingredients for maturity or stability for processing and finished products for safety, quality, and nutritional value. Confer with process engineers, plant operators, flavor experts, and packaging and marketing specialists to resolve problems in product development. Evaluate food processing and storage operations and assist in the development of quality-assurance programs for such operations. Study methods to improve aspects of foods such as chemical composition, flavor, color, texture, nutritional value, and convenience. Study the structure and composition of food or the changes foods undergo in storage and processing. Develop new or improved ways of preserving, processing, packaging, storing, and delivering foods, using knowledge of chemistry, microbiology, and other sciences. Develop food standards and production specifications, safety and sanitary regulations, and waste management and water supply specifications. Demonstrate products to clients. Inspect food processing areas in order to ensure compliance with government regulations and standards for sanitation, safety, quality, and waste management standards. Search for substitutes for harmful or undesirable additives, such as nitrites.

Personality Type: Investigative.

GOE—Interest Area: 01. Agriculture and Natural Resources. **Work Group:** 01.03. Resource Technologies for Plants, Animals, and the Environment. **Other Jobs in this Work Group:** Agricultural and Food Science Technicians; Agricultural Technicians;

Environmental Science and Protection Technicians, Including Health; Food Science Technicians; Geological and Petroleum Technicians; Geological Sample Test Technicians; Geophysical Data Technicians.

Skills: Quality Control Analysis; Science; Troubleshooting; Operation Monitoring; Mathematics; Reading Comprehension.

Education and Training Programs: Agriculture, General; International Agriculture; Food Science; Food Technology and Processing. **Related Knowledge/Courses:** Food Production; Chemistry; Production and Processing; Biology; Physics; Engineering and Technology.

Work Environment: Indoors; noisy; hazardous conditions; sitting.

Foreign Language and Literature Teachers, Postsecondary

- ❀ Education/Training Required: Doctoral degree
- ❀ Annual Earnings: $51,900
- ❀ Beginning Wage: $29,410
- ❀ Earnings Growth Potential: Very high
- ❀ Growth: 22.9%
- ❀ Annual Job Openings: 237,478
- ❀ Self-Employed: 0.4%
- ❀ Part-Time: 27.8%

Our sources did not provide separate job openings data for this occupation. The job openings listed here are shared with 35 other postsecondary teaching occupations. For a complete list, see the beginning of this section.

Industries with Greatest Employment: Educational Services, Public and Private.

Highest-Growth Industries (Projected Growth for This Job): Administrative and Support Services (48.3%); Amusement, Gambling, and Recreation Industries (45.3%); Social Assistance (38.6%); Support Activities for Transportation (32.8%); Religious, Grantmaking, Civic, Professional, and Similar

Organizations (29.9%); Professional, Scientific, and Technical Services (28.8%); Management of Companies and Enterprises (26.8%); Educational Services, Public and Private (22.9%); Hospitals, Public and Private (21.4%); Personal and Laundry Services (21.0%).

Lowest-Growth Industries (Projected Growth for This Job): Other Information Services (7.4%); Sporting Goods, Hobby, Book, and Music Stores (13.3%); Performing Arts, Spectator Sports, and Related Industries (13.4%); Insurance Carriers and Related Activities (13.9%).

Fastest-Growing Metropolitan Areas (Recent Growth for This Job): Atlanta–Sandy Springs–Marietta, GA (22.7%); San Antonio, TX (22.2%); Springfield, MA–CT (20.8%); San Diego–Carlsbad–San Marcos, CA (20.0%); Baton Rouge, LA (20.0%).

Other Considerations for Job Security: Retirements of current postsecondary teachers should create numerous openings for all types of postsecondary teachers, so job opportunities are generally expected to be very good. However, because students attend postsecondary institutions to prepare themselves for careers, the best job prospects for postsecondary teachers are likely to be in rapidly growing fields that offer many nonacademic career options—unlike foreign language and literature. On the other hand, foreign language courses are required for many majors. Community colleges and other institutions offering career and technical education have been among the most rapidly growing and are expected to offer some of the best opportunities for postsecondary teachers.

Teach courses in foreign (that is, other than English) languages and literature. Evaluate and grade students' classwork, assignments, and papers. Prepare course materials such as syllabi, homework assignments, and handouts. Initiate, facilitate, and moderate classroom discussions. Maintain student attendance records, grades, and other required records. Compile, administer, and grade examinations or assign this work to others. Plan, evaluate, and revise curricula, course content, course materials, and methods of instruction. Prepare and deliver lectures to undergraduate and graduate students on topics such as how to speak and write a foreign language and the cultural aspects of areas where a particular language is used. Maintain regularly scheduled office hours to advise and assist students. Select and obtain materials and supplies such as textbooks. Keep abreast of developments in their field by reading current literature, talking with colleagues, and participating in professional organizations and activities. Advise students on academic and vocational curricula and on career issues. Conduct research in a particular field of knowledge and publish findings in scholarly journals, books, and/or electronic media. Collaborate with colleagues to address teaching and research issues. Serve on academic or administrative committees that deal with institutional policies, departmental matters, and academic issues. Participate in student recruitment, registration, and placement activities. Compile bibliographies of specialized materials for outside reading assignments. Participate in campus and community events. Act as advisers to student organizations. Perform administrative duties such as serving as department head. Supervise undergraduate and graduate teaching, internships, and research work. Write grant proposals to procure external research funding. Provide professional consulting services to government or industry.

Personality Type: Artistic.

GOE—Interest Area: 05. Education and Training. **Work Group:** 05.03. Postsecondary and Adult Teaching and Instructing. **Other Jobs in this Work Group:** Adult Literacy, Remedial Education, and GED Teachers and Instructors; Agricultural Sciences Teachers, Postsecondary; Anthropology and Archeology Teachers, Postsecondary; Architecture Teachers, Postsecondary; Area, Ethnic, and Cultural Studies Teachers, Postsecondary; Art, Drama, and Music Teachers, Postsecondary; Atmospheric, Earth, Marine, and Space Sciences Teachers, Postsecondary; Biological Science Teachers, Postsecondary; Business Teachers, Postsecondary; Chemistry Teachers, Postsecondary; Communications Teachers, Postsecondary; Computer Science Teachers, Postsecondary; Criminal Justice and Law Enforcement Teachers, Postsecondary; Economics Teachers, Postsecondary; Education Teachers, Postsecondary; Engineering Teachers, Postsecondary; English Language and Literature Teachers, Postsecondary; Environmental Science Teachers, Postsecondary; Farm and Home Management Advisors; Forestry and Conservation Science Teachers, Postsecondary; Geography Teachers, Postsecondary; Graduate Teaching Assistants; Health Specialties Teachers, Postsecondary; History Teachers, Postsecondary; Home Economics Teachers, Postsecondary; Law Teachers, Postsecondary; Library Science Teachers, Postsecondary; Mathematical Science Teachers, Postsecondary; Nursing Instructors and Teachers, Postsecondary; Philosophy and Religion Teachers, Postsecondary; Physics Teachers, Postsecondary; Political Science Teachers, Postsecondary; Psychology Teachers, Postsecondary; Recreation and Fitness Studies Teachers, Postsecondary; Self-Enrichment Education Teachers; Social Work Teachers, Postsecondary; Sociology Teachers, Postsecondary; Vocational Education Teachers, Postsecondary.

Skills: Learning Strategies; Instructing; Writing; Reading Comprehension; Speaking; Persuasion.

Education and Training Programs: Latin Teacher Education; Foreign Languages and Literatures, General; Linguistics; Language Interpretation and Translation; African Languages, Literatures, and Linguistics; East Asian Languages, Literatures, and Linguistics, General; Chinese Language and Literature; Japanese Language and Literature; Korean Language and Literature; Tibetan Language and Literature; others. **Related Knowledge/Courses:** Foreign Language; Philosophy and Theology; History and Archeology; Sociology and Anthropology; Geography; English Language.

Work Environment: Indoors; sitting.

Forest Fire Fighters

* Education/Training Required: Long-term on-the-job training
* Annual Earnings: $41,190
* Beginning Wage: $20,660
* Earnings Growth Potential: Very high
* Growth: 12.1%
* Annual Job Openings: 18,887
* Self-Employed: 0.0%
* Part-Time: 1.3%

Our sources did not provide separate job openings data for this occupation. The job openings listed here are shared with Municipal Fire Fighters.

Industries with Greatest Employment: Professional, Scientific, and Technical Services; Performing Arts, Spectator Sports, and Related Industries; Support Activities for Agriculture and Forestry; Transportation Equipment Manufacturing; Fabricated Metal Product Manufacturing.

Highest-Growth Industries (Projected Growth for This Job): Performing Arts, Spectator Sports, and Related Industries (31.5%); Support Activities for Transportation (20.9%).

Lowest-Growth Industries (Projected Growth for This Job): Fabricated Metal Product Manufacturing (–11.2%); Hospitals, Public and Private (0.8%); Chemical Manufacturing (1.5%); Transportation Equipment Manufacturing (3.3%); Support Activities for Agriculture and Forestry (7.1%); Educational Services, Public and Private (11.4%); Professional, Scientific, and Technical Services (13.5%).

Fastest-Growing Metropolitan Areas (Recent Growth for This Job): Beaumont–Port Arthur, TX (330.0%); Green Bay, WI (103.6%); Tulsa, OK (62.7%); Fairbanks, AK (57.4%); Baton Rouge, LA (54.2%).

Other Considerations for Job Security: Prospective fire fighters are expected to face keen competition for available job openings. Many people are attracted to fire fighting because it is challenging and provides the opportunity to perform an essential public service; a high-school education is usually sufficient for entry; and a pension is usually guaranteed after 25 years of work. Consequently, the number of qualified applicants in most areas far exceeds the number of job openings, even though the written examination and physical requirements eliminate many applicants. This situation is expected to persist in coming years. Applicants with the best chances are those who are physically fit and score the highest on physical conditioning and mechanical aptitude exams. Those who have completed some fire-fighter education at a community college and have EMT or paramedic certification will have additional advantages.

Control and suppress fires in forests or vacant public land. Maintain contact with fire dispatchers at all times to notify them of the need for additional fire fighters and supplies or to detail any difficulties encountered. Rescue fire victims and administer emergency medical aid. Collaborate with other fire fighters as a member of a fire-fighting crew. Patrol burned areas after fires to locate and eliminate hot spots that may restart fires. Extinguish flames and embers to suppress fires, using shovels or engine- or hand-driven water or chemical pumps. Fell trees, cut and clear brush, and dig trenches to create firelines, using axes, chain saws, or shovels. Maintain knowledge of current fire-fighting practices by participating in drills and by attending seminars, conventions, and conferences. Operate pumps connected to high-pressure hoses. Participate in physical training to maintain high levels of physical fitness. Establish water supplies, connect hoses, and direct water onto fires. Maintain fire equipment and firehouse living quarters. Inform and educate the public about fire prevention. Take action to contain any hazardous chemicals that could catch fire, leak, or spill. Organize fire caches, positioning equipment for the most effective response. Transport personnel and cargo to and from fire areas. Participate in fire prevention and inspection programs. Perform forest maintenance and improvement tasks such as cutting brush, planting trees, building trails, and marking timber. Test and maintain tools, equipment, jump gear, and parachutes to ensure readiness for fire-suppression activities. Observe forest areas from fire lookout towers to spot potential problems. Orient self in relation to fire, using compass and map, and collect supplies and equipment dropped by parachute. Serve as fully trained lead helicopter crewmember and as helispot manager. Drop weighted paper streamers from aircraft to determine wind speed and direction at fire sites.

Personality Type: Realistic.

GOE—Interest Area: 12. Law and Public Safety. **Work Group:** 12.06. Emergency Responding. **Other Jobs in this Work Group:** Emergency Medical Technicians and Paramedics; Fire Fighters; Municipal Fire Fighters.

Skills: Management of Personnel Resources; Repairing; Equipment Maintenance; Operation Monitoring; Systems Analysis; Operation and Control.

Education and Training Programs: Fire Science/Fire Fighting; Fire Protection, Other. **Related Knowledge/Courses:** Geography; Customer and Personal Service; Mechanical Devices; Public Safety and Security; Education and Training; Psychology.

Work Environment: Outdoors; very hot or cold; contaminants; hazardous conditions; minor burns, cuts, bites, or stings; using hands on objects, tools, or controls.

Forest Fire Fighting and Prevention Supervisors

- ❋ Education/Training Required: Work experience in a related occupation
- ❋ Annual Earnings: $62,900
- ❋ Beginning Wage: $36,820
- ❋ Earnings Growth Potential: Very high
- ❋ Growth: 11.5%
- ❋ Annual Job Openings: 3,771
- ❋ Self-Employed: 0.0%
- ❋ Part-Time: 0.4%

Our sources did not provide separate job openings data for this occupation. The job openings listed here are shared with Municipal Fire Fighting and Prevention Supervisors.

Industries with Greatest Employment: Educational Services, Public and Private.

Highest-Growth Industries (Projected Growth for This Job): None met the criteria.

Lowest-Growth Industries (Projected Growth for This Job): Educational Services, Public and Private (11.9%).

Fastest-Growing Metropolitan Areas (Recent Growth for This Job): Canton–Massillon, OH (100.0%); Toledo, OH (100.0%); Cleveland–Elyria–Mentor, OH (95.7%); Memphis, TN–MS–AR (35.7%); Clarksville, TN–KY (33.3%).

Other Considerations for Job Security: Prospective fire fighters and their supervisors are expected to face keen competition for available job openings. Many people are attracted to fire fighting because it is challenging and provides the opportunity to perform an essential public service; a high-school education is usually sufficient for entry; and a pension is usually guaranteed after 25 of years work. Consequently, the number of qualified applicants in most areas far exceeds the number of job openings, even though the written examination and physical requirements eliminate many applicants. This situation is expected to persist in coming years. Applicants with the best chances are those who are physically fit and score the highest on physical conditioning and mechanical aptitude exams. Those who have completed some fire-fighter education at a community college and have EMT or paramedic certification will have additional advantages.

Supervise fire fighters who control and suppress fires in forests or vacant public land. Communicate fire details to superiors, subordinates, and interagency dispatch centers, using two-way radios. Serve as working leader of an engine, hand, helicopter, or prescribed fire crew of three or more fire fighters. Keep fire-suppression equipment in good condition, checking equipment periodically to ensure that it is ready for use. Evaluate size, location, and condition of forest fires to request and dispatch crews and position equipment so that fires can be contained safely and effectively. Operate wildland fire engines and hoselays. Direct and supervise prescribed burn projects and prepare post-burn reports, analyzing burn conditions and results. Monitor prescribed burns to ensure that they are conducted safely and effectively. Identify staff training and development needs to ensure that appropriate training can be arranged. Maintain knowledge of forest fire laws and fire prevention techniques and tactics. Recommend equipment modifications or new equipment purchases. Perform administrative duties such as compiling and maintaining records, completing forms, preparing reports, and composing correspondence. Recruit and hire forest fire-fighting personnel. Train workers in such skills as parachute jumping, fire suppression, aerial observation, and radio communication, both in the classroom and on the job. Review and evaluate employee performance. Observe fires and crews from air to determine fire-fighting force requirements and to note changing conditions that will affect fire-fighting efforts. Inspect all stations, uniforms, equipment, and recreation areas to ensure compliance with safety standards, taking corrective action as necessary. Schedule employee work assignments and set work priorities. Regulate open burning by issuing burning permits, inspecting problem sites, issuing citations for violations of laws and ordinances, and educating the public in proper burning practices. Direct investigations of suspected arsons in wildfires, working closely with other investigating agencies. Monitor fire suppression expenditures to ensure that they are necessary and reasonable.

Personality Type: Realistic.

GOE—Interest Area: 12. Law and Public Safety. **Work Group:** 12.01. Managerial Work in Law and Public Safety. **Other Jobs in this Work Group:** Emergency Management Specialists; First-Line Supervisors/Managers of Correctional Officers; First-Line Supervisors/Managers of Fire Fighting and Prevention Workers; First-Line Supervisors/Managers of

Police and Detectives; Municipal Fire Fighting and Prevention Supervisors.

Skills: Equipment Maintenance; Repairing; Management of Personnel Resources; Operation Monitoring; Operation and Control; Management of Material Resources.

Education and Training Programs: Fire Protection and Safety Technology/Technician; Fire Services Administration. **Related Knowledge/Courses:** Public Safety and Security; Building and Construction; Customer and Personal Service; Mechanical Devices; Personnel and Human Resources; Transportation.

Work Environment: Outdoors; noisy; very hot or cold; hazardous equipment; minor burns, cuts, bites, or stings; standing.

Forestry and Conservation Science Teachers, Postsecondary

- ✽ Education/Training Required: Doctoral degree
- ✽ Annual Earnings: $64,430
- ✽ Beginning Wage: $36,290
- ✽ Earnings Growth Potential: Very high
- ✽ Growth: 22.9%
- ✽ Annual Job Openings: 237,478
- ✽ Self-Employed: 0.4%
- ✽ Part-Time: 27.8%

Our sources did not provide separate job openings data for this occupation. The job openings listed here are shared with 35 other postsecondary teaching occupations. For a complete list, see the beginning of this section.

Industries with Greatest Employment: Educational Services, Public and Private.

Highest-Growth Industries (Projected Growth for This Job): Administrative and Support Services (48.3%); Amusement, Gambling, and Recreation Industries (45.3%); Social Assistance (38.6%); Support Activities for Transportation (32.8%); Religious, Grantmaking, Civic, Professional, and Similar

Organizations (29.9%); Professional, Scientific, and Technical Services (28.8%); Management of Companies and Enterprises (26.8%); Educational Services, Public and Private (22.9%); Hospitals, Public and Private (21.4%); Personal and Laundry Services (21.0%).

Lowest-Growth Industries (Projected Growth for This Job): Other Information Services (7.4%); Sporting Goods, Hobby, Book, and Music Stores (13.3%); Performing Arts, Spectator Sports, and Related Industries (13.4%); Insurance Carriers and Related Activities (13.9%).

Fastest-Growing Metropolitan Areas (Recent Growth for This Job): No data available.

Other Considerations for Job Security: Retirements of current postsecondary teachers should create numerous openings for all types of postsecondary teachers, so job opportunities are generally expected to be very good. Because students attend postsecondary institutions to prepare themselves for careers, the best job prospects for postsecondary teachers are likely to be in rapidly growing fields that offer many nonacademic career options. Community colleges and other institutions offering career and technical education have been among the most rapidly growing and are expected to offer some of the best opportunities for postsecondary teachers.

Teach courses in environmental and conservation science. Conduct research in a particular field of knowledge and publish findings in books, professional journals, and/or electronic media. Keep abreast of developments in their field by reading current literature, talking with colleagues, and participating in professional conferences. Prepare and deliver lectures to undergraduate and/or graduate students on topics such as forest resource policy, forest pathology, and mapping. Evaluate and grade students' classwork, assignments, and papers. Write grant proposals to procure external research funding. Supervise undergraduate and/or graduate teaching, internships, and research work. Plan, evaluate, and revise curricula, course content, course materials, and methods of instruction. Prepare course materials such as

syllabi, homework assignments, and handouts. Compile, administer, and grade examinations or assign this work to others. Advise students on academic and vocational curricula and on career issues. Initiate, facilitate, and moderate classroom discussions. Supervise students' laboratory work and fieldwork. Maintain student attendance records, grades, and other required records. Collaborate with colleagues to address teaching and research issues. Maintain regularly scheduled office hours to advise and assist students. Select and obtain materials and supplies such as textbooks and laboratory equipment. Participate in student recruitment, registration, and placement activities. Serve on academic or administrative committees that deal with institutional policies, departmental matters, and academic issues. Provide professional consulting services to government and/or industry. Perform administrative duties such as serving as department head. Compile bibliographies of specialized materials for outside reading assignments. Act as advisers to student organizations. Participate in campus and community events.

Personality Type: Investigative.

GOE—Interest Area: 05. Education and Training. **Work Group:** 05.03. Postsecondary and Adult Teaching and Instructing. **Other Jobs in this Work Group:** Adult Literacy, Remedial Education, and GED Teachers and Instructors; Agricultural Sciences Teachers, Postsecondary; Anthropology and Archeology Teachers, Postsecondary; Architecture Teachers, Postsecondary; Area, Ethnic, and Cultural Studies Teachers, Postsecondary; Art, Drama, and Music Teachers, Postsecondary; Atmospheric, Earth, Marine, and Space Sciences Teachers, Postsecondary; Biological Science Teachers, Postsecondary; Business Teachers, Postsecondary; Chemistry Teachers, Postsecondary; Communications Teachers, Postsecondary; Computer Science Teachers, Postsecondary; Criminal Justice and Law Enforcement Teachers, Postsecondary; Economics Teachers, Postsecondary; Education Teachers, Postsecondary; Engineering Teachers, Postsecondary; English Language and Literature Teachers, Postsecondary; Environmental Science Teachers, Postsecondary; Farm and Home Management Advisors; Foreign Language and Literature Teachers, Postsecondary; Geography Teachers, Postsecondary; Graduate Teaching Assistants; Health Specialties Teachers, Postsecondary; History Teachers, Postsecondary; Home Economics Teachers, Postsecondary; Law Teachers, Postsecondary; Library Science Teachers, Postsecondary; Mathematical Science Teachers, Postsecondary; Nursing Instructors and Teachers, Postsecondary; Philosophy and Religion Teachers, Postsecondary; Physics Teachers, Postsecondary; Political Science Teachers, Postsecondary; Psychology Teachers, Postsecondary; Recreation and Fitness Studies Teachers, Postsecondary; Self-Enrichment Education Teachers; Social Work Teachers, Postsecondary; Sociology Teachers, Postsecondary; Vocational Education Teachers, Postsecondary.

Skills: Science; Management of Financial Resources; Management of Personnel Resources; Writing; Instructing; Mathematics.

Education and Training Program: Science Teacher Education/General Science Teacher Education. **Related Knowledge/Courses:** Biology; Geography; Education and Training; Mathematics; Chemistry; History and Archeology.

Work Environment: Indoors; sitting.

Funeral Attendants

- ❋ Education/Training Required: Short-term on-the-job training
- ❋ Annual Earnings: $20,350
- ❋ Beginning Wage: $13,780
- ❋ Earnings Growth Potential: Very high
- ❋ Growth: 14.3%
- ❋ Annual Job Openings: 6,034
- ❋ Self-Employed: 0.6%
- ❋ Part-Time: 21.6%

Industries with Greatest Employment: Personal and Laundry Services.

Highest-Growth Industries (Projected Growth for This Job): None met the criteria.

Lowest-Growth Industries (Projected Growth for This Job): None met the criteria.

Fastest-Growing Metropolitan Areas (Recent Growth for This Job): Utica–Rome, NY (100.0%); Wichita, KS (80.0%); Atlanta–Sandy Springs–Marietta, GA (61.3%); Asheville, NC (55.6%); Parkersburg–Marietta–Vienna, WV–OH (50.0%).

Other Considerations for Job Security: No data available.

Perform tasks for funerals, such as placing caskets in parlor or chapel before service, arranging floral offerings or lights around caskets, directing or escorting mourners, closing caskets, and issuing and storing funeral equipment. Perform a variety of tasks during funerals to assist funeral directors and to ensure that services run smoothly and as planned. Greet people at funeral home. Offer assistance to mourners as they enter or exit limousines. Close caskets at appropriate point in services. Transfer the deceased to funeral homes. Obtain burial permits and register deaths. Direct or escort mourners to parlors or chapels in which wakes or funerals are being held. Place caskets in parlors or chapels before wakes or funerals. Clean and drive funeral vehicles such as cars or hearses in funeral processions. Carry flowers to hearses or limousines for transportation to places of interment. Clean funeral parlors and chapels. Arrange floral offerings or lights around caskets. Provide advice to mourners on how to make charitable donations in honor of the deceased. Perform general maintenance duties for funeral homes. Issue and store funeral equipment. Assist with cremations and with the processing and packaging of cremated remains. Act as pallbearers.

Personality Type: Social.

GOE—Interest Area: 10. Human Service. **Work Group:** 10.03. Child/Personal Care and Services. **Other Jobs in this Work Group:** Child Care Workers; Nannies; Personal and Home Care Aides.

Skills: No data available.

Education and Training Program: Funeral Service and Mortuary Science, General. **Related Knowledge/Courses:** Philosophy and Theology; Transportation; Customer and Personal Service; Psychology; Law and Government; Clerical Studies.

Work Environment: More often indoors than outdoors; standing.

Funeral Directors

- ❋ Education/Training Required: Associate degree
- ❋ Annual Earnings: $49,620
- ❋ Beginning Wage: $28,410
- ❋ Earnings Growth Potential: Very high
- ❋ Growth: 12.5%
- ❋ Annual Job Openings: 3,939
- ❋ Self-Employed: 19.7%
- ❋ Part-Time: 8.5%

Industries with Greatest Employment: Personal and Laundry Services.

Highest-Growth Industries (Projected Growth for This Job): None met the criteria.

Lowest-Growth Industries (Projected Growth for This Job): Personal and Laundry Services (14.3%).

Fastest-Growing Metropolitan Areas (Recent Growth for This Job): Portland–South Portland–Biddeford, ME (100.0%); Poughkeepsie–Newburgh–Middletown, NY (80.0%); Kansas City, MO–KS (71.4%); Rocky Mount, NC (66.7%); Chattanooga, TN–GA (50.0%).

Other Considerations for Job Security: Job opportunities are expected to be good, particularly for those who also embalm. Funeral directors are older, on average, than workers in most other occupations and are expected to retire in greater numbers over the coming decade. Also, some funeral directors leave the profession because of the long and irregular hours. Some mortuary science graduates relocate to get a job.

Perform various tasks to arrange and direct funeral services, such as coordinating transportation of body to mortuary for embalming, interviewing family or other authorized person to arrange details, selecting pallbearers, procuring official for religious rites, and providing transportation for mourners. Consult with families or friends of the deceased to arrange funeral details such as obituary notice wording, casket selection, and plans for services. Plan, schedule, and coordinate funerals, burials, and cremations, arranging such details as the time and place of services. Obtain information needed to complete legal documents such as death certificates and burial permits. Oversee the preparation and care of the remains of people who have died. Contact cemeteries to schedule the opening and closing of graves. Provide information on funeral service options, products, and merchandise and maintain a casket display area. Manage funeral home operations, including hiring and supervising embalmers, funeral attendants, and other staff. Offer counsel and comfort to bereaved families and friends. Close caskets and lead funeral corteges to churches or burial sites. Arrange for clergy members to perform needed services. Provide or arrange transportation between sites for the remains, mourners, pallbearers, clergy, and flowers. Perform embalming duties as necessary. Direct preparations and shipment of bodies for out-of-state burial. Discuss and negotiate prearranged funerals with clients. Inform survivors of benefits for which they may be eligible. Maintain financial records, order merchandise, and prepare accounts. Plan placement of caskets at funeral sites and place and adjust lights, fixtures, and floral displays. Arrange for pallbearers and inform pallbearers and honorary groups of their duties. Receive people and usher them to their seats for services.

Personality Type: Enterprising.

GOE—Interest Area: 14. Retail and Wholesale Sales and Service. **Work Group:** 14.01. Managerial Work in Retail/Wholesale Sales and Service. **Other Jobs in this Work Group:** Advertising and Promotions Managers; First-Line Supervisors/Managers of Non-Retail Sales Workers; First-Line Supervisors/

Managers of Retail Sales Workers; Marketing Managers; Property, Real Estate, and Community Association Managers; Purchasing Managers; Sales Managers.

Skills: Management of Financial Resources; Service Orientation; Social Perceptiveness; Management of Personnel Resources; Management of Material Resources; Coordination.

Education and Training Programs: Funeral Service and Mortuary Science, General; Funeral Direction/Service. **Related Knowledge/Courses:** Therapy and Counseling; Philosophy and Theology; Customer and Personal Service; Sales and Marketing; Clerical Studies; Psychology.

Work Environment: More often indoors than outdoors; contaminants; disease or infections; standing.

Gaming Surveillance Officers and Gaming Investigators

- ❈ Education/Training Required: Moderate-term on-the-job training
- ❈ Annual Earnings: $27,130
- ❈ Beginning Wage: $18,720
- ❈ Earnings Growth Potential: Very high
- ❈ Growth: 33.6%
- ❈ Annual Job Openings: 2,124
- ❈ Self-Employed: 0.7%
- ❈ Part-Time: 15.5%

Industries with Greatest Employment: Amusement, Gambling, and Recreation Industries; Accommodation, Including Hotels and Motels; Performing Arts, Spectator Sports, and Related Industries.

Highest-Growth Industries (Projected Growth for This Job): Amusement, Gambling, and Recreation Industries (83.1%); Performing Arts, Spectator Sports, and Related Industries (24.4%); Accommodation, Including Hotels and Motels (18.6%).

Lowest-Growth Industries (Projected Growth for This Job): None met the criteria.

Fastest-Growing Metropolitan Areas (Recent Growth for This Job): Albuquerque, NM (87.5%); Omaha–Council Bluffs, NE–IA (25.0%); St. Louis, MO–IL (16.7%).

Other Considerations for Job Security: Job prospects for gaming surveillance officers should be good, but they will be better for those with experience in the gaming industry. Casinos will continue to hire more surveillance officers as more states legalize gambling and as the number of casinos increases in states where gambling is already legal. Also, casino security forces will employ more technically trained personnel as technology becomes increasingly important in thwarting casino cheating and theft.

Act as oversight and security agent for management and customers. Observe casino or casino hotel operation for irregular activities such as cheating or theft by either employees or patrons. May utilize one-way mirrors above the casino floor and cashier's cage and from desk. Use of audio/video equipment is also common to observe operation of the business. Usually required to provide verbal and written reports of all violations and suspicious behavior to supervisor. Report all violations and suspicious behaviors to supervisors verbally or in writing. Monitor establishment activities to ensure adherence to all state gaming regulations and company policies and procedures. Act as oversight or security agents for management or customers. Supervise or train surveillance observers.

Personality Type: No data available.

GOE—Interest Area: 12. Law and Public Safety. **Work Group:** 12.05. Safety and Security. **Other Jobs in this Work Group:** Animal Control Workers; Crossing Guards; Lifeguards, Ski Patrol, and Other Recreational Protective Service Workers; Private Detectives and Investigators; Security Guards; Transportation Security Screeners.

Skills: Management of Personnel Resources; Active Listening; Writing; Negotiation; Social Perceptiveness; Learning Strategies.

Education and Training Program: Personal and Culinary Services, Other. **Related Knowledge/Courses:** Public Safety and Security; Computers and Electronics; Telecommunications; Law and Government; Clerical Studies; Education and Training.

Work Environment: Indoors; contaminants; sitting; using hands on objects, tools, or controls; repetitive motions.

Geography Teachers, Postsecondary

- ❋ Education/Training Required: Doctoral degree
- ❋ Annual Earnings: $59,000
- ❋ Beginning Wage: $34,300
- ❋ Earnings Growth Potential: Very high
- ❋ Growth: 22.9%
- ❋ Annual Job Openings: 237,478
- ❋ Self-Employed: 0.4%
- ❋ Part-Time: 27.8%

Our sources did not provide separate job openings data for this occupation. The job openings listed here are shared with 35 other postsecondary teaching occupations. For a complete list, see the beginning of this section.

Industries with Greatest Employment: Educational Services, Public and Private.

Highest-Growth Industries (Projected Growth for This Job): Administrative and Support Services (48.3%); Amusement, Gambling, and Recreation Industries (45.3%); Social Assistance (38.6%); Support Activities for Transportation (32.8%); Religious, Grantmaking, Civic, Professional, and Similar Organizations (29.9%); Professional, Scientific, and Technical Services (28.8%); Management of Companies and Enterprises (26.8%); Educational Services, Public and Private (22.9%); Hospitals, Public and Private (21.4%); Personal and Laundry Services (21.0%).

Lowest-Growth Industries (Projected Growth for This Job): Other Information Services (7.4%);

Sporting Goods, Hobby, Book, and Music Stores (13.3%); Performing Arts, Spectator Sports, and Related Industries (13.4%); Insurance Carriers and Related Activities (13.9%).

Fastest-Growing Metropolitan Areas (Recent Growth for This Job): Boston–Cambridge–Quincy, MA–NH (22.2%); New York–Northern New Jersey–Long Island, NY–NJ–PA (20.0%); San Diego–Carlsbad–San Marcos, CA (20.0%).

Other Considerations for Job Security: Retirements of current postsecondary teachers should create numerous openings for all types of postsecondary teachers. However, because students attend postsecondary institutions to prepare themselves for careers, the best job prospects for postsecondary teachers are likely to be in rapidly growing fields that offer many nonacademic career options. Community colleges and other institutions offering career and technical education have been among the most rapidly growing and are expected to offer some of the best opportunities for postsecondary teachers.

Teach courses in geography. Prepare and deliver lectures to undergraduate and/or graduate students on topics such as urbanization, environmental systems, and cultural geography. Evaluate and grade students' classwork, assignments, and papers. Compile, administer, and grade examinations or assign this work to others. Initiate, facilitate, and moderate classroom discussions. Maintain student attendance records, grades, and other required records. Prepare course materials such as syllabi, homework assignments, and handouts. Keep abreast of developments in their field by reading current literature, talking with colleagues, and participating in professional conferences. Supervise undergraduate and/or graduate teaching, internships, and research work. Plan, evaluate, and revise curricula, course content, course materials, and methods of instruction. Maintain regularly scheduled office hours to advise and assist students. Supervise students' laboratory work and fieldwork. Conduct research in a particular field of knowledge and publish findings in professional journals, books, and electronic media. Collaborate with colleagues to address teaching and research issues. Select and obtain materials and supplies such as textbooks. Advise students on academic and vocational curricula and on career issues. Serve on academic or administrative committees that deal with institutional policies, departmental matters, and academic issues. Participate in student recruitment, registration, and placement activities. Participate in campus and community events. Compile bibliographies of specialized materials for outside reading assignments. Perform administrative duties such as serving as department head. Write grant proposals to procure external research funding. Maintain geographic information systems laboratories, performing duties such as updating software. Perform spatial analysis and modeling, using geographic information system techniques. Act as advisers to student organizations. Provide professional consulting services to government and industry.

Personality Type: No data available.

GOE—Interest Area: 05. Education and Training. **Work Group:** 05.03. Postsecondary and Adult Teaching and Instructing. **Other Jobs in this Work Group:** Adult Literacy, Remedial Education, and GED Teachers and Instructors; Agricultural Sciences Teachers, Postsecondary; Anthropology and Archeology Teachers, Postsecondary; Architecture Teachers, Postsecondary; Area, Ethnic, and Cultural Studies Teachers, Postsecondary; Art, Drama, and Music Teachers, Postsecondary; Atmospheric, Earth, Marine, and Space Sciences Teachers, Postsecondary; Biological Science Teachers, Postsecondary; Business Teachers, Postsecondary; Chemistry Teachers, Postsecondary; Communications Teachers, Postsecondary; Computer Science Teachers, Postsecondary; Criminal Justice and Law Enforcement Teachers, Postsecondary; Economics Teachers, Postsecondary; Education Teachers, Postsecondary; Engineering Teachers, Postsecondary; English Language and Literature Teachers, Postsecondary; Environmental Science Teachers, Postsecondary; Farm and Home Management Advisors; Foreign Language and Literature Teachers, Postsecondary; Forestry and Conservation Science Teachers, Postsecondary; Graduate Teaching Assistants; Health Specialties

Teachers, Postsecondary; History Teachers, Postsecondary; Home Economics Teachers, Postsecondary; Law Teachers, Postsecondary; Library Science Teachers, Postsecondary; Mathematical Science Teachers, Postsecondary; Nursing Instructors and Teachers, Postsecondary; Philosophy and Religion Teachers, Postsecondary; Physics Teachers, Postsecondary; Political Science Teachers, Postsecondary; Psychology Teachers, Postsecondary; Recreation and Fitness Studies Teachers, Postsecondary; Self-Enrichment Education Teachers; Social Work Teachers, Postsecondary; Sociology Teachers, Postsecondary; Vocational Education Teachers, Postsecondary.

Skills: Science; Writing; Instructing; Learning Strategies; Reading Comprehension; Speaking.

Education and Training Programs: Geography Teacher Education; Geography. **Related Knowledge/Courses:** Geography; Sociology and Anthropology; History and Archeology; Philosophy and Theology; Education and Training; Communications and Media.

Work Environment: Indoors; sitting.

Geoscientists, Except Hydrologists and Geographers

- ✳ Education/Training Required: Master's degree
- ✳ Annual Earnings: $72,660
- ✳ Beginning Wage: $39,740
- ✳ Earnings Growth Potential: Very high
- ✳ Growth: 21.9%
- ✳ Annual Job Openings: 2,471
- ✳ Self-Employed: 2.2%
- ✳ Part-Time: 5.3%

Industries with Greatest Employment: Professional, Scientific, and Technical Services; Oil and Gas Extraction; Support Activities for Mining; Educational Services, Public and Private.

Highest-Growth Industries (Projected Growth for This Job): Professional, Scientific, and Technical

Services (45.2%); Securities, Commodity Contracts, and Other Financial Investments and Related Activities (40.7%); Waste Management and Remediation Services (32.1%); Administrative and Support Services (26.8%); Management of Companies and Enterprises (15.4%).

Lowest-Growth Industries (Projected Growth for This Job): Support Activities for Mining (–6.0%); Mining (except Oil and Gas) (6.5%); Oil and Gas Extraction (8.2%); Educational Services, Public and Private (11.7%).

Fastest-Growing Metropolitan Areas (Recent Growth for This Job): Austin–Round Rock, TX (165.4%); Richmond, VA (100.0%); San Antonio, TX (66.7%); Tucson, AZ (62.5%); Albuquerque, NM (55.6%).

Other Considerations for Job Security: Graduates with a master's degree can expect excellent job opportunities; very few geoscientist jobs are available to bachelor's-degree holders. Doctorates should face competition for basic research and college teaching jobs. Historically, employment of petroleum geologists, geophysicists, and some other geoscientists has been cyclical and affected considerably by the price of oil and gas. When prices are low, oil and gas producers curtail exploration activities and lay off geologists. When prices are higher, companies have the funds and incentive to renew exploration efforts and to hire geoscientists in larger numbers. In recent years, however, a growing worldwide demand for oil and gas and for new exploration and recovery techniques has created some stability in the petroleum industry. Geoscientists who speak foreign languages and who are willing to work abroad should enjoy the best opportunities.

Study the composition, structure, and other physical aspects of the earth. May use geological, physics, and mathematics knowledge in exploration for oil, gas, minerals, or underground water or in waste disposal, land reclamation, or other environmental problems. May study the earth's internal composition, atmospheres, and oceans and its magnetic, electrical, and gravitational forces.

Includes mineralogists, crystallographers, paleontologists, stratigraphers, geodesists, and seismologists. Analyze and interpret geological, geochemical, and geophysical information from sources such as survey data, well logs, bore holes, and aerial photos. Plan and conduct geological, geochemical, and geophysical field studies and surveys, sample collection, or drilling and testing programs used to collect data for research or application. Investigate the composition, structure, and history of the Earth's crust through the collection, examination, measurement, and classification of soils, minerals, rocks, or fossil remains. Prepare geological maps, cross-sectional diagrams, charts, and reports concerning mineral extraction, land use, and resource management, using results of field work and laboratory research. Locate and estimate probable natural gas, oil, and mineral ore deposits and underground water resources, using aerial photographs, charts, or research and survey results. Assess ground and surface water movement to provide advice regarding issues such as waste management, route and site selection, and the restoration of contaminated sites. Identify risks for natural disasters such as mud slides, earthquakes, and volcanic eruptions, providing advice on mitigation of potential damage. Conduct geological and geophysical studies to provide information for use in regional development, site selection, and development of public works projects. Inspect construction projects to analyze engineering problems, applying geological knowledge and using test equipment and drilling machinery. Advise construction firms and government agencies on dam and road construction, foundation design, or land use and resource management. Communicate geological findings by writing research papers, participating in conferences, or teaching geological science at universities. Measure characteristics of the Earth, such as gravity and magnetic fields, using equipment such as seismographs, gravimeters, torsion balances, and magnetometers. Test industrial diamonds and abrasives, soil, or rocks to determine their geological characteristics, using optical, X-ray, heat, acid, and precision instruments. Identify deposits of construction materials and assess their characteristics and suitability for use as concrete aggregates, as road fill, or in other applications.

Personality Type: Investigative.

GOE—Interest Area: 15. Scientific Research, Engineering, and Mathematics. **Work Group:** 15.02. Physical Sciences. **Other Jobs in this Work Group:** Astronomers; Atmospheric and Space Scientists; Chemists; Geographers; Hydrologists; Materials Scientists; Physicists.

Skills: Science; Management of Financial Resources; Active Learning; Time Management; Coordination; Mathematics.

Education and Training Programs: Geology/Earth Science, General; Geochemistry; Geophysics and Seismology; Paleontology; Geochemistry and Petrology; Oceanography, Chemical and Physical; Geological and Earth Sciences/Geosciences, Other. **Related Knowledge/Courses:** Geography; Physics; Chemistry; Biology; Engineering and Technology; Mathematics.

Work Environment: More often indoors than outdoors; sitting.

Graduate Teaching Assistants

- ❋ Education/Training Required: Bachelor's degree
- ❋ Annual Earnings: $27,840
- ❋ Beginning Wage: $15,830
- ❋ Earnings Growth Potential: Very high
- ❋ Growth: 22.9%
- ❋ Annual Job Openings: 237,478
- ❋ Self-Employed: 0.4%
- ❋ Part-Time: 27.8%

Our sources did not provide separate job openings data for this occupation. The job openings listed here are shared with 35 other postsecondary teaching occupations. For a complete list, see the beginning of this section.

Industries with Greatest Employment: Educational Services, Public and Private.

Highest-Growth Industries (Projected Growth for This Job): Administrative and Support Services (48.3%); Amusement, Gambling, and Recreation Industries (45.3%); Social Assistance (38.6%); Support Activities for Transportation (32.8%); Religious, Grantmaking, Civic, Professional, and Similar Organizations (29.9%); Professional, Scientific, and Technical Services (28.8%); Management of Companies and Enterprises (26.8%); Educational Services, Public and Private (22.9%); Hospitals, Public and Private (21.4%); Personal and Laundry Services (21.0%).

Lowest-Growth Industries (Projected Growth for This Job): Other Information Services (7.4%); Sporting Goods, Hobby, Book, and Music Stores (13.3%); Performing Arts, Spectator Sports, and Related Industries (13.4%); Insurance Carriers and Related Activities (13.9%).

Fastest-Growing Metropolitan Areas (Recent Growth for This Job): San Diego–Carlsbad–San Marcos, CA (20.0%); Riverside–San Bernardino–Ontario, CA (20.0%); Worcester, MA–CT (20.0%); New York–Northern New Jersey–Long Island, NY–NJ–PA (20.0%); Springfield, MA–CT (19.4%).

Other Considerations for Job Security: Retirements of current postsecondary teachers should create numerous openings for all types of postsecondary teachers, so job opportunities are generally expected to be very good. However, because students attend postsecondary institutions to prepare themselves for careers, the best job prospects for postsecondary teachers are likely to be in rapidly growing fields that offer many nonacademic career options. Community colleges and other institutions offering career and technical education have been among the most rapidly growing and are expected to offer some of the best opportunities for postsecondary teachers.

Assist department chairperson, faculty members, or other professional staff members in college or university by performing teaching or teaching-related duties, such as teaching lower-level courses, developing teaching materials, preparing and giving examinations, and grading examinations or papers. Graduate assistants must be enrolled in a graduate school program. Graduate assistants who primarily perform nonteaching duties, such as laboratory research, should be

reported in the occupational category related to the work performed. Lead discussion sections, tutorials, and laboratory sections. Evaluate and grade examinations, assignments, and papers and record grades. Return assignments to students according to established deadlines. Schedule and maintain regular office hours to meet with students. Inform students of the procedures for completing and submitting class work such as lab reports. Prepare and proctor examinations. Notify instructors of errors or problems with assignments. Meet with supervisors to discuss students' grades and to complete required grade-related paperwork. Copy and distribute classroom materials. Demonstrate use of laboratory equipment and enforce laboratory rules. Teach undergraduate-level courses. Complete laboratory projects before assigning them to students so that any needed modifications can be made. Develop teaching materials such as syllabi, visual aids, answer keys, supplementary notes, and course Web sites. Provide assistance to faculty members or staff with laboratory or field research. Arrange for supervisors to conduct teaching observations; meet with supervisors to receive feedback about teaching performance. Attend lectures given by the instructor whom they are assisting. Order or obtain materials needed for classes. Provide instructors with assistance in the use of audiovisual equipment. Assist faculty members or staff with student conferences.

Personality Type: Social.

GOE—Interest Area: 05. Education and Training. **Work Group:** 05.03. Postsecondary and Adult Teaching and Instructing. **Other Jobs in this Work Group:** Adult Literacy, Remedial Education, and GED Teachers and Instructors; Agricultural Sciences Teachers, Postsecondary; Anthropology and Archeology Teachers, Postsecondary; Architecture Teachers, Postsecondary; Area, Ethnic, and Cultural Studies Teachers, Postsecondary; Art, Drama, and Music Teachers, Postsecondary; Atmospheric, Earth, Marine, and Space Sciences Teachers, Postsecondary; Biological Science Teachers, Postsecondary; Business Teachers, Postsecondary; Chemistry Teachers, Postsecondary; Communications Teachers, Postsecondary; Computer Science Teachers, Postsecondary; Criminal Justice and Law Enforcement Teachers, Postsecondary; Economics Teachers, Postsecondary; Education Teachers, Postsecondary; Engineering Teachers, Postsecondary; English Language and Literature Teachers, Postsecondary; Environmental Science Teachers, Postsecondary; Farm and Home Management Advisors; Foreign Language and Literature Teachers, Postsecondary; Forestry and Conservation Science Teachers, Postsecondary; Geography Teachers, Postsecondary; Health Specialties Teachers, Postsecondary; History Teachers, Postsecondary; Home Economics Teachers, Postsecondary; Law Teachers, Postsecondary; Library Science Teachers, Postsecondary; Mathematical Science Teachers, Postsecondary; Nursing Instructors and Teachers, Postsecondary; Philosophy and Religion Teachers, Postsecondary; Physics Teachers, Postsecondary; Political Science Teachers, Postsecondary; Psychology Teachers, Postsecondary; Recreation and Fitness Studies Teachers, Postsecondary; Self-Enrichment Education Teachers; Social Work Teachers, Postsecondary; Sociology Teachers, Postsecondary; Vocational Education Teachers, Postsecondary.

Skills: Learning Strategies; Social Perceptiveness; Instructing; Reading Comprehension; Writing; Speaking.

Education and Training Program: Education, General. **Related Knowledge/Courses:** Sociology and Anthropology; Education and Training; English Language; Communications and Media; Philosophy and Theology; Psychology.

Work Environment: Indoors; sitting.

Hazardous Materials Removal Workers

- Education/Training Required: Moderate-term on-the-job training
- Annual Earnings: $35,450
- Beginning Wage: $22,910
- Earnings Growth Potential: Very high
- Growth: 11.2%
- Annual Job Openings: 1,933
- Self-Employed: 1.6%
- Part-Time: 5.7%

Industries with Greatest Employment: Waste Management and Remediation Services.

Highest-Growth Industries (Projected Growth for This Job): Professional, Scientific, and Technical Services (37.4%).

Lowest-Growth Industries (Projected Growth for This Job): Chemical Manufacturing (–20.4%); Transportation Equipment Manufacturing (–13.2%); Utilities (–12.4%); Specialty Trade Contractors (–5.3%); Educational Services, Public and Private (–4.4%); Hospitals, Public and Private (–4.1%); Administrative and Support Services (7.0%); Waste Management and Remediation Services (13.6%).

Fastest-Growing Metropolitan Areas (Recent Growth for This Job): Corpus Christi, TX (200.0%); New Orleans–Metairie–Kenner, LA (170.6%); Hartford–West Hartford–East Hartford, CT (150.0%); Sacramento–Arden–Arcade–Roseville, CA (106.7%); Columbia, SC (100.0%).

Other Considerations for Job Security: In addition to some job openings from employment growth, many openings are expected for hazardous materials removal workers because of the need to replace workers who leave the occupation, leading to good opportunities. The often dangerous aspects of the job lead to high turnover because many workers don't stay in the occupation long. Opportunities for decontamination technicians, radiation safety technicians, and decontamination workers should be particularly good.

Lead and asbestos workers will have some opportunities at specialty remediation companies as restoration of federal buildings and historic structures continues, although at a slower pace. The best employment opportunities for mold remediation workers will be in the Southeast and parts of the Northeast and Northwest, where mold tends to thrive. These workers aren't greatly affected by economic fluctuations because the facilities in which they work must operate, regardless of the state of the economy.

Identify, remove, pack, transport, or dispose of hazardous materials, including asbestos, lead-based paint, waste oil, fuel, transmission fluid, radioactive materials, contaminated soil, and so on. Specialized training and certification in hazardous materials handling or a confined entry permit are generally required. May operate earth-moving equipment or trucks. Follow prescribed safety procedures and comply with federal laws regulating waste-disposal methods. Record numbers of containers stored at disposal sites and specify amounts and types of equipment and waste disposed. Drive trucks or other heavy equipment to convey contaminated waste to designated sea or ground locations. Operate machines and equipment to remove, package, store, or transport loads of waste materials. Load and unload materials into containers and onto trucks, using hoists or forklifts. Clean contaminated equipment or areas for reuse, using detergents and solvents, sandblasters, filter pumps, and steam cleaners. Construct scaffolding or build containment areas before beginning abatement or decontamination work. Remove asbestos or lead from surfaces by using hand and power tools such as scrapers, vacuums, and high-pressure sprayers. Unload baskets of irradiated elements onto packaging machines that automatically insert fuel elements into canisters and secure lids. Apply chemical compounds to lead-based paint, allow compounds to dry, and then scrape the hazardous material into containers for removal or storage. Identify asbestos, lead, or other hazardous materials that need to be removed by using monitoring devices. Pull tram cars along underwater tracks and position cars to receive irradiated fuel elements; then pull loaded cars to mechanisms that automatically unload elements onto underwater tables. Package, store, and move irradiated fuel elements in underwater storage basin of nuclear reactor plant, using machines and equipment. Organize and track locations of hazardous items in landfills. Operate cranes to move and load baskets, casks, and canisters. Manipulate handgrips of mechanical arms to place irradiated fuel into baskets. Mix and pour concrete into forms to encase waste material for disposal.

Personality Type: Realistic.

GOE—Interest Area: 02. Architecture and Construction. **Work Group:** 02.04. Construction Crafts. **Other Jobs in this Work Group:** Boilermakers; Brickmasons and Blockmasons; Carpet Installers; Cement Masons and Concrete Finishers; Commercial Divers; Construction Carpenters; Crane and Tower Operators; Drywall and Ceiling Tile Installers; Electricians; Fence Erectors; Floor Layers, Except Carpet, Wood, and Hard Tiles; Floor Sanders and Finishers; Glaziers; Insulation Workers, Floor, Ceiling, and Wall; Insulation Workers, Mechanical; Manufactured Building and Mobile Home Installers; Operating Engineers and Other Construction Equipment Operators; Painters, Construction and Maintenance; Paperhangers; Paving, Surfacing, and Tamping Equipment Operators; Pile-Driver Operators; Pipe Fitters and Steamfitters; Pipelayers; Plasterers and Stucco Masons; Plumbers; Plumbers, Pipefitters, and Steamfitters; Rail-Track Laying and Maintenance Equipment Operators; Refractory Materials Repairers, Except Brickmasons; Reinforcing Iron and Rebar Workers; Riggers; Roofers; Rough Carpenters; Security and Fire Alarm Systems Installers; Segmental Pavers; Sheet Metal Workers; Stone Cutters and Carvers, Manufacturing; Stonemasons; Structural Iron and Steel Workers; Tapers; Terrazzo Workers and Finishers; Tile and Marble Setters.

Skills: Operation Monitoring; Equipment Maintenance; Repairing; Operation and Control; Troubleshooting; Science.

Education and Training Programs: Hazardous Materials Management and Waste Technology/

Technician; Construction Trades, Other; Mechanic and Repair Technologies/Technicians, Other. **Related Knowledge/Courses:** Chemistry; Mechanical Devices; Building and Construction; Transportation; Physics; Public Safety and Security.

Work Environment: Outdoors; very hot or cold; contaminants; hazardous conditions; using hands on objects, tools, or controls; repetitive motions.

Health Educators

- Education/Training Required: Bachelor's degree
- Annual Earnings: $41,330
- Beginning Wage: $24,750
- Earnings Growth Potential: Very high
- Growth: 26.2%
- Annual Job Openings: 13,707
- Self-Employed: 0.1%
- Part-Time: 12.0%

Industries with Greatest Employment: Hospitals, Public and Private; Social Assistance; Ambulatory Health Care Services; Religious, Grantmaking, Civic, Professional, and Similar Organizations; Educational Services, Public and Private.

Highest-Growth Industries (Projected Growth for This Job): Social Assistance (74.7%); Ambulatory Health Care Services (34.5%); Religious, Grantmaking, Civic, Professional, and Similar Organizations (29.7%); Administrative and Support Services (29.0%); Professional, Scientific, and Technical Services (27.5%); Nursing and Residential Care Facilities (23.3%); Management of Companies and Enterprises (15.2%).

Lowest-Growth Industries (Projected Growth for This Job): Insurance Carriers and Related Activities (3.7%); Hospitals, Public and Private (10.2%); Educational Services, Public and Private (13.1%).

Fastest-Growing Metropolitan Areas (Recent Growth for This Job): Winston-Salem, NC (175.0%); Scranton–Wilkes-Barre, PA (160.0%); Jackson, MS

(125.0%); Pittsfield, MA (114.3%); Columbia, SC (78.6%).

Other Considerations for Job Security: Rising health-care costs have increased the need for health educators. Demand for health educators will increase in most industries, but their employment may decrease in secondary schools. Many schools, facing budget cuts, ask teachers trained in other fields, such as science or physical education, to teach the subject of health education. Job prospects for health educators with bachelor's degrees will be favorable, but better for those who have acquired experience through internships or volunteer jobs. A graduate degree is preferred by many employers.

Promote, maintain, and improve individual and community health by helping individuals and communities adopt healthy behaviors. Collect and analyze data to identify community needs before planning, implementing, monitoring, and evaluating programs designed to encourage healthy lifestyles, policies, and environments. May also serve as a resource to assist individuals, other professionals, or the community and may administer fiscal resources for health education programs. Document activities, recording information such as the numbers of applications completed, presentations conducted, and persons assisted. Develop and present health education and promotion programs such as training workshops, conferences, and school or community presentations. Develop and maintain cooperative working relationships with agencies and organizations interested in public health care. Prepare and distribute health education materials, including reports; bulletins; and visual aids such as films, videotapes, photographs, and posters. Develop operational plans and policies necessary to achieve health education objectives and services. Collaborate with health specialists and civic groups to determine community health needs and the availability of services and to develop goals for meeting needs. Maintain databases, mailing lists, telephone networks, and other information to facilitate the functioning of health education programs. Supervise professional and technical staff in implementing health programs, objectives, and goals. Design and conduct evaluations and diagnostic studies to assess the quality and performance of health education programs. Provide program information to the public by preparing and presenting press releases, conducting media campaigns, and/or maintaining program-related Web sites. Develop, prepare, and coordinate grant applications and grant-related activities to obtain funding for health education programs and related work. Provide guidance to agencies and organizations in the assessment of health education needs and in the development and delivery of health education programs. Develop and maintain health education libraries to provide resources for staff and community agencies. Develop, conduct, or coordinate health needs assessments and other public health surveys.

Personality Type: Social.

GOE—Interest Area: 05. Education and Training. **Work Group:** 05.06. Counseling, Health, and Fitness Education. **Other Jobs in this Work Group:** Educational, Vocational, and School Counselors; Fitness Trainers and Aerobics Instructors.

Skills: Service Orientation; Social Perceptiveness; Monitoring; Learning Strategies; Speaking; Instructing.

Education and Training Programs: Health Communication; Community Health Services/Liaison/Counseling; Public Health Education and Promotion; Maternal and Child Health; International Public Health/International Health; Bioethics/Medical Ethics. **Related Knowledge/Courses:** Sociology and Anthropology; Customer and Personal Service; Education and Training; Personnel and Human Resources; Psychology; Therapy and Counseling.

Work Environment: Indoors; disease or infections; sitting; using hands on objects, tools, or controls.

Health Specialties Teachers, Postsecondary

- ❋ Education/Training Required: Doctoral degree
- ❋ Annual Earnings: $77,190
- ❋ Beginning Wage: $36,990
- ❋ Earnings Growth Potential: High
- ❋ Growth: 22.9%
- ❋ Annual Job Openings: 237,478
- ❋ Self-Employed: 0.4%
- ❋ Part-Time: 27.8%

Our sources did not provide separate job openings data for this occupation. The job openings listed here are shared with 35 other postsecondary teaching occupations. For a complete list, see the beginning of this section.

Industries with Greatest Employment: Educational Services, Public and Private.

Highest-Growth Industries (Projected Growth for This Job): Administrative and Support Services (48.3%); Amusement, Gambling, and Recreation Industries (45.3%); Social Assistance (38.6%); Support Activities for Transportation (32.8%); Religious, Grantmaking, Civic, Professional, and Similar Organizations (29.9%); Professional, Scientific, and Technical Services (28.8%); Management of Companies and Enterprises (26.8%); Educational Services, Public and Private (22.9%); Hospitals, Public and Private (21.4%); Personal and Laundry Services (21.0%).

Lowest-Growth Industries (Projected Growth for This Job): Other Information Services (7.4%); Sporting Goods, Hobby, Book, and Music Stores (13.3%); Performing Arts, Spectator Sports, and Related Industries (13.4%); Insurance Carriers and Related Activities (13.9%).

Fastest-Growing Metropolitan Areas (Recent Growth for This Job): Kansas City, MO–KS (29.6%); Fort Wayne, IN (29.6%); Tampa–St. Petersburg–Clearwater, FL (25.0%); Houston–Sugar Land–Baytown, TX (20.0%); Eau Claire, WI (20.0%).

Other Considerations for Job Security: Retirements of current postsecondary teachers should create numerous openings for all types of postsecondary teachers, so job opportunities are generally expected to be very good. However, because students attend postsecondary institutions to prepare themselves for careers, the best job prospects for postsecondary teachers are likely to be in rapidly growing fields that offer many nonacademic career options, such as the health sciences. Community colleges and other institutions offering career and technical education have been among the most rapidly growing and are expected to offer some of the best opportunities for postsecondary teachers.

Teach courses in health specialties, such as veterinary medicine, dentistry, pharmacy, therapy, laboratory technology, and public health. Initiate, facilitate, and moderate classroom discussions. Keep abreast of developments in their field by reading current literature, talking with colleagues, and participating in professional conferences. Compile, administer, and grade examinations or assign this work to others. Evaluate and grade students' classwork, assignments, and papers. Prepare course materials such as syllabi, homework assignments, and handouts. Prepare and deliver lectures to undergraduate or graduate students on topics such as public health, stress management, and worksite health promotion. Plan, evaluate, and revise curricula, course content, course materials, and methods of instruction. Supervise undergraduate or graduate teaching, internships, and research work. Conduct research in a particular field of knowledge and publish findings in professional journals, books, or electronic media. Collaborate with colleagues to address teaching and research issues. Supervise laboratory sessions. Maintain student attendance records, grades, and other required records. Maintain regularly scheduled office hours to advise and assist students. Advise students on academic and vocational curricula and on career issues. Participate in student recruitment, registration, and placement activities. Write grant proposals to procure external research funding. Serve on academic or administrative committees that deal with institutional policies, departmental matters, and academic issues. Select and obtain materials and supplies such as textbooks and laboratory equipment. Act as advisers to student organizations. Perform administrative duties such as serving as department head. Compile bibliographies of specialized materials for outside reading assignments. Provide professional consulting services to government and industry. Participate in campus and community events.

Personality Type: Investigative.

GOE—Interest Area: 05. Education and Training. **Work Group:** 05.03. Postsecondary and Adult Teaching and Instructing. **Other Jobs in this Work Group:** Adult Literacy, Remedial Education, and GED Teachers and Instructors; Agricultural Sciences Teachers, Postsecondary; Anthropology and Archeology Teachers, Postsecondary; Architecture Teachers, Postsecondary; Area, Ethnic, and Cultural Studies Teachers, Postsecondary; Art, Drama, and Music Teachers, Postsecondary; Atmospheric, Earth, Marine, and Space Sciences Teachers, Postsecondary; Biological Science Teachers, Postsecondary; Business Teachers, Postsecondary; Chemistry Teachers, Postsecondary; Communications Teachers, Postsecondary; Computer Science Teachers, Postsecondary; Criminal Justice and Law Enforcement Teachers, Postsecondary; Economics Teachers, Postsecondary; Education Teachers, Postsecondary; Engineering Teachers, Postsecondary; English Language and Literature Teachers, Postsecondary; Environmental Science Teachers, Postsecondary; Farm and Home Management Advisors; Foreign Language and Literature Teachers, Postsecondary; Forestry and Conservation Science Teachers, Postsecondary; Geography Teachers, Postsecondary; Graduate Teaching Assistants; History Teachers, Postsecondary; Home Economics Teachers, Postsecondary; Law Teachers, Postsecondary; Library Science Teachers, Postsecondary; Mathematical Science Teachers, Postsecondary; Nursing Instructors and Teachers, Postsecondary; Philosophy and Religion Teachers, Postsecondary; Physics Teachers, Postsecondary; Political Science Teachers, Postsecondary; Psychology Teachers, Postsecondary; Recreation and Fitness Studies Teachers, Postsecondary; Self-Enrichment Education Teachers; Social Work Teachers, Postsecondary; Sociology Teachers, Postsecondary; Vocational Education Teachers, Postsecondary.

Skills: Science; Instructing; Writing; Reading Comprehension; Learning Strategies; Complex Problem Solving.

Education and Training Programs: Health Occupations Teacher Education; Biostatistics; Epidemiology; Chiropractic (DC); Communication Disorders, General; Audiology/Audiologist and Hearing Sciences; Speech-Language Pathology/Pathologist; Audiology/Audiologist and Speech-Language Pathology/Pathologist; Dentistry (DDS, DMD); Dental Clinical Sciences, General (MS, PhD); Dental Assisting/Assistant; Dental Hygiene/Hygienist; others. **Related Knowledge/Courses:** Biology; Medicine and Dentistry; Education and Training; Therapy and Counseling; Sociology and Anthropology; Psychology.

Work Environment: Indoors; sitting.

History Teachers, Postsecondary

- ❋ Education/Training Required: Doctoral degree
- ❋ Annual Earnings: $57,390
- ❋ Beginning Wage: $32,150
- ❋ Earnings Growth Potential: Very high
- ❋ Growth: 22.9%
- ❋ Annual Job Openings: 237,478
- ❋ Self-Employed: 0.4%
- ❋ Part-Time: 27.8%

Our sources did not provide separate job openings data for this occupation. The job openings listed here are shared with 35 other postsecondary teaching occupations. For a complete list, see the beginning of this section.

Industries with Greatest Employment: Educational Services, Public and Private.

Highest-Growth Industries (Projected Growth for This Job): Administrative and Support Services (48.3%); Amusement, Gambling, and Recreation

Industries (45.3%); Social Assistance (38.6%); Support Activities for Transportation (32.8%); Religious, Grantmaking, Civic, Professional, and Similar Organizations (29.9%); Professional, Scientific, and Technical Services (28.8%); Management of Companies and Enterprises (26.8%); Educational Services, Public and Private (22.9%); Hospitals, Public and Private (21.4%); Personal and Laundry Services (21.0%).

Lowest-Growth Industries (Projected Growth for This Job): Other Information Services (7.4%); Sporting Goods, Hobby, Book, and Music Stores (13.3%); Performing Arts, Spectator Sports, and Related Industries (13.4%); Insurance Carriers and Related Activities (13.9%).

Fastest-Growing Metropolitan Areas (Recent Growth for This Job): Orlando–Kissimmee, FL (33.3%); Harrisburg–Carlisle, PA (28.6%).

Other Considerations for Job Security: Retirements of current postsecondary teachers should create numerous openings for all types of postsecondary teachers, so job opportunities are generally expected to be very good. However, because students attend postsecondary institutions to prepare themselves for careers, the best job prospects for postsecondary teachers are likely to be in rapidly growing fields that offer many nonacademic career options—unlike history. On the other hand, history courses are required for many majors. Community colleges and other institutions offering career and technical education have been among the most rapidly growing and are expected to offer some of the best opportunities for postsecondary teachers.

Teach courses in human history and historiography. Prepare and deliver lectures to undergraduate and/or graduate students on topics such as ancient history, postwar civilizations, and the history of third-world countries. Evaluate and grade students' classwork, assignments, and papers. Prepare course materials such as syllabi, homework assignments, and handouts. Compile, administer, and grade examinations or assign this work to others. Initiate, facilitate, and moderate classroom discussions. Keep abreast of developments in the field by reading current literature, talking with colleagues, and participating in professional conferences. Plan, evaluate, and revise curricula, course content, course materials, and methods of instruction. Maintain student attendance records, grades, and other required records. Maintain regularly scheduled office hours to advise and assist students. Conduct research in a particular field of knowledge and publish findings in professional journals, books, or electronic media. Select and obtain materials and supplies such as textbooks. Advise students on academic and vocational curricula and on career issues. Collaborate with colleagues to address teaching and research issues. Serve on academic or administrative committees that deal with institutional policies, departmental matters, and academic issues. Participate in campus and community events. Act as advisers to student organizations. Participate in student recruitment, registration, and placement activities. Compile bibliographies of specialized materials for outside reading assignments. Supervise undergraduate and graduate teaching, internships, and research work. Perform administrative duties such as serving as department head. Write grant proposals to procure external research funding. Provide professional consulting services to government, educational institutions, and industry.

Personality Type: Social.

GOE—Interest Area: 05. Education and Training. **Work Group:** 05.03. Postsecondary and Adult Teaching and Instructing. **Other Jobs in this Work Group:** Adult Literacy, Remedial Education, and GED Teachers and Instructors; Agricultural Sciences Teachers, Postsecondary; Anthropology and Archeology Teachers, Postsecondary; Architecture Teachers, Postsecondary; Area, Ethnic, and Cultural Studies Teachers, Postsecondary; Art, Drama, and Music Teachers, Postsecondary; Atmospheric, Earth, Marine, and Space Sciences Teachers, Postsecondary; Biological Science Teachers, Postsecondary; Business Teachers, Postsecondary; Chemistry Teachers, Postsecondary; Communications Teachers, Postsecondary; Computer Science Teachers, Postsecondary; Criminal Justice and Law Enforcement Teachers, Postsecondary; Economics Teachers, Postsecondary;

Education Teachers, Postsecondary; Engineering Teachers, Postsecondary; English Language and Literature Teachers, Postsecondary; Environmental Science Teachers, Postsecondary; Farm and Home Management Advisors; Foreign Language and Literature Teachers, Postsecondary; Forestry and Conservation Science Teachers, Postsecondary; Geography Teachers, Postsecondary; Graduate Teaching Assistants; Health Specialties Teachers, Postsecondary; Home Economics Teachers, Postsecondary; Law Teachers, Postsecondary; Library Science Teachers, Postsecondary; Mathematical Science Teachers, Postsecondary; Nursing Instructors and Teachers, Postsecondary; Philosophy and Religion Teachers, Postsecondary; Physics Teachers, Postsecondary; Political Science Teachers, Postsecondary; Psychology Teachers, Postsecondary; Recreation and Fitness Studies Teachers, Postsecondary; Self-Enrichment Education Teachers; Social Work Teachers, Postsecondary; Sociology Teachers, Postsecondary; Vocational Education Teachers, Postsecondary.

Skills: Writing; Instructing; Learning Strategies; Reading Comprehension; Speaking; Persuasion.

Education and Training Programs: History, General; American History (United States); European History; History and Philosophy of Science and Technology; Public/Applied History and Archival Administration; Asian History; Canadian History; History, Other. **Related Knowledge/Courses:** History and Archeology; Philosophy and Theology; Geography; Sociology and Anthropology; Education and Training; English Language.

Work Environment: Indoors; sitting.

Home Economics Teachers, Postsecondary

- ❋ Education/Training Required: Doctoral degree
- ❋ Annual Earnings: $55,310
- ❋ Beginning Wage: $27,090
- ❋ Earnings Growth Potential: High
- ❋ Growth: 22.9%
- ❋ Annual Job Openings: 237,478
- ❋ Self-Employed: 0.4%
- ❋ Part-Time: 27.8%

Our sources did not provide separate job openings data for this occupation. The job openings listed here are shared with 35 other postsecondary teaching occupations. For a complete list, see the beginning of this section.

Industries with Greatest Employment: Educational Services, Public and Private.

Highest-Growth Industries (Projected Growth for This Job): Administrative and Support Services (48.3%); Amusement, Gambling, and Recreation Industries (45.3%); Social Assistance (38.6%); Support Activities for Transportation (32.8%); Religious, Grantmaking, Civic, Professional, and Similar Organizations (29.9%); Professional, Scientific, and Technical Services (28.8%); Management of Companies and Enterprises (26.8%); Educational Services, Public and Private (22.9%); Hospitals, Public and Private (21.4%); Personal and Laundry Services (21.0%).

Lowest-Growth Industries (Projected Growth for This Job): Other Information Services (7.4%); Sporting Goods, Hobby, Book, and Music Stores (13.3%); Performing Arts, Spectator Sports, and Related Industries (13.4%); Insurance Carriers and Related Activities (13.9%).

Fastest-Growing Metropolitan Areas (Recent Growth for This Job): Los Angeles–Long Beach–Santa Ana, CA (18.2%); St. Louis, MO–IL (16.7%).

Other Considerations for Job Security: Retirements of current postsecondary teachers should create numerous openings for all types of postsecondary teachers, so job opportunities are generally expected to be very good. Because students attend postsecondary institutions to prepare themselves for careers, the best job prospects for postsecondary teachers are likely to be in rapidly growing fields that offer many nonacademic career options. Many home economics majors, such as textiles and culinary arts, are very career-oriented. Community colleges and other institutions offering career and technical education have been among the most rapidly growing and are expected to offer some of the best opportunities for postsecondary teachers.

Teach courses in child care, family relations, finance, nutrition, and related subjects as pertaining to home management. Evaluate and grade students' classwork, laboratory work, projects, assignments, and papers. Initiate, facilitate, and moderate classroom discussions. Prepare and deliver lectures to undergraduate or graduate students on topics such as food science, nutrition, and child care. Prepare course materials such as syllabi, homework assignments, and handouts. Keep abreast of developments in their field by reading current literature, talking with colleagues, and participating in professional conferences. Maintain student attendance records, grades, and other required records. Plan, evaluate, and revise curricula, course content, course materials, and methods of instruction. Compile, administer, and grade examinations or assign this work to others. Advise students on academic and vocational curricula and on career issues. Maintain regularly scheduled office hours to advise and assist students. Supervise undergraduate or graduate teaching, internships, and research work. Select and obtain materials and supplies such as textbooks. Conduct research in a particular field of knowledge and publish findings in professional journals, books, and/or electronic media. Collaborate with colleagues to address teaching and research issues. Act as advisers to student organizations. Participate in student recruitment, registration, and placement activities. Serve on academic or administrative committees that deal with institutional policies, departmental matters, and academic issues. Participate in campus and community events.

Compile bibliographies of specialized materials for outside reading assignments. Perform administrative duties such as serving as department head. Write grant proposals to procure external research funding. Provide professional consulting services to government and industry.

Personality Type: No data available.

GOE—Interest Area: 05. Education and Training. **Work Group:** 05.03. Postsecondary and Adult Teaching and Instructing. **Other Jobs in this Work Group:** Adult Literacy, Remedial Education, and GED Teachers and Instructors; Agricultural Sciences Teachers, Postsecondary; Anthropology and Archeology Teachers, Postsecondary; Architecture Teachers, Postsecondary; Area, Ethnic, and Cultural Studies Teachers, Postsecondary; Art, Drama, and Music Teachers, Postsecondary; Atmospheric, Earth, Marine, and Space Sciences Teachers, Postsecondary; Biological Science Teachers, Postsecondary; Business Teachers, Postsecondary; Chemistry Teachers, Postsecondary; Communications Teachers, Postsecondary; Computer Science Teachers, Postsecondary; Criminal Justice and Law Enforcement Teachers, Postsecondary; Economics Teachers, Postsecondary; Education Teachers, Postsecondary; Engineering Teachers, Postsecondary; English Language and Literature Teachers, Postsecondary; Environmental Science Teachers, Postsecondary; Farm and Home Management Advisors; Foreign Language and Literature Teachers, Postsecondary; Forestry and Conservation Science Teachers, Postsecondary; Geography Teachers, Postsecondary; Graduate Teaching Assistants; Health Specialties Teachers, Postsecondary; History Teachers, Postsecondary; Law Teachers, Postsecondary; Library Science Teachers, Postsecondary; Mathematical Science Teachers, Postsecondary; Nursing Instructors and Teachers, Postsecondary; Philosophy and Religion Teachers, Postsecondary; Physics Teachers, Postsecondary; Political Science Teachers, Postsecondary; Psychology Teachers, Postsecondary; Recreation and Fitness Studies Teachers, Postsecondary; Self-Enrichment Education Teachers; Social Work Teachers, Postsecondary; Sociology Teachers, Postsecondary; Vocational Education Teachers, Postsecondary.

Skills: Writing; Instructing; Learning Strategies; Service Orientation; Active Learning; Social Perceptiveness.

Education and Training Programs: Family and Consumer Sciences/Human Sciences, General; Business Family and Consumer Sciences/Human Sciences; Foodservice Systems Administration/Management; Human Development and Family Studies, General; Child Care and Support Services Management. **Related Knowledge/Courses:** Sociology and Anthropology; Philosophy and Theology; Education and Training; Therapy and Counseling; Psychology; English Language.

Work Environment: Indoors; sitting.

Hydrologists

- ❀ Education/Training Required: Master's degree
- ❀ Annual Earnings: $66,260
- ❀ Beginning Wage: $42,080
- ❀ Earnings Growth Potential: Very high
- ❀ Growth: 24.3%
- ❀ Annual Job Openings: 687
- ❀ Self-Employed: 2.4%
- ❀ Part-Time: 5.3%

Industries with Greatest Employment: Professional, Scientific, and Technical Services.

Highest-Growth Industries (Projected Growth for This Job): Professional, Scientific, and Technical Services (53.9%).

Lowest-Growth Industries (Projected Growth for This Job): Educational Services, Public and Private (11.5%).

Fastest-Growing Metropolitan Areas (Recent Growth for This Job): Tucson, AZ (142.9%); Albuquerque, NM (110.0%); Fort Collins–Loveland, CO (50.0%); Carson City, NV (33.3%); Jacksonville, FL (33.3%).

Other Considerations for Job Security: Job prospects for hydrologists should be favorable, particularly for those with field experience. Demand for hydrologists who understand both the scientific and engineering aspects of waste remediation should be strong. Few colleges and universities offer programs in hydrology, so the number of qualified workers may be limited. Funding for federal and state geological surveys depend largely on the political climate and the current budget. Thus, job security for hydrologists may vary. During periods of economic recession, layoffs of hydrologists may occur in consulting firms; layoffs are much less likely in government.

Research the distribution, circulation, and physical properties of underground and surface waters; study the form and intensity of precipitation, its rate of infiltration into the soil, its movement through the earth, and its return to the ocean and atmosphere. Study and document quantities, distribution, disposition, and development of underground and surface waters. Draft final reports describing research results, including illustrations, appendixes, maps, and other attachments. Coordinate and supervise the work of professional and technical staff, including research assistants, technologists, and technicians. Prepare hydrogeologic evaluations of known or suspected hazardous waste sites and land treatment and feedlot facilities. Design and conduct scientific hydrogeological investigations to ensure that accurate and appropriate information is available for use in water resource management decisions. Study public water supply issues, including flood and drought risks, water quality, wastewater, and impacts on wetland habitats. Collect and analyze water samples as part of field investigations and/or to validate data from automatic monitors. Apply research findings to help minimize the environmental impacts of pollution, water-borne diseases, erosion, and sedimentation. Measure and graph phenomena such as lake levels, stream flows, and changes in water volumes. Investigate complaints or conflicts related to the alteration of public waters, gathering information, recommending alternatives, informing participants of progress, and preparing draft orders. Develop or modify methods of conducting hydrologic studies.

Answer questions and provide technical assistance and information to contractors and/or the public regarding issues such as well drilling, code requirements, hydrology, and geology. Install, maintain, and calibrate instruments such as those that monitor water levels, rainfall, and sediments. Evaluate data and provide recommendations regarding the feasibility of municipal projects such as hydroelectric power plants, irrigation systems, flood warning systems, and waste treatment facilities. Conduct short- and long-term climate assessments and study storm occurrences. Study and analyze the physical aspects of the Earth in terms of the hydrological components, including atmosphere, hydrosphere, and interior structure. Conduct research and communicate information to promote the conservation and preservation of water resources.

Personality Type: Investigative.

GOE—Interest Area: 15. Scientific Research, Engineering, and Mathematics. **Work Group:** 15.02. Physical Sciences. **Other Jobs in this Work Group:** Astronomers; Atmospheric and Space Scientists; Chemists; Geographers; Geoscientists, Except Hydrologists and Geographers; Materials Scientists; Physicists.

Skills: Science; Programming; Management of Financial Resources; Mathematics; Management of Personnel Resources; Systems Analysis.

Education and Training Programs: Geology/Earth Science, General; Hydrology and Water Resources Science; Oceanography, Chemical and Physical. **Related Knowledge/Courses:** Geography; Physics; Engineering and Technology; Biology; Chemistry; Mathematics.

Work Environment: More often indoors than outdoors; sitting.

Immigration and Customs Inspectors

- ❀ Education/Training Required: Work experience in a related occupation
- ❀ Annual Earnings: $58,260
- ❀ Beginning Wage: $34,480
- ❀ Earnings Growth Potential: Very high
- ❀ Growth: 17.3%
- ❀ Annual Job Openings: 14,746
- ❀ Self-Employed: 0.3%
- ❀ Part-Time: 2.2%

Our sources did not provide separate job openings data for this occupation. The job openings listed here are shared with Criminal Investigators and Special Agents; Police Detectives; and Police Identification and Records Officers.

Industries with Greatest Employment: Educational Services, Public and Private.

Highest-Growth Industries (Projected Growth for This Job): None met the criteria.

Lowest-Growth Industries (Projected Growth for This Job): Educational Services, Public and Private (11.9%).

Fastest-Growing Metropolitan Areas (Recent Growth for This Job): Brownsville–Harlingen, TX (366.7%); Las Cruces, NM (350.0%); Bellingham, WA (183.3%); Jackson, MS (172.7%); Tucson, AZ (121.3%).

Other Considerations for Job Security: The level of government spending determines the level of employment for immigration and customs inspectors. The number of job opportunities, therefore, can vary from year to year. Concerns about homeland security may create a need for additional inspectors. Layoffs are rare because retirements enable most staffing cuts to be handled through attrition.

Investigate and inspect persons, common carriers, goods, and merchandise arriving in or departing

from the United States or moving between states to detect violations of immigration and customs laws and regulations. Examine immigration applications, visas, and passports and interview persons to determine eligibility for admission, residence, and travel in U.S. Detain persons found to be in violation of customs or immigration laws and arrange for legal action such as deportation. Locate and seize contraband or undeclared merchandise and vehicles, aircraft, or boats that contain such merchandise. Interpret and explain laws and regulations to travelers, prospective immigrants, shippers, and manufacturers. Inspect cargo, baggage, and personal articles entering or leaving U.S. for compliance with revenue laws and U.S. Customs Service regulations. Record and report job-related activities, findings, transactions, violations, discrepancies, and decisions. Institute civil and criminal prosecutions and cooperate with other law-enforcement agencies in the investigation and prosecution of those in violation of immigration or customs laws. Testify regarding decisions at immigration appeals or in federal court. Determine duty and taxes to be paid on goods. Collect samples of merchandise for examination, appraisal, or testing. Investigate applications for duty refunds and petition for remission or mitigation of penalties when warranted.

Personality Type: Conventional.

GOE—Interest Area: 07. Government and Public Administration. **Work Group:** 07.03. Regulations Enforcement. **Other Jobs in this Work Group:** Agricultural Inspectors; Aviation Inspectors; Compliance Officers, Except Agriculture, Construction, Health and Safety, and Transportation; Construction and Building Inspectors; Environmental Compliance Inspectors; Equal Opportunity Representatives and Officers; Financial Examiners; Fire Inspectors; Fish and Game Wardens; Forest Fire Inspectors and Prevention Specialists; Freight and Cargo Inspectors; Government Property Inspectors and Investigators; Licensing Examiners and Inspectors; Nuclear Monitoring Technicians; Occupational Health and Safety Specialists; Occupational Health and Safety Technicians; Tax Examiners, Collectors, and Revenue

Agents; Transportation Vehicle, Equipment, and Systems Inspectors, Except Aviation.

Skills: Persuasion; Negotiation; Speaking; Operations Analysis; Equipment Selection; Social Perceptiveness.

Education and Training Programs: Criminal Justice/Police Science; Criminalistics and Criminal Science. **Related Knowledge/Courses:** Public Safety and Security; Law and Government; Foreign Language; Geography; Customer and Personal Service; Sociology and Anthropology.

Work Environment: More often outdoors than indoors; noisy; contaminants; radiation; hazardous equipment.

Industrial-Organizational Psychologists

- ❋ Education/Training Required: Master's degree
- ❋ Annual Earnings: $86,420
- ❋ Beginning Wage: $48,380
- ❋ Earnings Growth Potential: Very high
- ❋ Growth: 21.3%
- ❋ Annual Job Openings: 118
- ❋ Self-Employed: 39.3%
- ❋ Part-Time: 24.0%

Industries with Greatest Employment: Professional, Scientific, and Technical Services; Educational Services, Public and Private.

Highest-Growth Industries (Projected Growth for This Job): Professional, Scientific, and Technical Services (49.6%).

Lowest-Growth Industries (Projected Growth for This Job): Educational Services, Public and Private (10.3%).

Fastest-Growing Metropolitan Areas (Recent Growth for This Job): Washington–Arlington–Alexandria, DC–VA–MD–WV (36.4%); New

York–Northern New Jersey–Long Island, NY–NJ–PA (16.7%).

Other Considerations for Job Security: Industrial-organizational psychologists will be in demand to help boost worker productivity and retention rates in a wide range of businesses. They will help companies deal with issues such as workplace diversity and antidiscrimination policies. Companies also will use their expertise in survey design, analysis, and research to develop tools for marketing evaluation and statistical analysis. Job prospects should be the best for people who have a doctorate from a leading university. Psychologists with extensive training in quantitative research methods and computer science may have a competitive edge over applicants without such background.

Apply principles of psychology to personnel, administration, management, sales, and marketing problems. Activities may include policy planning; employee screening, training, and development; and organizational development and analysis. May work with management to reorganize the work setting to improve worker productivity. Develop and implement employee selection and placement programs. Analyze job requirements and content to establish criteria for classification, selection, training, and other related personnel functions. Observe and interview workers to obtain information about jobs' physical, mental, and educational requirements as well as information about aspects such as job satisfaction. Write reports on research findings and implications to contribute to general knowledge and to suggest potential changes in organizational functioning. Advise management concerning personnel, managerial, and marketing policies and practices, as well as their potential effects on organizational effectiveness and efficiency. Identify training and development needs. Conduct research studies of physical work environments, organizational structures, communication systems, group interactions, morale, and motivation to assess organizational functioning. Formulate and implement training programs, applying principles of learning and individual differences. Develop interview techniques, rating scales, and psychological tests used to assess skills, abilities, and interests for the purpose of employee selection, placement, and promotion. Assess employee performance. Study organizational effectiveness, productivity, and efficiency, including the nature of workplace supervision and leadership. Facilitate organizational development and change. Analyze data, using statistical methods and applications, to evaluate the outcomes and effectiveness of workplace programs. Counsel workers about job and career-related issues. Study consumers' reactions to new products and package designs and to advertising efforts, using surveys and tests. Participate in mediation and dispute resolution.

Personality Type: Investigative.

GOE—Interest Area: 15. Scientific Research, Engineering, and Mathematics. **Work Group:** 15.04. Social Sciences. **Other Jobs in this Work Group:** Anthropologists; Anthropologists and Archeologists; Archeologists; Economists; Historians; Political Scientists; School Psychologists; Sociologists.

Skills: Science; Management of Personnel Resources; Systems Evaluation; Judgment and Decision Making; Writing; Complex Problem Solving.

Education and Training Programs: Psychology, General; Industrial and Organizational Psychology. **Related Knowledge/Courses:** Personnel and Human Resources; Psychology; Education and Training; Sales and Marketing; Sociology and Anthropology; Therapy and Counseling.

Work Environment: Indoors; sitting.

Inspectors, Testers, Sorters, Samplers, and Weighers

❋ Education/Training Required: Moderate-term on-the-job training
❋ Annual Earnings: $29,420
❋ Beginning Wage: $17,990
❋ Earnings Growth Potential: Very high
❋ Growth: –7.0%
❋ Annual Job Openings: 75,361
❋ Self-Employed: 1.5%
❋ Part-Time: 4.9%

Industries with Greatest Employment: Transportation Equipment Manufacturing; Administrative and Support Services; Fabricated Metal Product Manufacturing; Computer and Electronic Product Manufacturing; Plastics and Rubber Products Manufacturing.

Highest-Growth Industries (Projected Growth for This Job): Professional, Scientific, and Technical Services (27.1%); Warehousing and Storage (26.0%); Internet Service Providers, Web Search Portals, and Data Processing Services (23.7%); Ambulatory Health Care Services (23.3%); Telecommunications (22.2%); Administrative and Support Services (21.7%); Waste Management and Remediation Services (19.6%); Repair and Maintenance (19.3%); Social Assistance (16.0%).

Lowest-Growth Industries (Projected Growth for This Job): Apparel Manufacturing (–54.0%); Leather and Allied Product Manufacturing (–49.0%); Pipeline Transportation (–37.6%); Textile Mills (–34.3%); Primary Metal Manufacturing (–31.4%); Petroleum and Coal Products Manufacturing (–28.8%); Printing and Related Support Activities (–25.3%); Paper Manufacturing (–24.9%); Electrical Equipment, Appliance, and Component Manufacturing (–20.1%); Fabricated Metal Product Manufacturing (–20.1%).

Fastest-Growing Metropolitan Areas (Recent Growth for This Job): Ocala, FL (100.0%); Iowa City, IA (80.0%); Guayama, PR (68.8%); Farmington, NM (66.7%); El Centro, CA (60.0%).

Other Considerations for Job Security: Although numerous job openings will arise due to the need to replace workers who move out of this large occupation, many of these jobs will be open only to experienced workers with advanced skills. Because most inspectors, testers, sorters, samplers, and weighers work in the manufacturing sector, their outlook is greatly affected by what happens to manufacturing companies. As this sector becomes more automated and productive and as some production moves offshore, the number of inspectors, testers, sorters, samplers, and weighers is expected to decline. However, the continuing emphasis on producing quality goods and the need for accuracy in the growing medical and biotechnology fields will positively affect this occupation and moderate the decline.

Inspect, test, sort, sample, or weigh nonagricultural raw materials or processed, machined, fabricated, or assembled parts or products for defects, wear, and deviations from specifications. May use precision measuring instruments and complex test equipment. Discard or reject products, materials, and equipment not meeting specifications. Analyze and interpret blueprints, data, manuals, and other materials to determine specifications, inspection and testing procedures, adjustment and certification methods, formulas, and measuring instruments required. Inspect, test, or measure materials, products, installations, and work for conformance to specifications. Notify supervisors and other personnel of production problems and assist in identifying and correcting them. Discuss inspection results with those responsible for products and recommend necessary corrective actions. Record inspection or test data, such as weights, temperatures, grades, or moisture content and quantities inspected or graded. Mark items with details such as grade and acceptance or rejection status. Observe and monitor production operations and equipment to ensure conformance to specifications and make or order necessary process or assembly adjustments. Measure dimensions of products to verify conformance to specifications by using measuring instruments such as rulers, calipers, gauges, or micrometers. Analyze test data and make computations as necessary to determine test results. Collect or select samples for testing or for use as models. Check arriving materials to ensure that they match purchase orders and submit discrepancy reports when problems are found. Compare colors, shapes, textures, or grades of products or materials with color charts, templates, or samples to verify conformance to standards. Write test and inspection reports describing results, recommendations, and needed repairs. Read dials and meters to verify that equipment is functioning at specified levels. Remove defects, such as chips and burrs, and lap corroded or pitted surfaces. Clean, maintain, repair, and calibrate measuring instruments and test equipment such as dial indicators, fixed gauges, and height gauges. Adjust, clean, or repair products or processing equipment to correct defects found during inspections. Stack and arrange tested products for further processing, shipping, or packaging and transport products to other workstations as necessary.

Personality Type: Realistic.

GOE—Interest Area: 13. Manufacturing. **Work Group:** 13.07. Production Quality Control. **Other Jobs in this Work Group:** Graders and Sorters, Agricultural Products.

Skills: No data available.

Education and Training Program: Quality Control Technology/Technician. **Related Knowledge/Course:** Production and Processing.

Work Environment: Noisy; standing; using hands on objects, tools, or controls; repetitive motions.

Instructional Coordinators

- ❋ Education/Training Required: Master's degree
- ❋ Annual Earnings: $52,790
- ❋ Beginning Wage: $29,040
- ❋ Earnings Growth Potential: Very high
- ❋ Growth: 22.5%
- ❋ Annual Job Openings: 21,294
- ❋ Self-Employed: 3.1%
- ❋ Part-Time: 19.7%

Industries with Greatest Employment: Educational Services, Public and Private.

Highest-Growth Industries (Projected Growth for This Job): Internet Publishing and Broadcasting (40.9%); Museums, Historical Sites, and Similar Institutions (36.2%); Social Assistance (33.2%); Amusement, Gambling, and Recreation Industries (32.6%); Professional, Scientific, and Technical Services (31.9%); Administrative and Support Services (28.1%); Ambulatory Health Care Services (26.9%); Nursing and Residential Care Facilities (23.1%); Educational Services, Public and Private (22.8%); Performing Arts, Spectator Sports, and Related Industries (18.2%); Religious, Grantmaking, Civic, Professional, and Similar Organizations (17.5%); Management of Companies and Enterprises (15.3%).

Lowest-Growth Industries (Projected Growth for This Job): Crop Production (–33.7%); Computer and Electronic Product Manufacturing (–27.6%); Insurance Carriers and Related Activities (7.5%); Hospitals, Public and Private (10.8%); Publishing Industries (except Internet) (10.9%); Merchant Wholesalers, Durable Goods (14.8%).

Fastest-Growing Metropolitan Areas (Recent Growth for This Job): Salinas, CA (266.7%); Santa Barbara–Santa Maria, CA (138.5%); Olympia, WA (133.3%); Lawrence, KS (100.0%); York–Hanover, PA (80.0%).

Other Considerations for Job Security: Job opportunities generally should be favorable. Opportunities should be best for those who specialize in subjects targeted for improvement by the No Child Left Behind Act—namely, reading, math, and science. Also, more instructional coordinators will be needed to show teachers how to use technology in the classroom.

Develop instructional material, coordinate educational content, and incorporate current technology in specialized fields that provide guidelines to educators and instructors for developing curricula and conducting courses. Conduct or participate in workshops, committees, and conferences designed to promote students' intellectual, social, and physical welfare. Plan and conduct teacher training programs and conferences dealing with new classroom procedures, instructional materials and equipment, and teaching aids. Advise teaching and administrative staff in curriculum development, use of materials and equipment, and implementation of state and federal programs and procedures. Recommend, order, or authorize purchase of instructional materials, supplies, equipment, and visual aids designed to meet student educational needs and district standards. Interpret and enforce provisions of state education codes and rules and regulations of state education boards. Confer with members of educational committees and advisory groups to obtain knowledge of subject areas and to relate curriculum materials to specific subjects, individual student needs, and occupational areas. Organize production and design of curriculum materials. Research, evaluate, and prepare recommendations on curricula, instructional methods, and materials for school systems. Observe work of teaching staff to evaluate performance and to recommend changes that could strengthen teaching skills. Develop instructional materials to be used by educators and instructors. Prepare grant proposals, budgets, and program policies and goals or assist in their preparation. Develop tests, questionnaires, and procedures that measure the effectiveness of curricula and use these tools to determine whether program objectives are being met. Update the content of educational programs to ensure that students are being trained with technologically current equipment and processes. Address public audiences to explain program objectives and to elicit support. Advise and teach students. Prepare or approve manuals, guidelines, and reports on state educational policies and practices for distribution to school districts. Develop classroom-based and distance-learning training courses, using needs assessments and skill level analyses. Inspect instructional equipment to determine whether repairs are needed and authorize necessary repairs.

Personality Type: Social.

GOE—Interest Area: 05. Education and Training. **Work Group:** 05.01. Managerial Work in Education. **Other Jobs in this Work Group:** Education Administrators, Elementary and Secondary School; Education Administrators, Postsecondary; Education Administrators, Preschool and Child Care Center/Program.

Skills: Management of Financial Resources; Learning Strategies; Management of Personnel Resources; Monitoring; Social Perceptiveness; Coordination.

Education and Training Programs: Curriculum and Instruction; Educational/Instructional Media Design; International and Comparative Education. **Related Knowledge/Courses:** Education and Training; Sociology and Anthropology; Communications and Media; English Language; Personnel and Human Resources; Psychology.

Work Environment: Indoors; sitting.

Insurance Adjusters, Examiners, and Investigators

❋ Education/Training Required: Long-term on-the-job training
❋ Annual Earnings: $50,660
❋ Beginning Wage: $30,890
❋ Earnings Growth Potential: Very high
❋ Growth: 8.9%
❋ Annual Job Openings: 22,024
❋ Self-Employed: 3.5%
❋ Part-Time: 4.0%

Our sources did not provide separate job openings data for this occupation. The job openings listed here are shared with Claims Examiners, Property and Casualty Insurance.

Industries with Greatest Employment: Insurance Carriers and Related Activities.

Highest-Growth Industries (Projected Growth for This Job): Professional, Scientific, and Technical Services (48.0%); Securities, Commodity Contracts, and Other Financial Investments and Related Activities (44.8%); Social Assistance (44.3%); Internet Service Providers, Web Search Portals, and Data Processing Services (35.2%); Administrative and Support Services (27.7%); Real Estate (26.4%); Ambulatory Health Care Services (24.5%); Funds, Trusts, and Other Financial Vehicles (23.7%); Religious, Grantmaking, Civic, Professional, and Similar Organizations (17.7%); Repair and Maintenance (16.7%); Management of Companies and Enterprises (15.3%).

Lowest-Growth Industries (Projected Growth for This Job): Rail Transportation (–14.0%); Utilities (–11.1%); Hospitals, Public and Private (9.6%); Insurance Carriers and Related Activities (10.8%); Educational Services, Public and Private (11.8%); Truck Transportation (12.7%); Rental and Leasing Services (14.0%).

Fastest-Growing Metropolitan Areas (Recent Growth for This Job): Deltona–Daytona Beach–Ormond Beach, FL (233.3%); Beaumont–Port Arthur, TX (225.0%); Goldsboro, NC (200.0%); Tuscaloosa, AL (175.0%); Sarasota–Bradenton–Venice, FL (114.3%).

Other Considerations for Job Security: Keen competition is expected, especially in smaller, privately owned companies, with best opportunities for those with licenses and related experience. New technology is reducing the amount of time it takes for adjusters to complete claims, thereby increasing the number of claims that each adjuster can handle. The demand for these jobs will increase regardless of new technology, however, because they cannot be easily automated. Further, as the elderly population increases, there will be a greater need for health care, resulting in more health insurance claims.

Investigate, analyze, and determine the extent of insurance company's liability concerning personal, casualty, or property loss or damages and attempt to effect settlement with claimants. Correspond with or interview medical specialists, agents, witnesses, or claimants to compile information. Calculate benefit payments and approve payment of claims within a certain monetary limit. Interview or correspond with claimant and witnesses, consult police and hospital records, and inspect property damage to determine extent of liability. Investigate and assess property damage. Examine claims forms and other records to determine insurance coverage. Analyze information gathered by investigation and report findings and recommendations. Negotiate claim settlements and recommend litigation when settlement cannot be negotiated. Collect evidence to support contested claims in court. Prepare report of investigation findings. Interview or correspond with agents and claimants to correct errors or omissions and to investigate questionable claims. Refer questionable claims to investigator or claims adjuster for investigation or settlement. Examine titles to property to determine validity and act as company agent in transactions with property owners. Obtain credit information from banks and other credit services.

Communicate with former associates to verify employment record and to obtain background information regarding persons or businesses applying for credit.

Personality Type: Enterprising.

GOE—Interest Area: 06. Finance and Insurance. **Work Group:** 06.02. Finance/Insurance Investigation and Analysis. **Other Jobs in this Work Group:** Appraisers and Assessors of Real Estate; Appraisers, Real Estate; Assessors; Claims Adjusters, Examiners, and Investigators; Claims Examiners, Property and Casualty Insurance; Cost Estimators; Credit Analysts; Financial Analysts; Insurance Appraisers, Auto Damage; Insurance Underwriters; Loan Counselors; Loan Officers; Market Research Analysts; Survey Researchers.

Skills: Negotiation; Persuasion; Judgment and Decision Making; Time Management; Management of Financial Resources; Reading Comprehension.

Education and Training Program: Insurance. **Related Knowledge/Courses:** Customer and Personal Service; Clerical Studies; Computers and Electronics; Law and Government; Medicine and Dentistry; Therapy and Counseling.

Work Environment: Indoors; noisy; sitting; using hands on objects, tools, or controls; repetitive motions.

Insurance Appraisers, Auto Damage

- ❋ Education/Training Required: Postsecondary vocational training
- ❋ Annual Earnings: $49,180
- ❋ Beginning Wage: $34,220
- ❋ Earnings Growth Potential: Very high
- ❋ Growth: 12.5%
- ❋ Annual Job Openings: 1,030
- ❋ Self-Employed: 4.1%
- ❋ Part-Time: 4.0%

Industries with Greatest Employment: Insurance Carriers and Related Activities.

Highest-Growth Industries (Projected Growth for This Job): Administrative and Support Services (23.9%); Management of Companies and Enterprises (15.3%).

Lowest-Growth Industries (Projected Growth for This Job): Insurance Carriers and Related Activities (12.0%).

Fastest-Growing Metropolitan Areas (Recent Growth for This Job): Pittsburgh, PA (200.0%); Baltimore–Towson, MD (116.7%); Houston–Sugar Land–Baytown, TX (100.0%); San Juan–Caguas–Guaynabo, PR (66.7%); Louisville–Jefferson County, KY–IN (42.9%).

Other Considerations for Job Security: Keen competition is expected, with best opportunities for those who have some vocational training and previous auto body repair experience. The work of auto damage appraisers isn't easily automated because most appraisals require an on-site inspection, but new technology is making them somewhat more efficient. Also, some insurance companies are opening their own repair facilities, which may reduce the need for auto damage appraisers.

Appraise automobile or other vehicle damage to determine cost of repair for insurance claim settlement and seek agreement with automotive repair shop on cost of repair. Prepare insurance forms to indicate repair cost or cost estimates and recommendations. Estimate parts and labor to repair damage, using standard automotive labor and parts-cost manuals and knowledge of automotive repair. Review repair-cost estimates with automobile repair shop to secure agreement on cost of repairs. Examine damaged vehicle to determine extent of structural, body, mechanical, electrical, or interior damage. Evaluate practicality of repair as opposed to payment of market value of vehicle before accident. Determine salvage value on total-loss vehicle. Prepare insurance forms to indicate repair-cost estimates and recommendations. Arrange to have damage appraised by another appraiser to resolve disagreement with shop on repair cost.

Personality Type: Conventional.

GOE—Interest Area: 06. Finance and Insurance. **Work Group:** 06.02. Finance/Insurance Investigation and Analysis. **Other Jobs in this Work Group:** Appraisers and Assessors of Real Estate; Appraisers, Real Estate; Assessors; Claims Adjusters, Examiners, and Investigators; Claims Examiners, Property and Casualty Insurance; Cost Estimators; Credit Analysts; Financial Analysts; Insurance Adjusters, Examiners, and Investigators; Insurance Underwriters; Loan Counselors; Loan Officers; Market Research Analysts; Survey Researchers.

Skills: Negotiation; Service Orientation; Persuasion; Judgment and Decision Making; Active Listening; Time Management.

Education and Training Program: Insurance. **Related Knowledge/Courses:** Customer and Personal Service; Law and Government; Medicine and Dentistry; Computers and Electronics; Transportation; Telecommunications.

Work Environment: More often indoors than outdoors; noisy; very hot or cold; contaminants; sitting.

Insurance Underwriters

- ❋ Education/Training Required: Bachelor's degree
- ❋ Annual Earnings: $52,350
- ❋ Beginning Wage: $32,270
- ❋ Earnings Growth Potential: Very high
- ❋ Growth: 6.3%
- ❋ Annual Job Openings: 6,880
- ❋ Self-Employed: 0.0%
- ❋ Part-Time: 3.6%

Industries with Greatest Employment: Insurance Carriers and Related Activities.

Highest-Growth Industries (Projected Growth for This Job): Securities, Commodity Contracts, and Other Financial Investments and Related Activities (39.2%); Professional, Scientific, and Technical Services (23.1%); Administrative and Support Services

(16.4%); Funds, Trusts, and Other Financial Vehicles (16.2%).

Lowest-Growth Industries (Projected Growth for This Job): Insurance Carriers and Related Activities (5.6%); Credit Intermediation and Related Activities (8.6%); Management of Companies and Enterprises (8.7%); Religious, Grantmaking, Civic, Professional, and Similar Organizations (12.8%).

Fastest-Growing Metropolitan Areas (Recent Growth for This Job): Tulsa, OK (204.2%); Amarillo, TX (100.0%); New Haven, CT (90.0%); Springfield, MA–CT (73.3%); Worcester, MA–CT (52.4%).

Other Considerations for Job Security: Job prospects will remain good because of the continuous turnover experienced in this occupation. Underwriting software will continue to make workers more productive, but it doesn't do away with the need for human skills. Job opportunities should be best for those with experience in related insurance jobs, a background in finance, and strong computer and communication skills. Underwriters are needed particularly in the area of product development, where they assess risks and set the premiums for new lines of insurance.

Review individual applications for insurance to evaluate degree of risk involved and determine acceptance of applications. Examine documents to determine degree of risk from such factors as applicant financial standing and value and condition of property. Decline excessive risks. Write to field representatives, medical personnel, and others to obtain further information, quote rates, or explain company underwriting policies. Evaluate possibility of losses due to catastrophe or excessive insurance. Decrease value of policy when risk is substandard and specify applicable endorsements or apply rating to ensure safe profitable distribution of risks, using reference materials. Review company records to determine amount of insurance in force on single risk or group of closely related risks. Authorize reinsurance of policy when risk is high.

Personality Type: Conventional.

GOE—Interest Area: 06. Finance and Insurance. **Work Group:** 06.02. Finance/Insurance Investigation and Analysis. **Other Jobs in this Work Group:** Appraisers and Assessors of Real Estate; Appraisers, Real Estate; Assessors; Claims Adjusters, Examiners, and Investigators; Claims Examiners, Property and Casualty Insurance; Cost Estimators; Credit Analysts; Financial Analysts; Insurance Adjusters, Examiners, and Investigators; Insurance Appraisers, Auto Damage; Loan Counselors; Loan Officers; Market Research Analysts; Survey Researchers.

Skills: Writing; Service Orientation; Speaking; Active Listening; Active Learning; Learning Strategies.

Education and Training Program: Insurance. **Related Knowledge/Courses:** Clerical Studies; Customer and Personal Service; Sales and Marketing; Economics and Accounting; Computers and Electronics; Law and Government.

Work Environment: Indoors; sitting; using hands on objects, tools, or controls; repetitive motions.

Internists, General

* Education/Training Required: First professional degree
* Annual Earnings: More than $145,600
* Beginning Wage: $87,070
* Earnings Growth Potential: Cannot be calculated
* Growth: 14.2%
* Annual Job Openings: 38,027
* Self-Employed: 14.7%
* Part-Time: 8.1%

Our sources did not provide separate job openings data for this occupation. The job openings listed here are shared with Anesthesiologists; Family and General Practitioners; Obstetricians and Gynecologists; Pediatricians, General; Psychiatrists; and Surgeons.

Industries with Greatest Employment: Ambulatory Health Care Services; Hospitals, Public and Private.

Highest-Growth Industries (Projected Growth for This Job): Social Assistance (58.6%); Administrative and Support Services (26.8%); Professional, Scientific, and Technical Services (22.6%); Nursing and Residential Care Facilities (21.0%); Ambulatory Health Care Services (19.4%); Religious, Grantmaking, Civic, Professional, and Similar Organizations (16.7%); Management of Companies and Enterprises (15.3%).

Lowest-Growth Industries (Projected Growth for This Job): Insurance Carriers and Related Activities (4.6%); Health and Personal Care Stores (5.3%); Hospitals, Public and Private (9.9%); Educational Services, Public and Private (11.8%).

Fastest-Growing Metropolitan Areas (Recent Growth for This Job): St. Louis, MO–IL (52.6%); Greenville, SC (40.0%); Portland–South Portland–Biddeford, ME (35.0%); Chattanooga, TN–GA (33.3%); Washington–Arlington–Alexandria, DC–VA–MD–WV (33.3%).

Other Considerations for Job Security: Opportunities for individuals interested in becoming physicians and surgeons are expected to be very good. Unlike their predecessors, new physicians are much less likely to enter solo practice and more likely to take salaried jobs in group medical practices, clinics, and health networks. Reports of shortages in some specialties, such as general or family practice, internal medicine, and OB/GYN, or in rural or low-income areas should attract new entrants, encouraging schools to expand programs and hospitals to increase available residency slots. However, because physician training is so lengthy, employment change happens gradually. Opportunities should be particularly good in rural and low-income areas, as some physicians find these areas unattractive because of less control over work hours, isolation from medical colleagues, or other reasons.

Diagnose and provide nonsurgical treatment of diseases and injuries of internal organ systems. Provide care mainly for adults who have a wide range of problems associated with the internal organs. Treat internal disorders, such as hypertension;

heart disease; diabetes; and problems of the lung, brain, kidney, and gastrointestinal tract. Analyze records, reports, test results, or examination information to diagnose medical condition of patient. Prescribe or administer medication, therapy, and other specialized medical care to treat or prevent illness, disease, or injury. Provide and manage long-term, comprehensive medical care, including diagnosis and nonsurgical treatment of diseases, for adult patients in an office or hospital. Manage and treat common health problems, such as infections, influenza, and pneumonia, as well as serious, chronic, and complex illnesses in adolescents, adults, and the elderly. Monitor patients' conditions and progress and re-evaluate treatments as necessary. Collect, record, and maintain patient information, such as medical history, reports, and examination results. Make diagnoses when different illnesses occur together or in situations where the diagnosis may be obscure. Explain procedures and discuss test results or prescribed treatments with patients. Advise patients and community members concerning diet, activity, hygiene, and disease prevention. Refer patient to medical specialist or other practitioner when necessary. Immunize patients to protect them from preventable diseases. Advise surgeon of a patient's risk status and recommend appropriate intervention to minimize risk. Direct and coordinate activities of nurses, students, assistants, specialists, therapists, and other medical staff. Provide consulting services to other doctors caring for patients with special or difficult problems. Operate on patients to remove, repair, or improve functioning of diseased or injured body parts and systems. Plan, implement, or administer health programs in hospitals, businesses, or communities for prevention and treatment of injuries or illnesses. Conduct research to develop or test medications, treatments, or procedures to prevent or control disease or injury. Prepare government or organizational reports on birth, death, and disease statistics; workforce evaluations; or the medical status of individuals.

Personality Type: Investigative.

GOE—Interest Area: 08. Health Science. **Work Group:** 08.02. Medicine and Surgery. **Other Jobs**

in this Work Group: Anesthesiologists; Family and General Practitioners; Medical Assistants; Medical Transcriptionists; Obstetricians and Gynecologists; Pediatricians, General; Pharmacists; Pharmacy Aides; Pharmacy Technicians; Physician Assistants; Psychiatrists; Registered Nurses; Surgeons; Surgical Technologists.

Skills: Science; Judgment and Decision Making; Complex Problem Solving; Reading Comprehension; Social Perceptiveness; Management of Financial Resources.

Education and Training Programs: Cardiology; Critical Care Medicine; Endocrinology and Metabolism; Gastroenterology; Geriatric Medicine; Hematology; Infectious Disease; Internal Medicine; Nephrology; Neurology; Nuclear Medicine; Oncology; Pulmonary Disease; Rheumatology. **Related Knowledge/Courses:** Medicine and Dentistry; Biology; Therapy and Counseling; Psychology; Chemistry; Education and Training.

Work Environment: Indoors; disease or infections; standing.

Interpreters and Translators

* Education/Training Required: Long-term on-the-job training
* Annual Earnings: $35,560
* Beginning Wage: $20,550
* Earnings Growth Potential: Very high
* Growth: 23.6%
* Annual Job Openings: 6,630
* Self-Employed: 21.6%
* Part-Time: 28.5%

Industries with Greatest Employment: Educational Services, Public and Private; Professional, Scientific, and Technical Services; Hospitals, Public and Private; Social Assistance.

Highest-Growth Industries (Projected Growth for This Job): Social Assistance (62.8%); Museums, Historical Sites, and Similar Institutions (49.8%);

Administrative and Support Services (44.3%); Ambulatory Health Care Services (39.2%); Professional, Scientific, and Technical Services (37.4%); Nursing and Residential Care Facilities (33.3%); Religious, Grantmaking, Civic, Professional, and Similar Organizations (30.9%); Management of Companies and Enterprises (27.4%); Hospitals, Public and Private (21.8%); Educational Services, Public and Private (18.9%); Insurance Carriers and Related Activities (15.7%).

Lowest-Growth Industries (Projected Growth for This Job): Transportation Equipment Manufacturing (–7.1%); Telecommunications (5.1%); Publishing Industries (except Internet) (9.7%).

Fastest-Growing Metropolitan Areas (Recent Growth for This Job): Columbia, SC (133.3%); Santa Rosa–Petaluma, CA (133.3%); Riverside–San Bernardino–Ontario, CA (114.3%); Indianapolis–Carmel, IN (100.0%); Durham, NC (66.7%).

Other Considerations for Job Security: Growth in demand will be driven partly by strong demand in health-care settings and work related to homeland security. Job prospects for interpreters and translators vary by specialty. There should be demand for specialists in localization (adapting language content of products so that they can be used in foreign countries), driven by imports and exports and the expansion of the Internet; however, demand may be dampened somewhat by outsourcing of localization work to other countries. Demand is expected to be strong in other technical areas, such as medicine and law. Given the shortage of interpreters and translators meeting the desired skill level of employers, interpreters for the deaf will continue to have favorable employment prospects. On the other hand, job opportunities are expected to be limited for both conference interpreters and literary translators.

Translate or interpret written, oral, or sign-language text into another language for others. Follow ethical codes that protect the confidentiality of information. Identify and resolve conflicts related to the meanings of words, concepts, practices, or behaviors. Proofread, edit, and revise translated materials. Translate messages simultaneously or consecutively into specified languages orally or by using hand signs, maintaining message content, context, and style as much as possible. Check translations of technical terms and terminology to ensure that they are accurate and remain consistent throughout translation revisions. Read written materials such as legal documents, scientific works, or news reports and rewrite material into specified languages. Refer to reference materials such as dictionaries, lexicons, encyclopedias, and computerized terminology banks as needed to ensure translation accuracy. Compile terminology and information to be used in translations, including technical terms such as those for legal or medical material. Adapt translations to students' cognitive and grade levels, collaborating with educational team members as necessary. Listen to speakers' statements to determine meanings and to prepare translations, using electronic listening systems as necessary. Check original texts or confer with authors to ensure that translations retain the content, meaning, and feeling of the original material. Compile information about the content and context of information to be translated, as well as details of the groups for whom translation or interpretation is being performed. Discuss translation requirements with clients and determine any fees to be charged for services provided. Adapt software and accompanying technical documents to another language and culture. Educate students, parents, staff, and teachers about the roles and functions of educational interpreters. Train and supervise other translators/interpreters. Travel with or guide tourists who speak another language.

Personality Type: Artistic.

GOE—Interest Area: 03. Arts and Communication. **Work Group:** 03.03. News, Broadcasting, and Public Relations. **Other Jobs in this Work Group:** Broadcast News Analysts; Public Relations Specialists; Reporters and Correspondents.

Skills: No data available.

Education and Training Programs: Education/Teaching of Individuals with Hearing Impairments, Including Deafness; Foreign Languages and Literatures, General; Linguistics; Language Interpretation and Translation; African Languages, Literatures, and

Linguistics; East Asian Languages, Literatures, and Linguistics, General; Chinese Language and Literature; Japanese Language and Literature; Korean Language and Literature; Tibetan Language and Literature; others. **Related Knowledge/Courses:** Foreign Language; English Language; Geography; Sociology and Anthropology; Communications and Media; Computers and Electronics.

Work Environment: Indoors; sitting; repetitive motions.

Interviewers, Except Eligibility and Loan

- ❋ Education/Training Required: Short-term on-the-job training
- ❋ Annual Earnings: $26,290
- ❋ Beginning Wage: $17,370
- ❋ Earnings Growth Potential: Very high
- ❋ Growth: 9.5%
- ❋ Annual Job Openings: 54,060
- ❋ Self-Employed: 0.8%
- ❋ Part-Time: 23.4%

Industries with Greatest Employment: Hospitals, Public and Private; Professional, Scientific, and Technical Services; Ambulatory Health Care Services; Educational Services, Public and Private.

Highest-Growth Industries (Projected Growth for This Job): Social Assistance (54.4%); Securities, Commodity Contracts, and Other Financial Investments and Related Activities (40.4%); Internet Service Providers, Web Search Portals, and Data Processing Services (35.1%); General Merchandise Stores (32.1%); Ambulatory Health Care Services (27.0%); Funds, Trusts, and Other Financial Vehicles (26.3%); Nonstore Retailers (23.6%); Administrative and Support Services (23.0%); Nursing and Residential Care Facilities (19.6%); Religious, Grantmaking, Civic, Professional, and Similar Organizations (17.5%); Real Estate (17.4%); Credit Intermediation and Related Activities (15.6%); Management of Companies and Enterprises (15.3%).

Lowest-Growth Industries (Projected Growth for This Job): Publishing Industries (Except Internet) (–4.0%); Professional, Scientific, and Technical Services (–0.1%); Insurance Carriers and Related Activities (5.5%); Hospitals, Public and Private (10.9%); Educational Services, Public and Private (11.9%).

Fastest-Growing Metropolitan Areas (Recent Growth for This Job): Wilmington, NC (175.0%); Olympia, WA (85.7%); Atlantic City, NJ (82.4%); College Station–Bryan, TX (78.9%); Jonesboro, AR (77.8%).

Other Considerations for Job Security: Some job openings will come from employment growth, but most job openings should arise from the need to replace the numerous interviewers who leave the occupation each year. Prospects for filling these openings will be best for applicants with a broad range of job skills, including good customer service, math, and telephone skills. In addition to openings for full-time jobs, opportunities also should be available for part-time and temporary jobs.

Interview persons by telephone, by mail, in person, or by other means for the purpose of completing forms, applications, or questionnaires. Ask specific questions, record answers, and assist persons with completing form. May sort, classify, and file forms. Ask questions in accordance with instructions to obtain various specified information such as person's name, address, age, religious preference, and state of residency. Identify and resolve inconsistencies in interviewees' responses by means of appropriate questioning or explanation. Compile, record, and code results and data from interview or survey, using computer or specified form. Review data obtained from interview for completeness and accuracy. Contact individuals to be interviewed at home, place of business, or field location by telephone, by mail, or in person. Assist individuals in filling out applications or questionnaires. Ensure payment for services by verifying benefits with the person's insurance provider or working out financing options. Identify and report problems in obtaining valid data. Explain survey objectives and procedures to interviewees and interpret survey questions to help interviewees' comprehension. Perform patient services, such as answering the telephone and assisting patients with financial and medical questions. Prepare reports to provide answers in response to specific problems. Locate and list addresses and households. Perform other office duties as needed, such as telemarketing and customer service inquiries, billing patients, and receiving payments. Meet with supervisor daily to submit completed assignments and discuss progress. Collect and analyze data, such as studying old records; tallying the number of outpatients entering each day or week; or participating in federal, state, or local population surveys as a census enumerator.

Personality Type: Conventional.

GOE—Interest Area: 10. Human Service. **Work Group:** 10.04. Client Interviewing. **Other Jobs in this Work Group:** Eligibility Interviewers, Government Programs.

Skills: No data available.

Education and Training Program: Receptionist. **Related Knowledge/Courses:** Therapy and Counseling; Customer and Personal Service; Sales and Marketing; Psychology; Medicine and Dentistry; Education and Training.

Work Environment: Indoors; sitting; using hands on objects, tools, or controls; repetitive motions.

Judges, Magistrate Judges, and Magistrates

* Education/Training Required: Work experience plus degree
* Annual Earnings: $101,690
* Beginning Wage: $29,540
* Earnings Growth Potential: Low
* Growth: 5.1%
* Annual Job Openings: 1,567
* Self-Employed: 0.0%
* Part-Time: 5.9%

Industries with Greatest Employment: State Government, Excluding Education and Hospitals; Local Government, Excluding Education and Hospitals.

Highest-Growth Industries (Projected Growth for This Job): None met the criteria.

Lowest-Growth Industries (Projected Growth for This Job): None met the criteria.

Fastest-Growing Metropolitan Areas (Recent Growth for This Job): Jackson, MS (100.0%); Tulsa, OK (100.0%); Oklahoma City, OK (80.0%); Kingston, NY (75.0%); Lansing–East Lansing, MI (66.7%).

Other Considerations for Job Security: Judges and magistrates are expected to encounter competition for jobs because of the prestige associated with serving on the bench. Most job openings will arise as judges retire. However, additional openings will occur when new judgeships are authorized by law or when judges are elevated to higher judicial offices. Budgetary pressures at all levels of government are expected to hold down new openings of judges, despite rising caseloads, particularly in federal courts. However, the continued need to cope with crime and settle disputes, as well as the public's willingness to go to court to settle disputes, should spur demand for judges. Also, economic growth is expected to lead to more business contracts and transactions and, thus, more legal disputes.

Arbitrate, advise, adjudicate, or administer justice in a court of law. May sentence defendant in criminal cases according to government statutes. May determine liability of defendant in civil cases. May issue marriage licenses and perform wedding ceremonies. Instruct juries on applicable laws, direct juries to deduce the facts from the evidence presented, and hear their verdicts. Sentence defendants in criminal cases on conviction by jury according to applicable government statutes. Rule on admissibility of evidence and methods of conducting testimony. Preside over hearings and listen to allegations made by plaintiffs to determine whether the evidence supports the charges. Read documents on pleadings and motions to ascertain facts and issues. Interpret and enforce rules of procedure or establish new rules in situations where no procedures are already established by law. Monitor proceedings to ensure that all applicable rules and procedures are followed. Advise attorneys, juries, litigants, and court personnel regarding conduct, issues, and proceedings. Research legal issues and write opinions on them. Conduct preliminary hearings to decide issues such as whether there is reasonable and probable cause to hold defendants in felony cases. Write decisions on cases. Award compensation for damages to litigants in civil cases in relation to findings by juries or by the court. Settle disputes between opposing attorneys. Supervise other judges, court officers, and the court's administrative staff. Impose restrictions on parties in civil cases until trials can be held. Rule on custody and access disputes and enforce court orders regarding custody and support of children. Grant divorces and divide assets between spouses. Participate in judicial tribunals to help resolve disputes. Perform wedding ceremonies.

Personality Type: Enterprising.

GOE—Interest Area: 12. Law and Public Safety. **Work Group:** 12.02. Legal Practice and Justice Administration. **Other Jobs in this Work Group:** Administrative Law Judges, Adjudicators, and Hearing Officers; Arbitrators, Mediators, and Conciliators; Lawyers.

Skills: Judgment and Decision Making; Persuasion; Negotiation; Critical Thinking; Management of Personnel Resources; Active Listening.

Education and Training Programs: Law (LL.B., J.D.); Legal Professions and Studies, Other. **Related Knowledge/Courses:** Law and Government; Therapy and Counseling; Philosophy and Theology; English Language; Psychology; Sociology and Anthropology.

Work Environment: Indoors; sitting.

Kindergarten Teachers, Except Special Education

- ❋ Education/Training Required: Bachelor's degree
- ❋ Annual Earnings: $43,580
- ❋ Beginning Wage: $28,590
- ❋ Earnings Growth Potential: Very high
- ❋ Growth: 16.3%
- ❋ Annual Job Openings: 27,603
- ❋ Self-Employed: 1.1%
- ❋ Part-Time: 25.1%

Industries with Greatest Employment: Educational Services, Public and Private.

Highest-Growth Industries (Projected Growth for This Job): Social Assistance (25.8%); Religious, Grantmaking, Civic, Professional, and Similar Organizations (18.8%); Educational Services, Public and Private (15.9%).

Lowest-Growth Industries (Projected Growth for This Job): None met the criteria.

Fastest-Growing Metropolitan Areas (Recent Growth for This Job): Winston-Salem, NC (82.6%); St. Cloud, MN (77.8%); Lima, OH (75.0%); Janesville, WI (66.7%); Rochester–Dover, NH–ME (66.7%).

Other Considerations for Job Security: Job prospects are expected to be favorable, with particularly good prospects for teachers in less desirable urban or rural school districts and for those with licensure in more than one subject. Fast-growing states in the South and West—led by Nevada, Arizona, Texas, and Georgia—will experience the largest enrollment increases. Enrollments in the Midwest are expected to hold relatively steady, while those in the Northeast are expected to decline. The number of teachers employed depends on state and local expenditures for education and on the enactment of legislation to increase the quality and scope of public education. Education has received a large increase in federal funding, particularly for the hiring of qualified teachers in lower-income areas. Also, some states are instituting programs to improve early childhood education, such as offering full-day kindergarten and universal preschool.

Teach elemental natural and social science, personal hygiene, music, art, and literature to children aged 4 to 6 years old. Promote physical, mental, and social development. May be required to hold state certification. Teach basic skills such as color, shape, number, and letter recognition; personal hygiene; and social skills. Establish and enforce rules for behavior and policies and procedures to maintain order among students. Observe and evaluate children's performance, behavior, social development, and physical health. Instruct students individually and in groups, adapting teaching methods to meet students' varying needs and interests. Read books to entire classes or to small groups. Demonstrate activities to children. Provide a variety of materials and resources for children to explore, manipulate, and use, both in learning activities and in imaginative play. Plan and conduct activities for a balanced program of instruction, demonstration, and work time that provides students with opportunities to observe, question, and investigate. Confer with parents or guardians, other teachers, counselors, and administrators to resolve students' behavioral and academic problems. Prepare children for later grades by encouraging them to explore learning opportunities and to persevere with challenging tasks. Establish clear objectives for all lessons, units, and projects and communicate those objectives to children. Prepare and implement remedial programs for students requiring extra help. Meet with parents and guardians to discuss their children's progress and to determine priorities and resource needs for their children. Prepare objectives and outlines for courses of study, following curriculum guidelines or requirements of states and schools. Organize and lead activities designed to promote physical, mental, and social development such as games, arts and crafts, music, and storytelling. Guide and counsel students with adjustment or academic problems or special academic interests. Identify children showing signs of emotional, developmental, or health-related problems and discuss them with supervisors, parents or guardians, and child-development specialists. Instruct and monitor students in the use and care of equipment and materials to prevent injuries and damage. Assimilate arriving children to the school environment by greeting them, helping them remove outerwear, and selecting activities of interest to them.

Personality Type: Social.

GOE—Interest Area: 05. Education and Training. **Work Group:** 05.02. Preschool, Elementary, and Secondary Teaching and Instructing. **Other Jobs in this Work Group:** Elementary School Teachers, Except Special Education; Middle School Teachers, Except Special and Vocational Education; Preschool Teachers, Except Special Education; Secondary School Teachers, Except Special and Vocational Education; Special Education Teachers, Middle School; Special Education Teachers, Preschool, Kindergarten, and Elementary School; Special Education Teachers, Secondary School; Teacher Assistants; Vocational Education Teachers, Middle School; Vocational Education Teachers, Secondary School.

Skills: Learning Strategies; Instructing; Monitoring; Social Perceptiveness; Writing; Time Management.

Education and Training Programs: Montessori Teacher Education; Waldorf/Steiner Teacher Education; Kindergarten/Preschool Education and Teaching; Early Childhood Education and Teaching. **Related Knowledge/Courses:** History and Archeology; Geography; Sociology and Anthropology; Philosophy and Theology; Psychology; Education and Training.

Work Environment: Indoors; disease or infections; standing.

Law Teachers, Postsecondary

- ❋ Education/Training Required: First professional degree
- ❋ Annual Earnings: $87,240
- ❋ Beginning Wage: $40,080
- ❋ Earnings Growth Potential: High
- ❋ Growth: 22.9%
- ❋ Annual Job Openings: 237,478
- ❋ Self-Employed: 0.4%
- ❋ Part-Time: 27.8%

Our sources did not provide separate job openings data for this occupation. The job openings listed here are shared with 35 other postsecondary teaching occupations. For a complete list, see the beginning of this section.

Industries with Greatest Employment: Educational Services, Public and Private.

Highest-Growth Industries (Projected Growth for This Job): Administrative and Support Services (48.3%); Amusement, Gambling, and Recreation Industries (45.3%); Social Assistance (38.6%); Support Activities for Transportation (32.8%); Religious, Grantmaking, Civic, Professional, and Similar Organizations (29.9%); Professional, Scientific, and Technical Services (28.8%); Management of Companies and Enterprises (26.8%); Educational Services, Public and Private (22.9%); Hospitals, Public and Private (21.4%); Personal and Laundry Services (21.0%).

Lowest-Growth Industries (Projected Growth for This Job): Other Information Services (7.4%); Sporting Goods, Hobby, Book, and Music Stores (13.3%); Performing Arts, Spectator Sports, and Related Industries (13.4%); Insurance Carriers and Related Activities (13.9%).

Fastest-Growing Metropolitan Areas (Recent Growth for This Job): New York–Northern New Jersey–Long Island, NY–NJ–PA (12.5%).

Other Considerations for Job Security: Retirements of current postsecondary teachers should create numerous openings for all types of postsecondary teachers, so job opportunities are generally expected to be very good. Because students attend postsecondary institutions to prepare themselves for careers, the best job prospects for postsecondary teachers are likely to be in rapidly growing fields that offer many nonacademic career options. Enrollments in law schools seem likely to remain high.

Teach courses in law. Evaluate and grade students' classwork, assignments, papers, and oral presentations. Compile, administer, and grade examinations or assign this work to others. Prepare and deliver lectures to undergraduate or graduate students on topics such as civil procedure, contracts, and torts. Initiate, facilitate, and moderate classroom discussions. Prepare course materials such as syllabi, homework assignments, and handouts. Keep abreast of developments in the field by reading current literature, talking with colleagues, and participating in professional conferences. Plan, evaluate, and revise curricula, course content, course materials, and methods of instruction. Maintain regularly scheduled office hours to advise and assist students. Conduct research in a particular field of knowledge and publish findings in professional journals, books, or electronic media. Advise students on academic and vocational curricula and on career issues. Supervise undergraduate and/or graduate teaching, internships, and research work. Select and obtain materials and supplies such as textbooks. Maintain student attendance records, grades, and other required records. Serve on academic or administrative committees that deal with institutional policies, departmental matters, and academic issues. Perform administrative duties such as serving as department head. Collaborate with colleagues to address teaching and research issues. Participate in student recruitment, registration, and placement activities. Compile bibliographies of specialized materials for outside reading assignments. Participate in campus and community events. Act as advisers to student organizations. Assign cases for students to hear and try. Provide professional consulting services to government or industry. Write grant proposals to procure external research funding.

Personality Type: No data available.

GOE—**Interest Area:** 05. Education and Training. **Work Group:** 05.03. Postsecondary and Adult Teaching and Instructing. **Other Jobs in this Work Group:** Adult Literacy, Remedial Education, and GED Teachers and Instructors; Agricultural Sciences Teachers, Postsecondary; Anthropology and Archeology Teachers, Postsecondary; Architecture Teachers, Postsecondary; Area, Ethnic, and Cultural Studies Teachers, Postsecondary; Art, Drama, and Music Teachers, Postsecondary; Atmospheric, Earth, Marine, and Space Sciences Teachers, Postsecondary; Biological Science Teachers, Postsecondary; Business Teachers, Postsecondary; Chemistry Teachers, Postsecondary; Communications Teachers, Postsecondary; Computer Science Teachers, Postsecondary; Criminal Justice and Law Enforcement Teachers, Postsecondary; Economics Teachers, Postsecondary; Education Teachers, Postsecondary; Engineering Teachers, Postsecondary; English Language and Literature Teachers, Postsecondary; Environmental Science Teachers, Postsecondary; Farm and Home Management Advisors; Foreign Language and Literature Teachers, Postsecondary; Forestry and Conservation Science Teachers, Postsecondary; Geography Teachers, Postsecondary; Graduate Teaching Assistants; Health Specialties Teachers, Postsecondary; History Teachers, Postsecondary; Home Economics Teachers, Postsecondary; Library Science Teachers, Postsecondary; Mathematical Science Teachers, Postsecondary; Nursing Instructors and Teachers, Postsecondary; Philosophy and Religion Teachers, Postsecondary; Physics Teachers, Postsecondary; Political Science Teachers, Postsecondary; Psychology Teachers, Postsecondary; Recreation and Fitness Studies Teachers, Postsecondary; Self-Enrichment Education Teachers; Social Work Teachers, Postsecondary; Sociology Teachers, Postsecondary; Vocational Education Teachers, Postsecondary.

Skills: Instructing; Critical Thinking; Writing; Reading Comprehension; Persuasion; Speaking.

Education and Training Programs: Legal Studies, General; Law (LL.B., J.D.). **Related Knowledge/Courses:** Law and Government; English Language; History and Archeology; Education and Training;

Philosophy and Theology; Communications and Media.

Work Environment: Indoors; sitting.

Librarians

* Education/Training Required: Master's degree
* Annual Earnings: $49,060
* Beginning Wage: $30,930
* Earnings Growth Potential: Very high
* Growth: 3.6%
* Annual Job Openings: 18,945
* Self-Employed: 0.6%
* Part-Time: 21.2%

Industries with Greatest Employment: Educational Services, Public and Private.

Highest-Growth Industries (Projected Growth for This Job): Securities, Commodity Contracts, and Other Financial Investments and Related Activities (48.1%); Social Assistance (36.8%); Museums, Historical Sites, and Similar Institutions (36.1%); Administrative and Support Services (28.5%); Chemical Manufacturing (25.1%); Ambulatory Health Care Services (25.0%); Religious, Grantmaking, Civic, Professional, and Similar Organizations (18.5%); Professional, Scientific, and Technical Services (18.3%); Motion Picture, Video, and Sound Recording Industries (17.0%).

Lowest-Growth Industries (Projected Growth for This Job): Computer and Electronic Product Manufacturing (–9.1%); Publishing Industries (except Internet) (–7.3%); Other Information Services (–2.1%); Transportation Equipment Manufacturing (0.0%); Educational Services, Public and Private (3.9%); Performing Arts, Spectator Sports, and Related Industries (4.0%); Credit Intermediation and Related Activities (8.0%); Merchant Wholesalers, Nondurable Goods (8.4%); Hospitals, Public and Private (10.2%).

Fastest-Growing Metropolitan Areas (Recent Growth for This Job): Dayton, OH (115.4%); Fort Collins–Loveland, CO (75.0%); Merced, CA (75.0%); Pine Bluff, AR (75.0%); Cleveland–Elyria–Mentor, OH (66.9%).

Other Considerations for Job Security: More than two out of three librarians are aged 45 or older, which will result in many job openings over the next decade as many librarians retire. However, recent increases in enrollments in master's in library science programs will prepare a sufficient number of new librarians to fill these positions. Opportunities for public school librarians, who are usually drawn from the ranks of teachers, should be particularly favorable.

Administer libraries and perform related library services. Work in a variety of settings, including public libraries, schools, colleges and universities, museums, corporations, government agencies, law firms, nonprofit organizations, and health-care providers. Tasks may include selecting, acquiring, cataloging, classifying, circulating, and maintaining library materials and furnishing reference, bibliographical, and readers' advisory services. May perform in-depth, strategic research and synthesize, analyze, edit, and filter information. May set up or work with databases and information systems to catalog and access information. Search standard reference materials, including online sources, to answer patrons' reference questions. Analyze patrons' requests to determine needed information and assist in furnishing or locating that information. Teach library patrons to search for information by using databases. Keep records of circulation and materials. Supervise budgeting, planning, and personnel activities. Check books in and out of the library. Explain use of library facilities, resources, equipment, and services and provide information about library policies. Review and evaluate resource material, such as book reviews and catalogs, to select and order print, audiovisual, and electronic resources. Code, classify, and catalog books, publications, films, audiovisual aids, and other library materials based on subject matter or standard library classification systems. Locate unusual or unique information in response to specific requests. Direct and train library staff in duties such as receiving, shelving, researching, cataloging, and equipment use. Respond to customer complaints, taking action as necessary. Organize collections of books, publications, documents, audiovisual aids, and other reference materials for convenient access. Develop library policies and procedures. Evaluate materials to determine outdated or unused items to be discarded. Develop information access aids such as indexes and annotated bibliographies, Web pages, electronic pathfinders, and online tutorials. Plan and deliver client-centered programs and services such as special services for corporate clients, storytelling for children, newsletters, or programs for special groups. Compile lists of books, periodicals, articles, and audiovisual materials on particular subjects. Arrange for interlibrary loans of materials not available in a particular library. Assemble and arrange display materials. Confer with teachers, parents, and community organizations to develop, plan, and conduct programs in reading, viewing, and communication skills. Compile lists of overdue materials and notify borrowers that their materials are overdue.

Personality Type: Artistic.

GOE—Interest Area: 05. Education and Training. **Work Group:** 05.04. Library Services. **Other Jobs in this Work Group:** Library Assistants, Clerical; Library Technicians.

Skills: Management of Financial Resources; Management of Material Resources; Learning Strategies; Systems Evaluation; Service Orientation; Persuasion.

Education and Training Programs: School Librarian/School Library Media Specialist; Library Science/Librarianship; Library Science, Other. **Related Knowledge/Courses:** Communications and Media; Clerical Studies; Customer and Personal Service; Personnel and Human Resources; English Language; Computers and Electronics.

Work Environment: Indoors; sitting; using hands on objects, tools, or controls; repetitive motions.

Library Assistants, Clerical

- ❋ Education/Training Required: Short-term on-the-job training
- ❋ Annual Earnings: $21,640
- ❋ Beginning Wage: $14,070
- ❋ Earnings Growth Potential: Very high
- ❋ Growth: 7.9%
- ❋ Annual Job Openings: 18,961
- ❋ Self-Employed: 0.3%
- ❋ Part-Time: 52.5%

Industries with Greatest Employment: Educational Services, Public and Private; Other Information Services.

Highest-Growth Industries (Projected Growth for This Job): Museums, Historical Sites, and Similar Institutions (36.0%); Administrative and Support Services (31.3%); Social Assistance (30.1%); Religious, Grantmaking, Civic, Professional, and Similar Organizations (18.5%); Management of Companies and Enterprises (15.7%).

Lowest-Growth Industries (Projected Growth for This Job): Publishing Industries (except Internet) (–4.2%); Other Information Services (–2.1%); Educational Services, Public and Private (2.9%); Hospitals, Public and Private (10.9%); Professional, Scientific, and Technical Services (12.1%).

Fastest-Growing Metropolitan Areas (Recent Growth for This Job): Mobile, AL (266.7%); Stockton, CA (171.4%); Holland–Grand Haven, MI (133.3%); Lynchburg, VA (125.0%); Albuquerque, NM (100.0%).

Other Considerations for Job Security: Each year, many people leave this relatively low-paying occupation for other occupations that offer higher pay or full-time work. This creates good job opportunities for those who want to become library assistants. Efforts to contain costs in local governments and academic institutions of all types will slow overall growth in library services but may result in the hiring of more library support staff, who are paid less than librarians and who take on more responsibility. Because library assistants work for public institutions, they're not directly affected by the ups and downs of the business cycle, but they may be affected by changes in the level of government funding for libraries.

Compile records; sort and shelve books; and issue and receive library materials such as pictures, cards, slides, and microfilm. Locate library materials for loan and replace material in shelving area, stacks, or files according to identification number and title. Register patrons to permit them to borrow books, periodicals, and other library materials. Lend and collect books, periodicals, videotapes, and other materials at circulation desks. Enter and update patrons' records on computers. Process new materials, including books, audiovisual materials, and computer software. Sort books, publications, and other items according to established procedure and return them to shelves, files, or other designated storage areas. Locate library materials for patrons, including books, periodicals, tape cassettes, Braille volumes, and pictures. Instruct patrons on how to use reference sources, card catalogs, and automated information systems. Inspect returned books for condition and due-date status and compute any applicable fines. Answer routine inquiries and refer patrons in need of professional assistance to librarians. Maintain records of items received, stored, issued, and returned and file catalog cards according to system used. Perform clerical activities such as filing, typing, word processing, photocopying and mailing out material, and mail sorting. Provide assistance to librarians in the maintenance of collections of books, periodicals, magazines, newspapers, and audiovisual and other materials. Take action to deal with disruptive or problem patrons. Classify and catalog items according to content and purpose. Register new patrons and issue borrower identification cards that permit patrons to borrow books and other materials. Send out notices and accept fine payments for lost or overdue books. Operate small branch libraries under the direction of off-site librarian supervisors. Prepare, store, and retrieve classification and catalog information, lecture notes, or other information related to stored documents, using computers. Schedule and supervise clerical workers, volunteers, and student assistants. Operate and maintain audiovisual equipment. Review records, such as microfilm and issue cards, to identify titles of overdue materials and delinquent borrowers. Select substitute titles when requested materials are unavailable, following criteria such as age, education, and interests. Repair books, using mending tape, paste, and brushes.

Personality Type: Conventional.

GOE—Interest Area: 05. Education and Training. **Work Group:** 05.04. Library Services. **Other Jobs in this Work Group:** Librarians; Library Technicians.

Skills: No data available.

Education and Training Program: Library Assistant/Technician. **Related Knowledge/Courses:** Clerical Studies; Computers and Electronics.

Work Environment: Indoors; sitting; using hands on objects, tools, or controls; repetitive motions.

Library Science Teachers, Postsecondary

- ❋ Education/Training Required: Doctoral degree
- ❋ Annual Earnings: $54,570
- ❋ Beginning Wage: $33,120
- ❋ Earnings Growth Potential: Very high
- ❋ Growth: 22.9%
- ❋ Annual Job Openings: 237,478
- ❋ Self-Employed: 0.4%
- ❋ Part-Time: 27.8%

Our sources did not provide separate job openings data for this occupation. The job openings listed here are shared with 35 other postsecondary teaching occupations. For a complete list, see the beginning of this section.

Industries with Greatest Employment: Educational Services, Public and Private.

Highest-Growth Industries (Projected Growth for This Job): Administrative and Support Services (48.3%); Amusement, Gambling, and Recreation Industries (45.3%); Social Assistance (38.6%); Support Activities for Transportation (32.8%); Religious, Grantmaking, Civic, Professional, and Similar Organizations (29.9%); Professional, Scientific, and Technical Services (28.8%); Management of Companies and Enterprises (26.8%); Educational Services, Public and Private (22.9%); Hospitals, Public and Private (21.4%); Personal and Laundry Services (21.0%).

Lowest-Growth Industries (Projected Growth for This Job): Other Information Services (7.4%); Sporting Goods, Hobby, Book, and Music Stores (13.3%); Performing Arts, Spectator Sports, and Related Industries (13.4%); Insurance Carriers and Related Activities (13.9%).

Fastest-Growing Metropolitan Areas (Recent Growth for This Job): Washington–Arlington–Alexandria, DC–VA–MD–WV (50.0%); Los Angeles–Long Beach–Santa Ana, CA (42.9%); Philadelphia–Camden–Wilmington, PA–NJ–DE–MD (33.3%).

Other Considerations for Job Security: Retirements of current postsecondary teachers should create numerous openings for all types of postsecondary teachers. However, because students attend postsecondary institutions to prepare themselves for careers, the best job prospects for postsecondary teachers are likely to be in rapidly growing fields that offer many nonacademic career options. Community colleges and other institutions offering career and technical education have been among the most rapidly growing and are expected to offer some of the best opportunities for postsecondary teachers.

Teach courses in library science. Prepare course materials such as syllabi, homework assignments, and handouts. Prepare and deliver lectures to undergraduate or graduate students on topics such as collection development, archival methods, and indexing and abstracting. Evaluate and grade students' classwork, assignments, and papers. Keep abreast of developments in their field by reading current literature, talking with colleagues, and participating in professional conferences. Initiate, facilitate, and moderate classroom discussions. Plan, evaluate, and revise curricula, course content, course materials, and methods of instruction. Conduct research in a particular field of knowledge and publish findings in professional journals, books, and/or electronic media. Maintain student attendance records, grades, and other required records. Collaborate with colleagues to address teaching and research issues. Advise students on academic and vocational curricula and on career issues. Compile, administer, and grade examinations or assign this work to others. Supervise undergraduate or graduate teaching, internships, and research work. Maintain regularly scheduled office hours to advise and assist students. Write grant proposals to procure external research funding. Select and obtain materials and supplies such as textbooks. Serve on academic or administrative committees that deal with institutional policies, departmental matters, and academic issues. Compile bibliographies of specialized materials for outside reading assignments. Participate in student recruitment, registration, and placement activities. Perform administrative duties such as serving as department head. Participate in campus and community events. Act as advisers to student organizations. Provide professional consulting services to government and/or industry.

Personality Type: No data available.

GOE—Interest Area: 05. Education and Training. **Work Group:** 05.03. Postsecondary and Adult Teaching and Instructing. **Other Jobs in this Work Group:** Adult Literacy, Remedial Education, and GED Teachers and Instructors; Agricultural Sciences Teachers, Postsecondary; Anthropology and Archeology Teachers, Postsecondary; Architecture Teachers, Postsecondary; Area, Ethnic, and Cultural Studies Teachers, Postsecondary; Art, Drama, and Music Teachers, Postsecondary; Atmospheric, Earth, Marine, and Space Sciences Teachers, Postsecondary; Biological Science Teachers, Postsecondary; Business Teachers, Postsecondary; Chemistry Teachers, Postsecondary; Communications Teachers, Postsecondary; Computer Science Teachers, Postsecondary; Criminal Justice and Law Enforcement Teachers, Postsecondary; Economics Teachers, Postsecondary; Education Teachers, Postsecondary; Engineering Teachers, Postsecondary; English Language and Literature Teachers, Postsecondary; Environmental Science Teachers, Postsecondary; Farm and Home Management Advisors; Foreign Language and Literature Teachers, Postsecondary; Forestry and Conservation Science Teachers, Postsecondary; Geography Teachers, Postsecondary; Graduate Teaching Assistants; Health Specialties Teachers, Postsecondary; History Teachers, Postsecondary; Home Economics Teachers, Postsecondary; Law Teachers, Postsecondary; Mathematical Science Teachers, Postsecondary; Nursing Instructors and Teachers, Postsecondary; Philosophy and Religion Teachers, Postsecondary; Physics Teachers, Postsecondary; Political Science Teachers, Postsecondary; Psychology Teachers, Postsecondary; Recreation and Fitness Studies Teachers, Postsecondary; Self-Enrichment Education Teachers; Social Work Teachers, Postsecondary; Sociology Teachers, Postsecondary; Vocational Education Teachers, Postsecondary.

Skills: Writing; Learning Strategies; Instructing; Reading Comprehension; Active Learning; Systems Evaluation.

Education and Training Programs: Teacher Education and Professional Development, Specific Subject Areas, Other; Library Science/Librarianship. **Related Knowledge/Courses:** Education and Training; Sociology and Anthropology; Communications and Media; English Language; History and Archeology; Philosophy and Theology.

Work Environment: Indoors; sitting.

Library Technicians

- ✱ Education/Training Required: Postsecondary vocational training
- ✱ Annual Earnings: $26,560
- ✱ Beginning Wage: $15,820
- ✱ Earnings Growth Potential: Very high
- ✱ Growth: 8.5%
- ✱ Annual Job Openings: 29,075
- ✱ Self-Employed: 0.0%
- ✱ Part-Time: 65.0%

Industries with Greatest Employment: Educational Services, Public and Private; Other Information Services.

Highest-Growth Industries (Projected Growth for This Job): Museums, Historical Sites, and Similar Institutions (36.2%); Administrative and Support Services (33.4%); Professional, Scientific, and Technical Services (18.5%); Motion Picture, Video, and Sound Recording Industries (18.1%); Religious, Grantmaking, Civic, Professional, and Similar Organizations (17.4%).

Lowest-Growth Industries (Projected Growth for This Job): Publishing Industries (except Internet) (–11.0%); Other Information Services (–2.1%); Educational Services, Public and Private (4.6%); Hospitals, Public and Private (10.0%).

Fastest-Growing Metropolitan Areas (Recent Growth for This Job): Spartanburg, SC (220.0%); Boise City–Nampa, ID (124.3%); Augusta–Richmond County, GA–SC (100.0%); Bellingham, WA (100.0%); Cleveland–Elyria–Mentor, OH (100.0%).

Other Considerations for Job Security: Opportunities will be best for those with specialized postsecondary library training. Increased use of special libraries in businesses, hospitals, and other places should result in good job opportunities for library technicians in those settings.

Assist librarians by helping readers in the use of library catalogs, databases, and indexes to locate books and other materials and by answering questions that require only brief consultation of standard reference. Compile records; sort and shelve books; remove or repair damaged books; register patrons; check materials in and out of the circulation process. Replace materials in shelving area (stacks) or files. Includes bookmobile drivers who operate bookmobiles or light trucks that pull trailers to specific locations on a predetermined schedule and assist with providing services in mobile libraries. Reserve, circulate, renew, and discharge books and other materials. Enter and update patrons' records on computers. Provide assistance to teachers and students by locating materials and helping complete special projects. Guide patrons in finding and using library resources, including reference materials, audiovisual equipment, computers, and electronic resources. Answer routine reference inquiries and refer patrons needing further assistance to librarians. Train other staff, volunteers, or student assistants, and schedule and supervise their work. Sort books, publications, and other items according to procedure and return them to shelves, files, or other designated storage areas. Conduct reference searches, using printed materials and in-house and online databases. Deliver and retrieve items throughout the library by hand or by using pushcart. Take actions to halt disruption of library activities by problem patrons. Process interlibrary loans for patrons. Process print and nonprint library materials to prepare them for inclusion in library collections. Retrieve information from central databases for storage in library's computer. Organize and maintain periodicals and reference materials. Compile and maintain records relating to circulation, materials, and equipment. Collect fines and respond to complaints about fines. Issue identification cards to borrowers. Verify bibliographical data for materials, including author, title, publisher, publication date, and edition. Review subject matter of materials to be classified and select classification numbers and headings according to classification systems. Send out notices about lost or overdue books. Prepare order slips for materials to be acquired, checking prices and figuring costs. Design, customize, and maintain databases, Web pages, and local area networks. Operate and maintain audiovisual equipment such as projectors, tape recorders, and videocassette recorders. File catalog cards according to system used. Prepare volumes for binding. Conduct children's programs and other specialized programs such as library tours. Compose explanatory summaries of contents of books and other reference materials.

Personality Type: Conventional.

GOE—Interest Area: 05. Education and Training. **Work Group:** 05.04. Library Services. **Other Jobs in this Work Group:** Librarians; Library Assistants, Clerical.

Skills: No data available.

Education and Training Program: Library Assistant/Technician. **Related Knowledge/Courses:** Clerical Studies; Computers and Electronics; Customer and Personal Service; English Language; Administration and Management; Education and Training.

Work Environment: Indoors; sitting; using hands on objects, tools, or controls; repetitive motions.

Licensed Practical and Licensed Vocational Nurses

- ❋ Education/Training Required: Postsecondary vocational training
- ❋ Annual Earnings: $36,550
- ❋ Beginning Wage: $26,380
- ❋ Earnings Growth Potential: Very high
- ❋ Growth: 14.0%
- ❋ Annual Job Openings: 70,610
- ❋ Self-Employed: 1.5%
- ❋ Part-Time: 18.3%

Industries with Greatest Employment: Nursing and Residential Care Facilities; Hospitals, Public and Private; Ambulatory Health Care Services; Administrative and Support Services.

Highest-Growth Industries (Projected Growth for This Job): Social Assistance (50.0%); Professional, Scientific, and Technical Services (44.2%); Amusement, Gambling, and Recreation Industries (31.9%); Administrative and Support Services (26.9%); Ambulatory Health Care Services (23.4%); Nursing and Residential Care Facilities (23.4%); Religious, Grantmaking, Civic, Professional, and Similar Organizations (19.7%); Management of Companies and Enterprises (15.3%).

Lowest-Growth Industries (Projected Growth for This Job): Hospitals, Public and Private (–8.0%); Private Households (4.0%); Health and Personal Care Stores (4.0%); Primary and Secondary Jobs (4.0%); Insurance Carriers and Related Activities (5.1%); Educational Services, Public and Private (8.4%); Rental and Leasing Services (8.8%); Real Estate (10.5%); Food Manufacturing (13.6%).

Fastest-Growing Metropolitan Areas (Recent Growth for This Job): Hanford–Corcoran, CA (85.7%); Morristown, TN (64.5%); Prescott, AZ (50.0%); Altoona, PA (47.4%); Topeka, KS (42.5%).

Other Considerations for Job Security: Replacement needs will be a major source of job openings, as many workers leave the occupation permanently. Very good job opportunities are expected. Rapid employment growth is projected in most health-care industries, with the best job opportunities occurring in nursing care facilities and in home health-care services. However, applicants for hospital jobs may face competition as the number of hospital jobs for LPNs declines.

Care for ill, injured, convalescent, or disabled persons in hospitals, nursing homes, clinics, private homes, group homes, and similar institutions. May work under the supervision of a registered nurse. Licensing required. Observe patients, charting and reporting changes in patients' conditions, such as adverse reactions to medication or treatment, and taking any necessary action. Administer prescribed medications or start intravenous fluids and note times and amounts on patients' charts. Answer patients' calls and determine how to assist them. Measure and record patients' vital signs, such as height, weight, temperature, blood pressure, pulse, and respiration. Provide basic patient care and treatments, such as taking temperatures or blood pressures, dressing wounds, treating bedsores, giving enemas or douches, rubbing with alcohol, massaging, or performing catheterizations. Help patients with bathing, dressing, maintaining personal hygiene, moving in bed, or standing and walking. Supervise nurses' aides and assistants. Work as part of a health-care team to assess patient needs, plan and modify care, and implement interventions. Record food and fluid intake and output. Evaluate nursing intervention outcomes, conferring with other health-care team members as necessary. Assemble and use equipment such as catheters, tracheotomy tubes, and oxygen suppliers. Collect samples such as blood, urine, and sputum from patients and perform routine laboratory tests on samples. Prepare patients for examinations, tests, or treatments and explain procedures. Prepare food trays and examine them for conformance to prescribed diet. Apply compresses, ice bags, and hot-water bottles. Clean rooms and make beds. Inventory and requisition supplies and instruments. Provide medical treatment and personal care to patients in private home settings, such as cooking, keeping rooms orderly, seeing that patients are comfortable and in good spirits, and instructing family members in simple nursing tasks. Sterilize equipment and supplies, using germicides, sterilizer, or autoclave. Assist in delivery, care, and feeding of infants. Wash and dress bodies of deceased persons. Make appointments, keep records, and perform other clerical duties in doctors' offices and clinics. Set up equipment and prepare medical treatment rooms.

Personality Type: Social.

GOE—Interest Area: 08. Health Science. **Work Group:** 08.08. Patient Care and Assistance. **Other Jobs in this Work Group:** Home Health Aides; Nursing Aides, Orderlies, and Attendants; Psychiatric Aides; Psychiatric Technicians.

Skills: Science; Operation Monitoring; Service Orientation; Judgment and Decision Making; Management of Personnel Resources; Active Listening.

Education and Training Program: Licensed Practical /Vocational Nurse Training (LPN, LVN, Cert,

Dipl, AAS). **Related Knowledge/Courses:** Psychology; Therapy and Counseling; Medicine and Dentistry; Customer and Personal Service; Philosophy and Theology; Sociology and Anthropology.

Work Environment: Indoors; disease or infections; standing; walking and running.

Maintenance and Repair Workers, General

- ✷ Education/Training Required: Moderate-term on-the-job training
- ✷ Annual Earnings: $31,910
- ✷ Beginning Wage: $19,140
- ✷ Earnings Growth Potential: Very high
- ✷ Growth: 10.1%
- ✷ Annual Job Openings: 165,502
- ✷ Self-Employed: 1.5%
- ✷ Part-Time: 5.2%

Industries with Greatest Employment: Real Estate; Educational Services, Public and Private; Accommodation, Including Hotels and Motels; Administrative and Support Services; Religious, Grantmaking, Civic, Professional, and Similar Organizations.

Highest-Growth Industries (Projected Growth for This Job): Securities, Commodity Contracts, and Other Financial Investments and Related Activities (43.8%); Funds, Trusts, and Other Financial Vehicles (37.0%); Museums, Historical Sites, and Similar Institutions (36.2%); Social Assistance (35.9%); Professional, Scientific, and Technical Services (35.8%); Warehousing and Storage (33.6%); Amusement, Gambling, and Recreation Industries (32.5%); Scenic and Sightseeing Transportation (30.6%); Lessors of Nonfinancial Intangible Assets (except Copyrighted Works) (27.8%); Administrative and Support Services (27.6%); Waste Management and Remediation Services (27.4%); Performing Arts, Spectator Sports, and Related Industries (27.1%); Ambulatory Health Care Services (26.5%); Nursing and Residential Care Facilities (26.0%); Water Transportation (21.6%); Religious, Grantmaking, Civic, Professional, and

Similar Organizations (19.3%); Support Activities for Transportation (18.8%); Building Material and Garden Equipment and Supplies Dealers (18.5%); Real Estate (17.1%); others.

Lowest-Growth Industries (Projected Growth for This Job): Apparel Manufacturing (–47.5%); Leather and Allied Product Manufacturing (–44.4%); Pipeline Transportation (–33.8%); Crop Production (–33.7%); Primary Metal Manufacturing (–28.0%); Textile Mills (–27.1%); Petroleum and Coal Products Manufacturing (–24.5%); Paper Manufacturing (–21.9%); Printing and Related Support Activities (–20.8%); Nonstore Retailers (–20.8%).

Fastest-Growing Metropolitan Areas (Recent Growth for This Job): Brunswick, GA (61.5%); Idaho Falls, ID (51.9%); Ames, IA (42.2%); Provo–Orem, UT (31.9%); El Centro, CA (31.7%).

Other Considerations for Job Security: Job opportunities should be excellent, especially for those with experience in maintenance or related fields. General maintenance and repair is a large occupation, generating many job openings due to growth and the need to replace those who leave the occupation. Many job openings are expected to result from the retirement of experienced maintenance workers over the next decade. Employment is related to the number of buildings—for example, office and apartment buildings, stores, schools, hospitals, hotels, and factories—and the amount of equipment needing maintenance and repair. One factor limiting job growth is that computers allow buildings to be monitored more efficiently, partially reducing the need for workers.

Perform work involving the skills of two or more maintenance or craft occupations to keep machines, mechanical equipment, or the structure of an establishment in repair. Duties may involve pipefitting; boilermaking; insulating; welding; machining; carpentry; repairing electrical or mechanical equipment; installing, aligning, and balancing new equipment; and repairing buildings, floors, or stairs. Repair or replace defective equipment parts, using hand tools and power tools, and reassemble equipment. Perform routine preventive maintenance to ensure that machines

continue to run smoothly, building systems operate efficiently, and the physical condition of buildings doesn't deteriorate. Inspect drives, motors, and belts; check fluid levels; replace filters; and perform other maintenance actions, following checklists. Use tools ranging from common hand and power tools, such as hammers, hoists, saws, drills, and wrenches, to precision measuring instruments and electrical and electronic testing devices. Assemble, install, or repair wiring, electrical and electronic components, pipe systems and plumbing, machinery, and equipment. Diagnose mechanical problems and determine how to correct them, checking blueprints, repair manuals, and parts catalogs as necessary. Inspect, operate, and test machinery and equipment to diagnose machine malfunctions. Record maintenance and repair work performed and the costs of the work. Clean and lubricate shafts, bearings, gears, and other parts of machinery. Dismantle devices to gain access to and remove defective parts, using hoists, cranes, hand tools, and power tools. Plan and lay out repair work, using diagrams, drawings, blueprints, maintenance manuals, and schematic diagrams. Adjust functional parts of devices and control instruments, using hand tools, levels, plumb bobs, and straightedges. Order parts, supplies, and equipment from catalogs and suppliers or obtain them from storerooms. Paint and repair roofs, windows, doors, floors, woodwork, plaster, drywall, and other parts of building structures. Operate cutting torches or welding equipment to cut or join metal parts. Align and balance new equipment after installation. Inspect used parts to determine changes in dimensional requirements, using rules, calipers, micrometers, and other measuring instruments. Set up and operate machine tools to repair or fabricate machine parts, jigs and fixtures, and tools. Maintain and repair specialized equipment and machinery found in cafeterias, laundries, hospitals, stores, offices, and factories.

Personality Type: Realistic.

GOE—Interest Area: 02. Architecture and Construction. **Work Group:** 02.05. Systems and Equipment Installation, Maintenance, and Repair. **Other Jobs in this Work Group:** Electrical and Electronics Repairers, Powerhouse, Substation, and Relay;

Electrical Power-Line Installers and Repairers; Elevator Installers and Repairers; Heating and Air Conditioning Mechanics and Installers; Refrigeration Mechanics and Installers; Telecommunications Equipment Installers and Repairers, Except Line Installers; Telecommunications Line Installers and Repairers.

Skills: Equipment Maintenance; Installation; Repairing; Troubleshooting; Operation Monitoring; Operation and Control.

Education and Training Program: Building/Construction Site Management/Manager. **Related Knowledge/Courses:** Building and Construction; Mechanical Devices; Design; Physics; Engineering and Technology; Public Safety and Security.

Work Environment: Indoors; noisy; minor burns, cuts, bites, or stings; standing; walking and running; using hands on objects, tools, or controls.

Marriage and Family Therapists

- ❋ Education/Training Required: Master's degree
- ❋ Annual Earnings: $43,210
- ❋ Beginning Wage: $25,280
- ❋ Earnings Growth Potential: Very high
- ❋ Growth: 29.8%
- ❋ Annual Job Openings: 5,953
- ❋ Self-Employed: 6.2%
- ❋ Part-Time: 15.4%

Industries with Greatest Employment: Social Assistance; Ambulatory Health Care Services; Religious, Grantmaking, Civic, Professional, and Similar Organizations.

Highest-Growth Industries (Projected Growth for This Job): Social Assistance (63.4%); Nursing and Residential Care Facilities (23.6%); Ambulatory Health Care Services (20.4%); Religious, Grantmaking, Civic, Professional, and Similar Organizations (19.8%); Management of Companies and Enterprises (15.6%).

Lowest-Growth Industries (Projected Growth for This Job): Hospitals, Public and Private (4.7%); Educational Services, Public and Private (9.9%).

Fastest-Growing Metropolitan Areas (Recent Growth for This Job): Santa Rosa–Petaluma, CA (200.0%); Houston–Sugar Land–Baytown, TX (120.0%); Sacramento–Arden–Arcade–Roseville, CA (84.6%); Minneapolis–St. Paul–Bloomington, MN–WI (54.5%); Ocean City, NJ (50.0%).

Other Considerations for Job Security: Marriage and family therapists will experience fast growth in part because of an increased recognition of the field. It is more common now for people to seek help for their marital and family problems than it was in the past. Job prospects should be good due to growth and the need to replace people leaving the field.

Diagnose and treat mental and emotional disorders, whether cognitive, affective, or behavioral, within the context of marriage and family systems. Apply psychotherapeutic and family systems theories and techniques in the delivery of professional services to individuals, couples, and families for the purpose of treating such diagnosed nervous and mental disorders. Ask questions that will help clients identify their feelings and behaviors. Counsel clients on concerns such as unsatisfactory relationships, divorce and separation, child rearing, home management, and financial difficulties. Encourage individuals and family members to develop and use skills and strategies for confronting their problems constructively. Maintain case files that include activities, progress notes, evaluations, and recommendations. Collect information about clients, using techniques such as testing, interviewing, discussion, and observation. Develop and implement individualized treatment plans addressing family relationship problems. Determine whether clients should be counseled or referred to other specialists in such fields as medicine, psychiatry, and legal aid. Confer with clients to develop plans for post-treatment activities. Confer with other counselors to analyze individual cases and to coordinate counseling services. Follow up on results of counseling programs and clients' adjustments to determine effectiveness

M

of programs. Provide instructions to clients on how to obtain help with legal, financial, and other personal issues. Contact doctors, schools, social workers, juvenile counselors, law-enforcement personnel, and others to gather information in order to make recommendations to courts for the resolution of child custody or visitation disputes. Provide public education and consultation to other professionals or groups regarding counseling services, issues, and methods. Supervise other counselors, social service staff, and assistants. Provide family counseling and treatment services to inmates participating in substance abuse programs. Write evaluations of parents and children for use by courts deciding divorce and custody cases, testifying in court if necessary.

Personality Type: No data available.

GOE—Interest Area: 10. Human Service. **Work Group:** 10.01. Counseling and Social Work. **Other Jobs in this Work Group:** Child, Family, and School Social Workers; Clinical Psychologists; Clinical, Counseling, and School Psychologists; Counseling Psychologists; Medical and Public Health Social Workers; Mental Health and Substance Abuse Social Workers; Mental Health Counselors; Probation Officers and Correctional Treatment Specialists; Rehabilitation Counselors; Residential Advisors; Social and Human Service Assistants; Substance Abuse and Behavioral Disorder Counselors.

Skills: Social Perceptiveness; Negotiation; Active Listening; Persuasion; Service Orientation; Monitoring.

Education and Training Programs: Social Work; Marriage and Family Therapy/Counseling; Clinical Pastoral Counseling/Patient Counseling. **Related Knowledge/Courses:** Therapy and Counseling; Psychology; Philosophy and Theology; Sociology and Anthropology; Medicine and Dentistry; Customer and Personal Service.

Work Environment: Indoors; sitting.

Massage Therapists

- ❀ Education/Training Required: Postsecondary vocational training
- ❀ Annual Earnings: $33,400
- ❀ Beginning Wage: $15,550
- ❀ Earnings Growth Potential: High
- ❀ Growth: 20.3%
- ❀ Annual Job Openings: 9,193
- ❀ Self-Employed: 64.0%
- ❀ Part-Time: 42.9%

Industries with Greatest Employment: Personal and Laundry Services; Ambulatory Health Care Services; Accommodation, Including Hotels and Motels; Amusement, Gambling, and Recreation Industries.

Highest-Growth Industries (Projected Growth for This Job): Amusement, Gambling, and Recreation Industries (33.0%); Ambulatory Health Care Services (26.3%); Administrative and Support Services (26.1%); Nursing and Residential Care Facilities (18.5%); Accommodation, Including Hotels and Motels (16.1%).

Lowest-Growth Industries (Projected Growth for This Job): Health and Personal Care Stores (3.3%); General Merchandise Stores (9.0%); Personal and Laundry Services (10.2%); Educational Services, Public and Private (10.5%); Hospitals, Public and Private (12.3%); Religious, Grantmaking, Civic, Professional, and Similar Organizations (13.8%).

Fastest-Growing Metropolitan Areas (Recent Growth for This Job): Kansas City, MO–KS (183.3%); Cape Coral–Fort Myers, FL (160.0%); Baltimore–Towson, MD (135.7%); Virginia Beach–Norfolk–Newport News, VA–NC (133.3%); Deltona–Daytona Beach–Ormond Beach, FL (120.0%).

Other Considerations for Job Security: In states that regulate massage therapy, therapists who complete formal training programs and pass the national certification exam are likely to have very good opportunities. However, new massage therapists should expect to work only part-time in spas, hotels, hospitals, physical therapy centers, and other businesses until they can build their own client base. Because referrals are a very important source of work for massage therapists, networking will increase the number of job opportunities. Joining a state or local chapter of a professional association can also help build strong contacts and further increase the likelihood of steady work. Female massage therapists will continue to enjoy slightly better job prospects, as some clients—both male and female—are uncomfortable with male physical contact.

Massage customers for hygienic or remedial purposes. Confer with clients about their medical histories and any problems with stress or pain to determine whether massage would be helpful. Apply finger and hand pressure to specific points of the body. Massage and knead the muscles and soft tissues of the human body to provide courses of treatment for medical conditions and injuries or wellness maintenance. Maintain treatment records. Provide clients with guidance and information about techniques for postural improvement and stretching, strengthening, relaxation, and rehabilitative exercises. Assess clients' soft tissue condition, joint quality and function, muscle strength, and range of motion. Develop and propose client treatment plans that specify which types of massage are to be used. Refer clients to other types of therapists when necessary. Use complementary aids, such as infrared lamps, wet compresses, ice, and whirlpool baths, to promote clients' recovery, relaxation, and well-being. Treat clients in own office or travel to clients' offices and homes. Consult with other health-care professionals such as physiotherapists, chiropractors, physicians, and psychologists to develop treatment plans for clients. Prepare and blend oils and apply the blends to clients' skin.

Personality Type: No data available.

GOE—Interest Area: 08. Health Science. **Work Group:** 08.07. Medical Therapy. **Other Jobs in this Work Group:** Audiologists; Occupational Therapist Aides; Occupational Therapist Assistants; Occupational Therapists; Physical Therapist Aides; Physical Therapist Assistants; Physical Therapists; Radiation Therapists; Recreational Therapists; Respiratory

Therapists; Respiratory Therapy Technicians; Speech-Language Pathologists.

Skills: No data available.

Education and Training Programs: Massage Therapy/Therapeutic Massage; Asian Bodywork Therapy; Somatic Bodywork; Somatic Bodywork and Related Therapeutic Services, Other. **Related Knowledge/Courses:** Therapy and Counseling; Psychology; Sales and Marketing; Medicine and Dentistry; Chemistry; English Language.

Work Environment: Indoors; standing; using hands on objects, tools, or controls; repetitive motions.

Mathematical Science Teachers, Postsecondary

- Education/Training Required: Doctoral degree
- Annual Earnings: $56,420
- Beginning Wage: $31,580
- Earnings Growth Potential: Very high
- Growth: 22.9%
- Annual Job Openings: 237,478
- Self-Employed: 0.4%
- Part-Time: 27.8%

Our sources did not provide separate job openings data for this occupation. The job openings listed here are shared with 35 other postsecondary teaching occupations. For a complete list, see the beginning of this section.

Industries with Greatest Employment: Educational Services, Public and Private.

Highest-Growth Industries (Projected Growth for This Job): Administrative and Support Services (48.3%); Amusement, Gambling, and Recreation Industries (45.3%); Social Assistance (38.6%); Support Activities for Transportation (32.8%); Religious, Grantmaking, Civic, Professional, and Similar Organizations (29.9%); Professional, Scientific, and Technical Services (28.8%); Management of Companies and Enterprises (26.8%); Educational Services,

Public and Private (22.9%); Hospitals, Public and Private (21.4%); Personal and Laundry Services (21.0%).

Lowest-Growth Industries (Projected Growth for This Job): Other Information Services (7.4%); Sporting Goods, Hobby, Book, and Music Stores (13.3%); Performing Arts, Spectator Sports, and Related Industries (13.4%); Insurance Carriers and Related Activities (13.9%).

Fastest-Growing Metropolitan Areas (Recent Growth for This Job): Killeen–Temple–Fort Hood, TX (69.2%); Portland–Vancouver–Beaverton, OR–WA (50.0%); San Jose–Sunnyvale–Santa Clara, CA (50.0%); Augusta–Richmond County, GA–SC (48.3%); Kansas City, MO–KS (43.3%).

Other Considerations for Job Security: Retirements of current postsecondary teachers should create numerous openings for all types of postsecondary teachers, so job opportunities are generally expected to be very good. However, because students attend postsecondary institutions to prepare themselves for careers, the best job prospects for postsecondary teachers are likely to be in rapidly growing fields that offer many nonacademic career options. Community colleges and other institutions offering career and technical education have been among the most rapidly growing and are expected to offer some of the best opportunities for postsecondary teachers.

Teach courses pertaining to mathematical concepts, statistics, and actuarial science and to the application of original and standardized mathematical techniques in solving specific problems and situations. Evaluate and grade students' classwork, assignments, and papers. Compile, administer, and grade examinations or assign this work to others. Prepare and deliver lectures to undergraduate and/or graduate students on topics such as linear algebra, differential equations, and discrete mathematics. Prepare course materials such as syllabi, homework assignments, and handouts. Maintain student attendance records, grades, and other required records. Maintain regularly scheduled office hours to advise and assist students. Plan, evaluate, and revise

curricula, course content, course materials, and methods of instruction. Initiate, facilitate, and moderate classroom discussions. Select and obtain materials and supplies such as textbooks. Keep abreast of developments in their field by reading current literature, talking with colleagues, and participating in professional conferences. Advise students on academic and vocational curricula and on career issues. Collaborate with colleagues to address teaching and research issues. Serve on academic or administrative committees that deal with institutional policies, departmental matters, and academic issues. Participate in student recruitment, registration, and placement activities. Perform administrative duties such as serving as department head. Conduct research in a particular field of knowledge and publish findings in books, professional journals, and/or electronic media. Supervise undergraduate and/or graduate teaching, internships, and research work. Act as advisers to student organizations. Participate in campus and community events. Write grant proposals to procure external research funding. Compile bibliographies of specialized materials for outside reading assignments. Provide professional consulting services to government and/or industry.

Personality Type: Investigative.

GOE—Interest Area: 05. Education and Training. **Work Group:** 05.03. Postsecondary and Adult Teaching and Instructing. **Other Jobs in this Work Group:** Adult Literacy, Remedial Education, and GED Teachers and Instructors; Agricultural Sciences Teachers, Postsecondary; Anthropology and Archeology Teachers, Postsecondary; Architecture Teachers, Postsecondary; Area, Ethnic, and Cultural Studies Teachers, Postsecondary; Art, Drama, and Music Teachers, Postsecondary; Atmospheric, Earth, Marine, and Space Sciences Teachers, Postsecondary; Biological Science Teachers, Postsecondary; Business Teachers, Postsecondary; Chemistry Teachers, Postsecondary; Communications Teachers, Postsecondary; Computer Science Teachers, Postsecondary; Criminal Justice and Law Enforcement Teachers, Postsecondary; Economics Teachers, Postsecondary; Education Teachers, Postsecondary; Engineering

Teachers, Postsecondary; English Language and Literature Teachers, Postsecondary; Environmental Science Teachers, Postsecondary; Farm and Home Management Advisors; Foreign Language and Literature Teachers, Postsecondary; Forestry and Conservation Science Teachers, Postsecondary; Geography Teachers, Postsecondary; Graduate Teaching Assistants; Health Specialties Teachers, Postsecondary; History Teachers, Postsecondary; Home Economics Teachers, Postsecondary; Law Teachers, Postsecondary; Library Science Teachers, Postsecondary; Nursing Instructors and Teachers, Postsecondary; Philosophy and Religion Teachers, Postsecondary; Physics Teachers, Postsecondary; Political Science Teachers, Postsecondary; Psychology Teachers, Postsecondary; Recreation and Fitness Studies Teachers, Postsecondary; Self-Enrichment Education Teachers; Social Work Teachers, Postsecondary; Sociology Teachers, Postsecondary; Vocational Education Teachers, Postsecondary.

Skills: Mathematics; Instructing; Learning Strategies; Critical Thinking; Science; Complex Problem Solving.

Education and Training Programs: Mathematics, General; Algebra and Number Theory; Analysis and Functional Analysis; Geometry/Geometric Analysis; Topology and Foundations; Mathematics, Other; Applied Mathematics; Statistics, General; Mathematical Statistics and Probability; Mathematics and Statistics, Other; Logic; Business Statistics. **Related Knowledge/Courses:** Mathematics; Education and Training; Physics; Computers and Electronics; English Language; Communications and Media.

Work Environment: Indoors; more often standing than sitting.

Mathematicians

* Education/Training Required: Doctoral degree
* Annual Earnings: $86,930
* Beginning Wage: $43,500
* Earnings Growth Potential: High
* Growth: 10.2%
* Annual Job Openings: 473
* Self-Employed: 0.0%
* Part-Time: 5.6%

Industries with Greatest Employment: Professional, Scientific, and Technical Services; Educational Services, Public and Private.

Highest-Growth Industries (Projected Growth for This Job): Professional, Scientific, and Technical Services (26.3%).

Lowest-Growth Industries (Projected Growth for This Job): Educational Services, Public and Private (10.0%).

Fastest-Growing Metropolitan Area (Recent Growth for This Job): Baltimore–Towson, MD (14.3%).

Other Considerations for Job Security: Keen competition for jobs is expected because employment in this occupation is relatively small and few new jobs are expected. Master's degree and Ph.D. holders with a strong background in mathematics and a related discipline, such as engineering or computer science, and who apply mathematical theory to real-world problems will have the best job prospects in related occupations. Employment in theoretical mathematical research is sensitive to general economic fluctuations and to changes in government spending. Job prospects will be greatly influenced by changes in public and private funding for research and development.

Conduct research in fundamental mathematics or in application of mathematical techniques to science, management, and other fields. Solve or direct solutions to problems in various fields by mathematical methods. Apply mathematical theories and techniques to the solution of practical problems in business, engineering, the sciences, or other fields. Develop computational methods for solving problems that occur in areas of science and engineering or that come from applications in business or industry. Maintain knowledge in the field by reading professional journals, talking with other mathematicians, and attending professional conferences. Perform computations and apply methods of numerical analysis to data. Develop mathematical or statistical models of phenomena to be used for analysis or for computational simulation. Assemble sets of assumptions and explore the consequences of each set. Address the relationships of quantities, magnitudes, and forms by using numbers and symbols. Develop new principles and new relationships between existing mathematical principles to advance mathematical science. Design, analyze, and decipher encryption systems designed to transmit military, political, financial, or law-enforcement–related information in code. Conduct research to extend mathematical knowledge in traditional areas, such as algebra, geometry, probability, and logic.

Personality Type: Investigative.

GOE—Interest Area: 15. Scientific Research, Engineering, and Mathematics. **Work Group:** 15.06. Mathematics and Data Analysis. **Other Jobs in this Work Group:** Actuaries; Mathematical Technicians; Social Science Research Assistants; Statistical Assistants; Statisticians.

Skills: Programming; Mathematics; Science; Complex Problem Solving; Critical Thinking; Reading Comprehension.

Education and Training Programs: Mathematics, General; Algebra and Number Theory; Analysis and Functional Analysis; Geometry/Geometric Analysis; Topology and Foundations; Mathematics, Other; Applied Mathematics; Computational Mathematics; Applied Mathematics, Other; Mathematical Statistics and Probability; Mathematics and Statistics, Other; Logic. **Related Knowledge/Courses:** Mathematics; Physics; Computers and Electronics; Engineering and Technology; English Language.

Work Environment: Indoors; sitting.

Medical and Clinical Laboratory Technicians

- ❀ Education/Training Required: Associate degree
- ❀ Annual Earnings: $32,840
- ❀ Beginning Wage: $21,830
- ❀ Earnings Growth Potential: Very high
- ❀ Growth: 15.0%
- ❀ Annual Job Openings: 10,866
- ❀ Self-Employed: 0.7%
- ❀ Part-Time: 14.3%

Industries with Greatest Employment: Hospitals, Public and Private; Ambulatory Health Care Services; Educational Services, Public and Private.

Highest-Growth Industries (Projected Growth for This Job): Social Assistance (54.3%); Administrative and Support Services (26.9%); Chemical Manufacturing (25.1%); Nursing and Residential Care Facilities (23.4%); Merchant Wholesalers, Nondurable Goods (18.4%); Ambulatory Health Care Services (17.8%); Merchant Wholesalers, Durable Goods (17.0%); Religious, Grantmaking, Civic, Professional, and Similar Organizations (16.7%); Professional, Scientific, and Technical Services (15.2%).

Lowest-Growth Industries (Projected Growth for This Job): Miscellaneous Manufacturing (2.2%); Health and Personal Care Stores (2.9%); Educational Services, Public and Private (11.8%); Hospitals, Public and Private (14.0%).

Fastest-Growing Metropolitan Areas (Recent Growth for This Job): Cedar Rapids, IA (128.6%); Alexandria, LA (120.0%); Bridgeport–Stamford–Norwalk, CT (105.9%); Hickory–Lenoir–Morgantown, NC (91.7%); Pensacola–Ferry Pass–Brent, FL (72.7%).

Other Considerations for Job Security: Job opportunities are expected to be excellent because the number of job openings is expected to continue to exceed the number of job seekers. Although significant, job growth won't be the only source of opportunities. As in most occupations, many additional openings will result from the need to replace workers who transfer to other occupations, retire, or stop working for some other reason. The volume of laboratory tests continues to increase with both population growth and the development of new types of tests. Technological advances will continue to have opposing effects on employment. On the one hand, new, increasingly powerful diagnostic tests will encourage additional testing and spur employment. On the other, research and development efforts targeted at simplifying routine testing procedures may enhance the ability of nonlaboratory personnel—physicians and patients in particular—to perform tests now conducted in laboratories.

Perform routine medical laboratory tests for the diagnosis, treatment, and prevention of disease. May work under the supervision of a medical technologist. Conduct chemical analyses of body fluids, such as blood and urine, using microscope or automatic analyzer to detect abnormalities or diseases, and enter findings into computer. Set up, adjust, maintain, and clean medical laboratory equipment. Analyze the results of tests and experiments to ensure conformity to specifications, using special mechanical and electrical devices. Analyze and record test data to issue reports that use charts, graphs and narratives. Conduct blood tests for transfusion purposes and perform blood counts. Perform medical research to further control and cure disease. Obtain specimens, cultivating, isolating, and identifying microorganisms for analysis. Examine cells stained with dye to locate abnormalities. Collect blood or tissue samples from patients, observing principles of asepsis to obtain blood sample. Consult with pathologists to determine a final diagnosis when abnormal cells are found. Inoculate fertilized eggs, broths, or other bacteriological media with organisms. Cut, stain, and mount tissue samples for examination by pathologists. Supervise and instruct other technicians and laboratory assistants. Prepare standard volumetric solutions and reagents to be combined with samples, following standardized formulas or experimental procedures. Prepare vaccines and serums by standard laboratory methods, testing for virus inactivity and

sterility. Test raw materials, processes, and finished products to determine quality and quantity of materials or characteristics of a substance.

Personality Type: Realistic.

GOE—Interest Area: 08. Health Science. **Work Group:** 08.06. Medical Technology. **Other Jobs in this Work Group:** Biological Technicians; Cardiovascular Technologists and Technicians; Diagnostic Medical Sonographers; Medical and Clinical Laboratory Technologists; Medical Equipment Preparers; Medical Records and Health Information Technicians; Nuclear Medicine Technologists; Opticians, Dispensing; Orthotists and Prosthetists; Radiologic Technicians; Radiologic Technologists; Radiologic Technologists and Technicians.

Skills: Science; Equipment Maintenance; Troubleshooting; Operation Monitoring; Quality Control Analysis; Operation and Control.

Education and Training Programs: Clinical/Medical Laboratory Assistant; Blood Bank Technology Specialist; Hematology Technology/Technician; Clinical/Medical Laboratory Technician; Histologic Technician. **Related Knowledge/Courses:** Medicine and Dentistry; Therapy and Counseling; Biology; Clerical Studies.

Work Environment: Indoors; disease or infections; standing; walking and running; using hands on objects, tools, or controls.

Medical and Clinical Laboratory Technologists

- ❋ Education/Training Required: Bachelor's degree
- ❋ Annual Earnings: $49,700
- ❋ Beginning Wage: $34,660
- ❋ Earnings Growth Potential: Very high
- ❋ Growth: 12.4%
- ❋ Annual Job Openings: 11,457
- ❋ Self-Employed: 0.7%
- ❋ Part-Time: 14.3%

Industries with Greatest Employment: Hospitals, Public and Private; Ambulatory Health Care Services.

Highest-Growth Industries (Projected Growth for This Job): Social Assistance (46.7%); Ambulatory Health Care Services (36.8%); Professional, Scientific, and Technical Services (27.1%); Administrative and Support Services (26.5%); Chemical Manufacturing (26.1%); Nursing and Residential Care Facilities (15.7%); Management of Companies and Enterprises (15.3%).

Lowest-Growth Industries (Projected Growth for This Job): Miscellaneous Manufacturing (2.4%); Hospitals, Public and Private (3.1%); Educational Services, Public and Private (11.9%).

Fastest-Growing Metropolitan Areas (Recent Growth for This Job): Lafayette, LA (118.2%); Lancaster, PA (83.3%); Tyler, TX (75.0%); Boulder, CO (66.7%); Clarksville, TN–KY (60.0%).

Other Considerations for Job Security: Job opportunities are expected to be excellent because the number of job openings is expected to continue to exceed the number of job seekers. Although significant, job growth won't be the only source of opportunities. As in most occupations, many additional openings will result from the need to replace workers who transfer to other occupations, retire, or stop working for some other reason. The volume of laboratory tests continues to increase with both population growth and the development of new types of tests. Technological advances will continue to have opposing effects on employment. On the one hand, new, increasingly powerful diagnostic tests will encourage additional testing and spur employment. On the other, research and development efforts targeted at simplifying routine testing procedures may enhance the ability of nonlaboratory personnel—physicians and patients in particular—to perform tests now conducted in laboratories.

Perform complex medical laboratory tests for diagnosis, treatment, and prevention of disease. May train or supervise staff. Analyze laboratory findings to check the accuracy of the results.

Conduct chemical analysis of body fluids, including blood, urine, and spinal fluid, to determine presence of normal and abnormal components. Operate, calibrate, and maintain equipment used in quantitative and qualitative analysis, such as spectrophotometers, calorimeters, flame photometers, and computer-controlled analyzers. Enter data from analysis of medical tests and clinical results into computer for storage. Analyze samples of biological material for chemical content or reaction. Establish and monitor programs to ensure the accuracy of laboratory results. Set up, clean, and maintain laboratory equipment. Provide technical information about test results to physicians, family members, and researchers. Supervise, train, and direct lab assistants, medical and clinical laboratory technicians and technologists, and other medical laboratory workers engaged in laboratory testing. Develop, standardize, evaluate, and modify procedures, techniques, and tests used in the analysis of specimens and in medical laboratory experiments. Cultivate, isolate, and assist in identifying microbial organisms and perform various tests on these microorganisms. Study blood samples to determine the number of cells and their morphology, as well as the blood group, type, and compatibility for transfusion purposes, using microscopic technique. Obtain, cut, stain, and mount biological material on slides for microscopic study and diagnosis, following standard laboratory procedures. Select and prepare specimen and media for cell cultures, using aseptic technique and knowledge of medium components and cell requirements. Conduct medical research under direction of microbiologist or biochemist. Harvest cell cultures at optimum time based on knowledge of cell cycle differences and culture conditions.

Personality Type: Investigative.

GOE—Interest Area: 08. Health Science. **Work Group:** 08.06. Medical Technology. **Other Jobs in this Work Group:** Biological Technicians; Cardiovascular Technologists and Technicians; Diagnostic Medical Sonographers; Medical and Clinical Laboratory Technicians; Medical Equipment Preparers; Medical Records and Health Information Technicians; Nuclear Medicine Technologists; Opticians,

Dispensing; Orthotists and Prosthetists; Radiologic Technicians; Radiologic Technologists; Radiologic Technologists and Technicians.

Skills: Equipment Maintenance; Operation Monitoring; Quality Control Analysis; Science; Operation and Control; Repairing.

Education and Training Programs: Cytotechnology/Cytotechnologist; Clinical Laboratory Science/Medical Technology/Technologist; Histologic Technology/Histotechnologist; Cytogenetics/Genetics/Clinical Genetics Technology/Technologist; Renal/Dialysis Technologist/Technician; Clinical/Medical Laboratory Science and Allied Professions, Other. **Related Knowledge/Courses:** Biology; Chemistry; Mechanical Devices; Public Safety and Security; Computers and Electronics; Medicine and Dentistry.

Work Environment: Indoors; contaminants; disease or infections; hazardous conditions; using hands on objects, tools, or controls; repetitive motions.

Medical and Health Services Managers

- ❋ Education/Training Required: Work experience plus degree
- ❋ Annual Earnings: $73,340
- ❋ Beginning Wage: $45,050
- ❋ Earnings Growth Potential: Very high
- ❋ Growth: 16.4%
- ❋ Annual Job Openings: 31,877
- ❋ Self-Employed: 8.2%
- ❋ Part-Time: 5.5%

Industries with Greatest Employment: Hospitals, Public and Private; Ambulatory Health Care Services; Nursing and Residential Care Facilities.

Highest-Growth Industries (Projected Growth for This Job): Social Assistance (51.7%); Professional, Scientific, and Technical Services (35.2%); Ambulatory Health Care Services (31.0%); Administrative and Support Services (28.5%); Funds, Trusts, and

Other Financial Vehicles (23.2%); Nonstore Retailers (22.8%); Nursing and Residential Care Facilities (22.1%); Merchant Wholesalers, Nondurable Goods (18.8%); Religious, Grantmaking, Civic, Professional, and Similar Organizations (18.1%); Management of Companies and Enterprises (15.3%).

Lowest-Growth Industries (Projected Growth for This Job): Computer and Electronic Product Manufacturing (–6.5%); Transportation Equipment Manufacturing (–1.8%); Miscellaneous Manufacturing (2.2%); Insurance Carriers and Related Activities (4.9%); Health and Personal Care Stores (8.3%); Rental and Leasing Services (9.6%); Hospitals, Public and Private (10.3%); Educational Services, Public and Private (11.6%); Merchant Wholesalers, Durable Goods (12.7%); Real Estate (12.7%).

Fastest-Growing Metropolitan Areas (Recent Growth for This Job): Valdosta, GA (120.0%); Visalia–Porterville, CA (110.0%); Sherman–Denison, TX (90.9%); Fort Smith, AR–OK (80.0%); Champaign–Urbana, IL (62.5%).

Other Considerations for Job Security: Job opportunities for medical and health services managers should be good, especially for applicants with work experience in the health-care field and strong business management skills. Hospitals will continue to employ the most medical and health services managers, but the number of new jobs created is expected to increase at a slower rate in hospitals than in many other industries because of the growing use of clinics and other outpatient care sites. Despite relatively slow employment growth, a large number of new jobs will be created because of the industry's large size. Employment will grow fastest in practitioners' offices and in home health-care agencies. Medical and health services managers also will be employed by HMOs. Competition for jobs at the highest management levels will be keen because of the high pay and prestige.

Plan, direct, or coordinate medicine and health services in hospitals, clinics, managed-care organizations, public health agencies, or similar organizations. Direct, supervise, and evaluate work activities of medical, nursing, technical, clerical, service, maintenance, and other personnel. Establish objectives and evaluative or operational criteria for units they manage. Direct or conduct recruitment, hiring, and training of personnel. Develop and maintain computerized record management systems to store and process data such as personnel activities and information and to produce reports. Develop and implement organizational policies and procedures for the facility or medical unit. Conduct and administer fiscal operations, including accounting, planning budgets, authorizing expenditures, establishing rates for services, and coordinating financial reporting. Establish work schedules and assignments for staff according to workload, space, and equipment availability. Maintain communication between governing boards, medical staff, and department heads by attending board meetings and coordinating interdepartmental functioning. Monitor the use of diagnostic services, inpatient beds, facilities, and staff to ensure effective use of resources and assess the need for additional staff, equipment, and services. Maintain awareness of advances in medicine, computerized diagnostic and treatment equipment, data-processing technology, government regulations, health insurance changes, and financing options. Manage change in integrated health-care delivery systems, such as work restructuring, technological innovations, and shifts in the focus of care. Prepare activity reports to inform management of the status and implementation plans of programs, services, and quality initiatives. Plan, implement, and administer programs and services in a health-care or medical facility, including personnel administration, training, and coordination of medical, nursing, and physical plant staff. Consult with medical, business, and community groups to discuss service problems, respond to community needs, enhance public relations, coordinate activities and plans, and promote health programs. Inspect facilities and recommend building or equipment modifications to ensure emergency readiness and compliance to access, safety, and sanitation regulations.

Personality Type: Enterprising.

GOE—Interest Area: 08. Health Science. **Work Group:** 08.01. Managerial Work in Medical and

Health Services. **Other Jobs in this Work Group:** Coroners.

Skills: Management of Personnel Resources; Management of Material Resources; Systems Evaluation; Management of Financial Resources; Persuasion; Service Orientation.

Education and Training Programs: Health/Health Care Administration/Management; Hospital and Health Care Facilities Administration/Management; Health Unit Manager/Ward Supervisor; Health Information/Medical Records Administration/Administrator; Medical Staff Services Technology/Technician; Health and Medical Administrative Services, Other; Nursing Administration (MSN, MS, PhD); Public Health, General (MPH, DPH); Community Health and Preventive Medicine; others. **Related Knowledge/Courses:** Therapy and Counseling; Medicine and Dentistry; Philosophy and Theology; Biology; Sociology and Anthropology; Personnel and Human Resources.

Work Environment: Indoors; noisy; disease or infections; sitting.

Medical and Public Health Social Workers

* Education/Training Required: Bachelor's degree
* Annual Earnings: $43,040
* Beginning Wage: $27,280
* Earnings Growth Potential: Very high
* Growth: 24.2%
* Annual Job Openings: 16,429
* Self-Employed: 2.6%
* Part-Time: 9.4%

Industries with Greatest Employment: Hospitals, Public and Private; Ambulatory Health Care Services; Nursing and Residential Care Facilities; Social Assistance; Religious, Grantmaking, Civic, Professional, and Similar Organizations.

Highest-Growth Industries (Projected Growth for This Job): Ambulatory Health Care Services (57.1%); Social Assistance (56.4%); Administrative and Support Services (26.9%); Nursing and Residential Care Facilities (25.2%); Personal and Laundry Services (16.7%); Religious, Grantmaking, Civic, Professional, and Similar Organizations (16.0%); Professional, Scientific, and Technical Services (15.8%); Management of Companies and Enterprises (15.3%).

Lowest-Growth Industries (Projected Growth for This Job): Hospitals, Public and Private (–0.2%); Insurance Carriers and Related Activities (4.6%); Educational Services, Public and Private (12.9%).

Fastest-Growing Metropolitan Areas (Recent Growth for This Job): Chattanooga, TN–GA (300.0%); Utica–Rome, NY (233.3%); Lafayette, LA (140.0%); Lebanon, PA (100.0%); Oxnard–Thousand Oaks–Ventura, CA (100.0%).

Other Considerations for Job Security: Job prospects are generally expected to be favorable. Opportunities should be good in rural areas, which often find it difficult to attract and retain qualified staff. Hospitals continue to limit the length of patient stays, so the demand for social workers in hospitals will grow more slowly than in other areas. However, hospitals are releasing patients earlier than in the past, so social worker employment in home health-care services is growing. The expanding senior population is an even larger factor. Employment opportunities for social workers with backgrounds in gerontology should be good in the growing numbers of assisted-living and senior-living communities. The expanding senior population also will spur demand for social workers in nursing homes, long-term care facilities, and hospices. In these settings, however, other types of workers are often being given tasks that were previously done by social workers.

Provide persons, families, or vulnerable populations with the psychosocial support needed to cope with chronic, acute, or terminal illnesses, such as Alzheimer's, cancer, or AIDS. Services include advising family caregivers, providing patient education and counseling, and making necessary referrals for other social services. Collaborate with other professionals to evaluate patients' medical or physical condition and to assess client needs. Investigate child abuse or neglect cases and take authorized protective action when necessary. Refer patient, client, or family to community resources to assist in recovery from mental or physical illness and to provide access to services such as financial assistance, legal aid, housing, job placement, or education. Counsel clients and patients in individual and group sessions to help them overcome dependencies, recover from illness, and adjust to life. Organize support groups or counsel family members to help them understand, deal with, and support client or patient. Advocate for clients or patients to resolve crises. Identify environmental impediments to client or patient progress through interviews and review of patient records. Utilize consultation data and social work experience to plan and coordinate client or patient care and rehabilitation, following through to ensure service efficacy. Modify treatment plans to comply with changes in clients' status. Monitor, evaluate, and record client progress according to measurable goals described in treatment and care plan. Supervise and direct other workers providing services to clients or patients. Develop or advise on social policy and assist in community development. Oversee Medicaid- and Medicare-related paperwork and record keeping in hospitals. Conduct social research to advance knowledge in the social work field. Plan and conduct programs to combat social problems, prevent substance abuse, or improve community health and counseling services.

Personality Type: Social.

GOE—Interest Area: 10. Human Service. **Work Group:** 10.01. Counseling and Social Work. **Other Jobs in this Work Group:** Child, Family, and School Social Workers; Clinical Psychologists; Clinical, Counseling, and School Psychologists; Counseling Psychologists; Marriage and Family Therapists; Mental Health and Substance Abuse Social Workers; Mental Health Counselors; Probation Officers and Correctional Treatment Specialists; Rehabilitation

Counselors; Residential Advisors; Social and Human Service Assistants; Substance Abuse and Behavioral Disorder Counselors.

Skills: Social Perceptiveness; Service Orientation; Negotiation; Coordination; Active Listening; Writing.

Education and Training Program: Clinical/Medical Social Work. **Related Knowledge/Courses:** Therapy and Counseling; Psychology; Philosophy and Theology; Sociology and Anthropology; Medicine and Dentistry; Customer and Personal Service.

Work Environment: Indoors; noisy; disease or infections; sitting.

Medical Assistants

- Education/Training Required: Moderate-term on-the-job training
- Annual Earnings: $26,290
- Beginning Wage: $18,860
- Earnings Growth Potential: Very high
- Growth: 35.4%
- Annual Job Openings: 92,977
- Self-Employed: 0.0%
- Part-Time: 23.2%

Industries with Greatest Employment: Ambulatory Health Care Services; Hospitals, Public and Private.

Highest-Growth Industries (Projected Growth for This Job): Social Assistance (69.7%); Professional, Scientific, and Technical Services (40.5%); Administrative and Support Services (39.6%); Chemical Manufacturing (38.9%); Ambulatory Health Care Services (38.3%); Nursing and Residential Care Facilities (37.3%); Management of Companies and Enterprises (26.8%); Real Estate (22.6%); Educational Services, Public and Private (22.4%); Hospitals, Public and Private (21.9%); Insurance Carriers and Related Activities (19.9%).

Lowest-Growth Industries (Projected Growth for This Job): Animal Production (–2.5%); Health and Personal Care Stores (13.1%).

Fastest-Growing Metropolitan Areas (Recent Growth for This Job): Punta Gorda, FL (150.0%); Lawton, OK (112.5%); Oshkosh–Neenah, WI (100.0%); Utica–Rome, NY (100.0%); Pittsfield, MA (85.7%).

Other Considerations for Job Security: Job seekers who want to work as medical assistants should find excellent job prospects. Medical assistants are projected to account for a very large number of new jobs, and many other opportunities will come from the need to replace workers leaving the occupation. Those with formal training or experience—particularly those with certification—should have the best job opportunities.

Perform administrative and certain clinical duties under the direction of physician. Administrative duties may include scheduling appointments, maintaining medical records, billing, and coding for insurance purposes. Clinical duties may include taking and recording vital signs and medical histories, preparing patients for examination, drawing blood, and administering medications as directed by physician. Interview patients to obtain medical information and measure their vital signs, weight, and height. Show patients to examination rooms and prepare them for the physician. Record patients' medical history, vital statistics, and information such as test results in medical records. Prepare and administer medications as directed by physician. Collect blood, tissue, or other laboratory specimens; log the specimens; and prepare them for testing. Explain treatment procedures, medications, diets, and physicians' instructions to patients. Help physicians examine and treat patients, handing them instruments and materials or performing such tasks as giving injections or removing sutures. Authorize drug refills and provide prescription information to pharmacies. Prepare treatment rooms for patient examinations, keeping the rooms neat and clean. Clean and sterilize instruments and dispose of contaminated supplies. Schedule appointments for patients. Change dressings on wounds. Greet and log in patients arriving at office or clinic. Contact medical facilities or departments to schedule patients for tests or admission. Perform general office duties such as answering telephones, taking dictation, or completing insurance forms. Inventory and order medical, lab, or office supplies and equipment. Perform routine laboratory tests and sample analyses. Set up medical laboratory equipment. Keep financial records and perform other bookkeeping duties, such as handling credit and collections and mailing monthly statements to patients. Operate X-ray, electrocardiogram (EKG), and other equipment to administer routine diagnostic tests. Give physiotherapy treatments such as diathermy, galvanics, and hydrotherapy.

Personality Type: Social.

GOE—Interest Area: 08. Health Science. **Work Group:** 08.02. Medicine and Surgery. **Other Jobs in this Work Group:** Anesthesiologists; Family and General Practitioners; Internists, General; Medical Transcriptionists; Obstetricians and Gynecologists; Pediatricians, General; Pharmacists; Pharmacy Aides; Pharmacy Technicians; Physician Assistants; Psychiatrists; Registered Nurses; Surgeons; Surgical Technologists.

Skills: Social Perceptiveness; Service Orientation; Operation and Control; Operation Monitoring; Active Listening; Instructing.

Education and Training Programs: Medical Office Management/Administration; Medical Office Assistant/Specialist; Medical Reception/Receptionist; Medical Insurance Coding Specialist/Coder; Medical Administrative/Executive Assistant and Medical Secretary; Medical/Clinical Assistant; Anesthesiologist Assistant; Chiropractic Assistant/Technician; Allied Health and Medical Assisting Services, Other; Optomeric Technician/Assistant; others. **Related Knowledge/Courses:** Medicine and Dentistry; Therapy and Counseling; Clerical Studies; Psychology; Customer and Personal Service; English Language.

Work Environment: Indoors; disease or infections; standing; walking and running; using hands on objects, tools, or controls.

Medical Equipment Preparers

- ❋ Education/Training Required: Short-term on-the-job training
- ❋ Annual Earnings: $25,950
- ❋ Beginning Wage: $18,640
- ❋ Earnings Growth Potential: Very high
- ❋ Growth: 14.2%
- ❋ Annual Job Openings: 8,363
- ❋ Self-Employed: 2.8%
- ❋ Part-Time: 23.2%

Industries with Greatest Employment: Hospitals, Public and Private; Ambulatory Health Care Services.

Highest-Growth Industries (Projected Growth for This Job): Administrative and Support Services (41.9%); Chemical Manufacturing (26.0%); Ambulatory Health Care Services (23.7%); Professional, Scientific, and Technical Services (17.0%); Management of Companies and Enterprises (15.2%).

Lowest-Growth Industries (Projected Growth for This Job): Animal Production (–11.3%); Miscellaneous Manufacturing (2.0%); Health and Personal Care Stores (4.1%); Rental and Leasing Services (9.6%); Hospitals, Public and Private (11.1%); Educational Services, Public and Private (11.8%).

Fastest-Growing Metropolitan Areas (Recent Growth for This Job): Alexandria, LA (66.7%); Tampa–St. Petersburg–Clearwater, FL (66.7%); Albany–Schenectady–Troy, NY (57.1%); Birmingham–Hoover, AL (50.0%); Durham, NC (44.4%).

Other Considerations for Job Security: No data available.

Prepare, sterilize, install, or clean laboratory or health-care equipment. May perform routine laboratory tasks and operate or inspect equipment. Organize and assemble routine and specialty surgical instrument trays and other sterilized supplies, filling special requests as needed. Clean instruments to prepare them for sterilization. Operate and maintain steam autoclaves, keeping records of loads completed,

M

items in loads, and maintenance procedures performed. Record sterilizer test results. Disinfect and sterilize equipment such as respirators, hospital beds, and oxygen and dialysis equipment, using sterilizers, aerators, and washers. Start equipment and observe gauges and equipment operation to detect malfunctions and to ensure that equipment is operating to prescribed standards. Examine equipment to detect leaks, worn or loose parts, or other indications of disrepair. Report defective equipment to appropriate supervisors or staff. Check sterile supplies to ensure that they're not outdated. Maintain records of inventory and equipment usage. Attend hospital in-service programs related to areas of work specialization. Purge wastes from equipment by connecting equipment to water sources and flushing water through systems. Deliver equipment to specified hospital locations or to patients' residences. Assist hospital staff with patient care duties such as providing transportation or setting up traction. Install and set up medical equipment, using hand tools.

Personality Type: Realistic.

GOE—Interest Area: 08. Health Science. **Work Group:** 08.06. Medical Technology. **Other Jobs in this Work Group:** Biological Technicians; Cardiovascular Technologists and Technicians; Diagnostic Medical Sonographers; Medical and Clinical Laboratory Technicians; Medical and Clinical Laboratory Technologists; Medical Records and Health Information Technicians; Nuclear Medicine Technologists; Opticians, Dispensing; Orthotists and Prosthetists; Radiologic Technicians; Radiologic Technologists; Radiologic Technologists and Technicians.

Skills: Operation Monitoring; Management of Material Resources; Equipment Maintenance; Quality Control Analysis; Operation and Control; Management of Personnel Resources.

Education and Training Programs: Medical/Clinical Assistant; Allied Health and Medical Assisting Services, Other. **Related Knowledge/Courses:** Chemistry; Biology; Medicine and Dentistry; Production and Processing; Education and Training; Customer and Personal Service.

Work Environment: Indoors; contaminants; disease or infections; standing; using hands on objects, tools, or controls; repetitive motions.

Medical Records and Health Information Technicians

- ❊ Education/Training Required: Associate degree
- ❊ Annual Earnings: $28,030
- ❊ Beginning Wage: $19,060
- ❊ Earnings Growth Potential: Very high
- ❊ Growth: 17.8%
- ❊ Annual Job Openings: 39,048
- ❊ Self-Employed: 0.2%
- ❊ Part-Time: 12.5%

Industries with Greatest Employment: Hospitals, Public and Private; Ambulatory Health Care Services; Nursing and Residential Care Facilities.

Highest-Growth Industries (Projected Growth for This Job): Social Assistance (57.6%); Internet Service Providers, Web Search Portals, and Data Processing Services (32.7%); Professional, Scientific, and Technical Services (31.2%); Ambulatory Health Care Services (28.5%); Chemical Manufacturing (25.6%); Merchant Wholesalers, Nondurable Goods (18.9%); Religious, Grantmaking, Civic, Professional, and Similar Organizations (18.9%); Management of Companies and Enterprises (15.3%); Nursing and Residential Care Facilities (15.2%).

Lowest-Growth Industries (Projected Growth for This Job): Insurance Carriers and Related Activities (6.9%); Rental and Leasing Services (8.3%); Hospitals, Public and Private (10.4%); Health and Personal Care Stores (10.8%); Educational Services, Public and Private (11.8%).

Fastest-Growing Metropolitan Areas (Recent Growth for This Job): Cheyenne, WY (71.4%); Las Cruces, NM (66.7%); Waterbury, CT (66.7%); Altoona, PA (55.6%); Green Bay, WI (53.8%).

Other Considerations for Job Security: Job prospects should be very good. In addition to job growth, openings will result from the need to replace technicians who retire or leave the occupation permanently. Technicians with a strong background in medical coding will be in particularly high demand. Changing government regulations and the growth of managed care have increased the amount of paperwork involved in filing insurance claims. Also, health-care facilities are having some difficulty attracting qualified workers, primarily because employers prefer trained and experienced technicians prepared to work in an increasingly electronic environment with the integration of electronic health records. Job opportunities may be especially good for coders employed through temporary help agencies or by professional services firms.

Compile, process, and maintain medical records of hospital and clinic patients in a manner consistent with medical, administrative, ethical, legal, and regulatory requirements of the health-care system. Process, maintain, compile, and report patient information for health requirements and standards. Protect the security of medical records to ensure that confidentiality is maintained. Process patient admission and discharge documents. Review records for completeness, accuracy, and compliance with regulations. Compile and maintain patients' medical records to document condition and treatment and to provide data for research or cost control and care improvement efforts. Enter data such as demographic characteristics, history and extent of disease, diagnostic procedures, and treatment into computer. Release information to persons and agencies according to regulations. Plan, develop, maintain, and operate a variety of health record indexes and storage and retrieval systems to collect, classify, store, and analyze information. Manage medical records department and supervise clerical workers, directing and controlling activities of department personnel. Transcribe medical reports. Identify, compile, abstract, and code patient data, using standard classification systems. Resolve or clarify codes and diagnoses with conflicting, missing, or unclear information by consulting with doctors or others or

by participating in the coding team's regular meetings. Train medical records staff. Assign patients to diagnosis-related groups (DRGs), using appropriate computer software. Post medical insurance billings. Process and prepare business and government forms. Contact discharged patients, their families, and physicians to maintain registry with follow-up information, such as quality of life and length of survival of cancer patients. Prepare statistical reports, narrative reports, and graphic presentations of information such as tumor registry data for use by hospital staff, researchers, or other users. Consult classification manuals to locate information about disease processes. Compile medical care and census data for statistical reports on diseases treated, surgery performed, or use of hospital beds. Develop in-service educational materials.

Personality Type: Conventional.

GOE—Interest Area: 08. Health Science. **Work Group:** 08.06. Medical Technology. **Other Jobs in this Work Group:** Biological Technicians; Cardiovascular Technologists and Technicians; Diagnostic Medical Sonographers; Medical and Clinical Laboratory Technicians; Medical and Clinical Laboratory Technologists; Medical Equipment Preparers; Nuclear Medicine Technologists; Opticians, Dispensing; Orthotists and Prosthetists; Radiologic Technicians; Radiologic Technologists; Radiologic Technologists and Technicians.

Skills: No data available.

Education and Training Programs: Health Information/Medical Records Technology/Technician; Medical Insurance Coding Specialist/Coder. **Related Knowledge/Courses:** Clerical Studies; Personnel and Human Resources.

Work Environment: Indoors; noisy; sitting; using hands on objects, tools, or controls; repetitive motions.

Mental Health and Substance Abuse Social Workers

❋ Education/Training Required: Master's degree

❋ Annual Earnings: $35,410

❋ Beginning Wage: $22,490

❋ Earnings Growth Potential: Very high

❋ Growth: 29.9%

❋ Annual Job Openings: 17,289

❋ Self-Employed: 2.8%

❋ Part-Time: 9.4%

Industries with Greatest Employment: Ambulatory Health Care Services; Social Assistance; Nursing and Residential Care Facilities; Hospitals, Public and Private; Religious, Grantmaking, Civic, Professional, and Similar Organizations.

Highest-Growth Industries (Projected Growth for This Job): Professional, Scientific, and Technical Services (68.4%); Social Assistance (55.5%); Nursing and Residential Care Facilities (51.2%); Ambulatory Health Care Services (33.0%); Administrative and Support Services (29.6%); Religious, Grantmaking, Civic, Professional, and Similar Organizations (16.0%); Management of Companies and Enterprises (15.3%).

Lowest-Growth Industries (Projected Growth for This Job): Hospitals, Public and Private (–5.2%); Educational Services, Public and Private (10.4%).

Fastest-Growing Metropolitan Areas (Recent Growth for This Job): Weirton–Steubenville, WV–OH (333.3%); Gainesville, FL (125.0%); Green Bay, WI (125.0%); San Juan–Caguas–Guaynabo, PR (111.1%); Columbus, GA–AL (100.0%).

Other Considerations for Job Security: Job prospects are expected to be favorable, particularly for social workers who specialize in substance abuse. Substance abusers are increasingly being placed into treatment programs instead of being sentenced to prison. Also, growing numbers of the substance abusers sentenced to prison or probation are increasingly being required by correctional systems to have substance abuse treatment added as a condition to their sentence or probation. As this trend grows, demand will strengthen for treatment programs and social workers to assist abusers on the road to recovery.

Assess and treat individuals with mental, emotional, or substance abuse problems, including abuse of alcohol, tobacco, and/or other drugs. Activities may include individual and group therapy, crisis intervention, case management, client advocacy, prevention, and education. Counsel clients in individual and group sessions to help them deal with substance abuse, mental and physical illness, poverty, unemployment, or physical abuse. Interview clients, review records, and confer with other professionals to evaluate mental or physical condition of client or patient. Collaborate with counselors, physicians, and nurses to plan and coordinate treatment, drawing on social work experience and patient needs. Monitor, evaluate, and record client progress with respect to treatment goals. Refer patient, client, or family to community resources for housing or treatment to assist in recovery from mental or physical illness, following through to ensure service efficacy. Counsel and aid family members to help them understand, deal with, and support client or patient. Modify treatment plans according to changes in client status. Plan and conduct programs to prevent substance abuse, combat social problems, or improve health and counseling services in community. Supervise and direct other workers who provide services to clients or patients. Develop or advise on social policy and assist in community development. Conduct social research to advance knowledge in the social work field.

Personality Type: Social.

GOE—Interest Area: 10. Human Service. **Work Group:** 10.01. Counseling and Social Work. **Other Jobs in this Work Group:** Child, Family, and School Social Workers; Clinical Psychologists; Clinical, Counseling, and School Psychologists; Counseling Psychologists; Marriage and Family Therapists; Medical and Public Health Social Workers; Mental Health Counselors; Probation Officers and

Correctional Treatment Specialists; Rehabilitation Counselors; Residential Advisors; Social and Human Service Assistants; Substance Abuse and Behavioral Disorder Counselors.

Skills: Social Perceptiveness; Service Orientation; Negotiation; Judgment and Decision Making; Active Listening; Persuasion.

Education and Training Program: Clinical/Medical Social Work. **Related Knowledge/Courses:** Psychology; Therapy and Counseling; Sociology and Anthropology; Customer and Personal Service.

Work Environment: Indoors; noisy; sitting.

Mental Health Counselors

- ❋ Education/Training Required: Master's degree
- ❋ Annual Earnings: $34,380
- ❋ Beginning Wage: $21,890
- ❋ Earnings Growth Potential: Very high
- ❋ Growth: 30.0%
- ❋ Annual Job Openings: 24,103
- ❋ Self-Employed: 6.1%
- ❋ Part-Time: 15.4%

Industries with Greatest Employment: Ambulatory Health Care Services; Nursing and Residential Care Facilities; Social Assistance; Hospitals, Public and Private.

Highest-Growth Industries (Projected Growth for This Job): Social Assistance (57.9%); Nursing and Residential Care Facilities (39.2%); Ambulatory Health Care Services (33.1%); Administrative and Support Services (30.3%); Management of Companies and Enterprises (15.4%).

Lowest-Growth Industries (Projected Growth for This Job): Hospitals, Public and Private (–2.0%); Educational Services, Public and Private (10.8%).

Fastest-Growing Metropolitan Areas (Recent Growth for This Job): Salt Lake City, UT (200.0%); Memphis, TN–MS–AR (152.9%); Lewiston, ID–WA

(125.0%); Charleston, WV (100.0%); Eugene–Springfield, OR (100.0%).

Other Considerations for Job Security: Job prospects should be good due to growth and the need to replace people leaving the field. Employment of mental health counselors is expected to grow much faster than the average for all occupations. Mental health counselors will be needed to staff statewide networks being established to improve services for children and adolescents with serious emotional disturbances and for their families. Under managed care systems, insurance companies are increasingly providing for reimbursement of counselors as a less costly alternative to psychiatrists and psychologists.

Counsel with emphasis on prevention. Work with individuals and groups to promote optimum mental health. May help individuals deal with addictions and substance abuse; family, parenting, and marital problems; suicide; stress management; problems with self-esteem; and issues associated with aging and mental and emotional health. Maintain confidentiality of records relating to clients' treatment. Guide clients in the development of skills and strategies for dealing with their problems. Encourage clients to express their feelings and discuss what is happening in their lives and help them to develop insight into themselves and their relationships. Prepare and maintain all required treatment records and reports. Counsel clients and patients, individually and in group sessions, to assist in overcoming dependencies, adjusting to life, and making changes. Collect information about clients through interviews, observation, and tests. Act as client advocates to coordinate required services or to resolve emergency problems in crisis situations. Develop and implement treatment plans based on clinical experience and knowledge. Collaborate with other staff members to perform clinical assessments and develop treatment plans. Evaluate clients' physical or mental condition based on review of client information. Meet with families, probation officers, police, and other interested parties to exchange necessary information during the treatment process. Refer patients, clients, or family members to community resources or to specialists as necessary. Evaluate the effectiveness of counseling programs and clients' progress in resolving identified problems and moving toward defined objectives. Counsel family members to help them understand, deal with, and support clients or patients. Plan, organize, and lead structured programs of counseling, work, study, recreation, and social activities for clients. Modify treatment activities and approaches as needed to comply with changes in clients' status. Learn about new developments in the field by reading professional literature, attending courses and seminars, and establishing and maintaining contact with other social service agencies. Discuss with individual patients their plans for life after leaving therapy. Gather information about community mental-health needs and resources that could be used in conjunction with therapy. Monitor clients' use of medications. Supervise other counselors, social service staff, and assistants.

Personality Type: Social.

GOE—Interest Area: 10. Human Service. **Work Group:** 10.01. Counseling and Social Work. **Other Jobs in this Work Group:** Child, Family, and School Social Workers; Clinical Psychologists; Clinical, Counseling, and School Psychologists; Counseling Psychologists; Marriage and Family Therapists; Medical and Public Health Social Workers; Mental Health and Substance Abuse Social Workers; Probation Officers and Correctional Treatment Specialists; Rehabilitation Counselors; Residential Advisors; Social and Human Service Assistants; Substance Abuse and Behavioral Disorder Counselors.

Skills: Social Perceptiveness; Service Orientation; Negotiation; Persuasion; Active Listening; Learning Strategies.

Education and Training Programs: Substance Abuse/Addiction Counseling; Clinical/Medical Social Work; Mental Health Counseling/Counselor; Mental and Social Health Services and Allied Professions, Other. **Related Knowledge/Courses:** Therapy and Counseling; Psychology; Sociology and Anthropology; Philosophy and Theology; Medicine and Dentistry; Education and Training.

Work Environment: Indoors; noisy; sitting.

Middle School Teachers, Except Special and Vocational Education

* Education/Training Required: Bachelor's degree
* Annual Earnings: $46,300
* Beginning Wage: $31,450
* Earnings Growth Potential: Very high
* Growth: 11.2%
* Annual Job Openings: 75,270
* Self-Employed: 0.0%
* Part-Time: 9.5%

Industries with Greatest Employment: Educational Services, Public and Private.

Highest-Growth Industries (Projected Growth for This Job): Social Assistance (27.7%); Administrative and Support Services (26.6%); Nursing and Residential Care Facilities (22.4%); Religious, Grantmaking, Civic, Professional, and Similar Organizations (20.0%).

Lowest-Growth Industries (Projected Growth for This Job): Educational Services, Public and Private (11.1%).

Fastest-Growing Metropolitan Areas (Recent Growth for This Job): Saginaw–Saginaw Township North, MI (144.0%); Fajardo, PR (125.0%); Santa Barbara–Santa Maria, CA (124.3%); Medford, OR (91.7%); Corpus Christi, TX (73.8%).

Other Considerations for Job Security: Job prospects are expected to be favorable, with particularly good prospects for teachers in high-demand fields such as math, science, and bilingual education, or in less desirable urban or rural school districts. Fast-growing states in the South and West—led by Nevada, Arizona, Texas, and Georgia—will experience the largest enrollment increases. Enrollments in the Midwest are expected to hold relatively steady, while those in the Northeast are expected to decline. The number of teachers employed depends on state and local expenditures for education and on the enactment of legislation to increase the quality and scope of public education. At the federal level, there has been a large increase in funding for education, particularly for the hiring of qualified teachers in lower-income areas.

Teach students in public or private schools in one or more subjects at the middle, intermediate, or junior-high level, which falls between elementary and senior high school as defined by applicable state laws and regulations. Establish and enforce rules for behavior and procedures for maintaining order among the students for whom they are responsible. Adapt teaching methods and instructional materials to meet students' varying needs and interests. Instruct through lectures, discussions, and demonstrations in one or more subjects such as English, mathematics, or social studies. Prepare, administer, and grade tests and assignments to evaluate students' progress. Establish clear objectives for all lessons, units, and projects and communicate these objectives to students. Plan and conduct activities for a balanced program of instruction, demonstration, and work time that provides students with opportunities to observe, question, and investigate. Maintain accurate, complete, and correct student records as required by laws, district policies, and administrative regulations. Observe and evaluate students' performance, behavior, social development, and physical health. Assign lessons and correct homework. Prepare materials and classrooms for class activities. Enforce all administration policies and rules governing students. Confer with parents or guardians, other teachers, counselors, and administrators to resolve students' behavioral and academic problems. Prepare students for later grades by encouraging them to explore learning opportunities and to persevere with challenging tasks. Prepare objectives and outlines for courses of study, following curriculum guidelines or requirements of states and schools. Guide and counsel students with adjustment or academic problems or special academic interests. Meet with parents and guardians to discuss their children's progress and to determine their priorities for their children and their resource needs. Meet with other professionals to discuss individual students' needs and progress. Prepare and implement remedial programs for students requiring extra help. Prepare for assigned classes and show written evidence of preparation on request of immediate supervisors. Instruct and monitor students in the use and care of equipment and materials to prevent injury and damage.

Personality Type: Social.

GOE—Interest Area: 05. Education and Training. **Work Group:** 05.02. Preschool, Elementary, and Secondary Teaching and Instructing. **Other Jobs in this Work Group:** Elementary School Teachers, Except Special Education; Kindergarten Teachers, Except Special Education; Preschool Teachers, Except Special Education; Secondary School Teachers, Except Special and Vocational Education; Special Education Teachers, Middle School; Special Education Teachers, Preschool, Kindergarten, and Elementary School; Special Education Teachers, Secondary School; Teacher Assistants; Vocational Education Teachers, Middle School; Vocational Education Teachers, Secondary School.

Skills: Learning Strategies; Instructing; Monitoring; Social Perceptiveness; Time Management; Negotiation.

Education and Training Programs: Junior High/Intermediate/Middle School Education and Teaching; Montessori Teacher Education; Waldorf/Steiner Teacher Education; Art Teacher Education; English/Language Arts Teacher Education; Foreign Language Teacher Education; Health Teacher Education; Family and Consumer Sciences/Home Economics Teacher Education; Technology Teacher Education/Industrial Arts Teacher Education; Mathematics Teacher Education; others. **Related Knowledge/Courses:** Sociology and Anthropology; History and Archeology; Education and Training; Philosophy and Theology; Geography; Therapy and Counseling.

Work Environment: Indoors; noisy; standing.

Municipal Fire Fighters

- ❋ Education/Training Required: Long-term on-the-job training
- ❋ Annual Earnings: $41,190
- ❋ Beginning Wage: $20,660
- ❋ Earnings Growth Potential: Very high
- ❋ Growth: 12.1%
- ❋ Annual Job Openings: 18,887
- ❋ Self-Employed: 0.0%
- ❋ Part-Time: 1.3%

Our sources did not provide separate job openings data for this occupation. The job openings listed here are shared with Forest Fire Fighters.

Industries with Greatest Employment: Professional, Scientific, and Technical Services; Performing Arts, Spectator Sports, and Related Industries; Support Activities for Agriculture and Forestry; Transportation Equipment Manufacturing; Fabricated Metal Product Manufacturing.

Highest-Growth Industries (Projected Growth for This Job): Performing Arts, Spectator Sports, and Related Industries (31.5%); Support Activities for Transportation (20.9%).

Lowest-Growth Industries (Projected Growth for This Job): Fabricated Metal Product Manufacturing (–11.2%); Hospitals, Public and Private (0.8%); Chemical Manufacturing (1.5%); Transportation Equipment Manufacturing (3.3%); Support Activities for Agriculture and Forestry (7.1%); Educational Services, Public and Private (11.4%); Professional, Scientific, and Technical Services (13.5%).

Fastest-Growing Metropolitan Areas (Recent Growth for This Job): Beaumont–Port Arthur, TX (330.0%); Green Bay, WI (103.6%); Tulsa, OK (62.7%); Fairbanks, AK (57.4%); Baton Rouge, LA (54.2%).

Other Considerations for Job Security: Prospective fire fighters are expected to face keen competition for available job openings. Many people are attracted to fire fighting because it is challenging and provides the opportunity to perform an essential public service, a high-school education is usually sufficient for entry, and a pension is usually guaranteed after 25 years of work. Consequently, the number of qualified applicants in most areas far exceeds the number of job openings, even though the written examination and physical requirements eliminate many applicants. This situation is expected to persist in coming years. Applicants with the best chances are those who are physically fit and score the highest on physical conditioning and mechanical aptitude exams. Those who have completed some fire-fighter education at a community college and have EMT or paramedic certification will have additional advantages.

Control and extinguish municipal fires, protect life and property, and conduct rescue efforts. Administer first aid and cardiopulmonary resuscitation to injured persons. Rescue victims from burning buildings and accident sites. Search burning buildings to locate fire victims. Drive and operate fire-fighting vehicles and equipment. Move toward the source of a fire, using knowledge of types of fires, construction design, building materials, and physical layout of properties. Dress with equipment such as fire-resistant clothing and breathing apparatus. Position and climb ladders to gain access to upper levels of buildings or to rescue individuals from burning structures. Take action to contain hazardous chemicals that might catch fire, leak, or spill. Assess fires and situations and report conditions to superiors to receive instructions, using two-way radios. Respond to fire alarms and other calls for assistance, such as automobile and industrial accidents. Operate pumps connected to high-pressure hoses. Select and attach hose nozzles, depending on fire type, and direct streams of water or chemicals onto fires. Create openings in buildings for ventilation or entrance, using axes, chisels, crowbars, electric saws, or core cutters. Inspect fire sites after flames are extinguished to ensure that there is no further danger. Lay hose lines and connect them to water supplies. Protect property from water and smoke, using waterproof salvage covers, smoke ejectors, and deodorants. Participate in physical training activities to maintain a high level of physical fitness. Salvage property by removing broken glass, pumping out water, and ventilating buildings to remove smoke. Participate in fire drills and demonstrations of fire-fighting techniques. Clean and maintain fire stations and fire-fighting equipment and apparatus. Collaborate with police to respond to accidents, disasters, and arson investigation calls. Establish firelines to prevent unauthorized persons from entering areas near fires. Inform and educate the public on fire prevention. Inspect buildings for fire hazards and compliance with fire-prevention ordinances, testing and checking smoke alarms and fire suppression equipment as necessary.

Personality Type: Realistic.

GOE—Interest Area: 12. Law and Public Safety. **Work Group:** 12.06. Emergency Responding. **Other Jobs in this Work Group:** Emergency Medical Technicians and Paramedics; Fire Fighters; Forest Fire Fighters.

Skills: Equipment Maintenance; Service Orientation; Equipment Selection; Operation Monitoring; Social Perceptiveness; Complex Problem Solving.

Education and Training Programs: Fire Science/Fire Fighting; Fire Protection, Other. **Related Knowledge/Courses:** Medicine and Dentistry; Physics; Customer and Personal Service; Building and Construction; Chemistry; Public Safety and Security.

Work Environment: More often outdoors than indoors; noisy; contaminants; disease or infections; hazardous equipment.

Municipal Fire Fighting and Prevention Supervisors

* Education/Training Required: Work experience in a related occupation
* Annual Earnings: $62,900
* Beginning Wage: $36,820
* Earnings Growth Potential: Very high
* Growth: 11.5%
* Annual Job Openings: 3,771
* Self-Employed: 0.0%
* Part-Time: 0.4%

Our sources did not provide separate job openings data for this occupation. The job openings listed here are shared with Forest Fire Fighting and Prevention Supervisors.

Industries with Greatest Employment: Educational Services, Public and Private.

Highest-Growth Industries (Projected Growth for This Job): None met the criteria.

Lowest-Growth Industries (Projected Growth for This Job): Educational Services, Public and Private (11.9%).

Fastest-Growing Metropolitan Areas (Recent Growth for This Job): Canton–Massillon, OH (100.0%); Toledo, OH (100.0%); Cleveland–Elyria–Mentor, OH (95.7%); Memphis, TN–MS–AR (35.7%); Clarksville, TN–KY (33.3%).

Other Considerations for Job Security: Prospective fire fighters and their supervisors are expected to face keen competition for available job openings. Many people are attracted to fire fighting because it is challenging and provides the opportunity to perform an essential public service, a high-school education is usually sufficient for entry, and a pension is usually guaranteed after 25 years of work. Consequently, the number of qualified applicants in most areas far exceeds the number of job openings, even though the written examination and physical requirements eliminate many applicants. This situation is expected to persist in coming years. Applicants with the best chances are those who are physically fit and score the highest on physical conditioning and mechanical aptitude exams. Those who have completed some fire-fighter education at a community college and have EMT or paramedic certification will have additional advantages.

Supervise fire fighters who control and extinguish municipal fires, protect life and property, and conduct rescue efforts. Assign fire fighters to jobs at strategic locations to facilitate rescue of persons and maximize application of extinguishing agents. Provide emergency medical services as required and perform light to heavy rescue functions at emergencies. Assess nature and extent of fire, condition of building, danger to adjacent buildings, and water supply status to determine crew or company requirements. Instruct and drill fire department personnel in assigned duties, including fire fighting, medical care, hazardous materials response, fire prevention, and related subjects. Evaluate the performance of assigned fire-fighting personnel. Direct fire-fighter training, assigning instructors to training classes and providing supervisors with reports on training progress and status. Prepare activity reports listing fire call locations, actions taken, fire types and probable causes, damage estimates, and situation dispositions. Maintain required maps and records. Attend in-service training classes to remain current in knowledge of codes, laws, ordinances, and regulations. Evaluate fire station procedures to ensure efficiency and enforcement of departmental regulations. Direct fire fighters in station maintenance duties and participate in these duties. Compile and maintain equipment and personnel records, including accident reports. Direct investigation of cases of suspected arson, hazards, and false alarms, and submit reports outlining findings. Recommend personnel actions related to disciplinary procedures, performance, leaves of absence, and grievances. Supervise and participate in the inspection of properties to ensure that they are in compliance with applicable fire codes, ordinances, laws, regulations, and standards. Write and submit proposals for repair, modification, or replacement of fire-fighting equipment. Coordinate the distribution of fire-prevention promotional materials.

Identify corrective actions needed to bring properties into compliance with applicable fire codes and ordinances; conduct follow-up inspections to see whether corrective actions have been taken. Participate in creating fire safety guidelines and evacuation schemes for nonresidential buildings.

Personality Type: Realistic.

GOE—Interest Area: 12. Law and Public Safety. **Work Group:** 12.01. Managerial Work in Law and Public Safety. **Other Jobs in this Work Group:** Emergency Management Specialists; First-Line Supervisors/Managers of Correctional Officers; First-Line Supervisors/Managers of Fire Fighting and Prevention Workers; First-Line Supervisors/Managers of Police and Detectives; Forest Fire Fighting and Prevention Supervisors.

Skills: Management of Personnel Resources; Equipment Maintenance; Service Orientation; Operation Monitoring; Management of Material Resources; Coordination.

Education and Training Programs: Fire Protection and Safety Technology/Technician; Fire Services Administration. **Related Knowledge/Courses:** Public Safety and Security; Building and Construction; Medicine and Dentistry; Education and Training; Mechanical Devices; Customer and Personal Service.

Work Environment: More often outdoors than indoors; noisy; contaminants; disease or infections; hazardous equipment.

Museum Technicians and Conservators

- ❋ Education/Training Required: Bachelor's degree
- ❋ Annual Earnings: $34,340
- ❋ Beginning Wage: $20,600
- ❋ Earnings Growth Potential: Very high
- ❋ Growth: 15.9%
- ❋ Annual Job Openings: 1,341
- ❋ Self-Employed: 1.3%
- ❋ Part-Time: 18.4%

Industries with Greatest Employment: Museums, Historical Sites, and Similar Institutions; Educational Services, Public and Private.

Highest-Growth Industries (Projected Growth for This Job): Performing Arts, Spectator Sports, and Related Industries (39.4%); Museums, Historical Sites, and Similar Institutions (36.2%).

Lowest-Growth Industries (Projected Growth for This Job): Other Information Services (–2.2%); Educational Services, Public and Private (12.2%); Religious, Grantmaking, Civic, Professional, and Similar Organizations (12.6%).

Fastest-Growing Metropolitan Areas (Recent Growth for This Job): Houston–Sugar Land–Baytown, TX (230.0%); San Antonio, TX (100.0%); Tucson, AZ (66.7%); Virginia Beach–Norfolk–Newport News, VA–NC (62.5%); Albuquerque, NM (50.0%).

Other Considerations for Job Security: Keen competition is expected because qualified applicants generally outnumber job openings. Competition is stiff for the limited number of openings in conservation graduate programs, and applicants need a technical background. Conservation program graduates with knowledge of a foreign language and a willingness to relocate will have advantages over less qualified candidates. Public interest in science, art, history, and technology will continue, creating opportunities for curators, conservators, and museum technicians.

Museum attendance has held steady in recent years, many museums are financially healthy, and many have pursued building and renovation projects. There has been an increase in self-employment among conservators, as many museums move toward hiring these workers on contract rather than keeping them permanently on staff. This trend is expected to continue.

Prepare specimens, such as fossils, skeletal parts, lace, and textiles, for museum collection and exhibits. May restore documents or install, arrange, and exhibit materials. Install, arrange, assemble, and prepare artifacts for exhibition, ensuring the artifacts' safety, reporting their status and condition, and identifying and correcting any problems with the setup. Coordinate exhibit installations, assisting with design; constructing displays, dioramas, display cases, and models; and ensuring the availability of necessary materials. Determine whether objects need repair and choose the safest and most effective method of repair. Clean objects, such as paper, textiles, wood, metal, glass, rock, pottery, and furniture, using cleansers, solvents, soap solutions, and polishes. Prepare artifacts for storage and shipping. Supervise and work with volunteers. Present public programs and tours. Specialize in particular materials or types of object, such as documents and books, paintings, decorative arts, textiles, metals, or architectural materials. Recommend preservation procedures, such as control of temperature and humidity, to curatorial and building staff. Classify and assign registration numbers to artifacts and supervise inventory control. Direct and supervise curatorial and technical staff in the handling, mounting, care, and storage of art objects. Perform on-site fieldwork, which may involve interviewing people, inspecting and identifying artifacts, taking notes, viewing sites and collections, and repainting exhibition spaces. Repair, restore, and reassemble artifacts, designing and fabricating missing or broken parts, to restore them to their original appearance and to prevent deterioration. Prepare reports on the operation of conservation laboratories, documenting the condition of artifacts, treatment options, and the methods of preservation and repair used. Study object documentation or conduct standard chemical and physical tests to ascertain the object's age, composition, original appearance, need for treatment or restoration, and appropriate preservation method. Cut and weld metal sections in reconstruction or renovation of exterior structural sections and accessories of exhibits. Perform tests and examinations to establish storage and conservation requirements, policies, and procedures.

Personality Type: Artistic.

GOE—Interest Area: 05. Education and Training. **Work Group:** 05.05. Archival and Museum Services. **Other Jobs in this Work Group:** Archivists; Audio-Visual Collections Specialists; Curators.

Skills: Management of Material Resources; Repairing; Installation; Technology Design; Equipment Maintenance; Operations Analysis.

Education and Training Programs: Museology/Museum Studies; Art History, Criticism, and Conservation; Public/Applied History and Archival Administration. **Related Knowledge/Courses:** History and Archeology; Fine Arts; Sociology and Anthropology; Design; Clerical Studies; Building and Construction.

Work Environment: Indoors; standing; using hands on objects, tools, or controls.

Network and Computer Systems Administrators

- Education/Training Required: Bachelor's degree
- Annual Earnings: $62,130
- Beginning Wage: $38,610
- Earnings Growth Potential: Very high
- Growth: 27.0%
- Annual Job Openings: 37,010
- Self-Employed: 0.4%
- Part-Time: 3.1%

Our sources did not provide separate job openings data for this occupation. The job openings listed here are shared with Computer Security Specialists.

Industries with Greatest Employment: Professional, Scientific, and Technical Services; Educational Services, Public and Private; Management of Companies and Enterprises; Telecommunications; Credit Intermediation and Related Activities.

Highest-Growth Industries (Projected Growth for This Job): Amusement, Gambling, and Recreation Industries (66.1%); Social Assistance (58.3%); Securities, Commodity Contracts, and Other Financial Investments and Related Activities (58.2%); Internet Publishing and Broadcasting (54.3%); Museums, Historical Sites, and Similar Institutions (49.6%); Professional, Scientific, and Technical Services (47.2%); Warehousing and Storage (46.9%); Personal and Laundry Services (40.4%); Lessors of Nonfinancial Intangible Assets (except Copyrighted Works) (40.1%); Building Material and Garden Equipment and Supplies Dealers (39.8%); Waste Management and Remediation Services (39.7%); Administrative and Support Services (39.0%); Ambulatory Health Care Services (38.7%); Performing Arts, Spectator Sports, and Related Industries (38.0%); Nursing and Residential Care Facilities (37.4%); Support Activities for Transportation (34.5%); Water Transportation (33.7%); Real Estate (32.9%); Nonstore Retailers (31.7%); Religious, Grantmaking, Civic, Professional, and Similar Organizations (30.4%); others.

Lowest-Growth Industries (Projected Growth for This Job): Apparel Manufacturing (–51.5%); Textile Mills (–23.5%); Primary Metal Manufacturing (–20.6%); Petroleum and Coal Products Manufacturing (–16.8%); Paper Manufacturing (–15.8%); Printing and Related Support Activities (–12.8%); Electronics and Appliance Stores (–10.4%); Electrical Equipment, Appliance, and Component Manufacturing (–6.2%); Machinery Manufacturing (–5.5%); Rail Transportation (–5.5%).

Fastest-Growing Metropolitan Areas (Recent Growth for This Job): Billings, MT (150.0%);

Altoona, PA (125.0%); Jackson, MS (113.8%); Dalton, GA (100.0%); Lawton, OK (75.0%).

Other Considerations for Job Security: Although employment may be tempered somewhat by offshore outsourcing, strong employment growth combined with a limited supply of qualified workers will result in very good employment prospects for this occupation. Individuals with an advanced degree in computer science or computer engineering or with an MBA with a concentration in information systems should enjoy favorable employment prospects. College graduates with a bachelor's degree in computer science, computer engineering, information science, or MIS also should enjoy favorable prospects, particularly if they have supplemented their formal education with practical experience.

Install, configure, and support an organization's local area network (LAN), wide area network (WAN), and Internet system or a segment of a network system. Maintain network hardware and software. Monitor network to ensure its availability to all system users and perform necessary maintenance to support network availability. May supervise other network support and client server specialists and plan, coordinate, and implement network security measures. Diagnose hardware and software problems and replace defective components. Perform data backups and disaster recovery operations. Maintain and administer computer networks and related computing environments, including computer hardware, systems software, applications software, and all configurations. Plan, coordinate, and implement network security measures to protect data, software, and hardware. Operate master consoles to monitor the performance of computer systems and networks and to coordinate computer network access and use. Perform routine network startup and shutdown procedures and maintain control records. Design, configure, and test computer hardware, networking software, and operating system software. Recommend changes to improve systems and network configurations and determine hardware or software requirements related to such changes. Confer with network users about how to solve existing system problems. Monitor network performance to determine whether adjustments need to be made and to determine where changes will need to be made in the future. Train people in computer system use. Load computer tapes and disks and install software and printer paper or forms. Gather data pertaining to customer needs and use the information to identify, predict, interpret, and evaluate system and network requirements. Analyze equipment performance records to determine the need for repair or replacement. Maintain logs related to network functions as well as maintenance and repair records. Research new technology and implement it or recommend its implementation. Maintain an inventory of parts for emergency repairs. Coordinate with vendors and with company personnel to facilitate purchases.

Personality Type: Investigative.

GOE—Interest Area: 11. Information Technology. **Work Group:** 11.01. Managerial Work in Information Technology. **Other Jobs in this Work Group:** Computer and Information Systems Managers.

Skills: Installation; Troubleshooting; Programming; Repairing; Systems Evaluation; Systems Analysis.

Education and Training Programs: Computer and Information Sciences and Support Services, Other; Computer and Information Sciences, General; Computer and Information Systems Security; Computer Systems Analysis/Analyst; Computer Systems Networking and Telecommunications; Information Science/Studies; System Administration/Administrator; System, Networking, and LAN/WAN Management/Manager. **Related Knowledge/Courses:** Computers and Electronics; Telecommunications; Engineering and Technology; Customer and Personal Service; Education and Training; Communications and Media.

Work Environment: Indoors; sitting; using hands on objects, tools, or controls; repetitive motions.

Network Systems and Data Communications Analysts

❋ Education/Training Required: Bachelor's degree
❋ Annual Earnings: $64,600
❋ Beginning Wage: $38,410
❋ Earnings Growth Potential: Very high
❋ Growth: 53.4%
❋ Annual Job Openings: 35,086
❋ Self-Employed: 17.5%
❋ Part-Time: 8.6%

Industries with Greatest Employment: Professional, Scientific, and Technical Services; Telecommunications; Management of Companies and Enterprises; Administrative and Support Services; Educational Services, Public and Private.

Highest-Growth Industries (Projected Growth for This Job): Securities, Commodity Contracts, and Other Financial Investments and Related Activities (94.4%); Social Assistance (90.4%); Internet Publishing and Broadcasting (89.4%); Amusement, Gambling, and Recreation Industries (84.3%); Museums, Historical Sites, and Similar Institutions (83.8%); Professional, Scientific, and Technical Services (83.8%); Warehousing and Storage (80.4%); Waste Management and Remediation Services (76.9%); Personal and Laundry Services (72.9%); Lessors of Nonfinancial Intangible Assets (Except Copyrighted Works) (72.4%); Administrative and Support Services (71.7%); Funds, Trusts, and Other Financial Vehicles (70.9%); Ambulatory Health Care Services (70.0%); Nursing and Residential Care Facilities (69.3%); Performing Arts, Spectator Sports, and Related Industries (69.2%); Building Material and Garden Equipment and Supplies Dealers (66.7%); Nonstore Retailers (66.7%); Real Estate (64.7%); Support Activities for Transportation (62.4%); Religious, Grantmaking, Civic, Professional, and Similar Organizations (60.3%); others.

Lowest-Growth Industries (Projected Growth for This Job): Crop Production (–10.5%); Pipeline Transportation (–9.4%); Primary Metal Manufacturing (–3.8%); Paper Manufacturing (5.9%); Printing and Related Support Activities (6.9%); Electronics and Appliance Stores (10.4%); Electrical Equipment, Appliance, and Component Manufacturing (10.6%).

Fastest-Growing Metropolitan Areas (Recent Growth for This Job): Binghamton, NY (187.5%); Cedar Rapids, IA (133.3%); Winston-Salem, NC (106.3%); Lake Charles, LA (100.0%); Racine, WI (100.0%).

Other Considerations for Job Security: Strong employment growth combined with a limited supply of qualified workers will result in excellent employment prospects for this occupation and a high demand for their skills. Demand is growing for network systems and data communication analysts to help firms maximize their efficiency with available technology. Individuals with an advanced degree in computer science or computer engineering or with an MBA with a concentration in information systems should enjoy favorable employment prospects. College graduates with a bachelor's degree in computer science, computer engineering, information science, or MIS also should enjoy favorable prospects, particularly if they have supplemented their formal education with practical experience.

Analyze, design, test, and evaluate network systems, such as local area networks (LAN); wide area networks (WAN); and Internet, intranet, and other data communications systems. Perform network modeling, analysis, and planning. Research and recommend network and data communications hardware and software. Includes telecommunications specialists who deal with the interfacing of computer and communications equipment. May supervise computer programmers. Maintain needed files by adding and deleting them on the network server and backing them up to guarantee their safety in the event of network problems. Monitor system performance and provide security measures, troubleshooting, and maintenance as needed. Assist users to diagnose and solve data communication problems. Set up user accounts, regulating and monitoring file access to ensure confidentiality and proper use. Design and implement systems, network configurations, and network architecture, including hardware and software technology, site locations, and integration of technologies. Maintain the peripherals, such as printers, that are connected to the network. Identify areas of operation that need upgraded equipment such as modems, fiber-optic cables, and telephone wires. Train users in use of equipment. Develop and write procedures for installation, use, and troubleshooting of communications hardware and software. Adapt and modify existing software to meet specific needs. Work with other engineers, systems analysts, programmers, technicians, scientists, and top-level managers in the design, testing, and evaluation of systems. Test and evaluate hardware and software to determine efficiency, reliability, and compatibility with existing system and make purchase recommendations. Read technical manuals and brochures to determine which equipment meets establishment requirements. Consult customers, visit workplaces, or conduct surveys to determine present and future user needs. Visit vendors, attend conferences or training, and study technical journals to keep up with changes in technology.

Personality Type: Investigative.

GOE—Interest Area: 11. Information Technology. **Work Group:** 11.02. Information Technology Specialties. **Other Jobs in this Work Group:** Computer and Information Scientists, Research; Computer Operators; Computer Programmers; Computer Security Specialists; Computer Software Engineers, Applications; Computer Software Engineers, Systems Software; Computer Support Specialists; Computer Systems Analysts; Computer Systems Engineers/ Architects; Database Administrators; Network Designers; Software Quality Assurance Engineers and Testers; Web Administrators; Web Developers.

Skills: Installation; Systems Analysis; Technology Design; Troubleshooting; Systems Evaluation; Programming.

Education and Training Programs: Computer and Information Sciences, General; Information Technology; Computer Systems Analysis/Analyst; Computer Systems Networking and Telecommunications; System, Networking, and LAN/WAN Management/Manager; Computer and Information Systems Security. **Related Knowledge/Courses:** Telecommunications; Computers and Electronics; Customer and Personal Service; Engineering and Technology; Education and Training; Design.

Work Environment: Indoors; sitting.

Nuclear Medicine Technologists

- ❋ Education/Training Required: Associate degree
- ❋ Annual Earnings: $62,300
- ❋ Beginning Wage: $46,490
- ❋ Earnings Growth Potential: Very high
- ❋ Growth: 14.8%
- ❋ Annual Job Openings: 1,290
- ❋ Self-Employed: 1.0%
- ❋ Part-Time: 17.3%

Industries with Greatest Employment: Hospitals, Public and Private; Ambulatory Health Care Services.

Highest-Growth Industries (Projected Growth for This Job): Ambulatory Health Care Services (23.8%).

Lowest-Growth Industries (Projected Growth for This Job): Hospitals, Public and Private (11.0%); Educational Services, Public and Private (12.3%).

Fastest-Growing Metropolitan Areas (Recent Growth for This Job): Sarasota–Bradenton–Venice, FL (100.0%); Syracuse, NY (100.0%); Dallas–Fort Worth–Arlington, TX (52.2%); Birmingham–Hoover, AL (50.0%); Bridgeport–Stamford–Norwalk, CT (50.0%).

Other Considerations for Job Security: Despite fast growth in nuclear medicine, the number of openings into the occupation each year will be relatively low because of the small size of the occupation. Technologists with additional training in other diagnostic methods, such as radiologic technology or diagnostic medical sonography, will have the best prospects.

Prepare, administer, and measure radioactive isotopes in therapeutic, diagnostic, and tracer studies, utilizing a variety of radioisotope equipment. Prepare stock solutions of radioactive materials and calculate doses to be administered by radiologists. Subject patients to radiation. Execute blood volume, red cell survival, and fat absorption studies, following standard laboratory techniques. Calculate, measure, and record radiation dosage or radiopharmaceuticals received, used, and disposed, using computer and following physician's prescription. Detect and map radiopharmaceuticals in patients' bodies, using a camera to produce photographic or computer images. Explain test procedures and safety precautions to patients and provide them with assistance during test procedures. Administer radiopharmaceuticals or radiation to patients to detect or treat diseases, using radioisotope equipment, under direction of physician. Produce a computer-generated or film image for interpretation by a physician. Process cardiac function studies, using computer. Dispose of radioactive materials and store radiopharmaceuticals, following radiation safety procedures. Record and process results of procedures. Prepare stock radiopharmaceuticals, adhering to safety standards that minimize radiation exposure to workers and patients. Maintain and calibrate radioisotope and laboratory equipment. Gather information on patients' illnesses and medical history to guide the choice of diagnostic procedures for therapy. Measure glandular activity, blood volume, red cell survival, and radioactivity of patient, using scanners, Geiger counters, scintillometers, and other laboratory equipment. Train and supervise student or subordinate nuclear medicine technologists. Position radiation fields, radiation beams, and patient to allow for most effective treatment of patient's disease, using computer. Add radioactive substances to biological specimens, such as blood, urine, and feces, to determine therapeutic drug or hormone levels. Develop treatment procedures for nuclear medicine treatment programs.

Personality Type: Investigative.

GOE—Interest Area: 08. Health Science. **Work Group:** 08.06. Medical Technology. **Other Jobs in this Work Group:** Biological Technicians; Cardiovascular Technologists and Technicians; Diagnostic Medical Sonographers; Medical and Clinical Laboratory Technicians; Medical and Clinical Laboratory Technologists; Medical Equipment Preparers; Medical Records and Health Information Technicians; Opticians, Dispensing; Orthotists and Prosthetists; Radiologic Technicians; Radiologic Technologists; Radiologic Technologists and Technicians.

Skills: Science; Operation Monitoring; Operation and Control; Quality Control Analysis; Social Perceptiveness; Service Orientation.

Education and Training Programs: Nuclear Medical Technology/Technologist; Radiation Protection/Health Physics Technician. **Related Knowledge/Courses:** Medicine and Dentistry; Biology; Physics; Chemistry; Computers and Electronics; Customer and Personal Service.

Work Environment: Indoors; contaminants; radiation; disease or infections; standing; using hands on objects, tools, or controls.

Nuclear Power Reactor Operators

- Education/Training Required: Long-term on-the-job training
- Annual Earnings: $69,370
- Beginning Wage: $54,180
- Earnings Growth Potential: Very high
- Growth: 10.6%
- Annual Job Openings: 233
- Self-Employed: 0.0%
- Part-Time: 0.6%

Industries with Greatest Employment: Utilities.

Highest-Growth Industries (Projected Growth for This Job): None met the criteria.

Lowest-Growth Industries (Projected Growth for This Job): Utilities (10.3%).

Fastest-Growing Metropolitan Areas (Recent Growth for This Job): No data available.

Other Considerations for Job Security: Outlook information for nuclear power reactor operators is subsumed under the information for power plant operators, distributors, and dispatchers. Job opportunities are expected to be very good for people interested in becoming power plant operators. During the 1990s, the emphasis on cost cutting among utilities led to hiring freezes and the laying off of younger workers. The result is an aging workforce, half of which is expected to retire within the next 10 years. Utilities have responded by setting up new education programs at community colleges and high schools throughout the country. Prospects should be especially good for people with computer skills and a basic understanding of science and mathematics.

Control nuclear reactors. Adjust controls to position rod and to regulate flux level, reactor period, coolant temperature, and rate of power flow, following standard procedures. Respond to system or unit abnormalities, diagnosing the cause and recommending or taking corrective action. Monitor all systems for normal running conditions, performing activities such as checking gauges to assess output or assess the effects of generator loading on other equipment. Implement operational procedures such as those controlling startup and shutdown activities. Note malfunctions of equipment, instruments, or controls and report these conditions to supervisors. Monitor and operate boilers, turbines, wells, and auxiliary power plant equipment. Dispatch orders and instructions to personnel through radiotelephone or intercommunication systems to coordinate auxiliary equipment operation. Record operating data such as the results of surveillance tests. Participate in nuclear fuel element handling activities such as preparation, transfer, loading, and unloading. Conduct inspections and operations outside of control rooms as necessary. Direct reactor operators in emergency situations in accordance with emergency operating procedures.

Authorize maintenance activities on units and changes in equipment and system operational status.

Personality Type: Realistic.

GOE—Interest Area: 13. Manufacturing. **Work Group:** 13.16. Utility Operation and Energy Distribution. **Other Jobs in this Work Group:** Chemical Plant and System Operators; Gas Compressor and Gas Pumping Station Operators; Gas Plant Operators; Petroleum Pump System Operators, Refinery Operators, and Gaugers; Power Distributors and Dispatchers; Power Plant Operators; Ship Engineers; Stationary Engineers and Boiler Operators; Water and Liquid Waste Treatment Plant and System Operators.

Skills: Operation Monitoring; Operation and Control; Science; Systems Analysis; Troubleshooting; Equipment Maintenance.

Education and Training Program: Nuclear/Nuclear Power Technology/Technician. **Related Knowledge/Courses:** Physics; Engineering and Technology; Chemistry; Mechanical Devices; Public Safety and Security; Design.

Work Environment: Indoors; noisy; radiation; hazardous conditions; hazardous equipment; using hands on objects, tools, or controls.

Nursing Aides, Orderlies, and Attendants

- Education/Training Required: Postsecondary vocational training
- Annual Earnings: $22,180
- Beginning Wage: $16,190
- Earnings Growth Potential: Very high
- Growth: 18.2%
- Annual Job Openings: 321,036
- Self-Employed: 2.4%
- Part-Time: 24.0%

Industries with Greatest Employment: Nursing and Residential Care Facilities; Hospitals, Public and Private.

Highest-Growth Industries (Projected Growth for This Job): Social Assistance (55.0%); Ambulatory Health Care Services (42.3%); Administrative and Support Services (26.7%); Professional, Scientific, and Technical Services (24.4%); Hospitals, Public and Private (21.8%); Religious, Grantmaking, Civic, Professional, and Similar Organizations (19.9%); Management of Companies and Enterprises (15.3%).

Lowest-Growth Industries (Projected Growth for This Job): Private Households (4.3%); Educational Services, Public and Private (8.7%); Accommodation, Including Hotels and Motels (8.8%); Nursing and Residential Care Facilities (14.1%).

Fastest-Growing Metropolitan Areas (Recent Growth for This Job): Ponce, PR (116.7%); Dothan, AL (55.4%); Longview, WA (54.8%); Prescott, AZ (53.3%); Portsmouth, NH–ME (51.4%).

Other Considerations for Job Security: Excellent job opportunities for nursing, psychiatric, and home health aides will arise from a combination of rapid employment growth and the need to replace the many workers who leave the occupation each year. The occupation has high turnover because of the modest entry requirements, low pay, high physical and emotional demands, and limited opportunities for advancement within the occupation. For these same reasons, the number of people looking to enter the occupation will be limited. Many aides leave the occupation to attend training programs for other health-care occupations. Therefore, people who are interested in, and suited for, this work should have excellent job opportunities.

Provide basic patient care under direction of nursing staff. Perform duties such as feeding, bathing, dressing, grooming, or moving patients or changing linens. Turn and reposition bedridden patients, alone or with assistance, to prevent bedsores. Answer patients' call signals. Feed patients who cannot feed themselves. Observe patients' conditions, measuring and recording food and liquid intake and output and vital signs, and report changes to professional staff. Provide patient care by supplying and emptying bedpans, applying dressings, and supervising exercise routines. Provide patients with help walking, exercising, and moving in and out of bed. Bathe, groom, shave, dress, or drape patients to prepare them for surgery, treatment, or examination. Collect specimens such as urine, feces, or sputum. Prepare, serve, and collect food trays. Clean rooms and change linens. Transport patients to treatment units, using a wheelchair or stretcher. Deliver messages, documents, and specimens. Answer phones and direct visitors. Administer medications and treatments, such as catheterizations, suppositories, irrigations, enemas, massages, and douches, as directed by physician or nurse. Restrain patients if necessary. Maintain inventory by storing, preparing, sterilizing, and issuing supplies such as dressing packs and treatment trays. Explain medical instructions to patients and family members. Perform clerical duties such as processing documents and scheduling appointments. Work as part of a medical team that examines and treats clinic outpatients. Set up equipment such as oxygen tents, portable X-ray machines, and overhead irrigation bottles.

Personality Type: Social.

GOE—Interest Area: 08. Health Science. **Work Group:** 08.08. Patient Care and Assistance. **Other Jobs in this Work Group:** Home Health Aides; Licensed Practical and Licensed Vocational Nurses; Psychiatric Aides; Psychiatric Technicians.

Skills: Social Perceptiveness; Operation Monitoring; Time Management; Service Orientation; Monitoring; Instructing.

Education and Training Programs: Nurse/Nursing Assistant/Aide and Patient Care Assistant; Health Aide. **Related Knowledge/Courses:** Medicine and Dentistry; Psychology; Customer and Personal Service; Chemistry.

Work Environment: Indoors; disease or infections; standing; walking and running; using hands on objects, tools, or controls; bending or twisting the body.

Nursing Instructors and Teachers, Postsecondary

- ❋ Education/Training Required: Doctoral degree
- ❋ Annual Earnings: $55,280
- ❋ Beginning Wage: $34,140
- ❋ Earnings Growth Potential: Very high
- ❋ Growth: 22.9%
- ❋ Annual Job Openings: 237,478
- ❋ Self-Employed: 0.4%
- ❋ Part-Time: 27.8%

Our sources did not provide separate job openings data for this occupation. The job openings listed here are shared with 35 other postsecondary teaching occupations. For a complete list, see the beginning of this section.

Industries with Greatest Employment: Educational Services, Public and Private.

Highest-Growth Industries (Projected Growth for This Job): Administrative and Support Services (48.3%); Amusement, Gambling, and Recreation Industries (45.3%); Social Assistance (38.6%); Support Activities for Transportation (32.8%); Religious, Grantmaking, Civic, Professional, and Similar Organizations (29.9%); Professional, Scientific, and Technical Services (28.8%); Management of Companies and Enterprises (26.8%); Educational Services, Public and Private (22.9%); Hospitals, Public and Private (21.4%); Personal and Laundry Services (21.0%).

Lowest-Growth Industries (Projected Growth for This Job): Other Information Services (7.4%); Sporting Goods, Hobby, Book, and Music Stores (13.3%); Performing Arts, Spectator Sports, and Related Industries (13.4%); Insurance Carriers and Related Activities (13.9%).

Fastest-Growing Metropolitan Areas (Recent Growth for This Job): Scranton–Wilkes-Barre, PA (125.0%); Orlando–Kissimmee, FL (80.0%); Manchester, NH (50.0%); Tulsa, OK (28.6%).

Other Considerations for Job Security: Retirements of current postsecondary teachers should create numerous openings for all types of postsecondary teachers. However, because students attend postsecondary institutions to prepare themselves for careers, the best job prospects for postsecondary teachers are likely to be in rapidly growing fields that offer many nonacademic career options, such as nursing. The demand for nurses continues to grow, and many who are qualified to teach are finding work outside of education, so job opportunities should be excellent. Community colleges and other institutions offering career and technical education have been among the most rapidly growing and are expected to offer some of the best opportunities for postsecondary teachers.

Demonstrate and teach patient care in classroom and clinical units to nursing students. Includes both teachers primarily engaged in teaching and those who do a combination of teaching and research. Initiate, facilitate, and moderate classroom discussions. Prepare and deliver lectures to undergraduate or graduate students on topics such as pharmacology, mental-health nursing, and community health-care practices. Keep abreast of developments in their field by reading current literature, talking with colleagues, and participating in professional conferences. Prepare course materials such as syllabi, homework assignments, and handouts. Supervise students' laboratory and clinical work. Evaluate and grade students' classwork, laboratory and clinic work, assignments, and papers. Collaborate with colleagues to address teaching and research issues. Plan, evaluate, and revise curricula, course content, course materials, and methods of instruction. Assess clinical education needs and patient and client teaching needs, utilizing a variety of methods. Compile, administer, and grade examinations or assign this work to others. Advise students on academic and vocational curricula and on career issues. Maintain student attendance records, grades, and other required records. Maintain regularly scheduled office hours to advise and assist students. Supervise undergraduate or graduate teaching, internships, and research work. Conduct research in a particular field of knowledge and publish findings in professional journals, books, and/or electronic media. Participate in student recruitment, registration, and placement activities. Serve on academic or administrative committees that deal with institutional policies, departmental matters, and academic issues. Coordinate training programs with area universities, clinics, hospitals, health agencies, and/or vocational schools. Compile bibliographies of specialized materials for outside reading assignments. Select and obtain materials and supplies such as textbooks and laboratory equipment. Participate in campus and community events. Write grant proposals to procure external research funding. Act as advisers to student organizations. Demonstrate patient care in clinical units of hospitals. Perform administrative duties such as serving as department head.

Personality Type: Social.

GOE—Interest Area: 05. Education and Training. **Work Group:** 05.03. Postsecondary and Adult Teaching and Instructing. **Other Jobs in this Work Group:** Adult Literacy, Remedial Education, and GED Teachers and Instructors; Agricultural Sciences Teachers, Postsecondary; Anthropology and Archeology Teachers, Postsecondary; Architecture Teachers, Postsecondary; Area, Ethnic, and Cultural Studies Teachers, Postsecondary; Art, Drama, and Music Teachers, Postsecondary; Atmospheric, Earth, Marine, and Space Sciences Teachers, Postsecondary; Biological Science Teachers, Postsecondary; Business Teachers, Postsecondary; Chemistry Teachers, Postsecondary; Communications Teachers, Postsecondary; Computer Science Teachers, Postsecondary; Criminal Justice and Law Enforcement Teachers, Postsecondary; Economics Teachers, Postsecondary; Education Teachers, Postsecondary; Engineering Teachers, Postsecondary; English Language and Literature Teachers, Postsecondary; Environmental Science Teachers, Postsecondary; Farm and Home Management Advisors; Foreign Language and Literature Teachers, Postsecondary; Forestry and Conservation Science Teachers, Postsecondary; Geography Teachers, Postsecondary; Graduate Teaching Assistants; Health Specialties Teachers, Postsecondary; History Teachers, Postsecondary; Home Economics

Teachers, Postsecondary; Law Teachers, Postsecondary; Library Science Teachers, Postsecondary; Mathematical Science Teachers, Postsecondary; Philosophy and Religion Teachers, Postsecondary; Physics Teachers, Postsecondary; Political Science Teachers, Postsecondary; Psychology Teachers, Postsecondary; Recreation and Fitness Studies Teachers, Postsecondary; Self-Enrichment Education Teachers; Social Work Teachers, Postsecondary; Sociology Teachers, Postsecondary; Vocational Education Teachers, Postsecondary.

Skills: Science; Instructing; Writing; Social Perceptiveness; Reading Comprehension; Learning Strategies.

Education and Training Programs: Pre-Nursing Studies; Nursing—Registered Nurse Training (RN, ASN, BSN, MSN); Adult Health Nurse/Nursing; Nurse Anesthetist; Family Practice Nurse/Nurse Practitioner; Maternal/Child Health and Neonatal Nurse/Nursing; Nurse Midwife/Nursing Midwifery; Nursing Science (MS, PhD); Pediatric Nurse/Nursing; Psychiatric/Mental Health Nurse/Nursing; Public Health/Community Nurse/Nursing; others. **Related Knowledge/Courses:** Therapy and Counseling; Sociology and Anthropology; Biology; Medicine and Dentistry; Philosophy and Theology; Psychology.

Work Environment: Indoors; disease or infections; sitting.

Obstetricians and Gynecologists

- ❈ Education/Training Required: First professional degree
- ❈ Annual Earnings: More than $145,600
- ❈ Beginning Wage: $103,070
- ❈ Earnings Growth Potential: Cannot be calculated
- ❈ Growth: 14.2%
- ❈ Annual Job Openings: 38,027
- ❈ Self-Employed: 14.7%
- ❈ Part-Time: 8.1%

Our sources did not provide separate job openings data for this occupation. The job openings listed here are shared with Anesthesiologists; Family and General Practitioners; Internists, General; Pediatricians, General; Psychiatrists; and Surgeons.

Industries with Greatest Employment: Ambulatory Health Care Services; Hospitals, Public and Private.

Highest-Growth Industries (Projected Growth for This Job): Social Assistance (58.6%); Administrative and Support Services (26.8%); Professional, Scientific, and Technical Services (22.6%); Nursing and Residential Care Facilities (21.0%); Ambulatory Health Care Services (19.4%); Religious, Grantmaking, Civic, Professional, and Similar Organizations (16.7%); Management of Companies and Enterprises (15.3%).

Lowest-Growth Industries (Projected Growth for This Job): Insurance Carriers and Related Activities (4.6%); Health and Personal Care Stores (5.3%); Hospitals, Public and Private (9.9%); Educational Services, Public and Private (11.8%).

Fastest-Growing Metropolitan Areas (Recent Growth for This Job): Indianapolis–Carmel, IN (50.0%); Phoenix–Mesa–Scottsdale, AZ (50.0%); St. Louis, MO–IL (40.0%); Milwaukee–Waukesha–West Allis, WI (33.3%); San Diego–Carlsbad–San Marcos, CA (33.3%).

Other Considerations for Job Security: Opportunities for individuals interested in becoming physicians and surgeons are expected to be very good. Unlike their predecessors, new physicians are much less likely to enter solo practice and more likely to take salaried jobs in group medical practices, clinics, and health networks. Reports of shortages in some specialties, such as general or family practice, internal medicine, and OB/GYN, or in rural or low-income areas should attract new entrants, encouraging schools to expand programs and hospitals to increase available residency slots. However, because physician training is so lengthy, employment change happens gradually. Opportunities should be particularly good in rural and low-income areas, as some physicians find these areas unattractive because of less control over work hours, isolation from medical colleagues, or other reasons.

Diagnose, treat, and help prevent diseases of women, especially those affecting the reproductive system and the process of childbirth. Care for and treat women during prenatal, natal, and postnatal periods. Explain procedures and discuss test results or prescribed treatments with patients. Treat diseases of female organs. Monitor patients' condition and progress and re-evaluate treatments as necessary. Perform Caesarean sections or other surgical procedures as needed to preserve patients' health and deliver babies safely. Prescribe or administer therapy, medication, and other specialized medical care to treat or prevent illness, disease, or injury. Analyze records, reports, test results, or examination information to diagnose medical condition of patient. Collect, record, and maintain patient information, such as medical histories, reports, and examination results. Advise patients and community members concerning diet, activity, hygiene, and disease prevention. Refer patient to medical specialist or other practitioner when necessary. Consult with, or provide consulting services to, other physicians. Direct and coordinate activities of nurses, students, assistants, specialists, therapists, and other medical staff. Plan, implement, or administer health programs in hospitals, businesses, or communities for prevention and treatment of injuries or illnesses. Prepare government and organizational reports on birth, death, and disease statistics; workforce evaluations; or the medical status of individuals. Conduct research to develop or test medications, treatments, or procedures to prevent or control disease or injury.

Personality Type: Investigative.

GOE—Interest Area: 08. Health Science. **Work Group:** 08.02. Medicine and Surgery. **Other Jobs in this Work Group:** Anesthesiologists; Family and General Practitioners; Internists, General; Medical Assistants; Medical Transcriptionists; Pediatricians, General; Pharmacists; Pharmacy Aides; Pharmacy Technicians; Physician Assistants;

Psychiatrists; Registered Nurses; Surgeons; Surgical Technologists.

Skills: Science; Judgment and Decision Making; Reading Comprehension; Complex Problem Solving; Active Learning; Social Perceptiveness.

Education and Training Programs: Neonatal-Perinatal Medicine; Obstetrics and Gynecology. **Related Knowledge/Courses:** Medicine and Dentistry; Therapy and Counseling; Biology; Psychology; Sociology and Anthropology; Chemistry.

Work Environment: Indoors; disease or infections; standing; using hands on objects, tools, or controls.

Occupational Therapist Assistants

- ❋ Education/Training Required: Associate degree
- ❋ Annual Earnings: $42,060
- ❋ Beginning Wage: $26,050
- ❋ Earnings Growth Potential: Very high
- ❋ Growth: 25.4%
- ❋ Annual Job Openings: 2,634
- ❋ Self-Employed: 3.5%
- ❋ Part-Time: 17.8%

Industries with Greatest Employment: Hospitals, Public and Private; Ambulatory Health Care Services; Nursing and Residential Care Facilities; Educational Services, Public and Private; Social Assistance.

Highest-Growth Industries (Projected Growth for This Job): Ambulatory Health Care Services (45.3%); Social Assistance (36.6%); Administrative and Support Services (26.6%); Hospitals, Public and Private (20.2%); Management of Companies and Enterprises (15.1%).

Lowest-Growth Industries (Projected Growth for This Job): Educational Services, Public and Private (6.5%); Nursing and Residential Care Facilities (14.4%).

Fastest-Growing Metropolitan Areas (Recent Growth for This Job): Chicago–Naperville–Joliet, IL–IN–WI (91.0%); Tyler, TX (66.7%); Salt Lake City, UT (60.0%); Portland–Vancouver–Beaverton, OR–WA (55.6%); Hickory–Lenoir–Morgantown, NC (50.0%).

Other Considerations for Job Security: Opportunities for individuals interested in becoming occupational therapist assistants are expected to be very good. In addition to employment growth, job openings will result from the need to replace occupational therapist assistants and aides who leave the occupation permanently over the 2006 to 2016 period. Occupational therapist assistants and aides with prior experience working in an occupational therapy office or other health-care setting will have the best job opportunities. However, individuals with only a high-school diploma may face keen competition for occupational therapist aide jobs.

Assist occupational therapists in providing occupational therapy treatments and procedures. May, in accordance with state laws, assist in development of treatment plans, carry out routine functions, direct activity programs, and document the progress of treatments. Generally requires formal training. Observe and record patients' progress, attitudes, and behavior and maintain this information in client records. Maintain and promote a positive attitude toward clients and their treatment programs. Monitor patients' performance in therapy activities, providing encouragement. Select therapy activities to fit patients' needs and capabilities. Instruct, or assist in instructing, patients and families in home programs, basic living skills, and the care and use of adaptive equipment. Evaluate the daily living skills and capacities of physically, developmentally, or emotionally disabled clients. Aid patients in dressing and grooming themselves. Implement, or assist occupational therapists with implementing, treatment plans designed to help clients function independently. Report to supervisors, verbally or in writing, on patients' progress, attitudes, and behavior. Alter treatment programs to obtain better results if treatment isn't having the intended effect. Work under the direction of occupational therapists to plan, implement, and administer educational, vocational, and recreational programs that restore and enhance performance in individuals with functional impairments. Design, fabricate, and repair assistive devices and make adaptive changes to equipment and environments. Assemble, clean, and maintain equipment and materials for patient use. Teach patients how to deal constructively with their emotions. Perform clerical duties such as scheduling appointments, collecting data, and documenting health insurance billings. Transport patients to and from the occupational therapy work area. Demonstrate therapy techniques such as manual and creative arts or games. Order any needed educational or treatment supplies. Assist educational specialists or clinical psychologists in administering situational or diagnostic tests to measure client's abilities or progress.

Personality Type: Social.

GOE—Interest Area: 08. Health Science. **Work Group:** 08.07. Medical Therapy. **Other Jobs in this Work Group:** Audiologists; Massage Therapists; Occupational Therapist Aides; Occupational Therapists; Physical Therapist Aides; Physical Therapist Assistants; Physical Therapists; Radiation Therapists; Recreational Therapists; Respiratory Therapists; Respiratory Therapy Technicians; Speech-Language Pathologists.

Skills: Social Perceptiveness; Operations Analysis; Service Orientation; Writing; Persuasion; Monitoring.

Education and Training Program: Occupational Therapist Assistant. **Related Knowledge/Courses:** Therapy and Counseling; Psychology; Sociology and Anthropology; Philosophy and Theology; Medicine and Dentistry; Biology.

Work Environment: Indoors; disease or infections; standing; walking and running; using hands on objects, tools, or controls; bending or twisting the body.

Occupational Therapists

- ❋ Education/Training Required: Master's degree
- ❋ Annual Earnings: $60,470
- ❋ Beginning Wage: $40,840
- ❋ Earnings Growth Potential: Very high
- ❋ Growth: 23.1%
- ❋ Annual Job Openings: 8,338
- ❋ Self-Employed: 8.6%
- ❋ Part-Time: 29.8%

Industries with Greatest Employment: Hospitals, Public and Private; Ambulatory Health Care Services; Educational Services, Public and Private; Nursing and Residential Care Facilities; Social Assistance.

Highest-Growth Industries (Projected Growth for This Job): Professional, Scientific, and Technical Services (64.0%); Social Assistance (38.0%); Ambulatory Health Care Services (37.2%); Administrative and Support Services (26.6%); Nursing and Residential Care Facilities (23.9%); Hospitals, Public and Private (21.5%); Management of Companies and Enterprises (15.3%).

Lowest-Growth Industries (Projected Growth for This Job): Insurance Carriers and Related Activities (3.5%); Educational Services, Public and Private (6.5%); Religious, Grantmaking, Civic, Professional, and Similar Organizations (14.7%).

Fastest-Growing Metropolitan Areas (Recent Growth for This Job): Leominster–Fitchburg–Gardner, MA (100.0%); Stockton, CA (83.3%); Oxnard–Thousand Oaks–Ventura, CA (80.0%); Scranton–Wilkes-Barre, PA (78.6%); Shreveport–Bossier City, LA (77.8%).

Other Considerations for Job Security: Job opportunities should be good for licensed occupational therapists in all settings, particularly in acute hospital, rehabilitation, and orthopedic settings because the elderly receive most of their treatment in these settings. Occupational therapists with specialized knowledge in a treatment area also will have increased job prospects. Driver rehabilitation and fall-prevention training for the elderly are emerging practice areas for occupational therapy.

Assess, plan, organize, and participate in rehabilitative programs that help restore vocational, home-making, and daily living skills, as well as general independence, to disabled persons. Complete and maintain necessary records. Evaluate patients' progress and prepare reports that detail progress. Test and evaluate patients' physical and mental abilities and analyze medical data to determine realistic rehabilitation goals for patients. Select activities that will help individuals learn work and life-management skills within limits of their mental and physical capabilities. Plan, organize, and conduct occupational therapy programs in hospital, institutional, or community settings to help rehabilitate those impaired because of illness, injury or psychological or developmental problems. Recommend changes in patients' work or living environments consistent with their needs and capabilities. Consult with rehabilitation team to select activity programs and coordinate occupational therapy with other therapeutic activities. Help clients improve decision making, abstract reasoning, memory, sequencing, coordination, and perceptual skills, using computer programs. Develop and participate in health promotion programs, group activities, or discussions to promote client health, facilitate social adjustment, alleviate stress, and prevent physical or mental disability. Provide training and supervision in therapy techniques and objectives for students and nurses and other medical staff. Design and create, or requisition, special supplies and equipment, such as splints, braces, and computer-aided adaptive equipment. Plan and implement programs and social activities to help patients learn work and school skills and adjust to handicaps. Lay out materials such as puzzles, scissors, and eating utensils for use in therapy; clean and repair these tools after therapy sessions. Advise on health risks in the workplace and on health-related transition to retirement. Conduct research in occupational therapy. Provide patients with assistance in locating and holding jobs.

Personality Type: Social.

GOE—Interest Area: 08. Health Science. **Work Group:** 08.07. Medical Therapy. **Other Jobs in this Work Group:** Audiologists; Massage Therapists; Occupational Therapist Aides; Occupational Therapist Assistants; Physical Therapist Aides; Physical Therapist Assistants; Physical Therapists; Radiation Therapists; Recreational Therapists; Respiratory Therapists; Respiratory Therapy Technicians; Speech-Language Pathologists.

Skills: Social Perceptiveness; Service Orientation; Science; Technology Design; Reading Comprehension; Writing.

Education and Training Program: Occupational Therapy/Therapist. **Related Knowledge/Courses:** Therapy and Counseling; Psychology; Medicine and Dentistry; Biology; Customer and Personal Service; Sociology and Anthropology.

Work Environment: Indoors; disease or infections; standing.

Optometrists

* Education/Training Required: First professional degree
* Annual Earnings: $91,040
* Beginning Wage: $45,030
* Earnings Growth Potential: High
* Growth: 11.3%
* Annual Job Openings: 1,789
* Self-Employed: 25.5%
* Part-Time: 20.8%

Industries with Greatest Employment: Ambulatory Health Care Services; Health and Personal Care Stores.

Highest-Growth Industries (Projected Growth for This Job): Administrative and Support Services (23.6%); Ambulatory Health Care Services (16.4%).

Lowest-Growth Industries (Projected Growth for This Job): Miscellaneous Manufacturing (–1.6%); Health and Personal Care Stores (–0.4%); General Merchandise Stores (4.3%); Educational Services,

Public and Private (7.9%); Hospitals, Public and Private (8.2%); Management of Companies and Enterprises (11.6%).

Fastest-Growing Metropolitan Areas (Recent Growth for This Job): Austin–Round Rock, TX (225.0%); Boulder, CO (100.0%); Riverside–San Bernardino–Ontario, CA (70.6%); Oklahoma City, OK (70.0%); Portland–Vancouver–Beaverton, OR–WA (62.5%).

Other Considerations for Job Security: Job opportunities for optometrists should be very good over the next decade. Demand is expected to be much higher, and because there are only 16 schools of optometry, the number of students who can get a degree in optometry is limited. In addition to growth, the need to replace optometrists who retire or leave the occupation for other reasons will create more employment opportunities.

Diagnose, manage, and treat conditions and diseases of the human eye and visual system. Examine eyes and visual system, diagnose problems or impairments, prescribe corrective lenses, and provide treatment. May prescribe therapeutic drugs to treat specific eye conditions. Examine eyes, using observation, instruments, and pharmaceutical agents, to determine visual acuity and perception, focus, and coordination and to diagnose diseases and other abnormalities such as glaucoma or color-blindness. Analyze test results and develop a treatment plan. Prescribe, supply, fit, and adjust eyeglasses, contact lenses, and other vision aids. Prescribe medications to treat eye diseases if state laws permit. Educate and counsel patients on contact lens care, visual hygiene, lighting arrangements, and safety factors. Consult with and refer patients to ophthalmologist or other health-care practitioner if additional medical treatment is determined necessary. Remove foreign bodies from the eye. Provide patients undergoing eye surgeries, such as cataract and laser vision correction, with pre- and post-operative care. Prescribe therapeutic procedures to correct or conserve vision. Provide vision therapy and low vision rehabilitation.

Personality Type: Investigative.

GOE—Interest Area: 08. Health Science. **Work Group:** 08.04. Health Specialties. **Other Jobs in this Work Group:** Chiropractors; Podiatrists.

Skills: Science; Judgment and Decision Making; Management of Personnel Resources; Active Listening; Reading Comprehension; Management of Material Resources.

Education and Training Program: Optometry (OD). **Related Knowledge/Courses:** Medicine and Dentistry; Biology; Psychology; Economics and Accounting; Therapy and Counseling; Sales and Marketing.

Work Environment: Indoors; disease or infections; sitting; using hands on objects, tools, or controls; repetitive motions.

Pediatricians, General

- ❋ Education/Training Required: First professional degree
- ❋ Annual Earnings: $138,130
- ❋ Beginning Wage: $66,480
- ❋ Earnings Growth Potential: High
- ❋ Growth: 14.2%
- ❋ Annual Job Openings: 38,027
- ❋ Self-Employed: 14.7%
- ❋ Part-Time: 8.1%

Our sources did not provide separate job openings data for this occupation. The job openings listed here are shared with Anesthesiologists; Family and General Practitioners; Internists, General; Obstetricians and Gynecologists; Psychiatrists; and Surgeons.

Industries with Greatest Employment: Ambulatory Health Care Services; Hospitals, Public and Private.

Highest-Growth Industries (Projected Growth for This Job): Social Assistance (58.6%); Administrative and Support Services (26.8%); Professional, Scientific, and Technical Services (22.6%); Nursing and Residential Care Facilities (21.0%); Ambulatory

Health Care Services (19.4%); Religious, Grantmaking, Civic, Professional, and Similar Organizations (16.7%); Management of Companies and Enterprises (15.3%).

Lowest-Growth Industries (Projected Growth for This Job): Insurance Carriers and Related Activities (4.6%); Health and Personal Care Stores (5.3%); Hospitals, Public and Private (9.9%); Educational Services, Public and Private (11.8%).

Fastest-Growing Metropolitan Areas (Recent Growth for This Job): San Francisco–Oakland–Fremont, CA (66.7%); Springfield, MA–CT (50.0%); Detroit–Warren–Livonia, MI (50.0%); San Diego–Carlsbad–San Marcos, CA (47.8%); Minneapolis–St. Paul–Bloomington, MN–WI (40.0%).

Other Considerations for Job Security: Opportunities for individuals interested in becoming physicians and surgeons are expected to be very good. Unlike their predecessors, new physicians are much less likely to enter solo practice and more likely to take salaried jobs in group medical practices, clinics, and health networks. Reports of shortages in some specialties, such as general or family practice, internal medicine, and OB/GYN, or in rural or low-income areas should attract new entrants, encouraging schools to expand programs and hospitals to increase available residency slots. However, because physician training is so lengthy, employment change happens gradually. Opportunities should be particularly good in rural and low-income areas, as some physicians find these areas unattractive because of less control over work hours, isolation from medical colleagues, or other reasons.

Diagnose, treat, and help prevent children's diseases and injuries. Examine patients or order, perform, and interpret diagnostic tests to obtain information on medical condition and determine diagnosis. Examine children regularly to assess their growth and development. Prescribe or administer treatment, therapy, medication, vaccination, and other specialized medical care to treat or prevent illness, disease, or injury in infants and children. Collect, record, and maintain patient information, such as medical history, reports, and examination results. Advise patients, parents or guardians, and community members concerning diet, activity, hygiene, and disease prevention. Treat children with minor illnesses, acute and chronic health problems, and growth and development concerns. Explain procedures and discuss test results or prescribed treatments with patients and parents or guardians. Monitor patients' condition and progress and re-evaluate treatments as necessary. Plan and execute medical care programs to aid in the mental and physical growth and development of children and adolescents. Refer patient to medical specialist or other practitioner when necessary. Direct and coordinate activities of nurses, students, assistants, specialists, therapists, and other medical staff. Provide consulting services to other physicians. Plan, implement, or administer health programs or standards in hospital, business, or community for information, prevention, or treatment of injury or illness. Operate on patients to remove, repair, or improve functioning of diseased or injured body parts and systems. Conduct research to study anatomy and develop or test medications, treatments, or procedures to prevent or control disease or injury. Prepare reports for government or management of birth, death, and disease statistics; workforce evaluations; or medical status of individuals.

Personality Type: Investigative.

GOE—Interest Area: 08. Health Science. **Work Group:** 08.02. Medicine and Surgery. **Other Jobs in this Work Group:** Anesthesiologists; Family and General Practitioners; Internists, General; Medical Assistants; Medical Transcriptionists; Obstetricians and Gynecologists; Pharmacists; Pharmacy Aides; Pharmacy Technicians; Physician Assistants; Psychiatrists; Registered Nurses; Surgeons; Surgical Technologists.

Skills: Science; Social Perceptiveness; Active Learning; Persuasion; Critical Thinking; Reading Comprehension.

Education and Training Programs: Child/Pediatric Neurology; Family Medicine; Neonatal-Perinatal Medicine; Pediatric Cardiology; Pediatric

Endocrinology; Pediatric Hemato-Oncology; Pediatric Nephrology; Pediatric Orthopedics; Pediatric Surgery; Pediatrics. **Related Knowledge/Courses:** Medicine and Dentistry; Therapy and Counseling; Biology; Psychology; Chemistry; Sociology and Anthropology.

Work Environment: Indoors; disease or infections; standing; using hands on objects, tools, or controls.

Pest Control Workers

- ❋ Education/Training Required: Moderate-term on-the-job training
- ❋ Annual Earnings: $27,880
- ❋ Beginning Wage: $18,460
- ❋ Earnings Growth Potential: Very high
- ❋ Growth: 15.5%
- ❋ Annual Job Openings: 6,006
- ❋ Self-Employed: 8.7%
- ❋ Part-Time: 4.4%

Industries with Greatest Employment: Administrative and Support Services.

Highest-Growth Industries (Projected Growth for This Job): Nursing and Residential Care Facilities (48.0%); Administrative and Support Services (16.7%); Accommodation, Including Hotels and Motels (16.0%).

Lowest-Growth Industries (Projected Growth for This Job): Food Manufacturing (–5.1%); Educational Services, Public and Private (8.8%); Food Services and Drinking Places (14.7%).

Fastest-Growing Metropolitan Areas (Recent Growth for This Job): Bridgeport–Stamford–Norwalk, CT (58.3%); Topeka, KS (50.0%); Yuma, AZ (50.0%); Akron, OH (42.9%); Merced, CA (40.0%).

Other Considerations for Job Security: Job prospects should be favorable for qualified applicants because of relatively fast job growth and because many people don't find the nature of pest control work appealing. In addition to job openings arising from employment growth, opportunities will result from the need to replace workers who leave the occupation. Demand for pest control workers is projected to increase for a number of reasons. Population growth will generate new residential and commercial buildings that will require inspections by pest control workers. Also, more people are expected to use pest control services as environmental and health concerns, greater numbers of dual-income households, and improvements in the standard of living convince more people to hire professionals rather than attempt pest control work themselves. Moreover, tougher regulations limiting pesticide use will demand more complex integrated pest management strategies.

Spray or release chemical solutions or toxic gases and set traps to kill pests and vermin, such as mice, termites, and roaches, that infest buildings and surrounding areas. Record work activities performed. Inspect premises to identify infestation source and extent of damage to property, wall and roof porosity, and access to infested locations. Spray or dust chemical solutions, powders, or gases into rooms; onto clothing, furnishings, or wood; and over marshlands, ditches, and catch-basins. Clean work site after job completion. Direct or assist other workers in treatment and extermination processes to eliminate and control rodents, insects, and weeds. Drive truck equipped with power-spraying equipment. Measure area dimensions requiring treatment, using rule; calculate fumigant requirements; and estimate service cost. Post warning signs and lock building doors to secure area to be fumigated. Cut or bore openings in building or surrounding concrete, access infested areas, insert nozzle, and inject pesticide to impregnate ground. Study preliminary reports and diagrams of infested area and determine treatment type required to eliminate and prevent recurrence of infestation. Dig up and burn or spray weeds with herbicides. Set mechanical traps and place poisonous paste or bait in sewers, burrows, and ditches. Clean and remove blockages from infested areas to facilitate spraying procedure and provide drainage, using broom, mop, shovel, and rake. Position and fasten edges of tarpaulins over building and tape vents to ensure airtight environment and check for leaks.

Personality Type: Realistic.

GOE—Interest Area: 01. Agriculture and Natural Resources. **Work Group:** 01.05. Nursery, Groundskeeping, and Pest Control. **Other Jobs in this Work Group:** Landscaping and Groundskeeping Workers; Nursery Workers; Pesticide Handlers, Sprayers, and Applicators, Vegetation; Tree Trimmers and Pruners.

Skills: Persuasion; Service Orientation; Equipment Selection; Social Perceptiveness; Management of Material Resources; Active Learning.

Education and Training Program: Agricultural/Farm Supplies Retailing and Wholesaling. **Related Knowledge/Courses:** Sales and Marketing; Chemistry; Biology; Customer and Personal Service; Building and Construction; Law and Government.

Work Environment: More often outdoors than indoors; very hot or cold; contaminants; hazardous conditions; using hands on objects, tools, or controls.

Pharmacists

- ❋ Education/Training Required: First professional degree
- ❋ Annual Earnings: $94,520
- ❋ Beginning Wage: $67,860
- ❋ Earnings Growth Potential: Very high
- ❋ Growth: 21.7%
- ❋ Annual Job Openings: 16,358
- ❋ Self-Employed: 0.5%
- ❋ Part-Time: 18.1%

Industries with Greatest Employment: Health and Personal Care Stores; Hospitals, Public and Private; General Merchandise Stores; Food and Beverage Stores.

Highest-Growth Industries (Projected Growth for This Job): Social Assistance (62.8%); Nonstore Retailers (50.1%); Professional, Scientific, and Technical Services (48.3%); Warehousing and Storage (33.7%); Ambulatory Health Care Services (31.7%);

Administrative and Support Services (27.8%); General Merchandise Stores (26.2%); Chemical Manufacturing (26.0%); Health and Personal Care Stores (22.1%); Hospitals, Public and Private (21.1%); Food and Beverage Stores (20.0%); Merchant Wholesalers, Nondurable Goods (18.9%); Religious, Grantmaking, Civic, Professional, and Similar Organizations (18.8%); Nursing and Residential Care Facilities (17.2%); Merchant Wholesalers, Durable Goods (16.6%).

Lowest-Growth Industries (Projected Growth for This Job): Rental and Leasing Services (11.0%); Educational Services, Public and Private (11.9%); Wholesale Electronic Markets and Agents and Brokers (13.5%).

Fastest-Growing Metropolitan Areas (Recent Growth for This Job): Flagstaff, AZ (133.3%); Lewiston–Auburn, ME (116.7%); Dalton, GA (100.0%); Boise City–Nampa, ID (75.0%); Yuba City, CA (75.0%).

Other Considerations for Job Security: Excellent opportunities are expected for pharmacists over the 2006 to 2016 period. Job openings will result from rapid employment growth, and from the need to replace workers who retire or leave the occupation for other reasons. As the use of prescription drugs increases, demand for pharmacists will grow in most practice settings, such as community pharmacies, hospital pharmacies, and mail-order pharmacies. As the population ages, assisted living facilities and home care organizations should see particularly rapid growth. Demand will also increase as cost-conscious insurers, in an attempt to improve preventative care, use pharmacists in areas such as patient education and vaccination administration.

Compound and dispense medications, following prescriptions issued by physicians, dentists, or other authorized medical practitioners. Review prescriptions to assure accuracy, to ascertain the needed ingredients, and to evaluate their suitability. Provide information and advice regarding drug interactions, side effects, dosage, and proper medication storage. Analyze prescribing trends to monitor patient compliance and to prevent excessive usage or harmful interactions. Order and purchase pharmaceutical supplies, medical supplies, and drugs, maintaining stock and storing and handling it properly. Maintain records, such as pharmacy files; patient profiles; charge system files; inventories; control records for radioactive nuclei; and registries of poisons, narcotics, and controlled drugs. Provide specialized services to help patients manage conditions such as diabetes, asthma, smoking cessation, or high blood pressure. Advise customers on the selection of medication brands, medical equipment, and health-care supplies. Collaborate with other health-care professionals to plan, monitor, review, and evaluate the quality and effectiveness of drugs and drug regimens, providing advice on drug applications and characteristics. Compound and dispense medications as prescribed by doctors and dentists by calculating, weighing, measuring, and mixing ingredients or oversee these activities. Offer health promotion and prevention activities—for example, training people to use devices such as blood-pressure or diabetes monitors. Refer patients to other health professionals and agencies when appropriate. Prepare sterile solutions and infusions for use in surgical procedures, emergency rooms, or patients' homes. Plan, implement, and maintain procedures for mixing, packaging, and labeling pharmaceuticals according to policy and legal requirements to ensure quality, security, and proper disposal. Assay radiopharmaceuticals, verify rates of disintegration, and calculate the volume required to produce the desired results to ensure proper dosages. Manage pharmacy operations, hiring and supervising staff, performing administrative duties, and buying and selling nonpharmaceutical merchandise. Work in hospitals, clinics, or for health maintenance organizations (HMOs), dispensing prescriptions, serving as a medical team consultant, or specializing in specific drug therapy areas such as oncology or nuclear pharmacotherapy.

Personality Type: Investigative.

GOE—Interest Area: 08. Health Science. **Work Group:** 08.02. Medicine and Surgery. **Other Jobs in this Work Group:** Anesthesiologists; Family and General Practitioners; Internists, General; Medical Assistants; Medical Transcriptionists; Obstetricians and Gynecologists; Pediatricians, General; Pharmacy Aides; Pharmacy Technicians; Physician Assistants; Psychiatrists; Registered Nurses; Surgeons; Surgical Technologists.

Skills: Science; Reading Comprehension; Social Perceptiveness; Active Listening; Instructing; Mathematics.

Education and Training Programs: Pharmacy (PharmD [USA] PharmD, BS/BPharm [Canada]); Pharmacy Administration and Pharmacy Policy and Regulatory Affairs (MS, PhD); Pharmaceutics and Drug Design (MS, PhD); Medicinal and Pharmaceutical Chemistry (MS, PhD); Natural Products Chemistry and Pharmacognosy (MS, PhD); Clinical and Industrial Drug Development (MS, PhD); Pharmacoeconomics/Pharmaceutical Economics (MS, PhD); Clinical, Hospital, and Managed Care Pharmacy (MS, PhD); others. **Related Knowledge/Courses:** Medicine and Dentistry; Chemistry; Therapy and Counseling; Biology; Psychology; Mathematics.

Work Environment: Indoors; disease or infections; standing; repetitive motions.

Pharmacy Technicians

* Education/Training Required: Moderate-term on-the-job training
* Annual Earnings: $25,630
* Beginning Wage: $17,800
* Earnings Growth Potential: Very high
* Growth: 32.0%
* Annual Job Openings: 54,453
* Self-Employed: 0.2%
* Part-Time: 20.8%

Industries with Greatest Employment: Hospitals, Public and Private; General Merchandise Stores; Food and Beverage Stores; Ambulatory Health Care Services.

Highest-Growth Industries (Projected Growth for This Job): Nonstore Retailers (50.1%); General Merchandise Stores (41.0%); Professional, Scientific, and Technical Services (39.4%); Warehousing and Storage (33.3%); Hospitals, Public and Private (31.9%); Ambulatory Health Care Services (31.1%); Food and Beverage Stores (30.9%); Merchant Wholesalers, Nondurable Goods (18.9%); Nursing and Residential Care Facilities (17.3%); Merchant Wholesalers, Durable Goods (16.6%); Management of Companies and Enterprises (15.3%).

Lowest-Growth Industries (Projected Growth for This Job): Gasoline Stations (–10.4%); Insurance Carriers and Related Activities (5.6%); Rental and Leasing Services (10.0%); Educational Services, Public and Private (11.9%); Wholesale Electronic Markets and Agents and Brokers (13.5%).

Fastest-Growing Metropolitan Areas (Recent Growth for This Job): Ocean City, NJ (166.7%); Lewiston–Auburn, ME (128.6%); Coeur d'Alene, ID (100.0%); Lewiston, ID–WA (100.0%); Pittsfield, MA (100.0%).

Other Considerations for Job Security: Good job opportunities are expected for full- and part-time work, especially for technicians with formal training or previous experience. Job openings for pharmacy technicians will result from employment growth, and from the need to replace workers who transfer to other occupations or leave the labor force. Almost all states have legislated the maximum number of technicians who can safely work under a pharmacist at one time. Changes in these laws could directly affect employment.

Prepare medications under the direction of a pharmacist. May measure, mix, count out, label, and record amounts and dosages of medications. Receive written prescription or refill requests and verify that information is complete and accurate. Maintain proper storage and security conditions for drugs. Answer telephones, responding to questions or requests. Fill bottles with prescribed medications and type and affix labels. Assist customers by answering simple questions, locating items, or referring them to the pharmacist for medication information. Price and file filled prescriptions. Clean and help maintain equipment and work areas and sterilize glassware according to prescribed methods. Establish and maintain patient profiles, including lists of medications taken by individual patients. Order, label, and count stock of medications, chemicals, and supplies and enter inventory data into computer. Receive and store incoming supplies, verify quantities against invoices, and inform supervisors of stock needs and shortages. Transfer medication from vials to the appropriate number of sterile disposable syringes, using aseptic techniques. Under pharmacist supervision, add measured drugs or nutrients to intravenous solutions under sterile conditions to prepare intravenous (IV) packs. Supply and monitor robotic machines that dispense medicine into containers and label the containers. Prepare and process medical insurance claim forms and records. Mix pharmaceutical preparations according to written prescriptions. Operate cash registers to accept payment from customers. Compute charges for medication and equipment dispensed to hospital patients and enter data in computer. Deliver medications and pharmaceutical supplies to patients, nursing stations, or surgery. Price stock and mark items for sale. Maintain and merchandise home health-care products and services.

Personality Type: Conventional.

GOE—Interest Area: 08. Health Science. **Work Group:** 08.02. Medicine and Surgery. **Other Jobs in this Work Group:** Anesthesiologists; Family and General Practitioners; Internists, General; Medical Assistants; Medical Transcriptionists; Obstetricians and Gynecologists; Pediatricians, General; Pharmacists; Pharmacy Aides; Physician Assistants; Psychiatrists; Registered Nurses; Surgeons; Surgical Technologists.

Skills: No data available.

Education and Training Program: Pharmacy Technician/Assistant. **Related Knowledge/Courses:** Medicine and Dentistry; Chemistry; Customer and Personal Service; Mathematics; Clerical Studies.

Work Environment: Indoors; standing; using hands on objects, tools, or controls; repetitive motions.

Philosophy and Religion Teachers, Postsecondary

- ❋ Education/Training Required: Doctoral degree
- ❋ Annual Earnings: $54,880
- ❋ Beginning Wage: $31,660
- ❋ Earnings Growth Potential: Very high
- ❋ Growth: 22.9%
- ❋ Annual Job Openings: 237,478
- ❋ Self-Employed: 0.4%
- ❋ Part-Time: 27.8%

Our sources did not provide separate job openings data for this occupation. The job openings listed here are shared with 35 other postsecondary teaching occupations. For a complete list, see the beginning of this section.

Industries with Greatest Employment: Educational Services, Public and Private.

Highest-Growth Industries (Projected Growth for This Job): Administrative and Support Services (48.3%); Amusement, Gambling, and Recreation Industries (45.3%); Social Assistance (38.6%); Support Activities for Transportation (32.8%); Religious, Grantmaking, Civic, Professional, and Similar Organizations (29.9%); Professional, Scientific, and Technical Services (28.8%); Management of Companies and Enterprises (26.8%); Educational Services, Public and Private (22.9%); Hospitals, Public and Private (21.4%); Personal and Laundry Services (21.0%).

Lowest-Growth Industries (Projected Growth for This Job): Other Information Services (7.4%); Sporting Goods, Hobby, Book, and Music Stores (13.3%); Performing Arts, Spectator Sports, and Related Industries (13.4%); Insurance Carriers and Related Activities (13.9%).

Fastest-Growing Metropolitan Areas (Recent Growth for This Job): Portland–Vancouver–Beaverton, OR–WA (50.0%); Durham, NC (50.0%); Honolulu, HI (50.0%); Orlando–Kissimmee, FL (50.0%); Scranton–Wilkes-Barre, PA (42.9%).

Other Considerations for Job Security: Retirements of current postsecondary teachers should create numerous openings for all types of postsecondary teachers, so job opportunities are generally expected to be very good. However, because students attend postsecondary institutions to prepare themselves for careers, the best job prospects for postsecondary teachers are likely to be in rapidly growing fields that offer many nonacademic career options, unlike philosophy and religious studies. Community colleges and other institutions offering career and technical education have been among the most rapidly growing and are expected to offer some of the best opportunities for postsecondary teachers.

Teach courses in philosophy, religion, and theology. Evaluate and grade students' classwork, assignments, and papers. Initiate, facilitate, and moderate classroom discussions. Prepare and deliver lectures to undergraduate and graduate students on topics such as ethics, logic, and contemporary religious thought. Prepare course materials such as syllabi, homework assignments, and handouts. Compile, administer, and grade examinations or assign this work to others. Keep abreast of developments in their field by reading current literature, talking with colleagues, and participating in professional conferences. Maintain student attendance records, grades, and other required records. Plan, evaluate, and revise curricula, course content, course materials, and methods of instruction. Maintain regularly scheduled office hours to advise and assist students. Select and obtain materials and supplies such as textbooks. Advise students on academic and vocational curricula and on career issues. Conduct research in a particular field of knowledge and publish findings in professional journals, books, or electronic media. Perform administrative duties such as serving as department head. Serve on academic or administrative committees that deal with institutional policies, departmental matters, and academic issues. Collaborate with colleagues to address teaching and research issues. Participate in campus and community events. Participate in student recruitment, registration, and placement activities. Compile bibliographies of specialized materials for outside reading assignments. Supervise undergraduate and graduate teaching, internships, and research work. Act as advisers to student organizations. Write grant proposals to procure external research funding. Provide professional consulting services to government or industry.

Personality Type: No data available.

GOE—Interest Area: 05. Education and Training. **Work Group:** 05.03. Postsecondary and Adult Teaching and Instructing. **Other Jobs in this Work Group:** Adult Literacy, Remedial Education, and GED Teachers and Instructors; Agricultural Sciences Teachers, Postsecondary; Anthropology and Archeology Teachers, Postsecondary; Architecture Teachers, Postsecondary; Area, Ethnic, and Cultural Studies Teachers, Postsecondary; Art, Drama, and Music Teachers, Postsecondary; Atmospheric, Earth, Marine, and Space Sciences Teachers, Postsecondary; Biological Science Teachers, Postsecondary; Business Teachers, Postsecondary; Chemistry Teachers, Postsecondary; Communications Teachers, Postsecondary; Computer Science Teachers, Postsecondary; Criminal Justice and Law Enforcement Teachers, Postsecondary; Economics Teachers, Postsecondary; Education Teachers, Postsecondary; Engineering Teachers, Postsecondary; English Language and Literature Teachers, Postsecondary; Environmental Science Teachers, Postsecondary; Farm and Home Management Advisors; Foreign Language and Literature Teachers, Postsecondary; Forestry and Conservation Science Teachers, Postsecondary; Geography Teachers, Postsecondary; Graduate Teaching Assistants; Health Specialties Teachers, Postsecondary; History Teachers, Postsecondary; Home Economics Teachers, Postsecondary; Law Teachers, Postsecondary; Library Science Teachers, Postsecondary; Mathematical Science Teachers, Postsecondary; Nursing Instructors and Teachers, Postsecondary; Physics Teachers, Postsecondary; Political Science Teachers, Postsecondary; Psychology Teachers, Postsecondary; Recreation and Fitness Studies Teachers, Postsecondary; Self-Enrichment Education Teachers; Social Work Teachers, Postsecondary; Sociology Teachers, Postsecondary; Vocational Education Teachers, Postsecondary.

Skills: Writing; Instructing; Reading Comprehension; Critical Thinking; Speaking; Learning Strategies.

Education and Training Programs: Philosophy; Ethics; Philosophy, Other; Religion/Religious Studies; Buddhist Studies; Christian Studies.; Hindu Studies; Philosophy and Religious Studies, Other; Bible/Biblical Studies; Missions/Missionary Studies and Missiology; Religious Education; Religious/Sacred Music; Theology/Theological Studies; Divinity/Ministry (BD, MDiv.); Pre-Theology/Pre-Ministerial Studies; others. **Related Knowledge/Courses:** Philosophy and Theology; History and Archeology; Sociology and Anthropology; Foreign Language; English Language; Education and Training.

Work Environment: Indoors; sitting.

Physical Therapist Aides

- ❀ Education/Training Required: Short-term on-the-job training
- ❀ Annual Earnings: $22,060
- ❀ Beginning Wage: $15,850
- ❀ Earnings Growth Potential: Very high
- ❀ Growth: 24.4%
- ❀ Annual Job Openings: 4,092
- ❀ Self-Employed: 0.2%
- ❀ Part-Time: 27.1%

Industries with Greatest Employment: Ambulatory Health Care Services; Hospitals, Public and Private; Nursing and Residential Care Facilities.

Highest-Growth Industries (Projected Growth for This Job): Ambulatory Health Care Services (32.5%); Social Assistance (28.8%).

Lowest-Growth Industries (Projected Growth for This Job): Educational Services, Public and Private (10.4%); Hospitals, Public and Private (13.6%); Nursing and Residential Care Facilities (14.7%).

Fastest-Growing Metropolitan Areas (Recent Growth for This Job): Columbus, OH (212.5%); Augusta–Richmond County, GA–SC (200.0%); Austin–Round Rock, TX (153.8%); Greensboro–High Point, NC (150.0%); Omaha–Council Bluffs, NE–IA (150.0%).

Other Considerations for Job Security: Physical therapist aides may face keen competition from the large pool of qualified individuals. Physical therapist aides with prior experience working in a physical therapy office or other health-care setting will have the best job opportunities. The increasing number of people who need therapy reflects, in part, the increasing elderly population, which is particularly vulnerable to chronic and debilitating conditions that require therapeutic services. These patients often need additional assistance in their treatment, making the roles of assistants and aides vital. Also, the large baby-boom generation is entering the prime age for heart attacks and strokes, further increasing the demand for cardiac and physical rehabilitation. Moreover, future medical developments should permit an increased percentage of trauma victims to survive, creating added demand for therapy services.

Under close supervision of a physical therapist or physical therapy assistant, perform only delegated, selected, or routine tasks in specific situations. These duties include preparing the patient and the treatment area. Clean and organize work area and disinfect equipment after treatment. Observe patients during treatment to compile and evaluate data on patients' responses and progress and report to physical therapist. Instruct, motivate, safeguard, and assist patients practicing exercises and functional activities under direction of medical staff. Secure patients into or onto therapy equipment. Transport patients to and from treatment areas, using wheelchairs or providing standing support. Confer with physical therapy staff or others to discuss and evaluate patient information for planning, modifying, and coordinating treatment. Record treatment given and equipment used. Perform clerical duties, such as taking inventory, ordering supplies, answering telephone, taking messages, and filling out forms. Maintain equipment and furniture to keep it in good working condition, including performing the assembly and disassembly of equipment and accessories. Administer active and passive manual therapeutic exercises; therapeutic massage; and heat, light, sound, water, or electrical modality treatments such as ultrasound. Change linens, such as bed sheets and pillowcases. Arrange treatment supplies to keep them in order. Assist patients to dress; undress; and put on and remove supportive devices, such as braces, splints, and slings. Measure patient's range of joint motion, body parts, and vital signs to determine effects of treatments or for patient evaluations. Train patients to use orthopedic braces, prostheses, or supportive devices. Fit patients for orthopedic braces, prostheses, or supportive devices, adjusting fit as needed. Participate in patient-care tasks, such as assisting with passing food trays, feeding residents, or bathing residents on bed rest. Administer traction to relieve neck and back pain, using intermittent and static traction equipment.

Personality Type: Social.

GOE—Interest Area: 08. Health Science. **Work Group:** 08.07. Medical Therapy. **Other Jobs in this Work Group:** Audiologists; Massage Therapists; Occupational Therapist Aides; Occupational Therapist Assistants; Occupational Therapists; Physical Therapist Assistants; Physical Therapists; Radiation Therapists; Recreational Therapists; Respiratory Therapists; Respiratory Therapy Technicians; Speech-Language Pathologists.

Skills: No data available.

Education and Training Program: Physical Therapist Assistant. **Related Knowledge/Courses:** Psychology; Medicine and Dentistry; Therapy and Counseling; Customer and Personal Service; Clerical Studies; Education and Training.

Work Environment: Indoors; disease or infections; standing; walking and running; using hands on objects, tools, or controls; repetitive motions.

Physical Therapist Assistants

* Education/Training Required: Associate degree
* Annual Earnings: $41,360
* Beginning Wage: $26,190
* Earnings Growth Potential: Very high
* Growth: 32.4%
* Annual Job Openings: 5,957
* Self-Employed: 0.2%
* Part-Time: 27.1%

Industries with Greatest Employment: Ambulatory Health Care Services; Hospitals, Public and Private; Nursing and Residential Care Facilities.

Highest-Growth Industries (Projected Growth for This Job): Ambulatory Health Care Services (36.4%); Amusement, Gambling, and Recreation Industries (33.3%); Social Assistance (32.9%); Hospitals, Public and Private (32.1%); Administrative and Support Services (26.6%); Nursing and Residential Care Facilities (23.7%); Management of Companies and Enterprises (15.5%).

Lowest-Growth Industries (Projected Growth for This Job): Educational Services, Public and Private (11.1%).

Fastest-Growing Metropolitan Areas (Recent Growth for This Job): Blacksburg–Christiansburg–Radford, VA (100.0%); Deltona–Daytona Beach–Ormond Beach, FL (87.5%); Erie, PA (71.4%); Springfield, MO (71.4%); Salt Lake City, UT (66.7%).

Other Considerations for Job Security: Opportunities are expected to be very good. Physical therapist aides with prior experience working in a physical therapy office or other health-care setting will have the best job opportunities. The increasing number of people who need therapy reflects, in part, the increasing elderly population.

Assist physical therapists in providing physical therapy treatments and procedures. May, in accordance with state laws, assist in the development of treatment plans, carry out routine functions, document treatment progress, and modify specific treatments in accordance with patient status and within the scope of treatment plans established by a physical therapist. Generally requires formal training. Instruct, motivate, safeguard, and assist patients as they practice exercises and functional activities. Confer with physical therapy staff or others to discuss and evaluate patient information for planning, modifying, and coordinating treatment. Administer active and passive manual therapeutic exercises; therapeutic massage; and heat, light, sound, water, and electrical modality treatments such as ultrasound. Observe patients during treatments to compile and evaluate data on patients' responses and progress and report to physical therapist. Measure patients' range of joint motion, body parts, and vital signs to determine effects of treatments or for patient evaluations. Secure patients into or onto therapy equipment. Fit patients for orthopedic braces, prostheses, and supportive devices such as crutches. Train patients in the use of orthopedic braces, prostheses, or supportive devices. Transport patients to and from treatment areas, lifting and transferring them according to positioning requirements. Monitor operation of equipment and record use of equipment and administration of treatment. Clean work area and check and store equipment after treatment. Assist patients to dress; undress; or put on and remove supportive devices such as braces, splints, and slings. Administer traction to relieve neck and back pain, using intermittent and static traction equipment. Perform clerical duties, such as taking inventory, ordering supplies, answering telephone, taking messages, and filling out forms. Prepare treatment areas and electrotherapy equipment for use by physiotherapists. Perform postural drainage, percussions, and vibrations and teach deep breathing exercises to treat respiratory conditions.

Personality Type: Social.

GOE—Interest Area: 08. Health Science. **Work Group:** 08.07. Medical Therapy. **Other Jobs in this Work Group:** Audiologists; Massage Therapists; Occupational Therapist Aides; Occupational Therapist Assistants; Occupational Therapists; Physical Therapist Aides; Physical Therapists; Radiation Therapists; Recreational Therapists; Respiratory Therapists; Respiratory Therapy Technicians; Speech-Language Pathologists.

Skills: Science; Social Perceptiveness; Service Orientation; Writing; Speaking; Time Management.

Education and Training Program: Physical Therapist Assistant. **Related Knowledge/Courses:** Therapy and Counseling; Psychology; Medicine and Dentistry; Biology; Sociology and Anthropology; Education and Training.

Work Environment: Indoors; disease or infections; standing; walking and running; using hands on objects, tools, or controls; bending or twisting the body.

Physical Therapists

* Education/Training Required: Master's degree
* Annual Earnings: $66,200
* Beginning Wage: $46,510
* Earnings Growth Potential: Very high
* Growth: 27.1%
* Annual Job Openings: 12,072
* Self-Employed: 8.4%
* Part-Time: 22.7%

Industries with Greatest Employment: Ambulatory Health Care Services; Hospitals, Public and Private; Nursing and Residential Care Facilities.

Highest-Growth Industries (Projected Growth for This Job): Social Assistance (39.7%); Ambulatory Health Care Services (37.2%); Amusement, Gambling, and Recreation Industries (33.0%);

Administrative and Support Services (26.6%); Nursing and Residential Care Facilities (23.8%); Hospitals, Public and Private (22.1%); Management of Companies and Enterprises (15.2%).

Lowest-Growth Industries (Projected Growth for This Job): Educational Services, Public and Private (7.5%).

Fastest-Growing Metropolitan Areas (Recent Growth for This Job): Naples–Marco Island, FL (233.3%); Prescott, AZ (166.7%); Augusta–Richmond County, GA–SC (78.9%); Rockford, IL (77.8%); Missoula, MT (76.9%).

Other Considerations for Job Security: Job opportunities will be good for licensed physical therapists in all settings. Opportunities should be particularly good in acute hospital, rehabilitation, and orthopedic settings, where the elderly are most often treated. Physical therapists with specialized knowledge of particular types of treatment also will have excellent job prospects. The increasing elderly population will drive growth in the demand for physical therapy services. The elderly population is particularly vulnerable to chronic and debilitating conditions that require therapeutic services. Also, the baby-boom generation is entering the prime age for heart attacks and strokes, increasing the demand for cardiac and physical rehabilitation. Moreover, increasing numbers of children will need physical therapy as technological advances save the lives of a larger proportion of newborns with severe birth defects.

Assess, plan, organize, and participate in rehabilitative programs that improve mobility, relieve pain, increase strength, and decrease or prevent deformity of patients suffering from disease or injury. Plan, prepare, and carry out individually designed programs of physical treatment to maintain, improve, or restore physical functioning; alleviate pain; and prevent physical dysfunction in patients. Perform and document an initial exam, evaluating data to identify problems and determine a diagnosis before intervention. Evaluate effects of treatment at various stages and adjust treatments to achieve maximum benefit. Administer manual exercises, massage, or traction to help relieve pain, increase patient strength, or decrease or prevent deformity or crippling. Instruct patient and family in treatment procedures to be continued at home. Confer with the patient, medical practitioners, and appropriate others to plan, implement, and assess the intervention program. Review physician's referral and patient's medical records to help determine diagnosis and physical therapy treatment required. Obtain patients' informed consent to proposed interventions. Record prognosis, treatment, response, and progress in patient's chart or enter information into computer. Discharge patient from physical therapy when goals or projected outcomes are attained and provide for appropriate follow-up care or referrals. Test and measure patient's strength, motor development and function, sensory perception, functional capacity, and respiratory and circulatory efficiency and record data. Identify and document goals, anticipated progress, and plans for re-evaluation. Provide information to the patient about the proposed intervention, its material risks and expected benefits, and any reasonable alternatives. Inform patients when diagnosis reveals findings outside physical therapy and refer to appropriate practitioners. Direct, supervise, assess, and communicate with supportive personnel. Administer treatment involving application of physical agents, using equipment, moist packs, ultraviolet and infrared lamps, and ultrasound machines. Teach physical therapy students as well as those in other health professions. Evaluate, fit, and adjust prosthetic and orthotic devices and recommend modification to orthotist. Provide educational information about physical therapy and physical therapists, injury prevention, ergonomics, and ways to promote health.

Personality Type: Social.

GOE—Interest Area: 08. Health Science. **Work Group:** 08.07. Medical Therapy. **Other Jobs in this Work Group:** Audiologists; Massage Therapists; Occupational Therapist Aides; Occupational Therapist Assistants; Occupational Therapists; Physical Therapist Aides; Physical Therapist Assistants; Radiation Therapists; Recreational Therapists; Respiratory Therapists; Respiratory Therapy Technicians; Speech-Language Pathologists.

Skills: Science; Reading Comprehension; Social Perceptiveness; Learning Strategies; Service Orientation; Instructing.

Education and Training Programs: Physical Therapy/Therapist; Kinesiotherapy/Kinesiotherapist. **Related Knowledge/Courses:** Therapy and Counseling; Medicine and Dentistry; Psychology; Biology; Sociology and Anthropology; Customer and Personal Service.

Work Environment: Indoors; contaminants; disease or infections; standing; walking and running; bending or twisting the body.

Physician Assistants

- ✸ Education/Training Required: Master's degree
- ✸ Annual Earnings: $74,980
- ✸ Beginning Wage: $43,100
- ✸ Earnings Growth Potential: Very high
- ✸ Growth: 27.0%
- ✸ Annual Job Openings: 7,147
- ✸ Self-Employed: 1.8%
- ✸ Part-Time: 15.6%

Industries with Greatest Employment: Ambulatory Health Care Services; Hospitals, Public and Private.

Highest-Growth Industries (Projected Growth for This Job): Ambulatory Health Care Services (36.5%); Administrative and Support Services (26.9%); Management of Companies and Enterprises (15.2%).

Lowest-Growth Industries (Projected Growth for This Job): Hospitals, Public and Private (10.7%); Educational Services, Public and Private (11.9%); Professional, Scientific, and Technical Services (13.4%).

Fastest-Growing Metropolitan Areas (Recent Growth for This Job): Modesto, CA (133.3%); Roanoke, VA (125.0%); Fresno, CA (120.0%); Madison, WI (111.1%); Nashville–Davidson–Murfreesboro, TN (93.3%).

Other Considerations for Job Security: Job opportunities for PAs should be good, particularly in rural and inner-city clinics because those settings have difficulty attracting physicians. In addition to job openings from employment growth, openings will result from the need to replace physician assistants who retire or leave the occupation permanently during the 2006 to 2016 decade. Opportunities will be best in states that allow PAs a wider scope of practice, such as allowing PAs to prescribe medications. Physicians and institutions are expected to employ more PAs to provide primary care and to assist with medical and surgical procedures because PAs are cost-effective and productive members of the health-care team. Physician assistants can relieve physicians of routine duties and procedures. Telemedicine—using technology to facilitate interactive consultations between physicians and physician assistants—also will expand the use of physician assistants.

Under the supervision of a physician, provide health-care services typically performed by a physician. Conduct complete physicals, provide treatment, and counsel patients. May, in some cases, prescribe medication. Must graduate from an accredited educational program for physician assistants. Examine patients to obtain information about their physical condition. Make tentative diagnoses and decisions about management and treatment of patients. Interpret diagnostic test results for deviations from normal. Obtain, compile, and record patient medical data, including health history, progress notes, and results of physical examination. Administer or order diagnostic tests, such as X-ray, electrocardiogram, and laboratory tests. Prescribe therapy or medication with physician approval. Perform therapeutic procedures, such as injections, immunizations, suturing and wound care, and infection management. Instruct and counsel patients about prescribed therapeutic regimens, normal growth and development, family planning, emotional problems of daily living, and health maintenance. Provide physicians with assistance during surgery or complicated medical procedures. Supervise and coordinate activities of technicians and technical assistants. Visit and observe patients on hospital rounds or house calls, updating charts, ordering therapy, and reporting back to physician. Order medical and laboratory supplies and equipment.

Personality Type: Investigative.

GOE—Interest Area: 08. Health Science. **Work Group:** 08.02. Medicine and Surgery. **Other Jobs in this Work Group:** Anesthesiologists; Family and General Practitioners; Internists, General; Medical Assistants; Medical Transcriptionists; Obstetricians and Gynecologists; Pediatricians, General; Pharmacists; Pharmacy Aides; Pharmacy Technicians; Psychiatrists; Registered Nurses; Surgeons; Surgical Technologists.

Skills: Science; Social Perceptiveness; Reading Comprehension; Critical Thinking; Active Listening; Writing.

Education and Training Program: Physician Assistant. **Related Knowledge/Courses:** Medicine and Dentistry; Biology; Therapy and Counseling; Psychology; Chemistry; Customer and Personal Service.

Work Environment: Indoors; disease or infections; standing.

Physicians and Surgeons

See *Anesthesiologists, Family and General Practitioners; Internists, General; Obstetricians and Gynecologists; Pediatricians, General; Psychiatrists; and Surgeons, described separately.*

Physics Teachers, Postsecondary

- ❋ Education/Training Required: Doctoral degree
- ❋ Annual Earnings: $68,170
- ❋ Beginning Wage: $39,580
- ❋ Earnings Growth Potential: Very high
- ❋ Growth: 22.9%
- ❋ Annual Job Openings: 237,478
- ❋ Self-Employed: 0.4%
- ❋ Part-Time: 27.8%

Our sources did not provide separate job openings data for this occupation. The job openings listed here are shared with 35 other postsecondary teaching occupations. For a complete list, see the beginning of this section.

Industries with Greatest Employment: Educational Services, Public and Private.

Highest-Growth Industries (Projected Growth for This Job): Administrative and Support Services (48.3%); Amusement, Gambling, and Recreation Industries (45.3%); Social Assistance (38.6%); Support Activities for Transportation (32.8%); Religious, Grantmaking, Civic, Professional, and Similar Organizations (29.9%); Professional, Scientific, and Technical Services (28.8%); Management of Companies and Enterprises (26.8%); Educational Services, Public and Private (22.9%); Hospitals, Public and Private (21.4%); Personal and Laundry Services (21.0%).

Lowest-Growth Industries (Projected Growth for This Job): Other Information Services (7.4%); Sporting Goods, Hobby, Book, and Music Stores (13.3%); Performing Arts, Spectator Sports, and Related Industries (13.4%); Insurance Carriers and Related Activities (13.9%).

Fastest-Growing Metropolitan Areas (Recent Growth for This Job): Virginia Beach–Norfolk–Newport News, VA–NC (12.5%); Portland–Vancouver–Beaverton, OR–WA (12.5%).

Other Considerations for Job Security: Retirements of current postsecondary teachers should create numerous openings for all types of postsecondary teachers, so job opportunities are generally expected to be very good. Because students attend postsecondary institutions to prepare themselves for careers, the best job prospects for postsecondary teachers are likely to be in rapidly growing fields that offer many nonacademic career options. Physics is a key part of the curriculum for many technician majors and some health-care majors. Community colleges and other institutions offering career and technical education have been among the most rapidly growing and are expected to offer some of the best opportunities for postsecondary teachers.

Teach courses pertaining to the laws of matter and energy. Includes both teachers primarily engaged in teaching and those who do both teaching and research. Evaluate and grade students' classwork, laboratory work, assignments, and papers. Prepare and deliver lectures to undergraduate and/or graduate students on topics such as quantum mechanics, particle physics, and optics. Compile, administer, and grade examinations or assign this work to others. Maintain student attendance records, grades, and other required records. Supervise students' laboratory work. Prepare course materials such as syllabi, homework assignments, and handouts. Maintain regularly scheduled office hours to advise and assist students. Supervise undergraduate and/or graduate teaching, internships, and research work. Keep abreast of developments in their field by reading current literature, talking with colleagues, and participating in professional conferences. Plan, evaluate, and revise curricula, course content, course materials, and methods of instruction. Initiate, facilitate, and moderate classroom discussions. Conduct research in a particular field of knowledge and publish findings in professional journals, books, and/or electronic media. Advise students on academic and vocational curricula and on career issues. Select and obtain materials and supplies such as textbooks and laboratory equipment. Collaborate with colleagues to address teaching and research issues. Participate in student recruitment, registration, and placement activities. Serve on academic or administrative committees that deal with institutional policies, departmental matters, and academic issues. Write grant proposals to procure external research funding. Perform administrative duties such as serving as department head. Act as advisers to student organizations. Provide professional consulting services to government and/or industry. Compile bibliographies of specialized materials for outside reading assignments. Participate in campus and community events.

Personality Type: Investigative.

GOE—Interest Area: 05. Education and Training. **Work Group:** 05.03. Postsecondary and Adult

Teaching and Instructing. **Other Jobs in this Work Group:** Adult Literacy, Remedial Education, and GED Teachers and Instructors; Agricultural Sciences Teachers, Postsecondary; Anthropology and Archeology Teachers, Postsecondary; Architecture Teachers, Postsecondary; Area, Ethnic, and Cultural Studies Teachers, Postsecondary; Art, Drama, and Music Teachers, Postsecondary; Atmospheric, Earth, Marine, and Space Sciences Teachers, Postsecondary; Biological Science Teachers, Postsecondary; Business Teachers, Postsecondary; Chemistry Teachers, Postsecondary; Communications Teachers, Postsecondary; Computer Science Teachers, Postsecondary; Criminal Justice and Law Enforcement Teachers, Postsecondary; Economics Teachers, Postsecondary; Education Teachers, Postsecondary; Engineering Teachers, Postsecondary; English Language and Literature Teachers, Postsecondary; Environmental Science Teachers, Postsecondary; Farm and Home Management Advisors; Foreign Language and Literature Teachers, Postsecondary; Forestry and Conservation Science Teachers, Postsecondary; Geography Teachers, Postsecondary; Graduate Teaching Assistants; Health Specialties Teachers, Postsecondary; History Teachers, Postsecondary; Home Economics Teachers, Postsecondary; Law Teachers, Postsecondary; Library Science Teachers, Postsecondary; Mathematical Science Teachers, Postsecondary; Nursing Instructors and Teachers, Postsecondary; Philosophy and Religion Teachers, Postsecondary; Political Science Teachers, Postsecondary; Psychology Teachers, Postsecondary; Recreation and Fitness Studies Teachers, Postsecondary; Self-Enrichment Education Teachers; Social Work Teachers, Postsecondary; Sociology Teachers, Postsecondary; Vocational Education Teachers, Postsecondary.

Skills: Science; Programming; Mathematics; Instructing; Writing; Reading Comprehension.

Education and Training Programs: Physics, General; Atomic/Molecular Physics; Elementary Particle Physics; Plasma and High-Temperature Physics; Nuclear Physics; Optics/Optical Sciences; Solid State and Low-Temperature Physics; Acoustics; Theoretical and Mathematical Physics; Physics, Other. **Related Knowledge/Courses:** Physics; Mathematics; Chemistry; Engineering and Technology; Education and Training; Computers and Electronics.

Work Environment: Indoors; sitting.

Podiatrists

- Education/Training Required: First professional degree
- Annual Earnings: $108,220
- Beginning Wage: $44,500
- Earnings Growth Potential: Medium
- Growth: 9.5%
- Annual Job Openings: 648
- Self-Employed: 23.9%
- Part-Time: 23.6%

Industries with Greatest Employment: Ambulatory Health Care Services.

Highest-Growth Industries (Projected Growth for This Job): None met the criteria.

Lowest-Growth Industries (Projected Growth for This Job): Ambulatory Health Care Services (4.4%); Hospitals, Public and Private (9.5%).

Fastest-Growing Metropolitan Areas (Recent Growth for This Job): Atlanta–Sandy Springs–Marietta, GA (375.0%); Riverside–San Bernardino–Ontario, CA (75.0%); Chicago–Naperville–Joliet, IL–IN–WI (73.7%); Los Angeles–Long Beach–Santa Ana, CA (50.0%); Detroit–Warren–Livonia, MI (43.8%).

Other Considerations for Job Security: Although the occupation is small and most podiatrists continue to practice until retirement, job opportunities should be good for entry-level graduates of accredited podiatric medicine programs. Job growth and replacement needs should create enough job openings for the supply of new podiatric medicine graduates. Opportunities will be better for board-certified podiatrists because many managed-care organizations require board certification. Newly trained podiatrists will find more opportunities in group medical practices, clinics, and health networks than in traditional solo practices. Establishing a practice will be most difficult in the areas surrounding colleges of podiatric medicine, where podiatrists concentrate.

Diagnose and treat diseases and deformities of the human foot. Treat bone, muscle, and joint disorders affecting the feet. Diagnose diseases and deformities of the foot, using medical histories, physical examinations, X rays, and laboratory test results. Prescribe medications, corrective devices, physical therapy, or surgery. Treat conditions such as corns, calluses, ingrown nails, tumors, shortened tendons, bunions, cysts, and abscesses by surgical methods. Advise patients about treatments and foot-care techniques necessary for prevention of future problems. Refer patients to physicians when symptoms indicative of systemic disorders, such as arthritis or diabetes, are observed in feet and legs. Correct deformities by means of plaster casts and strapping. Make and fit prosthetic appliances. Perform administrative duties such as hiring employees, ordering supplies, and keeping records. Educate the public about the benefits of foot care through techniques such as speaking engagements, advertising, and other forums. Treat deformities, using mechanical methods such as whirlpool or paraffin baths and electrical methods such as shortwave and low-voltage currents.

Personality Type: Social.

GOE—Interest Area: 08. Health Science. **Work Group:** 08.04. Health Specialties. **Other Jobs in this Work Group:** Chiropractors; Optometrists.

Skills: Science; Complex Problem Solving; Active Listening; Management of Financial Resources; Reading Comprehension; Equipment Selection.

Education and Training Program: Podiatric Medicine/Podiatry (DPM). **Related Knowledge/Courses:** Medicine and Dentistry; Biology; Therapy and Counseling; Sales and Marketing; Chemistry; Psychology.

Work Environment: Indoors; contaminants; disease or infections; sitting; using hands on objects, tools, or controls; repetitive motions.

Police and Sheriff's Patrol Officers

See *Police Patrol Officers and Sheriffs and Deputy Sheriffs, described separately.*

Police Detectives

- ❋ Education/Training Required: Work experience in a related occupation
- ❋ Annual Earnings: $58,260
- ❋ Beginning Wage: $34,480
- ❋ Earnings Growth Potential: Very high
- ❋ Growth: 17.3%
- ❋ Annual Job Openings: 14,746
- ❋ Self-Employed: 0.3%
- ❋ Part-Time: 2.2%

Our sources did not provide separate job openings data for this occupation. The job openings listed here are shared with Criminal Investigators and Special Agents; Immigration and Customs Inspectors; and Police Identification and Records Officers.

Industries with Greatest Employment: Educational Services, Public and Private.

Highest-Growth Industries (Projected Growth for This Job): None met the criteria.

Lowest-Growth Industries (Projected Growth for This Job): Educational Services, Public and Private (11.9%).

Fastest-Growing Metropolitan Areas (Recent Growth for This Job): Brownsville–Harlingen, TX (366.7%); Las Cruces, NM (350.0%); Bellingham, WA (183.3%); Jackson, MS (172.7%); Tucson, AZ (121.3%).

Other Considerations for Job Security: Overall, opportunities in local police departments will be excellent for individuals who meet the psychological, personal, and physical qualifications. There will be more competition for jobs in federal and state law-enforcement agencies than for jobs in local agencies. Less competition for jobs will occur in departments that offer relatively low salaries or those in urban communities where the crime rate is relatively high. Applicants with military experience or college training in police science will have the best opportunities in local and state departments. Applicants with a bachelor's degree and several years of law-enforcement or military experience, especially investigative experience, will have the best opportunities in federal agencies. The level of government spending determines the level of employment for police and detectives, but layoffs are rare because retirements enable most staffing cuts to be handled through attrition.

Conduct investigations to prevent crimes or solve criminal cases. Examine crime scenes to obtain clues and evidence, such as loose hairs, fibers, clothing, or weapons. Secure deceased body and obtain evidence from it, preventing bystanders from tampering with it before medical examiner's arrival. Obtain evidence from suspects. Provide testimony as a witness in court. Analyze completed police reports to determine what additional information and investigative work is needed. Prepare charges, responses to charges, or information for court cases according to formalized procedures. Note, mark, and photograph location of objects found, such as footprints, tire tracks, bullets, and bloodstains, and take measurements of the scene. Obtain facts or statements from complainants, witnesses, and accused persons and record interviews, using recording device. Obtain summary of incident from officer in charge at crime scene, taking care to avoid disturbing evidence. Examine records and governmental agency files to find identifying data about suspects. Prepare and serve search and arrest warrants. Block or rope off scene and check perimeter to ensure that entire scene is secured. Summon medical help for injured individuals and alert medical personnel to take statements from them. Provide information to lab personnel concerning the source of an item of evidence and tests to be performed. Monitor conditions of unconscious victims so that arrangements can be made to take statements if consciousness is regained. Secure persons at scene, keeping witnesses from conversing or leaving the scene before investigators arrive. Preserve, process, and analyze items of evidence obtained from crime scenes and suspects, placing them in proper containers and destroying evidence no longer needed. Record progress of investigation, maintain informational files on suspects, and submit reports to commanding officer or magistrate to authorize warrants. Organize scene search, assigning specific tasks and areas of search to individual officers and obtaining adequate lighting as necessary. Take photographs from all angles of relevant parts of a crime scene, including entrance and exit routes and streets and intersections.

Personality Type: Enterprising.

GOE—Interest Area: 12. Law and Public Safety. **Work Group:** 12.04. Law Enforcement and Public Safety. **Other Jobs in this Work Group:** Bailiffs; Correctional Officers and Jailers; Criminal Investigators and Special Agents; Detectives and Criminal Investigators; Fire Investigators; Forensic Science Technicians; Parking Enforcement Workers; Police and Sheriff's Patrol Officers; Police Identification and Records Officers; Police Patrol Officers; Sheriffs and Deputy Sheriffs; Transit and Railroad Police.

Skills: Persuasion; Negotiation; Social Perceptiveness; Speaking; Coordination; Active Listening.

Education and Training Programs: Criminal Justice/Police Science; Criminalistics and Criminal Science. **Related Knowledge/Courses:** Public Safety and Security; Law and Government; Psychology; Therapy and Counseling; Philosophy and Theology; Sociology and Anthropology.

Work Environment: More often indoors than outdoors; very hot or cold; sitting.

P

Police Identification and Records Officers

※ Education/Training Required: Work experience in a related occupation
※ Annual Earnings: $58,260
※ Beginning Wage: $34,480
※ Earnings Growth Potential: Very high
※ Growth: 17.3%
※ Annual Job Openings: 14,746
※ Self-Employed: 0.3%
※ Part-Time: 2.2%

Our sources did not provide separate job openings data for this occupation. The job openings listed here are shared with Criminal Investigators and Special Agents; Immigration and Customs Inspectors; and Police Detectives.

Industries with Greatest Employment: Educational Services, Public and Private.

Highest-Growth Industries (Projected Growth for This Job): None met the criteria.

Lowest-Growth Industries (Projected Growth for This Job): Educational Services, Public and Private (11.9%).

Fastest-Growing Metropolitan Areas (Recent Growth for This Job): Brownsville–Harlingen, TX (366.7%); Las Cruces, NM (350.0%); Bellingham, WA (183.3%); Jackson, MS (172.7%); Tucson, AZ (121.3%).

Other Considerations for Job Security: Overall, opportunities in local police departments will be excellent for individuals who meet the psychological, personal, and physical qualifications. There will be more competition for jobs in federal and state law-enforcement agencies than for jobs in local agencies. Less competition for jobs will occur in departments that offer relatively low salaries or those in urban communities where the crime rate is relatively high. Applicants with military experience or college training in police science will have the best opportunities in local and state departments. Applicants with a bachelor's degree and several years of law-enforcement or military experience, especially investigative experience, will have the best opportunities in federal agencies. The level of government spending determines the level of employment for police and detectives, but layoffs are rare because retirements enable most staffing cuts to be handled through attrition.

Collect evidence at crime scene, classify and identify fingerprints, and photograph evidence for use in criminal and civil cases. Photograph crime or accident scenes for evidence records. Analyze and process evidence at crime scenes and in the laboratory, wearing protective equipment and using powders and chemicals. Look for trace evidence, such as fingerprints, hairs, fibers, or shoe impressions, using alternative light sources when necessary. Dust selected areas of crime scene and lift latent fingerprints, adhering to proper preservation procedures. Testify in court and present evidence. Package, store, and retrieve evidence. Serve as technical advisor and coordinate with other law-enforcement workers to exchange information on crime scene collection activities. Perform emergency work during off hours. Submit evidence to supervisors. Process film and prints from crime or accident scenes. Identify, classify, and file fingerprints, using systems such as the Henry Classification system.

Personality Type: Conventional.

GOE—Interest Area: 12. Law and Public Safety. **Work Group:** 12.04. Law Enforcement and Public Safety. **Other Jobs in this Work Group:** Bailiffs; Correctional Officers and Jailers; Criminal Investigators and Special Agents; Detectives and Criminal Investigators; Fire Investigators; Forensic Science Technicians; Parking Enforcement Workers; Police and Sheriff's Patrol Officers; Police Detectives; Police Patrol Officers; Sheriffs and Deputy Sheriffs; Transit and Railroad Police.

Skills: Persuasion; Judgment and Decision Making; Negotiation; Service Orientation; Social Perceptiveness; Critical Thinking.

Education and Training Programs: Criminal Justice/Police Science; Criminalistics and Criminal Science. **Related Knowledge/Courses:** Law and Government; Public Safety and Security; Telecommunications; Customer and Personal Service; Psychology; Computers and Electronics.

Work Environment: More often outdoors than indoors; noisy; very hot or cold; contaminants; using hands on objects, tools, or controls.

Police Patrol Officers

- ❋ Education/Training Required: Long-term on-the-job training
- ❋ Annual Earnings: $47,460
- ❋ Beginning Wage: $27,310
- ❋ Earnings Growth Potential: Very high
- ❋ Growth: 10.8%
- ❋ Annual Job Openings: 37,842
- ❋ Self-Employed: 0.0%
- ❋ Part-Time: 1.1%

Our sources did not provide separate job openings data for this occupation. The job openings listed here are shared with Sheriffs and Deputy Sheriffs.

Industries with Greatest Employment: Educational Services, Public and Private; Hospitals, Public and Private.

Highest-Growth Industries (Projected Growth for This Job): None met the criteria.

Lowest-Growth Industries (Projected Growth for This Job): Hospitals, Public and Private (11.3%); Educational Services, Public and Private (11.7%).

Fastest-Growing Metropolitan Areas (Recent Growth for This Job): Beaumont–Port Arthur, TX (95.7%); Lafayette, IN (92.3%); Houma–Bayou Cane–Thibodaux, LA (89.5%); Waterloo–Cedar Falls, IA (69.2%); Kennewick–Richland–Pasco, WA (57.1%).

Other Considerations for Job Security: Overall, opportunities in local police departments will be excellent for individuals who meet the psychological, personal, and physical qualifications. There will be more competition for jobs in federal and state law-enforcement agencies than for jobs in local agencies. Less competition for jobs will occur in departments that offer relatively low salaries or those in urban communities where the crime rate is relatively high. Applicants with military experience or college training in police science will have the best opportunities in local and state departments. Applicants with a bachelor's degree and several years of law-enforcement or military experience, especially investigative experience, will have the best opportunities in federal agencies. The level of government spending determines the level of employment for police and detectives, but layoffs are rare because retirements enable most staffing cuts to be handled through attrition.

Patrol assigned area to enforce laws and ordinances, regulate traffic, control crowds, prevent crime, and arrest violators. Provide for public safety by maintaining order, responding to emergencies, protecting people and property, enforcing motor vehicle and criminal laws, and promoting good community relations. Identify, pursue, and arrest suspects and perpetrators of criminal acts. Record facts to prepare reports that document incidents and activities. Review facts of incidents to determine whether criminal act or statute violations were involved. Render aid to accident victims and other persons requiring first aid for physical injuries. Testify in court to present evidence or act as witness in traffic and criminal cases. Evaluate complaint and emergency-request information to determine response requirements. Patrol specific area on foot, horseback, or motorized conveyance, responding promptly to calls for assistance. Monitor, note, report, and investigate suspicious persons and situations, safety hazards, and unusual or illegal activity in patrol area. Investigate traffic accidents and other accidents to determine causes and to determine whether a crime has been committed. Photograph or draw diagrams of crime or accident scenes and interview principals and eyewitnesses. Monitor traffic to ensure that motorists observe traffic regulations and exhibit safe driving procedures. Relay complaint and emergency-request information to appropriate agency dispatchers. Issue citations or warnings to violators of motor vehicle ordinances. Direct traffic flow and reroute traffic in case of emergencies. Inform citizens of community services and recommend options to facilitate longer-term problem resolution. Provide road information to assist motorists. Process detainees and prepare and maintain records of their bookings and their status during booking and pre-trial process. Inspect public establishments to ensure compliance with rules and regulations. Act as official escorts, such as when leading funeral processions or fire fighters.

Personality Type: Social.

GOE—Interest Area: 12. Law and Public Safety. **Work Group:** 12.04. Law Enforcement and Public Safety. **Other Jobs in this Work Group:** Bailiffs; Correctional Officers and Jailers; Criminal Investigators and Special Agents; Detectives and Criminal Investigators; Fire Investigators; Forensic Science Technicians; Parking Enforcement Workers; Police and Sheriff's Patrol Officers; Police Detectives; Police Identification and Records Officers; Sheriffs and Deputy Sheriffs; Transit and Railroad Police.

Skills: Negotiation; Persuasion; Judgment and Decision Making; Social Perceptiveness; Service Orientation; Complex Problem Solving.

Education and Training Programs: Criminal Justice/Police Science; Criminalistics and Criminal Science. **Related Knowledge/Courses:** Public Safety and Security; Law and Government; Psychology; Therapy and Counseling; Telecommunications; Customer and Personal Service.

Work Environment: Outdoors; noisy; very hot or cold; contaminants; hazardous equipment; using hands on objects, tools, or controls.

Police, Fire, and Ambulance Dispatchers

* Education/Training Required: Moderate-term on-the-job training
* Annual Earnings: $31,470
* Beginning Wage: $20,010
* Earnings Growth Potential: Very high
* Growth: 13.6%
* Annual Job Openings: 17,628
* Self-Employed: 1.2%
* Part-Time: 6.3%

Industries with Greatest Employment: Ambulatory Health Care Services; Educational Services, Public and Private; Hospitals, Public and Private; Administrative and Support Services.

Highest-Growth Industries (Projected Growth for This Job): Professional, Scientific, and Technical Services (35.6%); Ambulatory Health Care Services (29.7%); Waste Management and Remediation Services (26.2%); Administrative and Support Services (21.7%).

Lowest-Growth Industries (Projected Growth for This Job): Hospitals, Public and Private (11.5%); Educational Services, Public and Private (12.4%).

Fastest-Growing Metropolitan Areas (Recent Growth for This Job): Medford, OR (100.0%); Merced, CA (100.0%); Seattle–Tacoma–Bellevue, WA (97.4%); Houston–Sugar Land–Baytown, TX (88.7%); St. Joseph, MO–KS (50.0%).

Other Considerations for Job Security: In addition to openings due to growth, job openings will result from the need to replace workers who transfer to other occupations or leave the labor force. Many districts are consolidating their communications centers into a shared area-wide facility. As the equipment becomes more complex, individuals with computer skills and experience will have greater opportunities for employment as public-safety dispatchers. Public-safety dispatchers are unlikely to be affected by economic downturns.

Receive complaints from the public concerning crimes and police emergencies. Broadcast orders to police patrol units in vicinity of complaint to investigate. Operate radio, telephone, or computer equipment to receive reports of fires and medical emergencies and relay information or orders to proper officials. Determine response requirements and relative priorities of situations and dispatch units in accordance with established procedures. Record details of calls, dispatches, and messages. Question callers to determine their locations and the nature of their problems to determine type of response needed. Enter, update, and retrieve information from teletype networks and computerized data systems regarding such things as wanted persons, stolen property, vehicle registration, and stolen vehicles. Scan status charts and computer screens and contact emergency response field units to determine units available for dispatch. Relay information and messages to and from emergency sites, to law-enforcement agencies, and to all other individuals or groups requiring notification. Receive incoming telephone or alarm system calls regarding emergency and non-emergency police and fire service, emergency ambulance service, information, and after-hours calls for departments within a city. Maintain access to, and security of, highly sensitive materials. Observe alarm registers and scan maps to determine whether a specific emergency is in the dispatch service area. Maintain files of information relating to emergency calls such as personnel rosters and emergency call-out and pager files. Monitor various radio frequencies such as those used by public works departments, school security, and civil defense to keep apprised of developing situations. Learn material and pass required tests for certification. Read and effectively interpret small-scale maps and information from a computer screen to determine locations and provide directions. Answer routine inquiries and refer calls not requiring dispatches to appropriate departments and agencies. Provide emergency medical instructions to callers. Monitor alarm systems to detect emergencies such as fires and illegal entry into establishments. Test and adjust communication and alarm systems and report malfunctions to maintenance units. Operate and maintain mobile dispatch vehicles and equipment.

Personality Type: Social.

GOE—Interest Area: 03. Arts and Communication. **Work Group:** 03.10. Communications Technology. **Other Jobs in this Work Group:** Air Traffic Controllers; Airfield Operations Specialists; Dispatchers, Except Police, Fire, and Ambulance; Telephone Operators.

Skills: No data available.

Related Knowledge/Courses: Telecommunications; Customer and Personal Service; Clerical Studies; Public Safety and Security; Law and Government; Computers and Electronics.

Work Environment: Indoors; noisy; sitting; using hands on objects, tools, or controls; repetitive motions.

Political Science Teachers, Postsecondary

- Education/Training Required: Doctoral degree
- Annual Earnings: $61,820
- Beginning Wage: $35,730
- Earnings Growth Potential: Very high
- Growth: 22.9%
- Annual Job Openings: 237,478
- Self-Employed: 0.4%
- Part-Time: 27.8%

Our sources did not provide separate job openings data for this occupation. The job openings listed here are shared with 35 other postsecondary teaching occupations. For a complete list, see the beginning of this section.

Industries with Greatest Employment: Educational Services, Public and Private.

Highest-Growth Industries (Projected Growth for This Job): Administrative and Support Services (48.3%); Amusement, Gambling, and Recreation

Industries (45.3%); Social Assistance (38.6%); Support Activities for Transportation (32.8%); Religious, Grantmaking, Civic, Professional, and Similar Organizations (29.9%); Professional, Scientific, and Technical Services (28.8%); Management of Companies and Enterprises (26.8%); Educational Services, Public and Private (22.9%); Hospitals, Public and Private (21.4%); Personal and Laundry Services (21.0%).

Lowest-Growth Industries (Projected Growth for This Job): Other Information Services (7.4%); Sporting Goods, Hobby, Book, and Music Stores (13.3%); Performing Arts, Spectator Sports, and Related Industries (13.4%); Insurance Carriers and Related Activities (13.9%).

Fastest-Growing Metropolitan Areas (Recent Growth for This Job): Kansas City, MO–KS (20.0%); San Antonio, TX (17.6%); Miami–Fort Lauderdale–Miami Beach, FL (16.7%); Honolulu, HI (16.7%); Virginia Beach–Norfolk–Newport News, VA–NC (16.7%).

Other Considerations for Job Security: Retirements of current postsecondary teachers should create numerous openings for all types of postsecondary teachers, so job opportunities are generally expected to be very good. However, because students attend postsecondary institutions to prepare themselves for careers, the best job prospects for postsecondary teachers are likely to be in rapidly growing fields that offer many nonacademic career options—unlike political science. Community colleges and other institutions offering career and technical education have been among the most rapidly growing and are expected to offer some of the best opportunities for postsecondary teachers.

Teach courses in political science, international affairs, and international relations. Initiate, facilitate, and moderate classroom discussions. Prepare and deliver lectures to undergraduate or graduate students on topics such as classical political thought, international relations, and democracy and citizenship. Evaluate and grade students' classwork, assignments, and papers. Compile, administer, and grade examinations or assign this work to others. Prepare course materials such as syllabi, homework assignments, and handouts. Keep abreast of developments in their field by reading current literature, talking with colleagues, and participating in professional conferences. Plan, evaluate, and revise curricula, course content, course materials, and methods of instruction. Maintain student attendance records, grades, and other required records. Maintain regularly scheduled office hours to advise and assist students. Advise students on academic and vocational curricula and on career issues. Select and obtain materials and supplies such as textbooks. Conduct research in a particular field of knowledge and publish findings in professional journals, books, and electronic media. Supervise undergraduate and graduate teaching, internships, and research work. Collaborate with colleagues to address teaching and research issues. Serve on academic or administrative committees that deal with institutional policies, departmental matters, and academic issues. Participate in student recruitment, registration, and placement activities. Participate in campus and community events. Compile bibliographies of specialized materials for outside reading assignments. Act as advisers to student organizations. Perform administrative duties such as serving as department head. Write grant proposals to procure external research funding. Provide professional consulting services to government and industry.

Personality Type: Social.

GOE—Interest Area: 05. Education and Training. **Work Group:** 05.03. Postsecondary and Adult Teaching and Instructing. **Other Jobs in this Work Group:** Adult Literacy, Remedial Education, and GED Teachers and Instructors; Agricultural Sciences Teachers, Postsecondary; Anthropology and Archeology Teachers, Postsecondary; Architecture Teachers, Postsecondary; Area, Ethnic, and Cultural Studies Teachers, Postsecondary; Art, Drama, and Music Teachers, Postsecondary; Atmospheric, Earth, Marine, and Space Sciences Teachers, Postsecondary; Biological Science Teachers, Postsecondary; Business Teachers, Postsecondary; Chemistry Teachers, Postsecondary; Communications Teachers,

Postsecondary; Computer Science Teachers, Postsecondary; Criminal Justice and Law Enforcement Teachers, Postsecondary; Economics Teachers, Postsecondary; Education Teachers, Postsecondary; Engineering Teachers, Postsecondary; English Language and Literature Teachers, Postsecondary; Environmental Science Teachers, Postsecondary; Farm and Home Management Advisors; Foreign Language and Literature Teachers, Postsecondary; Forestry and Conservation Science Teachers, Postsecondary; Geography Teachers, Postsecondary; Graduate Teaching Assistants; Health Specialties Teachers, Postsecondary; History Teachers, Postsecondary; Home Economics Teachers, Postsecondary; Law Teachers, Postsecondary; Library Science Teachers, Postsecondary; Mathematical Science Teachers, Postsecondary; Nursing Instructors and Teachers, Postsecondary; Philosophy and Religion Teachers, Postsecondary; Physics Teachers, Postsecondary; Psychology Teachers, Postsecondary; Recreation and Fitness Studies Teachers, Postsecondary; Self-Enrichment Education Teachers; Social Work Teachers, Postsecondary; Sociology Teachers, Postsecondary; Vocational Education Teachers, Postsecondary.

Skills: Writing; Instructing; Persuasion; Reading Comprehension; Learning Strategies; Critical Thinking.

Education and Training Programs: Social Science Teacher Education; Political Science and Government, General; American Government and Politics (United States); Political Science and Government, Other. **Related Knowledge/Courses:** History and Archeology; Philosophy and Theology; Sociology and Anthropology; Geography; Law and Government; English Language.

Work Environment: Indoors; sitting.

Political Scientists

* Education/Training Required: Master's degree
* Annual Earnings: $90,140
* Beginning Wage: $36,730
* Earnings Growth Potential: Medium
* Growth: 5.3%
* Annual Job Openings: 318
* Self-Employed: 7.5%
* Part-Time: 20.1%

Industries with Greatest Employment: Professional, Scientific, and Technical Services; Religious, Grantmaking, Civic, Professional, and Similar Organizations; Educational Services, Public and Private.

Highest-Growth Industries (Projected Growth for This Job): Professional, Scientific, and Technical Services (21.0%); Religious, Grantmaking, Civic, Professional, and Similar Organizations (20.0%).

Lowest-Growth Industries (Projected Growth for This Job): Educational Services, Public and Private (11.7%).

Fastest-Growing Metropolitan Areas (Recent Growth for This Job): Seattle–Tacoma–Bellevue, WA (14.3%).

Other Considerations for Job Security: Political scientists will find jobs mainly in policy or research. Demand for political science research is growing because of increasing interest about politics and foreign affairs, including social and environmental policy issues and immigration. Political scientists will use their knowledge of political institutions to further the interests of nonprofit, political lobbying, and social organizations. Those with higher educational attainment will have the best prospects. There will be keen competition for tenured college-teaching positions.

Study the origin, development, and operation of political systems. Research a wide range of subjects, such as relations between the United States and foreign countries, the beliefs and institutions

of foreign nations, or the politics of small towns or a major metropolis. May study topics such as public opinion, political decision making, and ideology. May analyze the structure and operation of governments, as well as various political entities. May conduct public opinion surveys, analyze election results, or analyze public documents. Teach political science. Disseminate research results through academic publications, written reports, or public presentations. Identify issues for research and analysis. Develop and test theories, using information from interviews, newspapers, periodicals, case law, historical papers, polls, and/or statistical sources. Maintain current knowledge of government policy decisions. Collect, analyze, and interpret data such as election results and public opinion surveys; report on findings, recommendations, and conclusions. Interpret and analyze policies; public issues; legislation; and the operations of governments, businesses, and organizations. Evaluate programs and policies and make related recommendations to institutions and organizations. Write drafts of legislative proposals and prepare speeches, correspondence, and policy papers for governmental use. Forecast political, economic, and social trends. Consult with and advise government officials, civic bodies, research agencies, the media, political parties, and others concerned with political issues. Provide media commentary and/or criticism related to public policy and political issues and events.

Personality Type: Investigative.

GOE—Interest Area: 15. Scientific Research, Engineering, and Mathematics. **Work Group:** 15.04. Social Sciences. **Other Jobs in this Work Group:** Anthropologists; Anthropologists and Archeologists; Archeologists; Economists; Historians; Industrial-Organizational Psychologists; School Psychologists; Sociologists.

Skills: Writing; Reading Comprehension; Critical Thinking; Speaking; Active Learning; Instructing.

Education and Training Programs: International/Global Studies; Political Science and Government, General; American Government and Politics (United States); Canadian Government and Politics; Political

Science and Government, Other. **Related Knowledge/Courses:** History and Archeology; Law and Government; Philosophy and Theology; Sociology and Anthropology; Foreign Language; Geography.

Work Environment: Indoors; sitting.

Postal Service Clerks

- ❋ Education/Training Required: Short-term on-the-job training
- ❋ Annual Earnings: $44,800
- ❋ Beginning Wage: $38,980
- ❋ Earnings Growth Potential: Very high
- ❋ Growth: 1.2%
- ❋ Annual Job Openings: 3,703
- ❋ Self-Employed: 0.0%
- ❋ Part-Time: 4.2%

Industries with Greatest Employment: Postal Service.

Highest-Growth Industries (Projected Growth for This Job): None met the criteria.

Lowest-Growth Industries (Projected Growth for This Job): None met the criteria.

Fastest-Growing Metropolitan Areas (Recent Growth for This Job): Wilmington, NC (71.4%); Columbus, GA–AL (66.7%); Las Cruces, NM (66.7%); Bremerton–Silverdale, WA (50.0%); Lubbock, TX (50.0%).

Other Considerations for Job Security: Those seeking postal service jobs can expect to encounter keen competition. The number of applicants usually exceeds the number of job openings because of the occupation's low entry requirements and attractive wages and benefits. The postal service's role as a government-approved monopoly continues to be a topic of debate. However, in 2003 the Presidential Commission on Postal Services and in 2006 the Congress both rejected the idea of privatizing the U.S. Postal Service. Employment and schedules in the postal service fluctuate with the seasonal demand for its services. When mail volume is high, full-time employees work overtime, part-time workers get additional hours, and casual workers may be hired. When mail volume is low, overtime is curtailed, part-timers work fewer hours, and casual workers are discharged.

Perform any combination of tasks in a post office, such as receiving letters and parcels; selling postage and revenue stamps, postal cards, and stamped envelopes; filling out and selling money orders; placing mail in pigeonholes of mail rack or in bags according to state, address, or other scheme; and examining mail for correct postage. Keep money drawers in order and record and balance daily transactions. Weigh letters and parcels; compute mailing costs based on type, weight, and destination; and affix correct postage. Obtain signatures from recipients of registered or special-delivery mail. Register, certify, and insure letters and parcels. Sell and collect payment for products such as stamps, prepaid mail envelopes, and money orders. Check mail to ensure correct postage and that packages and letters are in proper condition for mailing. Answer questions regarding mail regulations and procedures, postage rates, and post-office boxes. Complete forms regarding address changes, theft or loss of mail, or special services such as registered or priority mail. Provide assistance to the public in complying with federal regulations of U.S. Postal Service and other federal agencies. Sort incoming and outgoing mail according to type and destination by hand or by operating electronic mail-sorting and scanning devices. Cash money orders. Rent post-office boxes to customers. Put undelivered parcels away, retrieve them when customers come to claim them, and complete any related documentation. Provide customers with assistance in filing claims for mail theft or lost or damaged mail. Respond to complaints regarding mail theft, delivery problems, and lost or damaged mail, filling out forms and making appropriate referrals for investigation. Receive letters and parcels and place mail into bags. Feed mail into postage-canceling devices or hand-stamp mail to cancel postage. Transport mail from one workstation to another. Set postage meters and calibrate them to ensure correct operation. Post announcements or government information on public bulletin boards.

Personality Type: Conventional.

GOE—Interest Area: 04. Business and Administration. **Work Group:** 04.07. Records and Materials Processing. **Other Jobs in this Work Group:** Correspondence Clerks; File Clerks; Human Resources Assistants, Except Payroll and Timekeeping; Marking Clerks; Meter Readers, Utilities; Office Clerks, General; Order Fillers, Wholesale and Retail Sales; Postal Service Mail Sorters, Processors, and Processing Machine Operators; Procurement Clerks; Production, Planning, and Expediting Clerks; Shipping, Receiving, and Traffic Clerks; Stock Clerks and Order Fillers; Stock Clerks, Sales Floor; Stock Clerks—Stockroom, Warehouse, or Storage Yard; Weighers, Measurers, Checkers, and Samplers, Recordkeeping.

Skills: No data available.

Education and Training Program: General Office Occupations and Clerical Services. **Related Knowledge/Courses:** Sales and Marketing; Transportation; Clerical Studies; Public Safety and Security.

Work Environment: Indoors; noisy; contaminants; standing; bending or twisting the body; repetitive motions.

Postal Service Mail Carriers

- ✳ Education/Training Required: Short-term on-the-job training
- ✳ Annual Earnings: $44,350
- ✳ Beginning Wage: $34,810
- ✳ Earnings Growth Potential: Very high
- ✳ Growth: 1.0%
- ✳ Annual Job Openings: 16,710
- ✳ Self-Employed: 0.0%
- ✳ Part-Time: 7.1%

Industries with Greatest Employment: Postal Service.

Highest-Growth Industries (Projected Growth for This Job): None met the criteria.

Lowest-Growth Industries (Projected Growth for This Job): None met the criteria.

Fastest-Growing Metropolitan Areas (Recent Growth for This Job): Hinesville–Fort Stewart, GA (20.0%); Wichita Falls, TX (13.3%); Hanford–Corcoran, CA (12.5%); Lawton, OK (11.1%); St. George, UT (11.1%).

Other Considerations for Job Security: Those seeking postal service jobs can expect to encounter keen competition. The number of applicants usually exceeds the number of job openings because of the occupation's low entry requirements and attractive wages and benefits. The postal service's role as a government-approved monopoly continues to be a topic of debate. However, in 2003 the Presidential Commission on Postal Services and in 2006 the Congress both rejected the idea of privatizing the U.S. Postal Service. Employment and schedules in the postal service fluctuate with the seasonal demand for its services. When mail volume is high, full-time employees work overtime, part-time workers get additional hours, and casual workers may be hired. When mail volume is low, overtime is curtailed, part-timers work fewer hours, and casual workers are discharged.

Sort mail for delivery, arranging it in delivery sequence. Deliver mail on established route by vehicle or on foot. Obtain signed receipts for registered, certified, and insured mail; collect associated charges; and complete any necessary paperwork. Deliver mail to residences and business establishments along specified routes by walking or driving, using a combination of satchels, carts, cars, and small trucks. Return to the post office with mail collected from homes, businesses, and public mailboxes. Turn in money and receipts collected along mail routes. Sign for cash-on-delivery and registered mail before leaving the post office. Record address changes and redirect mail for those addresses. Hold mail for customers who are away from delivery locations. Bundle mail in preparation for delivery or transportation to relay boxes. Leave notices telling patrons where to collect mail that couldn't be delivered. Meet schedules for the collection and return of mail. Return incorrectly addressed mail to senders. Maintain accurate records of deliveries. Answer customers' questions about postal services and regulations. Provide customers with change-of-address cards and other forms. Report any unusual circumstances concerning mail delivery, including the condition of street letter boxes. Register, certify, and insure parcels and letters. Travel to post offices to pick up the mail for routes or pick up mail from postal relay boxes. Enter change-of-address orders into computers that process forwarding address stickers. Complete forms that notify publishers of address changes. Sell stamps and money orders.

Personality Type: Conventional.

GOE—Interest Area: 16. Transportation, Distribution, and Logistics. **Work Group:** 16.06. Other Services Requiring Driving. **Other Jobs in this Work Group:** Ambulance Drivers and Attendants, Except Emergency Medical Technicians; Bus Drivers, School; Bus Drivers, Transit and Intercity; Couriers and Messengers; Driver/Sales Workers; Parking Lot Attendants; Taxi Drivers and Chauffeurs.

Skills: No data available.

Education and Training Program: General Office Occupations and Clerical Services. **Related Knowledge/Courses:** Transportation; Public Safety and Security.

Work Environment: Outdoors; very hot or cold; contaminants; standing; using hands on objects, tools, or controls; repetitive motions.

Postal Service Mail Sorters, Processors, and Processing Machine Operators

- ❈ Education/Training Required: Short-term on-the-job training
- ❈ Annual Earnings: $43,900
- ❈ Beginning Wage: $25,770
- ❈ Earnings Growth Potential: Very high
- ❈ Growth: –8.4%
- ❈ Annual Job Openings: 6,855
- ❈ Self-Employed: 0.0%
- ❈ Part-Time: 3.8%

Industries with Greatest Employment: Postal Service.

Highest-Growth Industries (Projected Growth for This Job): None met the criteria.

Lowest-Growth Industries (Projected Growth for This Job): None met the criteria.

Fastest-Growing Metropolitan Areas (Recent Growth for This Job): Ogden–Clearfield, UT (66.7%); Baton Rouge, LA (63.2%); Santa Fe, NM (50.0%); Vallejo–Fairfield, CA (33.3%); Alexandria, LA (25.0%).

Other Considerations for Job Security: Those seeking postal service jobs can expect to encounter keen competition. The number of applicants usually exceeds the number of job openings because of the occupation's low entry requirements and attractive wages and benefits. The postal service's role as a government-approved monopoly continues to be a topic of debate. However, in 2003 the Presidential Commission on Postal Services and in 2006 the Congress both rejected the idea of privatizing the U.S. Postal Service. Employment and schedules in the postal service fluctuate with the seasonal demand for its services. When mail volume is high, full-time employees work overtime, part-time workers get additional hours, and casual workers may be hired. When mail volume is low, overtime is curtailed, part-timers work fewer hours, and casual workers are discharged.

Prepare incoming and outgoing mail for distribution. Examine, sort, and route mail by state, type, or other scheme. Load, operate, and occasionally adjust and repair mail-processing, -sorting, and -canceling machinery. Keep records of shipments, pouches, and sacks and perform other duties related to mail handling within the postal service. Must complete a competitive exam. Direct items according to established routing schemes, using computer-controlled keyboards or voice-recognition equipment. Bundle, label, and route sorted mail to designated areas depending on destinations and according to established procedures and deadlines. Serve the public at counters or windows, such as by selling stamps and weighing parcels. Supervise other mail sorters. Train new workers. Distribute incoming mail into the correct boxes or pigeonholes. Operate various types of equipment, such as computer scanning equipment, addressographs, mimeographs, optical-character readers, and bar-code sorters. Search directories to find correct addresses for redirected mail. Clear jams in sorting equipment. Open and label mail containers. Check items to ensure that addresses are legible and correct, that sufficient postage has been paid or the appropriate documentation is attached, and that items are in a suitable condition for processing. Rewrap soiled or broken parcels. Weigh articles to determine required postage. Move containers of mail, using equipment such as forklifts and automated "trains." Sort odd-sized mail by hand, sort mail that other workers have been unable to sort, and segregate items requiring special handling. Accept and check containers of mail from large-volume mailers, couriers, and contractors. Load and unload mail trucks, sometimes lifting containers of mail onto equipment that transports items to sorting stations. Cancel letter or parcel post stamps by hand. Dump sacks of mail onto conveyors for culling and sorting.

Personality Type: No data available.

GOE—Interest Area: 04. Business and Administration. **Work Group:** 04.07. Records and Materials Processing. **Other Jobs in this Work Group:** Correspondence Clerks; File Clerks; Human Resources

Assistants, Except Payroll and Timekeeping; Marking Clerks; Meter Readers, Utilities; Office Clerks, General; Order Fillers, Wholesale and Retail Sales; Postal Service Clerks; Procurement Clerks; Production, Planning, and Expediting Clerks; Shipping, Receiving, and Traffic Clerks; Stock Clerks and Order Fillers; Stock Clerks, Sales Floor; Stock Clerks—Stockroom, Warehouse, or Storage Yard; Weighers, Measurers, Checkers, and Samplers, Recordkeeping.

Skills: No data available.

Education and Training Program: General Office Occupations and Clerical Services. **Related Knowledge/Courses:** Geography; Public Safety and Security.

Work Environment: Indoors; noisy; contaminants; standing; using hands on objects, tools, or controls; repetitive motions.

Postmasters and Mail Superintendents

* Education/Training Required: Work experience in a related occupation
* Annual Earnings: $55,790
* Beginning Wage: $38,230
* Earnings Growth Potential: Very high
* Growth: –0.8%
* Annual Job Openings: 1,627
* Self-Employed: 0.0%
* Part-Time: 3.2%

Industries with Greatest Employment: Postal Service.

Highest-Growth Industries (Projected Growth for This Job): None met the criteria.

Lowest-Growth Industries (Projected Growth for This Job): None met the criteria.

Fastest-Growing Metropolitan Areas (Recent Growth for This Job): Asheville, NC (33.3%); Charlottesville, VA (33.3%); Jackson, MS (33.3%);

Sioux Falls, SD (33.3%); Wheeling, WV–OH (33.3%).

Other Considerations for Job Security: Those seeking postal service jobs can expect to encounter keen competition. The number of applicants usually exceeds the number of job openings because of the occupation's low entry requirements and attractive wages and benefits. The postal service's role as a government-approved monopoly continues to be a topic of debate. However, in 2003 the Presidential Commission on Postal Services and in 2006 the Congress both rejected the idea of privatizing the U.S. Postal Service. Employment and schedules in the postal service fluctuate with the seasonal demand for its services. When mail volume is high, full-time employees work overtime, part-time workers get additional hours, and casual workers may be hired. When mail volume is low, overtime is curtailed, part-timers work fewer hours, and casual workers are discharged.

Direct and coordinate operational, administrative, management, and supportive services of a U.S. post office or coordinate activities of workers engaged in postal and related work in assigned post office. Organize and supervise activities such as the processing of incoming and outgoing mail. Direct and coordinate operational, management, and supportive services of one or a number of postal facilities. Resolve customer complaints. Hire and train employees and evaluate their performance. Prepare employee work schedules. Negotiate labor disputes. Prepare and submit detailed and summary reports of post-office activities to designated supervisors. Collect rents for post-office boxes. Issue and cash money orders. Inform the public of available services and of postal laws and regulations. Select and train postmasters and managers of associate postal units. Confer with suppliers to obtain bids for proposed purchases and to requisition supplies; disburse funds according to federal regulations.

Personality Type: Enterprising.

GOE—Interest Area: 16. Transportation, Distribution, and Logistics. **Work Group:** 16.01. Managerial

Work in Transportation. **Other Jobs in this Work Group:** Aircraft Cargo Handling Supervisors; First-Line Supervisors/Managers of Transportation and Material-Moving Machine and Vehicle Operators; Railroad Conductors and Yardmasters; Storage and Distribution Managers; Transportation Managers; Transportation, Storage, and Distribution Managers.

Skills: Negotiation; Management of Personnel Resources; Persuasion; Monitoring; Management of Financial Resources; Service Orientation.

Education and Training Program: Public Administration. **Related Knowledge/Courses:** Production and Processing; Personnel and Human Resources; Public Safety and Security; Clerical Studies; Economics and Accounting; Psychology.

Work Environment: Indoors; contaminants; standing.

Power Plant Operators

- ❋ Education/Training Required: Long-term on-the-job training
- ❋ Annual Earnings: $55,000
- ❋ Beginning Wage: $35,590
- ❋ Earnings Growth Potential: Very high
- ❋ Growth: 2.7%
- ❋ Annual Job Openings: 1,796
- ❋ Self-Employed: 0.0%
- ❋ Part-Time: 0.6%

Industries with Greatest Employment: Utilities.

Highest-Growth Industries (Projected Growth for This Job): Administrative and Support Services (42.9%); Professional, Scientific, and Technical Services (24.5%); Management of Companies and Enterprises (15.2%).

Lowest-Growth Industries (Projected Growth for This Job): Paper Manufacturing (–30.1%); Primary Metal Manufacturing (–30.1%); Chemical Manufacturing (–14.5%); Food Manufacturing (–7.8%);

Utilities (0.9%); Hospitals, Public and Private (4.7%); Educational Services, Public and Private (11.7%).

Fastest-Growing Metropolitan Areas (Recent Growth for This Job): Nashville–Davidson–Murfreesboro, TN (60.0%); Evansville, IN–KY (38.7%); Allentown–Bethlehem–Easton, PA–NJ (36.4%); Chico, CA (25.0%); Buffalo–Niagara Falls, NY (20.0%).

Other Considerations for Job Security: Job opportunities are expected to be very good for people interested in becoming power plant operators. During the 1990s, the emphasis on cost cutting among utilities led to hiring freezes and the laying off of younger workers. The result is an aging workforce, half of which is expected to retire within the next 10 years. Utilities have responded by setting up new education programs at community colleges and high schools throughout the country. Prospects should be especially good for people with computer skills and a basic understanding of science and mathematics.

Control, operate, or maintain machinery to generate electric power. Includes auxiliary equipment operators. Monitor and inspect power-plant equipment and indicators to detect evidence of operating problems. Adjust controls to generate specified electrical power or to regulate flow of power between generating stations and substations. Operate or control power-generating equipment, including boilers, turbines, generators, and reactors, via control boards or semi-automatic equipment. Regulate equipment operations and conditions such as water levels based on data from recording and indicating instruments or from computers. Take readings from charts, meters, and gauges at established intervals and take corrective steps as necessary. Inspect records and logbook entries and communicate with other plant personnel to assess equipment operating status. Start or stop generators, auxiliary pumping equipment, turbines, and other power plant equipment; connect or disconnect equipment from circuits. Control and maintain auxiliary equipment, such as pumps, fans, compressors, condensers, feedwater heaters, filters, and chlorinators, to supply water, fuel, lubricants, air, and auxiliary power. Clean, lubricate, and maintain equipment such as generators, turbines, pumps, and compressors to prevent equipment failure or deterioration. Communicate with systems operators to regulate and coordinate transmission loads, frequencies, and line voltages. Record and compile operational data, completing and maintaining forms, logs, and reports. Open and close valves and switches in sequence on signals from other workers to start or shut down auxiliary units. Collect oil, water, and electrolyte samples for laboratory analysis. Make adjustments or minor repairs, such as tightening leaking gland and pipe joints; report any needs for major repairs. Control generator output to match phase, frequency, and voltage of electricity supplied to panels. Place standby electrical generators on line during emergencies and monitor system's temperature, output, and lubrication. Receive outage calls and call in necessary personnel during power outages and emergencies.

Personality Type: Realistic.

GOE—Interest Area: 13. Manufacturing. **Work Group:** 13.16. Utility Operation and Energy Distribution. **Other Jobs in this Work Group:** Chemical Plant and System Operators; Gas Compressor and Gas Pumping Station Operators; Gas Plant Operators; Nuclear Power Reactor Operators; Petroleum Pump System Operators, Refinery Operators, and Gaugers; Power Distributors and Dispatchers; Ship Engineers; Stationary Engineers and Boiler Operators; Water and Liquid Waste Treatment Plant and System Operators.

Skills: Operation Monitoring; Equipment Maintenance; Operation and Control; Technology Design; Systems Evaluation; Coordination.

Education and Training Programs: No related CIP programs; this job is learned through long-term on-the-job training. **Related Knowledge/Courses:** Physics; Mechanical Devices; Chemistry; Engineering and Technology; Public Safety and Security; Computers and Electronics.

Work Environment: Indoors; noisy; very hot or cold; contaminants; high places; hazardous conditions.

Preschool Teachers, Except Special Education

- ❋ Education/Training Required: Postsecondary vocational training
- ❋ Annual Earnings: $22,680
- ❋ Beginning Wage: $14,870
- ❋ Earnings Growth Potential: Very high
- ❋ Growth: 26.3%
- ❋ Annual Job Openings: 78,172
- ❋ Self-Employed: 1.1%
- ❋ Part-Time: 25.1%

Industries with Greatest Employment: Social Assistance; Religious, Grantmaking, Civic, Professional, and Similar Organizations; Educational Services, Public and Private.

Highest-Growth Industries (Projected Growth for This Job): Amusement, Gambling, and Recreation Industries (32.2%); Social Assistance (31.8%); Administrative and Support Services (26.8%); Professional, Scientific, and Technical Services (26.2%); Ambulatory Health Care Services (26.2%); Nursing and Residential Care Facilities (19.6%); Religious, Grantmaking, Civic, Professional, and Similar Organizations (18.5%); Educational Services, Public and Private (16.0%); Management of Companies and Enterprises (15.2%).

Lowest-Growth Industries (Projected Growth for This Job): Sporting Goods, Hobby, Book, and Music Stores (–19.1%); Hospitals, Public and Private (10.6%).

Fastest-Growing Metropolitan Areas (Recent Growth for This Job): Farmington, NM (233.3%); Alexandria, LA (225.0%); Missoula, MT (200.0%); Palm Bay–Melbourne–Titusville, FL (172.7%); Odessa, TX (135.7%).

Other Considerations for Job Security: Job prospects are expected to be favorable, with particularly good prospects for teachers in less desirable urban or rural school districts and for those with licensure in more than one subject. Fast-growing states in the

South and West—led by Nevada, Arizona, Texas, and Georgia—will experience the largest enrollment increases. Enrollments in the Midwest are expected to hold relatively steady, while those in the Northeast are expected to decline. The number of teachers employed depends on state and local expenditures for education and on the enactment of legislation to increase the quality and scope of public education. Education has received a large increase in federal funding, particularly for the hiring of qualified teachers in lower-income areas. Also, some states are instituting programs to improve early childhood education.

Instruct children (normally up to 5 years old) in activities designed to promote social, physical, and intellectual growth needed for primary school in preschool, daycare center, or other child-development facility. May be required to hold state certification. Provide a variety of materials and resources for children to explore, manipulate, and use, both in learning activities and in imaginative play. Attend to children's basic needs by feeding them, dressing them, and changing their diapers. Establish and enforce rules for behavior and procedures for maintaining order. Read books to entire classes or to small groups. Teach basic skills such as color, shape, number, and letter recognition; personal hygiene; and social skills. Organize and lead activities designed to promote physical, mental, and social development, such as games, arts and crafts, music, storytelling, and field trips. Observe and evaluate children's performance, behavior, social development, and physical health. Meet with parents and guardians to discuss their children's progress and needs, determine their priorities for their children, and suggest ways that they can promote learning and development. Identify children showing signs of emotional, developmental, or health-related problems and discuss them with supervisors, parents or guardians, and child-development specialists. Enforce all administration policies and rules governing students. Prepare materials and classrooms for class activities. Serve meals and snacks in accordance with nutritional guidelines. Teach proper eating habits and personal hygiene. Assimilate arriving children to the school environment by greeting them, helping them remove outerwear, and selecting activities of interest to them. Adapt teaching methods and instructional materials to meet students' varying needs and interests. Establish clear objectives for all lessons, units, and projects and communicate those objectives to children. Demonstrate activities to children. Arrange indoor and outdoor space to facilitate creative play, motor-skill activities, and safety. Plan and conduct activities for a balanced program of instruction, demonstration, and work time that provides students with opportunities to observe, question, and investigate. Maintain accurate and complete student records as required by laws, district policies, and administrative regulations.

Personality Type: Social.

GOE—Interest Area: 05. Education and Training. **Work Group:** 05.02. Preschool, Elementary, and Secondary Teaching and Instructing. **Other Jobs in this Work Group:** Elementary School Teachers, Except Special Education; Kindergarten Teachers, Except Special Education; Middle School Teachers, Except Special and Vocational Education; Secondary School Teachers, Except Special and Vocational Education; Special Education Teachers, Middle School; Special Education Teachers, Preschool, Kindergarten, and Elementary School; Special Education Teachers, Secondary School; Teacher Assistants; Vocational Education Teachers, Middle School; Vocational Education Teachers, Secondary School.

Skills: No data available.

Education and Training Programs: Montessori Teacher Education; Early Childhood Education and Teaching; Child Care and Support Services Management. **Related Knowledge/Courses:** Philosophy and Theology; Sociology and Anthropology; Psychology; Customer and Personal Service; Education and Training.

Work Environment: Indoors; standing; walking and running; bending or twisting the body.

Private Detectives and Investigators

- ❀ Education/Training Required: Work experience in a related occupation
- ❀ Annual Earnings: $33,750
- ❀ Beginning Wage: $19,720
- ❀ Earnings Growth Potential: Very high
- ❀ Growth: 18.2%
- ❀ Annual Job Openings: 7,329
- ❀ Self-Employed: 29.7%
- ❀ Part-Time: 11.1%

Industries with Greatest Employment: Administrative and Support Services; Professional, Scientific, and Technical Services; Credit Intermediation and Related Activities.

Highest-Growth Industries (Projected Growth for This Job): Amusement, Gambling, and Recreation Industries (62.3%); Administrative and Support Services (32.5%); Professional, Scientific, and Technical Services (29.8%); Accommodation, Including Hotels and Motels (16.9%); Management of Companies and Enterprises (15.3%).

Lowest-Growth Industries (Projected Growth for This Job): Utilities (–11.7%); Telecommunications (1.5%); Transportation Equipment Manufacturing (1.9%); Electronics and Appliance Stores (3.2%); Clothing and Clothing Accessories Stores (4.4%); Hospitals, Public and Private (5.9%); Internet Service Providers, Web Search Portals, and Data Processing Services (6.6%); Sporting Goods, Hobby, Book, and Music Stores (7.2%); Credit Intermediation and Related Activities (8.1%); Educational Services, Public and Private (8.1%).

Fastest-Growing Metropolitan Areas (Recent Growth for This Job): Kansas City, MO–KS (114.3%); Albuquerque, NM (91.7%); Charlotte–Gastonia–Concord, NC–SC (83.3%); Dayton, OH (71.4%); Hartford–West Hartford–East Hartford, CT (66.7%).

Other Considerations for Job Security: Keen competition is expected for most jobs because private detective and investigator careers attract many qualified people, including relatively young retirees from law-enforcement and military careers. The best opportunities for new jobseekers will be in entry-level jobs in detective agencies or stores, particularly large chain and discount stores that hire detectives on a part-time basis. Opportunities are expected to be excellent for qualified computer forensic investigators. Increased demand for private detectives and investigators will result from heightened security concerns, increased litigation, and the need to protect confidential information and property of all kinds.

Detect occurrences of unlawful acts or infractions of rules in private establishment or seek, examine, and compile information for client. Question persons to obtain evidence for cases of divorce, child custody, or missing persons or information about individuals' character or financial status. Conduct private investigations on a paid basis. Confer with establishment officials, security departments, police, or postal officials to identify problems, provide information, and receive instructions. Observe and document activities of individuals to detect unlawful acts or to obtain evidence for cases, using binoculars and still or video cameras. Investigate companies' financial standings or locate funds stolen by embezzlers, using accounting skills. Monitor industrial or commercial properties to enforce conformance to establishment rules and to protect people or property. Search computer databases, credit reports, public records, tax and legal filings, and other resources to locate persons or to compile information for investigations. Write reports and case summaries to document investigations. Count cash and review transactions, sales checks, and register tapes to verify amounts and to identify shortages. Perform undercover operations such as evaluating employee performance and honesty by posing as customers or employees. Expose fraudulent insurance claims or stolen funds. Alert appropriate personnel to suspects' locations. Conduct background investigations of individuals, such as pre-employment checks, to obtain information about an individual's character, financial status, or personal history. Testify at hearings and court trials to present evidence. Warn troublemakers causing problems on establishment premises and eject them from premises when necessary. Obtain and analyze information on suspects, crimes, and disturbances to solve cases, identify criminal activity, and gather information for court cases. Apprehend suspects and release them to law-enforcement authorities or security personnel.

Personality Type: Enterprising.

GOE—Interest Area: 12. Law and Public Safety. **Work Group:** 12.05. Safety and Security. **Other Jobs in this Work Group:** Animal Control Workers; Crossing Guards; Gaming Surveillance Officers and Gaming Investigators; Lifeguards, Ski Patrol, and Other Recreational Protective Service Workers; Security Guards; Transportation Security Screeners.

Skills: Management of Financial Resources; Persuasion; Time Management; Writing; Service Orientation; Speaking.

Education and Training Program: Criminal Justice/Police Science. **Related Knowledge/Courses:** Clerical Studies; Law and Government; Customer and Personal Service; Computers and Electronics; Sales and Marketing; Mathematics.

Work Environment: Outdoors; noisy; very hot or cold; very bright or dim lighting; sitting; using hands on objects, tools, or controls.

Probation Officers and Correctional Treatment Specialists

- ❈ Education/Training Required: Bachelor's degree
- ❈ Annual Earnings: $42,500
- ❈ Beginning Wage: $28,000
- ❈ Earnings Growth Potential: Very high
- ❈ Growth: 10.9%
- ❈ Annual Job Openings: 18,335
- ❈ Self-Employed: 0.1%
- ❈ Part-Time: 12.0%

Industries with Greatest Employment: Social Assistance; Administrative and Support Services; Nursing and Residential Care Facilities; Hospitals, Public and Private; Religious, Grantmaking, Civic, Professional, and Similar Organizations.

Highest-Growth Industries (Projected Growth for This Job): Social Assistance (65.6%); Administrative and Support Services (47.5%); Nursing and Residential Care Facilities (19.8%); Religious, Grantmaking, Civic, Professional, and Similar Organizations (15.3%).

Lowest-Growth Industries (Projected Growth for This Job): Hospitals, Public and Private (–1.4%); Educational Services, Public and Private (12.2%); Ambulatory Health Care Services (14.8%).

Fastest-Growing Metropolitan Areas (Recent Growth for This Job): Durham, NC (225.0%); Minneapolis–St. Paul–Bloomington, MN–WI (69.7%); Fresno, CA (61.5%); Buffalo–Niagara Falls, NY (60.9%); Columbia, SC (41.7%).

Other Considerations for Job Security: Job outlook depends primarily on the amount of government funding allocated to corrections, especially to probation systems. Although community supervision is far less expensive than keeping offenders in prison, a change in political trends toward more imprisonment and away from community supervision could result in reduced employment opportunities. In addition to openings due to growth, many openings will be created by replacement needs, especially openings due to the large number of these workers who are expected to retire. This occupation isn't attractive to some potential entrants due to relatively low earnings, heavy workloads, and high stress. For these reasons, job opportunities are expected to be excellent.

Provide social services to assist in rehabilitation of law offenders in custody or on probation or parole. Recommend actions involving formulation of rehabilitation plan and treatment of offender, including conditional release and education and employment stipulations. Prepare and maintain case folder for each assigned inmate or offender. Write reports describing offenders' progress.

Inform offenders or inmates of requirements of conditional release, such as office visits, restitution payments, or educational and employment stipulations. Discuss with offenders how such issues as drug and alcohol abuse and anger management problems might have played roles in their criminal behavior. Gather information about offenders' backgrounds by talking to offenders, their families and friends, and other people with relevant information. Develop rehabilitation programs for assigned offenders or inmates, establishing rules of conduct, goals, and objectives. Develop liaisons and networks with other parole officers, community agencies, staff in correctional institutions, psychiatric facilities, and after-care agencies to make plans for helping offenders with life adjustments. Arrange for medical, mental-health, or substance-abuse treatment services according to individual needs and court orders. Provide offenders or inmates with assistance in matters concerning detainers, sentences in other jurisdictions, writs, and applications for social assistance. Arrange for post-release services such as employment, housing, counseling, education, and social activities. Recommend remedial action or initiate court action when terms of probation or parole aren't complied with. Interview probationers and parolees regularly to evaluate their progress in accomplishing goals and maintaining the terms specified in their probation contracts and rehabilitation plans. Supervise people on community-based sentences, including people on electronically monitored home detention. Assess the suitability of penitentiary inmates for release under parole and statutory release programs and submit recommendations to parole boards. Investigate alleged parole violations, using interviews, surveillance, and search and seizure. Conduct prehearing and presentencing investigations and testify in court regarding offenders' backgrounds and recommended sentences and sentencing conditions.

Personality Type: Social.

GOE—Interest Area: 10. Human Service. **Work Group:** 10.01. Counseling and Social Work. **Other Jobs in this Work Group:** Child, Family, and School Social Workers; Clinical Psychologists; Clinical, Counseling, and School Psychologists; Counseling Psychologists; Marriage and Family Therapists; Medical and Public Health Social Workers; Mental Health and Substance Abuse Social Workers; Mental Health Counselors; Rehabilitation Counselors; Residential Advisors; Social and Human Service Assistants; Substance Abuse and Behavioral Disorder Counselors.

Skills: Social Perceptiveness; Persuasion; Management of Personnel Resources; Negotiation; Time Management; Monitoring.

Education and Training Program: Social Work. **Related Knowledge/Courses:** Therapy and Counseling; Psychology; Sociology and Anthropology; Philosophy and Theology; Law and Government; Public Safety and Security.

Work Environment: More often indoors than outdoors; very hot or cold; disease or infections; sitting.

Psychiatrists

- ❋ Education/Training Required: First professional degree
- ❋ Annual Earnings: More than $145,600
- ❋ Beginning Wage: $60,900
- ❋ Earnings Growth Potential: Cannot be calculated
- ❋ Growth: 14.2%
- ❋ Annual Job Openings: 38,027
- ❋ Self-Employed: 14.7%
- ❋ Part-Time: 8.1%

Our sources did not provide separate job openings data for this occupation. The job openings listed here are shared with Anesthesiologists; Family and General Practitioners; Internists, General; Obstetricians and Gynecologists; Pediatricians, General; and Surgeons.

Industries with Greatest Employment: Ambulatory Health Care Services; Hospitals, Public and Private.

Highest-Growth Industries (Projected Growth for This Job): Social Assistance (58.6%); Administrative and Support Services (26.8%); Professional, Scientific, and Technical Services (22.6%); Nursing and Residential Care Facilities (21.0%); Ambulatory Health Care Services (19.4%); Religious, Grantmaking, Civic, Professional, and Similar Organizations (16.7%); Management of Companies and Enterprises (15.3%).

Lowest-Growth Industries (Projected Growth for This Job): Insurance Carriers and Related Activities (4.6%); Health and Personal Care Stores (5.3%); Hospitals, Public and Private (9.9%); Educational Services, Public and Private (11.8%).

Fastest-Growing Metropolitan Areas (Recent Growth for This Job): Columbia, SC (180.0%); San Juan–Caguas–Guaynabo, PR (28.6%).

Other Considerations for Job Security: Opportunities for individuals interested in becoming physicians and surgeons are expected to be very good. Unlike their predecessors, new physicians are much less likely to enter solo practice and more likely to take salaried jobs in group medical practices, clinics, and health networks. Reports of shortages in some specialties, such as general or family practice, internal medicine, and OB/GYN, or in rural or low-income areas should attract new entrants, encouraging schools to expand programs and hospitals to increase available residency slots. However, because physician training is so lengthy, employment change happens gradually. Opportunities should be particularly good in rural and low-income areas, as some physicians find these areas unattractive because of less control over work hours, isolation from medical colleagues, or other reasons.

Diagnose, treat, and help prevent disorders of the mind. Analyze and evaluate patient data and test findings to diagnose nature and extent of mental disorder. Prescribe, direct, and administer psychotherapeutic treatments or medications to treat mental, emotional, or behavioral disorders. Collaborate with physicians, psychologists, social workers, psychiatric nurses, or other professionals to discuss treatment plans and progress. Gather and maintain patient information and records, including social and medical history obtained from patients, relatives, and other professionals. Counsel outpatients and other patients during office visits. Design individualized care plans, using a variety of treatments. Examine or conduct laboratory or diagnostic tests on patient to provide information on general physical condition and mental disorder. Advise and inform guardians, relatives, and significant others of patients' conditions and treatment. Review and evaluate treatment procedures and outcomes of other psychiatrists and medical professionals. Teach, conduct research, and publish findings to increase understanding of mental, emotional, and behavioral states and disorders. Prepare and submit case reports and summaries to government and mental-health agencies. Serve on committees to promote and maintain community mental-health services and delivery systems.

Personality Type: Investigative.

GOE—Interest Area: 08. Health Science. **Work Group:** 08.02. Medicine and Surgery. **Other Jobs in this Work Group:** Anesthesiologists; Family and General Practitioners; Internists, General; Medical Assistants; Medical Transcriptionists; Obstetricians and Gynecologists; Pediatricians, General; Pharmacists; Pharmacy Aides; Pharmacy Technicians; Physician Assistants; Registered Nurses; Surgeons; Surgical Technologists.

Skills: Social Perceptiveness; Science; Systems Analysis; Persuasion; Active Learning; Active Listening.

Education and Training Programs: Child Psychiatry; Psychiatry; Physical Medical and Rehabilitation/Psychiatry. **Related Knowledge/Courses:** Therapy and Counseling; Medicine and Dentistry; Psychology; Biology; Philosophy and Theology; Sociology and Anthropology.

Work Environment: Indoors; disease or infections; sitting.

P

Psychology Teachers, Postsecondary

- ❋ Education/Training Required: Doctoral degree
- ❋ Annual Earnings: $58,670
- ❋ Beginning Wage: $32,800
- ❋ Earnings Growth Potential: Very high
- ❋ Growth: 22.9%
- ❋ Annual Job Openings: 237,478
- ❋ Self-Employed: 0.4%
- ❋ Part-Time: 27.8%

Our sources did not provide separate job openings data for this occupation. The job openings listed here are shared with 35 other postsecondary teaching occupations. For a complete list, see the beginning of this section.

Industries with Greatest Employment: Educational Services, Public and Private.

Highest-Growth Industries (Projected Growth for This Job): Administrative and Support Services (48.3%); Amusement, Gambling, and Recreation Industries (45.3%); Social Assistance (38.6%); Support Activities for Transportation (32.8%); Religious, Grantmaking, Civic, Professional, and Similar Organizations (29.9%); Professional, Scientific, and Technical Services (28.8%); Management of Companies and Enterprises (26.8%); Educational Services, Public and Private (22.9%); Hospitals, Public and Private (21.4%); Personal and Laundry Services (21.0%).

Lowest-Growth Industries (Projected Growth for This Job): Other Information Services (7.4%); Sporting Goods, Hobby, Book, and Music Stores (13.3%); Performing Arts, Spectator Sports, and Related Industries (13.4%); Insurance Carriers and Related Activities (13.9%).

Fastest-Growing Metropolitan Areas (Recent Growth for This Job): None growing over 10 percent.

Other Considerations for Job Security: Retirements of current postsecondary teachers should create

numerous openings for all types of postsecondary teachers, so job opportunities are generally expected to be very good. However, because students attend postsecondary institutions to prepare themselves for careers, the best job prospects for postsecondary teachers are likely to be in rapidly growing fields that offer many nonacademic career options. Psychology is a course requirement in many health-care majors. Community colleges and other institutions offering career and technical education have been among the most rapidly growing and are expected to offer some of the best opportunities for postsecondary teachers.

Teach courses in psychology, such as child, clinical, and developmental psychology, and psychological counseling. Prepare and deliver lectures to undergraduate and/or graduate students on topics such as abnormal psychology, cognitive processes, and work motivation. Evaluate and grade students' classwork, laboratory work, assignments, and papers. Initiate, facilitate, and moderate classroom discussions. Compile, administer, and grade examinations or assign this work to others. Keep abreast of developments in their field by reading current literature, talking with colleagues, and participating in professional conferences. Prepare course materials such as syllabi, homework assignments, and handouts. Plan, evaluate, and revise curricula, course content, course materials, and methods of instruction. Maintain student attendance records, grades, and other required records. Supervise undergraduate and/or graduate teaching, internships, and research work. Maintain regularly scheduled office hours to advise and assist students. Conduct research in a particular field of knowledge and publish findings in professional journals, books, and electronic media. Advise students on academic and vocational curricula and on career issues. Select and obtain materials and supplies such as textbooks. Collaborate with colleagues to address teaching and research issues. Serve on academic or administrative committees that deal with institutional policies, departmental matters, and academic issues. Compile bibliographies of specialized materials for outside reading assignments. Participate in student recruitment, registration, and placement activities. Supervise students' laboratory work. Perform administrative duties such as serving as department head. Act as advisers to student organizations. Write grant proposals to procure external research funding. Participate in campus and community events. Provide professional consulting services to government and industry.

Personality Type: Social.

GOE—Interest Area: 05. Education and Training. **Work Group:** 05.03. Postsecondary and Adult Teaching and Instructing. **Other Jobs in this Work Group:** Adult Literacy, Remedial Education, and GED Teachers and Instructors; Agricultural Sciences Teachers, Postsecondary; Anthropology and Archeology Teachers, Postsecondary; Architecture Teachers, Postsecondary; Area, Ethnic, and Cultural Studies Teachers, Postsecondary; Art, Drama, and Music Teachers, Postsecondary; Atmospheric, Earth, Marine, and Space Sciences Teachers, Postsecondary; Biological Science Teachers, Postsecondary; Business Teachers, Postsecondary; Chemistry Teachers, Postsecondary; Communications Teachers, Postsecondary; Computer Science Teachers, Postsecondary; Criminal Justice and Law Enforcement Teachers, Postsecondary; Economics Teachers, Postsecondary; Education Teachers, Postsecondary; Engineering Teachers, Postsecondary; English Language and Literature Teachers, Postsecondary; Environmental Science Teachers, Postsecondary; Farm and Home Management Advisors; Foreign Language and Literature Teachers, Postsecondary; Forestry and Conservation Science Teachers, Postsecondary; Geography Teachers, Postsecondary; Graduate Teaching Assistants; Health Specialties Teachers, Postsecondary; History Teachers, Postsecondary; Home Economics Teachers, Postsecondary; Law Teachers, Postsecondary; Library Science Teachers, Postsecondary; Mathematical Science Teachers, Postsecondary; Nursing Instructors and Teachers, Postsecondary; Philosophy and Religion Teachers, Postsecondary; Physics Teachers, Postsecondary; Political Science Teachers, Postsecondary; Recreation and Fitness Studies Teachers, Postsecondary; Self-Enrichment Education Teachers; Social Work Teachers, Postsecondary;

Sociology Teachers, Postsecondary; Vocational Education Teachers, Postsecondary.

Skills: Science; Learning Strategies; Instructing; Social Perceptiveness; Writing; Reading Comprehension.

Education and Training Programs: Social Science Teacher Education; Psychology Teacher Education; Psychology, General; Clinical Psychology; Cognitive Psychology and Psycholinguistics; Community Psychology; Comparative Psychology; Counseling Psychology; Developmental and Child Psychology; Experimental Psychology; Industrial and Organizational Psychology; Personality Psychology; Physiological Psychology/Psychobiology; others. **Related Knowledge/Courses:** Therapy and Counseling; Psychology; Sociology and Anthropology; Philosophy and Theology; Education and Training; English Language.

Work Environment: Indoors; sitting.

Public Relations Specialists

- Education/Training Required: Bachelor's degree
- Annual Earnings: $47,350
- Beginning Wage: $28,080
- Earnings Growth Potential: Very high
- Growth: 17.6%
- Annual Job Openings: 51,216
- Self-Employed: 4.9%
- Part-Time: 13.9%

Industries with Greatest Employment: Religious, Grantmaking, Civic, Professional, and Similar Organizations; Professional, Scientific, and Technical Services; Educational Services, Public and Private; Management of Companies and Enterprises; Administrative and Support Services.

Highest-Growth Industries (Projected Growth for This Job): Social Assistance (44.1%); Securities, Commodity Contracts, and Other Financial Investments and Related Activities (42.9%); Internet

Publishing and Broadcasting (40.3%); Amusement, Gambling, and Recreation Industries (38.6%); Museums, Historical Sites, and Similar Institutions (36.1%); Ambulatory Health Care Services (35.0%); Warehousing and Storage (34.0%); Funds, Trusts, and Other Financial Vehicles (32.0%); Professional, Scientific, and Technical Services (30.8%); Lessors of Nonfinancial Intangible Assets (Except Copyrighted Works) (27.6%); Nursing and Residential Care Facilities (26.8%); Waste Management and Remediation Services (26.7%); Administrative and Support Services (25.1%); Building Material and Garden Equipment and Supplies Dealers (22.6%); Personal and Laundry Services (22.5%); Performing Arts, Spectator Sports, and Related Industries (21.6%); Support Activities for Transportation (20.8%); Real Estate (19.8%); Nonstore Retailers (19.5%); others.

Lowest-Growth Industries (Projected Growth for This Job): Crop Production (–33.5%); Petroleum and Coal Products Manufacturing (–24.3%); Electrical Equipment, Appliance, and Component Manufacturing (–21.8%); Printing and Related Support Activities (–20.8%); Computer and Electronic Product Manufacturing (–18.9%); Rail Transportation (–13.6%); Machinery Manufacturing (–12.5%); Fabricated Metal Product Manufacturing (–12.3%); Furniture and Related Product Manufacturing (–12.3%); Monetary Authorities–Central Bank (–12.3%).

Fastest-Growing Metropolitan Areas (Recent Growth for This Job): Ogden–Clearfield, UT (260.0%); Ames, IA (225.0%); Barnstable Town, MA (116.7%); Canton–Massillon, OH (108.3%); Erie, PA (83.3%).

Other Considerations for Job Security: Keen competition likely will continue for entry-level PR jobs, as the number of qualified applicants is expected to exceed the number of job openings. Many people are attracted to this profession because of the high-profile nature of the work. Opportunities should be best for college graduates who combine a degree in journalism, public relations, advertising, or another communications-related field with a PR internship or other related work experience. Applicants without the appropriate educational background or work experience will face the toughest obstacles.

Engage in promoting or creating good will for individuals, groups, or organizations by writing or selecting favorable publicity material and releasing it through various communications media. May prepare and arrange displays and make speeches. Prepare or edit organizational publications for internal and external audiences, including employee newsletters and stockholders' reports. Respond to requests for information from the media or designate another appropriate spokesperson or information source. Establish and maintain cooperative relationships with representatives of community, consumer, employee, and public interest groups. Plan and direct development and communication of informational programs to maintain favorable public and stockholder perceptions of an organization's accomplishments and agenda. Confer with production and support personnel to produce or coordinate production of advertisements and promotions. Arrange public appearances, lectures, contests, or exhibits for clients to increase product and service awareness and to promote goodwill. Study organizations' objectives, promotional policies, and needs to develop public-relations strategies that will influence public opinion or promote ideas, products, and services. Consult with advertising agencies or staff to arrange promotional campaigns in all types of media for products, organizations, or individuals. Confer with other managers to identify trends and key group interests and concerns or to provide advice on business decisions. Coach client representatives in effective communication with the public and with employees. Prepare and deliver speeches to further public-relations objectives. Purchase advertising space and time as required to promote client's product or agenda. Plan and conduct market and public opinion research to test products or determine potential for product success, communicating results to client or management.

Personality Type: Enterprising.

GOE—Interest Area: 03. Arts and Communication. **Work Group:** 03.03. News, Broadcasting, and Public Relations. **Other Jobs in this Work Group:**

Broadcast News Analysts; Interpreters and Translators; Reporters and Correspondents.

Skills: Management of Financial Resources; Service Orientation; Persuasion; Negotiation; Writing; Social Perceptiveness.

Education and Training Programs: Communication Studies/Speech Communication and Rhetoric; Public Relations/Image Management; Political Communication; Health Communication; Family and Consumer Sciences/Human Sciences Communication. **Related Knowledge/Courses:** Sales and Marketing; Communications and Media; Customer and Personal Service; Sociology and Anthropology; Clerical Studies; Administration and Management.

Work Environment: Indoors; sitting.

Radiation Therapists

- ❋ Education/Training Required: Associate degree
- ❋ Annual Earnings: $66,170
- ❋ Beginning Wage: $44,840
- ❋ Earnings Growth Potential: Very high
- ❋ Growth: 24.8%
- ❋ Annual Job Openings: 1,461
- ❋ Self-Employed: 0.0%
- ❋ Part-Time: 10.3%

Industries with Greatest Employment: Hospitals, Public and Private; Ambulatory Health Care Services.

Highest-Growth Industries (Projected Growth for This Job): Ambulatory Health Care Services (34.9%); Hospitals, Public and Private (22.1%).

Lowest-Growth Industries (Projected Growth for This Job): Educational Services, Public and Private (12.1%).

Fastest-Growing Metropolitan Areas (Recent Growth for This Job): Oklahoma City, OK (140.0%); Houston–Sugar Land–Baytown, TX (80.0%); New York–Northern New Jersey–Long Island, NY–NJ–PA (40.6%); St. Louis, MO–IL (37.5%); Baltimore–Towson, MD (33.3%).

Other Considerations for Job Security: Job prospects are expected to be good. Openings will result from employment growth and from the need to replace workers who retire or leave the occupation for other reasons. Certified applicants should have the best opportunities. As the U.S. population grows and an increasing share of it is in the older age groups, the number of people needing treatment is expected to increase and to spur demand for radiation therapists. Also, as radiation technology advances and is able to treat more types of cancer, radiation therapy will be prescribed more often.

Provide radiation therapy to patients as prescribed by a radiologist according to established practices and standards. Duties may include reviewing prescription and diagnosis; acting as liaison with physician and supportive care personnel; preparing equipment, such as immobilization, treatment, and protection devices; and maintaining records, reports, and files. May assist in dosimetry procedures and tumor localization. Administer prescribed doses of radiation to specific body parts, using radiation therapy equipment according to established practices and standards. Position patients for treatment with accuracy according to prescription. Enter data into computer and set controls to operate and adjust equipment and regulate dosage. Follow principles of radiation protection for patient, self, and others. Maintain records, reports and files as required, including such information as radiation dosages, equipment settings, and patients' reactions. Review prescription, diagnosis, patient chart, and identification. Conduct most treatment sessions independently in accordance with the long-term treatment plan and under the general direction of the patient's physician. Check radiation therapy equipment to ensure proper operation. Observe and reassure patients during treatment and report unusual reactions to physician or turn equipment off if unexpected adverse reactions occur. Check for side effects such as skin irritation, nausea, and hair loss to assess patients' reaction to treatment. Educate, prepare,

R

and reassure patients and their families by answering questions, providing physical assistance, and reinforcing physicians' advice regarding treatment reactions and post-treatment care. Calculate actual treatment dosages delivered during each session. Prepare and construct equipment, such as immobilization, treatment, and protection devices. Photograph treated area of patient and process film. Help physicians, radiation oncologists, and clinical physicists to prepare physical and technical aspects of radiation treatment plans, using information about patient condition and anatomy. Train and supervise student or subordinate radiotherapy technologists. Provide assistance to other health-care personnel during dosimetry procedures and tumor localization. Implement appropriate follow-up care plans. Act as liaison with physicist and supportive care personnel. Store, sterilize, or prepare the special applicators containing the radioactive substance implanted by the physician. Assist in the preparation of sealed radioactive materials, such as cobalt, radium, cesium, and isotopes, for use in radiation treatments.

Personality Type: Social.

GOE—Interest Area: 08. Health Science. **Work Group:** 08.07. Medical Therapy. **Other Jobs in this Work Group:** Audiologists; Massage Therapists; Occupational Therapist Aides; Occupational Therapist Assistants; Occupational Therapists; Physical Therapist Aides; Physical Therapist Assistants; Physical Therapists; Recreational Therapists; Respiratory Therapists; Respiratory Therapy Technicians; Speech-Language Pathologists.

Skills: Operation Monitoring; Operation and Control; Technology Design; Time Management; Science; Management of Personnel Resources.

Education and Training Program: Medical Radiologic Technology/Science—Radiation Therapist. **Related Knowledge/Courses:** Medicine and Dentistry; Biology; Physics; Therapy and Counseling; Psychology; Customer and Personal Service.

Work Environment: Indoors; disease or infections; standing; walking and running; using hands on objects, tools, or controls; repetitive motions.

Radiologic Technicians

* Education/Training Required: Associate degree
* Annual Earnings: $48,170
* Beginning Wage: $32,750
* Earnings Growth Potential: Very high
* Growth: 15.1%
* Annual Job Openings: 12,836
* Self-Employed: 1.1%
* Part-Time: 17.3%

Our sources did not provide separate job openings data for this occupation. The job openings listed here are shared with Radiologic Technologists.

Industries with Greatest Employment: Hospitals, Public and Private; Ambulatory Health Care Services.

Highest-Growth Industries (Projected Growth for This Job): Professional, Scientific, and Technical Services (37.7%); Administrative and Support Services (26.7%); Ambulatory Health Care Services (23.7%); Management of Companies and Enterprises (15.2%).

Lowest-Growth Industries (Projected Growth for This Job): Insurance Carriers and Related Activities (5.0%); Hospitals, Public and Private (11.0%); Educational Services, Public and Private (11.8%).

Fastest-Growing Metropolitan Areas (Recent Growth for This Job): Kingston, NY (160.0%); Tyler, TX (75.0%); Sebastian–Vero Beach, FL (66.7%); Utica–Rome, NY (66.7%); Alexandria, LA (63.6%).

Other Considerations for Job Security: In addition to job growth, job openings also will arise from the need to replace technicians who leave the occupation. Radiologic technicians who are willing to relocate and who also are experienced in more than one diagnostic imaging procedure—such as CT, MR, and mammography—will have the best employment opportunities as employers seek to control costs by using multi-credentialed employees. CT is becoming a frontline diagnosis tool. Instead of X rays being taken to decide whether a CT is needed, as was the practice before, CT is often the first choice for imaging because of its accuracy. MR also is increasing in frequency of use. Techncians with credentialing in either of these specialties will be very marketable to employers.

Maintain and use equipment and supplies necessary to demonstrate portions of the human body on X-ray film or fluoroscopic screen for diagnostic purposes. Use beam-restrictive devices and patient-shielding techniques to minimize radiation exposure to patient and staff. Position X-ray equipment and adjust controls to set exposure factors, such as time and distance. Position patient on examining table and set up and adjust equipment to obtain optimum view of specific body area as requested by physician. Determine patients' X-ray needs by reading requests or instructions from physicians. Make exposures necessary for the requested procedures, rejecting and repeating work that doesn't meet established standards. Process exposed radiographs, using film processors or computer-generated methods. Explain procedures to patients to reduce anxieties and obtain cooperation. Perform procedures such as linear tomography; mammography; sonograms; joint and cyst aspirations; routine contrast studies; routine fluoroscopy; and examinations of the head, trunk, and extremities under physician supervision. Prepare and set up X-ray room for patient. Assure that sterile supplies, contrast materials, catheters, and other required equipment are present and in working order, requisitioning materials as necessary. Maintain records of patients examined, examinations performed, views taken, and technical factors used. Provide assistance to physicians or other technologists in the performance of more complex procedures. Monitor equipment operation and report malfunctioning equipment to supervisor. Provide students and other technologists with suggestions of additional views, alternate positioning, or improved techniques to ensure the images produced are of the highest quality. Coordinate work of other technicians or technologists when procedures require more than one person. Assist with on-the-job training of new employees and students and provide input to supervisors regarding training performance. Maintain a current file of examination protocols. Operate mobile X-ray equipment in operating room, in emergency room, or at patient's bedside. Provide assistance in radiopharmaceutical administration, monitoring patients' vital signs and notifying the radiologist of any relevant changes.

Personality Type: Realistic.

GOE—Interest Area: 08. Health Science. **Work Group:** 08.06. Medical Technology. **Other Jobs in this Work Group:** Biological Technicians; Cardiovascular Technologists and Technicians; Diagnostic Medical Sonographers; Medical and Clinical Laboratory Technicians; Medical and Clinical Laboratory Technologists; Medical Equipment Preparers; Medical Records and Health Information Technicians; Nuclear Medicine Technologists; Opticians, Dispensing; Orthotists and Prosthetists; Radiologic Technologists; Radiologic Technologists and Technicians.

Skills: Science; Operation Monitoring; Operation and Control; Equipment Selection; Service Orientation; Negotiation.

Education and Training Programs: Medical Radiologic Technology/Science—Radiation Therapist; Radiologic Technology/Science—Radiographer; Allied Health Diagnostic, Intervention, and Treatment Professions, Other. **Related Knowledge/Courses:** Medicine and Dentistry; Clerical Studies; Psychology; Physics; Biology; Chemistry.

Work Environment: Indoors; radiation; disease or infections; standing; walking and running; using hands on objects, tools, or controls.

Radiologic Technologists

- ✷ Education/Training Required: Associate degree
- ✷ Annual Earnings: $48,170
- ✷ Beginning Wage: $32,750
- ✷ Earnings Growth Potential: Very high
- ✷ Growth: 15.1%
- ✷ Annual Job Openings: 12,836
- ✷ Self-Employed: 1.1%
- ✷ Part-Time: 17.3%

Our sources did not provide separate job openings data for this occupation. The job openings listed here are shared with Radiologic Technicians.

Industries with Greatest Employment: Hospitals, Public and Private; Ambulatory Health Care Services.

Highest-Growth Industries (Projected Growth for This Job): Professional, Scientific, and Technical Services (37.7%); Administrative and Support Services (26.7%); Ambulatory Health Care Services (23.7%); Management of Companies and Enterprises (15.2%).

Lowest-Growth Industries (Projected Growth for This Job): Insurance Carriers and Related Activities (5.0%); Hospitals, Public and Private (11.0%); Educational Services, Public and Private (11.8%).

Fastest-Growing Metropolitan Areas (Recent Growth for This Job): Kingston, NY (160.0%); Tyler, TX (75.0%); Sebastian–Vero Beach, FL (66.7%); Utica–Rome, NY (66.7%); Alexandria, LA (63.6%).

Other Considerations for Job Security: In addition to job growth, job openings also will arise from the need to replace technologists who leave the occupation. Radiologic technologists who are willing to relocate and who also are experienced in more than one diagnostic imaging procedure—such as CT, MR, and mammography—will have the best employment opportunities as employers seek to control costs by using multi-credentialed employees. CT is becoming a frontline diagnosis tool. Instead of X rays being taken to decide whether a CT is needed, as was the practice before, CT is often the first choice for imaging because of its accuracy. MR also is increasing in frequency of use. Technologists with credentialing in either of these specialties will be very marketable to employers.

Take X rays and Computerized Axial Tomography (CAT or CT) scans or administer nonradioactive materials into patient's bloodstream for diagnostic purposes. Includes technologists who specialize in other modalities, such as computed tomography, ultrasound, and magnetic resonance. Review and evaluate developed X rays, videotape, or computer-generated information to determine whether images are satisfactory for diagnostic purposes. Use radiation safety measures and protection devices to comply with government regulations and to ensure safety of patients and staff. Explain procedures and observe patients to ensure safety and comfort during scan. Operate or oversee operation of radiologic and magnetic imaging equipment to produce images of the body for diagnostic purposes. Position and immobilize patient on examining table. Position imaging equipment and adjust controls to set exposure time and distance according to specification of examination. Key commands and data into computer to document and specify scan sequences, adjust transmitters and receivers, or photograph certain images. Monitor video display of area being scanned and adjust density or contrast to improve picture quality. Monitor patients' conditions and reactions, reporting abnormal signs to physician. Prepare and administer oral or injected contrast media to patients. Set up examination rooms, ensuring that all necessary equipment is ready. Take thorough and accurate patient medical histories. Remove and process film. Record, process, and maintain patient data and treatment records and prepare reports. Coordinate work with clerical personnel or other technologists. Demonstrate new equipment, procedures, and techniques to staff and provide technical assistance. Provide assistance in dressing or changing seriously ill, injured, or disabled patients. Move ultrasound scanner over patient's body and watch pattern produced on video screen. Measure thickness of section to be radiographed, using instruments similar to measuring tapes. Operate fluoroscope to aid physician to view and guide wire or catheter through blood vessels to area of interest. Assign duties to radiologic staff to maintain patient flows and achieve production goals. Collaborate with other medical team members, such as physicians and nurses, to conduct angiography or special vascular procedures. Perform administrative duties such as developing departmental operating budget, coordinating purchases of supplies and equipment, and preparing work schedules.

Personality Type: Realistic.

GOE—Interest Area: 08. Health Science. **Work Group:** 08.06. Medical Technology. **Other Jobs in this Work Group:** Biological Technicians; Cardiovascular Technologists and Technicians; Diagnostic Medical Sonographers; Medical and Clinical Laboratory Technicians; Medical and Clinical Laboratory Technologists; Medical Equipment Preparers; Medical Records and Health Information Technicians; Nuclear Medicine Technologists; Opticians, Dispensing; Orthotists and Prosthetists; Radiologic Technicians; Radiologic Technologists and Technicians.

Skills: Operation Monitoring; Social Perceptiveness; Reading Comprehension; Instructing; Service Orientation; Active Listening.

Education and Training Programs: Medical Radiologic Technology/Science—Radiation Therapist; Radiologic Technology/Science—Radiographer; Allied Health Diagnostic, Intervention, and Treatment Professions, Other. **Related Knowledge/Courses:** Medicine and Dentistry; Biology; Physics; Psychology; Chemistry; Customer and Personal Service.

Work Environment: Indoors; disease or infections; standing; walking and running; using hands on objects, tools, or controls; repetitive motions.

Radiologic Technologists and Technicians

See *Radiologic Technicians and Radiologic Technologists, described separately.*

Recreation and Fitness Studies Teachers, Postsecondary

* Education/Training Required: Doctoral degree
* Annual Earnings: $49,270
* Beginning Wage: $25,140
* Earnings Growth Potential: Very high
* Growth: 22.9%
* Annual Job Openings: 237,478
* Self-Employed: 0.4%
* Part-Time: 27.8%

Our sources did not provide separate job openings data for this occupation. The job openings listed here are shared with 35 other postsecondary teaching occupations. For a complete list, see the beginning of this section.

Industries with Greatest Employment: Educational Services, Public and Private.

Highest-Growth Industries (Projected Growth for This Job): Administrative and Support Services (48.3%); Amusement, Gambling, and Recreation Industries (45.3%); Social Assistance (38.6%); Support Activities for Transportation (32.8%); Religious, Grantmaking, Civic, Professional, and Similar Organizations (29.9%); Professional, Scientific, and Technical Services (28.8%); Management of Companies and Enterprises (26.8%); Educational Services, Public and Private (22.9%); Hospitals, Public and Private (21.4%); Personal and Laundry Services (21.0%).

Lowest-Growth Industries (Projected Growth for This Job): Other Information Services (7.4%); Sporting Goods, Hobby, Book, and Music Stores (13.3%); Performing Arts, Spectator Sports, and Related

Industries (13.4%); Insurance Carriers and Related Activities (13.9%).

Fastest-Growing Metropolitan Areas (Recent Growth for This Job): New York–Northern New Jersey–Long Island, NY–NJ–PA (16.7%); Miami–Fort Lauderdale–Miami Beach, FL (16.4%); Dallas–Fort Worth–Arlington, TX (14.3%); Phoenix–Mesa–Scottsdale, AZ (14.3%); Pittsburgh, PA (14.3%).

Other Considerations for Job Security: Retirements of current postsecondary teachers should create numerous openings for all types of postsecondary teachers, so job opportunities are generally expected to be very good. However, because students attend postsecondary institutions to prepare themselves for careers, the best job prospects for postsecondary teachers are likely to be in rapidly growing fields that offer many nonacademic career options, such as recreation and fitness studies. Community colleges and other institutions offering career and technical education have been among the most rapidly growing and are expected to offer some of the best opportunities for postsecondary teachers.

Teach courses pertaining to recreation, leisure, and fitness studies, including exercise physiology and facilities management. Evaluate and grade students' classwork, assignments, and papers. Maintain student attendance records, grades, and other required records. Prepare and deliver lectures to undergraduate and graduate students on topics such as anatomy, therapeutic recreation, and conditioning theory. Prepare course materials such as syllabi, homework assignments, and handouts. Maintain regularly scheduled office hours to advise and assist students. Compile, administer, and grade examinations or assign this work to others. Plan, evaluate, and revise curricula, course content, course materials, and methods of instruction. Initiate, facilitate, and moderate classroom discussions. Keep abreast of developments in their field by reading current literature, talking with colleagues, and participating in professional conferences. Advise students on academic and vocational curricula and on career issues. Participate in student recruitment, registration, and placement activities. Collaborate with colleagues

to address teaching and research issues. Select and obtain materials and supplies such as textbooks. Participate in campus and community events. Serve on academic or administrative committees that deal with institutional policies, departmental matters, and academic issues. Compile bibliographies of specialized materials for outside reading assignments. Supervise undergraduate or graduate teaching, internships, and research work. Perform administrative duties such as serving as department heads. Prepare students to act as sports coaches. Conduct research in a particular field of knowledge and publish findings in professional journals, books, or electronic media. Act as advisers to student organizations. Write grant proposals to procure external research funding. Provide professional consulting services to government or industry.

Personality Type: No data available.

GOE—Interest Area: 05. Education and Training. **Work Group:** 05.03. Postsecondary and Adult Teaching and Instructing. **Other Jobs in this Work Group:** Adult Literacy, Remedial Education, and GED Teachers and Instructors; Agricultural Sciences Teachers, Postsecondary; Anthropology and Archeology Teachers, Postsecondary; Architecture Teachers, Postsecondary; Area, Ethnic, and Cultural Studies Teachers, Postsecondary; Art, Drama, and Music Teachers, Postsecondary; Atmospheric, Earth, Marine, and Space Sciences Teachers, Postsecondary; Biological Science Teachers, Postsecondary; Business Teachers, Postsecondary; Chemistry Teachers, Postsecondary; Communications Teachers, Postsecondary; Computer Science Teachers, Postsecondary; Criminal Justice and Law Enforcement Teachers, Postsecondary; Economics Teachers, Postsecondary; Education Teachers, Postsecondary; Engineering Teachers, Postsecondary; English Language and Literature Teachers, Postsecondary; Environmental Science Teachers, Postsecondary; Farm and Home Management Advisors; Foreign Language and Literature Teachers, Postsecondary; Forestry and Conservation Science Teachers, Postsecondary; Geography Teachers, Postsecondary; Graduate Teaching Assistants; Health Specialties Teachers, Postsecondary;

History Teachers, Postsecondary; Home Economics Teachers, Postsecondary; Law Teachers, Postsecondary; Library Science Teachers, Postsecondary; Mathematical Science Teachers, Postsecondary; Nursing Instructors and Teachers, Postsecondary; Philosophy and Religion Teachers, Postsecondary; Physics Teachers, Postsecondary; Political Science Teachers, Postsecondary; Psychology Teachers, Postsecondary; Self-Enrichment Education Teachers; Social Work Teachers, Postsecondary; Sociology Teachers, Postsecondary; Vocational Education Teachers, Postsecondary.

Skills: Instructing; Learning Strategies; Science; Social Perceptiveness; Persuasion; Time Management.

Education and Training Programs: Parks, Recreation and Leisure Studies; Health and Physical Education, General; Sport and Fitness Administration/ Management. **Related Knowledge/Courses:** Education and Training; Philosophy and Theology; Psychology; Therapy and Counseling; Medicine and Dentistry; Sociology and Anthropology.

Work Environment: More often indoors than outdoors; standing.

Registered Nurses

- ✳ Education/Training Required: Associate degree
- ✳ Annual Earnings: $57,280
- ✳ Beginning Wage: $40,250
- ✳ Earnings Growth Potential: Very high
- ✳ Growth: 23.5%
- ✳ Annual Job Openings: 233,499
- ✳ Self-Employed: 0.8%
- ✳ Part-Time: 21.8%

Industries with Greatest Employment: Hospitals, Public and Private; Ambulatory Health Care Services; Nursing and Residential Care Facilities.

Highest-Growth Industries (Projected Growth for This Job): Social Assistance (51.0%); Professional,

Scientific, and Technical Services (44.8%); Ambulatory Health Care Services (37.5%); Internet Service Providers, Web Search Portals, and Data Processing Services (34.3%); Amusement, Gambling, and Recreation Industries (32.5%); Administrative and Support Services (26.7%); Nursing and Residential Care Facilities (25.2%); Nonstore Retailers (25.0%); Funds, Trusts, and Other Financial Vehicles (23.6%); Performing Arts, Spectator Sports, and Related Industries (23.3%); Hospitals, Public and Private (21.6%); Religious, Grantmaking, Civic, Professional, and Similar Organizations (19.3%); Merchant Wholesalers, Nondurable Goods (18.8%); Real Estate (18.8%); Personal and Laundry Services (15.5%); Management of Companies and Enterprises (15.3%).

Lowest-Growth Industries (Projected Growth for This Job): Primary Metal Manufacturing (–29.7%); Paper Manufacturing (–26.3%); Electrical Equipment, Appliance, and Component Manufacturing (–16.8%); Fabricated Metal Product Manufacturing (–13.3%); Computer and Electronic Product Manufacturing (–11.4%); Machinery Manufacturing (–9.6%); Transportation Equipment Manufacturing (–8.0%); Publishing Industries (except Internet) (–5.1%); Chemical Manufacturing (0.0%); Miscellaneous Manufacturing (0.0%).

Fastest-Growing Metropolitan Areas (Recent Growth for This Job): College Station–Bryan, TX (60.7%); Midland, TX (43.4%); Elkhart–Goshen, IN (32.9%); Prescott, AZ (28.4%); Visalia–Porterville, CA (24.4%).

Other Considerations for Job Security: Overall, job opportunities are expected to be excellent for registered nurses, but they can vary by employment setting. Generally, RNs with at least a bachelor's degree will have better job prospects than those without a bachelor's. Also, all four advanced practice specialties—clinical nurse specialists, nurse practitioners, nurse-midwives, and nurse anesthetists—will be in high demand, particularly in medically underserved areas such as inner cities and rural areas. Relative to physicians, these RNs increasingly serve as lower-cost primary care providers.

Assess patient health problems and needs, develop and implement nursing care plans, and maintain medical records. Administer nursing care to ill, injured, convalescent, or disabled patients. May advise patients on health maintenance and disease prevention or provide case management. Licensing or registration required. Includes advance practice nurses, such as nurse practitioners, clinical nurse specialists, certified nurse midwives, and certified registered nurse anesthetists. Advanced practice nursing is performed by RNs with specialized formal, post-basic education and who function in highly autonomous and specialized roles. Maintain accurate, detailed reports and records. Monitor, record, and report symptoms and changes in patients' conditions. Record patients' medical information and vital signs. Modify patient treatment plans as indicated by patients' responses and conditions. Consult and coordinate with health-care team members to assess, plan, implement, and evaluate patient care plans. Order, interpret, and evaluate diagnostic tests to identify and assess patient's condition. Monitor all aspects of patient care, including diet and physical activity. Direct and supervise less-skilled nursing or health-care personnel or supervise a particular unit. Prepare patients for, and assist with, examinations and treatments. Observe nurses and visit patients to ensure proper nursing care. Assess the needs of individuals, families, or communities, including assessment of individuals' home or work environments, to identify potential health or safety problems. Instruct individuals, families, and other groups on topics such as health education, disease prevention, and childbirth; develop health-improvement programs. Prepare rooms, sterile instruments, equipment, and supplies and ensure that stock of supplies is maintained. Inform physician of patient's condition during anesthesia. Deliver infants and provide prenatal and postpartum care and treatment under obstetrician's supervision. Administer local, inhalation, intravenous, and other anesthetics. Provide health care, first aid, immunizations, and assistance in convalescence and rehabilitation in locations such as schools, hospitals, and industry. Conduct specified laboratory tests. Perform physical examinations, make tentative diagnoses, and treat patients en route to hospitals or at disaster-site triage centers. Hand items to surgeons during operations. Prescribe or recommend drugs; medical devices; or other forms of treatment, such as physical therapy, inhalation therapy, or related therapeutic procedures. Direct and coordinate infection-control programs, advising and consulting with specified personnel about necessary precautions. Perform administrative and managerial functions, such as taking responsibility for a unit's staff, budget, planning, and long-range goals.

Personality Type: Social.

GOE—Interest Area: 08. Health Science. **Work Group:** 08.02. Medicine and Surgery. **Other Jobs in this Work Group:** Anesthesiologists; Family and General Practitioners; Internists, General; Medical Assistants; Medical Transcriptionists; Obstetricians and Gynecologists; Pediatricians, General; Pharmacists; Pharmacy Aides; Pharmacy Technicians; Physician Assistants; Psychiatrists; Surgeons; Surgical Technologists.

Skills: Social Perceptiveness; Service Orientation; Science; Time Management; Monitoring; Reading Comprehension.

Education and Training Programs: Nursing—Registered Nurse Training (RN, ASN, BSN, MSN); Adult Health Nurse/Nursing; Nurse Anesthetist; Family Practice Nurse/Nurse Practitioner; Maternal/Child Health and Neonatal Nurse/Nursing; Nurse Midwife/Nursing Midwifery; Nursing Science (MS, PhD); Pediatric Nurse/Nursing; Psychiatric/Mental Health Nurse/Nursing; Public Health/Community Nurse/Nursing; others. **Related Knowledge/Courses:** Medicine and Dentistry; Psychology; Therapy and Counseling; Biology; Sociology and Anthropology; Philosophy and Theology.

Work Environment: Indoors; noisy; contaminants; disease or infections; standing; using hands on objects, tools, or controls.

Rehabilitation Counselors

- ❀ Education/Training Required: Master's degree
- ❀ Annual Earnings: $29,200
- ❀ Beginning Wage: $19,260
- ❀ Earnings Growth Potential: Very high
- ❀ Growth: 23.0%
- ❀ Annual Job Openings: 32,081
- ❀ Self-Employed: 5.9%
- ❀ Part-Time: 15.4%

Industries with Greatest Employment: Social Assistance; Nursing and Residential Care Facilities.

Highest-Growth Industries (Projected Growth for This Job): Professional, Scientific, and Technical Services (55.6%); Social Assistance (34.6%); Administrative and Support Services (34.5%); Nursing and Residential Care Facilities (26.8%); Ambulatory Health Care Services (21.5%); Management of Companies and Enterprises (15.3%).

Lowest-Growth Industries (Projected Growth for This Job): Hospitals, Public and Private (–0.7%); Educational Services, Public and Private (11.2%); Miscellaneous Store Retailers (12.5%); Real Estate (13.9%); Religious, Grantmaking, Civic, Professional, and Similar Organizations (14.7%); Insurance Carriers and Related Activities (14.9%).

Fastest-Growing Metropolitan Areas (Recent Growth for This Job): Pittsburgh, PA (127.7%); Mobile, AL (100.0%); Canton–Massillon, OH (77.8%); Rapid City, SD (75.0%); Akron, OH (73.3%).

Other Considerations for Job Security: The number of people who will need rehabilitation counseling is expected to grow as advances in medical technology allow more people to survive injury or illness and live independently again. Also, legislation requiring equal employment rights for disabled people will spur demand for counselors, who not only help these people make a transition to the workforce but also help companies comply with the law. Prospects for rehabilitation counselors are excellent because many people are leaving the field or retiring.

Counsel individuals to maximize the independence and employability of persons coping with personal, social, and vocational difficulties that result from birth defects, illness, disease, accidents, or the stress of daily life. Coordinate activities for residents of care and treatment facilities. Assess client needs and design and implement rehabilitation programs that may include personal and vocational counseling, training, and job placement. Monitor and record clients' progress to ensure that goals and objectives are met. Confer with clients to discuss their options and goals so that rehabilitation programs and plans for accessing needed services can be developed. Prepare and maintain records and case files, including documentation such as clients' personal and eligibility information, services provided, narratives of client contacts, and relevant correspondence. Arrange for physical, mental, academic, vocational, and other evaluations to obtain information for assessing clients' needs and developing rehabilitation plans. Analyze information from interviews, educational and medical records, consultation with other professionals, and diagnostic evaluations to assess clients' abilities, needs, and eligibility for services. Develop rehabilitation plans that fit clients' aptitudes, education levels, physical abilities, and career goals. Maintain close contact with clients during job training and placements to resolve problems and evaluate placement adequacy. Locate barriers to client employment, such as inaccessible work sites, inflexible schedules, and transportation problems, and work with clients to develop strategies for overcoming these barriers. Develop and maintain relationships with community referral sources such as schools and community groups. Arrange for on-site job coaching or assistive devices such as specially equipped wheelchairs to help clients adapt to work or school environments. Confer with physicians, psychologists, occupational therapists, and other professionals to develop and implement client rehabilitation programs. Develop diagnostic procedures for determining clients' needs. Participate in job development and placement programs, contacting prospective employers, placing clients in jobs, and evaluating the success of placements. Collaborate with clients' families to implement rehabilitation plans that include behavioral, residential, social, and/or employment goals. Collaborate with community agencies to establish facilities and programs to assist persons with disabilities.

Personality Type: No data available.

GOE—Interest Area: 10. Human Service. **Work Group:** 10.01. Counseling and Social Work. **Other Jobs in this Work Group:** Child, Family, and School Social Workers; Clinical Psychologists; Clinical, Counseling, and School Psychologists; Counseling Psychologists; Marriage and Family Therapists; Medical and Public Health Social Workers; Mental Health and Substance Abuse Social Workers; Mental Health Counselors; Probation Officers and Correctional Treatment Specialists; Residential Advisors; Social and Human Service Assistants; Substance Abuse and Behavioral Disorder Counselors.

Skills: Management of Financial Resources; Social Perceptiveness; Writing; Service Orientation; Monitoring; Coordination.

Education and Training Programs: Vocational Rehabilitation Counseling/Counselor; Assistive/Augmentative Technology and Rehabiliation Engineering. **Related Knowledge/Courses:** Psychology; Therapy and Counseling; Philosophy and Theology; Education and Training; Personnel and Human Resources; Sociology and Anthropology.

Work Environment: More often indoors than outdoors; sitting; walking and running.

Respiratory Therapists

- ❀ Education/Training Required: Associate degree
- ❀ Annual Earnings: $47,420
- ❀ Beginning Wage: $35,200
- ❀ Earnings Growth Potential: Very high
- ❀ Growth: 22.6%
- ❀ Annual Job Openings: 5,563
- ❀ Self-Employed: 1.1%
- ❀ Part-Time: 15.0%

Industries with Greatest Employment: Hospitals, Public and Private.

Highest-Growth Industries (Projected Growth for This Job): Professional, Scientific, and Technical Services (71.7%); Ambulatory Health Care Services (32.5%); Rental and Leasing Services (29.9%); Hospitals, Public and Private (22.6%); Nursing and Residential Care Facilities (22.1%); Administrative and Support Services (19.5%); Merchant Wholesalers, Durable Goods (16.5%); Management of Companies and Enterprises (15.4%).

Lowest-Growth Industries (Projected Growth for This Job): Health and Personal Care Stores (6.3%); Educational Services, Public and Private (11.8%).

Fastest-Growing Metropolitan Areas (Recent Growth for This Job): Austin–Round Rock, TX (130.8%); Rochester, NY (71.4%); Norwich–New London, CT–RI (50.0%); Montgomery, AL (42.9%); Greensboro–High Point, NC (42.1%).

Other Considerations for Job Security: Job opportunities are expected to be very good. The vast majority of job openings will continue to be in hospitals. However, a growing number of openings are expected to be outside hospitals, especially in home health-care services, offices of physicians or other health practitioners, consumer-goods rental firms, or in the employment services industry as a temporary worker in various settings. The increasing demand will come from substantial growth in the middle-aged and elderly population—a development that will heighten the incidence of cardiopulmonary disease. Growth in demand also will result from the expanding role of respiratory therapists in case management, disease prevention, emergency care, and the early detection of pulmonary disorders.

Assess, treat, and care for patients with breathing disorders. Assume primary responsibility for all respiratory care modalities, including the supervision of respiratory therapy technicians. Initiate and conduct therapeutic procedures; maintain patient records; and select, assemble, check, and operate equipment. Set up and operate devices such as mechanical ventilators, therapeutic gas administration apparatus, environmental control systems, and aerosol generators, following specified parameters of treatment. Provide emergency care, including artificial respiration, external cardiac massage, and assistance with cardiopulmonary resuscitation. Determine requirements for treatment, such as type, method, and duration of therapy; precautions to be taken; and medication and dosages, compatible with physicians' orders. Monitor patient's physiological responses to therapy, such as vital signs, arterial blood gases, and blood chemistry changes, and consult with physician if adverse reactions occur. Read prescriptions, measure arterial blood gases, and review patient information to assess patient condition. Work as part of a team of physicians, nurses, and other health-care professionals to manage patient care. Enforce safety rules and ensure careful adherence to physicians' orders. Maintain charts that contain patients' pertinent identification and therapy information. Inspect, clean, test, and maintain respiratory therapy equipment to ensure equipment is functioning safely and efficiently, ordering repairs when necessary. Educate patients and their families about their conditions and teach appropriate disease-management techniques, such as breathing exercises and the use of medications and respiratory equipment. Explain treatment procedures to patients to gain cooperation and allay fears. Relay blood analysis results to a physician. Perform pulmonary function and adjust equipment to obtain optimum results in therapy. Perform bronchopulmonary drainage and assist or instruct patients in performance of breathing exercises. Demonstrate respiratory care procedures to trainees and other health-care personnel. Teach, train, supervise, and utilize the help of students, respiratory therapy technicians, and assistants. Make emergency visits to resolve equipment problems. Use a variety of testing techniques to assist doctors in cardiac and pulmonary research and to diagnose disorders. Conduct tests, such as electrocardiograms (EKGs), stress testing, and lung capacity tests, to evaluate patients' cardiopulmonary functions.

Personality Type: Investigative.

GOE—Interest Area: 08. Health Science. **Work Group:** 08.07. Medical Therapy. **Other Jobs in this Work Group:** Audiologists; Massage Therapists; Occupational Therapist Aides; Occupational Therapist Assistants; Occupational Therapists; Physical Therapist Aides; Physical Therapist Assistants; Physical Therapists; Radiation Therapists; Recreational Therapists; Respiratory Therapy Technicians; Speech-Language Pathologists.

Skills: Science; Operation Monitoring; Mathematics; Reading Comprehension; Active Learning; Instructing.

Education and Training Program: Respiratory Care Therapy/Therapist. **Related Knowledge/Courses:** Medicine and Dentistry; Biology; Psychology; Customer and Personal Service; Therapy and Counseling; Chemistry.

Work Environment: Indoors; disease or infections; standing.

School Psychologists

* Education/Training Required: Doctoral degree
* Annual Earnings: $59,440
* Beginning Wage: $35,280
* Earnings Growth Potential: Very high
* Growth: 15.8%
* Annual Job Openings: 8,309
* Self-Employed: 34.2%
* Part-Time: 24.0%

Our sources did not provide separate job openings data for this occupation. The job openings listed here are shared with Clinical Psychologists and with Counseling Psychologists.

Industries with Greatest Employment: Educational Services, Public and Private; Ambulatory Health Care Services; Hospitals, Public and Private; Social Assistance.

Highest-Growth Industries (Projected Growth for This Job): Social Assistance (56.2%); Professional, Scientific, and Technical Services (34.6%); Ambulatory Health Care Services (26.8%); Nursing and Residential Care Facilities (24.8%); Funds, Trusts, and Other Financial Vehicles (23.3%); Religious, Grantmaking, Civic, Professional, and Similar Organizations (19.4%); Management of Companies and Enterprises (15.2%).

Lowest-Growth Industries (Projected Growth for This Job): Hospitals, Public and Private (–3.5%); Educational Services, Public and Private (6.9%).

Fastest-Growing Metropolitan Areas (Recent Growth for This Job): Augusta–Richmond County, GA–SC (100.0%); Memphis, TN–MS–AR (100.0%); Peoria, IL (90.0%); Greenville, SC (87.5%); Oklahoma City, OK (86.2%).

Other Considerations for Job Security: Growing awareness of how students' mental health and behavioral problems, such as bullying, affect learning will increase demand for school psychologists to offer student counseling and mental-health services. Job prospects should be the best for people with a specialist or doctoral degree in school psychology. Opportunities directly related to psychology will be limited for bachelor's-degree holders. Those who meet state certification requirements may become high-school psychology teachers.

Investigate processes of learning and teaching and develop psychological principles and techniques applicable to educational problems. Compile and interpret students' test results, along with information from teachers and parents, to diagnose conditions and to help assess eligibility for special services. Report any pertinent information to the proper authorities in cases of child endangerment, neglect, or abuse. Assess an individual child's needs, limitations, and potential, using observation, review of school records, and consultation with parents and school personnel. Select, administer, and score psychological tests. Provide consultation to parents, teachers, administrators, and others on topics such as learning styles and behavior-modification techniques. Promote an understanding of child development and its relationship to learning and behavior. Collaborate with other educational professionals to develop teaching strategies and school programs. Counsel children and families to help solve conflicts and problems in learning and adjustment. Develop individualized educational plans in collaboration with teachers and other staff members. Maintain student records, including special education reports, confidential records, records of services provided, and behavioral data. Serve as a resource to help families and schools deal with crises, such as separation and loss. Attend workshops, seminars, or professional meetings to remain informed of new developments in school psychology. Design classes and programs to meet the needs of special students. Refer students and their families to appropriate community agencies for medical, vocational, or social services. Initiate and direct efforts to foster tolerance, understanding, and appreciation of diversity in school communities. Collect and analyze data to evaluate the effectiveness of academic programs and other services, such as behavioral management systems. Provide educational programs on topics such as classroom management, teaching strategies, or parenting skills. Conduct research to generate new knowledge that can be used to address learning and behavior issues.

Personality Type: Investigative.

GOE—Interest Area: 15. Scientific Research, Engineering, and Mathematics. **Work Group:** 15.04. Social Sciences. **Other Jobs in this Work Group:** Anthropologists; Anthropologists and Archeologists; Archeologists; Economists; Historians; Industrial-Organizational Psychologists; Political Scientists; Sociologists.

Skills: Social Perceptiveness; Negotiation; Learning Strategies; Persuasion; Writing; Active Listening.

Education and Training Programs: Educational Assessment, Testing, and Measurement; Psychology, General; Clinical Psychology; Counseling Psychology; Developmental and Child Psychology; School Psychology; Psychoanalysis and Psychotherapy. **Related Knowledge/Courses:** Therapy and Counseling; Psychology; Sociology and Anthropology; Philosophy and Theology; Education and Training; Customer and Personal Service.

Work Environment: Indoors; sitting.

Secondary School Teachers, Except Special and Vocational Education

- ✳ Education/Training Required: Bachelor's degree
- ✳ Annual Earnings: $47,740
- ✳ Beginning Wage: $31,760
- ✳ Earnings Growth Potential: Very high
- ✳ Growth: 5.6%
- ✳ Annual Job Openings: 93,166
- ✳ Self-Employed: 0.0%
- ✳ Part-Time: 7.8%

Industries with Greatest Employment: Educational Services, Public and Private.

Highest-Growth Industries (Projected Growth for This Job): Social Assistance (50.4%); Administrative and Support Services (26.7%); Nursing and Residential Care Facilities (21.6%).

Lowest-Growth Industries (Projected Growth for This Job): Hospitals, Public and Private (–10.1%); Educational Services, Public and Private (5.5%).

Fastest-Growing Metropolitan Areas (Recent Growth for This Job): Battle Creek, MI (109.5%); Ithaca, NY (79.2%); Memphis, TN–MS–AR (58.1%); Harrisburg–Carlisle, PA (47.2%); Chico, CA (45.5%).

Other Considerations for Job Security: Job prospects are expected to be favorable, with particularly good prospects for teachers in high-demand fields such as math, science, and bilingual education, in less desirable urban or rural school districts, and for those who obtain licensure in more than one subject. Fast-growing states in the South and West—led by Nevada, Arizona, Texas, and Georgia—will experience the largest enrollment increases. Enrollments in the Midwest are expected to hold relatively steady, while those in the Northeast are expected to decline. Teachers who are geographically mobile and who obtain licensure in more than one subject should have a distinct advantage in finding a job. The number of teachers employed depends on state and local expenditures for education and on the enactment of legislation to increase the quality and scope of public education. At the federal level, there has been a large increase in funding for education, particularly for the hiring of qualified teachers in lower-income areas.

Instruct students in secondary public or private schools in one or more subjects at the secondary level, such as English, mathematics, or social studies. May be designated according to subject matter specialty, such as typing instructors, commercial teachers, or English teachers. Establish and enforce rules for behavior and procedures for maintaining order among the students for whom they are responsible. Instruct through lectures, discussions, and demonstrations in one or more subjects such as English, mathematics, or social studies. Establish clear objectives for all lessons, units, and projects and communicate those objectives to students. Prepare, administer, and grade tests and assignments to evaluate students' progress. Prepare materials and classrooms for class activities. Adapt teaching methods and instructional materials to meet students' varying needs and interests. Assign and grade classwork and homework. Maintain accurate and complete student records as required by laws, district policies, and administrative regulations. Enforce all administration policies and rules governing students. Observe and evaluate students' performance, behavior, social development, and physical health. Plan and conduct activities for a balanced program of instruction, demonstration, and work time that provides students with opportunities to observe, question, and investigate. Prepare students for later grades by encouraging them to explore learning opportunities and to persevere with challenging tasks. Guide and counsel students with adjustment and/or academic problems or special academic interests. Instruct and monitor students in the use and care of equipment and materials to prevent injuries and damage. Prepare for assigned classes and show written evidence of preparation on request of immediate supervisors. Meet with parents and guardians to discuss their children's progress and to determine their priorities for their children and their resource needs. Confer with parents or guardians, other teachers, counselors, and administrators to resolve students' behavioral and academic problems. Use computers, audiovisual aids, and other equipment and materials to supplement presentations. Prepare objectives and outlines for courses of study, following curriculum guidelines or state and school requirements. Meet with other professionals to discuss individual students' needs and progress.

Personality Type: Social.

GOE—Interest Area: 05. Education and Training. **Work Group:** 05.02. Preschool, Elementary, and Secondary Teaching and Instructing. **Other Jobs in this Work Group:** Elementary School Teachers, Except Special Education; Kindergarten Teachers, Except Special Education; Middle School Teachers, Except Special and Vocational Education; Preschool Teachers, Except Special Education; Special Education Teachers, Middle School; Special Education Teachers, Preschool, Kindergarten, and Elementary School; Special Education Teachers, Secondary School; Teacher Assistants; Vocational Education Teachers, Middle School; Vocational Education Teachers, Secondary School.

Skills: Learning Strategies; Social Perceptiveness; Persuasion; Monitoring; Instructing; Time Management.

Education and Training Programs: Junior High/Intermediate/Middle School Education and Teaching; Secondary Education and Teaching; Teacher

Education, Multiple Levels; Waldorf/Steiner Teacher Education; Agricultural Teacher Education; Art Teacher Education; Business Teacher Education; Driver and Safety Teacher Education; English/Language Arts Teacher Education; Foreign Language Teacher Education; Health Teacher Education; others. **Related Knowledge/Courses:** History and Archeology; Philosophy and Theology; Sociology and Anthropology; Education and Training; Geography; Therapy and Counseling.

Work Environment: Indoors; noisy; standing.

Self-Enrichment Education Teachers

- ❋ Education/Training Required: Work experience in a related occupation
- ❋ Annual Earnings: $33,440
- ❋ Beginning Wage: $17,740
- ❋ Earnings Growth Potential: Very high
- ❋ Growth: 23.1%
- ❋ Annual Job Openings: 64,449
- ❋ Self-Employed: 21.5%
- ❋ Part-Time: 41.3%

Industries with Greatest Employment: Educational Services, Public and Private; Religious, Grantmaking, Civic, Professional, and Similar Organizations; Social Assistance.

Highest-Growth Industries (Projected Growth for This Job): Social Assistance (38.7%); Museums, Historical Sites, and Similar Institutions (36.2%); Amusement, Gambling, and Recreation Industries (31.0%); Scenic and Sightseeing Transportation (30.1%); Administrative and Support Services (28.3%); Professional, Scientific, and Technical Services (25.1%); Nursing and Residential Care Facilities (23.9%); Educational Services, Public and Private (23.1%); Ambulatory Health Care Services (22.2%); Support Activities for Transportation (20.9%); Religious, Grantmaking, Civic, Professional, and Similar Organizations (19.0%); Management of Companies and Enterprises (15.3%).

Lowest-Growth Industries (Projected Growth for This Job): Electronics and Appliance Stores (–8.7%); Sporting Goods, Hobby, Book, and Music Stores (3.0%); Private Households (3.9%); Miscellaneous Store Retailers (6.9%); Hospitals, Public and Private (8.2%); Performing Arts, Spectator Sports, and Related Industries (9.2%); Personal and Laundry Services (10.6%); Air Transportation (13.1%); Accommodation, Including Hotels and Motels (14.5%).

Fastest-Growing Metropolitan Areas (Recent Growth for This Job): Lakeland, FL (300.0%); Salem, OR (250.0%); Danbury, CT (160.0%); Pittsburgh, PA (151.4%); Lewiston–Auburn, ME (133.3%).

Other Considerations for Job Security: Job prospects should be favorable as increasing demand and high turnover creates many opportunities, but opportunities may vary as some fields have more prospective teachers than others. Opportunities should be best for teachers of subjects that aren't easily researched on the Internet and those that benefit from hands-on experiences, such as cooking, crafts, and the arts. Classes on self-improvement, personal finance, and computer and Internet-related subjects are also expected to be popular.

Teach or instruct courses other than those that normally lead to an occupational objective or degree. Courses may include self-improvement, nonvocational, and nonacademic subjects. Teaching may or may not take place in a traditional educational institution. Adapt teaching methods and instructional materials to meet students' varying needs and interests. Conduct classes, workshops, and demonstrations and provide individual instruction to teach topics and skills such as cooking, dancing, writing, physical fitness, photography, personal finance, and flying. Monitor students' performance to make suggestions for improvement and to ensure that they satisfy course standards, training requirements, and objectives. Observe students to determine qualifications, limitations, abilities, interests, and other individual characteristics. Instruct students individually and in groups, using various teaching methods such as lectures, discussions, and demonstrations. Establish clear objectives for all lessons, units, and projects and communicate those objectives to students. Instruct and monitor students in use and care of equipment and materials to prevent injury and damage. Prepare students for further development by encouraging them to explore learning opportunities and to persevere with challenging tasks. Prepare materials and classrooms for class activities. Enforce policies and rules governing students. Plan and conduct activities for a balanced program of instruction, demonstration, and work time that provides students with opportunities to observe, question, and investigate. Prepare instructional program objectives, outlines, and lesson plans. Maintain accurate and complete student records as required by administrative policy. Participate in publicity planning and student recruitment. Plan and supervise class projects, field trips, visits by guest speakers, contests, or other experiential activities and guide students in learning from those activities. Attend professional meetings, conferences, and workshops to maintain and improve professional competence. Meet with other instructors to discuss individual students and their progress. Confer with other teachers and professionals to plan and schedule lessons promoting learning and development. Attend staff meetings and serve on committees as required. Prepare and administer written, oral, and performance tests and issue grades in accordance with performance.

Personality Type: Social.

GOE—Interest Area: 05. Education and Training. **Work Group:** 05.03. Postsecondary and Adult Teaching and Instructing. **Other Jobs in this Work Group:** Adult Literacy, Remedial Education, and GED Teachers and Instructors; Agricultural Sciences Teachers, Postsecondary; Anthropology and Archeology Teachers, Postsecondary; Architecture Teachers, Postsecondary; Area, Ethnic, and Cultural Studies Teachers, Postsecondary; Art, Drama, and Music Teachers, Postsecondary; Atmospheric, Earth, Marine, and Space Sciences Teachers, Postsecondary; Biological Science Teachers, Postsecondary; Business Teachers, Postsecondary; Chemistry Teachers, Postsecondary; Communications Teachers, Postsecondary; Computer Science Teachers, Postsecondary;

Criminal Justice and Law Enforcement Teachers, Postsecondary; Economics Teachers, Postsecondary; Education Teachers, Postsecondary; Engineering Teachers, Postsecondary; English Language and Literature Teachers, Postsecondary; Environmental Science Teachers, Postsecondary; Farm and Home Management Advisors; Foreign Language and Literature Teachers, Postsecondary; Forestry and Conservation Science Teachers, Postsecondary; Geography Teachers, Postsecondary; Graduate Teaching Assistants; Health Specialties Teachers, Postsecondary; History Teachers, Postsecondary; Home Economics Teachers, Postsecondary; Law Teachers, Postsecondary; Library Science Teachers, Postsecondary; Mathematical Science Teachers, Postsecondary; Nursing Instructors and Teachers, Postsecondary; Philosophy and Religion Teachers, Postsecondary; Physics Teachers, Postsecondary; Political Science Teachers, Postsecondary; Psychology Teachers, Postsecondary; Recreation and Fitness Studies Teachers, Postsecondary; Social Work Teachers, Postsecondary; Sociology Teachers, Postsecondary; Vocational Education Teachers, Postsecondary.

Skills: No data available.

Education and Training Program: Adult and Continuing Education and Teaching. **Related Knowledge/Courses:** Fine Arts; Education and Training; Psychology; Customer and Personal Service; Sales and Marketing; Administration and Management.

Work Environment: Indoors; standing.

Sheriffs and Deputy Sheriffs

* Education/Training Required: Long-term on-the-job training
* Annual Earnings: $47,460
* Beginning Wage: $27,310
* Earnings Growth Potential: Very high
* Growth: 10.8%
* Annual Job Openings: 37,842
* Self-Employed: 0.0%
* Part-Time: 1.1%

Our sources did not provide separate job openings data for this occupation. The job openings listed here are shared with Police Patrol Officers.

Industries with Greatest Employment: Educational Services, Public and Private; Hospitals, Public and Private.

Highest-Growth Industries (Projected Growth for This Job): None met the criteria.

Lowest-Growth Industries (Projected Growth for This Job): Hospitals, Public and Private (11.3%); Educational Services, Public and Private (11.7%).

Fastest-Growing Metropolitan Areas (Recent Growth for This Job): Beaumont–Port Arthur, TX (95.7%); Lafayette, IN (92.3%); Houma–Bayou Cane–Thibodaux, LA (89.5%); Waterloo–Cedar Falls, IA (69.2%); Kennewick–Richland–Pasco, WA (57.1%).

Other Considerations for Job Security: Overall, opportunities for sheriffs will be excellent for individuals who meet the psychological, personal, and physical qualifications. There will be more competition for jobs in federal and state law-enforcement agencies than for jobs in local agencies. Less competition for jobs will occur in departments that offer relatively low salaries or those in urban communities where the crime rate is relatively high. Applicants with military experience or college training in police science will have the best opportunities in local and state departments. The level of government spending determines the level of employment for sheriffs, police, and detectives, but layoffs are rare because retirements enable most staffing cuts to be handled through attrition.

Enforce law and order in rural or unincorporated districts or serve legal processes of courts. May patrol courthouse, guard court or grand jury, or escort defendants. Drive vehicles or patrol specific areas to detect law violators, issue citations, and make arrests. Investigate illegal or suspicious activities. Verify that the proper legal charges have been made against law offenders. Execute arrest warrants, locating and taking persons into custody. Record daily activities and submit logs and other related reports and paperwork to appropriate authorities. Patrol and guard courthouses, grand jury rooms, or assigned areas to provide security, enforce laws, maintain order, and arrest violators. Notify patrol units to take violators into custody or to provide needed assistance or medical aid. Place people in protective custody. Serve statements of claims, subpoenas, summonses, jury summonses, orders to pay alimony, and other court orders. Take control of accident scenes to maintain traffic flow, to assist accident victims, and to investigate causes. Question individuals entering secured areas to determine their business, directing and rerouting individuals as necessary. Transport or escort prisoners and defendants en route to courtrooms, prisons or jails, attorneys' offices, or medical facilities. Locate and confiscate real or personal property, as directed by court order. Manage jail operations and tend to jail inmates.

Personality Type: Social.

GOE—Interest Area: 12. Law and Public Safety. **Work Group:** 12.04. Law Enforcement and Public Safety. **Other Jobs in this Work Group:** Bailiffs; Correctional Officers and Jailers; Criminal Investigators and Special Agents; Detectives and Criminal Investigators; Fire Investigators; Forensic Science Technicians; Parking Enforcement Workers; Police and Sheriff's Patrol Officers; Police Detectives; Police Identification and Records Officers; Police Patrol Officers; Transit and Railroad Police.

Skills: Negotiation; Persuasion; Social Perceptiveness; Service Orientation; Complex Problem Solving; Judgment and Decision Making.

Education and Training Programs: Criminal Justice/Police Science; Criminalistics and Criminal Science. **Related Knowledge/Courses:** Public Safety and Security; Law and Government; Telecommunications; Psychology; Therapy and Counseling; Philosophy and Theology.

Work Environment: More often outdoors than indoors; very hot or cold; contaminants; disease or infections; sitting.

Social and Community Service Managers

- ✸ Education/Training Required: Bachelor's degree
- ✸ Annual Earnings: $52,070
- ✸ Beginning Wage: $31,050
- ✸ Earnings Growth Potential: Very high
- ✸ Growth: 24.7%
- ✸ Annual Job Openings: 23,788
- ✸ Self-Employed: 5.9%
- ✸ Part-Time: 11.6%

Industries with Greatest Employment: Social Assistance; Religious, Grantmaking, Civic, Professional, and Similar Organizations; Nursing and Residential Care Facilities.

Highest-Growth Industries (Projected Growth for This Job): Social Assistance (47.2%); Professional, Scientific, and Technical Services (38.5%); Museums, Historical Sites, and Similar Institutions (35.9%); Amusement, Gambling, and Recreation Industries (31.2%); Administrative and Support Services (28.7%); Ambulatory Health Care Services (24.8%); Nursing and Residential Care Facilities (24.3%); Real Estate (20.7%); Performing Arts, Spectator Sports, and Related Industries (18.8%); Religious, Grantmaking, Civic, Professional, and Similar Organizations (15.9%); Management of Companies and Enterprises (15.3%).

Lowest-Growth Industries (Projected Growth for This Job): Insurance Carriers and Related Activities (3.5%); Hospitals, Public and Private (7.3%); Miscellaneous Store Retailers (10.0%); Educational Services, Public and Private (13.3%); Accommodation, Including Hotels and Motels (14.2%).

Fastest-Growing Metropolitan Areas (Recent Growth for This Job): Santa Fe, NM (200.0%); Olympia, WA (100.0%); Evansville, IN–KY (90.0%); Norwich–New London, CT–RI (76.9%); Waterloo–Cedar Falls, IA (75.0%).

Other Considerations for Job Security: No data available.

Plan, organize, or coordinate the activities of a social service program or community outreach organization. Oversee the program or organization's budget and policies regarding participant involvement, program requirements, and benefits. Work may involve directing social workers, counselors, or probation officers. Establish and maintain relationships with other agencies and organizations in community to meet community needs and to ensure that services aren't duplicated. Prepare and maintain records and reports, such as budgets, personnel records, or training manuals. Direct activities of professional and technical staff members and volunteers. Evaluate the work of staff and volunteers to ensure that programs are of appropriate quality and that resources are used effectively. Establish and oversee administrative procedures to meet objectives set by boards of directors or senior management. Participate in the determination of organizational policies regarding such issues as participant eligibility, program requirements, and program benefits. Research and analyze member or community needs to determine program directions and goals. Speak to community groups to explain and interpret agency purposes, programs, and policies. Recruit, interview, and hire or sign up volunteers and staff. Represent organizations in relations with governmental and media institutions. Plan and administer budgets for programs, equipment, and support services. Analyze proposed legislation, regulations, or rule changes to determine how agency services could be impacted. Act as consultants to agency staff and other community programs regarding the interpretation of program-related federal, state, and county regulations and policies. Implement and evaluate staff training programs. Direct fundraising activities and the preparation of public relations materials.

Personality Type: Social.

GOE—Interest Area: 07. Government and Public Administration. **Work Group:** 07.01. Managerial Work in Government and Public Administration.

Other Jobs in this Work Group: No other jobs in this group.

Skills: Management of Personnel Resources; Social Perceptiveness; Systems Evaluation; Negotiation; Service Orientation; Persuasion.

Education and Training Programs: Human Services, General; Community Organization and Advocacy; Public Administration; Business/Commerce, General; Business Administration and Management, General; Nonprofit/Public/Organizational Management; Entrepreneurship/Entrepreneurial Studies; Business, Management, Marketing, and Related Support Services, Other. **Related Knowledge/Courses:** Sociology and Anthropology; Therapy and Counseling; Psychology; Philosophy and Theology; Clerical Studies; Education and Training.

Work Environment: Indoors; noisy; sitting.

Social and Human Service Assistants

- ✳ Education/Training Required: Moderate-term on-the-job training
- ✳ Annual Earnings: $25,580
- ✳ Beginning Wage: $16,180
- ✳ Earnings Growth Potential: Very high
- ✳ Growth: 33.6%
- ✳ Annual Job Openings: 80,142
- ✳ Self-Employed: 0.1%
- ✳ Part-Time: 12.0%

Industries with Greatest Employment: Social Assistance; Nursing and Residential Care Facilities; Ambulatory Health Care Services; Religious, Grantmaking, Civic, Professional, and Similar Organizations; Hospitals, Public and Private.

Highest-Growth Industries (Projected Growth for This Job): Social Assistance (73.8%); Professional, Scientific, and Technical Services (57.3%); Nursing and Residential Care Facilities (37.3%); Administrative and Support Services (27.8%); Ambulatory

Health Care Services (27.6%); Management of Companies and Enterprises (15.3%).

Lowest-Growth Industries (Projected Growth for This Job): Hospitals, Public and Private (−0.4%); Religious, Grantmaking, Civic, Professional, and Similar Organizations (9.2%); Educational Services, Public and Private (10.9%); Miscellaneous Store Retailers (12.3%); Real Estate (13.9%).

Fastest-Growing Metropolitan Areas (Recent Growth for This Job): Dalton, GA (216.7%); Hot Springs, AR (183.3%); Las Cruces, NM (166.7%); Grand Forks, ND–MN (118.2%); Shreveport–Bossier City, LA (100.0%).

Other Considerations for Job Security: Job prospects are expected to be excellent, particularly for applicants with appropriate postsecondary education. Urban areas will have more job competition than rural ones, but qualified applicants should have little difficulty finding employment. Demand for social services will expand with the growing elderly population, who are more likely to need adult daycare, meal delivery programs, support during medical crises, and other services. Also, more social and human service assistants will be needed to provide services to pregnant teenagers, people who are homeless, people who are mentally disabled or developmentally challenged, and people who are substance abusers.

Assist professionals from a wide variety of fields, such as psychology, rehabilitation, or social work, to provide client services, as well as support for families. May assist clients in identifying available benefits and social and community services and help clients obtain them. May assist social workers with developing, organizing, and conducting programs to prevent and resolve problems relevant to substance abuse, human relationships, rehabilitation, or adult daycare. Provide information and refer individuals to public or private agencies or community services for assistance. Keep records and prepare reports for owner or management concerning visits with clients. Visit individuals in homes or attend group meetings to provide information on agency services, requirements, and procedures.

Advise clients regarding food stamps, child care, food, money management, sanitation, or housekeeping. Submit reports and review reports or problems with superior. Oversee day-to-day group activities of residents in institution. Interview individuals and family members to compile information on social, educational, criminal, institutional, or drug history. Meet with youth groups to acquaint them with consequences of delinquent acts. Transport and accompany clients to shopping areas or to appointments, using automobile. Explain rules established by owner or management, such as sanitation and maintenance requirements and parking regulations. Observe and discuss meal preparation and suggest alternative methods of food preparation. Demonstrate use and care of equipment for tenant use. Consult with supervisor concerning programs for individual families. Monitor free supplementary meal program to ensure cleanliness of facility and that eligibility guidelines are met for persons receiving meals. Observe clients' food selections and recommend alternative economical and nutritional food choices. Inform tenants of facilities such as laundries and playgrounds. Care for children in client's home during client's appointments. Assist in locating housing for displaced individuals. Assist clients with preparation of forms, such as tax or rent forms. Assist in planning of food budget, using charts and sample budgets.

Personality Type: Social.

GOE—Interest Area: 10. Human Service. **Work Group:** 10.01. Counseling and Social Work. **Other Jobs in this Work Group:** Child, Family, and School Social Workers; Clinical Psychologists; Clinical, Counseling, and School Psychologists; Counseling Psychologists; Marriage and Family Therapists; Medical and Public Health Social Workers; Mental Health and Substance Abuse Social Workers; Mental Health Counselors; Probation Officers and Correctional Treatment Specialists; Rehabilitation Counselors; Residential Advisors; Substance Abuse and Behavioral Disorder Counselors.

Skills: Social Perceptiveness; Management of Financial Resources; Service Orientation; Speaking; Judgment and Decision Making; Active Listening.

Education and Training Program: Mental and Social Health Services and Allied Professions, Other. **Related Knowledge/Courses:** Therapy and Counseling; Psychology; Sociology and Anthropology; Philosophy and Theology; Clerical Studies; Customer and Personal Service.

Work Environment: Indoors; noisy; sitting.

Social Work Teachers, Postsecondary

- ❋ Education/Training Required: Doctoral degree
- ❋ Annual Earnings: $54,340
- ❋ Beginning Wage: $31,410
- ❋ Earnings Growth Potential: Very high
- ❋ Growth: 22.9%
- ❋ Annual Job Openings: 237,478
- ❋ Self-Employed: 0.4%
- ❋ Part-Time: 27.8%

Our sources did not provide separate job openings data for this occupation. The job openings listed here are shared with 35 other postsecondary teaching occupations. For a complete list, see the beginning of this section.

Industries with Greatest Employment: Educational Services, Public and Private.

Highest-Growth Industries (Projected Growth for This Job): Administrative and Support Services (48.3%); Amusement, Gambling, and Recreation Industries (45.3%); Social Assistance (38.6%); Support Activities for Transportation (32.8%); Religious, Grantmaking, Civic, Professional, and Similar Organizations (29.9%); Professional, Scientific, and Technical Services (28.8%); Management of Companies and Enterprises (26.8%); Educational Services, Public and Private (22.9%); Hospitals, Public and Private (21.4%); Personal and Laundry Services (21.0%).

Lowest-Growth Industries (Projected Growth for This Job): Other Information Services (7.4%); Sporting Goods, Hobby, Book, and Music Stores (13.3%); Performing Arts, Spectator Sports, and Related Industries (13.4%); Insurance Carriers and Related Activities (13.9%).

Fastest-Growing Metropolitan Areas (Recent Growth for This Job): Boston–Cambridge–Quincy, MA–NH (170.0%); Washington–Arlington–Alexandria, DC–VA–MD–WV (83.9%); Tampa–St. Petersburg–Clearwater, FL (81.8%); Chicago–Naperville–Joliet, IL–IN–WI (58.9%); Detroit–Warren–Livonia, MI (37.5%).

Other Considerations for Job Security: Retirements of current postsecondary teachers should create numerous openings for all types of postsecondary teachers, so job opportunities are generally expected to be very good. Because students attend postsecondary institutions to prepare themselves for careers, the best job prospects for postsecondary teachers are likely to be in rapidly growing fields that offer many nonacademic career options. Community colleges and other institutions offering career and technical education have been among the most rapidly growing and are expected to offer some of the best opportunities for postsecondary teachers.

Teach courses in social work. Initiate, facilitate, and moderate classroom discussions. Evaluate and grade students' classwork, assignments, and papers. Prepare and deliver lectures to undergraduate or graduate students on topics such as family behavior, child and adolescent mental health, and social intervention evaluation. Keep abreast of developments in their field by reading current literature, talking with colleagues, and participating in professional conferences. Supervise students' laboratory work and fieldwork. Conduct research in a particular field of knowledge and publish findings in professional journals, books, or electronic media. Prepare course materials such as syllabi, homework assignments, and handouts. Maintain regularly scheduled office hours to advise and assist students. Supervise undergraduate or graduate teaching, internships, and research work. Plan, evaluate, and revise curricula, course content, course materials, and methods of instruction. Collaborate with colleagues and with community agencies to address teaching and research issues. Compile, administer, and grade examinations or assign this work to others. Advise students on academic and vocational curricula and on career issues. Maintain student attendance records, grades, and other required records. Write grant proposals to procure external research funding. Serve on academic or administrative committees that deal with institutional policies, departmental matters, and academic issues. Perform administrative duties such as serving as department head. Compile bibliographies of specialized materials for outside reading assignments. Select and obtain materials and supplies such as textbooks and laboratory equipment. Participate in student recruitment, registration, and placement activities. Participate in campus and community events. Provide professional consulting services to government and industry. Act as advisers to student organizations.

Personality Type: No data available.

GOE—Interest Area: 05. Education and Training. **Work Group:** 05.03. Postsecondary and Adult Teaching and Instructing. **Other Jobs in this Work Group:** Adult Literacy, Remedial Education, and GED Teachers and Instructors; Agricultural Sciences Teachers, Postsecondary; Anthropology and Archeology Teachers, Postsecondary; Architecture Teachers, Postsecondary; Area, Ethnic, and Cultural Studies Teachers, Postsecondary; Art, Drama, and Music Teachers, Postsecondary; Atmospheric, Earth, Marine, and Space Sciences Teachers, Postsecondary; Biological Science Teachers, Postsecondary; Business Teachers, Postsecondary; Chemistry Teachers, Postsecondary; Communications Teachers, Postsecondary; Computer Science Teachers, Postsecondary; Criminal Justice and Law Enforcement Teachers, Postsecondary; Economics Teachers, Postsecondary; Education Teachers, Postsecondary; Engineering Teachers, Postsecondary; English Language and Literature Teachers, Postsecondary; Environmental Science Teachers, Postsecondary; Farm and Home Management Advisors; Foreign Language and Literature Teachers, Postsecondary; Forestry and Conservation Science Teachers, Postsecondary; Geography Teachers, Postsecondary; Graduate

Teaching Assistants; Health Specialties Teachers, Postsecondary; History Teachers, Postsecondary; Home Economics Teachers, Postsecondary; Law Teachers, Postsecondary; Library Science Teachers, Postsecondary; Mathematical Science Teachers, Postsecondary; Nursing Instructors and Teachers, Postsecondary; Philosophy and Religion Teachers, Postsecondary; Physics Teachers, Postsecondary; Political Science Teachers, Postsecondary; Psychology Teachers, Postsecondary; Recreation and Fitness Studies Teachers, Postsecondary; Self-Enrichment Education Teachers; Sociology Teachers, Postsecondary; Vocational Education Teachers, Postsecondary.

Skills: Social Perceptiveness; Service Orientation; Instructing; Learning Strategies; Writing; Complex Problem Solving.

Education and Training Programs: Teacher Education and Professional Development, Specific Subject Areas, Other; Social Work; Clinical/Medical Social Work. **Related Knowledge/Courses:** Therapy and Counseling; Sociology and Anthropology; Psychology; Philosophy and Theology; Education and Training; English Language.

Work Environment: Indoors; sitting.

Sociologists

- ❋ Education/Training Required: Master's degree
- ❋ Annual Earnings: $60,290
- ❋ Beginning Wage: $36,790
- ❋ Earnings Growth Potential: Very high
- ❋ Growth: 10.0%
- ❋ Annual Job Openings: 403
- ❋ Self-Employed: 0.0%
- ❋ Part-Time: 24.0%

Industries with Greatest Employment: Professional, Scientific, and Technical Services; Educational Services, Public and Private.

Highest-Growth Industries (Projected Growth for This Job): None met the criteria.

Lowest-Growth Industries (Projected Growth for This Job): Professional, Scientific, and Technical Services (8.6%); Educational Services, Public and Private (11.1%).

Fastest-Growing Metropolitan Areas (Recent Growth for This Job): Phoenix–Mesa–Scottsdale, AZ (100.0%); Sacramento–Arden–Arcade–Roseville, CA (25.0%); Washington–Arlington–Alexandria, DC–VA–MD–WV (18.2%); Madison, WI (12.5%).

Other Considerations for Job Security: Job seekers may face competition, and those with higher educational attainment will have the best prospects. The incorporation of sociology into research in other fields will continue to increase the need for sociologists. They may find work conducting policy research for consulting firms and nonprofit organizations, and their knowledge of society and social behavior may be used by various companies in product development, marketing, and advertising. Keen competition is expected for tenured positions as university faculty. The growing importance and popularity of social science subjects in secondary schools also is strengthening the demand for social science teachers at that level.

Study human society and social behavior by examining the groups and social institutions that people form, as well as various social, religious, political, and business organizations. May study the behavior and interaction of groups, trace their origin and growth, and analyze the influence of group activities on individual members. Analyze and interpret data to increase the understanding of human social behavior. Prepare publications and reports containing research findings. Plan and conduct research to develop and test theories about societal issues such as crime, group relations, poverty, and aging. Collect data about the attitudes, values, and behaviors of people in groups, using observation, interviews, and review of documents. Develop, implement, and evaluate methods of data collection, such as questionnaires or interviews. Teach sociology. Direct work of statistical clerks, statisticians, and others who compile and evaluate research data. Consult with and advise individuals such as administrators, social workers, and legislators regarding social issues and policies, as well as the implications of research findings. Collaborate with research workers in other disciplines. Develop approaches to the solution of groups' problems based on research findings in sociology and related disciplines. Observe group interactions and role affiliations to collect data, identify problems, evaluate progress, and determine the need for additional change. Develop problem intervention procedures, utilizing techniques such as interviews, consultations, role-playing, and participant observation of group interactions.

Personality Type: Investigative.

GOE—Interest Area: 15. Scientific Research, Engineering, and Mathematics. **Work Group:** 15.04. Social Sciences. **Other Jobs in this Work Group:** Anthropologists; Anthropologists and Archeologists; Archeologists; Economists; Historians; Industrial-Organizational Psychologists; Political Scientists; School Psychologists.

Skills: Science; Writing; Management of Financial Resources; Reading Comprehension; Critical Thinking; Management of Personnel Resources.

Education and Training Programs: Criminology; Demography and Population Studies; Sociology; Urban Studies/Affairs. **Related Knowledge/Courses:** Sociology and Anthropology; Philosophy and Theology; History and Archeology; Psychology; English Language; Mathematics.

Work Environment: Indoors; sitting.

Sociology Teachers, Postsecondary

- ❋ Education/Training Required: Doctoral degree
- ❋ Annual Earnings: $56,620
- ❋ Beginning Wage: $30,880
- ❋ Earnings Growth Potential: Very high
- ❋ Growth: 22.9%
- ❋ Annual Job Openings: 237,478
- ❋ Self-Employed: 0.4%
- ❋ Part-Time: 27.8%

Our sources did not provide separate job openings data for this occupation. The job openings listed here are shared with 35 other postsecondary teaching occupations. For a complete list, see the beginning of this section.

Industries with Greatest Employment: Educational Services, Public and Private.

Highest-Growth Industries (Projected Growth for This Job): Administrative and Support Services (48.3%); Amusement, Gambling, and Recreation Industries (45.3%); Social Assistance (38.6%); Support Activities for Transportation (32.8%); Religious, Grantmaking, Civic, Professional, and Similar Organizations (29.9%); Professional, Scientific, and Technical Services (28.8%); Management of Companies and Enterprises (26.8%); Educational Services, Public and Private (22.9%); Hospitals, Public and Private (21.4%); Personal and Laundry Services (21.0%).

Lowest-Growth Industries (Projected Growth for This Job): Other Information Services (7.4%); Sporting Goods, Hobby, Book, and Music Stores (13.3%); Performing Arts, Spectator Sports, and Related Industries (13.4%); Insurance Carriers and Related Activities (13.9%).

Fastest-Growing Metropolitan Areas (Recent Growth for This Job): Dallas–Fort Worth–Arlington, TX (12.5%).

Other Considerations for Job Security: Retirements of current postsecondary teachers should create numerous openings for all types of postsecondary teachers. However, because students attend postsecondary institutions to prepare themselves for careers, the best job prospects for postsecondary teachers are likely to be in rapidly growing fields that offer many nonacademic career options, unlike sociology. Community colleges and other institutions offering career and technical education have been among the most rapidly growing and are expected to offer some of the best opportunities for postsecondary teachers.

Teach courses in sociology. Evaluate and grade students' classwork, assignments, and papers. Prepare and deliver lectures to undergraduate and graduate students on topics such as race and ethnic relations, measurement and data collection, and workplace social relations. Initiate, facilitate, and moderate classroom discussions. Prepare course materials such as syllabi, homework assignments, and handouts. Compile, administer, and grade examinations or assign this work to others. Keep abreast of developments in their field by reading current literature, talking with colleagues, and participating in professional conferences. Maintain student attendance records, grades, and other required records. Maintain regularly scheduled office hours to advise and assist students. Plan, evaluate, and revise curricula, course content, course materials, and methods of instruction. Advise students on academic and vocational curricula and on career issues. Collaborate with colleagues to address teaching and research issues. Conduct research in a particular field of knowledge and publish findings in professional journals, books, or electronic media. Select and obtain materials and supplies such as textbooks and laboratory equipment. Supervise undergraduate and graduate teaching, internships, and research work. Serve on academic or administrative committees that deal with institutional policies, departmental matters, and academic issues. Participate in student recruitment, registration, and placement activities. Perform administrative duties such as serving as department head. Supervise students' laboratory work and fieldwork. Write grant proposals to procure external research funding. Act as advisers to student organizations. Compile bibliographies of specialized materials for outside reading assignments. Participate in campus and community events. Provide professional consulting services to government and industry.

Personality Type: Social.

GOE—Interest Area: 05. Education and Training. **Work Group:** 05.03. Postsecondary and Adult Teaching and Instructing. **Other Jobs in this Work Group:** Adult Literacy, Remedial Education, and GED Teachers and Instructors; Agricultural Sciences Teachers, Postsecondary; Anthropology and Archeology Teachers, Postsecondary; Architecture Teachers, Postsecondary; Area, Ethnic, and Cultural Studies Teachers, Postsecondary; Art, Drama, and

Music Teachers, Postsecondary; Atmospheric, Earth, Marine, and Space Sciences Teachers, Postsecondary; Biological Science Teachers, Postsecondary; Business Teachers, Postsecondary; Chemistry Teachers, Postsecondary; Communications Teachers, Postsecondary; Computer Science Teachers, Postsecondary; Criminal Justice and Law Enforcement Teachers, Postsecondary; Economics Teachers, Postsecondary; Education Teachers, Postsecondary; Engineering Teachers, Postsecondary; English Language and Literature Teachers, Postsecondary; Environmental Science Teachers, Postsecondary; Farm and Home Management Advisors; Foreign Language and Literature Teachers, Postsecondary; Forestry and Conservation Science Teachers, Postsecondary; Geography Teachers, Postsecondary; Graduate Teaching Assistants; Health Specialties Teachers, Postsecondary; History Teachers, Postsecondary; Home Economics Teachers, Postsecondary; Law Teachers, Postsecondary; Library Science Teachers, Postsecondary; Mathematical Science Teachers, Postsecondary; Nursing Instructors and Teachers, Postsecondary; Philosophy and Religion Teachers, Postsecondary; Physics Teachers, Postsecondary; Political Science Teachers, Postsecondary; Psychology Teachers, Postsecondary; Recreation and Fitness Studies Teachers, Postsecondary; Self-Enrichment Education Teachers; Social Work Teachers, Postsecondary; Vocational Education Teachers, Postsecondary.

Skills: Instructing; Science; Writing; Learning Strategies; Social Perceptiveness; Critical Thinking.

Education and Training Programs: Social Science Teacher Education; Sociology. **Related Knowledge/Courses:** Sociology and Anthropology; Philosophy and Theology; History and Archeology; Education and Training; English Language; Psychology.

Work Environment: Indoors; sitting.

Soil and Plant Scientists

- ❋ Education/Training Required: Bachelor's degree
- ❋ Annual Earnings: $56,080
- ❋ Beginning Wage: $33,650
- ❋ Earnings Growth Potential: Very high
- ❋ Growth: 8.4%
- ❋ Annual Job Openings: 850
- ❋ Self-Employed: 19.5%
- ❋ Part-Time: 11.4%

Industries with Greatest Employment: Professional, Scientific, and Technical Services; Educational Services, Public and Private; Merchant Wholesalers, Nondurable Goods; Support Activities for Agriculture and Forestry; Crop Production.

Highest-Growth Industries (Projected Growth for This Job): Professional, Scientific, and Technical Services (28.4%); Administrative and Support Services (16.8%); Management of Companies and Enterprises (15.4%).

Lowest-Growth Industries (Projected Growth for This Job): Crop Production (–33.7%); Merchant Wholesalers, Nondurable Goods (5.2%); Support Activities for Agriculture and Forestry (7.1%); Educational Services, Public and Private (11.8%).

Fastest-Growing Metropolitan Areas (Recent Growth for This Job): Miami–Fort Lauderdale–Miami Beach, FL (175.0%); Salinas, CA (100.0%); Atlanta–Sandy Springs–Marietta, GA (50.0%); Sacramento–Arden-Arcade–Roseville, CA (40.0%); Philadelphia–Camden–Wilmington, PA–NJ–DE–MD (37.5%).

Other Considerations for Job Security: Agricultural scientists will be needed to balance increased agricultural output with protection and preservation of soil, water, and ecosystems. Opportunities should be good for agricultural scientists with a master's degree, particularly those seeking applied research positions in a laboratory. Master's degree candidates also can seek to become certified crop advisors, helping farmers better manage their crops. Those with a doctorate in agricultural science will experience the best opportunities, especially in basic research and teaching positions at colleges and universities. The federal government hires bachelor's-degree holders to work as soil scientists. Employment of agricultural scientists is relatively stable during periods of economic recession because food is a staple item and its demand fluctuates very little with economic activity.

Conduct research in breeding, physiology, production, yield, and management of crops and agricultural plants, their growth in soils, and control of pests or study the chemical, physical, biological, and mineralogical composition of soils as they relate to plant or crop growth. May classify and map soils and investigate effects of alternative practices on soil and crop productivity. Communicate research and project results to other professionals and the public or teach related courses, seminars, or workshops. Provide information and recommendations to farmers and other landowners regarding ways in which they can best use land, promote plant growth, and avoid or correct problems such as erosion. Investigate responses of soils to specific management practices to determine the use capabilities of soils and the effects of alternative practices on soil productivity. Develop methods of conserving and managing soil that can be applied by farmers and forestry companies. Conduct experiments to develop new or improved varieties of field crops, focusing on characteristics such as yield, quality, disease resistance, nutritional value, or adaptation to specific soils or climates. Investigate soil problems and poor water quality to determine sources and effects. Study soil characteristics to classify soils based on factors such as geographic location, landscape position, and soil properties. Develop improved measurement techniques, soil conservation methods, soil sampling devices, and related technology. Conduct experiments investigating how soil forms and changes and how it interacts with land-based ecosystems and living organisms. Identify degraded or contaminated soils and develop plans to improve their chemical, biological, and physical characteristics. Survey undisturbed and disturbed lands for classification, inventory, mapping, environmental impact assessments, environmental protection planning, and conservation and reclamation planning. Plan and supervise land conservation and reclamation programs for industrial development projects and waste-management programs for composting and farming. Perform chemical analyses of the microorganism content of soils to determine microbial reactions and chemical mineralogical relationships to plant growth. Provide advice regarding the development of regulatory standards for land reclamation and soil conservation. Develop new or improved methods and products for controlling and eliminating weeds, crop diseases, and insect pests.

Personality Type: Investigative.

GOE—Interest Area: 01. Agriculture and Natural Resources. **Work Group:** 01.02. Resource Science/Engineering for Plants, Animals, and the Environment. **Other Jobs in this Work Group:** Agricultural Engineers; Animal Scientists; Conservation Scientists; Environmental Engineers; Foresters; Mining and Geological Engineers, Including Mining Safety Engineers; Petroleum Engineers; Range Managers; Soil and Water Conservationists; Zoologists and Wildlife Biologists.

Skills: Science; Management of Financial Resources; Management of Personnel Resources; Writing; Management of Material Resources; Reading Comprehension.

Education and Training Programs: Soil Science and Agronomy, General; Soil Chemistry and Physics; Soil Microbiology. **Related Knowledge/Courses:** Biology; Food Production; Geography; Chemistry; Physics; Communications and Media.

Work Environment: More often indoors than outdoors; sitting.

Special Education Teachers, Middle School

* Education/Training Required: Bachelor's degree
* Annual Earnings: $47,650
* Beginning Wage: $32,420
* Earnings Growth Potential: Very high
* Growth: 15.8%
* Annual Job Openings: 8,846
* Self-Employed: 0.3%
* Part-Time: 9.6%

Industries with Greatest Employment: Educational Services, Public and Private.

Highest-Growth Industries (Projected Growth for This Job): Social Assistance (39.2%); Nursing and Residential Care Facilities (26.9%); Ambulatory Health Care Services (18.2%); Educational Services, Public and Private (16.0%).

Lowest-Growth Industries (Projected Growth for This Job): None met the criteria.

Fastest-Growing Metropolitan Areas (Recent Growth for This Job): New Bedford, MA (140.0%); Yuba City, CA (133.3%); Sioux City, IA–NE–SD (83.3%); Ithaca, NY (66.7%); Birmingham–Hoover, AL (60.0%).

Other Considerations for Job Security: Special education teachers should have excellent job prospects. The job outlook varies by geographic area and specialty. Although most areas of the country report difficulty finding qualified applicants, positions in inner cities and rural areas usually are more plentiful than in suburban or wealthy urban areas. Student population growth will be highest in the South and West. Also, job opportunities may be better in certain specialties—such as teachers who work with children with multiple disabilities or severe disabilities such as autism. Bilingual special education teachers and those with multicultural experience also are needed.

Teach middle school subjects to educationally and physically handicapped students. Includes teachers who specialize and work with audibly and visually handicapped students and those who teach basic academic and life processes skills to the mentally impaired. Establish and enforce rules for behavior and policies and procedures to maintain order among students. Maintain accurate and complete student records and prepare reports on children and activities as required by laws, district policies, and administrative regulations. Prepare materials and classrooms for class activities. Confer with parents, administrators, testing specialists, social workers, and professionals to develop individual educational plans designed to promote students' educational, physical, and social development. Develop and implement strategies to meet the needs of students with various handicapping conditions. Teach socially acceptable behavior, employing techniques such as behavior modification and positive reinforcement. Modify the general education curriculum for special-needs students based on various instructional techniques and instructional technology. Employ special educational strategies and techniques during instruction to improve the development of sensory- and perceptual-motor skills, language, cognition, and memory. Confer with parents or guardians, other teachers, counselors, and administrators to resolve students' behavioral and academic problems. Instruct through lectures, discussions, and demonstrations in one or more subjects such as English, mathematics, or social studies. Coordinate placement of students with special needs into mainstream classes. Meet with parents and guardians to discuss their children's progress and to determine their priorities for their children and their resource needs. Guide and counsel students with adjustment or academic problems or special academic interests. Prepare, administer, and grade tests and assignments to evaluate students' progress. Observe and evaluate students' performance, behavior, social development, and physical health. Establish clear objectives for all lessons, units, and projects and communicate those objectives to students. Teach students personal development skills such as goal setting, independence, and self-advocacy. Plan and conduct activities for a balanced program of instruction, demonstration, and work time that provides students with opportunities to observe, question, and investigate.

Personality Type: Social.

GOE—Interest Area: 05. Education and Training. **Work Group:** 05.02. Preschool, Elementary, and Secondary Teaching and Instructing. **Other Jobs in this Work Group:** Elementary School Teachers, Except Special Education; Kindergarten Teachers, Except Special Education; Middle School Teachers, Except Special and Vocational Education; Preschool Teachers, Except Special Education; Secondary School Teachers, Except Special and Vocational Education; Special Education Teachers, Preschool, Kindergarten, and Elementary School; Special Education Teachers, Secondary School; Teacher Assistants; Vocational Education Teachers, Middle School; Vocational Education Teachers, Secondary School.

Skills: Learning Strategies; Social Perceptiveness; Instructing; Monitoring; Persuasion; Writing.

Education and Training Programs: Special Education and Teaching, General; Education/Teaching of the Gifted and Talented; Education/Teaching of Individuals Who are Developmentally Delayed; Education/Teaching of Individuals in Early Childhood Special Education Programs. **Related Knowledge/Courses:** Geography; History and Archeology; Psychology; Therapy and Counseling; Sociology and Anthropology; Education and Training.

Work Environment: Indoors; noisy; standing.

Special Education Teachers, Secondary School

* Education/Training Required: Bachelor's degree
* Annual Earnings: $48,330
* Beginning Wage: $32,760
* Earnings Growth Potential: Very high
* Growth: 8.5%
* Annual Job Openings: 10,601
* Self-Employed: 0.3%
* Part-Time: 9.6%

Industries with Greatest Employment: Educational Services, Public and Private.

Highest-Growth Industries (Projected Growth for This Job): Social Assistance (48.1%); Nursing and Residential Care Facilities (25.8%); Ambulatory Health Care Services (23.1%).

Lowest-Growth Industries (Projected Growth for This Job): Hospitals, Public and Private (–14.3%); Educational Services, Public and Private (8.1%).

Fastest-Growing Metropolitan Areas (Recent Growth for This Job): Baltimore–Towson, MD (128.6%); Topeka, KS (80.0%); Oxnard–Thousand Oaks–Ventura, CA (73.3%); San Jose–Sunnyvale–Santa Clara, CA (71.4%); Fresno, CA (69.2%).

Other Considerations for Job Security: Special education teachers should have excellent job prospects. The job outlook varl by geographic area and specialty. Although most areas of the country report difficulty finding qualified applicants, positions in inner cities and rural areas usually are more plentiful than in suburban or wealthy urban areas. Student population growth will be highest in the South and West. Also, job opportunities may be better in certain specialties—such as teachers who work with children with multiple disabilities or severe disabilities like autism. Bilingual special education teachers and those with multicultural experience also are needed.

Part III: Descriptions of the Best Recession-Proof Jobs

Teach secondary school subjects to educationally and physically handicapped students. Includes teachers who specialize and work with audibly and visually handicapped students and those who teach basic academic and life processes skills to the mentally impaired. Maintain accurate and complete student records and prepare reports on children and activities as required by laws, district policies, and administrative regulations. Prepare materials and classrooms for class activities. Teach socially acceptable behavior, employing techniques such as behavior modification and positive reinforcement. Establish and enforce rules for behavior and policies and procedures to maintain order among students. Confer with parents, administrators, testing specialists, social workers, and professionals to develop individual educational plans designed to promote students' educational, physical, and social development. Instruct through lectures, discussions, and demonstrations in one or more subjects such as English, mathematics, or social studies. Employ special educational strategies and techniques during instruction to improve the development of sensory- and perceptual-motor skills, language, cognition, and memory. Plan and conduct activities for a balanced program of instruction, demonstration, and work time that provides students with opportunities to observe, question, and investigate. Prepare students for later grades by encouraging them to explore learning opportunities and to persevere with challenging tasks. Teach personal development skills such as goal setting, independence, and self-advocacy. Establish clear objectives for all lessons, units, and projects and communicate those objectives to students. Develop and implement strategies to meet the needs of students with various handicapping conditions. Modify the general education curriculum for special-needs students based on various instructional techniques and technologies. Meet with other professionals to discuss individual students' needs and progress. Confer with parents or guardians, other teachers, counselors, and administrators to resolve students' behavioral and academic problems. Meet with parents and guardians to discuss their children's progress and to determine their priorities for their children and their resource needs.

Guide and counsel students with adjustment or academic problems or special academic interests.

Personality Type: Social.

GOE—Interest Area: 05. Education and Training. **Work Group:** 05.02. Preschool, Elementary, and Secondary Teaching and Instructing. **Other Jobs in this Work Group:** Elementary School Teachers, Except Special Education; Kindergarten Teachers, Except Special Education; Middle School Teachers, Except Special and Vocational Education; Preschool Teachers, Except Special Education; Secondary School Teachers, Except Special and Vocational Education; Special Education Teachers, Middle School; Special Education Teachers, Preschool, Kindergarten, and Elementary School; Teacher Assistants; Vocational Education Teachers, Middle School; Vocational Education Teachers, Secondary School.

Skills: Learning Strategies; Social Perceptiveness; Negotiation; Persuasion; Instructing; Service Orientation.

Education and Training Programs: Special Education and Teaching, General; Education/Teaching of the Gifted and Talented; Education/Teaching of Individuals Who are Developmentally Delayed; Education/Teaching of Individuals in Early Childhood Special Education Programs. **Related Knowledge/Courses:** Therapy and Counseling; History and Archeology; Geography; Psychology; Philosophy and Theology; Sociology and Anthropology.

Work Environment: Indoors; noisy; standing.

Speech-Language Pathologists

- Education/Training Required: Master's degree
- Annual Earnings: $57,710
- Beginning Wage: $37,970
- Earnings Growth Potential: Very high
- Growth: 10.6%
- Annual Job Openings: 11,160
- Self-Employed: 8.8%
- Part-Time: 24.6%

Industries with Greatest Employment: Educational Services, Public and Private; Ambulatory Health Care Services; Hospitals, Public and Private.

Highest-Growth Industries (Projected Growth for This Job): Social Assistance (40.5%); Administrative and Support Services (26.5%); Ambulatory Health Care Services (16.2%); Nursing and Residential Care Facilities (15.5%); Management of Companies and Enterprises (15.2%); Religious, Grantmaking, Civic, Professional, and Similar Organizations (15.1%).

Lowest-Growth Industries (Projected Growth for This Job): Educational Services, Public and Private (6.2%); Hospitals, Public and Private (13.6%).

Fastest-Growing Metropolitan Areas (Recent Growth for This Job): Muskegon–Norton Shores, MI (100.0%); Prescott, AZ (100.0%); Racine, WI (100.0%); Las Vegas–Paradise, NV (87.5%); Boise City–Nampa, ID (75.0%).

Other Considerations for Job Security: The combination of growth in the occupation and an expected increase in retirements over the coming years should create excellent job opportunities for speech-language pathologists. Opportunities should be particularly favorable for those with the ability to speak a second language, such as Spanish. Job prospects also are expected to be especially favorable for those who are willing to relocate, particularly to areas experiencing difficulty in attracting and hiring speech-language pathologists.

Assess and treat persons with speech, language, voice, and fluency disorders. May select alternative communication systems and teach their use. May perform research related to speech and language problems. Monitor patients' progress and adjust treatments accordingly. Evaluate hearing and speech/language test results and medical or background information to diagnose and plan treatment for speech, language, fluency, voice, and swallowing disorders. Administer hearing or speech and language evaluations, tests, or examinations to patients to collect information on type and degree of impairments, using written and oral tests and special instruments. Record information on the initial evaluation, treatment, progress, and discharge of clients. Develop and implement treatment plans for problems such as stuttering, delayed language, swallowing disorders, and inappropriate pitch or harsh voice problems, based on own assessments and recommendations of physicians, psychologists, or social workers. Develop individual or group programs in schools to deal with speech or language problems. Instruct clients in techniques for more effective communication, including sign language, lip reading, and voice improvement. Teach clients to control or strengthen tongue, jaw, face muscles, and breathing mechanisms. Develop speech exercise programs to reduce disabilities. Consult with and advise educators or medical staff on speech or hearing topics, such as communication strategies or speech and language stimulation. Instruct patients and family members in strategies to cope with or avoid communication-related misunderstandings. Design, develop, and employ alternative diagnostic or communication devices and strategies. Conduct lessons and direct educational or therapeutic games to assist teachers dealing with speech problems. Refer clients to additional medical or educational services if needed. Participate in conferences or training, or publish research results, to share knowledge of new hearing or speech disorder treatment methods or technologies. Communicate with nonspeaking students, using sign language or computer technology. Provide communication instruction to dialect speakers or students with limited English proficiency. Use computer applications to identify and assist with communication disabilities.

S

Personality Type: Social.

GOE—Interest Area: 08. Health Science. **Work Group:** 08.07. Medical Therapy. **Other Jobs in this Work Group:** Audiologists; Massage Therapists; Occupational Therapist Aides; Occupational Therapist Assistants; Occupational Therapists; Physical Therapist Aides; Physical Therapist Assistants; Physical Therapists; Radiation Therapists; Recreational Therapists; Respiratory Therapists; Respiratory Therapy Technicians.

Skills: Instructing; Learning Strategies; Social Perceptiveness; Speaking; Monitoring; Service Orientation.

Education and Training Programs: Communication Disorders, General; Speech-Language Pathology/Pathologist; Audiology/Audiologist and Speech-Language Pathology/Pathologist; Communication Disorders Sciences and Services, Other. **Related Knowledge/Courses:** Therapy and Counseling; Psychology; Sociology and Anthropology; Medicine and Dentistry; Education and Training; English Language.

Work Environment: Indoors; disease or infections; sitting.

Statisticians

- ❋ Education/Training Required: Master's degree
- ❋ Annual Earnings: $65,720
- ❋ Beginning Wage: $37,010
- ❋ Earnings Growth Potential: Very high
- ❋ Growth: 8.5%
- ❋ Annual Job Openings: 3,433
- ❋ Self-Employed: 6.0%
- ❋ Part-Time: 13.1%

Industries with Greatest Employment: Professional, Scientific, and Technical Services; Educational Services, Public and Private; Insurance Carriers and Related Activities; Management of Companies and Enterprises; Chemical Manufacturing.

Highest-Growth Industries (Projected Growth for This Job): Social Assistance (47.1%); Securities, Commodity Contracts, and Other Financial Investments and Related Activities (42.4%); Ambulatory Health Care Services (27.2%); Chemical Manufacturing (25.7%); Administrative and Support Services (23.8%); Professional, Scientific, and Technical Services (19.9%); Religious, Grantmaking, Civic, Professional, and Similar Organizations (18.8%); Management of Companies and Enterprises (15.2%).

Lowest-Growth Industries (Projected Growth for This Job): Computer and Electronic Product Manufacturing (–12.6%); Fabricated Metal Product Manufacturing (–11.7%); Publishing Industries (except Internet) (1.4%); Miscellaneous Manufacturing (1.6%); Insurance Carriers and Related Activities (5.2%); Internet Service Providers, Web Search Portals, and Data Processing Services (10.0%); Hospitals, Public and Private (11.9%); Educational Services, Public and Private (12.1%); Credit Intermediation and Related Activities (14.7%).

Fastest-Growing Metropolitan Areas (Recent Growth for This Job): San Antonio, TX (100.0%); Salt Lake City, UT (75.0%); Nashville–Davidson–Murfreesboro, TN (66.7%); Houston–Sugar Land–Baytown, TX (62.5%); Kansas City, MO–KS (60.0%).

Other Considerations for Job Security: Individuals with a degree in statistics should have opportunities in a variety of fields. Among graduates with a master's degree in statistics, those with a strong background in an allied field, such as finance, biology, engineering, or computer science, should have the best prospects of finding jobs related to their field of study.

Engage in the development of mathematical theory or apply statistical theory and methods to collect, organize, interpret, and summarize numerical data to provide usable information. May specialize in fields such as biostatistics, agricultural statistics, business statistics, economic statistics, or other fields. Report results of statistical analyses, including information in the form of graphs, charts, and tables. Process large amounts of data for statistical modeling and graphic analysis, using computers. Identify relationships and trends in data, as well as any factors that could affect research results. Analyze and interpret statistical data to identify significant differences in relationships among sources of information. Prepare data for processing by organizing information, checking for any inaccuracies, and adjusting and weighting raw data. Evaluate statistical methods and procedures used to obtain data to ensure validity, applicability, efficiency, and accuracy. Evaluate sources of information to determine any limitations in terms of reliability or usability. Plan data-collection methods for specific projects and determine the types and sizes of sample groups to be used. Design research projects that apply valid scientific techniques and utilize information obtained from baselines or historical data to structure uncompromised and efficient analyses. Develop an understanding of fields to which statistical methods are to be applied to determine whether methods and results are appropriate. Supervise and provide instructions for workers collecting and tabulating data. Apply sampling techniques or utilize complete enumeration bases to determine and define groups to be surveyed. Adapt statistical methods to solve specific problems in many fields, such as economics, biology, and engineering. Develop and test experimental designs, sampling techniques, and analytical methods. Examine theories, such as those of probability and inference, to discover mathematical bases for new or improved methods of obtaining and evaluating numerical data.

Personality Type: Investigative.

GOE—Interest Area: 15. Scientific Research, Engineering, and Mathematics. **Work Group:** 15.06. Mathematics and Data Analysis. **Other Jobs in this Work Group:** Actuaries; Mathematical Technicians; Mathematicians; Social Science Research Assistants; Statistical Assistants.

Skills: Programming; Science; Mathematics; Writing; Active Learning; Negotiation.

Education and Training Programs: Biostatistics; Mathematics, General; Applied Mathematics; Statistics, General; Mathematical Statistics and Probability; Statistics, Other; Business Statistics. **Related Knowledge/Courses:** Mathematics; Computers and Electronics; English Language; Law and Government; Education and Training.

Work Environment: Indoors; sitting; using hands on objects, tools, or controls; repetitive motions.

Substance Abuse and Behavioral Disorder Counselors

- ❋ Education/Training Required: Bachelor's degree
- ❋ Annual Earnings: $34,040
- ❋ Beginning Wage: $22,600
- ❋ Earnings Growth Potential: Very high
- ❋ Growth: 34.3%
- ❋ Annual Job Openings: 20,821
- ❋ Self-Employed: 5.8%
- ❋ Part-Time: 15.4%

Industries with Greatest Employment: Ambulatory Health Care Services; Nursing and Residential Care Facilities; Social Assistance; Hospitals, Public and Private; Educational Services, Public and Private.

Highest-Growth Industries (Projected Growth for This Job): None met the criteria.

Lowest-Growth Industries (Projected Growth for This Job): Hospitals, Public and Private (0.2%); Insurance Carriers and Related Activities (3.3%); Educational Services, Public and Private (9.9%).

Fastest-Growing Metropolitan Areas (Recent Growth for This Job): Springfield, MO (157.1%); Chattanooga, TN–GA (137.5%); Lincoln, NE (133.3%); Modesto, CA (133.3%); Boise City–Nampa, ID (125.0%).

Other Considerations for Job Security: Employment of substance abuse and behavioral disorder counselors is expected to grow much faster than the average for all occupations. As society becomes more knowledgeable about addiction, it is increasingly common for people to seek treatment. Furthermore, drug offenders are increasingly being sent to treatment programs rather than jail. Job opportunities are very good because relatively low wages and long hours make recruiting new entrants difficult.

Counsel and advise individuals with alcohol; tobacco; drug; or other problems, such as gambling and eating disorders. May counsel individuals, families, or groups or engage in prevention programs. Counsel clients and patients individually and in group sessions to assist in overcoming dependencies, adjusting to life, and making changes. Complete and maintain accurate records and reports regarding the patients' histories and progress, services provided, and other required information. Develop client treatment plans based on research, clinical experience, and client histories. Review and evaluate clients' progress in relation to measurable goals described in treatment and care plans. Interview clients, review records, and confer with other professionals to evaluate individuals' mental and physical condition and to determine their suitability for participation in a specific program. Intervene as advocate for clients or patients to resolve emergency problems in crisis situations. Provide clients or family members with information about addiction issues and about available services and programs, making appropriate referrals when necessary. Modify treatment plans to comply with changes in client status. Coordinate counseling efforts with mental-health professionals and other health professionals such as doctors, nurses, and social workers. Attend training sessions to increase knowledge and skills. Plan and implement follow-up and aftercare programs for clients to be discharged from treatment programs. Conduct chemical dependency program orientation sessions. Counsel family members to help them understand, deal with, and support clients or patients. Participate in case conferences and staff meetings. Act as liaisons between clients and medical staff. Coordinate activities with courts, probation officers, community services, and other post-treatment agencies. Confer with family members or others close to clients

to keep them informed of treatment planning and progress. Instruct others in program methods, procedures, and functions. Follow progress of discharged patients to determine effectiveness of treatments. Develop, implement, and evaluate public education, prevention, and health promotion programs, working in collaboration with organizations, institutions, and communities.

Personality Type: Social.

GOE—Interest Area: 10. Human Service. **Work Group:** 10.01. Counseling and Social Work. **Other Jobs in this Work Group:** Child, Family, and School Social Workers; Clinical Psychologists; Clinical, Counseling, and School Psychologists; Counseling Psychologists; Marriage and Family Therapists; Medical and Public Health Social Workers; Mental Health and Substance Abuse Social Workers; Mental Health Counselors; Probation Officers and Correctional Treatment Specialists; Rehabilitation Counselors; Residential Advisors; Social and Human Service Assistants.

Skills: Social Perceptiveness; Persuasion; Service Orientation; Negotiation; Active Listening; Learning Strategies.

Education and Training Programs: Substance Abuse/Addiction Counseling; Clinical/Medical Social Work; Mental and Social Health Services and Allied Professions, Other. **Related Knowledge/Courses:** Therapy and Counseling; Psychology; Sociology and Anthropology; Philosophy and Theology; Customer and Personal Service; Education and Training.

Work Environment: Indoors; disease or infections; sitting.

Surgeons

- ❀ Education/Training Required: First professional degree
- ❀ Annual Earnings: More than $145,600
- ❀ Beginning Wage: $116,850
- ❀ Earnings Growth Potential: Cannot be calculated
- ❀ Growth: 14.2%
- ❀ Annual Job Openings: 38,027
- ❀ Self-Employed: 14.7%
- ❀ Part-Time: 8.1%

Our sources did not provide separate job openings data for this occupation. The job openings listed here are shared with Anesthesiologists; Family and General Practitioners; Internists, General; Obstetricians and Gynecologists; Pediatricians, General; and Psychiatrists.

Industries with Greatest Employment: Ambulatory Health Care Services; Hospitals, Public and Private.

Highest-Growth Industries (Projected Growth for This Job): Social Assistance (58.6%); Administrative and Support Services (26.8%); Professional, Scientific, and Technical Services (22.6%); Nursing and Residential Care Facilities (21.0%); Ambulatory Health Care Services (19.4%); Religious, Grantmaking, Civic, Professional, and Similar Organizations (16.7%); Management of Companies and Enterprises (15.3%).

Lowest-Growth Industries (Projected Growth for This Job): Insurance Carriers and Related Activities (4.6%); Health and Personal Care Stores (5.3%); Hospitals, Public and Private (9.9%); Educational Services, Public and Private (11.8%).

Fastest-Growing Metropolitan Areas (Recent Growth for This Job): Omaha–Council Bluffs, NE–IA (22.0%); Portland–South Portland–Biddeford, ME (20.0%); Springfield, MA–CT (19.6%); San Jose–Sunnyvale–Santa Clara, CA (19.0%); Phoenix–Mesa–Scottsdale, AZ (19.0%).

Other Considerations for Job Security: Opportunities for individuals interested in becoming physicians and surgeons are expected to be very good. Unlike their predecessors, new physicians are much less likely to enter solo practice and more likely to take salaried jobs in group medical practices, clinics, and health networks. Reports of shortages in some specialties, such as general or family practice, internal medicine, and OB/GYN, or in rural or low-income areas should attract new entrants, encouraging schools to expand programs and hospitals to increase available residency slots. However, because physician training is so lengthy, employment change happens gradually. Opportunities should be particularly good in rural and low-income areas, as some physicians find these areas unattractive because of less control over work hours, isolation from medical colleagues, or other reasons.

Treat diseases, injuries, and deformities by invasive methods, such as manual manipulation, or by using instruments and appliances. Analyze patient's medical history, medication allergies, physical condition, and examination results to verify operation's necessity and to determine best procedure. Operate on patients to correct deformities, repair injuries, prevent and treat diseases, or improve or restore patients' functions. Follow established surgical techniques during the operation. Prescribe preoperative and postoperative treatments and procedures, such as sedatives, diets, antibiotics, and preparation and treatment of the patient's operative area. Examine patient to provide information on medical condition and surgical risk. Diagnose bodily disorders and orthopedic conditions and provide treatments, such as medicines and surgeries, in clinics, hospital wards, and operating rooms. Direct and coordinate activities of nurses, assistants, specialists, residents, and other medical staff. Provide consultation and surgical assistance to other physicians and surgeons. Refer patient to medical specialist or other practitioners when necessary. Examine instruments, equipment, and operating room to ensure sterility. Prepare case histories. Manage surgery services, including planning, scheduling and coordination, determination of procedures, and procurement of supplies and equipment.

Conduct research to develop and test surgical techniques that can improve operating procedures and outcomes.

Personality Type: Investigative.

GOE—Interest Area: 08. Health Science. **Work Group:** 08.02. Medicine and Surgery. **Other Jobs in this Work Group:** Anesthesiologists; Family and General Practitioners; Internists, General; Medical Assistants; Medical Transcriptionists; Obstetricians and Gynecologists; Pediatricians, General; Pharmacists; Pharmacy Aides; Pharmacy Technicians; Physician Assistants; Psychiatrists; Registered Nurses; Surgical Technologists.

Skills: Science; Reading Comprehension; Judgment and Decision Making; Complex Problem Solving; Management of Financial Resources; Critical Thinking.

Education and Training Programs: Colon and Rectal Surgery; Critical Care Surgery; General Surgery; Hand Surgery; Neurological Surgery/Neurosurgery; Orthopedics/Orthopedic Surgery; Otolaryngology; Pediatric Orthopedics; Pediatric Surgery; Plastic Surgery; Sports Medicine; Thoracic Surgery; Urology; Vascular Surgery; Adult Reconstructive Orthopedics (Orthopedic Surgery); Orthopedic Surgery of the Spine. **Related Knowledge/Courses:** Medicine and Dentistry; Biology; Therapy and Counseling; Psychology; Chemistry; Customer and Personal Service.

Work Environment: Indoors; contaminants; radiation; disease or infections; standing; using hands on objects, tools, or controls.

Surgical Technologists

* Education/Training Required: Postsecondary vocational training
* Annual Earnings: $36,080
* Beginning Wage: $25,490
* Earnings Growth Potential: Very high
* Growth: 24.5%
* Annual Job Openings: 15,365
* Self-Employed: 0.2%
* Part-Time: 20.8%

Industries with Greatest Employment: Hospitals, Public and Private.

Highest-Growth Industries (Projected Growth for This Job): Professional, Scientific, and Technical Services (43.5%); Administrative and Support Services (32.4%); Hospitals, Public and Private (21.9%).

Lowest-Growth Industries (Projected Growth for This Job): Educational Services, Public and Private (11.9%); Management of Companies and Enterprises (14.3%).

Fastest-Growing Metropolitan Areas (Recent Growth for This Job): Waco, TX (62.5%); Panama City–Lynn Haven, FL (57.1%); Erie, PA (50.0%); Cleveland–Elyria–Mentor, OH (49.1%); Deltona–Daytona Beach–Ormond Beach, FL (45.5%).

Other Considerations for Job Security: Job opportunities will be best for certified technologists. The number of surgical procedures is expected to rise as the population grows and ages. Hospitals will continue to be the primary employer of surgical technologists, although much faster employment growth is expected in offices of physicians and in outpatient care centers, including ambulatory surgical centers.

Assist in operations under the supervision of surgeons, registered nurses, or other surgical personnel. May help set up operating room; prepare and transport patients for surgery; adjust lights and equipment; pass instruments and other supplies to surgeons and surgeon's assistants; hold retractors; cut sutures; and help count sponges, needles,

supplies, and instruments. Count sponges, needles, and instruments before and after operation. Hand instruments and supplies to surgeons and surgeons' assistants, hold retractors and cut sutures, and perform other tasks as directed by surgeon during operation. Scrub arms and hands and assist the surgical team in scrubbing and putting on gloves, masks, and surgical clothing. Position patients on the operating table and cover them with sterile surgical drapes to prevent exposure. Provide technical assistance to surgeons, surgical nurses, and anesthesiologists. Wash and sterilize equipment, using germicides and sterilizers. Prepare, care for, and dispose of tissue specimens taken for laboratory analysis. Clean and restock the operating room, placing equipment and supplies and arranging instruments according to instruction. Prepare dressings or bandages and apply or assist with their application following surgery. Operate, assemble, adjust, or monitor sterilizers, lights, suction machines, and diagnostic equipment to ensure proper operation. Monitor and continually assess operating room conditions, including patient and surgical team needs. Observe patients' vital signs to assess physical condition. Maintain supply of fluids, such as plasma, saline, blood, and glucose, for use during operations. Maintain files and records of surgical procedures.

Personality Type: Realistic.

GOE—Interest Area: 08. Health Science. Work Group: 08.02. Medicine and Surgery. Other Jobs in this Work Group: Anesthesiologists; Family and General Practitioners; Internists, General; Medical Assistants; Medical Transcriptionists; Obstetricians and Gynecologists; Pediatricians, General; Pharmacists; Pharmacy Aides; Pharmacy Technicians; Physician Assistants; Psychiatrists; Registered Nurses; Surgeons.

Skills: Troubleshooting; Equipment Selection; Science; Operation Monitoring; Instructing; Reading Comprehension.

Education and Training Programs: Pathology/Pathologist Assistant; Surgical Technology/Technologist. Related Knowledge/Courses: Medicine and

Dentistry; Chemistry; Philosophy and Theology; Psychology; Therapy and Counseling; Customer and Personal Service.

Work Environment: Indoors; contaminants; disease or infections; hazardous conditions; standing; using hands on objects, tools, or controls.

Tax Examiners, Collectors, and Revenue Agents

- ✸ Education/Training Required: Bachelor's degree
- ✸ Annual Earnings: $45,620
- ✸ Beginning Wage: $27,290
- ✸ Earnings Growth Potential: Very high
- ✸ Growth: 2.1%
- ✸ Annual Job Openings: 4,465
- ✸ Self-Employed: 0.0%
- ✸ Part-Time: 3.9%

Industries with Greatest Employment: State Government, excluding Education and Hospitals; Local Government, excluding Education and Hospitals.

Highest-Growth Industries (Projected Growth for This Job): None met the criteria.

Lowest-Growth Industries (Projected Growth for This Job): None met the criteria.

Fastest-Growing Metropolitan Areas (Recent Growth for This Job): Jackson, MS (157.1%); Kingston, NY (100.0%); Shreveport–Bossier City, LA (100.0%); Tucson, AZ (100.0%); Santa Fe, NM (83.3%).

Other Considerations for Job Security: Demand for tax examiners, revenue agents, and tax collectors will stem from changes in government policy toward tax enforcement and from growth in the number of businesses. Workers with knowledge of tax laws and experience working with complex tax issues will have the best opportunities. The work of tax examiners is especially well suited to automation, adversely affecting demand for these workers in particular. Also, more than 40 states and many local tax agencies contract out their tax collection functions to private-sector collection agencies to reduce costs, and this trend is likely to continue. Employment at the state and local levels may fluctuate with the overall state of the economy. When the economy is contracting, state and local governments are likely to freeze hiring and lay off workers in response to budgetary constraints.

Determine tax liability or collect taxes from individuals or business firms according to prescribed laws and regulations. Collect taxes from individuals or businesses according to prescribed laws and regulations. Maintain knowledge of tax code changes and of accounting procedures and theory to properly evaluate financial information. Maintain records for each case, including contacts, telephone numbers, and actions taken. Confer with taxpayers or their representatives to discuss the issues, laws, and regulations involved in returns and to resolve problems with returns. Contact taxpayers by mail or telephone to address discrepancies and to request supporting documentation. Send notices to taxpayers when accounts are delinquent. Notify taxpayers of any overpayment or underpayment and either issue refunds or request further payments. Conduct independent field audits and investigations of income tax returns to verify information or to amend tax liabilities. Review filed tax returns to determine whether claimed tax credits and deductions are allowed by law. Review selected tax returns to determine the nature and extent of audits to be performed on them. Enter tax return information into computers for processing. Examine accounting systems and records to determine whether accounting methods used were appropriate and in compliance with statutory provisions. Process individual and corporate income tax returns and sales and excise tax returns. Impose payment deadlines on delinquent taxpayers and monitor payments to ensure that deadlines are met. Check tax forms to verify that names and taxpayer identification numbers are correct, that computations have been performed correctly, or that amounts match those on supporting documentation. Examine and analyze tax assets and liabilities to determine resolution of delinquent tax problems. Recommend

criminal prosecutions or civil penalties. Determine appropriate methods of debt settlement, such as offers of compromise, wage garnishment, or seizure and sale of property. Secure a taxpayer's agreement to discharge a tax assessment or submit contested determinations to other administrative or judicial conferees for appeals hearings. Prepare briefs and assist in searching and seizing records to prepare charges and documentation for court cases.

Personality Type: Conventional.

GOE—Interest Area: 07. Government and Public Administration. **Work Group:** 07.03. Regulations Enforcement. **Other Jobs in this Work Group:** Agricultural Inspectors; Aviation Inspectors; Compliance Officers, Except Agriculture, Construction, Health and Safety, and Transportation; Construction and Building Inspectors; Environmental Compliance Inspectors; Equal Opportunity Representatives and Officers; Financial Examiners; Fire Inspectors; Fish and Game Wardens; Forest Fire Inspectors and Prevention Specialists; Freight and Cargo Inspectors; Government Property Inspectors and Investigators; Immigration and Customs Inspectors; Licensing Examiners and Inspectors; Nuclear Monitoring Technicians; Occupational Health and Safety Specialists; Occupational Health and Safety Technicians; Transportation Vehicle, Equipment, and Systems Inspectors, Except Aviation.

Skills: Service Orientation; Mathematics; Speaking; Active Learning; Complex Problem Solving; Instructing.

Education and Training Programs: Accounting; Taxation. **Related Knowledge/Courses:** Law and Government; Customer and Personal Service; Computers and Electronics; Economics and Accounting; Clerical Studies; Mathematics.

Work Environment: Indoors; sitting; repetitive motions.

Taxi Drivers and Chauffeurs

- ❋ Education/Training Required: Short-term on-the-job training
- ❋ Annual Earnings: $20,350
- ❋ Beginning Wage: $14,250
- ❋ Earnings Growth Potential: Very high
- ❋ Growth: 13.0%
- ❋ Annual Job Openings: 35,954
- ❋ Self-Employed: 29.5%
- ❋ Part-Time: 17.7%

Industries with Greatest Employment: Transit and Ground Passenger Transportation; Motor Vehicle and Parts Dealers; Social Assistance; Nursing and Residential Care Facilities; Personal and Laundry Services.

Highest-Growth Industries (Projected Growth for This Job): Social Assistance (45.6%); Securities, Commodity Contracts, and Other Financial Investments and Related Activities (42.2%); Amusement, Gambling, and Recreation Industries (37.2%); Nursing and Residential Care Facilities (30.8%); Scenic and Sightseeing Transportation (30.1%); Repair and Maintenance (24.9%); Professional, Scientific, and Technical Services (24.7%); Ambulatory Health Care Services (23.2%); Administrative and Support Services (22.6%); Personal and Laundry Services (21.4%); Support Activities for Transportation (15.5%).

Lowest-Growth Industries (Projected Growth for This Job): Rail Transportation (–14.7%); Private Households (2.6%); Insurance Carriers and Related Activities (6.2%); Credit Intermediation and Related Activities (7.2%); Hospitals, Public and Private (7.3%); Food and Beverage Stores (7.5%); Couriers and Messengers (7.8%); Educational Services, Public and Private (8.8%); Air Transportation (9.7%); Food Services and Drinking Places (9.7%).

Fastest-Growing Metropolitan Areas (Recent Growth for This Job): Grand Rapids–Wyoming, MI (175.0%); Lawrence, KS (166.7%); Weirton–Steubenville, WV–OH (133.3%); Chattanooga, TN–GA (128.6%); Lafayette, IN (120.0%).

Other Considerations for Job Security: People seeking jobs as taxi drivers and chauffeurs are expected to have plentiful opportunities because of the need to replace the many people who work in this occupation for short periods and then transfer to other occupations or leave the labor force. Applicants with good driving records, good customer service instincts, and the ability to work flexible schedules should have the best prospects. The number of job opportunities can fluctuate during economic slowdowns, but drivers seldom are laid off. Rapidly growing metropolitan areas and cities experiencing economic growth should offer the best job opportunities.

Drive automobiles, vans, or limousines to transport passengers. May occasionally carry cargo. Test vehicle equipment such as lights, brakes, horns, or windshield wipers to ensure proper operation. Notify dispatchers or company mechanics of vehicle problems. Drive taxicabs, limousines, company cars, or privately owned vehicles to transport passengers. Follow regulations governing taxi operation and ensure that passengers follow safety regulations. Pick up passengers at prearranged locations, at taxi stands, or by cruising streets in high-traffic areas. Perform routine vehicle maintenance such as regulating tire pressure and adding gasoline, oil, and water. Communicate with dispatchers by radio, telephone, or computer to exchange information and receive requests for passenger service. Record name, date, and taxi identification information on trip sheets, along with trip information such as time and place of pickup and dropoff and total fee. Complete accident reports when necessary. Provide passengers with assistance entering and exiting vehicles and help them with any luggage. Arrange to pick up particular customers or groups on a regular schedule. Vacuum and clean interiors and wash and polish exteriors of automobiles. Pick up or meet employers according to requests, appointments, or schedules. Operate vans with special equipment such as wheelchair lifts to transport people with special needs. Collect fares or vouchers from passengers and make change or issue receipts as necessary. Determine fares based on trip distances and times, using taximeters and fee schedules, and announce fares to passengers. Perform minor vehicle repairs such as cleaning spark plugs or take vehicles to mechanics for servicing. Turn the taximeter on when passengers enter the cab and turn it off when they reach their final destination. Report to taxicab services or garages to receive vehicle assignments. Perform errands for customers or employers, such as delivering or picking up mail and packages. Provide passengers with information about the local area and points of interest or give advice on hotels and restaurants.

Personality Type: Realistic.

GOE—Interest Area: 16. Transportation, Distribution, and Logistics. **Work Group:** 16.06. Other Services Requiring Driving. **Other Jobs in this Work Group:** Ambulance Drivers and Attendants, Except Emergency Medical Technicians; Bus Drivers, School; Bus Drivers, Transit and Intercity; Couriers and Messengers; Driver/Sales Workers; Parking Lot Attendants; Postal Service Mail Carriers.

Skills: No data available.

Education and Training Program: Truck and Bus Driver/Commercial Vehicle Operation. **Related Knowledge/Courses:** Transportation; English Language.

Work Environment: Outdoors; contaminants; sitting; using hands on objects, tools, or controls.

Teacher Assistants

- ❋ Education/Training Required: Short-term on-the-job training
- ❋ Annual Earnings: $20,740
- ❋ Beginning Wage: $13,910
- ❋ Earnings Growth Potential: Very high
- ❋ Growth: 10.4%
- ❋ Annual Job Openings: 193,986
- ❋ Self-Employed: 0.2%
- ❋ Part-Time: 38.0%

Industries with Greatest Employment: Educational Services, Public and Private; Social Assistance.

Highest-Growth Industries (Projected Growth for This Job): Professional, Scientific, and Technical Services (38.6%); Social Assistance (37.2%); Museums, Historical Sites, and Similar Institutions (36.1%); Ambulatory Health Care Services (28.9%); Nursing and Residential Care Facilities (24.0%); Religious, Grantmaking, Civic, Professional, and Similar Organizations (18.4%); Management of Companies and Enterprises (15.3%).

Lowest-Growth Industries (Projected Growth for This Job): Educational Services, Public and Private (6.5%); Hospitals, Public and Private (10.1%).

Fastest-Growing Metropolitan Areas (Recent Growth for This Job): Lebanon, PA (100.0%); Morristown, TN (96.3%); San Luis Obispo–Paso Robles, CA (76.1%); St. Joseph, MO–KS (59.3%); Rockford, IL (58.4%).

Other Considerations for Job Security: Favorable job prospects are expected. Opportunities for teacher assistant jobs should be best for those with at least two years of formal postsecondary education, those with experience in helping special education students, or those who can speak foreign languages. Demand is expected to vary by region of the country. Regions in which the population and school enrollments are expected to grow faster, such as many communities in the South and West, should have rapid growth in the demand for teacher assistants.

Perform duties that are instructional in nature or deliver direct services to students or parents. Serve in a position for which a teacher or another professional has ultimate responsibility for the design and implementation of educational programs and services. Provide extra assistance to students with special needs, such as non-English–speaking students or those with physical and mental disabilities. Tutor and assist children individually or in small groups to help them master assignments and to reinforce learning concepts presented by teachers. Supervise students in classrooms, halls, cafeterias, school yards, and gymnasiums or on field trips. Enforce administration policies and rules governing students. Observe students' performance and record relevant data to assess progress. Discuss assigned duties with classroom teachers to coordinate instructional efforts. Instruct and monitor students in the use and care of equipment and materials to prevent injuries and damage. Present subject matter to students under the direction and guidance of teachers, using lectures, discussions, or supervised role-playing methods. Organize and label materials and display students' work in a manner appropriate for their eye levels and perceptual skills. Distribute tests and homework assignments and collect them when they are completed. Type, file, and duplicate materials. Distribute teaching materials such as textbooks, workbooks, papers, and pencils to students. Use computers, audiovisual aids, and other equipment and materials to supplement presentations. Attend staff meetings and serve on committees as required. Prepare lesson materials, bulletin board displays, exhibits, equipment, and demonstrations. Carry out therapeutic regimens such as behavior modification and personal development programs under the supervision of special education instructors, psychologists, or speech-language pathologists. Provide disabled students with assistive devices, supportive technology, and assistance accessing facilities such as restrooms. Assist in bus loading and unloading. Take class attendance and maintain attendance records. Grade homework and tests, and compute and record results, using answer sheets or electronic marking devices. Organize and supervise games and other recreational activities to promote physical, mental, and social development.

Personality Type: Social.

GOE—Interest Area: 05. Education and Training. **Work Group:** 05.02. Preschool, Elementary, and Secondary Teaching and Instructing. **Other Jobs in this Work Group:** Elementary School Teachers, Except Special Education; Kindergarten Teachers, Except Special Education; Middle School Teachers, Except Special and Vocational Education; Preschool Teachers, Except Special Education; Secondary School Teachers, Except Special and Vocational Education; Special Education Teachers, Middle School; Special

Education Teachers, Preschool, Kindergarten, and Elementary School; Special Education Teachers, Secondary School; Vocational Education Teachers, Middle School; Vocational Education Teachers, Secondary School.

Skills: No data available.

Education and Training Programs: Teacher Assistant/Aide; Teaching Assistants/Aides, Other. **Related Knowledge/Courses:** Geography; History and Archeology; Psychology; Therapy and Counseling; Sociology and Anthropology; English Language.

Work Environment: Indoors; noisy; standing.

Teachers, Postsecondary

See *Agricultural Sciences Teachers, Postsecondary; Anthropology and Archeology Teachers, Postsecondary; Architecture Teachers, Postsecondary; Area, Ethnic, and Cultural Studies Teachers, Postsecondary; Art, Drama, and Music Teachers, Postsecondary; Atmospheric, Earth, Marine, and Space Sciences Teachers, Postsecondary; Biological Science Teachers, Postsecondary; Business Teachers, Postsecondary; Chemistry Teachers, Postsecondary; Communications Teachers, Postsecondary; Computer Science Teachers, Postsecondary; Criminal Justice and Law Enforcement Teachers, Postsecondary; Economics Teachers, Postsecondary; Education Teachers, Postsecondary; Engineering Teachers, Postsecondary; English Language and Literature Teachers, Postsecondary; Environmental Science Teachers, Postsecondary; Foreign Language and Literature Teachers, Postsecondary; Forestry and Conservation Science Teachers, Postsecondary; Geography Teachers, Postsecondary; Graduate Teaching Assistants; Health Specialties Teachers, Postsecondary; History Teachers, Postsecondary; Home Economics Teachers, Postsecondary; Law Teachers, Postsecondary; Library Science Teachers, Postsecondary; Mathematical Science Teachers, Postsecondary; Nursing Instructors and Teachers, Postsecondary; Philosophy and Religion Teachers, Postsecondary; Physics Teachers, Postsecondary; Political Science Teachers, Postsecondary; Psychology Teachers, Postsecondary; Recreation and Fitness Studies Teachers, Postsecondary; Social Work Teachers,*

Postsecondary; Sociology Teachers, Postsecondary; and Vocational Education Teachers, Postsecondary, described separately.

Veterinarians

- ❋ Education/Training Required: First professional degree
- ❋ Annual Earnings: $71,990
- ❋ Beginning Wage: $43,530
- ❋ Earnings Growth Potential: Very high
- ❋ Growth: 35.0%
- ❋ Annual Job Openings: 5,301
- ❋ Self-Employed: 17.1%
- ❋ Part-Time: 13.4%

Industries with Greatest Employment: Professional, Scientific, and Technical Services.

Highest-Growth Industries (Projected Growth for This Job): Professional, Scientific, and Technical Services (45.1%); Amusement, Gambling, and Recreation Industries (38.8%); Museums, Historical Sites, and Similar Institutions (36.8%); Personal and Laundry Services (31.9%); Chemical Manufacturing (26.1%); Performing Arts, Spectator Sports, and Related Industries (23.6%); Religious, Grantmaking, Civic, Professional, and Similar Organizations (15.5%).

Lowest-Growth Industries (Projected Growth for This Job): Animal Production (–11.3%); Educational Services, Public and Private (11.9%).

Fastest-Growing Metropolitan Areas (Recent Growth for This Job): Ocala, FL (150.0%); Harrisburg–Carlisle, PA (88.9%); Asheville, NC (80.0%); Lansing–East Lansing, MI (80.0%); Erie, PA (66.7%).

Other Considerations for Job Security: Excellent job opportunities are expected because there are only 28 accredited schools of veterinary medicine in the United States, resulting in a limited number of graduates—about 2,700—each year. However, applicants face keen competition for admission to veterinary school. New graduates continue to be attracted to companion-animal medicine. Employment opportunities are good in cities and suburbs, but even better in rural areas because fewer veterinarians compete to work there. Although the number of jobs for large-animal veterinarians is likely to grow more slowly than jobs for companion-animal veterinarians, job prospects should be better for veterinarians who specialize in farm animals. Veterinarians with training in food safety and security, animal health and welfare, and public health and epidemiology should have the best opportunities for careers in the federal government.

Diagnose and treat diseases and dysfunctions of animals. May engage in a particular function, such as research and development, consultation, administration, technical writing, sale or production of commercial products, or rendering of technical services to commercial firms or other organizations. Includes veterinarians who inspect livestock. Examine animals to detect and determine the nature of diseases or injuries. Treat sick or injured animals by prescribing medication, setting bones, dressing wounds, or performing surgery. Inoculate animals against various diseases such as rabies and distemper. Collect body tissue, feces, blood, urine, or other body fluids for examination and analysis. Operate diagnostic equipment such as radiographic and ultrasound equipment and interpret the resulting images. Advise animal owners regarding sanitary measures, feeding, and general care necessary to promote health of animals. Educate the public about diseases that can be spread from animals to humans. Train and supervise workers who handle and care for animals. Provide care to a wide range of animals or specialize in a particular species, such as horses or exotic birds. Euthanize animals. Establish and conduct quarantine and testing procedures that prevent the spread of diseases to other animals or to humans and that comply with applicable government regulations. Conduct postmortem studies and analyses to determine the causes of animals' deaths. Perform administrative duties such as scheduling appointments, accepting payments from clients, and maintaining business records. Drive mobile clinic vans to farms so that health problems can be treated or prevented. Direct the overall operations of animal hospitals, clinics, or mobile services to farms. Specialize in a particular type of treatment such as dentistry, pathology, nutrition, surgery, microbiology, or internal medicine. Inspect and test horses, sheep, poultry, and other animals to detect the presence of communicable diseases. Research diseases to which animals could be susceptible. Plan and execute animal nutrition and reproduction programs. Inspect animal housing facilities to determine their cleanliness and adequacy. Determine the effects of drug therapies, antibiotics, or new surgical techniques by testing them on animals.

Personality Type: Investigative.

GOE—Interest Area: 08. Health Science. **Work Group:** 08.05. Animal Care. **Other Jobs in this Work Group:** Animal Breeders; Animal Trainers; Nonfarm Animal Caretakers; Veterinary Assistants and Laboratory Animal Caretakers; Veterinary Technologists and Technicians.

Skills: Science; Management of Financial Resources; Management of Personnel Resources; Reading Comprehension; Judgment and Decision Making; Complex Problem Solving.

Education and Training Programs: Veterinary Medicine (DVM); Veterinary Sciences/Veterinary Clinical Sciences, General (Cert, MS, PhD); Veterinary Anatomy (Cert, MS, PhD); Veterinary Physiology (Cert, MS, PhD); Veterinary Microbiology and Immunobiology (Cert, MS, PhD); Veterinary Pathology and Pathobiology (Cert, MS, PhD); Veterinary Toxicology and Pharmacology (Cert, MS, PhD); Large Animal/Food Animal and Equine Surgery and Medicine (Cert, MS, PhD); others. **Related Knowledge/Courses:** Biology; Medicine and Dentistry; Chemistry; Therapy and Counseling; Sales and Marketing; Customer and Personal Service.

Work Environment: Indoors; noisy; contaminants; disease or infections; standing; using hands on objects, tools, or controls.

Veterinary Technologists and Technicians

* Education/Training Required: Associate degree
* Annual Earnings: $26,780
* Beginning Wage: $18,280
* Earnings Growth Potential: Very high
* Growth: 41.0%
* Annual Job Openings: 14,674
* Self-Employed: 0.2%
* Part-Time: 20.8%

Industries with Greatest Employment: Professional, Scientific, and Technical Services.

Highest-Growth Industries (Projected Growth for This Job): Professional, Scientific, and Technical Services (44.2%); Museums, Historical Sites, and Similar Institutions (24.7%); Personal and Laundry Services (20.0%); Administrative and Support Services (16.0%); Chemical Manufacturing (15.1%).

Lowest-Growth Industries (Projected Growth for This Job): Educational Services, Public and Private (2.1%); Religious, Grantmaking, Civic, Professional, and Similar Organizations (4.6%); Hospitals, Public and Private (13.3%).

Fastest-Growing Metropolitan Areas (Recent Growth for This Job): Deltona–Daytona Beach–Ormond Beach, FL (116.7%); Youngstown–Warren–Boardman, OH–PA (100.0%); Harrisburg–Carlisle, PA (81.8%); Medford, OR (75.0%); Rochester–Dover, NH–ME (75.0%).

Other Considerations for Job Security: Excellent job opportunities are expected because of the relatively few veterinary technology graduates each year. The number of two-year programs has recently grown to 131, but due to small class sizes, fewer than 3,000 graduates are anticipated each year, which isn't expected to meet demand. Also, many veterinary technicians remain in the field for only seven or eight years, so the need to replace workers who leave the occupation each year also will produce many job opportunities. Employment of veterinary technicians and technologists is relatively stable during periods of economic recession. Layoffs are less likely to occur among veterinary technologists and technicians than in some other occupations because animals will continue to require medical care.

Perform medical tests in a laboratory environment for use in the treatment and diagnosis of diseases in animals. Prepare vaccines and serums for prevention of diseases. Prepare tissue samples; take blood samples; and execute laboratory tests, such as urinalysis and blood counts. Clean and sterilize instruments and materials and maintain equipment and machines. Administer anesthesia to animals, under the direction of a veterinarian, and monitor animals' responses to anesthetics so that dosages can be adjusted. Care for and monitor the condition of animals recovering from surgery. Prepare and administer medications, vaccines, serums, and treatments as prescribed by veterinarians. Perform laboratory tests on blood, urine, and feces, such as urinalyses and blood counts, to assist in the diagnosis and treatment of animal health problems. Administer emergency first aid, such as performing emergency resuscitation or other life-saving procedures. Collect, prepare, and label samples for laboratory testing, culture, or microscopic examination. Clean and sterilize instruments, equipment, and materials. Provide veterinarians with the correct equipment and instruments as needed. Fill prescriptions, measuring medications and labeling containers. Prepare animals for surgery, performing such tasks as shaving surgical areas. Take animals into treatment areas and assist with physical examinations by performing such duties as obtaining temperature, pulse, and respiration data. Observe the behavior and condition of animals and monitor their clinical symptoms. Take and develop diagnostic radiographs, using X-ray equipment. Maintain laboratory, research, and treatment records, as well as inventories of pharmaceuticals, equipment, and supplies. Give enemas and perform catheterizations, ear flushes, intravenous feedings, and gavages. Prepare treatment rooms for surgery. Maintain instruments, equipment, and machinery to ensure proper working condition. Perform dental work such as cleaning, polishing, and extracting teeth. Clean kennels, animal holding areas, surgery suites, examination rooms, and animal loading/unloading facilities to control the spread of disease. Provide information and counseling regarding issues such as animal health care, behavior problems, and nutrition. Provide assistance with animal euthanasia and the disposal of remains. Dress and suture wounds and apply splints and other protective devices. Perform various office, clerical, and accounting duties, such as reception, billing, bookkeeping, or selling products.

Personality Type: No data available.

GOE—Interest Area: 08. Health Science. **Work Group:** 08.05. Animal Care. **Other Jobs in this Work Group:** Animal Breeders; Animal Trainers; Nonfarm Animal Caretakers; Veterinarians; Veterinary Assistants and Laboratory Animal Caretakers.

Skills: Science; Operation Monitoring; Instructing; Equipment Maintenance; Social Perceptiveness; Operation and Control.

Education and Training Program: Veterinary/Animal Health Technology/Technician and Veterinary Assistant. **Related Knowledge/Courses:** Biology; Medicine and Dentistry; Chemistry; Sales and Marketing; Customer and Personal Service; Mathematics.

Work Environment: Indoors; contaminants; radiation; disease or infections; minor burns, cuts, bites, or stings; standing.

Vocational Education Teachers, Postsecondary

* ❋ Education/Training Required: Work experience in a related occupation
* ❋ Annual Earnings: $43,900
* ❋ Beginning Wage: $25,420
* ❋ Earnings Growth Potential: Very high
* ❋ Growth: 22.9%
* ❋ Annual Job Openings: 237,478
* ❋ Self-Employed: 0.4%
* ❋ Part-Time: 27.8%

Our sources did not provide separate job openings data for this occupation. The job openings listed here are shared with 35 other postsecondary teaching occupations. For a complete list, see the beginning of this section.

Industries with Greatest Employment: Educational Services, Public and Private.

Highest-Growth Industries (Projected Growth for This Job): Administrative and Support Services (48.3%); Amusement, Gambling, and Recreation Industries (45.3%); Social Assistance (38.6%); Support Activities for Transportation (32.8%); Religious, Grantmaking, Civic, Professional, and Similar Organizations (29.9%); Professional, Scientific, and Technical Services (28.8%); Management of Companies and Enterprises (26.8%); Educational Services, Public and Private (22.9%); Hospitals, Public and Private (21.4%); Personal and Laundry Services (21.0%).

Lowest-Growth Industries (Projected Growth for This Job): Other Information Services (7.4%); Sporting Goods, Hobby, Book, and Music Stores (13.3%); Performing Arts, Spectator Sports, and Related Industries (13.4%); Insurance Carriers and Related Activities (13.9%).

Fastest-Growing Metropolitan Areas (Recent Growth for This Job): None growing over 10 percent.

Other Considerations for Job Security: Retirements of current postsecondary teachers should create numerous openings for all types of postsecondary teachers, so job opportunities are generally expected to be very good. However, because students attend postsecondary institutions to prepare themselves for careers, the best job prospects for postsecondary teachers are likely to be in rapidly growing fields that offer many nonacademic career options. Community colleges and other institutions offering career and technical education have been among the most rapidly growing and are expected to offer some of the best opportunities for postsecondary teachers.

Teach or instruct vocational or occupational subjects at the postsecondary (but less than baccalaureate) level to students who have graduated or left high school. Includes correspondence school instructors; industrial, commercial, and government training instructors; and adult education teachers and instructors who prepare persons to operate industrial machinery and equipment and transportation and communications equipment. Teaching may take place in public or private schools whose primary business is education or in schools associated with organizations whose primary business is other than education. Supervise and monitor students' use of tools and equipment. Observe and evaluate students' work to determine progress, provide feedback, and make suggestions for improvement. Present lectures and conduct discussions to increase students' knowledge and competence, using visual aids such as graphs, charts, videotapes, and slides. Administer oral, written, or performance tests to measure progress and to evaluate training effectiveness. Prepare reports and maintain records such as student grades, attendance rolls, and training activity details. Supervise independent or group projects, field placements, laboratory work, or other training. Determine training needs of students or workers. Provide individualized instruction and tutorial or remedial instruction. Conduct on-the-job training, classes, or training sessions to teach and demonstrate principles, techniques, procedures, and methods of designated subjects. Develop curricula and plan course content and methods of instruction. Prepare outlines of instructional programs and training schedules and establish course goals. Integrate academic and vocational curricula so that students can obtain a variety of skills. Develop teaching aids such as instructional software, multimedia visual aids, or study materials. Select and assemble books, materials, supplies, and equipment for training, courses, or projects. Advise students on course selection, career decisions, and other academic and vocational concerns. Participate in conferences, seminars, and training sessions to keep abreast of developments in the field and integrate relevant information into training programs. Serve on faculty and school committees concerned with budgeting, curriculum revision, and course and diploma requirements. Review enrollment applications and correspond with applicants to obtain additional information. Arrange for lectures by experts in designated fields.

Personality Type: Social.

GOE—Interest Area: 05. Education and Training. **Work Group:** 05.03. Postsecondary and Adult Teaching and Instructing. **Other Jobs in this Work Group:** Adult Literacy, Remedial Education, and GED Teachers and Instructors; Agricultural Sciences Teachers, Postsecondary; Anthropology and Archeology Teachers, Postsecondary; Architecture Teachers, Postsecondary; Area, Ethnic, and Cultural Studies Teachers, Postsecondary; Art, Drama, and Music Teachers, Postsecondary; Atmospheric, Earth, Marine, and Space Sciences Teachers, Postsecondary; Biological Science Teachers, Postsecondary; Business Teachers, Postsecondary; Chemistry Teachers, Postsecondary; Communications Teachers, Postsecondary; Computer Science Teachers, Postsecondary; Criminal Justice and Law Enforcement Teachers, Postsecondary; Economics Teachers, Postsecondary; Education Teachers, Postsecondary; Engineering Teachers, Postsecondary; English Language and Literature Teachers, Postsecondary; Environmental Science Teachers, Postsecondary; Farm and Home Management Advisors; Foreign Language and Literature Teachers, Postsecondary; Forestry and Conservation Science Teachers, Postsecondary; Geography Teachers, Postsecondary; Graduate Teaching Assistants; Health Specialties Teachers, Postsecondary; History Teachers, Postsecondary; Home Economics

Teachers, Postsecondary; Law Teachers, Postsecondary; Library Science Teachers, Postsecondary; Mathematical Science Teachers, Postsecondary; Nursing Instructors and Teachers, Postsecondary; Philosophy and Religion Teachers, Postsecondary; Physics Teachers, Postsecondary; Political Science Teachers, Postsecondary; Psychology Teachers, Postsecondary; Recreation and Fitness Studies Teachers, Postsecondary; Self-Enrichment Education Teachers; Social Work Teachers, Postsecondary; Sociology Teachers, Postsecondary; Teachers, Postsecondary.

Skills: Instructing; Learning Strategies; Social Perceptiveness; Speaking; Service Orientation; Time Management.

Education and Training Programs: Agricultural Teacher Education; Business Teacher Education; Technology Teacher Education/Industrial Arts Teacher Education; Sales and Marketing Operations/Marketing and Distribution Teacher Education; Technical Teacher Education; Trade and Industrial Teacher Education; Health Occupations Teacher Education; Teacher Education and Professional Development, Specific Subject Areas, Other. **Related Knowledge/Courses:** Education and Training; Psychology; Therapy and Counseling; Computers and Electronics; Sales and Marketing; Communications and Media.

Work Environment: Indoors; standing; using hands on objects, tools, or controls.

Vocational Education Teachers, Secondary School

- ❋ Education/Training Required: Work experience plus degree
- ❋ Annual Earnings: $48,690
- ❋ Beginning Wage: $33,070
- ❋ Earnings Growth Potential: Very high
- ❋ Growth: –4.6%
- ❋ Annual Job Openings: 7,639
- ❋ Self-Employed: 0.0%
- ❋ Part-Time: 7.8%

Industries with Greatest Employment: Educational Services, Public and Private.

Highest-Growth Industries (Projected Growth for This Job): Social Assistance (41.8%); Nursing and Residential Care Facilities (21.3%).

Lowest-Growth Industries (Projected Growth for This Job): Educational Services, Public and Private (–4.9%).

Fastest-Growing Metropolitan Areas (Recent Growth for This Job): Morristown, TN (100.0%); Salt Lake City, UT (55.6%); Kennewick–Richland–Pasco, WA (50.0%); Rochester, MN (50.0%); San Diego–Carlsbad–San Marcos, CA (50.0%).

Other Considerations for Job Security: Job prospects are expected to be favorable, with particularly good prospects for teachers in less desirable urban or rural school districts and for those and who obtain licensure in more than one subject. Fast-growing states in the South and West—led by Nevada, Arizona, Texas, and Georgia—will experience the largest enrollment increases. Enrollments in the Midwest are expected to hold relatively steady, while those in the Northeast are expected to decline. The number of teachers employed depends on state and local expenditures for education and on the enactment of legislation to increase the quality and scope of public education. At the federal level, there has been a large increase in funding for education, particularly for the hiring of qualified teachers in lower-income areas. Qualified vocational teachers are currently in demand in a variety of fields at both the middle school and secondary school levels.

Teach or instruct vocational or occupational subjects at the secondary-school level. Prepare materials and classroom for class activities. Maintain accurate and complete student records as required by law, district policy, and administrative regulations. Instruct students individually and in groups, using various teaching methods such as lectures, discussions, and demonstrations. Observe and evaluate students' performance, behavior, social development, and physical health. Establish and enforce rules for behavior and procedures for maintaining order among the students for whom they are responsible. Instruct and monitor students in the use and care of equipment and materials to prevent injury and damage. Plan and conduct activities for a balanced program of instruction, demonstration, and work time that provides students with opportunities to observe, question, and investigate. Prepare, administer, and grade tests and assignments to evaluate students' progress. Enforce all administration policies and rules governing students. Assign and grade classwork and homework. Instruct students in the knowledge and skills required in a specific occupation or occupational field, using a systematic plan of lectures; discussions; audiovisual presentations; and laboratory, shop, and field studies. Establish clear objectives for all lessons, units, and projects and communicate those objectives to students. Use computers, audiovisual aids, and other equipment and materials to supplement presentations. Plan and supervise work-experience programs in businesses, industrial shops, and school laboratories. Prepare students for later grades by encouraging them to explore learning opportunities and to persevere with challenging tasks. Confer with parents or guardians, other teachers, counselors, and administrators to resolve students' behavioral and academic problems. Guide and counsel students with adjustment or academic problems or special academic interests. Prepare objectives and outlines for courses of study, following curriculum guidelines or requirements of states and schools. Keep informed about trends in education and subject matter specialties.

Personality Type: Social.

GOE—Interest Area: 05. Education and Training. **Work Group:** 05.02. Preschool, Elementary, and Secondary Teaching and Instructing. **Other Jobs in this Work Group:** Elementary School Teachers, Except Special Education; Kindergarten Teachers, Except Special Education; Middle School Teachers, Except Special and Vocational Education; Preschool Teachers, Except Special Education; Secondary School Teachers, Except Special and Vocational Education; Special Education Teachers, Middle School; Special Education Teachers, Preschool, Kindergarten, and Elementary School; Special Education Teachers,

Secondary School; Teacher Assistants; Vocational Education Teachers, Middle School.

Skills: Management of Financial Resources; Management of Personnel Resources; Management of Material Resources; Learning Strategies; Social Perceptiveness; Instructing.

Education and Training Program: Technology Teacher Education/Industrial Arts Teacher Education. **Related Knowledge/Courses:** Education and Training; Therapy and Counseling; Sociology and Anthropology; Psychology; Design; Mechanical Devices.

Work Environment: Indoors; noisy; standing; using hands on objects, tools, or controls.

Water and Liquid Waste Treatment Plant and System Operators

- ❋ Education/Training Required: Long-term on-the-job training
- ❋ Annual Earnings: $36,070
- ❋ Beginning Wage: $21,860
- ❋ Earnings Growth Potential: Very high
- ❋ Growth: 13.8%
- ❋ Annual Job Openings: 9,575
- ❋ Self-Employed: 1.3%
- ❋ Part-Time: 3.4%

Industries with Greatest Employment: Utilities; Waste Management and Remediation Services; Food Manufacturing.

Highest-Growth Industries (Projected Growth for This Job): Professional, Scientific, and Technical Services (58.0%); Administrative and Support Services (38.7%); Waste Management and Remediation Services (27.8%); Utilities (26.6%); Religious, Grantmaking, Civic, Professional, and Similar Organizations (20.9%); Management of Companies and Enterprises (15.9%).

Lowest-Growth Industries (Projected Growth for This Job): Textile Mills (–30.1%); Primary Metal Manufacturing (–28.1%); Paper Manufacturing (–27.4%); Fabricated Metal Product Manufacturing (–17.3%); Machinery Manufacturing (–12.2%); Computer and Electronic Product Manufacturing (–11.1%); Beverage and Tobacco Product Manufacturing (–8.4%); Transportation Equipment Manufacturing (–7.6%); Chemical Manufacturing (–2.7%); Plastics and Rubber Products Manufacturing (–2.7%).

Fastest-Growing Metropolitan Areas (Recent Growth for This Job): San Juan–Caguas–Guaynabo, PR (560.0%); Parkersburg–Marietta–Vienna, WV–OH (171.4%); Santa Barbara–Santa Maria, CA (140.0%); Dover, DE (133.3%); Harrisburg–Carlisle, PA (100.0%).

Other Considerations for Job Security: Job opportunities should be excellent because the retirement of the baby-boom generation will require that many operators with years of experience be replaced. Further, the number of applicants for these jobs is normally low, due primarily to the physically demanding and unappealing nature of some of the work. Opportunities should be best for persons with mechanical aptitude and problem-solving skills. An increasing population and economic growth are expected to boost demand for water and wastewater treatment services. As new plants are constructed to meet this demand, new water and wastewater treatment plant and system operator new jobs will arise.

Operate or control an entire process or system of machines, often through the use of control boards, to transfer or treat water or liquid waste. Add chemicals such as ammonia, chlorine, or lime to disinfect and deodorize water and other liquids. Operate and adjust controls on equipment to purify and clarify water, process or dispose of sewage, and generate power. Inspect equipment or monitor operating conditions, meters, and gauges to determine load requirements and detect malfunctions. Collect and test water and sewage samples, using test equipment and color analysis standards. Record operational data, personnel attendance, or meter and gauge readings on specified forms. Maintain, repair, and lubricate equipment, using hand tools and power tools.

Clean and maintain tanks and filter beds, using hand tools and power tools. Direct and coordinate plant workers engaged in routine operations and maintenance activities.

Personality Type: Realistic.

GOE—Interest Area: 13. Manufacturing. **Work Group:** 13.16. Utility Operation and Energy Distribution. **Other Jobs in this Work Group:** Chemical Plant and System Operators; Gas Compressor and Gas Pumping Station Operators; Gas Plant Operators; Nuclear Power Reactor Operators; Petroleum Pump System Operators, Refinery Operators, and Gaugers; Power Distributors and Dispatchers; Power Plant Operators; Ship Engineers; Stationary Engineers and Boiler Operators.

Skills: Operation Monitoring; Operation and Control; Installation; Troubleshooting; Management of Material Resources; Operations Analysis.

Education and Training Program: Water Quality and Wastewater Treatment Management and Recycling Technology/Technician. **Related Knowledge/Courses:** Biology; Chemistry; Physics; Public Safety and Security; Mechanical Devices; Law and Government.

Work Environment: More often outdoors than indoors; noisy; very hot or cold; contaminants; minor burns, cuts, bites, or stings.

APPENDIX A

Resources for Further Exploration

The facts and pointers in this book provide a good beginning to the subject of recession-proof jobs. If you want additional details, we suggest that you consult some of the resources listed here.

Facts About Careers

The *Occupational Outlook Handbook* (or the *OOH*) (JIST): Updated every two years by the U.S. Department of Labor, this book provides descriptions for 270 major jobs covering more than 85 percent of the workforce. In each job description, a section titled "Job Outlook" explains how, why, and—in many cases—where employment in the job is growing or shrinking, how much competition for jobs can be expected, and which kinds of job hunters have the greatest advantage. A section titled "Projections Data" presents a chart showing job growth statistics. In cases where the job is an aggregation of several specializations, you can see which specializations are expected to grow fastest.

The *Enhanced Occupational Outlook Handbook* (JIST): This book includes all descriptions in the *OOH* plus descriptions of more than 6,000 more-specialized jobs related to them.

The *O*NET Dictionary of Occupational Titles* (JIST): The only printed source of the 950 jobs described in the U.S. Department of Labor's Occupational Information Network database, it covers all the jobs in the book you're now reading, but it offers more topics than we could fit here.

The *New Guide for Occupational Exploration* (JIST): This important career reference allows you to explore all major O*NET jobs based on your interests. (An outline of the included Interest Areas and Work Groups appears in Appendix B.)

Career Decision Making and Planning

Overnight Career Choice, by Michael Farr (JIST): This book can help you choose a career goal based on a variety of criteria, including skills, interests, and values. As part of the *Help in a Hurry* series, it is designed to produce quick results.

50 Best Jobs for Your Personality, by Michael Farr and Laurence Shatkin, Ph.D. (JIST): Built around the six Holland personality types, this book includes an assessment to help you identify your dominant and secondary personality types, plus lists and descriptions of high-paying and high-growth jobs linked to those personality types.

Job Hunting

Same-Day Resume, by Michael Farr (JIST): Learn in an hour how to write an effective resume. This book includes dozens of sample resumes from professional writers and even offers advice on cover letters, online resumes, and more.

Seven-Step Job Search, by Michael Farr (JIST): In seven easy steps, learn what it takes to land the right job fast. Quick worksheets will help you identify your skills, define your ideal job, use the most effective job search methods, write a superior resume, organize your time to get two interviews a day, dramatically improve your interviewing skills, and follow up on all job leads effectively.

Job Banks by Occupation: This is a set of links offered by America's Career InfoNet. At www.acinet.org, find the Career Tools box, click Career Resource Library, and then click Job & Resume Banks. The Job Banks by Occupation link leads you to job groupings such as "Construction and Extraction Occupations" and "Arts, Design, Entertainment, Sports and Media Occupations," which in turn lead you to more specific job titles and occupation-specific job-listing sites maintained by various organizations.

APPENDIX B

The GOE Interest Areas and Work Groups

As Part II explains, the GOE organizes the world of work into large interest areas and more specific work groups containing jobs with a lot in common. Part II defines the 16 GOE interest areas, but Part III also lists the work groups for each job described. We thought you would want to see the complete GOE taxonomy so you would understand how any job that interests you fits into this structure.

Interest areas have two-digit code numbers; work groups have four-digit code numbers beginning with the code number for the interest area in which they are classified. These are the 16 GOE interest areas and work groups:

01 Agriculture and Natural Resources

    01.01 Managerial Work in Agriculture and Natural Resources

    01.02 Resource Science/Engineering for Plants, Animals, and the Environment

    01.03 Resource Technologies for Plants, Animals, and the Environment

    01.04 General Farming

    01.05 Nursery, Groundskeeping, and Pest Control

    01.06 Forestry and Logging

    01.07 Hunting and Fishing

    01.08 Mining and Drilling

02 Architecture and Construction

    02.01 Managerial Work in Architecture and Construction

    02.02 Architectural Design

    02.03 Architecture/Construction Engineering Technologies

    02.04 Construction Crafts

02.05 Systems and Equipment Installation, Maintenance, and Repair

02.06 Construction Support/Labor

03 Arts and Communication

03.01 Managerial Work in Arts and Communication

03.02 Writing and Editing

03.03 News, Broadcasting, and Public Relations

03.04 Studio Art

03.05 Design

03.06 Drama

03.07 Music

03.08 Dance

03.09 Media Technology

03.10 Communications Technology

03.11 Musical Instrument Repair

04 Business and Administration

04.01 Managerial Work in General Business

04.02 Managerial Work in Business Detail

04.03 Human Resources Support

04.04 Secretarial Support

04.05 Accounting, Auditing, and Analytical Support

04.06 Mathematical Clerical Support

04.07 Records and Materials Processing

04.08 Clerical Machine Operation

05 Education and Training

05.01 Managerial Work in Education

05.02 Preschool, Elementary, and Secondary Teaching and Instructing

05.03 Postsecondary and Adult Teaching and Instructing

05.04 Library Services

05.05 Archival and Museum Services

05.06 Counseling, Health, and Fitness Education

06 Finance and Insurance

06.01 Managerial Work in Finance and Insurance

06.02 Finance/Insurance Investigation and Analysis

06.03 Finance/Insurance Records Processing

06.04 Finance/Insurance Customer Service

06.05 Finance/Insurance Sales and Support

07 Government and Public Administration

07.01 Managerial Work in Government and Public Administration

07.02 Public Planning

07.03 Regulations Enforcement

07.04 Public Administration Clerical Support

08 Health Science

08.01 Managerial Work in Medical and Health Services

08.02 Medicine and Surgery

08.03 Dentistry

08.04 Health Specialties

08.05 Animal Care

08.06 Medical Technology

08.07 Medical Therapy

08.08 Patient Care and Assistance

08.09 Health Protection and Promotion

09 Hospitality, Tourism, and Recreation

09.01 Managerial Work in Hospitality and Tourism

09.02 Recreational Services

09.03 Hospitality and Travel Services

09.04 Food and Beverage Preparation

09.05 Food and Beverage Service

09.06 Sports

09.07 Barber and Beauty Services

10 Human Service

10.01 Counseling and Social Work

10.02 Religious Work

10.03 Child/Personal Care and Services

10.04 Client Interviewing

11 Information Technology

11.01 Managerial Work in Information Technology

11.02 Information Technology Specialties

11.03 Digital Equipment Repair

12 Law and Public Safety

    12.01 Managerial Work in Law and Public Safety

    12.02 Legal Practice and Justice Administration

    12.03 Legal Support

    12.04 Law Enforcement and Public Safety

    12.05 Safety and Security

    12.06 Emergency Responding

    12.07 Military

13 Manufacturing

    13.01 Managerial Work in Manufacturing

    13.02 Machine Setup and Operation

    13.03 Production Work, Assorted Materials Processing

    13.04 Welding, Brazing, and Soldering

    13.05 Production Machining Technology

    13.06 Production Precision Work

    13.07 Production Quality Control

    13.08 Graphic Arts Production

    13.09 Hands-On Work, Assorted Materials

    13.10 Woodworking Technology

    13.11 Apparel, Shoes, Leather, and Fabric Care

    13.12 Electrical and Electronic Repair

    13.13 Machinery Repair

    13.14 Vehicle and Facility Mechanical Work

    13.15 Medical and Technical Equipment Repair

    13.16 Utility Operation and Energy Distribution

    13.17 Loading, Moving, Hoisting, and Conveying

14 Retail and Wholesale Sales and Service

    14.01 Managerial Work in Retail/Wholesale Sales and Service

    14.02 Technical Sales

    14.03 General Sales

    14.04 Personal Soliciting

    14.05 Purchasing

    14.06 Customer Service

15 Scientific Research, Engineering, and Mathematics

        15.01 Managerial Work in Scientific Research, Engineering, and Mathematics

        15.02 Physical Sciences

        15.03 Life Sciences

        15.04 Social Sciences

        15.05 Physical Science Laboratory Technology

        15.06 Mathematics and Data Analysis

        15.07 Research and Design Engineering

        15.08 Industrial and Safety Engineering

        15.09 Engineering Technology

16 Transportation, Distribution, and Logistics

        16.01 Managerial Work in Transportation

        16.02 Air Vehicle Operation

        16.03 Truck Driving

        16.04 Rail Vehicle Operation

        16.05 Water Vehicle Operation

        16.06 Other Services Requiring Driving

        16.07 Transportation Support Work

APPENDIX C

Skills Referenced in This Book

Following are the definitions of the 35 skills that the O*NET database uses to characterize jobs and that this book uses in the Part III job descriptions.

Active Learning	Working with new material or information to grasp its implications.
Active Listening	Listening to what other people are saying and asking questions as appropriate.
Critical Thinking	Using logic and analysis to identify the strengths and weaknesses of different approaches.
Complex Problem Solving	Identifying complex problems, reviewing options, and implementing solutions.
Coordination	Adjusting actions in relation to others' actions.
Equipment Maintenance	Performing routine maintenance and determining when and what kind of maintenance is needed.
Equipment Selection	Determining the kind of tools and equipment needed to do a job.
Installation	Installing equipment, machines, wiring, or programs to meet specifications.
Instructing	Teaching others how to do something.
Judgment and Decision Making	Weighing the relative costs and benefits of a potential action.
Learning Strategies	Using multiple approaches when learning or teaching new things.
Management of Financial Resources	Determining how money will be spent to get work done and accounting for these expenditures.
Management of Material Resources	Obtaining and seeing to the appropriate use of equipment, facilities, and materials needed to do certain work.

Management of Personnel Resources	Motivating, developing, and directing people as they work; identifying the best people for the job.
Mathematics	Using mathematics to solve problems.
Monitoring	Assessing how well one is doing when learning or doing something.
Negotiation	Bringing others together and trying to reconcile differences.
Operation and Control	Controlling operations of equipment or systems.
Operation Monitoring	Watching gauges, dials, or other indicators to make sure a machine is working properly.
Operations Analysis	Analyzing needs and product requirements to create a design.
Persuasion	Persuading others to approach things differently.
Programming	Writing computer programs for various purposes.
Quality Control Analysis	Evaluating the quality or performance of products, services, or processes.
Repairing	Repairing machines or systems, using the needed tools.
Reading Comprehension	Understanding written sentences and paragraphs in work-related documents.
Science	Using scientific methods to solve problems.
Service Orientation	Actively looking for ways to help people.
Social Perceptiveness	Being aware of others' reactions and understanding why they react the way they do.
Speaking	Talking to others to effectively convey information.
Systems Analysis	Determining how a system should work and how changes will affect outcomes.
Systems Evaluation	Looking at many indicators of system performance and taking into account their accuracy.
Technology Design	Generating or adapting equipment and technology to serve user needs.
Time Management	Managing one's own time and the time of others.
Troubleshooting	Determining what is causing an operating error and deciding what to do about it.
Writing	Communicating effectively with others in writing as indicated by the needs of the audience.

APPENDIX D

Knowledge Areas Referenced in This Book

Following are definitions of the 33 areas of knowledge that the O*NET database uses to characterize jobs. They often are subjects that are studied in school, college, or training courses, so in the Part III job descriptions they are referred to as "knowledges/courses."

Administration and Management	Knowledge of principles and processes involved in business and organizational planning, coordination, and execution. This includes strategic planning, resource allocation, manpower modeling, leadership techniques, and production methods.
Biology	Knowledge of plant and animal living tissue, cells, organisms, and entities, including their functions, interdependencies, and interactions with each other and the environment.
Building and Construction	Knowledge of materials, methods, and the appropriate tools to construct objects, structures, and buildings.
Chemistry	Knowledge of the composition, structure, and properties of substances and of the chemical processes and transformations that they undergo. This includes uses of chemicals and their interactions, danger signs, production techniques, and disposal methods.
Clerical Studies	Knowledge of administrative and clerical procedures and systems such as word-processing systems, filing and records management systems, stenography and transcription, forms, design principles, and other office procedures and terminology.
Communications and Media	Knowledge of media production, communication, and dissemination techniques and methods, including alternative ways to inform and entertain via written, oral, and visual media.
Computers and Electronics	Knowledge of electric circuit boards, processors, chips, and computer hardware and software, including applications and programming.
Customer and Personal Service	Knowledge of principles and processes for providing customer and personal services, including needs assessment techniques, quality service standards,

alternative delivery systems, and customer satisfaction evaluation techniques.

Design
: Knowledge of design techniques, principles, tools, and instruments involved in the production and use of precision technical plans, blueprints, drawings, and models.

Economics and Accounting
: Knowledge of economic and accounting principles and practices, the financial markets, banking, and the analysis and reporting of financial data.

Education and Training
: Knowledge of instructional methods and training techniques, including curriculum design principles, learning theory, group and individual teaching techniques, design of individual development plans, and test design principles.

Engineering and Technology
: Knowledge of equipment, tools, and mechanical devices and their uses to produce motion, light, power, technology, and other applications.

English Language
: Knowledge of the structure and content of the English language, including the meaning and spelling of words, rules of composition, and grammar.

Fine Arts
: Knowledge of theory and techniques required to produce, compose, and perform works of music, dance, visual arts, drama, and sculpture.

Foreign Language
: Knowledge of the structure and content of a foreign (non-English) language, including the meaning and spelling of words, rules of composition and grammar, and pronunciation.

Food Production
: Knowledge of techniques and equipment for planting, growing, and harvesting of food for consumption, including crop rotation methods, animal husbandry, and food storage/handling techniques.

Geography
: Knowledge of various methods for describing the location and distribution of land, sea, and air masses, including their physical locations, relationships, and characteristics.

History and Archeology
: Knowledge of historical events and their causes, indicators, and impact on particular civilizations and cultures.

Law and Government
: Knowledge of laws, legal codes, court procedures, precedents, government regulations, executive orders, agency rules, and the democratic political process.

Mathematics
: Knowledge of numbers and their operations and interrelationships, including arithmetic, algebra, geometry, calculus, and statistics and their applications.

Mechanical Devices
: Knowledge of machines and tools, including their designs, uses, benefits, repair, and maintenance.

Medicine and Dentistry	Knowledge of the information and techniques needed to diagnose and treat injuries, diseases, and deformities. This includes symptoms, treatment alternatives, drug properties and interactions, and preventive health-care measures.
Personnel and Human Resources	Knowledge of policies and practices involved in personnel/human resource functions. This includes recruitment, selection, training, and promotion regulations and procedures; compensation and benefits packages; labor relations and negotiation strategies; and personnel information systems.
Philosophy and Theology	Knowledge of different philosophical systems and religions, including their basic principles, values, ethics, ways of thinking, customs, and practices and their impact on human culture.
Physics	Knowledge and prediction of physical principles, laws, and applications, including air, water, material dynamics, light, atomic principles, heat, electric theory, earth formations, and meteorological and related natural phenomena.
Production and Processing	Knowledge of inputs, outputs, raw materials, waste, quality control, costs, and techniques for maximizing the manufacture and distribution of goods.
Psychology	Knowledge of human behavior and performance, mental processes, psychological research methods, and the assessment and treatment of behavioral and affective disorders.
Public Safety and Security	Knowledge of weaponry; public safety; security operations, rules, regulations, precautions, and prevention; and the protection of people, data, and property.
Sales and Marketing	Knowledge of principles and methods involved in showing, promoting, and selling products or services. This includes marketing strategies and tactics, product demonstration and sales techniques, and sales control systems.
Sociology and Anthropology	Knowledge of group behavior and dynamics; societal trends and influences; and cultures and their history, migrations, ethnicity, and origins.
Telecommunications	Knowledge of transmission, broadcasting, switching, control, and operation of telecommunications systems.
Therapy and Counseling	Knowledge of information and techniques needed to rehabilitate physical and mental ailments and to provide career guidance, including alternative treatments, rehabilitation equipment and its proper use, and methods to evaluate treatment effects.
Transportation	Knowledge of principles and methods for moving people or goods by air, rail, sea, or road, including their relative costs, advantages, and limitations.

Index

M